THE ELEMENTARY SCHOOL TEACHER

THE UNIVERSITY OF CHICAGO PRESS
CHICAGO, ILLINOIS

Agents

THE CAMBRIDGE UNIVERSITY PRESS
LONDON AND EDINBURGH

THE MARUZEN-KABUSHIKI-KAISHA
TOKYO, OSAKA, KYOTO

KARL W. HIERSEMANN
LEIPZIG

THE BAKER & TAYLOR COMPANY
NEW YORK

THE

ELEMENTARY SCHOOL TEACHER

VOLUME XIV

SEPTEMBER, 1913—JUNE, 1914

THE UNIVERSITY OF CHICAGO PRESS
CHICAGO, ILLINOIS

Published
September, October, November, December, 1913
January, February, March, April, May, June, 1914

Composed and Printed By
The University of Chicago Press
Chicago, Illinois, U.S.A.

INDEX TO VOLUME XIV

INDEX TO ARTICLES

[The asterisk indicates authors of books reviewed]

INDEX TO AUTHORS

[The asterisk indicates authors of books reviewed]

VOLUME XIV NUMBER I

THE ELEMENTARY SCHOOL TEACHER

SEPTEMBER 1913

EDUCATIONAL NEWS AND EDITORIAL COMMENT

Departmental Teaching

The Bureau of Education recently conducted an inquiry regarding the prevalence of departmental teaching in the elementary school and the conclusions as to its value reached by those who have had experience with this type of organization. The following table presents the summary of the answers received from cities of 5,000 population and over. All told, there are 813 replies, distributed in the fashion indicated in the table. Following the table there are eighteen typical comments which are copied from the reports indicating the attitude of various workers in the field.

	Departmental Teaching		Is the Percentage of Failures Less?			Do a Larger Percentage Enter High School?			Are Pupils Better Able to Do High-School Work?		
	Yes	No	Yes	No	No Data	Yes	No	No Data	Yes	No	No Data
Total..........	461	352	240	78	143	250	61	150	302	34	125

1. Succeeds with the strong and industrious pupils and fails with the weak and lazy.

2. Tends to develop independence and self-reliance.

3. Danger of teachers making their subjects of more importance than their pupils.

4. Have had departmental teaching since 1896–97 and have found that it is more economical; that it requires pupils to be independent of the teacher; that they are better able to express their ideas, and that promotion can be made by subject.

5. English should be distributed among the different teachers so that it may be co-ordinated with other subjects.

6. Better teaching and discipline; more interest; less loss between grades.

7. Satisfactory on the whole, but open to faults such as overtaxing the child.

8. Efficiency of pupils higher; discipline suffers.

9. Makes the break between the grades and high school less sudden.

10. All right if child does not meet too many teachers.

11. Very superior; teachers more interested; pupils develop broader ideas.

12. Excellent if teaching force is prepared and in favor of the plan.

13. If there is a poor teacher in the departmental corps pupils do not have her all the time.

14. Will abandon the plan, as we secure better results with one teacher to a grade; discipline easier, and teachers prefer old method of having a room of their own.

15. Gave the plan a fair trial but it proved an absolute failure; perhaps the novelty of the plan causes some to think it a good scheme.

16. Difficult to co-ordinate the work properly; moral hold of teacher not so strong; supervision by principal more difficult.

17. Will abolish or greatly modify it this year; pupils are not taught individually.

18. Do not care for it; would rather have one-teacher plan in first-year high school than extend departmental system to the grades.

The following item is condensed from an article in the *New York Globe:*

A Permanent Educational Exhibit

In the fall there will be opened in this city what is planned to be the greatest and most complete exhibit of modern school equipment ever brought together. Space to the extent of two floors has been reserved in the new Educational Building at 70 Fifth Avenue, corner of Thirteenth Street, to display the remarkable collection of samples and the best models of everything belonging to the equipment and supply of educational institutions. Teachers College has announced that it has made arrangements to transfer its museum interests to this permanent educational exhibit.

It is planned that the Educational Building, now in course of construction, will make it possible to arrange the display in one building of everything for the school, from the engaging of its architect to the selection of its teachers. With economy of time the educational public can procure schoolbooks, desks and seats, laboratory apparatus, and manual training equipment. Floors and offices have already been engaged by textbook publishers, teachers' agencies, and dealers in school supplies, as well as by illustrators of schoolbooks and agents for printers and paper mills.

For the convenience of teachers from out of town an attractive room will be provided with library facilities. Here members of school committees or school principals can chat comfortably with prospective teachers or keep other business appointments.

The upper floors will be subdivided and arranged to suit the needs of tenants. Two or more of these floors will be devoted to the Permanent Educational Exhibit Company and to salesrooms where everything pertaining to school construction and equipment of the most modern type may be seen. The first portion of the building (70×103 feet) is now ready for occupancy.

The Exhibit Company will to a certain extent act as a sales agent, and a bureau of information regarding construction and equipment of school buildings throughout the country will be open for the benefit of exhibitors.

Information in regard to the Permanent Exhibit Company can be secured from Charles C. Stimets, manager, Educational Building, Fifth Avenue and Thirteenth Street.

Compulsory Education in Ohio

The state of Ohio has a new compulsory-education act. This act is distinctly in advance of any of the laws under which even the northern states are operating. Some question having arisen as to the exact meaning and interpretation of the law, the attorney-general has given the following interpretation to this law as now amended:

That every boy between eight and fifteen years, and every girl between eight and sixteen years must attend school.

That every boy between fifteen and sixteen years not engaged in some regular employment must attend school.

That such attendance must begin the first week of the school term and continue for the full time that the school attended is in session, which in no case shall be for less than 28 weeks.

That no person, firm, or corporation shall employ any child under fifteen in any business whatsoever during any of the hours when the public schools are in session.

That no boy under sixteen and no girl under eighteen shall be employed unless such child presents an age certificate approved by the superintendent of the public schools.

That no boy under sixteen years of age shall receive a certificate until he is fifteen and has passed a satisfactory sixth-grade test, and no girl until she is sixteen and has passed a satisfactory seventh-grade test.

That any boy between fifteen and sixteen who ceases to work must return to school within two weeks unless he secures other employment within such time.

Some of the Problems of the National Education Association

At the summer meeting of the National Education Association the plan to raise one million dollars endowment was passed upon by the trustees and directors. Mr. T. W. Bicknell of Providence, R.I., was authorized to go ahead and try to collect this sum. The statement is made that if the money can be secured the income will be distributed among the departments of the Association in proportion to their needs. The department and the general offices of the Association will be housed in a proposed national home in Washington. The federal government will be asked to supply the money necessary for the erection of a building to be used for this general purpose and also to house a museum of pedagogy. The museum and the national home will, it is pointed out, become the center of education in the United States. Establishment of such an institution will duplicate the work of no other department of the United States government and it will not parallel the work of any other organization. It is said in connection with the announcement of this campaign for one million dollars that at present the Association is seriously handicapped because of lack of funds. There is no adequate income from the annual meeting, especially this year, when the number of members was very small indeed. The membership of the Association has shown itself so unstable in recent years that it is impossible from year to year to determine how much work can be undertaken by the Association.

The *Elementary School Teacher* has commented before on this endowment fund for the National Education Association. It still believes that the policy of trying to secure funds before there is a definite plan of organization which would appeal to those who might contribute the money is a mistake. The National Education Association is at the present time facing a very large problem. Its organization is by no means adequate to meet the needs of the teaching profession of this country. The committees which are investigating educational problems are of very different types and very different degrees of energy and efficiency. Some need money and would use it productively; others give no evidence of ability to use either time or money properly. The general Board of Directors which deals with these various committees has a curious way of making appropriations in some directions and finding it impossible to support other lines of work. If the money of this endowment is to be adequately expended, there must be back of the endowment an association with a perfectly clear definition of its own policies and of its relation to other agencies which throughout the nation are undertaking to promote educational investigation and educational publication.

In this connection it is interesting to note that the president of the National Education Association made it the theme of his address at the annual meeting to discuss the possible reorganization of the Association. It has long been recognized that the Association is not representative. The members who come from the particular locality where the meeting is held have a very undue weight in determining the policies of that particular meeting of the Association. In any case, the numbers in actual attendance at the meeting are so small as compared with the teaching profession of the whole country that the question naturally arises of organizing a better means of communicating with all the teachers of the nation. Shall there be a general representative council of the whole profession? Shall there be local groups of directors for the different states? Shall the meeting be divided in such a way that various meetings are held in different parts of the country? Shall the meeting be held only at long intervals, say once every three or four years? These and various other questions are facing the Association as important questions of organization. The competition of the regular summer schools giving university credit for the work of teachers, the failure of the railroads to give rates, and other considerations are making inroads into the summer meeting. The winter meeting of the Department of Superintendence is coming to be educationally very much more significant than the general summer meeting. The whole problem of reorganizing the National Education Association therefore looms up as the chief problem before this Association.

The next meeting of the Association is to be held in St. Paul. It will be remembered that the meeting once before was voted for St. Paul, but for reasons best known to the board of directors of that date the meeting was brought to Chicago. In the year 1915 the Association will go back to California and will join with the Panama Exposition in the city of San Francisco. The actual seat of the meeting of the National Education Association for that year is voted to be Oakland, Cal. The new president of the National Education Association for the coming year is President Swain of Swarthmore College.

Importance of Policies regarding Promotion

The following paragraph is quoted from a pamphlet by Dr. L. C. Ayres, published by the Russell Sage Foundation. The pamphlet is entitled *The Effect of Promotion Rates on School Efficiency*. In this pamphlet Dr. Ayres has shown the importance to the pupils and to the community of changes in the rate of promotion. The paragraph here quoted puts the matter in a very concrete and striking form.

WHAT A CHANGE OF 1 PER CENT MEANS

The importance of small changes in promotion rates may be best illustrated by figuring the results of a change of 1 per cent, say for example from 80 per cent to 81 per cent, in the promotion rate in the elementary schools of a small city. Let us suppose that 1,000 children enter the elementary schools each year, the annual per capita cost for schooling is $40, and the buildings, grounds, and equipment have a value of $200 per child.

Under these conditions, the change in the promotion rate from 80 per cent to 81 per cent will have the following results: The time saved by each 1,000 children if they complete the elementary course will amount to 130 years of schooling, which means a saving of $5,200 annually. The plant required to accommodate the children will be decreased by about $25,600 worth, and the salaries of four teachers will be saved. The number of failures among the 1,000 children during eight years of school life will be reduced by 70, while the number of children failing during that period will be lessened by 19. The number of over-age children in the grades will be reduced by 220. These figures strikingly illustrate the importance of even the smallest changes in promotion rates.

Summer Schools

The summer-school movement for both pupils and teachers has come to be a commonly recognized feature of American education. Mr. Perry, writing for the Russell Sage Foundation of New York City, finds that 141 municipalities report vacation schools in one or more buildings in 1912. An aggregate appropriation of over $300,000 was made for the maintenance of these schools. Reports from all parts of the country show that the movement was more vigorous this summer than last. For example, a clipping from the *Los Angeles Examiner* states that the summer schools opened for a term of six weeks and over 7,000 pupils enrolled for the vocational and academic branches. The vocational work is emphasized in these schools somewhat more than in the regular sessions. From St. Paul, Minn., comes a statement that 540 pupils enrolled in a summer school and are prepared to go forward with the regular work; 180 were in the high-school department and 360 in the grades. They are here allowed to make up the failures that they have accumulated throughout the year or they are at liberty to work in advance. From Savannah, Ga., there is a statement to the effect that the high school has for the first time undertaken to give an opportunity to those who failed of promotion to make up the work during the summer. In Chicago the summer school opened with a very large registration. A number of the schools are undertaking to try work outdoors and are chiefly recreational and vocational schools. On the other hand, the high schools are undertaking to give students an opportunity to make advanced standing as well as to make up their credits. In Omaha, Neb., open-air study is a feature of the high school. It is introduced for the first time in the vacation schools. "High-school boys and girls may now take Caesar and geometry out under the trees on the lawn. Others have found cool stations at tables in the corridors, in quiet corners on the main floor." All of these different kinds of experimentation with summer work find in the public press comments of a favorable type. The following editorials indicate the attitudes of various editorial writers:

"Geographically and climatically it is desirable that we should have some suitable pastime and occupation for the children who are unable to leave the city."

Another comment is to the effect that "nowhere in the world is there more need of some good place to which children may resort than in the cities." Still another comment points out that "children in the summer are no longer employed on the farm as they used to be generations ago and it would be well for them to have the opportunity of working under a teacher who would give them regular instruction as they used to receive it in the older days on the farm."

It is not only the pupils, however, who are afforded the opportunity of attending summer schools. So widespread has the movement of summer schools for teachers become that universities regard the success of their summer schools as among the most important items in their annual reports. Columbia University had this year a very large addition to its summer enrolment. The same is true of the various university summer schools throughout the Middle West. The University of Chicago and the University of Wisconsin both had large additions to their registration. The same report comes from the Pacific Coast, where the University of California had an unusual record. The Summer School of the South, which has long been one of the centers around which southern education has been focused, had a slightly smaller registration than usual this year, but carried on a very enthusiastic session. Summer schools at the normal schools also show large increases in attendance. These summer schools satisfy a demand which is different from that which is met by the university summer schools in that immature rural teachers and others who are taking their first certificates here have an opportunity to get review courses and to get some training in the principles of teaching. In addition to training immature students, the normal schools also furnish an opportunity for teachers who have been out in the service for some time to come back and get training even if they are not able to go to the remoter centers where the universities are holding their summer quarters.

Consulting Psychologists

Some years ago Professor Royce in a vigorous article advocated the appointment in all the leading school systems of a consulting psychologist. At that time the probability seemed very remote that school boards would take the step suggested by Professor Royce. In many of the large systems, however, since that time child-study departments have been organized and have been put in the charge of technically trained psychologists. These child-study departments have very commonly devoted their whole attention to the discovery of abnormal children. A somewhat broader program is outlined in the following statement, which comes from Los Angeles, Cal.:

> To bring every boy and girl attending the public schools of Los Angeles to the highest degree of efficiency, and to develop the individual child according to his capacity, is the purpose of a new departure in pedagogy taken by the board of education yesterday.
>
> The board created the position of clinical psychologist, and appointed Professor George L. Leslie to fill the office for the year 1913–14.
>
> Dr. Leslie's work will be to visit every class of every school in the city and determine the mental status of every pupil. By scientific methods he will ascertain whether a boy or girl is normal, abnormal, or subnormal as to mental faculties.
>
> To this end Dr. Leslie will employ the Binet test, invented by a noted French scientist. Without instruments or any paraphernalia calculated to bewilder the pupil, he will, by oral test, determine the status of each child. If a boy who is sixteen years old is found to be twelve or eighteen years in mental development, special studies and mental treatment will be prescribed for him that will tend to bring him to normal.
>
> The position of clinical psychologist carries a salary of $2,700 a year. This feature will be entirely separate from the health and development department of the schools.

Training of Music Teachers

The music teachers of the state of Ohio at their annual convention in the latter part of June took vigorous action looking toward the improvement of standards within their own profession. They considered the advisability of securing some kind of state supervision for the private instruction which is given in music throughout the state. They also recognized the importance of raising the requirements imposed on special teachers of music in public schools.

The teaching of music has not been taken very seriously in this country. Sometimes it is assumed that anyone can add a little teaching of music to the rest of the grade work. Sometimes it is assumed that a special teacher with a natural taste for music and a little training in the art of music can do all that is necessary without attempting in any way to mix music and the "regular" school work.

The qualification of special teachers of music are often very meager. Very often the only special training they have had for their professional work has been secured at a short summer training school of three weeks' duration. The result is that music has not commanded respect and has never taken the place that it should in the course of study. It is gratifying to see that the Ohio teachers of music have realized that the way to improve the situation is to raise standards within the profession. It was a like conviction which led the physical education teachers of the Middle West at their last annual meeting to draft an elaborate scheme for the raising of the professional standards within their group. It is to be hoped that this consciousness of the teaching profession of its obligation to itself will spread rapidly, so that it will be impossible in the special branches for teachers to secure positions and influence school policy with regard to these special subjects unless they have the qualifications that give them a right to represent the subject adequately in school councils.

THE IDEALS WHICH LED TO THE FOUNDING OF THE SCHOOL OF EDUCATION[1]

ANITA McCORMICK BLAINE

This, our school, had its original and only true foundation in the mind and heart—in the purpose, of Col. Francis W. Parker. In its second phase, in which it was intended to be freed of all trammels for its work, it was founded (at the first instance of my wish, and Col. Parker's consent) by the efforts of its Trustees, Owen F. Aldis, Henry B. Favill, Cyrus Bentley, Stanley McCormick, and myself; and of Col. Parker and of his faculty.

In its third phase it had its foundation in a great concourse of elements—the appreciation of its work and of its principles and of its possibilities by President William R. Harper—the sympathetic joining with it of the faculties of three of the University's schools and of the University's Department of Education—and the consent to join the University, of all of its own authorities—which included its whole faculty.

To present to you all of the ideals which determined this broad foundation—and they make collectively a force which must surely help to move on this old world—is more than I am able to do.

I realize that in asking me to speak to you on this subject you have had in mind the limitations which I have in dealing with it. For that reason I am not staggered by the thought. For another reason I am not staggered by it. As I have known this work in education, its aims and its ideals have not been divergent. I do not need to analyze for you widely separating threads with their actions and interactions. With all the varying ideas and viewpoints of such a great concourse of so many active and independent minds, the purposes of this work have been in one great stream—the goals have all been at one great end. So that if I lead you to this stream, even though it be down one small rivulet, it is still to one large stream I bring you. For, in this current of educational effort, clashing and warring and disputing as the ideas have been—

[1] Address to the United Grades Meeting of the University Elementary School.

just as clashing and warring and disputing as ideas must be that are vital to the individual and to the world—they have been below that, as I have known the work, singularly and deeply harmonious.

I take it that currents that are deep are swept onward so much more irresistibly that the eddies do not stay the progress, nor separate nor retard the flow. And so, though I bring you to the ideals that dominated the work of the school, through my own medium, I have not the feeling that this is out of harmony with the greater force you find there.

However, I must ask you, as I go on, to bear clearly in mind that what I am giving you is my own standpoint, from which I have viewed this great school work.

At the outset of taking up the subject you have given me, it came to me to try wholly to depict Col. Parker's viewpoint toward his school—and then perhaps to add, of my own, views about the work, and parts of the work, which I should particularly want to emphasize.

The difficulty about this process is that I am inadequate for the description of Col. Parker's viewpoint toward his own school. Many others could give you that much better than I could—notably Miss Cooke, who carries on Col. Parker's work on the North Side—and equally notably, many members of his faculty whom you have with you.

I eagerly suggest that you gain an opportunity of hearing the statement of the school work which Miss Cooke gave to the Parker School this spring. We felt that it was as vivid and comprehensive a statement of this complex subject as we had had.

Leaving you in anticipation of that possibility as a reward of patience, may I then draw you on with me for the moment?

The composite seeming not a hopeful attempt, I shall not try then to separate myself from my own view of Col. Parker's school work.

So I will ask you, to remember that it does not necessarily follow from my statement that the more responsible factors in the school work would be represented therein, and if you promise to keep this in mind, I shall go freely forward and give you what seems the only thing to attempt—the ideals of our school as seen in the foundation of it by one factor in that great and comprehensive process.

One other preliminary word is quite necessary to say—that I shall not attempt at all points to make clear wherein the school did not fulfil its whole ideal in its performance.

It is unnecessary to state that it did not do so. To speak of its ideals is to indicate that it reached out toward goals beyond its grasp which it had not yet perfectly attained. What you ask for today is a picture of those goals. To analyze the shortcomings and find the reasons and cures for those is the process of school work. This I am not attempting to describe in this moment. I am but trying to pass on to you—and I fear it will be but faintly—that alluring picture which I got a glimpse of when I first entered Col. Parker's school—the ideal growing ground for a child—a picture that itself has grown and grown as one gazes on it and dwells in it.

The ideals—the aims of its existence—of this school which was Col. Parker's—now yours—and ours by affection and courtesy! Let me once and for all entreat you whenever you approach this vital subject of the work of a school that is trying to set a standard for children, that you take great care to make the distinctions which give the essential idea. This move in education in general has been open, naturally and rightly, to a vast amount of criticism. We cannot approach the subject without meeting it on every hand. This school has challenged attention by its fundamental importance, and also more or less by its power to attract attention by its results. Its real upholders have always welcomed criticism—courted suggestion as a great avenue of help—and ignored the carping criticism which was manifestly trying to pick flaws for the pleasure of that interesting occupation, for which new territory always offers so many easy and attractive opportunities. But there is a vast amount of keenly interested criticism which shoots wide of the mark, because it proceeds from a lack of understanding of the real ideas contained in the terms used. I have often been engulfed by the hopeless and helpless feeling that that situation leaves one in, when it is realized that a word will not straighten the issue, and that the critic will not give more than passing attention to the matter. The confusion is often deeper and more important, however, than the momentary missing of the point by casual beholders. For real criticism is the meat and drink of constructive work in education, or in anything else and we can ill afford to have it mixed with the poison of a misunderstanding of the real idea.

It is the frequent vision of this confusion which leads me to beg you to make the correct distinctions in dealing with this subject.

A serious effort to advance education a point further in its evolution is worth clear thinking.

Loose thought does more to becloud issues than we are aware of. So much so-called thought is but a game of follow-the-leader that it becomes an important matter for the leaders not to perpetuate side-tracking lines of mistake. This, no doubt, is an unnecessary reflection or suggestion to make within a university atmosphere. I must be pardoned for making it, on the score of coming into the sacred precincts from the philistine, plebeian sections of the city—of the country—of the world. But even in coming out of the outer darkness—or because of that—it seems worth while to point out the pitfalls that may catch the steps of the unwary, who may stray from the pure light of university thought.

Such familiar battlegrounds due to varied interpretations come at once to mind—as in the common error of making the poor, jaded word discipline do service for the birch rod and an intellectual development of the power of the will, alike, the idea is torn limb from limb in separating these two impersonations of it. The result in the casual beholder is, nine times out of ten, the retention of the more dramatic fact of the relegation of the birch rod to the dust heap—and the conclusion, immediate and final, that discipline—all discipline—is gone bag and baggage to the same quarter.

An equally ready to hand spot of confusion is the well worn topic of interest. Because interest in the mind of the child may be considered a *sine qua non* of good work, therefore your non-distinction-drawer, whipping poor interest around the stump of all of his own preconceived ideas, pictures your education as tied to the apron string of every passing whim of each separate and individual child of every group—a confusing enough result, surely, in the mind of the believer, if not in the actual fact.

These errors of the common herd are, as we have said, irrelevant n this presence. But they serve to illustrate common mistakes which can be corrected only by the uncommon clearness of the thinking few—and therefore they may be alluded to pleadingly by a commoner.

May I then proceed to draw one distinction which I think lies at the root of the whole matter?

The first aim of this school, as I have seen it, was to improve the conditions of school life for all children—to improve them by its immediate discoveries for its own pupils and, by that demonstration, and its influence, for all the children in the world—if possible to reach so far.

This does not fall within the territory of just trying to do what is and has been done in a yet better or more perfect way. It has in it a very different meaning, viz., to change more or less radically, as the case may be, the existing conditions in schools for children; and it clearly involves a choice. If the former idea is quite right, then the other is not to be followed. If the latter idea is right, then the former idea is in some sense wrong. This division or choice is not always a clear one by any means. Known schools would not necessarily fall into the one category or the other. But yet in what Col. Parker set forth to do for children in schools is involved in an essential way an element of choice—an element of negativing another way which largely obtained and which he found to be not the right condition for children's education, and which his purpose was to supersede as largely as possible.

Thus, in the aim of his school to improve the conditions for children is contained an arraignment of a former, and what it would have been his life hope to call an outgrown, idea in the education of children. I think any understanding of the ideas of this school must proceed from a realization of that former state and those elements in it which Col. Parker's work set forth to eradicate—it must proceed from an arraignment!

Holding the former way, then, at the bar, we must make counts against it—in all solemnity.

It received the pupil from the hands of its parents, but it did not take all of him. At the gate of the school he, like the Gaul he was to learn so much about, was divided into three parts. His parents were told to retain two of them, keeping entire charge of his character formation and his physical well-being. The school assumed the task of developing his head machine.

Due notice being thus given of what the school attempted and what it did not attempt to do, it could with perfect good faith wash its hands of all it had not undertaken—and this it proceeded to do. It held its pupils then as little integers for head work, and its educational work went on, on that theory. It became then an irrelevant—almost an impertinent—question if one ventured to inquire, whether such and such a part of school work was a salutary influence on the pupil's character—or whether the school life was conducive to the pupil's health.

Those were questions for the home to deal with wholly! Any particularly benign teacher might enter that realm with her advice. But it was by no possible construction her responsibility.

It is strange to stop to consider, in this conception of the school's function for children, what a large proportion of time and influence the school was willing to assume in the lives of children, on this basis of partial responsibility.

By this division the school took no particular account of the pupil's physical development, and the pupil had no particular way through the school of acquiring a greater store of strength than nature had started him with. The quota of gymnastics in schools in general would hardly make an appreciable limit to this statement. It is quite fair to say that it was not considered the school's especial business to conserve or increase the pupil's store of physical vigor.

Dealing, as the school set forth to do, then, with the head work of the child, it would be fair to hope that that would be done with enlightenment. But it is more in keeping to expect that a narrow and partial conception of the whole realm of school work would be followed by a limited conception in the field which it did assume. And this we find to be the case.

In the *ancien régime* the pedagogic process must be declared to be faulty.

It consisted mainly in the stuffing of the pupil's mind with the thoughts and conclusions of others, and the requirement from him of the repetition of these—too often word for word—as his contribution.

It was not only the stuffing of his mind with foreign material, but in such unrelated nuggets as to make no mass which he could by any process of his own assimilate.

The result of this pedagogic conception was no thinking process on the part of the pupil—and no possession by him of such material as he had succeeded in uttering by rote.

The standards set up by the schools of yesterday were in every case the standards set by others. They were labeled by names made sacred by an awe, which severed them from all real connection with the mind of the pupil.

With the leverage of distance and the power of superstitious reverence, the hold they gained over the pupil was absolute—so that it would never occur to a pupil to have any confidence in any departure whatever of his own. These standards became an absolute measure of excellence—not from intrinsic appreciation, but from artificial stamp and acceptance. The result was a complete stoppage of any originality and a prime emphasis on imitation.

Discipline in the olden time was a method invented for dealing with inevitably refractory human nature—a means of catching the refraction in the shoot, and bringing it into line for the easement of trouble for the population in general, and for individual teachers in particular. It was a method applied on the outside—prickers of one sort or another, which the refractory one would come up against and wish for his own comfort in the end to steer clear of—a process convenient enough for an ease-loving and thought-shirking adulthood, but not producing in the pupil any real control whatsoever.

From the foregoing elements, it is not a surprise to reach the predicament the old education found itself in. With no physical joy to expect, no work of one's own, but only plodding through the repetition of the work of others, no free play to find one's own *métier*, nothing wanted but strict adherence to a stamped pattern—with spikes of tongues and glances, reprimands and marks (meaning other reprimands) on every side to prevent any deviation from the lines as laid down, an incentive for such work was needed—and needed badly.

And, alas, the school—which should flash the beacon light of high motive from hilltop to hilltop for humanity—fell into the device, common to all authorities needing to hold their populace within their power—resorted to the appeal to the lower elements of human nature—the fear of punishment and the hope of gain—the appeal to the selfish desire to escape censure, and to excel above others.

It does not follow from a clear seeing of these elements in the old education, that all school-rooms or all schools contained them.

Minds in all ages have done their part within systems on plans wholly of their own inspiration—minds have found themselves, in spite of all barriers forcing the contrary.

Schools have always been full of the surprises of minds coming upon revivifying connections of ideas—on their own unbounded uprising personality—on one and another teacher, who sees and inspires—and lives have been built on the foundations laid by such chance teachers.

But that does not go so far as to negative the statement that, in the ordinary course and by the accepted plan, at the last end of the old education, all was but left to be overcome. The end was but to begin, and perhaps the best result was the common cry that nothing was remembered.

In the realm of the physical, it was to put an adult mind on the subject and get out of the circumstances what could be rescued—and the effort probably too late at that.

If to think was needed, it was to begin by getting out of and forgetting well-worn ruts.

If a personality demanded recognition, it was at the cost of eradicating the almost ineradicable stamp. If control was to be reached, it was needed to begin all over again in the school of experience.

If co-operation could hold sway (instead of fierce rivalry and competition), it was only by uprooting that sturdy plant of selfishness, developed by careful cultivation through all the period of youth.

We are used to crying out against human nature and railing against our civilization. I wonder if it often enough occurs to us that our civilization is made by the people of it—and that we are making in turn the civilization of tomorrow.

The minds that must mount, will. How many more might soar if we gave them the chance! How many thousands and millions may be losing their lights, in the treadmill of educational process!

It is no doubt divinely true that we must be born again—but if so is it within reason that our educational process should consider that divine necessity so wholly outside of its sphere? Might there not be a gradual rebirth in which our education should play the leading part?

It is a thankless task to arraign with no outlook of possibility and hope.

We are never driven to this necessity in scoring ways past for children—for there are always ways to come. For them, ever and anon, teachers arise—prophets—to hold aloft torches to light new paths, and while we spur our search by glancing at the steps we wish to leave, we may concentrate our efforts more on that better way of discerning the footsteps traced ahead and, by the flicker of the light in advance, find which steps are the ones to follow and which to improve.

Col. Parker was one such prophet.

He founded our school in the spirit of a prophet for the purpose of seeking and finding light to shed on the path of mankind.

[*To be continued*]

SEVEN, EIGHT, AND NINE YEARS IN THE ELEMENTARY SCHOOL

E. C. BROOKS
Professor of Education, Trinity College, Durham, N.C.

Can a four-year high school resting on a seven-year grammar school give a preparation equal to that of a four-year high school resting on an eight-year grammar school? It is not so much the purpose of my investigation to answer this question as it is to present some facts relative to the grammar schools especially and the high school incidentally, which are sufficient to prove this, that there is no general rule governing the length of the grammar school, and no strong reason why either a seven-, eight-, or nine-year school, as a class, exists in its present form. Each seems to be the result of accident or imitation, and, in many instances, an eight-year grammar school might, without at all detracting therefrom, or adding thereto, be labeled with equal accuracy a nine-year school, or a seven-year school.

The efficiency of any school system must be judged (1) by its content, that is, the quality and the quantity of subject-matter presented, and (2) by its organization, that is, how this content is distributed through the years, how it is adjusted to the age, ability, and experience of the child, and what opportunity it gives the child for the best development, consequently the best progress from year to year. In studying the content and the organization of the grammar school, this question naturally presents itself: Is there an exact amount of subject-matter necessary for all children before they can begin the work of the high school? Or can we measure the content of the grammar school in terms of units? Whenever a definite number of years is adopted, whether it be seven, eight, or nine, the quality and quantity of the content of the grammar school must be made more nearly uniform. When this is done we are close to a unit basis.

In this investigation of the content and the organization of the grammar school, I have endeavored to learn as much as possible about: (1) The courses of study in a number of schools—their length in years as they exist and the preferred length; at what legal age pupils enter school; the number of daily recitations for each grade; the length of the recitation and the school day for each grade; and the amount of work that each grade is supposed to do out of school. (2) The promotion of students—what percentage of each grade completes more than the work outlined for the whole grade; how students are promoted from grade to grade; how much time is saved by this method; and what per cent of each grade repeats more than half the work of the grade.

In order to obtain this information I sent out more than two hundred blanks, including in each a return stamped envelope. I was guided by the list of schools found in the last number of the *Report of the United States Commissioner of Education* showing the number of schools in towns of more than eight thousand population that contain seven-, eight-, and nine-year grammar schools. I sent about five to a state, three to superintendents of the eight- and nine-year grammar schools, and two to those of a seven-year grammar school. From these two hundred blanks sent out I have received about seventy replies from thirty-nine states. They contain such interesting information, that, in order to be as accurate as possible about one feature of the report, I wrote about thirty personal letters to as many superintendents in as many states.

The information obtained shows that the seven-year grammar school is found in nearly every state of the union; but as a rule it prevails more generally in the South. In New England the eight- and nine-year schools are found in about equal ratio in the larger cities, but the tendency is to reduce all to eight years; while in the West, the eight-year school prevails with a tendency in many sections to reduce it to seven years. Is a seven-year school better for the New England states? Is the quality and the quantity of the content the same? And is the organization of the one as well adjusted as that of the other? In other words, what determines the length of the grammar school?

If we can for the present omit the personal inclination of the superintendent, it would appear that the length of the grammar school is governed by (1) the age of students entering the first grade, (2) the number of subjects taught daily in each grade, (3) the opportunity offered by the school organization for the promotion of students, and (4) the character of the population in the community of the school. Yet in the same state where all these conditions are similar, we find grammar schools of different lengths, showing that the personal inclination of the superintendent is a strong factor.

I. THE LEGAL AGE OF ENTRANCE

This question was asked each school: If three students, ages respectively five, six, and seven, enter the first grade at the same time, will they reach the high school at the same time, granting equal capacities at the same age? The answers to this question were almost unanimous in the opinion that the seven-year-old child would reach the high school at least a year before the others; and, if an opportunity is given for the capacity of each to express itself, the six-year-old child will reach the high school ahead of the five-year-old child. Yet only a few of the schools exhibit any scheme by which one student can progress more rapidly than another.

The first opinion is verified by the reports, for in the schools of Alabama, Texas, Virginia, and Tennessee the age of admission is seven, and the length of the grammar school is seven years. In Tennessee the grammar school in one city is eight years, and the high school three years, but high-school work is probably done in the last year of the grammar school, as is the case in many eight-year grammar schools in the South.

Students entering at six years of age in Arkansas, California, Colorado, Florida, Georgia, Idaho, Illinois, Indiana, Kentucky, Missouri, Montana, North Carolina, New Hampshire, Ohio, Oklahoma, Oregon, Pennsylvania, South Carolina, South Dakota, Utah, and Washington show different results. In Colorado, one city has a seven-year course, but prefers an eight-year course. On the other hand another city in the same state has an eight-year course which "under present conditions," it says, is advisabl . Florida has eight, Georgia, seven; Idaho, eight, but prefers seven; Indiana, eight; Kentucky, eight; Missouri, two eight, one seven; Montana, eight; North Carolina, seven; New Hampshire, eight;

Oklahoma, eight; Oregon, eight; Pennsylvania reports three schools—one seven, another eight, and the third nine; South Carolina, seven; Utah, eight; Washington, eight under present conditions; California, eight; Ohio, eight; Illinois, eight.

Students entering at five years of age in Connecticut, Iowa, Massachusetts, Michigan, Mississippi, Nebraska, New Jersey, New York, Rhode Island, Vermont, and Wisconsin show likewise different results. One school in Connecticut has eight years, but would give students opportunity to complete the work in seven years. But in another school the course is nine years. In Iowa, Des Moines has eight, but would reduce it if the school year were longer. It is now one hundred and ninety days. In an Iowa city the course is eight and one-half years. In Massachusetts it is nine years, with a few exceptions. In Mississippi it is eight years; Nebraska, eight years; New Jersey, eight, "as a rule"; New York, eight; Rhode Island, nine with one exception; Vermont, nine; Wisconsin, eight, but in favor of a reduction.[1]

It would appear then that the progress of students through the grammar-school years is not influenced as much as it should be by the age of the pupils. There may be a vast difference in the ages, yet the progress may be the same. An extreme case, to use as an illustration, is a young man now at Trinity College, Durham, N.C., who had, all told, only five years' training when he entered college. He brought a diploma from one of the best high schools in the state that maintains a four-year course carrying fourteen units. The young man entered the high school at twenty-five years of age, having had only two years' preparation beforehand, and he completed the high-school course in three years. If this young man had entered a city school where the number of daily recitations are counted with two figures, it is quite probable that he would have been ten of the twelve years at least passing through the grammar school and the high school. And the end of his schooling would have been reached even before he could pass into the high school. His age would have aided but little in his progress through the years.

[1] The reader will keep in mind that these facts are taken from an average of three reports from a state.

The reports lead one to believe that it does not make much difference whether the work of the grammar school is called six, seven, eight, or nine years in length. In fact, this tells so little about a school that the grouping of the courses by years might very well be dropped. For instance, one superintendent writes: "In seventeen years as superintendent I have had only one pupil, entering at six, who finished the grammar and high school on required time." The two make only a nine-year course.

The superintendent of a certain school in Connecticut says: "The really vital test of the school system is not how many grades below the high school, but how many years does it take the average pupil to reach the high school." He believes it will take nine years; but "popular clamor will compel us all to have an eight-grade system, I suppose." Here students enter at five years of age, but he believes that if students entered at seven they would gain more than a year.

The most perplexing problem, then, of the city school systems is not the length of term, the age of pupils, nor governing boards, but it seems to be one or both of the following: (1) the number of daily subjects or recitations, and (2) the lack of opportunity for individual progress.

II. THE NUMBER OF DAILY RECITATIONS

The number of subjects taught daily in each grade of the grammar school, the order of their appearance, the prominence given to each, and the amount of time devoted to each furnish a chapter in the study of present-day education that is no less astonishing than it is unique. In studying the reports I was struck with this most interesting feature that one school in New England requires each pupil of the third grade to recite nineteen times daily; while another school in the same state requires its pupils of the same grade to recite only four times daily. In order, then, that these figures might be better understood, I wrote personal letters to the superintendents of about thirty schools asking each to define the term "recitation," and to send me a copy of the daily program of the different grades; for it was clear to me that a grade which attempts to instruct pupils in four subjects daily should show different results from one that attempts to instruct pupils in nineteen subjects daily. The superintendents, as a rule, replied promptly to my letters giving me their ideas of the recitation and sending me also copies of the daily program.

I was aware of the fact that the term "recitation" included in many schools the time spent by the teacher in assigning a subject to a class and in aiding the class to overcome the difficulties of the lesson in order that the class on the following day might be well prepared to recite that lesson; for the clamor against home study has forced teachers to some such practice as this. Let me add here that home study is prohibited in some cities by the authority of governing boards; and, in one instance, the state law prohibits assigning home work to pupils under fourteen years of age. And it is at fourteen that high-school work begins as a rule. Having these facts in mind I asked for a definition of the "recitation"; and I quote one which is typical. "So far as my observation and experience go, the word recitation, as used in school work, means the time in which the group of children recite directly to the teacher and is exclusive of preparation periods." Other schools that included the preparation in the number of daily recitations designated the same in the daily program sent to me, so it is not difficult to study this subject.

I have selected from the number received four daily programs. One is taken from New England, one from north of the Ohio, one west of the Mississippi, and one from the South Atlantic States. Practically a duplicate of each, however, could be found in modified forms in the North, South, East, and West.

Program I, given on the following page, shows the content of a seventh grade in a New England school:

This "Order of Exercises" shows that the day's work is divided into sixteen periods, exclusive of all recesses; two of these periods are devoted to individual study or preparation; while fourteen are given over to recitations or some order of exercise. A student entering the first grade at five years of age would be eleven years old when he reached the seventh grade. Suppose this pupil is in the first division of the history class, he is on recitation continuously from the period of opening exercises to 1:45 o'clock in the afternoon, save the recess periods. He has been on nine exercises. When did he make his preparation for the various exercises? At 1:45 he has twenty minutes study period in which to prepare his geography lesson. Then come reading and written work in order, followed by another period of fifteen minutes for individual work, and the day closes with music. The content here is great indeed,

PROGRAM I

ORDER OF EXERCISES

Of the Seventh Grade .... School
Fall Term, 1909 .... Teacher

Time			Recitations		Study	
	From	To	Class	Subject	Class	Subject
A.M.	8.30	8.40	Opening	Exercises Talks	on Phys	iology and Manners
	8.40	9.30	All	Arithmetic	All	Arithmetic
	9.30	9.35	All	Gymnastics	....	....
	9.35	10.00	All	Language	All	Language
	10.00	10.15	All	Recess	....	....
	10.15	10.40	1st Div.	History	2d Div.	History
	10.40	11.00	All	Penmanship	All	Penmanship
	11.00	11.10	All	Mental Arithmetic	....	....
	11.10	11.30	All	Spelling	All	Spelling
Thurs.	11.00	11.30	All	Drawing	....	....
P.M.	1.30	1.45	All	Music	....	....
	1.45	2.05	2d Div.	History	1st Div.	Geography
	2.05	2.30	All	Geography	....	....
	2.30	2.35	All	Recess	....	....
	2.35	2.55	1st Div.	Reading	2d Div.	Written Work
	2.55	3.15	2d Div.	Reading	1st Div.	Written Work
	2.15	2.30	All	Individual Work	....	....
	2.30	3.00	All	Music	....	....

but the quality can only be approached approximately. Here the organization keeps all the pupils together in all subjects except those of history and reading; and it is quite probable that in these exercises they all recite the same lessons, although there are two divisions of the grade.

Program II, given below, exhibits a "Daily Program" of the fifth grade, which comes from a school north of the Ohio.

Here the content, or the number of subjects for each child, is about the same as that in Program I, but the organization is vastly different. The grade is divided into two sections, and one recites while the other studies. The length of the day here is two hundred and eighty minutes, against two hundred and fifty in Program I. In arithmetic, history, physiology, geography, grammar, and reading, the two sections recite separately; but in literature, writing, music, calisthenics, spelling, individual assistance they are all grouped together. In all subjects, therefore, that require

PROGRAM II

DAILY PROGRAM

Grades 5A and 5B ....School ....Teacher

Hour			Recitation Period	Study Period
A.M.	8.45	8.50	Opening Exercises	
	8.50	9.20	Literature, Writing	Drawing
	9.20	9.40	B. Arithmetic	A. Read., Spell., Def.
	9.40	10.00	A. Arithmetic	B. Arithmetic
	10.00	10.15	B. Hist. or Physiol.	A. Arithmetic
	10.15	10.25	A. Hist. or Physiol.	B. Hist. or Physics
	10.25	10.40	Recess	
	10.40	11.00	A. and B. Music	
	11.00	11.20	B. Geography	A. Hist. or Physiol.
	11.20	11.30	Calisthenics	
	11.30	11.45	A. Geography	B. Geography
	11.45	11.55	Individual Assistance	or General Work
P.M.	1.30	1.40	Spelling	......
	1.40	2.00	B. Grammar	A. Geography
	2.00	2.20	A. Grammar	B. Grammar
	2.20	2.35	Calisthenics and Rest	......
	2.35	2.55	B. Def., Reading	A. Grammar
	2.55	3.15	A. Def., Reading	Read., Spell., and Def.
	3.15	3.25	General Work and In	dividual Instruction

much previous preparation, there are two sections; and one studies while the other recites; but in the exercises that do not demand previous preparation, except spelling, they are all grouped together. It is interesting to notice how the emphasis is placed. Twenty minutes are devoted to arithmetic; ten minutes to history; twenty minutes to music; fifteen minutes to geography; ten minutes to spelling; twenty minutes to grammar; thirty minutes to literature writing; ten minutes to calisthenics; and ten minutes to individual assistance. While one class is reciting history in the ten minutes allowed, the other class is devoting the same time to preparation; and thus the day is spent in short periods.

Program III is from the seventh grade of a school west of the Mississippi. It is as follows:

PROGRAM III

Sections 1 and 2 Seventh Grade

Time			Recite	Prepare
9.00	9.15	15	Music	
9.15	9.40	25	2. Arithmetic	1. Spelling
9.40	10.05	25	1. Arithmetic	2. Grammar
10.05	10.30	25	2. Grammar	1. Grammar
10.45	11.10	25	1. Grammar	2. History
11.10	11.35	25	2. History	1. History
11.35	12.00	25	Drawing, Tues, Thurs., Fri.	Mental Arith., Wed.; Penmanship, Fri.
1.15	1.40	25	1. History	2. Geography
1.40	2.05	25	2. Geography	1. Geography
2.05	2.30	25	1. Geography	2. Reading
2.45	3.10	25	2. Reading	1. Reading
3.10	3.35	25	1. Reading	2. Spelling
3.35	4.00	25	Spelling, Mon., Tues., Wed.	Mental Arith., Thurs., Fri.

This grade is divided into two sections, and while one recites the other prepares. The emphasis is placed on five subjects: arithmetic, grammar, history, geography, and reading. The time devoted to each subject is fifty minutes, twenty-five for study and twenty-five for recitation. Here the number of daily recitations is considerably less than is found in the other two; yet the organization of the classes is very similar to those found in Program II. The length of the school day, exclusive of all recesses, is three hundred and fifteen minutes. Although the number of subjects taught daily in this school is smaller than in either of the above, the school day is the longest.

[*To be continued*]

A STUDY OF ERRORS IN TESTS OF ADDING ABILITY[1]

C. L. PHELPS
Leland Stanford Junior University

In some of the recent tests of adding ability the results have been based almost entirely on the rapidity with which combinations were attempted and not much attention has been given to the errors that were made in taking the tests. Justification of this failure to make a careful study of errors is found in the claim that speed and accuracy show such a close positive correlation in these tests that checking for errors can safely be neglected. If this claim is true, the only remaining reason for making an analysis of errors is for diagnostic purposes. But this reason alone seemed sufficient to justify the writer in making an examination of a large amount of data in order to find out how often errors are made on the various combinations, what per cent of a group make them, how the combinations rank in difficulty, and what kind of mistakes are made on them.

SOURCE AND DESCRIPTION OF DATA

The material upon which this study is based was collected by Otis and Davidson[2] for their investigation of the reliability of standard scores as a measure of adding ability. It was collected from the eighth grade of eight of the larger grammar schools of San Jose, California, a city of about 50,000 population. It will be seen by reference to their study that their tests consisted of 25 arrangements of the combinations varying slightly in order from the Courtis Test No. 1, that the tests were one minute in length, that five were given each day for five days, that they were all given by the same person in exactly the same way, and that 270 children were thus examined.

[1] This study was suggested and guided by Professor Percy E. Davidson of Leland Stanford Junior University.

[2] "The Reliability of Standard Scores in Adding Ability," *Elementary School Teacher*, October, 1912.

Of this material the papers of 238 children have been checked for errors and the results studied. Of the 32 sets of papers rejected for this study 20 were five tests short of the full number and twelve were eliminated because they were not representative and would have vitiated the results if they had been included. For example, when it was found that the lower figure had been written for the total of several combinations in succession, it indicated that no attempt had been made to add and the sets of papers containing this error were left out. This type of error, with others which could not in fairness be included, resulted in the elimination of the twelve sets referred to as not representative. The 238 sets remaining, consisting of 5,950 tests, are considered entirely fair for the purposes of this study.

METHOD OF MARKING ERRORS AND TABULATING RESULTS

In checking the errors each paper was examined carefully and all mistakes marked. At first a separate marking was made of combinations which had been missed at the first stroke of the pencil and corrected by a second stroke. But this was later abandoned and only those errors were counted which had not been corrected at all.

When the errors were all marked, a system of tabulation was arranged in such a way that the errors on each combination could easily be totaled for each pupil as well as for the whole group. This was done for each school separately, and then the results were collected into one table which is here presented as Table I.

DISPLAY AND DISCUSSION OF TABLES

This table shows gross results just as they appeared when the first tabulation was completed. It is reproduced here in order to show how the errors were distributed among the eight schools and on the various combinations. On examination several things can be seen in regard to this point. One is that there is a rather erratic distribution of errors in the ones and twos; another is that there is a more regular distribution in the other combinations; a third is that the number of errors increases with the increase in size of the combinations; and a final one is that the errors on the doubles are almost as erratic in their distribution as on the ones and twos.

Table I takes no account, however, of the fact that in any arrangement of combinations for tests having a time limit certain

TABLE I

SHOWING ERRORS ON EACH COMBINATION FOR EACH SCHOOL AND FOR THE WHOLE GROUP

COMBINATIONS	SCHOOL No. 1	SCHOOL No. 2	SCHOOL No. 3	SCHOOL No. 4	SCHOOL No. 5	SCHOOL No. 6	SCHOOL No. 7	SCHOOL No. 8	TOTAL
	40 Pupils	12 Pupils	14 Pupils	23 Pupils	33 Pupils	48 Pupils	28 Pupils	40 Pupils	
0+0	2	2	0	0	19	0	0	0	23
0+1	1	1	0	2	5	2	3	1	15
0+2	1	1	1	1	6	1	2	3	16
0+3	0	2	1	2	5	6	1	0	17
0+4	2	1	0	1	6	1	3	0	14
0+5	4	1	2	2	9	4	7	2	31
0+6	1	1	0	0	1	0	0	0	3
0+7	0	3	0	1	5	4	1	0	14
0+8	5	1	2	2	5	12	4	6	37
0+9	0	0	0	0	4	4	1	0	9
1+1	1	4	1	1	2	1	5	1	16
1+2	1	4	0	8	8	5	4	8	38
1+3	4	2	1	7	6	18	8	7	53
1+4	8	8	7	24	22	43	12	30	154
1+5	10	16	8	11	6	16	7	12	86
1+6	22	15	4	16	21	16	21	17	132
1+7	21	17	22	19	12	19	16	18	144
1+8	6	6	2	4	3	9	5	2	37
1+9	9	6	3	4	17	11	9	6	65
2+2	6	1	3	1	4	4	0	3	22
2+3	8	7	1	4	3	3	5	1	32
2+4	6	11	2	10	5	8	7	10	59
2+5	19	9	5	8	20	14	9	18	102
2+6	7	2	3	3	10	3	11	3	42
2+7	8	17	8	11	19	32	22	41	158
2+8	3	7	1	5	8	11	6	11	52
2+9	7	6	0	7	10	13	15	13	71
3+3	15	4	2	15	5	12	19	15	87
3+4	5	1	2	1	7	13	8	3	40
3+5	10	8	14	11	9	12	8	6	78
3+6	12	15	7	6	4	11	12	4	71
3+7	8	30	11	11	7	36	11	6	120
3+8	23	34	9	21	30	44	59	11	231
3+9	48	46	16	19	39	45	52	39	304
4+4	1	2	0	0	3	0	1	0	7
4+5	3	3	2	3	4	9	12	7	43
4+6	2	12	2	7	6	4	4	4	41
4+7	21	52	12	8	8	44	50	37	232
4+8	30	23	7	14	11	21	19	17	142
4+9	32	56	23	19	11	19	22	10	192

TABLE I—*Continued*

Combinations	School No. 1 40 Pupils	School No. 2 12 Pupils	School No. 3 14 Pupils	School No. 4 23 Pupils	School No. 5 33 Pupils	School No. 6 48 Pupils	School No. 7 28 Pupils	School No. 8 40 Pupils	Total
5+5	0	0	1	1	1	0	1	0	4
5+6	17	23	5	10	15	18	22	25	135
5+7	16	35	6	11	16	13	26	11	134
5+8	78	63	26	51	24	44	58	25	369
5+9	32	41	21	47	19	30	78	30	298
6+6	2	1	1	3	1	7	1	5	21
6+7	81	11	10	13	14	24	12	21	186
6+8	14	15	0	1	6	3	18	5	62
6+9	32	98	7	35	23	50	42	33	320
7+7	2	3	2	1	5	1	2	0	16
7+8	35	11	16	6	9	18	19	23	137
7+9	71	75	5	38	61	64	40	41	395
8+8	14	11	8	20	6	22	25	12	118
8+9	14	27	3	13	31	21	20	16	145
9+9	3	0	0	3	3	3	1	5	18
Total	783	851	295	542	619	848	826	624	5,388

combinations will be attempted oftener than others because some pupils will work more rapidly than others. For this reason only approximate results can be obtained for those combinations which, in the arrangement of the tests, fall beyond the average number of attempts made by the pupils tested. Accurate results can be obtained, however, for all those combinations which fall safely within this limit. These will all receive practically an equal number of trials because of the slight variation in the order of the combinations for the different tests and because the average deviation from the central tendency with regard to the number of combinations is not high, except in one school where it amounts to 10.6 combinations. But in this case the average for the school is so far above the average for the whole group that results are not affected. In the other cases they would be affected but slightly. For combinations which do not fall within the range of average number of attempts, a certain amount of data is available and fairly accurate conclusions might be drawn concerning some of them. But it is perhaps safer to eliminate them from this consideration. Combinations affected in this way are: 0+0; 1+1; 4+4; 4+9; 5+5, and 6+8. There are also certain combinations which are repeated in inverse order within the limits noted. These have all been credited with twice as many trials as the others.

These explanations prepare the reader for Table II, which is derived from Table I. In this is shown the percentage of error made on each combination, the basis for calculation being the actual number of times it was attempted. This table is considered as fair an index to the relative difficulty of the combinations as can be derived by this method from the data at hand.

TABLE II

SHOWING PERCENTAGE OF ERRORS BASED ON THE NUMBER OF TRIALS FOR EACH COMBINATION

Combinations	Errors in Percentage	Combinations	Errors in Percentage	Combinations	Errors in Percentage
0+0	.39	2+2	.37	4+8	2.38
0+1	.25	2+3	.54	4+9	*
0+2	.14	2+4	.50	5+5	.07
0+3	.28	2+5	.86	5+6	2.27
0+4	.24	2+6	.71	5+7	2.25
0+5	.52	2+7	1.33	5+8	3.10
0+6	.05	2+8	.88	5+9	2.50
0+7	.24	2+9	1.19	6+6	.35
0+8	.62	3+3	1.46	6+7	1.56
0+9	.15	3+4	.67	6+8	1.04
1+1	.27	3+5	1.31	6+9	2.60
1+2	.64	3+6	1.19	7+7	.14
1+3	.45	3+7	2.02	7+8	2.30
1+4	1.30	3+8	1.94	7+9	3.32
1+5	.72	3+9	2.55	8+8	1.98
1+6	2.22	4+4	.12	8+9	2.44
1+7	2.42	4+5	.72	9+9	.30
1+8	.62	4+6	.69		
1+9	1.09	4+7	1.95		

* Unsatisfactory data.

But it may be held by some that the method used here is not a fair one because it is based entirely on the *number of errors* made and does not take into account the *number of children* making the errors. It may further be held that, because of the large number of trials possible, a very few repeaters could make the entire number of mistakes credited to any combination. When such a possibility suggested itself all the papers were checked again to see exactly what the facts were concerning this possibility. The findings in this search were tabulated by schools so as to show how many children missed each combination a single time and how many missed it two or more times. This table is not reproduced here, on account of lack of space, but two condensed ones, showing the rank of 20 of the combinations above the ones, are taken from it along with a similar table taken from Table II. In these three tables 20 combinations are ranked in difficulty in accord with (1) the number of times they were missed, (2) the number of children that missed them, and (3) the number of children that missed them two or more times. These tables are presented, for purposes of comparison, as Tables III*A*, III*B*, and III*C*, respectively.

TABLE III*A*

Rank	Combinations	Errors in Percentage of Attempts
1....	9+7	3.32
2....	8+5	3.10
3....	9+6	2.69
4....	9+3	2.55
5....	9+5	2.50
6....	9+8	2.44
7....	8+4	2.38
8....	8+7	2.30
9....	6+5	2.27
10....	7+5	2.25
11....	7+3	2.02
12....	8+8	1.98
13....	7+4	1.95
14....	8+3	1.94
15....	7+6	1.56
16....	3+3	1.46
17....	7+2	1.33
18....	5+3	1.31
19....	6+3	1.19
19....	9+2	1.19

TABLE III*B*

Rank	Combinations	No. of Children Making Errors	Percentage of Children Making Errors
1....	9+7	120	50.42
2....	9+3	109	45.80
3....	9+6	94	39.49
4....	8+5	91	38.23
5....	9+5	86	36.13
6....	7+6	79	33.19
6....	7+2	79	33.19
7....	8+3	74	31.09
8....	7+4	72	30.25
9....	8+8	71	29.83
10....	9+8	67	28.15
10....	8+7	67	28.15
11....	9+4	60	25.21
12....	5+2	59	24.79
13....	6+5	58	24.37
14....	8+4	52	21.85
14....	9+2	52	21.85
15....	7+5	48	20.17
15....	7+3	48	20.17
16....	6+3	44	18.48

TABLE III*C*

Rank	Combinations	No. of Children Making 2 or More Errors	Percentage of Children Making 2 or More Errors
1....	9+7	63	26.47
2....	9+3	59	24.79
3....	9+5	49	20.59
4....	8+5	47	19.75
5....	9+6	38	15.96
6....	7+4	37	15.55
7....	9+4	33	13.86
8....	8+3	32	13.44
9....	7+2	31	13.02
9....	8+7	31	13.02
10....	9+8	26	10.92
11....	7+6	25	10.50
11....	6+5	25	10.50
12....	8+8	24	10.08
13....	7+3	23	9.66
14....	8+4	21	8.82
14....	5+2	21	8.82
15....	7+5	20	8.40
16....	9+2	17	7.14
17....	8+6	15	6.30

From these tables it can be seen that there is a close correspondence in results, regardless of whether they are based on the number of times the combination was missed, on the number of children who missed it, or on the number who missed it two or more times.

It can also be seen that the higher combinations make the greatest showing of difficulty from all three points of consideration. The totals for the number of mistakes, the number of children who made them, and the number who made them repeatedly are all highest for the higher combinations.

The fact that the tests were repeated 25 times is significant in this connection. We may assume that any child might miss a combination once in 25 times on account of a slip of the pen or for some reason other than lack of knowledge of the combination, but it is not to be supposed that this would be done repeatedly. It may not be of the highest importance to note that 120 children out of 238 missed the combination 9+7, but it certainly is significant to know that 63 of them missed it two or more times. If an arbitrary standard were to be set up and it should be agreed that two or more errors in 25 chances on any combination should be taken to mean uncertainty concerning that combination, then it could be stated that from 6 per cent to 26 per cent of the children taking these tests were uncertain about some one or more of the twenty combinations included in the tables above. This would indicate that there are many children who make mistakes on the higher combinations because of lack of knowledge of them or uncertainty concerning them.

The errors on some of the combinations, especially on the ones and the doubles, seem to be out of proportion to the general indications of their difficulty, but this is because of the existence of certain *type errors*. Table IV shows the principal errors of this kind found in this study and indicates the explanation of the erratic showing of errors on certain of the combinations previously referred to.

One form of these errors is multiplication which is found mainly in the ones, though it is also found in certain other combinations. The 3+3 combination is a striking example of this. In three of the eight schools tested no other kind of mistake was made on it, while only 8 out of a total of 87 errors were due to any other cause. This kind of type error is not found in any other double, unless it is in the 2+2 where it makes no difference in the result.

In 8+8=18 a different form of type error is found which

accounts for nearly all of the mistakes made on the 8+8 combination. For example in School No. 7, 16 out of 28 children made this error one or more times.

TABLE IV

SHOWING PRINCIPAL TYPE ERRORS AS INDICATED BY THE NUMBER OF TIMES THE SAME MISTAKE WAS MADE IN EACH CASE

Combinations	School No. 1	School No. 2	School No. 3	School No. 4	School No. 5	School No. 6	School No. 7	School No. 8	Total
1+4=6	5	2	1	18	17	26	7	24	100
1+4=4	3	5	3	3	3	14	5	4	40
Miscellaneous	0	1	3	3	2	3	0	2	14
1+6=6	19	9	4	11	11	11	17	11	93
1+6=8	3	4	0	3	7	3	3	2	25
Miscellaneous	0	2	0	2	3	1	1	4	13
1+7=9	11	15	21	17	8	13	9	12	106
1+7=7	8	2	1	1	3	5	4	4	28
Miscellaneous	2	0	0	1	1	1	3	2	10
2+7=7	4	5	5	6	9	14	13	31	87
2+7=8	1	11	3	4	2	8	6	3	38
2+7=11	0	0	0	0	3	4	2	6	15
Miscellaneous	3	1	0	1	5	6	1	1	18
3+3=9	14	3	2	14	5	9	17	15	79
Miscellaneous	1	1	0	1	0	3	2	0	8
3+9=11	34	24	13	12	25	35	41	27	211
3+9=13	2	18	0	4	5	4	3	2	38
3+9=9	10	2	3	2	8	3	5	9	42
Miscellaneous	2	2	0	1	1	3	3	1	13
8+8=18	13	9	8	17	5	20	22	10	104
Miscellaneous	1	2	0	3	1	2	3	2	14

The 9+3 combination also presents peculiar results. Theoretically, 9+3 should equal 13 as often as 11. Practically, it does not. In every school 11 is strongly the favorite error, while the total shows more than 5 to 1 in its favor.

Another point of interest is shown by Table V. It can be seen from this that there is a considerable difference in the number of errors made by the different groups, the average number per child varying from 15.60 in School No. 8 to 70.92 in School No. 2. It seems significant that there should be such a wide range, but the real importance of the table becomes apparent when it is noticed that the school which had the *smallest number of errors* per pupil had the *slowest speed record*, and that the school which had the *largest number of errors* had the *highest record for speed*.

TABLE V

SHOWING AVERAGE NUMBER OF ERRORS PER PUPIL, AVERAGE NUMBER OF COMBINATIONS ATTEMPTED, AND RANK OF THE SCHOOLS ACCORDING TO SPEED AND ACCURACY

Schools	Average Number of Errors per Pupil	Rank Based on Accuracy	Average Number of Combinations per Pupil	Rank Based on Speed
1	19.57	4	69.77	5
2	70.92	8	76.08	1
3	21.07	5	71.78	3
4	23.56	6	70.13	4
5	18.76	3	73.75	2
6	17.67	2	62.04	7
7	29.50	7	68.50	6
8	15.60	1	59.82	8

From this table it is apparent that if the San Jose schools were ranked according to the number of combinations attempted in these tests and according to the errors made in the tests, the order of the schools would be almost reversed.

SUMMARY AND DISCUSSION OF RESULTS

In the introduction of this paper it was stated that this study was undertaken to find out how often errors are made on the combinations, what percentage of the group make them, how the combinations rank in difficulty, and what kind of mistakes are made on them. Something has been learned about all of these questions and the results have been presented in the foregoing tables and discussions. They may be summarized as follows:

1. Except in the zero combinations, where the errors were few, and in the ones where they were erratic because of the influence of type errors, *a fairly regular increase was found in the number of errors made and in the number of children making them as the combinations increased in size.* This finding indicates either that not enough attention has been given to the teaching of the higher combinations or that their inherent difficulty is greater than has been supposed. The fact in the case could be definitely determined

by experimentation, to the very great advantage of practice in teaching the combinations.

2. It was found that not only was there an increase in mistakes and the number of children making them as the combinations increased in size but that *a large percentage of the children* made mistakes on each of the larger combinations. On certain combinations from a *third* to a *half* made mistakes, while about half of this number made *two or more mistakes on the same combination.*

3. The rank in difficulty of the higher combinations is fairly well shown. For example, 9+7 was missed 3.32 per cent of the times it was attempted and 50.42 per cent of the children missed it. From this it can be seen that half of the children must have missed it, on the average, twice the percentage of the times credited to all. It can therefore be said that half the children taking these tests missed this combination about 6⅔ per cent of the times they attempted it. Practically the same can be said of 8+5. A third or more missed 9+6, 9+3, and 9+5 an average of at least 7½ per cent of their trials. And a fourth or more missed 9+8, 8+4, 8+7, 6+5, 7+5, 7+3, 8+8, and 7+4 an average of more than 7 per cent of their attempts. These results are derived from Tables III*A* and III*B* and, besides giving an idea of their relative difficulty, demonstrate rather clearly the lack of knowledge of the higher combinations.

4. It was found that *there were certain kinds of errors which were peculiar to certain combinations throughout all the schools tested.* These were called *type errors.* They were found to occur on several combinations and to account for a large part of the errors made on those combinations. Pedagogically, this finding is important, for, while the mere knowledge that a certain error is a *type* error may not suggest to the teacher the best method of dealing with it, it ought to prevent the ignoring of it as a slip of the pen or an accident.

In conclusion, the fact must be noted that some of the results found in this study are not in harmony with certain statements concerning tests of this kind that are widely known and relied upon. Reference is made here to two statements made by Courtis in his "Instructions for Making and Recording Scores" in giving the Courtis Standard Tests. The first statement, which applies to four of eight of the Courtis Tests, is that "Ignorance is shown, not by incorrect answers, but by reduced speed." That is, he holds that speed and accuracy in such tests show a close positive correlation. In this study no such correlation was found. *The slowest group did the most accurate work and the fastest group made the most errors.* The second statement is that "Mistakes, except for the zero combinations, are very few." In this study, mistakes were found to be *fewest in the zero combinations and to gradually increase in number as the combinations increased in size*, with certain exceptions which have been noted. And, finally, the results of this study do not justify the ranking of groups by scoring their speed record without taking into account the errors made on the tests taken. On the other hand, they indicate that speed records alone may be unfair and sometimes directly opposed, as they were in some cases in this study, to the findings of a tabulation of errors.

BOOK REVIEWS

Francis W. Parker School Year Book, Vol. II, June, 1913, 198 pages, 54 illustrations. Francis W. Parker School, Chicago.

This volume, prepared by the faculty of the Francis W. Parker School, Chicago, deals with "The Morning Exercise As a Socializing Influence in the School." It is a distinctive contribution to the literature on social education, and gives a very vivid picture of certain phases of social education as they have been worked out in this school.

This publication is not of the character of the ordinary school reports, but consists of concrete, illustrated descriptions of different pieces of work in the school as they have actually been carried on. The Francis W. Parker School, being unhampered by traditions that beset the average school, and free to experiment in the carrying-out of educational theories, constitutes a sort of educational laboratory. Through the medium of the *Year Book*, the results of the experiments are given from year to year to the educational public.

One of the chief features of the work in this school is the utilization of the social motive in the teaching of the various subjects of the curriculum, and in all the activities of the children.

In the general school assembly, or "morning exercise," the children of the various grades and groups share their experiences and knowledge with the entire school through descriptions and summaries of the work they have been doing, their games, travel, etc. Here questions relating to the school community are worked out in the "town meeting," and other forms of exercises. The great floods of inspiration that go coursing through the school find their chief origin here. And through the morning exercises the big children and little, as well as the entire faculty, are brought together and their interests molded into those of one big family.

Volume II of the *Year Book* describes the morning exercises as they are conducted in the school. It contains a brief history of the morning exercise, an article on the purposes and values of the morning exercise, six articles showing concretely types of preparation of morning exercises that have been given in the school, verbatim reports of a large number of exercises, exercises for special days, a classified list of nearly three hundred typical exercises that have been given in the school, and other valuable material.

The Authors

Sixth Annual Report on the Medical Inspection of School Children in Dunfermline, 1911–12. By L. D. Cruikshank, M.D. Pp. 120. Published under Carnegie Dunfermline Trust by Turnbull & Spears, Edinburgh.

The public-school system of Dunfermline, Scotland, with a population of 5,417 school children showing a percentage of attendance of 90.2 is represented in this report. The medical service of these schools consists of inspection of the physical condition of the children, each child having a careful medical examination upon entrance, upon passing into the Senior division, at 11 years of age, and just before leaving school.

The examination includes height, weight, nutrition, cleanliness, the skin, adenoids, tonsils, glands, hearing, speech, mentality, heart and circulation, lungs, and nervous system. Special attention is given to tuberculosis and other infectious diseases, deformities, and the eyes.

After medical inspection, the case is followed up in the home by the school nurse and by the Civic Guild, a voluntary body organized to look after the social well-being of the citizens of Dunfermline, especially "the necessitous and suffering children." There were 556 such visits paid. When the routine school examination cannot be made sufficiently thorough, the child is sent to the School Clinic, where the case is studied in the medical, dental, or eye department. If there is no family physician the Clinic advises with the parents, teachers, or others directly interested in the child and institutes necessary treatment—the Clinic being equipped to provide medicine, to prescribe and furnish eye-glasses, and to handle orthopedic defects by special medical gymnastics in a department well appointed with Swedish apparatus for the work. Medical gymnastics is regarded as supplementary to the educational gymnastics which is systematically carried on in all the schools. Dunfermline is fortunate in the assistance of the Trustees of the Carnegie Fund, who have voted £20,000 for the establishment of a fully equipped School Clinic and College of Hygiene.

Careful survey is made of the school buildings by the architect and medical inspector with especial regard to overcrowding, sanitary conveniences, lavatories, drinking-water, cloak rooms, and the doors, desks, seats, gangways, heating, lighting, ventilation, and schoolroom apparatus of the classrooms and gymnasia.

The report urges the importance of providing experimental and open-air schools for the prevention of tuberculosis and its cure, emphasizing the battle note of modern medicine—prevention, and in conclusion raises the hygienic ideal for every growing child to that of "abundant health."

Josephine Young

University of Chicago

The Newton Public Schools, Annual Report of Superintendent F. E. Spaulding to the School Committee. Published by the School Committee, Newton, Mass., 1912. Pp. 151. Paper.

The Annual Report of Mr. F. E. Spaulding, superintendent of the schools of Newton, Massachusetts, has just appeared. In this report, he not only holds to the high standard set by his reports for several years past, but here surpasses his own previous best work in many ways. So far as it goes—and as compared with the usual report it goes a very long way—it is a model of what a school report should be. It is a publicity message from the superintendent of the city schools to his constituency which shows simply, accurately, and clearly just what the schools are attempting, where the emphases are being placed, where the moneys are being expended, where economies are being attempted, and the plans that are being made for the future.

The report presents certain questions in terms that the layman can understand; it answers those that the superintendent is expected to answer, and presents the facts needed by the layman for answering the questions asked of him. Some of the questions are: What are the Newton schools trying to do? With what success? Do you approve their policy? Is it carried out economically? Is it administered efficiently? Can we afford to continue it? Can we afford not to continue it?

Mr. Spaulding prefaces the chapter which deals with the efficiency of the schools with a statement that is remarkable for its practical and scientific—the two are one—modernity:

"The progressive improvement of a school system demands that the following essentials of scientific management be applied incessantly: (1) the measurement and comparison of comparable results; (2) the analysis and comparison of conditions under which given results are secured—especially of the means and time employed in securing given results; (3) the consistent adoption and use of those means that justify themselves most fully by their results, abandoning those that fail so to justify themselves. The measurement of measurable educational results by suitable standards need limit those results to the dimensions of the standards no more than the measurement of a child's height limits his growth to the dimensions of the yard-stick."

As our profession carries out the implications of these principles, we shall during the process develop educational science to the degree that will permit for educational labor that of which we now hear much and see little, namely, scientific management.

J. F. Bobbitt

University of Chicago

BOOKS RECEIVED

MACMILLAN, NEW YORK

Everyday English. Book Two. By Franklin L. Baker and Ashley H. Thorndike. Cloth. Pp. 336. Illustrated.

The Way to the Heart of the Pupil. By Dr. Hermann Weimer. Authorized Translation by J. Remsen Bishop and Adolph Neiderpruem. Cloth. Pp. 178.

Moral Training in the School and Home. By E. Hershey Sneath and George Hodges. Cloth. Pp. 219.

The Golden Deed Book (The Golden Rule Series). By E. Hershey Sneath, George Hodges, and Edward Lawrence Stevens. Cloth. Pp. 351. Illustrated.

The Idea of the Industrial School. By Georg Kerschensteiner. Translated by Rudolf Pintner. Cloth. Pp. 110. Price $0.50 net.

Stories of the Spanish Main. Adapted from Frank R. Stockton's *Buccaneers and Pirates of Our Coast.* Cloth. Pp. 232. Illustrated. Price $0.40 net.

RAND McNALLY & CO., NEW YORK

Lucita, A Child's Story of Old Mexico. By Ruth Gaines. Cloth. Pp. 127. Illustrated. Price $0.50.

Southern Literary Readings. Edited by Leonidas Warren Payne, Jr. Cloth. Pp. 501. Illustrated. Price $0.75.

HOUGHTON MIFFLIN CO., BOSTON

Eighth Reader (The Riverside Readers). By James Van Sickle and Wilhelmina Seegmiller. Cloth. Pp. 310. Illustrated. Price $0.60.

The Home School (Riverside Educational Monographs). By Ada Wilson Trowbridge. Cloth. Pp. 95. Price $0.60.

LAIRD & LEE, CHICAGO

Webster's New Standard Dictionary. Students' Common High-School Edition. Half Leather. Pp. 752.

Webster's New Standard Dictionary. High-School and Collegiate Edition. Flexible Leather. Pp. 1049. Illustrated. Price $3.50.

George Washington (Historic Americans Series). By EUGENE PARSONS. Cloth. Pp. 184. Illustrated. Price $0.75.

Thomas Jefferson (Historic Americans Series). By EDWARD S. ELLIS, A.M. Cloth. Pp. 180. Illustrated. Price $0.75.

Abraham Lincoln (Historic Americans Series). By ROBERT DICKINSON SHEPPARD, D.D. Cloth. Pp. 179. Price $0.75.

William McKinley (Historic Americans Series). By EDWARD T. ROE, LL.B. Cloth. Pp. 193. Illustrated. Price $0.75.

HENRY HOLT & CO., NEW YORK

Rhetoric and the Study of Literature. By ALFRED M. HITCHCOCK. Cloth. Pp. 410. Price $1.00.

CHARLES E. MERRILL CO., NEW YORK

Stories from the Far East. Translated and arranged by ROLAND G. KENT, PH.D., and I. FREEMAN HALL. Cloth. Pp. 153. Illustrated. Price $0.30.

THE CENTURY CO., NEW YORK

Arithmetic by Practice. By D. W. WERREMEYER. Cloth. Pp. 80.

PUTNAM, NEW YORK

The Vikings. By ALLEN MAWER, M.A. Cloth. Pp. 150. Illustrated. Price $0.40 net.

The Icelandic Sagas. By W. A. CRAIGIE, LL.D. Cloth. Pp. 120. Illustrated. Price $0.40 net.

CURRENT EDUCATIONAL LITERATURE IN THE PERIODICALS[1]

IRENE WARREN
Librarian, School of Education, University of Chicago

Aldrich, F. R. Industrial education in the early nineteenth century. El. School T. 13:478–85. (Je. '13.)

Atwood, Wallace W. A new way of studying astronomy. Sci. Am. 108:557–58. (21 Je. '13.)

Bagley, W. C. Do the high schools need reconstruction for social ends? Relig. Educa. 8:176–83. (Je. '13.)

Bailey, Thomas P. Mood in monologue. Pedagog. Sem. 20:222–28. (Je. '13.)

Bancroft, Jessie H. New efficiency methods for training the posture of school children. Am. Phys. Educa. R. 18:309–12. (My. '13.)

Bawden, William T. Wentworth Institute. Voca. Educa. 2:357–73. (My. '13.)

Belcher, Katharine F. The Sabbatical year for the public school teacher. Educa. R. 45:471–84. (My. '13.)

Beulah Miller as a scientist saw her. Lit. D. 46:1087–91. (10 My. '13.)

Bevard, Katherine H. Progress of repeaters of the class of 1912 of the public schools of Washington, D.C. Psychol. Clinic 7:68–83. (My. '13.)

Brandon, Edgar Ewing. The largest Latin-American university. Educa. R. 46:31–38. (Je. '13.)

Brereton, Cloudesley. The character-forming influence of vocational education. Educa. R. 45:501–6. (My. '13.)

Butler, Nathaniel. Report of the Twenty-fifth Educational Conference of the Secondary Schools in Relations with the University of Chicago. School R. 21:398–411. (Je. '13.)

[1] *Abbreviations:*—Am. J. of Psychol., American Journal of Psychology; Am. Phys. Educa. R., American Physical Educational Review; Educa., Education; Educa. R., Educational Review; El. School T., Elementary School Teacher; Geographical T., Geographical Teacher; Harp. W., Harper's Weekly; J. of Educa. (Bost.), Journal of Education (Boston); J. of Educa. Psychol., Journal of Educational Psychology; J. of Home Econ., Journal of Home Economics; Lit. D., Literary Digest; Liv. Age, Living Age; Man. Train. M., Manual Training Magazine; Outl., Outlook; Pedagog. Sem., Pedagogical Seminary; Pop. Sci. Mo., Popular Science Monthly; Pri. Educa., Primary Education; Psychol. Clinic, Psychological Clinic; Relig. Educa., Religious Education; School R., School Review; School W., School World; Sci. Am., Scientific American; Teach. Coll. Rec., Teachers College Record; Tech. World M., Technical World Magazine; Voca. Educa., Vocational Education.

Carmichael, R. D. The meaning of graduate study. Science 37:738–43. (16 My. '13.)

Chickering, Edward C. Efficiency methods in Latin teaching. Educa. R. 46:15–24. (Je. '13.)

Children's reading. Harp. W. 57:6. (31 My. '13.)

(The) coming International Congress on School Hygiene. Pedagog. Sem. 20: 267–70. (Je. '13.)

Cook, W. A. The problem of sex education. J. of Educa. Psychol. 4:253–60. (My. '13.)

Cope, Henry F. Ten years progress in religious education. Relig. Educa. 8:117–49. (Je. '13.)

Courtis, S. A. The reliability of single measurements with standard tests. El. School T. 13:486–504. (Je. '13.)

Crawshaw, Fred D., and Phillips, J. D. Report of a committee on mechanical drawing for high schools. II. Man. Train. M. 14:458–65. (Je. '13.)

Curry, H. Ida. County agencies for dependent children of state charities aid association of New York. Child (Chicago) 2:22–24. (Jl. '13.)

Dearborn, George V. N. Notes on school-life hygiene. Pedagog. Sem. 20: 209–21. (Je. '13.)

Dewey, John. An undemocratic proposal. Voca. Educa. 2:374–77. (My. '13.)

Donovan, M. E., and Thorndike, Edward L. Improvement in a practice experiment under school conditions. Am. J. of Psychol. 24:426–28. (Jl. '13.)

Enright, H. G. Census to save the babies. Tech. World M. 19:539–42. (Je. '13.)

(The) eye and the printed page. Educa. 33:552–69. (My. '13.)

Whipple, Guy Montrose. The eye movements in reading.
Briggs, Thomas H. The right way to read.
Koopman, Harry Lyman. How students actually read.

Faddis, Jennie Rebecca. Our play day. Pri. Educa. 21:331–33. (Je. '13.)

Frederick, Frank Forrest. Co-operation between the school and the shop. Voca. Educa. 2:414–17. (My. '13.)

Grady, William E. Curriculum making. Psychol. Clinic 7:57–67. (My. '13.)

Greater flexibility in college entrance requirements. Educa. 33:527–51. (My. '13.)

Holmes, William H. The needs of the high school.
Huntington, Henry B. The attitude of the colleges.
Davis, Harvey N. The new Harvard plan.

Hadley, Arthur T. The relation of science to higher education in America. Science 37:775–79. (23 My. '13.)

Hall, Winfield S. Conservation of the child as related to social ethics. Child (Chicago) 2:7–14. (Jl. '13.)

Handschin, Charles Hart. The American college as it looks from the inside. Pop. Sci. Mo. 82:556–58. (Je. '13.)

Harper, Carrie A. A feminine professorial viewpoint. Educa. R. 46:47–51. (Je. '13.)

Hemmingway, William. Building men—not champions. Harp. W. 57:11. (14 Je. '13.)

Hirshberg, Leonard Keene. "Dog Latin" and sparrow languages used by Baltimore children. Pedagog. Sem. 20:257–58. (Je. '13.)

Hodgkins, Louise Manning. The higher education of women in 1912. Educa. 33:610–15. (Je. '13.)

Holbrook, Sara M. The home environment as affecting the physical and mental growth of school children. J. of Home Econ. 5:211–17. (Je. '13.)

Horace Mann Elementary School Teachers. Curriculum of the Horace Mann Elementary School. Arithmetic, geography, history and music. Teach. Coll. Rec. 14:1–76. (Mr. '13.)

Howard, Frank E. Psychological differences between children and adults. Pedagog. Sem. 20:236–53. (Je. '13.)

Hurt, Huber William. Vocational guidance in college. Voca. Educa. 2:411–13. (My. '13.)

Kelly, Amy. Novel-reading for high-school girls. Home Progress 2:34–40. (Jl. '13.)

Kuhlmann, F. The results of grading thirteen hundred feeble-minded children with the Binet-Simon tests. J. of Educa. Psychol. 4:261–68. (My. '13.)

Kuo, P. W. Effect of the revolution upon educational system of China. Educa. R. 45:457–70. (My. '13.)

Leavitt, Frank M. The reorganization of secondary education. III. J. of Educa. (Boston) 78:44–45. (10 Jl. '13.)

———. Vocational guidance and the manual arts. Man. Train. M. 14:423–30. (Je. '13.)

Lindsey, Ben S., and Creel, George. Children in bondage. Good Housekeeping 57:15–22. (Jl. '13.)

Macdonald, Greville. The fairy tale in education. Liv. Age 277:783–90. (28 Je. '13.)

Mackinder, H. J. The teaching of geography and history as a combined subject. Geographical T. 7:4–19. (Spring, 1913.)

MacLear, Martha. My mind and I and the kindergarten. Pedagog. Sem. 20:254–56. (Je. '13.)

Mall, F. P. University education in London. Science 38:33–39. (11 Jl. '13.)

Mangold, George B. A new line of attack on infant mortality. Child (Chicago) 2:25–27. (Jl. '13.)

Marrinan, John J. The children and religion. Pedagog. Sem. 20:229–35. (Je. '13.)

———. Vocational education for the rural school. Educa. R. 44:39–46. (Je. '13.)

Meighan, Charles W. Where schools make men. Tech. World M. 19:692–95. (Jl. '13.)

Mentre, Francois. The A B C of a philosophy of handwork. Man. Train. M. 14:431–33. (Je. '13.)

Model for rural open air school. Child (Chicago) 2:34–36. (Jl. '13.)

Moore, E. S. Lecture and recitation methods in university instruction. Science 37:929–32. (20 Je. '13.)

More, Paul E. The paradox of Oxford. School R. 21:369–87. (Je. '13.)

Morrison, Richard. Bringing the stars to earth. Tech. World M. 19:772–75. (Jl. '13.)

Muir, James N. How to determine normal progress in school. Educa. R. 46:10–14. (Je. '13.)

Munroe, James P. The business man and the high-school graduate. Pop. Sci. Mo. 83:73–80. (Jl. '13.)

Oliphant, James. Secretarial training for girls. School W. 15:241–43. (Jl. '13.)

Papillon, Thomas L. What is going on at Oxford. Educa. R. 45:433–43. (My. '13.)

Pintner, Rudolf. Oral and silent reading of fourth grade pupils. J. of Educa. Psychol. 4:333–37. (Je. '13.)

Pope, Elfrieda Hochbaum. Women teachers and equal pay. Pop. Sci. Mo. 83:65–72. (Jl. '13.)

Prosser, Charles A. The meaning of industrial education. Voca. Educa. 2:401–10. (My. '13.)

Pulsifer, Harold Trowbridge. Poetry and the school. Outl. 104:521–23. (5 Jl. '13.)

Putnam, George A. The women's institutes of Ontario. J. of Home Econ. 5:197–203. (Je. '13.)

Roman, Frederick W. Control of the industrial schools of Germany once more. El. School T. 13:469–74. (Je. '13.)

Roosevelt, Theodore. The high school and the college. Outl. 104:66–68. (10 My. '13.)

Rowe, Eugene C., and Rowe, Helen Niles. The vocabulary of a child at four and six years of age. Pedagog. Sem. 20:187–208. (Je. '13.)

Rynearson, Edward. Do the high schools need reconstruction for social ends? Relig. Educa. 8:176–83. (Je. '13.)

Schuster, Arthur. The National Academy of Sciences: international co-operation in research. Science 37:691–701. (9 My. '13.)

Scott, Jonathan F. Economic reasons for vocational education. Pedagog. Sem. 20:259–67. (Je. '13.)

Selvidge, Robert W. The culture elements in the manual arts. Man. Train. M. 14:413–16. (Je. '13.)

Should he have told? A question of conduct. Outl. 104:563–68. (12 Jl. '13.)

Slingerland, W. H. The defective child of the twentieth century. Child (Chicago) 2:37–43. (Jl.' 13.)

Social service and the public schools. Lit. D. 46:1230. (31 My. '13.)

Stearns, Wallace N. What does it cost to build a college? Educa. 33:616–18. (Je. '13.)

Stevens, Ellen Yale. The Montessori movement in America. McClure 41:84, 86, 89, 92, 94. (Je. '13.)

Sutton, William S. Some principles of moral instruction. Educa. R. 46:1–9. (Je. '13.)

Talbot, Marion. The vocational and cultural value of domestic science. J. of Home Econ. 5:232–36. (Je. '13.)

Tassin, Algernon. The disclosures of a college elocution class. Educa. R. 45:485–500. (My. '13.)

Terman, Lewis M., and Hocking, Adeline. The sleep of school children, its distribution according to age, and its relation to physical and mental efficiency. J. of Educa. Psychol. 4:269–82. (My. '13.)

Tests of school efficiency. By an ex-teacher. Educa. 33:604–9. (Je. '13.)

Titchener, E. B. The method of examination. Am. J. of Psychol. 2:429–40. (Jl. '13.)

Tombo, Rudolph, Jr. German and Swiss university statistics. Science 38: 77–78. (18 Jl. '13.)

Vaughn, S. J. The moral significance of the vocational motive. Educa. 33:591–603. (Je. '13.)

Weeks, Arland D. A summer school poet. Educa. R. 46:25–30. (Je. '13.)

Wheeler, Charles G. A manual training workshop built by grammar school pupils. Man. Train. M. 14:417–22. (Je. '13.)

When corporal punishment for children is right. Outl. 104:523–26. (5 Jl. '13.)

White, Frank R. Industrial education in the Philippine Islands. II. Voca. Educa. 2:378–400. (My. '13.)

Wilkin, Robert J. Children's courts. Child (Chicago) 2:28–29. (Jl. '13.)

Willard, Meriel W. Training high-school girls for trade work. J. of Home Econ. 5:219–23. (Je. '13.)

Winship, A. E. Rural Cook County's leadership. J. of Educa. (Bost.) 77:693–96, 707–8. (19 Je. '13.)

Witter, John H. The Chicago boy's club. Child (Chicago) 2:30–32. (Jl. '13.)

Wolfson, Arthur M. Efficiency of the history recitation. Educa. R. 45:444–56. (My. '13.)

Yamada, Soshichi. A study of questioning. Pedagog. Sem. 20:129–86. (Je. '13.)

Yoakum, C. S., and Calfee, Marguerite. An analysis of the mirror drawing experiment. J. of Educa. Psychol. 4:283–92. (My. '13.)

VOLUME XIV NUMBER 2

THE ELEMENTARY SCHOOL TEACHER

OCTOBER 1913

EDUCATIONAL NEWS AND EDITORIAL COMMENT

A statement of the work of the Educational Museum of St. Louis is given as follows by the director of this museum:

Educational Museums

The Educational Museum of the St. Louis public schools has now been in existence for six or seven years and is providing a service of increasing importance to schools by furnishing various kinds of teaching materials for use in schoolrooms. The collections are stored in a central warehouse, are made accessible to the individual grade teacher by a catalogue, and are sent out on requisition. The demand for exhibits is growing rapidly as is evidenced by the following figures: 26,123, 1909–10; 38,803, 1910–11; 50,042, 1911–12.

A similar statement is clipped from the *Register* of Des Moines, Ia., indicating that the movement of equipping schools with concrete material is spreading:

The Des Moines public schools will have an educational museum according to an announcement made yesterday.

The museum which will be established at a central station, probably at the Garfield school building, will be transferred from school to school when desired for supplementary classroom work. It will be so arranged as to be of interest to older persons. The American Society of Physical Research will aid Des Moines in the establishment of this permanent museum of mineral, animal, and plant life.

The museum will revolutionize the study of geography in the public schools. Formerly when a pupil studied the products of Iowa he depended upon a book to tell him that this was a great corn state but could, in emergency, produce its share of wheat and other things. He recited from the book and promptly forgot it.

In the future the teacher will turn in an order for the chief products of Iowa. There will be a relief map to show the topography, and the children begin by reasoning out what ought to be the industries of the state. They will take into consideration the climate and soil and the facts they have learned of neighboring states. They will naturally decide that Iowa produces corn and wheat or will decide or be told that it mines large quantities of soft coal. Here is an opportunity for a lesson on corn. It may happen that all of the coal and wheat exhibits are in use elsewhere.

The teacher will have a great deal of latitude in the selection of the point which she wishes to emphasize, and in this way a small number of sets of each material can be made to serve the sixty-eight schools. The friends and enemies of wheat and corn—insect pests and the birds that destroy these insects—will be studied. This brings in the bird and entomology collections.

The teacher sends in a request for mounted specimens of the birds that frequent the corn fields. There is the crow that pulls up the young corn for the sake of eating the sprouting grain. Then there will be the meadow lark, the thrush, and the quail.

Improving the Teaching Profession

The following note, extracted from the bulletin issued by the Bureau of Education on *Special Features in City Schools*, is of general interest because it deals with the problem of the professional standing of teacher and the returns which can be made to teachers for their services in forms other than through the increase in salary. Superintendent Brubacher, of the schools of Schenectady, reports that in order to promote the standard of teaching the teachers of Schenectady are allowed a sabbatical year for study and travel with one-third payment of salary. The conditions are as follows:

The teacher must map out a course of study in some recognized institution of learning and have it approved by the superintendent of schools in advance. In cases of travel her itinerary must be approved in the same way. A teacher may have such sabbatical year once in ten years and in exceptional cases once in seven years.

Each teacher accepting such leave of absence agrees to teach in the Schenectady schools for at least three years. If she fails to return after the leave of absence she refunds the amount of salary advanced. If she leaves after less than three years' service she refunds a pro rata amount of the salary advanced. These provisions have been accepted by many of the Schenectady teachers.

Such a device for making the teaching profession attractive undoubtedly is wise in all respects. It gives teachers the kind of training which will increase their efficiency, and at the same time gives them a privilege which will be appreciated by many who can afford to take advantage of the temporary reduction in salary if they feel sure that they can come back to an assured position in the schools that they have been serving.

The same bulletin gives several statements from different parts of the country with regard to the grounds on which teachers may be promoted, including among other qualifications professional ability and length of experience. Superintendent J. H. Risley, of Owensboro, Ky., presents the following classification which may be selected as worth quoting in detail:

CLASS C

To be eligible to class C, a teacher must have the following qualifications:

1. Graduation from an accredited high school or recognized equivalent.

2. A minimum of 20 weeks' study in some standard normal school or college. The course must include some observation work or practice teaching.

3. A state or city certificate.

CLASS B

To be eligible to class B, the teacher must have the following qualifications:

1. Graduation from an accredited high school or recognized equivalent.

2. A minimum of 36 weeks' study in a standard normal school or college. At least one-fourth of this work must be along professional lines and must include both observation work and practice teaching.

3. Experience of 27 months or more in Owensboro city schools or schools of equal standing.

4. A success grade of 85 or above.

5. A state or city certificate.

CLASS A

To be eligible to class A, the teacher must have the following qualifications:

1. Graduation from an accredited high school or recognized equivalent.

2. Graduation from an accredited normal school or college requiring at least a two years' course above the accredited high school. One-fourth of this work must be along professional lines and must include at least 20 weeks of observation work and practice teaching.

3. Experience, 45 months or more in Owensboro schools or schools of equal standing.

4. A success grade of 95 or above.

5. A life state diploma or certificate.

Class B carries $15 more per month than class C for grades 1, 5, 6, 7, 8, and $12.50 more for grades 2, 3, 4.

Class A carries $10 more per month than class B for grades 1, 5, 6, 7, 8, and $7.50 more for grades 2, 3, 4.

The only feature of this classification which does not commend itself to immediate approval is the discrimination against grades 2, 3, and 4.

School Social Centers

Three hundred and thirty-eight schools in 101 cities of the United States were used as social centers during the past season, according to a report compiled by Clarence Arthur Perry for the Sage Foundation. Officials of the United States Bureau of Education, who have examined the report, declare that it is bound to stimulate interest in this rapidly developing phase of the movement for wider use of the school plant.

Mr. Perry finds that in 44 of the 101 cities social centers were directed by paid workers. New York had 48 such centers and Chicago 16, while Philadelphia, Boston, Columbus, Detroit, Jersey City, Louisville, Rochester, and Trenton are also among the cities included in this list. There is wide variation in the length of the season, from five or six weeks in some localities to the full school term in others. In fact, little uniformity prevails as to what constitutes a social center. Mr. Perry presents in the report a tentative definition of a social center as follows: "A community may be said to have a schoolhouse social center if one of its school buildings is thrown open to the public on one or more fixed nights a week, for at least twelve weeks a year, for activities of a social, recreational, or civic character, regularly directed by one or more trained leaders."

The report also presents data on the growing use of school buildings for political meetings. In Cleveland, Ohio, meetings were held in the schools to discuss the new constitutional provisions that were before the people for adoption. In Jersey City the public schools were opened to partisan political meetings with gratifying results; eight public-school auditoriums in New York City were also opened for the same purpose, and in Chicago the assembly halls were employed for political rallies and proved a distinctly popular innovation. Milwaukee, Wis., and Worcester, Mass., are cities where the schools have for some time been used for political meeting places.

The use of schools as polling-places is another recent development. Thirty schools in Los Angeles were used for this purpose in 1911. In the past year Milwaukee began using the basements of school buildings as polling-places. In New York the commissioner of accounts recommended that the school buildings be used for registration booths throughout the city, declaring that the plan would mean the saving of a considerable part of the hundred thousand dollars expended for rental every year. Definite adoption of the idea of schools as polling-places is reported from Boston, Mass., Berkeley and Long Beach, Cal., Grand Rapids, Mich., Madison, Wis., and Salt Lake City, Utah.

Preservation of Health as a Profession

This autumn Harvard University and Massachusetts School of Technology will join in a school for the training of health officers. This school is not designed to do merely the work of a medical school, nor, on the other hand, will it confine itself to the training of engineers. It will issue a certificate which will be called the Certificate of Public Health. Candidates for this certificate need not necessarily have a medical degree, but it is expected that in the majority of cases a medical degree will precede the training given in this special school. Students taking the courses will be prepared to organize communities from the engineering and medical point of view for the purpose of preventing disease and for the purpose of removing all of the conditions of disease. In connection with the hygiene movement in the schools and throughout the country it is very significant that two of the leading institutions of the country should join in adopting vigorous measures for the training of a special group of officers. Doubtless communities will find it in the future quite as important to have such officers as these as to provide the regular civic officers now known in city and town organization.

A Course for Vocational Schools

The state department of education of Indiana has issued, in compliance with the requirements of the new law, a statement of those courses which satisfy the demands of this new law for industrial and agricultural work throughout the state. The book is compiled by the state department under the immediate direction of the deputy superintendent of education, Mr. William F. Book. Mr. Book brings to the task the training of a scientific student. He has had the co-operation of the other members of the state department. This general outline of an industrial course will undoubtedly be scrutinized with great interest by students of the problem throughout the United States. Indiana promises to stand as the conspicuous example of a vigorous effort to solve this problem by co-operation of the state with the local schools under the general supervision of a strong state department. It is too early to pass judgment upon the courses here outlined. It will undoubtedly be of interest to many of the readers of this journal to secure copies of this statement for purposes of careful study.

Circulating Educational Library

The state department of education in Pennsylvania has prepared a special circulating library for teachers and others who are interested in educational matters. In making announcement about this library the state department calls attention to the fact that many people who are interested in education find it difficult to get the latest sources of information. Not only are teachers and superintendents desirous of this information at times for purposes of presenting the information to their communities, but laymen as well are frequently desirous of referring to recent educational literature. This literature is now to be made accessible in the form of special books, pamphlets, and even clippings and reference lists which will be supplied by the state department to all students of education throughout the state. The library will also furnish teachers with the opportunity of continuing their professional study. The books will be circulated from Harrisburg on request sent to the state department.

State Aid

No better simple illustration could be given of the relation between state aid and local schools than that which is presented in the following news item clipped from the *Star*, of Kansas City:

> Those Kansas school districts which have been hit hardest by the dry weather will not shorten the school terms. Kansas is insisting upon every boy and girl being allowed to attend a good school for not less than seven months in the year.

The state will pay a part of the expenses of the school districts of western Kansas where the crops have not been good this year and were not the best for the last two seasons. The state has $50,000 a year to spend helping these school districts to see that they provide a good teacher for seven months of a school term. It doesn't make any difference how many pupils there are in the district, everyone of school age is to have an opportunity to go to school whether or not there are good crops.

"Don't worry about the school money," Superintendent Ross has told the school officials. "The state wants every boy and girl to have opportunities for a good education. The state has a fund appropriated by each legislature to help out school districts in your condition. Each school district should obtain as much money as it can for school purposes. If that isn't enough to pay the salary of a good teacher and the running expenses of the school for the entire seven months the state and county will help out by paying the balance. The state pays two-thirds of whatever additional money is required, and the county will pay the other third."

The state as a whole is so much concerned with the education of the child in any district in the state that when a given district finds itself financially embarrassed it becomes the function of the state as a whole to provide the means of carrying on regular and efficient schools. Indeed the presentation of the Page bill to the Congress of the United States raises the general question whether in many respects the federal government is not related to the various states exactly as in this particular instance the state department of Kansas is related to the local communities that are not able to conduct, during the coming year, schools of a degree of efficiency to be satisfactory to the state government.

The Lengthened School Year

Superintendent L. J. Montgomery, of South Bend, Ind., reports the following details of an experiment carried on during the past summer in conducting the work of the public schools so as to lengthen the school year:

We opened all grades and high-school work the Monday following the close of regular school year and continued for eight weeks. Work was offered in every department except kindergarten and this was only because of lack of funds. Those who failed or had done rather weak work during the year were especially urged to attend this summer term, but all others were welcomed and as much individual attention was given to each pupil as possible. Classes were somewhat smaller than during the regular term. A total of 2,400 pupils were enrolled with an average daily attendance of 1,762. This large percentage of attendance was obtained, of course, without the use of any truancy officers, which I think shows not only the great need of such work, but also the interest and willingness of children and parents. In the grades 927 credits were obtained, which otherwise would have been obtained this next semester, and in addition to this, 140 credits in high school. Seventy-five teachers in all were employed and on no day did the attendance run below 1,550. Teachers who were employed feel that the children received a great deal of help and will do much better work the following term. No great inconvenience was felt on account of the excessive heat, as we had only forenoon sessions from eight to twelve. The greatest result, and perhaps the one which is the least likely to attract attention, will be found in the better work done by the children in September. Considering the cost which is necessary to obtain such number of credits during the regular school year, the school city was saved something over $5,000 by obtaining these credits during the summer session when there was no additional expense for light, heat, and janitor service.

Ninth Year in Elementary Schools

Two news items from different parts of the country indicate the interest of elementary school officers in the general question of the upper grades. In Harrisburg, Pa., the school system is dropping the ninth year from the elementary-school course. Up to this time there have been nine grades in the elementary school. Under the new course the fifth grade of next year wi l be given some sixth-grade work to do along with the usual fifth-grade work. Each year more advanced work will be added, until in 1916 the class that will enter the high school will be made up of the present fifth and sixth grades. In many parts of the country it will seem very curious to consider the possibility of a nine-year school course. Such a long course, as indicated in the last number of the *Elementary School Teacher*, is now, however, still carried on in many quarters. On the other hand, an interesting effort to develop the elementary school beyond its present compass is reported from Hutchinson, Kan. The following statement of the case indicates the necessity in that part of the country of more work in the district schools:

Because a large percentage of the boys and girls who finish the district schools of the country do not go on into the high school, County Superintendent S. P. Rowland has decided to inaugurate an innovation in the country school this year.

A postgraduate course will be added to the district schools, and all common-school graduates who for some reason or other do not go on into the high school can take another year of work in the district school, in the home district.

"If the pupil is going on into the high school our common-school course is complete enough, but if he is going to quit school, if this common-school course is to be the extent of his education, he should have a more thorough finishing, what we might call a postgraduate course," said the county superintendent.

This will include the regular work in arithmetic, plus a course in special farm arithmetic; and regular work in civics, agriculture, grammar, classics, and United States history, plus additional work in each.

The postgraduate course will not require any additional teachers in the schools, but will be a great advantage to the common-school graduates. They will be required to take the examination in the spring, the same as the regular graduates, and on getting a minimum of 80 and an average of 90 they will be given certificates of attainment.

There were 218 graduates last spring from the district schools of the county. Only a part of these will go on into the high school, either in the county high school at Nickerson, or in the high schools of Hutchinson or other towns.

It is for the benefit of the rest, those who will not round out their public-school education with the high-school course, that this extra year's work in the district school is intended.

Mr. Rowland will keep a close check on the 218 boys and girls who finished the district school work this spring.

"I want to find out just what they are doing, whether they are going on into high school, or quitting school entirely," said the county superintendent. "I would encourage every one to go on through high school. But if they can't, they ought, by all means, to take this extra year's work in the district school."

Such an organization of an additional grade as this makes a nine-year school of an entirely different type from that which is being discontinued at Harrisburg, Pa. There is a groove here which is to be compared to the original development of the American academy or the American high school, the elementary school providing in this case somewhat further work for those who cannot go into a regularly organized secondary school. This movement for the recognition of a local need of more popular education can properly be compared also to another movement which is widespread. The movement here referred to is that of segregating the upper grades of the elementary school into a separate school. A good illustration of this is to be found in New York City, where two of the new schools that are just being provided will be devoted entirely to the upper grades. The upper grades will be drawn from neighboring schools so as to make up here an intermediate school for older pupils. Evidently the beginnings of a junior high-school movement are to be seen in this specialization of elementary schools in New York City.

The Boy Scout Movement

The President of the United States has interested himself during the summer in the Boy Scout movement. He is the honorary president of this organization and in that position has sent to all the boys who are beginning school work this autumn the following message:

THE WHITE HOUSE
WASHINGTON, D.C.

Boys' Life, 200 Fifth Avenue, New York City:

My warmest greetings to the boys on their return to school. May the year bring them every good thing and strengthen them in all the ideals of their service. It is a pleasure to me to be their chief, because I know that good citizens without number will come out of their ranks to counsel and serve the country we love.

WOODROW WILSON

The Boy Scout committee asks that this message be read as widely as possible in all the schools so that boys may feel the influence of the President's interest in the work which they are doing.

The publication issued by the Boy Scout movement known as *Boys' Life* is full of valuable and stimulating information for boys. The September number gives advice on how to deal with fires and panics. It also gives a very interesting and clear statement of the cost of public schools in the United States and the reasons why a boy should seek an education. There is an article on how to influence boys to deal with the problem of "cribbing" in the schools and an account of the Gettysburg experiences of some of the Boy Scouts who were present during the celebration of the summer.

In general it may be said that the literature which is being produced by the Boy Scout movement cannot be neglected by any teacher who is interested in surrounding the boys in his school with wholesome influences of the type cultivated by this movement.

FACTS ABOUT THE WORKING CHILDREN OF CINCINNATI, AND THEIR BEARING UPON EDUCATIONAL PROBLEMS

HELEN T. WOOLLEY
Cincinnati, Ohio

This paper deals with the following series of facts about the working children of Cincinnati: the number who have left the schools to go to work each year since records have been kept; a classification of the children who left during the year September 1, 1911, to September 1, 1912, showing the type and location of the schools from which they come; their age, their sex, and their school grade; a tabulation of the kinds of occupations they engaged in; a study of wages; and an investigation of economic necessity as a factor in child labor.[1]

The office which issues working certificates in Cincinnati is—like all similar offices in Ohio—a subdivision of the office of the Superintendent of Schools. When the Child Labor law of 1910 went into effect, a bureau of research to investigate various phases of the problems of child labor, vocational guidance, and industrial education was formed through the agency of Miss M. Edith Campbell of the Schmidlapp Bureau, and Mr. E. N. Clopper, of the National Child Labor Committee. Mr. Schmidlapp contributed half the funds for this new bureau, and a group of public-spirited business men made up the other half. To this Bureau, which we sometimes call the Vocation Bureau when pressed for a name, Mr. Dyer, who was then superintendent of schools, turned over the management of the work certificate office.

[1] The tabulations presented in this paper are the work of many hands. For the original classification, month by month, I am chiefly indebted to volunteer workers—Miss Lisette Friend, Miss Claire Nelter, and Miss Alice Eichberg. Another volunteer worker, Mrs. Agnes Senior Seasongood, did most of the work of tabulating wages. Miss Rose Rankins and Mr. William Spencer, of the office force, made out and verified the final tables. Miss Louise Boswell, with the assistance of Mrs. Charlotte Rust Fischer, both of the office force, made the study of economic necessity as a factor in child labor.

The scope of the investigation includes, first, working out a good office system[1] to accord with the provisions of the new law, and keeping careful records to show the effect of the law; and secondly, carrying out a comprehensive investigation with a limited series of children, an investigation which involves a study of their physical and mental growth under conditions of industry, a study of the industries in which they are employed, a careful and detailed industrial history for each child studied, and an investigation of the homes. The present paper deals only with results obtained in working out the system for the office, not with those of the special research.

The Child Labor law of Ohio, requires that a child shall be at least fourteen years of age,[2] and shall have completed the fifth grade in school before he is allowed to begin work. Each work certificate must be issued to a definitely named employer, on the authority of a contract signed by that employer. When the child changes his position, the previous employer is required to return the certificate to the issuing office, which then reissues it to the new employer upon the receipt from him of a signed contract. These regulations thus give the work certificate office a large measure of supervision of all working children until the sixteenth birthday, when a certificate is no longer required.

Through careful co-operation with the schools, the truancy department, and the factory inspectors, the law is well enforced, so that we feel confident that the records in the office are now fairly complete for all the working children of the city under sixteen years of age. The office is keeping not only the necessary records, but many additional notes with regard to wages and conditions of employment. Only a small part of the information on our cards has as yet been tabulated, but enough facts to be of interest, and we hope of value, to teachers, are now at hand.

NUMBER OF WORK CERTIFICATES ISSUED EACH YEAR SINCE 1904

The old books used in issuing certificates, containing a stub for each certificate issued, are in the possession of the office, and

[1] For a more detailed account of the method of administering the Child Labor law, see *The Survey*, August 9, 1912.

[2] In August, 1913, a new law went into effect which raises the age to sixteen for girls and fifteen for boys. The school grade was raised proportionately.

the figures presented are taken directly from the books. The first records are dated, March, 1903. The number of certificates issued during the first sixteen months was 1,018, a number so small that it means no attempt to enforce the law. The continuous record begins in September, 1904, and the numbers for each year, from September 1 to September 1, are as follows:

1904–5	2,550	1908–9	2,856
1905–6	2,623	1909–10	3,348
1906–7	4,218	1910–11	2,800
1907–8	2,053	1911–12	2,366

The totals for the years previous to the year 1908–9 are of doubtful significance, since during that period there was very little systematic effort to enforce the child labor laws. The state factory inspector spent several months of the year 1906–7 in Cincinnati investigating the conditions of child labor, and with the assistance of the truant officers, he sent to the certificate office a large number of children who had been working without certificates—hence the very large number of certificates for that year, 4,218, which is almost a thousand more than in any other year. The very small number issued in 1907–8, 2,053, is thought to be the effect of the panic, which closed so many industries, thus lessening the chances of employment. From 1907–8 to 1909–10, the numbers increased again, an increase due to the two factors of greater business prosperity and better factory inspection. From the year 1909–10, down to the present time, one can be sure that the numbers correspond closely to the number of children actually at work. The drop from 3,348 in 1909–10, to 2,800 in 1910–11, is the effect of the Child Labor law which went into effect in July, 1910. This law reduced the number of eligible children by establishing a higher educational requirement (i.e., the completion of the fifth grade in school). It also limited the number of children to the number of available positions, since it required every child to present a written promise of work before he was allowed to take out a certificate. At the same time, it served to decrease the number of positions open to children. Many employers preferred to dispense with juvenile labor, rather than to bother with signing cards, returning certificates, and making reports about the children.

The establishment of the compulsory continuation schools in September, 1911, reduced the number of working children still further—to 2,366 in 1911–12. The continuation school acted in two ways. It reduced yet more the number of positions open to children, since some employers are unwilling to excuse the children from work for the required four hours a week of school. The regulation which exempts children who have completed the eighth grade from attendance on continuation schools, gives a practical value to the completion of the grammar-school course which serves to hold many children in school for that purpose. An increase in the proportion of children who had completed the eighth grade from 13 per cent in 1910–11 to 19 per cent in 1911–12, demonstrates this tendency. Doubtless the greater number of fifteen-year-old children (22 per cent in 1911–11 and 27 per cent in 1911–12) is another expression of the same fact. It is probable that when the readjustment to the new requirements is complete, the total number of certificates issued will increase again. The first few months of the year beginning September, 1912, show an increase in numbers over the corresponding months of the previous year. It will be interesting to see whether the totals under the new system will, within a few years, equal the totals under the old.

STATISTICS FOR THE YEAR 1911–12

(Table I; Charts I, II, III, and IV)

The statistics for the year 1911–12 have been tabulated more in detail, and more accurately, than those for any previous year. Cross-classifications were made which served as checks on one another, and insured absolute correctness. The important facts are as follows:

The type and location of the schools from which the Working Children came, and the sex and age of the children (Table I; Charts I, II, III, and IV).

Of the 2,366 working certificates issued during the year, 1,996, or 84.4 per cent, were to children from the schools of the city of Cincinnati, and 370, or 15.6 per cent, to those from schools outside of the city (Chart I).

There is but a slight difference in sex, 52.8 per cent boys and

TABLE I

SHOWING THE TYPE AND LOCATION OF THE SCHOOLS FROM WHICH THE WORKING CHILDREN CAME, AND THE SEX AND AGE OF THE CHILDREN

Month	Cincinnati Schools										Other Schools										Grand Total
	Public					Parochial					Public					Parochial					
	Boys		Girls		Total	Boys		Girls		Total	Boys		Girls		Total	Boys		Girls		Total	
	14	15	14	15		14	15	14	15		14	15	14	15		14	15	14	15		
September	85	33	62	18	198	62	17	49	10	138	5	5	13	9	32	3	6	14	2	25	393
October	47	19	37	20	123	40	5	38	8	91	3	3	7	2	15	5	1	17	4	27	256
November	28	16	29	15	88	29	4	29	7	69	3	3	4	6	16	3	2	8	0	13	186
December	15	6	13	7	41	14	4	18	2	38	1	2	3	6	12	4	0	3	1	8	99
January	24	10	19	7	60	33	3	23	5	64	5	3	3	1	12	2	0	5	0	7	143
February	19	11	20	13	63	22	7	29	9	67	1	7	3	2	13	2	1	2	3	8	151
March	25	16	24	9	74	18	8	19	4	49	2	1	4	3	10	2	2	5	0	9	142
April	30	16	16	14	76	24	1	16	5	46	5	4	2	0	11	6	2	3	3	14	147
May	24	18	18	10	70	28	2	15	4	49	7	1	3	3	14	2	3	6	3	14	147
June	70	31	27	24	152	39	7	38	5	89	17	5	14	3	39	3	3	7	1	14	294
July	46	20	37	22	125	24	2	35	7	68	6	2	3	3	14	3	4	4	2	13	220
August	32	12	32	15	91	30	7	24	6	67	4	4	4	2	14	7	1	8	0	16	188
Total	445	208	334	174	1,161	363	67	333	72	835	59	40	63	40	202	42	25	82	19	168	2,366

47.2 per cent girls (Chart II). In the previous year, the girls were slightly in excess of the boys—50.7 per cent girls and 49.3 per cent boys.

The public schools furnished 1,363, or 57.6 per cent of the whole number, and the church schools 1,003, or 42.4 per cent (Chart III).

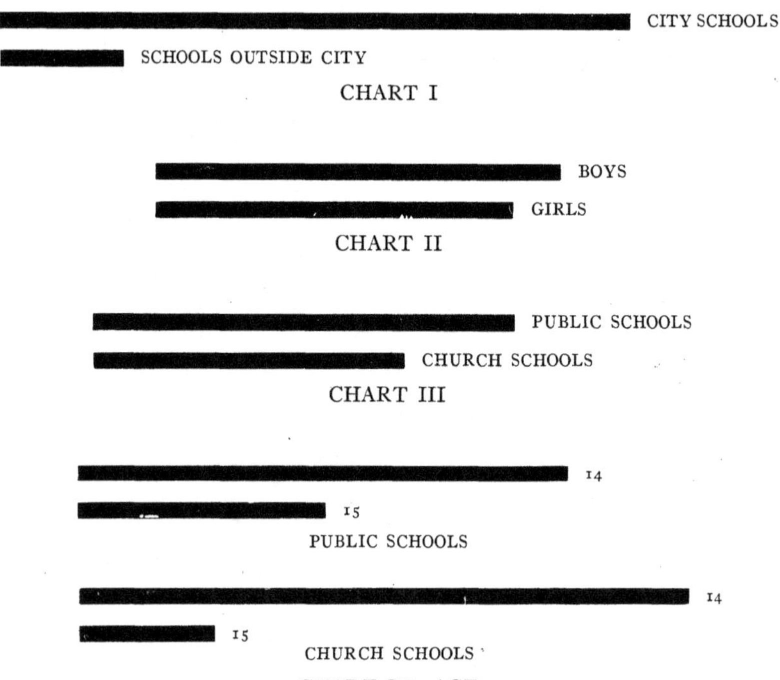

CHART I

CHART II

CHART III

CHART IV—AGE

Since the total enrolment of the church schools is not made public, it is impossible to compare exactly the proportion of those leaving, to the total enrolment in the two cases. The usual estimate is that the public schools have at least twice and perhaps more than twice as many children as the church schools. Since the total number from the church schools is only 15 per cent less than the number from the public schools, the proportion of those leaving the church schools must be from one and one-half to two times as great as the proportion leaving the public schools. For the sake of comparisons with other cities, it may be of interest to state that the proportion of children who left the public schools of the city to go to work was 3 per cent of the total enrolment of the grades below the high school.

Certificates may be taken out at any time between the fourteenth and the sixteenth birthdays. In making the classification of age, any child who took out his certificate before the fifteenth birthday is classified as fourteen, and any who took it out on or after the fifteenth birthday, as fifteen. Of the total number, 1,721, or 72.7 per cent, were fourteen years of age, and 645, or 27.3 per cent, were fifteen. This proportion figured separately for boys and girls remains the same to a tenth of 1 per cent. A decided difference in proportion appears, however, when it is figured separately for the two types of school. There were 1,363 public-school children, of whom 901, or 66.1 per cent, were fourteen years, and 462, or 33.9 per cent, fifteen. Of the 1,003 church-school children, 820, or 81.7 per cent, were fourteen years of age, and 183, or 18.3 per cent, fifteen (Chart III). Reference has already been made to the increase in the proportion of fifteen-year-old children from 22 per cent in 1910–11 to 27 per cent in 1911–12, but since the record has never before been made out separately for the two types of school, we have no way of knowing how this increase is apportioned between them.

THE SCHOOL GRADE COMPLETED BY WORKING CHILDREN
(Tables II, III, and IV; Chart V)

The facts with regard to the grade completed by these children can be seen in detail in Table II for the public-school children, and Table III for the church-school children. They are summed up in Table IV. If one considers only the totals including both types of school (Table IV, last two columns), it appears that approximately equal numbers came from the fifth, sixth, and seventh grades. The same relationship holds for the year 1910–11. Previous to that year, statistics are based, not upon the grade completed, but upon the grade in which the child was registered when he left school, and are, therefore, not comparable.

The analysis of grade carried a step farther to the two types of school, shows an interesting difference between them. In the case

TABLE II

SHOWING THE GRADE COMPLETED BY CHILDREN LEAVING THE PUBLIC SCHOOLS TO GO TO WORK

PUBLIC SCHOOLS

Grade	5				6				7				8				9 and 10				Total
	Boys		Girls		Boys		Girls		Boys		Girls		Boys		Girls		Boys		Girls		
	14	15	14	15	14	15	14	15	14	15	14	15	14	15	14	15	14	15	14	15	
September	38	14	18	2	23	12	21	8	21	5	19	10	7	6	16	5	1	1	1	2	230
October	12	9	5	6	12	2	19	7	15	9	11	6	11	2	9	3	0	0	0	0	138
November	9	9	11	5	8	0	11	1	12	4	8	6	2	3	3	7	0	3	0	2	104
December	8	1	6	2	5	1	3	1	2	3	5	6	1	3	2	3	0	0	0	1	53
January	13	3	5	2	9	3	12	4	4	7	4	1	2	0	1	1	1	0	0	0	72
February	7	6	11	5	4	7	5	2	6	3	4	7	3	2	2	0	0	0	1	1	76
March	9	8	11	4	10	6	10	4	4	2	2	2	4	0	5	2	0	1	0	0	84
April	13	9	5	5	15	7	7	3	6	3	4	5	1	1	2	1	0	0	0	0	87
May	6	8	4	3	19	7	12	3	3	4	2	2	2	0	3	5	1	0	0	0	84
June	21	13	6	10	24	8	16	4	19	4	10	5	20	8	8	6	3	3	1	2	191
July	20	7	16	9	10	4	7	3	12	4	7	1	7	5	10	8	3	2	0	4	139
August	6	4	16	5	8	6	12	2	8	4	3	2	13	1	5	5	1	1	0	3	105
Totals	162	91	114	58	147	63	135	42	112	52	79	55	73	31	66	46	10	11	3	15	1,363

TABLE III

SHOWING THE GRADE COMPLETED BY CHILDREN LEAVING THE CHURCH SCHOOLS TO GO TO WORK

CHURCH SCHOOLS

Grade	5				6				7				8				9 and 10				Total
	Boys		Girls		Boys		Girls		Boys		Girls		Boys		Girls		Boys		Girls		
	14	15	14	15	14	15	14	15	14	15	14	15	14	15	14	15	14	15	14	15	
September	13	5	8	2	12	5	21	1	23	5	17	6	17	6	15	3	0	2	2	0	163
October	12	2	15	2	16	1	11	1	13	2	22	6	4	1	7	3	0	0	0	0	118
November	5	0	5	0	14	1	12	3	7	2	14	2	6	3	6	2	0	0	0	0	82
December	7	0	3	1	4	1	7	0	4	0	9	0	3	2	2	1	0	1	0	1	46
January	13	1	4	1	11	0	6	1	5	1	10	2	6	1	7	1	0	0	1	0	71
February	5	4	8	1	8	2	8	3	5	1	12	3	6	0	3	5	0	1	0	0	75
March	3	3	3	0	6	3	6	0	8	3	9	3	3	1	6	1	0	0	0	0	58
April	1	1	6	2	11	0	6	1	12	0	3	2	6	2	4	3	0	0	0	0	60
May	11	0	3	2	6	0	8	1	6	1	5	1	7	3	5	3	0	1	0	0	63
June	9	3	14	1	5	1	13	0	14	2	10	3	11	3	8	2	3	1	0	0	103
July	5	1	4	1	7	2	6	0	5	0	16	4	10	3	12	3	0	0	1	1	81
August	9	1	7	1	6	1	9	0	9	2	6	1	12	4	8	4	1	0	2	0	83
Total	93	21	80	14	106	17	113	11	111	19	133	33	91	29	83	31	4	6	6	2	1,003

of the public school, the largest number of children—31.2 per cent—left from the fifth grade, and the numbers decreased steadily to the eighth grade. In the case of the church school, the smallest number

TABLE IV

A Summary of the Grade Completed by Children Leaving School to Go to Work

Grade	Public Schools						Church Schools						All Schools	
	Boys		Girls		Total	Percentage	Boys		Girls		Total	Percentage	Total	Percentage
	14	15	14	15			14	15	14	15				
5	162	91	114	58	425	31.2	93	21	80	14	208	20.8	633	26.7
6	147	63	135	42	387	28.4	106	17	113	11	247	24.6	634	26.8
7	112	52	79	53	296	21.7	111	19	133	33	296	29.5	592	25.1
8	73	31	66	46	216	15.8	91	29	83	31	234	23.3	450	19.0
9 and 10	10	11	3	15	39	2.9	4	6	6	2	18	1.8	57	2.4
Total	504	248	397	214	1,363	100.0	405	92	415	91	1,003	100.0	2,366	100.0

left from the fifth grade (20.8 per cent), the numbers increased to the seventh grade, and then dropped a bit to the eighth (Table IV; Chart V). In spite, then, of the fact that the children from the

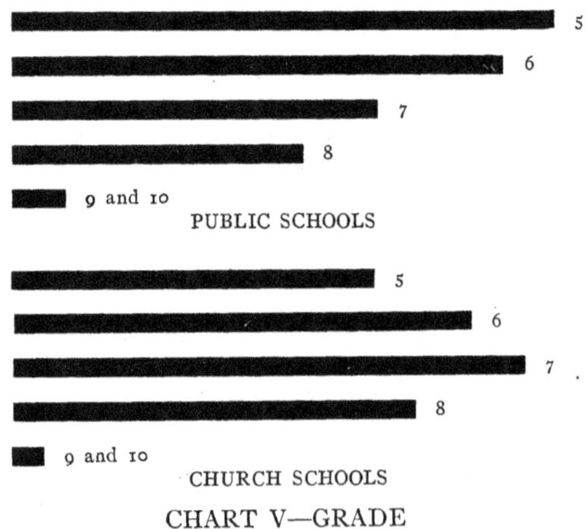

CHART V—GRADE

church schools were younger than those from the public schools, there were many more of them in the higher grades. The difference is not easy to interpret. Doubtless one element in it is the fact that a larger proportion of the total enrolment of the church schools left to go to work than in the case of the public schools. While the public schools sent us chiefly retarded children, the church schools sent us more of the children who were up to grade. It is possible that differences in the method of grading children are also a factor in the result.

THE RETARDATION OF WORKING CHILDREN

(Table V; Chart VI)

The facts about the school grade of working children have been figured out more accurately in terms of retardation (Table V). The basis of computing retardation allows a leeway of more than a year. Only those children are called retarded who have completed the sixth grade or less at fourteen years. It is to be borne in mind

TABLE V

SHOWING AMOUNT OF RETARDATION AMONG CHILDREN LEAVING SCHOOL TO GO TO WORK

	Public Schools							Church Schools							Grand Total
	Normal		Retarded		Ahead		Total	Normal		Retarded		Ahead		Total	
	No.	Percentage	No.	Percentage	No.	Percentage		No.	Percentage	No.	Percentage	No.	Percentage		
Boys......	226	30.1	515	68.5	11	1.4	752	237	47.7	256	51.5	4	0.8	497	1,249
Girls......	204	33.4	402	65.8	5	0.8	611	249	49.2	251	49.6	6	1.2	506	1,117
Totals.....	430	31.5	917	67.3	16	1.2	1,363	486	48.5	507	50.5	10	1.0	1,003	2,366

that in this case, fourteen may indicate any point between the fourteenth and fifteenth birthdays. In the same way, a child who has completed not more than the seventh grade at fifteen is retarded. A child who has completed the seventh or eighth grades at fourteen is considered normal; likewise a child who has completed a grade above the eighth at fourteen is called ahead of grade. On this basis, 67 per cent of the public-school children, and 50 per cent of the church-school children who left school to go to work were retarded. We do not know the retardation within the church schools, but within the public school during the same year, the retardation for the group of children under sixteen years, and in the ninth grade and below, was 28.7 per cent.[1] Of this same group 67.1 per cent were normal, and 4.2 per cent ahead of grade. The

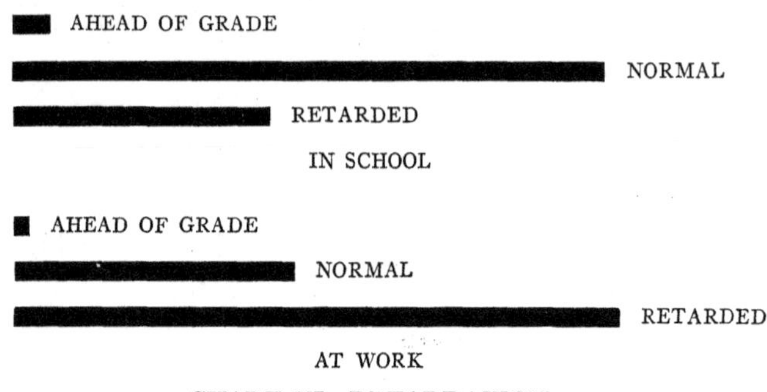

CHART VI—RETARDATION

percentage of retardation among those who leave the public school to go to work, is, then, more than twice as great as that among the children who are in school.

OCCUPATIONS ENTERED BY THE WORKING CHILDREN OF 1911–12

Let us consider for a moment what these children receive in exchange for school. Table VI shows the occupations which they entered. In Cincinnati, the shoe factories employ more children than any other one industry. Of the 2,366 children who began work during the year, 19 per cent entered shoe factories; 17.2 per cent became errand boys and girls for a large variety of business firms; 15.5 per cent went into department stores as cash or stock boys and girls, wrappers, or inside messengers; 8.7 per cent entered the tailoring and sewing trades; 6.8 per cent worked at home helping their parents; 5.2 per cent became telegraph messengers; 3.9 per cent entered paper-box factories; between 1 and 2 per cent were employed in each of the following: candy factories, office work, and private families; and the remaining 20 per cent were scattered over a wide range of occupations, no

[1] Calculated from the advance sheets of the "Age Report of Pupils for Year Ending June, 1912," from the *Report of the Superintendent of Schools of Cincinnati*, for the year 1911–12.

one of which comprised as many as 1 per cent of the children. Almost half of these miscellaneous occupations were in factories of various kinds. Eighty-seven per cent of the working children can, then, be ranged in five groups; working in factories, 33 per cent; running errands, 22.5 per cent; working in department stores, 15.5 per cent; sewing trades, 8.7 per cent, and assisting at home, 6.8 per cent.

TABLE VI

OCCUPATIONS ENTERED BY CHILDREN BEGINNING TO WORK

Occupations	Boys		Girls		Totals	Percentage
	14	15	14	15		
Department stores	111	37	160	58	366	15.5
Errands	287	87	26	7	407	17.2
Tailoring and sewing	7	4	153	43	207	8.7
Shoe factories	167	74	149	59	449	19.0
Telegraph messenger	85	38	0	0	123	5.2
Office work	21	16	9	1	47	1.9
Paper box and paper goods	6	3	67	16	92	3.9
Candy factories	3	1	23	9	36	1.5
Working for parents	24	9	84	42	159	6.8
Private families	0	0	14	11	25	1.1
Miscellaneous	198	71	127	59	455	19.2
	909	340	812	305	2,366	100

A few of the occupations on this list include skilled work—for instance the shoe factories, the sewing trades, and the department stores. In many of the factories represented, in the messenger service, and in most that is included under the head of helping at home, there is no skilled work. But even in those industries which include skilled work, the first two years of employment for those who begin at fourteen are not made periods of training for skilled work, or apprenticeships in which the industry as a whole is learned. A child in a shoe factory, for instance, is taught but one or two of the one hundred and fifty or more processes involved in making a shoe. The children in the sewing trades pull bastings, or baste one kind of a seam. Apprenticeships in the dressmaking and millinery trades are rarely open to children under sixteen. In the department stores, the children run errands inside the store, or wrap packages. Many of the best department stores and most of the skilled trades are entirely closed to children under sixteen.

There is, then, very little that counts as training in the occupations for children under sixteen—a fact which the children themselves realize. Many of them tell us that they hope to enter trades at sixteen and are meanwhile just earning a little money. It is a conservative statement to say that only a small proportion of these children find themselves any better fitted to earn a living at sixteen than they were when they began work at fourteen. Some of them, particularly those in the messenger service, are of less value in the industrial world as a result of these two years of work.

[*To be continued*]

THE IDEALS WHICH LED TO THE FOUNDING OF THE SCHOOL OF EDUCATION.—*Concluded*

ANITA McCORMICK BLAINE

Col. Parker's school was designed to touch the lives of as many children as it could reach, with its magic wand; but more than that, to be a school of the prophets, where new light should ever be sought and found—tested and disseminated—by new minds marching on and on—drawn by the irresistible call of the children—giving new and new waves of light, in devotion to them.

It was in this part of the picture of the future that Col. Parker chiefly exulted when he came with his school within this University—the vision of the stream of young things setting forth for their life work, catching sight of the teacher's vision, coming within these gates, and his being able to add of his store to the storehouse of the University, for their preparation for a high mission.

Children were a mission to Col. Parker. To teach them, really, as they might be taught, he held out to his students as the highest mission on this earth. He could not touch the question of teaching in any other spirit.

Children were received from their parents in his school as a sacred trust. There was no dividing of territory here—no separating of functions which left the real child falling between two. The child was in himself a trinity—yes, physical, intellectual, spiritual—but one godhead.

There was no agreement for division of duties. When the child was the school's, he was one whole splendid opportunity and responsibility. It was not that the school would do all for him—but that what it did do it would do wholly for all of him—and if it did not thus help the home to do the same, in its still higher ground, it failed.

The child was considered first as a physical being. It was realized that his whole life up to the adult point is based on growth.

It is the first necessity to rate power from the physical standpoint. How unscientific we are—how dull! We take growing things whose chief element is growth—no two of whom grow precisely alike—each one being a law unto himself—yet we rate and grade them for work by arbitrary years, and erect standards for each year by which they must toe the mark. Then we give them the totally false feeling that at such and such moments, such and such things, arbitrarily decided, must be accomplished, and we call them forward or backward as they go beyond or behind these nicely adjusted facts of our own making, and—by so doing—cut away all chance of a right adjustment by hopelessly twisting their own ideas of themselves.

The school must rate the children's work as it would fit their clothes, to their physical proportions—and then, having the right adjustment, build in all ways to conserve and increase their physical store—taking account at all points of their need for physical overflow and a chance for physical exuberance. Gymnastics and dancing and physical games, for development in different kinds, all made part of the school day.

Free periods, even for a few moments between classes, for a run, it seems to me, should be brought about.

One of the dreams of the second foundation of the school was a great playground where perhaps all of the second half of the school day could be spent out of doors in work and play.

I am sure that it is a serious and important thing for our country, with our more and more rushing life and our concentration in cities, that the schools should take big hold of the physical side of children's lives and build for the future a sturdier race than we can say we are today.

In the pedagogic field, how shall we describe Col. Parker in his school? The thought of it reminds me of a new elemental thing in its beginnings; and his exuberant joy, in the freedom and courage of his experiments, makes me think of the god Pan with his reeds—finding every day new and diviner sounds and giving them forth to the listening, waiting earth.

He set forth on his quest to overturn school methods. He had no pattern to move by. He studied under the leaders of thought in Germany in his studying days—but that only furnished him with food for thought, not with a plan. Where was the school in this country that was making departures?

In our most vital spots, as of our children, we are most conservative, perhaps to their detriment.

Col. Parker truly set forth alone. Your own John Dewey—and his—came next in time, came equal in courage and initiative, and alongside in plan.

Col. Parker broke into unploughed territory and verily broke the ground. He discarded all precedents. His school practice was determined by two factors: (1) the prime fundamental principles he clung to for children; (2) these, guided in their application, by his own fine intuitive sense for children.

Col. Parker's principles for teaching were few and clear—as I understand them.

He held that the child is the unit, for teaching—not society. He aimed for the development of the individual to all of his highest powers, to serve and to make society, not the training of individuals necessarily to fit society—the finished product of today.

He held that the child's mind is as a plant to let grow—not as a box to fill.

He held that thinking is the growth process, and developed thinking the result to attain—that there is no learning without thinking—and that, therefore, all teaching is but to put the mind in contact—real contact—with a subject in order to let the mind act. He held that a recitation without thought on the part of the child was no recitation.

He held that activity was a necessary condition of thinking and also a necessary product of thinking—therefore activity must be present in the child's attitude toward his work—and also as an outcome of his work, in expression of some kind.

He held that freedom is a necessary condition of activity, and therefore trammels must be taken away.

He held that interest is a concomitant of activity of thinking, in freedom, and therefore a test to apply to the whole. If real interest in the work was lacking, something was wrong—and then his way would be, not to sugar-coat, to tickle the palate, but to diagnose.

He held that to enable the mind to grow by thinking, it must have intellectual food; that this must be fitted in kind and variety to the child's place in his intellectual development, and chosen with a view to growth—not to filling.

The function of the teacher was to lead to the pastures green and the still waters—to spread the table—to furnish the opportunity and let the child feed and grow.

He held that the whole round world belonged to every child, and that to bring that circle aright to the child was the great realm of the teacher—not in unrelated, incoherent masses could it break on the child, without overwhelming and confusing him—but in correlated contacts, with man and nature, in ever enlarging circles, could he at last possess the whole earth.

He held that all of the child's powers should be used toward the gradual but complete possession of nature—including man in that category—and to this end, that the acquiring of all necessary intellectual tools and facilities should be in the course of this thought-building process, in order to prevent waste of energy and time.

Col. Parker would not have given up one of his intellectual dogmas for any person—but he would have given them all up for a child!

The second—but truly the chief and most final and determining factor in his school work—was his intuitive sense of child nature—what it wanted—what it needed—what dwarfed it or twisted it—what expanded it—and any preconceived ideas that did not measure, in practice, the manifest good of the children, would not have been held for a moment. He was like a gardener tending beloved plants as he went about his school—and he put his finger unerringly on the needed elements—a little more sunshine here or shade there—and the plants throve wondrously and grew apace.

What did this sense for children consist of? It is difficult to say, but into it went an unbounded belief in them—a sympathetic understanding of them and joy in them—a love of them which included them all.

In teaching, there is the intellectual element and there is the spiritual—and I think we must come to see that the spiritual must be the predominating element in the end. It must have the real ascendancy—the final decisive voice—the ultimate authority. This is most important nearest to the beginnings of life, where the foundations are laid, in the impressionable years. But I wonder if the age comes at all, during education, when it is not equally true. With Col. Parker this was the guiding star of his whole work.

I am keenly aware, as I have tried to speak of these elements in education, that I have not stated them in technical terms. I am almost as keenly aware that I have no great wish to do so.

It is undoubtedly necessary and serviceable, when one is closely analyzing psychological processes, or pulling one nerve filament from another, to distinguish between them, to have exact technical terms for the true understanding of the matter.

But the adoption of them, without that close, urgent need of their use, is a dangerous and hampering thing. And when one is talking about the teaching of children, there are broader issues involved than these close analyses, and I have a feeling that to try to closely analyze and condense, into technical statements, matters that are too big and broad for that treatment, is to arrive at more of falsehood than of truth.

I do not think that Col. Parker stated well his principles and beliefs in education. He always said that John Dewey spoke for him better than he could speak for himself.

But he saw—and one difficulty in his promulgating what he saw, was that he said it so inadequately. But he carried out his views for the children in a marvelous fashion, and the main point for the children was not the phrasing but the doing.

Did Col. Parker hold with pride some of his intellectual dogmas?

There is hardly a point in the world where that archenemy of the best and highest good does not gain some foothold. I do not know—I could not say that he had none. It might be that his intellectual creed, like other creeds, had fences built around some of its tenets—holding some regions untouchable.

But if this were so, it boots not.

If so, it would only mean that what he held for children was so great, that it was too great for his own grasp. For the deepest fundamental principles of Col. Parker's school were on such truly untouchable ground that to put any mere intellectual theories into the same category must be to lower them.

It may be that, with a touch of pride, Col. Parker hedged about some of the lesser holdings of his pedagogic doctrine—and if so, all would suffer from a disturbed proportion—but even if so, we cannot let that rob us of the greatness of his greatest.

The great, the pre-eminent, the undying part of Col. Parker's move in education was to free, to lift, the soul of the child—therefore the soul of humanity. I do not want to use that term in such a way that it could provoke the discussion of what is the soul, and whether there is a soul. If I could ask you, each one, to supply your own term, to mean the highest development of the inner nature of man—that is what I should like to do. I use soul only because I know no better term.

The great move in education that he made was to put that soul—that highest possible character development—as the one standard, the one aim, the one goal, of school work—its accomplishment the one final test of the work. He put his school at the disposal of that achievement. All that would further it might stand—all that would help it must be had, if possible—anything that would hinder it must be done away with.

I am afraid that Col. Parker did not live and work long enough to let us realize what that truly meant—the vital difference between that and the basis that most of our educational institutions are on—young and old alike.

They are doing the expected thing, the accepted work, and are doing, in addition, as much as they can toward improvement of the ideas in education, and of the individual pupils.

Discussion of betterings of school processes for children is very apt to come to a close with, "We would do so and so, if we could."

It does not follow that we should all be pace-setters—we may not have the conviction or the power for that. But it helps all, when one can be such. It is worth while to see what such a one is really doing. Even so much, it sometimes seems, it is difficult to grasp the full force of.

Col. Parker in his school could do all things that he was convinced were for the good of the children, because he would. And it was really doing—not only saying, or writing in a catalogue. All interests—all authorities even—himself, his whole school, and everything connected with it, were subjected to the one purpose to find the best—the very best—thing for children—and no other purpose was admitted within the walls—to stay.

And of the best, that best of the best—the child's soul—was paramount. Neither angels nor principalities could have kept in that school a measure that would injure a child's soul, so far as its head could know it.

Of what would injure a child's soul he took all counsel—of his faculty primarily. They being his chosen counselors and in the heart of the machine, their advice was weighty with him.

All and any light Col. Parker courted from far or near. Any who could contribute thought for a child had a hearing. And from it all, and the depths of his own convictions, conclusions were reached—and then there was never a question about action.

Artificiality of every sort was swept away. The only standard that was set for a child was that child's best. The world's leaders were not brought to him as arbiters, but as friends. Each child was made a king in his own domain, and what he gave of that princely possession was a gift to all.

Discipline, as all else, was evoked from within, not laid on from without—and it was evoked wholly on the basis of usefulness to the community—the real basis.

If it became necessary at any point to protect the community arbitrarily, that could be done. It is amazing how seldom it was needed. With all the forces working toward self-control, how could it otherwise than come about—rightly and completely—developing a true responsibility?

The finest flower of Col. Parker's work was in his final appeal to the child's motive and incentive. He never allowed an appeal to be made directly or indirectly to the lower, selfish instinct of a human being in his care—unless it might be in a humor which would dispose of it, as a serious consideration, perhaps more effectually than silence.

Thus all competition—that is, of the get-ahead-of-the-other-fellow sort—was wiped out.

When he took this stand, it took more courage than it would today—although I cannot say that even today education has declared competition an outworn way.

In that day, to abolish rating marks among pupils would have been considered a step toward pandemonium. But Col. Parker would have said that even if so, pandemonium would have been better than creating greed for glory, and at another's expense.

But of course it did not produce pandemonium—the courage of the right step never does. It produced only added fervor in the pupil—greater interest in the real issue of one's work, when the false issue of its rating by someone else, in comparison with someone else, was eliminated. And competition (except in the field of the friendly rivalry of play where the gamboling spirit makes it a thing of joy!), competition took its proper place, and became competition with oneself to do ever better and better work. Vulgar, sordid competition was wiped out of existence in its selfish aspects—and co-operation came to take its place.

The question for every pupil at every turn was not, how much can I get ahead of my brother? but, how much can I help my brother to do also?

If Col. Parker's school had no other reason for existence in fact or in memory, this alone would furnish cause for its continuance—need that it should live and not die—that in one spot, in the world, credits for self were not counted up for miserly, selfish gain; inches or dots or lines or figures were not closely estimated in order to rate one ahead of another.

Competition was lost sight of in the effort to help, and to do better oneself, in order to help more—co-operation loomed up big and beautiful for a cause—for work and the joy of it—with others in a community spirit—where contribution was so diverse and so overflowing that efforts to rate it became an absurdity, efforts to increase it a joy.

Can the ideals of our school be told in words?

They flow from the purpose of the foundation. They change in shape and color—in detail—as they go forward—as a river finds new channels from its very force.

They are to build on the old—losing none of its strengths—but, with reverence, to add forever new lights.

They are to make that great art of teaching come to seem the greatest thing in the world, so that ideals may become realities in all schools.

They are to take the child—all children—and build them better bodies—keener, truer minds—and through all, at all moments and in all experiences, lead them to be finer spirits.

And the saving clause, as we think of how we cannot, perhaps, do it all ourselves, is that, as we drop even stray gems of ideals, the children pick them up and play with them and weave them into their lives to do it all better.

I feel sure that when the millennium comes, it will come to us through the ideals of our schools.

SEVEN, EIGHT, AND NINE YEARS IN THE ELEMENTARY SCHOOL.—*Concluded*

E. C. BROOKS
Professor of Education, Trinity College, Durham, N.C.

Program IV is from the sixth grade of a school in the South Atlantic States. It is shown in table on p. 83.

Here we find an entirely different program. The grade is divided into two sections. The recitation period for all subjects except spelling is thirty minutes, and the study period thirty minutes. The total number of daily exercises for each section, exclusive of opening exercises, is six. In four of these the sections recite together, and in two, separately. This is true for every day except Friday, when the number of recitations is seven, but the two sections recite together on four subjects. Three of them, however, require no previous preparation.

This program exhibits the work of a one-session school which runs from 9 A.M to 2 P.M., with only one recess during the day. The same number of subjects is found here that is exhibited in the other programs, but they are distributed through the week, and all do not appear daily. Whenever they do come, however, more time is devoted to each. For instance, the B section devotes thirty minutes to the preparation of arithmetic and thirty minutes to the recitation, making an hour to this subject, but arithmetic appears only four times a week. In Program III fifty minutes are devoted to arithmetic, including the study period, and it comes five times a week. History alternates with geography, each coming three times a week.

Any schoolman can compare these daily programs and draw his own conclusions. Evidently this has been done already, and the results are individual rather than general conclusions. Going from the first to the last program, both the content and the organization are vastly different, and the results must be different. In these four schools the working-out of the courses of study is as

PROGRAM IV

Time	9:15–9:30	9:30–10:00	10:00–10:30	10:30–11:00	11:00–11:30	11:30–12:00	12:00–12:30	12:30–1:00	1:00–1:30	1:30–2:00
Monday	A and B Writing	A Math.	B Math.	A and B Comp.	A Gram.	B Gram.	Recess	A Geog.	B Geog.	A and B 15 15 Spelling
Tuesday	A and B Writing	A Math.	B Math.	A and B Drawing	A Lit.	B Lit.	Recess	A History	B History	A and B 15 15 Spelling
Wednesday	A and B Writing	A Math.	B Math.	A and B 15 15 Spelling	A Gram.	B Gram.	Recess	A Geog.	B Geog.	A and B Drawing
Thursday	A and B Writing	A Math.	B Math.	A and B 15 15 Spelling	A Lit.	B Lit.	Recess	A and B Music	A History	B History
Friday	A and B Writing	A and B Comp.	A History	B History	A and B 15 15 Spelling	A and B Music	Recess	A Geog.	B Geog.	A and B Drawing

different as if they came from different nations with different purposes and ideals. The first school presents twelve different subjects, placing much emphasis on arithmetic, and about equal emphasis on all other subjects. The organization of the day's work is such that the child has very little time for private study or individual work. He has little opportunity to try his strength. The excessive number of recitations makes it impossible for him to prepare all the work out of school, and little opportunity is given for preparation in school. Such a condition makes it necessary for the teacher to aid considerably in the daily preparation.

In the second school the number of subjects is somewhat reduced. Here we find eight subjects emphasized, but there are six other periods when the classes are engaged in some kind of work or exercise; and, notwithstanding the reduction, the number of recitation periods is about the same, if we include gymnastics and general work as a recitation period. So the attempt is made to get in the same number of subjects, or to make the content about the same. In order to do it the recitation period is reduced, ranging from ten to twenty minutes, with the same time devoted to study. Notwithstanding the two sections, it would appear from the short recitation periods that they are kept about together.

The third school swings still farther away. Here the content is materially different. Five subjects are emphasized, and fifty minutes are devoted to each. The other three subjects require little or no preparation. One of them is included in the opening exercises. The fourth school resembles to some extent the third type; but it makes the difference between the extremes still more pronounced.

These four types are not confined to sections or localities. Take New England for instance. In one school we find nineteen daily recitations in the third grade, while another, less than two hours' journey, almost the next neighboring town, has only five daily recitations for the same grade. If we go west of the Rocky Mountains we could spend the morning in a school with only five daily recitations in the eighth grade, and in the afternoon of the same day visit another with twelve daily recitations in the same grade. If we should come south we can select a school with four daily recitations in the fifth grade, and almost within speaking distance select another with ten daily recitations in the same grade. Likewise we find the one-session plan as well as the two-session plan in different parts of the country. The size of the town, the age of entrance, and the length of the grammar school have little influence on the number of daily recitations.

This is not the only interesting aspect of the grammar school, and here again we could make some classifications: (1) Those schools that begin with only three or four daily recitations in the first grade and increase the number each year until we find in the eighth year eleven and twelve daily recitations; (2) those schools that begin with a large number like fifteen, eighteen, or nineteen, and reduce the number gradually to four or five in the eighth grade; (3) those that retain the same number in all grades. Some run four or five throughout the eight grades, while others run as many as eleven and twelve; and again we are unable to make a local application of these several divisions, for we find them in every section of the country.

I wish to notice only one other classification: (1) Those that devote only about two and one-half hours a day to the first grade and gradually increase the length of the day until it registers about five hours; and (2) those that have the same length of day for each grade. And thus we might go on classifying until we have as many classifications as there are schools.

III. THE PROMOTION OF STUDENTS

In the long run of years from the first grade to the last year of the high school, this question naturally arises: What opportunity is given students to pass from one grade to another? All admit that a seven-year-old child will reach the high school ahead of the six-year-old child, and the six-year-old child ahead of the five-year-old child. The amount of work for each grade is different in different schools. If in the fifth grade of one school there are five different subjects daily, and in the fifth grade of another school twelve different subjects daily, what is the relative standing of these two sets of pupils? Suppose this difference continues, and we find that it does, through the sixth, seventh, and eighth grades, there is necessarily a better opportunity for the former set to reach the high school earlier, and to know more of these five particular subjects than the students of the other school, for more than twice the time is devoted to them. If these five subjects should be reading, language, mathematics, history, and geography, the former students would probably be better able to continue these subjects through the high school than would the latter, for they would have more knowledge of them when they enter the high school. But this in itself is not the greatest blessing; for another group of subjects might be selected that would enrich the life of the pupil just as much and give him a background that would be just as helpful in pursuing the high-school work.

This question may be asked: What influence do these systems have on the mental habits of the child? Do they all give him power and skill as well as knowledge? Is it better to present short lessons on many subjects? Or, in other words, is it better to know a little about many things than much about a few things? Which produces more knowledge, power, skill, and character?

When a child has twelve recitations without a break, less the recesses, the teacher must necessarily do the greater part of the work for the child. She drops into the lecture method or the telling method and does much that the child should do unaided and alone. And whenever and wherever this is done, the child is robbed of a certain amount of mental activity, and he is thereby the weaker, since he is deprived of the skill in doing things and the pleasure that come to one conscious of the fact that he is doing things.

As a rule the method of advancing pupils from one grade to another is by semiannual promotions; but this fact conveys very little information. In the first three schools mentioned above we find semiannual promotions. In the school with thirteen daily periods we find ten minutes devoted to history; and in the school with eight periods we find twenty-five minutes devoted to the same subject. In the one a broad curriculum is run eight years, in the other a narrow curriculum is run eight years.

The older schools when they were established had probably only a few subjects for the child to study. We know something about the history of the course of study, since the last twenty-five years have crowded a number of new studies into the curriculum. They have been forced in, so to speak, and the schoolman in many instances, not knowing how to make his selections, nor how to group his subjects, has put them all in the curriculum, and has given them all equal importance. By degrees the study period has been taken away, and the child is put through the mill of nineteen daily recitations. It is impossible, then, for one child to proceed faster than another. The content has choked the organization. The length of the term has been increased from six years to seven years, to eight years, to nine years, in order that they all may go through together and the wonder to me is, when I observe the crowded curriculum, that it is not ten years, eleven years, twelve years, and so on indefinitely. But the study of child development has taught us this, that a child when it reaches thirteen or fourteen years of age is capable of doing work found in the high school, and this has probably stopped the lengthening of the grammar school.

The old teacher confined the school to mere getting knowledge. All teaching reduced itself to an examination of the child's knowledge, to be sure that it got the exact amount prescribed, and there was generally a stern incentive to meet the demands. In the growth of the graded schools a new idea entered, that of assimilating what has been acquired. Many of the graded schools then swung to the other extreme and ceased to emphasize the value of the self-activity of the child in acquiring knowledge, losing sight of the fact that its mental activity in acquiring knowledge within the scope of its experience and understanding will so facilitate the assimilation of this knowledge that much less extra assistance from the teacher is necessary. The child by its own efforts makes the teacher's efforts much more fruitful. The immature mind has many ways of developing itself through its own reactive power. It responds to numerous stimuli from without, and many of the strongest stimuli can come to the child when it is not on recitation. This fact is ignored by many of the schools, which have followed the line of least resistance in securing knowledge, being led far afield by that *ignis fatuus*, the doctrine of interest, and leaving the child basking in a lazy sunshine of soft pedagogics.

In tracing the course of study as it works through the grades, another very interesting fact is noted. Here are two schools, each claiming to be eight years in length. It is not unusual to find the content of the third grade of one in the fourth grade of the other, and if we trace them into the eighth grade we notice that the differences vanish, and they march together through the last year. Equal lengths here would appear to be the result of imitation. If we compare the course in a seven-year school with that of an eight-year school we shall find in almost every case that the course in the fourth year of the one is nearly or quite a year higher than that of the other, which leads me to quote what one superintendent of a seven-year grammar school says: "About two-thirds of the pupils entering my first grade are held two years in this grade." This is really an eight-year school labeled a seven-year school. Suppose we take this curriculum that requires two years for two-thirds of the pupils (this is in the state of North Carolina where pupils enter at six) and put it in a Massachusetts school, where students enter at five years of age, and where a large percentage of the first-year pupils come from homes where the English language is barely spoken, and I suspect that the difference in the time of working out this curriculum through the grades would be more than a year. It is impossible to discuss here the influence of foreign-born population on the school. There seems to be, however, no general plan, really no guide save the personal opinion of the superintendent, possibly influenced by some favorite school or schoolman.

A very interesting fact in studying the progress of pupils through the grades is the absence of anything like definite information; yet from that furnished we find the widest possible variations. Many schools can tell the number of pupils that repeat as much as or more than half of a grade, and lose a year or more; but only a few have any information about the time gained. In one school, 25 per cent of the pupils repeat a year's work, and the superintendent, although he has a seven-year course, prefers an eight-year course. Another school shows that 30 per cent of the pupils gain a year, yet this school has an eight-year course and prefers an eight-year course. And instances like these might be multiplied indefinitely.

An interesting situation is found in one western school. In the first grade, 50 per cent repeat a year; second grade, 40 per cent; third grade, 30 per cent; fourth grade, 25 per cent; fifth grade, 20 per cent; sixth grade, 15 per cent; seventh grade, 10 per cent; and eighth grade, 5 per cent. Here we find an eight-year grammar school. We find similar conditions elsewhere, although the percentage is not quite so large. In a certain Pennsylvania school, 39 per cent gain more than a year, while 15 per cent lose more than a year. Here the length of the grammar school is eight years; but, in another school of the same state, 20 per cent lose on an average a year's work; but the length here is seven years. In one school in Massachusetts the length is nine years, and 20 per cent lose a year, yet the superintendent prefers an eight-year course. In a southern school we find another peculiar situation. In the first grade, 6 per cent lose a year; second grade, 6 per cent; third grade, 7 per cent; fourth grade, 6 per cent; fifth grade, 16 per cent; sixth grade, 16 per cent; seventh grade, 25 per cent. And a number of instances similar to this might be quoted.

All of this seems to prove nothing except that the individual superintendent has various and sundry perplexing questions that beset his soul, and results are as they are because of these soul perplexities. The child, the content, the organization, aye, there's the rub! Child nature is being studied; the content of the school is being analyzed; and the organization of the whole machinery is being worked over. The three should be studied together, not separately, for it is in the combination that we detect gross errors.

SUMMARY

After observing these many facts relative to the grammar school we come back to the question, is a four-year high school that rests on a seven-year grammar school equal to a four-year high school that rests on an eight-year grammar school? If the seven-year grammar school presented only a few subjects daily to students who enter the first grade at seven years of age, and should give the students opportunity to do the greatest amount of work in these subjects and to grow as rapidly as their health and capacity would permit; and if the eight-year grammar school should present fifteen or eighteen subjects daily; should permit students to enter the first grade at five years of age; should give the students only ten or fifteen minutes on recitation, and offer no opportunity for promotion beyond the mass; then I should say that a seven-year grammar school would be superior to an eight-year grammar school.

On the contrary, if an eight-year grammar school should present only a few subjects daily; should require steady, vigorous work of all pupils in these few subjects; and should permit students to complete the entire work as their several capacities would permit; and if the seven-year grammar school should present the other conditions—of a large number of subjects, no study periods, no possible means of advancing faster than the mass; then I should say that the eight-year grammar school would be superior. But we are unable to make any such classifications. All the evils and defects of all the schools can be found in either class—those of a seven-, eight,- or a nine-year grammar school. Again, it is difficult to tell what is a seven-year grammar school or an eight-year grammar school; for it is frequently the case that the seven-year school holds pupils in the first grade two years, while it is equally true that the eight-year school permits a large percentage of its pupils to complete the course in seven years; therefore a seven-year grammar school may be really an eight-year school, and a so-called eight-year grammar school may be really a seven-year grammar school.

But this seems to be a fair conclusion, that we do not yet know the meaning of education, and what children are capable of doing; for if it is the right process to take a class of forty pupils thirteen years of age and present the complete circle of knowledge to them in a list of subjects that numbers fifteen, eighteen, or nineteen, and to keep the pupils turning from subject to subject, giving them largely impressions and entertainment, and to prohibit all home work, then it is not the right process to confine the same pupils to a curriculum containing only five subjects, with long study periods, both in school and at home; yet both of these plans prevail to such an extent and under so many different conditions that it is next to impossible to take the results of the school and tell which is the better process.

Our personal opinions may be very pronounced. Certainly, the men who supervise these courses have personal opinions, but they are largely personal and not general. Therefore, I am leaving the question where I asked it. The answer is an individual one, not general. It may be wrong, it may be right, and there are instances enough to prove either. Let me say here that we find in every section of the country schools that seem to be working away and trying to understand the reason for the large or the small number of subjects; and the tendency seems to be toward the smaller number.

INFLUENCE ON THE HIGH SCHOOL

We come with these varying results from so many varying conditions to the high school. Here we find some uniformity. There are enough contrasts, however, to attract attention; but these are in the main confined to the city schools where the grammar school has had such a checkered career. Since the States have become alive to the necessity of public high schools there is a distinct tendency toward uniformity. This question has been thoroughly discussed, however, by Dr. Edwin R. Snyder, of Teachers College, Columbia University, in "The Legal Status of the Rural High School." Colleges for years have published their entrance requirements, and high-school men have planned their courses to meet them. This has had a tendency to carry college methods into high-school classes. And here the two extremes meet—the grammar-school methods of thirteen or nineteen recitations a day, and college methods of three or four recitations a day. So our high schools have one of these tendencies. We find them carrying six and seven daily recitations of forty to fifty minutes each. This fills the entire day, and there is no break from opening exercise to the last recitation period. This is a continuation of certain grammar-school methods. On the other hand, we find high schools carrying only three or four recitations a day, each followed by a study period. This is approaching college methods. One superintendent of an eleven-year system writes that his four-year high school can present seventeen units certainly, eighteen possibly. That means that his pupils carry thirty to thirty-five recitations weekly, an impossible task; while another high school that has a nine-year grammar school carries in the high school only three periods daily, and takes five years to complete the courses. But the tendency is toward uniformity in high schools. Fifteen hours a week seems to be the average—that means three hours a day in the high school against five hours in the grammar school.

Another noticeable fact is that the grammar school comes up to the high school with fifteen daily recitations, and then drops to three and four daily recitations. Likewise, students come up to the high school having been accustomed to a recitation period of about fifteen or twenty minutes and then rise to a recitation period of forty-five minutes. The pupils come to the high school having had the teacher to aid in the preparation. In fact, the recitation period has been of such a nature in many instances that the teacher did the greater part of the thinking for the class until the class moved into the high school; here pupils are required to make individual preparation with little assistance from the teacher.

Taking a general view of the entire "educational ladder" from the first grade of the grammar school to the senior year of the college, we are confronted with a loss of students in the fifth and sixth grades, especially; another break comes in the first year of the high school. We notice a distinct falling-off through the four years of the high school; we are told over and over again that the character of the college student has defects sufficient to cause many writers and speakers to question the efficiency of the college. In it all and through it all this seems to be a very pertinent question: Do we yet know how to handle large numbers of students? Do we know the value of a subject, how it enters the life current of the individual, and what influence it has on the child? In making this study of the grammar school, this final question may be asked: What influence does this disorganized and seemingly purposeless work of the grammar school have on the subsequent years of the child when he is found in the high school and in the college?

BOOK REVIEWS

Helping School Children: Suggestions for Efficient Co-operation with the Public Schools. By ELSA DENISON. New York: Harper & Brothers, 1912. Pp. xxii+352.

In this carefully compiled volume, which draws its facts from hundreds of sources, Miss Denison shows the channels through which the general public in America expends voluntarily some $10,000,000 annually by way of supplementing the so-called regular work of the public schools. The book is of the type already made familiar by Perry's *Wider Use of the School Plant;* the scope, however, is much wider, inasmuch as it includes the activities of all sorts of supplementary educational agencies outside of the school plant as well. While many of the facts have already appeared in periodical literature and non-professional publications, it is the first appearance for most of them in sifted, balanced form in a carefully compiled educational volume. The work ought to be widely read.

The book enumerates the multitude of things that can be done for schools by parents and parents' associations, mothers' clubs, women's clubs, physicians, dentists, churches, business men's organizations, civic leagues, philanthropic bequests, libraries, newspapers, together with many other voluntary organizations of various types; and shows through concrete examples just how the work may be done, and the kind of results that may be expected.

The book shows that the importance of these forms of voluntary assistance is not to be measured by the amount of money expended. The $10,000,000 is only about 2 per cent of the $450,000,000 annually expended on public education—a relatively insignificant amount. Its importance is not so much in what it purchases as in the interest aroused in the community in the movements so fostered, an interest which results in large annual increases in the regular school budget.

JOHN F. BOBBITT

UNIVERSITY OF CHICAGO

Educational Administration: Quantitative Studies. By GEORGE DRAYTON STRAYER and EDWARD L. THORNDIKE. New York: Macmillan, 1913. Pp. xii+392. $2.00 net.

One of the large obstacles to progress in educational thought of the scientific type is the relative inaccessibility of its literature. It is to be found scattered through hundreds of books, bulletins, monographs, educational journals, and reports of countless organizations. It is time that this literature be sifted and summarized so that the best of all be made accessible to all, and the 95 per cent of repetitious matter be discarded.

Even the notable series of "Contributions to Educations" put out at Columbia University is mostly inaccessible to all except those in immediate contact with large educational libraries; and even then they can be used only for individual library reference, and not for class use, where they are most needed, owing to the almost universal lack of duplicate copies, and the impossibility of the students' purchasing so many expensive monographs.

In this volume, Professors Strayer and Thorndike have sifted out the materials of essential value that relate to educational administration from about a score of these monographs, and have presented them in so compact a compass that every educational administrator can have a copy for his desk, and in such a form, too, that the busy man will have time to read it. It permits also an effective use of these materials for class discussion, since the book can be in the hands of the students as a reference text.

For the most part, the volume does not attempt to show the relations of the various topics discussed to the field of education in general, or to show general administrative perspective. It is expected that the educational administrator is already familiar with these matters, and that where the book is used as a text, comment and perspective will be supplied by lectures and readings from other books already in the field. The volume consistently adheres to its plan of presenting only the essentials of the monographs; and it makes the valuable suggestion, which we hope will be heeded, "that similar volumes will be prepared adapting for students' use the work done by other natural groups of investigators."

Five kinds of topics are discussed. Part I presents "Studies of the Students": enrolment and attendance as related to ages and grades, elimination, promotion, retardation, and variations among students. Part II is made up of "Studies of the Teaching Staff": causes and conditions of teaching efficiency, social and economic status, special supervision, secondary teachers, and the influence of sex balance upon enrolment. Part III discusses the "Organization of Schools and Courses of Study": the elementary school curriculum, relation of size of school to effectiveness, the inefficiency of college entrance examinations, studies actually taken for the A.B. degree. Part IV considers "Means of Measuring Educational Products": scales in handwriting, composition, and arithmetic, achievements, school records and reports. Part V presents studies of "School Finance": city school expenditures, relation of these expenditures to other municipal expenditures, and the apportionment of school funds.

JOHN F. BOBBITT

UNIVERSITY OF CHICAGO

The Social Factors Affecting Special Supervision in the Public Schools of the United States. By WALTER ALBERT JESSUP. New York: Teachers College, Columbia University, 1911. Pp. viii+124.

Where education consciously attempts to prepare for active life in the world of affairs, schools find their tasks determined by the needs of this outside world. But the latter is always changing. For some time it has been growing more complicated. This results, on the one hand, in heavier demands upon the schools in subjects already included; and on the other hand in the inclusion of many things that hitherto were satisfactorily taken care of in extra-scholastic ways. Mr. Jessup's study covers this second aspect of growth of the curricula. It is a study of the genesis of the newer subjects in our public-school curricula, and of certain aspects of the present situation as regards these subjects. The subjects considered are music, drawing, manual training, domestic science, physical education, and penmanship.

Matters considered in connection with each subject are: the origin of the social demand, whether within or without the school; the sanctions on the basis of which the subject was justified, social, industrial, psychological; typical ways in which the new matter becomes a part of the curriculum; the modifications which the subject tends to undergo because of the intellectualistic predilections of the pedagogic mind; the spread of the subject through the schools of the country; the mode of teaching, whether by class teacher, special teacher, or co-operative effort on the part of both; sex and salaries of teachers of each of the subjects.

JOHN F. BOBBITT

UNIVERSITY OF CHICAGO

CURRENT EDUCATIONAL LITERATURE IN THE PERIODICALS[1]

IRENE WARREN
Librarian, School of Education, University of Chicago

Andrews, E. B. Education through reading. Pop. Sci. Mo. 83:139–49. (Ag. '13.)

Blaine, Anita McCormick. The ideals which led to the foundation of the School of Education. El. School T. 14:11–19. (S. '13.)

Brooks, E. C. Seven, eight, and nine years in the elementary school. El. School T. 14:20–28. (S. '13.)

Carrington, Thomas. Outdoor schools. Harp. W. 57:12. (26 Jl. '13.)

Dean, Arthur D. The new education: nature, the community, and the home are today combining with the school to train children for an industrial democracy. Craftsman 24:463–71. (Ag. '13.)

Doctorates conferred by American universities. Science 38:259–67. (22 Ag. '13.)

Gray, Mary Richards. The education of children in the school gardens of Los Angeles. Craftsman 24:472–79. (Ag. '13.)

Hanmer, Lee F. The schoolhouse evening centre—what it is, what it costs and what it pays. J. of Educa. (Bost.) 78:117–18. (14 Ag. '13.)

Harris, James H. Vacation schools. J. of Educa. (Bost.) 78:148–49. (21 Ag. '13.)

Human stock shows. Lit.D. 47:127–28. (26 Jl. '13.)

Judson, Harry Pratt. Economy in education. School R. 21:441–45. (S. '13.)

Key, Ellen. Education for motherhood. II. Atlan. 112:191–97. (Ag. '13.)

Leupp, Francis E. The progressive ideal in school management. Scrib. M. 54:388–94. (S. '13.)

Main, Josiah. Sequence of sciences in the high school. Pop. Sci. Mo. 83:158–63. (Ag. '13.)

(A) new laboratory for research in optics and photography. Sci. Am. Sup. 76:56–57. (26 Jl. '13.)

(An) open-window school. Lit.D. 47:241–42. (16 Ag. '13.)

Phelps, C. L. A study of errors in tests of adding ability. El. School T. 14:29–39. (S. '13.)

(The) traveling university. J. of Educa. (Bost.) 78:124–25. (14 Ag. '13.)

Walcott, Gregory D. The final examination of seniors in American colleges. Science 38:179–85. (8 Ag. '13.)

Wells, Frederic Lyman. The principle of mental tests. Science 38:221–24. (15 Ag. '13.)

[1] *Abbreviations.*—Atlan., Atlantic Monthly; El. School T., Elementary School Teacher; Harp. W., Harper's Weekly; J. of Educa. (Bost.), Journal of Education (Boston); Lit.D., Literary Digest; Pop. Sci. Mo., Popular Science Monthly; School R., School Review; Sci. Am. Sup., Scientific American Supplement; Scrib. M., Scribner's Magazine.

VOLUME XIV NUMBER 3

THE ELEMENTARY SCHOOL TEACHER

NOVEMBER 1913

EDUCATIONAL NEWS AND EDITORIAL COMMENT

Stuttering

The Board of Superintendents of the city schools of New York has issued a circular addressed to parents of children who stutter. There is no question at all that the early years of training in the school are of very great importance in avoiding this difficulty. Stuttering is a very serious handicap to any child, and if proper attention is given early in the school course to the cultivation of correct, distinct articulation the danger is very much decreased, if not, indeed, entirely removed. One of the specialists in this country who has had more experience with stuttering than most teachers or physicians has asserted with emphasis that if every child who has a disposition to stutter could be trained properly in the primary years he could be relieved entirely of this defect. There are some cases where surgical operations are necessary, but in most cases the difficulty is a functional difficulty in breathing and in the proper control of the vocal organs. The circular issued by the Board of Superintendents is therefore a very timely encouragement to parents to give their children proper training.

Your child has formed incorrect habits of speech. He will not speak correctly until he has been carefully trained in correct speech and has formed the habit of correct natural speech.

The speech improvement class has been formed for the purpose of systematically training pupils in correct natural speech and is in charge of a teacher who has made a thorough study of the principles of speech. Your child should become a member of that class. You should visit the class occasionally and co-operate with the teacher, that you may continue the work of building correct speech habits when the child is at home. This is very important, as he can have at best only a very small part of each day under instruction for speech, and he is constantly using his former bad habits, which are altogether too firmly fixed at present.

The physical, breathing, and vocal exercises are excellent material for home practice, but the application of these to his everyday speech is a very important factor in his training. Your co-operation with the teacher will more than repay you and the child by the results obtained.

Though progress seems to be slow, do not lose confidence in the teacher, or fail to encourage the child in his efforts. Do not try scolding, threatening, or ridicule as a means of cure. Never unduly excite him. Never indulge a child because of his stuttering. All stutterers are despondent at times, and hence the attitude toward the child should always be a cheerful one. Stutterers, almost without exception, talk too rapidly; therefore encourage slow, deliberate, and modulated speech. Singing tones can be used to advantage. The child should be led to acquire correct speaking by observing, listening to, and imitating slow, distinct, well-spoken conversations.

Try to get the child to breathe naturally. It is not necessary to say a full sentence in a single breath. Let the child feel free to pause for breath at the end of any phrase.

Pay particular attention to correct articulation of sounds. When any sound has been learned, see that the child uses the correct form in his daily speech.

Let the child frequently read aloud or tell an incident to one or more members of the family, or let him recite from memory. Call attention to any improvement, have patience, and do not attempt to correct all mistakes at once.

He should be carefully kept away from stutterers outside of school.

The physical condition of the child is of the highest importance. He needs nourishing diet, with no stimulants (tea or coffee), and plenty of exercise in the open air. The greatest help toward a cure is perfect health.

Pennsylvania Normal Schools

The normal-school situation in the state of Pennsylvania has been the subject of investigation and of much discussion of late. The following statement from the *Philadelphia Ledger* is therefore interesting as indicating the changes which are being worked out in these institutions:

A beginning has been made of standardizing the dozen or more normal schools of this state by the purchase of the West Chester Normal School for a consideration of $12,900.

It is not generally known that most of the training schools for teachers of Pennsylvania—those in this city and Pittsburgh being notable exceptions—have remained distinctively private academies whose courses of instruction and budget systems are only secondarily under the authority of the state. Private ownership and personal gains too frequently take precedence of educational standards. Consequently, no two of the schools offer diplomas which have precisely the same face value throughout the commonwealth.

All this is to be changed by the wise provisions of the new school law which provides for the purchase of the schools from their stockholders. In this first instance of transfer the deal was consummated without any of the sharp bargaining which over-shrewd holders of stock might have felt inclined to resort to at the expense of the public-school treasury. All trustees and stockholders of the other normal schools are expected to show the same fidelity to the cause of public education and relinquish their ownership claims to the state at the earliest practical moment for a proper compensation.

There should be no delay in raising all these training schools for teachers to the level of the high plane established by the Normal School for Girls and the School of Pedagogy of this city. The face value of every normal-school certificate should be approximately the same and should always represent throughout this state and elsewhere sound scholarship and the most complete pedagogic equipment obtainable.

The *Elementary School Teacher* is very glad indeed to give publicity to the following notice and request:

A School Exhibit

During the late fall and early winter the City Club of Chicago will hold in its clubrooms an exhibit of public buildings and grounds for the purpose of stimulating municipalities to make improvements in police stations, streets and alleys, playgrounds, schools, etc. A large space will be devoted to school buildings and grounds and it is the desire of the subcommittee in charge of the school exhibit to secure helpful suggestions from all persons interested in the success of the public schools.

The general purpose is to show the functions of school buildings and grounds and the adequacy of the buildings and grounds for the performance of these functions. Particular attention will be paid to heating, lighting, ventilating, seating, and general care of buildings. All persons interested are asked to send suggestions to William J. Bogan, Chairman, Subcommittee of School Buildings and Grounds.

Compulsory Education in Tennessee

The last legislature of Tennessee passed a compulsory attendance law. There was much discussion during the meeting of the legislature as to the probable effect of that law in increasing the attendance of children on the public schools of the state. An answer to these questions comes with the opening of the schools this autumn. The following clipping from Columbia, Tenn., is typical of news items which are appearing in the public press in different parts of that state:

More and more the effects of the compulsory school law are becoming apparent in every section of the state, and these effects have not missed Maury County.

The principal and most noticeable effect, perhaps, is the shortage of the school books. The local depository for the school books recently made out its order for books, based on the estimate of the demands for the opening of the schools in the county, and this order was only partially filled, being some three hundred books or more short, in spellers and primers.

The explanation of this shortage from the state agent was that the compulsory school law had had the effect of increasing the estimated demand for the books that were short.

It will be noticed that the shortage is in the primary grades, just the ones that would be effected by the school law referred to. It will probably be August 20 to 25 before this shortage can be supplied.

Other sections of the state have been disappointed even worse than the local depository. While the books were short on the recent order, the schools in the county that have already opened are not suffering, and only the schools that are to open later may be subjected to some inconvenience for a short time for the books with which to supply the primary grades.

According to the state superintendent of public instruction the county schools all over Tennessee are raising the Macedonian cry for more teachers to meet the necessities of the increased daily attendance.

C. H. J.

International Congress on School Hygiene

The Buffalo meeting of the International Congress on School Hygiene, August 25–30, was a big event. Hundreds of delegates from all over the world crowded the hotel corridors and the various rooms in which the sessions were held. Some five hundred papers were presented during the week on a great variety of topics. The following outline taken from the exhibit that was part of the Congress gives an idea of the scope of health direction now undertaken in public schools:

Child Study: Eugenics; Lectures and Exhibits; Special Schools for Defectives; Trained Psychologist; Laboratory for Examinations.

Preventive Hygiene: Sex Hygiene; Care of Eyes, Ears, and Teeth; Food and Adequate Rest; Cleanliness.

Physical Training: Gymnasiums; Games and Dancing; Corrective Gymnastics under a Competent Director.

Wider Use of the School Plant: For Lectures and Exhibits; School Lunches; Summer Supply of Pure Milk; Child Welfare Work; Little Mothers' Clubs.

Medical Inspection: With Adequate Dispensary Service; Co-operation of

Family Physician, of Principal, Teachers, and Parents; Home Visitation; School Nurses; Contact with Juvenile Court.

Preventive Measures: Proper Buildings with Adequate Light, Heat, Ventilation; Correct Furniture; Teachers' Restrooms; Sanitary Toilets, Sterilized Towels, Drinking-Fountains; Open-Air Rooms; Well-printed Books; Curriculum That Is Correct from Health Standpoint; Matron for the High School.

Personal Hygiene: Bathing, Food, Air, Exercise, Rest, Clothing; Care of Eyes, Nose, Throat, Teeth. Infection and Immunity; Study Habits; Beauty; Efficiency.

It is impossible to report the proceedings in limited space. A few excerpts may be given:

"We have in this country 183,000 students in colleges and universities; 187,000 patients in hospitals for the insane. Do the results justify our methods of education?"—Potter.

"The acquisition of good habits and not of information is our educational aim."—Burnham.

"The schools should develop a rudimentary philosophy of life."—Burnham.

"Free eyeglasses are an economy, not a charity."—Wessels.

"With an epidemic of contagious disease existing," said Dr. McLaughlin, "there is a tendency in most communities to close the schools. In the Philippines, on the contrary, it is the policy of the Bureau of Health to keep the schools open because of their extraordinary value in teaching the precepts of disease prevention.

"They are used in cholera epidemics as demonstrating stations where the children were taught how to protect themselves and their parents against cholera. The same principle is used in combating tuberculosis, hookworm, dysentery, and beri-beri. The children are taught how these diseases are contracted and how they may be prevented."

Dr. Charles V. Chapin maintained that, generally speaking, the schoolroom is not a factor in the spread of many contagious diseases.

"Because scarlet fever and diphtheria are much less prevalent in summer and increase during the autumn," he said, "it is argued that the increase must be due to school attendance. It is, however, clearly shown by figures, derived from various cities, that there is no real correlation between these diseases and school attendance, but rather between them and seasonal temperature.

"Detailed study of cases also shows that very few cases of scarlet fever and diphtheria are contracted in school. It is otherwise with measles and whooping cough, the spread of which seems to be greatly facilitated by school attendance. That other contagious diseases are spread in schools, we have no evidence.

"The way to prevent infection in school is to teach personal cleanliness. Abolish the drinking-cup and the towel in common use. Keep careful watch of contagious diseases and exclude them. The fumigation of schoolrooms is a concession to prejudices of the past."

Dr. Walter W. Roach told of an interesting experiment with two classes of third-grade pupils in Philadelphia. One class occupied a room heated and ventilated in the usual way. The second class studied all winter in a classroom with the windows wide open.

"The windows of the one room were kept constantly down from the top and up from the bottom, and the room was cut off from the regular heating plant of the building. The ordinary desks were removed, and replaced with chair desks which could easily be moved by the pupils themselves to clear the floor space for frequent physical exercises. As cold weather approached, the children were provided with woolen sweaters, worsted caps, soft woolen blankets, and knitted woolen gloves. Thus their lower extremities were protected from the cold floor with no disturbance of the circulation.

"Week by week during the fall and winter and spring we weighed and examined these pupils, watched their study and their play, and compared their scholarship with that of the children in the warm-air room. The children from both rooms came from the same kind of homes, so that the test was as fair and as accurate and searching as possible. As might have been expected, we found at the end that the pupils in the open-window room had gained on an average more than twice as much in weight as those in the warm-air room. They kept wholly free from colds, and were much more regular in attendance than the others."

E. R. D.

School Hygiene

The International Congress on Hygiene, which convened at Buffalo and which is reported in another section, has aroused very widespread discussion throughout the country on the problems of hygiene in the school.

Open-Air Schools

A number of cities and institutions are experimenting with open-air schools as a means of improving the health of pupils. The project which is being organized at Bryn Mawr has received wide currency. This plan, in brief, consists in giving a complete outdoor education for seven years to a number of girls. They enter the school at ten and continue until they finish their college career. This thoroughgoing experiment will be watched with interest. A number of school systems are introducing open-air schools for children who suffer from tuberculosis, undernourishment, or some other physical disability. The *Harrisburg, Pa., Independent* has the following note in regard to a school to be opened in that city:

If the plans of the medical inspector of the Harrisburg school district are carried out, a second open-air school for the education of tubercular pupils will be established in Harrisburg this fall. Money for such a school was appropriated in the annual budget this spring and active steps are now being made to establish the school.

An open-air school is also to be started in Portland, Ore.

A Supervisor of Hygienics

Another symptom of the increased interest in the hygiene of school children is the appointment of a new officer in the city of Houston, Tex., as reported in the *Houston Post:*

Supervisor of hygienics is the newest office in the Houston city school system. It was created at a meeting of the School Board Monday night, when it was decided that a regular physician should be employed for that position to be placed on the pay-rolls at a salary of about $300 per month and to have entire supervision of all matters pertaining to health, sanitation, and hygiene in the various schools.

The spread of psychological clinics in connection with public-school systems or under other auspices is a further evidence of the attention which is given to the mental abnormalities of children. According to a note sent out by the Bureau of Education there are now forty psychological clinics in the United States. The first clinic for the examination of deficient children was founded by Dr. Witmer at the University of Pennsylvania in 1896.

A Trial of Slanting Desks

An attempt to improve the physical conditions of the schoolroom in such a way as to prevent physical abnormalities is reported from Chicago. According to the *Chicago Tribune* the superintendent of schools is about to instal in several rooms desks with a top having a slant of 35 degrees. Educational theorists have for a long time condemned the flat-top desk for children. The slanting top favors a more erect posture in reading, writing, drawing, etc., but the practical difficulties have thus far prevented the adoption of a desk with much slant. The results of this experiment will therefore be of much interest.

Another modification of the physical equipment of the schoolroom is reported by the *Detroit News:*

The new Sampson School at Ironwood and Begole Streets, in the Sixteenth Ward, has been equipped with movable chairs and tables similar to those in use in the ordinary business office. The pupils who flock to the new school this morning will be the first public-school children who have not been forced to absorb the rudiments of education at the nailed-to-the-floor desk and bench. The experiment of substituting movable chairs and tables will be watched with interest outside of Detroit, for it is new to the country, generally, as well as to this city.

The Problem of Congestion

The opening of the school year with the increase in pupils over the past year has caused attention to be particularly directed toward the insufficient accommodations of the school buildings. Various means are being adopted to meet the problem which arises from the congestion of the schools. The *Globe and Commercial Advertiser* of New York reports a method of taking care of two sets of children in the same school without unduly reducing the length of the school day for the pupils. The plan is the so-called Ettinger plan with some modifications.

Unless present plans are changed when the Board of Education meets this afternoon, and that does not now appear likely, the last act necessary to carry into effect the plan for reducing part time approved unanimously by the board two weeks ago will be taken. It is to amend the by-laws to reduce the school day for all young children from five to four hours, and to authorize double sessions of five hours each in the upper grades. The Brooklyn Teachers' Association has asked for a hearing, but it is too late. The Public Education Association has followed its usual policy of seeking delay. The members of the Board of Education are convinced that a careful study has been made of the problem by the superintendents, that prompt action is necessary, and that after the plan has been tried out any changes found to be necessary can be made. There isn't any evidence at present that any will be.

Everything is in readiness to put the plan into operation without delay. In anticipation of favorable action by the board today, City Superintendent Maxwell, by direction of the board of superintendents, ordered district superintendents and principals that to put the proposed plan into operation it is necessary to act promptly. "There should be no delay," he says in his circular to them, "in making preparations to put into operation the recommendations."

It is significant to note that teachers and principals in general have not regarded this plan with great favor for reasons which are obvious. It appears, however, to be a better expedient than to reduce the school day in length.

Another method of relieving congestion consists in expanding the available school space by means of providing portable buildings. This plan has been in operation in Chicago for some time and is to be extended this year by the addition of a hundred portable buildings containing 188 rooms. A similar plan is being put into operation in Cleveland, Toledo, and Columbus, Ohio, Racine, Wis., South Bend, Ind., and Long Beach, Cal., among other places. The time will doubtless come when school boards will have sufficient foresight to provide for the increasing needs of the school population, but until such time comes school administrators will find it necessary to adopt such temporary expedients.

Cost of Living and Teachers' Salaries

A report which is made by a committee of the National Education Association and published by the Bureau of Education has called attention to the relation between the increase in cost of living and the salaries received by teachers. Part of the report is thus summarized by the *Northwest Journal of Education:*

Dr. Robert C. Brooks, executive secretary for the National Education Association committee, which prepared the report, shows by Bureau of Labor figures that wholesale prices in 1911 were 44.1 per cent higher than in 1907; that retail prices had increased 50.2 per cent in the same period; while in June, 1912, retail food prices were 61.7 per cent higher than in 1896. With these figures as a basis he analyzes teachers' salaries in five cities in different parts of the United States and demonstrates the plight of the teachers in the problem of increased cost of living.

The natural consequence of the diminishing returns from the salaries is the agitation of many teachers' associations for increased salary. Another symptom of the same attitude of mind is the effort which is being made toward pensions for retired teachers. A circular from the chairman of the Committee to Advance Insurance Legislation for Teachers of Illinois has for its purpose the awakening of interest in a bill which is to be introduced into the Illinois legislature. This is known as the Illinois Teachers' Insurance and Retirement Fund Bill and was framed by a committee of Freeport teachers. The provisions of the bill are briefly summarized in the circular as follows:

1. Its name, Insurance. It is a better investment than ordinary life insurance, as the benefit is *annual, for life,* instead of a single endowment.

2. It requires twenty-five years of service, fifteen in Illinois. No age limit is stated.

3. It provides for illness and other loss of time (Secs. 548, 549, 551, 554, 555).

4. If a teacher leaves the profession, it allows her to withdraw three-fourths of all money paid in.

5. If a teacher dies before completing twenty-five years of service, her estate receives three-fourths of all money paid in.

6. It provides that the fund shall be in the custody of the state treasurer and subject to the same requirements.

7. It requires the state to make an annual appropriation to the fund.

Salaries and Qualifications

That there is another side to the question of teachers' salaries is indicated by the action of the Board of Education of Philadelphia in limiting the attendance of students at the normal school. The *Philadelphia Inquirer* reports the action in the following words:

Drastic regulations to limit the attendance of students at the Normal School and thus reduce the number of applicants for positions as teachers in the local system, it was stated yesterday, would result from the present controversy as to whether graduates of the classes of 1912 or 1913 should be given preference in appointments by the Board of Education.

The school body has been divided for several months over the problem of supplying places for all available teachers and, it was declared by officials yesterday, it will endeavor to avoid these differences in the future by keeping the supply in proportion to the demand.

If this action in limiting the number who enter the normal school is accompanied by raising the standard of entrance, it deals with the fundamental principle affecting salaries. It is obvious that salaries are dependent, not merely upon the efforts of the interested individuals to obtain compensation adequate to meet their needs, but also upon the relation between supply and demand and upon the professional equipment of those who offer themselves for service. The legislature of Wisconsin recognizes this fact in the recent law in which a minimum salary of $400 for teachers was fixed. In the same law in which a minimum salary was fixed, a minimum requirement of education and equipment was also included.

F. N. F.

THE RELATION BETWEEN AND THE CONTROL OF MANUAL ARTS AND VOCATIONAL EDUCATION[1]

F. D. CRAWSHAW
University of Wisconsin

The purpose of this paper is to show how the present public-school facilities may be reorganized to meet the demands, not only of public-school manual arts, but of vocational education as well.

The public from time to time hears of some wonderful discovery, for example in the field of medicine. Immediately a new class of doctors appears, and the claim set forth by them is this: We have found a new way to treat people for an old disease. We are the only physicians who can effect a cure.

In our educational progress at the present time the new doctor is the man who is advocating vocational education as the only means of keeping boys in school. He is the physician of *general* practice, however. But there is the specialist. He does not treat the boy who has any one or all of many aches and pains and who would relieve himself by quitting school. He is the man who prescribes for the boy who has just one particular kind of a pain, viz., a heartache to do real industrial work. This boy has taken medicine that we call manual training, but because it has not been given in large, allopathic, bitter-pill doses he has not entirely recovered from his trouble. His pain is simply reduced by this treatment; or perhaps, as in the case of many a misapplied potion, it has been aggravated thereby. The only way to cure him, says the industrial educationalist, is to give him an old-fashioned dose of sulphur and molasses without any peppermint in it. Hard work and long hours with eyes always fixed upon the one goal—a wage-earning job—is the ultimatum.

Now I take it that very few people believe there is *only one way* to cure a boy from wishing to leave school, any more than we

[1] Address before the Northeastern Minnesota Teachers' Association, December, 1912.

believe there is only one way to cure one from some physical ailment. Neither do I think that many of us believe it necessary always to prescribe *an entirely new method* in education any more than I believe we think it is always necessary to prescribe an entirely new and perhaps drastic means of curing some ailment of the body.

What I do believe is this: Most of us feel certain that in old methods which have had some degree of success in producing desired results there must be something worth while, even though the conditions under which the means have been used have changed; also, that in many well-thought-out new methods there must be much that deserves consideration. Consequently with reference to our present educational problem, "How shall we provide for vocational education?" I assume that, with me, you may believe two things, viz., (1) that in the old method of securing motor activity of an industrial type, that is, manual training, there must be something good, even at the present time when industrial education is the advocated cure-all for most educational ills, and (2) that in industrial education there is subject-matter, and method too, perhaps, which should be regarded as the best we know at the present time and therefore should be used.

These assumptions are made partly because school teachers are known to be of conservative mind—a mind, which, however, is not ultra-conservative, for it is not only willing but eager to respond to all that is new, if the new has in it the promise of reliability.

The statement printed upon the front page of an educational program which I saw recently suggests the attitude of teachers toward transition in educational matters. The statement follows: "Our system of education must be continually modified to meet new conditions, if it is to train boys and girls to meet the emergencies and seize the opportunities of modern life. The ideal system is the one which best meets the vital problems of the present and the future!" If we are all in accord with the underlying thought in this quotation, particularly in two essentials, viz., (1) that the present system must be "continually modified" and (2) "that the ideal system must meet *both present and near-future problems*," we shall be sympathetic in this discussion.

Before entering upon the main part of my theme, may I give briefly, and in a non-technical way, a few definitions:

1. *Manual arts* means what we usually think of as the subject-matter of public-school drawing and shop work.

2. *Manual training* is the method or process involved in teaching the manual arts.

3. *Vocational education* is that form of education the purpose of which is to prepare for particular productive service.

4. *Industrial education* is that part of vocational education which prepares for industrial service.

It will be seen upon reflection that the real difference between the manual arts and vocational education, if the above definitions are correct, is about, if not quite, the same as the difference between multiplying 2×4 for the sake of mental discipline and multiplying 2×4 to find out what four two-cent postage stamps cost. In the first case we have an example of generalization; in the second case we have an example of specialization. You reach the conclusion—a correct one I believe—that manual arts is a form of *general education* while vocational education is a form of *special education*, or education for a particular end.

It is because the manual arts in our public schools have not been properly differentiated and specialized that they have not been vocational. If we wish to make them vocational then we shall differentiate them and make them special in character.

Can we do this and if so shall we in our existing public schools?

My answer is that *we can* and that *we should*.

The agitation for vocational education has been vital to our American people for five years past. It is vital for three reasons:

1. It is vital because it is the result of an economic demand. We are told by the manufacturers through the National Association of Manufacturers that America is running far behind its competitors in the Old World in the race for industrial supremacy. We no longer have skilled labor in America they tell us. We are further told by this association that through industrial training as a form of vocational education we may hope to secure a sufficient number of skilled mechanics to meet the demand. In the process, also, at least one-half of the school population beyond the age of fourteen

will be saved from a precarious livelihood—the result of an unskilled and consequently, truly speaking, unproductive labor—a form of labor in which boys and girls engage as soon as the state permits them to leave school and go to work.

2. It is vital because it is the result of a social demand. No less a personage than Miss Jane Addams of Hull House, Chicago, has quite conclusively proven this. All associations for civic and social betterment are agreed that the man or woman who possesses skill in some form of industry is a happier, a more helpful social being and a better citizen thereby. Formerly, the distinction between the "cultural" and "bread-and-butter" aims in education was drawn sharply. It was considered unsocial and even sordid to pursue knowledge with the hope of improving one's career in a financial way. Today this idea is changed. Instead of being sordid or basely utilitarian, Professor Frank Leavitt of the University of Chicago says about vocational education, or the education for utilitarian ends, that it "represents one of the finest ideals which the human mind has conceived, and sets forth a philosophy of life which can be fully realized under no other conditions than complete solidarity."

3. It is vital because it is the result of an educational demand. It may be that the educational workers of the country are always a little behind the economic and social workers in seeing the real need of the masses and adjusting their machinery to meet the need. However, the adjustment is always made. It has been made in the past to line up with political changes and it will be made now to accord with industrial changes. The National Education Association and every state and local educational association is keyed up to the point which demands adjustment in educational means and methods to solve the great educational problem of the hour.

Now both the manufacturers and the labor unions have tried to solve the problem of vocational education in the form of industrial education by each organizing schools to make better industrial workers and likewise better citizens. The result has been conflict growing out of misunderstanding and perhaps prejudice and jealousy. The manufacturer has accused the labor union, as the labor union has accused the manufacturer, of exploiting youth in the specially endowed school for the special interest represented by the organization which established the school.

So, does it not become a public-school problem? It would seem so to me, and I think it must seem so to all of us who are charged with the problem of educating the American youth, without reference to the special interests of any particular individual or set of individuals save the boys and girls themselves. Their interests we must certainly regard and conserve. Have we done so in the past? Yes, to the best of our ability. But have we constantly kept in mind the fact that with each new year our younger companions in school are surrounded by a changed social and economic atmosphere? Perhaps so, but it has not always been evident from the adjustments we have made from year to year. On the dynamic side of our education we have fortified ourselves with what we have called the vocational studies: the commercial branches, agriculture, domestic science, and the manual arts, and then with the conviction of the man who trusts in the Almighty for his daily sustenance without himself making an effort to provide for the needs of the day, we have failed to exert ourselves further. The result has been stagnation. It has come through so-called vocational work, but in the guise of manual training for "cultural" ends alone. Gradually these vocational subjects have become more and more formal until by main force, as it were, interests outside of the school system have aroused us from our apathy.

Again we are given the opportunity truly to vitalize and motivate our vocational work and make it *real.*

I would not in this apparent arraignment of our past methods even suggest that what we have called manual training, for example, has not been worth while. It has; but as a general educational means, not as a vocational means. What we are now called upon to do, if we will, is to make it both educational and vocational. And I truly believe that if we do not accept this opportunity—one which the educators of twenty-five or thirty years ago had but failed to accept—we shall not be given a similar opportunity again. If we but read the signs we cannot but see that some way, somehow, the estimated 85 per cent who will not accept our methods of the past are to be given methods adapted to their environment—one which is largely industrial, we are told. The fathers and mothers of these boys and girls are engaged in an economic struggle in which industrial activity plays an important part.

Now, "necessity is the mother of invention." We have been confronted with the necessity for vocational education; we have invented a means of giving it. And what is the invention? State laws for vocational education in twenty-nine of the states of the Union with several others seeking the enactment of vocational education bills into laws during the legislative sessions of the present year. And what is the result of the inventions—these laws? Vocational schools of *two kinds:* (1) those placed under the administrative control of existing boards of education; (2) those placed under the administrative control of new boards, usually called industrial education boards.

In general it may be said that the first of these t[illegible]s seeks to utilize present resources and facilities by extending and expanding them so that there shall be a reformation rather than a revolution. The second of these two schools for the most part fails to recognize anything good in the schools as they exist and works upon the theory that nothing good can come out of Nazareth; therefore we must create anew.

In the particular field of educational work in which I am especially interested the first school says to its manual-arts director: "Here is a new problem. I believe you can solve it. We will give you the benefit of the judgment of our representative manufacturers and industrial workmen. You may employ expert commercial workmen, purchase new machinery, and have more time in which to do your work. Your problem is one of *adjustment.* In making the adjustment, maintain *not* the traditions of the past, but the vitalizing educational *purpose* of the work of the past which has been found lacking in subject-matter only."

The second school will have nothing to do with the manual-arts teacher of the past. In the spirit of revolution, rather than evolution, it sets up an entirely new organization. It employs a man from the shops who may be and probably is an excellent workman, but who may not be and usually is not a teacher. It purchases an entirely new equipment, puts it into a new building, and says to the prospective instructor: "Here is a class of boys who have tired and sickened of the public school and its *play*. Put them to work. Train them (mind you, train them, not educate), train them to be skilled workers in your occupation."

My illustration is an extreme one, but by it I wish more clearly and surely to make my point, viz., each school is attempting to solve a *single* problem: the most effective education of the boys (or girls in the case of girls' vocational schools) who need vocational work to satisfy their craving for instruction which will do two things: (1) prepare them directly for productive employment, and (2) prepare them for better living.

Now, as is the case with almost everything that exists, there is good in both of these schools and in their methods. The question we have to answer is this: Which one has the greatest possibility in [illegible] boys and girls themselves? Each one of us must answer this question for himself, but we may be helped in reaching a conclusion if we will consider a somewhat similar question, but one which takes us out of the schoolroom and away from its atmosphere.

Would you or would I, if we had a large sum of money to invest in some new enterprise, put it into the hands of a number of trained men who had the reputation of being honest, earnest, and capable in the conduct of general business, and who would join with them experts in the particular new business to be undertaken, that they might counsel with these new members and perhaps allow their judgment to carry in the case of special or new points which were carefully considered by all? Or would we put our money into the hands of a special committee whom we also knew to be honest and earnest, but whose business ability had been tested in the handling of their own special affairs and in a way which had little or no relation to the general affairs under community control in which the first group of men were well versed?

Again, perhaps, my illustration is not well chosen, but you see the point of it I am sure.

Are we going to intrust vocational education to a fair-minded board of education with a special committee made up of men experienced in both the management and actual operation of the vocations concerned, or are we going to have this special committee or board, disconnected with the existing school organization, act alone? It is the much-mooted question—a debatable one—whether vocational education shall be administered by a unit or a dual system of control.

For the manual arts, it means this: Shall we continue to utilize our present facilities both in physicial equipment and individual instructors for an extended and expanded manual arts which shall either become vocational in character, or include vocational education, or are we going to encourage and finally allow, without effort on our part, manual arts for vocational ends to be controlled by administrators who have little or no immediate knowledge of the educational significance of this important connecting link between book work and the work of productive labor? And shall we allow this work to be taught by men who come from the shops without their having some training for the great work of teaching?

The question is already being answered and answered by the very natural means of practical experiments. In Wisconsin we are experimenting—I think I can say no more than this—with the *dual system* of control and the shop man as teacher. In New York, New Jersey, Ohio, and other states the unit system of control is in vogue, and in these states, as in Wisconsin to a degree, both manual-arts teachers and shop men are acting as teachers. From what observation I am able to make—and I come in contact with a good many schools and teachers of industrial work every year—the idea of unit control is in the ascendency. I cannot speak as positively with reference to the teacher. As Dr. David Snedden, commissioner of education for Massachusetts says: "We are obtaining teachers much as the early settlers obtained their food—we are trusting to an accidental and variable supply produced by no effort of our own."

And yet it is perfectly evident now as it proved to be when manual training was first introduced in our schools that the man of actual shop experience, who has been trained to teach, is meeting with much more success than is the shop man who may perform his daily work at the bench or machine with great success, and who may be able to train an individual apprentice but who cannot secure a systematic development in the same work with a *class of boys*. It is the old problem of turning the trick by having the power of organization and the ability to impart knowledge.

I would not be understood to say that the shop man cannot teach. My experience during the past two years in a continuation school for mechanics in which they are being trained for industrial teaching makes me feel certain that intelligent shop men properly trained may make some of our best teachers. I most thoroughly believe, however, that the wide-awake manual-arts teacher who has had some good commercial shop experience has much the advantage over the shop man unless the latter will spend a larger time in academic and professional teaching preparation than the manual-arts teacher will need to spend in a commercial shop. I cannot agree with Mr. C. A. Prosser, secretary of the National Society for the Promotion of Industrial Education, that a man must spend not less than five years in the commercial shop to be prepared to teach industrial work.

Nor would I be understood to say that the manual-arts department to retain its educational significance, nor the industrial school to maintain an educational atmosphere, must not have in it a shop man. To my mind unless the manual-arts teacher is a man of considerable commercial shop experience he must have associated with him in his work, not only advisers from the shops, but men from the commercial shops who will teach with him.

What is needed on the side of administration is a combination of manufacturers or employers of labor, employees, and school men in the administrative body which now exists, viz., the public-school board, and what is needed in the teaching is a combination of the school teacher and the shop workman. Get him in one person, if possible, either from the ranks of manual-arts teachers or from the commercial shop. What is needed is a man of commercial shop experience with teaching ability coupled with good character, virility, and the proper sympathy with the work he is doing for boys. He must have a burning desire to make them both good workmen and good citizens.

Furthermore, it must always be true that every boy, whether

he differentiates, and to a degree specializes, in his school work, either in a regular or a special public school, must have the opportunity *to advance as far as his abilities will permit him.* If he is a permit boy in a continuation school he should first be trained both in vocational and non-vocational work to be a *better workman.* If he is a boy in a regular public school he should likewise be trained, at the time when his desire for active community life makes it necessary, to work hard and long at the thing in which he wishes to become proficient, but this thing should be of the applied and concrete type, not the formal and abstract. Herein lies the chief suggestion for our public-school manual arts.

It is all a part of the great problem of universal education, and as Dean Eugene Davenport of the University of Illinois has said: "The best results will always follow when as many subjects as possible and as many vocations as may be are taught together in the same school, under the same management, and to the same body of men."

Differentiation and a certain amount of specialization is needed as early as the sixth grade. It should be preceded by a type of work, both vocational and non-vocational, and this prevocational work should be furnished in applied, concrete problems, if possible, that will show the connection between school and the work-a-day world. *But the exploitation of youth must always be a moral and therefore an educational impossibility.*

ADDRESSES BY CITIZENS TO SCHOOL BOYS

Various citizens of Winnipeg have made addresses before the public-school boys. These addresses have been printed in pamphlet form by the Winnipeg Industrial Bureau. That Bureau gave permission to the *Elementary School Teacher* to print several of the addresses as examples of what can be done in the way of bringing industrial information into the schools. There is no community where similar addresses are not possible.

APPRENTICESHIP

E. E. E. BAILEY
Supervisor of Apprentices, Canadian Pacific Railway Shops, Winnipeg

This afternoon I have been asked to talk to you, boys, on the way to become an apprentice. Several papers were read to you last season on the choice of a trade and how to commence and follow it, and I want now to go a little farther and tell you of the steps necessary to be taken, once you have decided on the trade to follow, should you wish to be apprenticed with us at Weston.

But first I want to point out, as so many gentlemen did in their addresses in the early part of the year, how very necessary it is that you should not suddenly drop, at the age of twelve or fourteen, all schooling. You will see why in a moment.

We have thirteen distinct and separate trades for you to choose from, namely, machinist, electrical machinist, boiler-maker, blacksmith, molder, pipe-fitter, airbrake-fitter, brass-finisher, pattern-maker, tinsmith, painter, tool-maker, and coach-carpenter, so you see there is plenty of choice.

But we expect a boy, once he has selected the trade he thinks he would like to follow, and has been duly apprenticed to it, to stick to it and not to switch round and tell us he does not like what he has chosen and that he wants to change to something else.

However, telling you that now, is rather like putting the cart before the horse, and you will want to know what to do first.

First, then, when you apply at the shops, you will have to pass an entrance examination in simple arithmetic, such as sums in fractions and decimals, freehand drawing, and English composition, because we are going to teach you more than that before we turn you out a tradesman, and we have not time to instruct you in all primary subjects.

Now, it is just here where so many applicants fail (and if you don't pass the examination you don't get made an apprentice), and that is why I said, at the beginning, it was so necessary to keep up, at any rate in some degree, the schooling that many boys leave behind them for a couple of years. Many boys come along thinking it easy enough to remember what they learned three or four years back, and are surprised when they get stuck with what used to be simple sums. That is where the advantage of keeping up your schooling comes in, for it is only by constant practice that you can keep your mind trained to acquire and retain knowledge.

It does not follow, in fact it very rarely happens, that there is an immediate vacancy for an apprentice in any of the trades, even if he is successful in passing the entrance examination. We have so many boys anxious to serve their time with the company that a waiting list is kept for each trade, and boys enter in rotation as vacancies occur. So it is better for a boy to present himself some months before he is sixteen (which is the minimum age at which apprenticeships are started), in order that he will be able to complete the obligatory five years at the time, or soon after, he is twenty-one.

Next, supposing the vacancy occurs. The senior boy on the list is written to, generally about a fortnight beforehand (so that, if he is in a job he can give convenient notice), and instructed to obtain a medical certificate of suitability from the company's doctor—and, I may say, that no boy is accepted who is a cigarette smoker. Armed with this, and accompanied by his parent or guardian, he comes up to the shops, and, provided the certificate is satisfactory, he is duly indentured or apprenticed. These indentures are simple documents, consisting practically of two clauses, one that he shall serve an apprenticeship of five years, and the other that he shall not become a member of a trades union until he is out of his time, when he can please himself.

All these preliminary things being settled, the boy is now fairly launched into the way of learning his trade. The training in every department is very careful and thorough and, beyond his shop work, each boy in his first year takes up for two hours a week, in the company's time, his arithmetic where he left off at school, and one or two other elementary subjects, such as freehand drawing. The next two years he is given more extended technical instruction for four hours per week, and each year the company donates scholarships to the five boys gaining the highest marks in the annual examinations on the year's work. These scholarships consist of some technical course chosen by the successful boy as most useful in increasing his theoretical knowledge of the trade he is learning, and a special class is held each week for them.

Now, there are only one or two things the company expects from an apprentice in return for the care, time, and trouble that is expended on him. First, he must be punctual, and, second, he must apply himself to his work and seek to learn all he can. Idleness is not allowed, nor is inattention or incivility. As regards punctuality, he is allowed two "lates" in a month, with a maximum of twelve a year, and he may have one hundred hours off per annum without affecting his annual increase. Anything over this number he has to make up before he can obtain an increase in pay.

The rates of wages during apprenticeship are the same for all trades and run as follows: first year, 13 cents per hour; second year, 17 cents; third year, 20 cents; fourth year, 23 cents, and the fifth year, 26 cents per hour. Free holiday transportation is granted on an ascending scale, starting with a short distance the first year and finishing in the fifth over all the Canadian Pacific Railway system, foreign continental lines and a three-quarter rate on Canadian Pacific Railway boats to and from England.

On completion of a satisfactory apprenticeship the apprentice receives a certificate and passes at once on to the current rate of pay for the trade he has learnt.

The company takes a great interest in the present system of

training, which has now been in existence for over three years, and very careful records are kept of each boy's progress and adaptability, because we expect that as a result of our training the majority of our apprentices will, before long, be very excellent material from which to select officers, and it therefore rests entirely with each boy as to what he will make of himself. You will all readily understand that with the enormous and constantly increasing mileage of the Canadian Pacific Railways, the demand for well-trained and ambitious young men is large, and our vice-president, Mr. George Bury, told the public high-school boys in his paper some time ago: "I am continually looking around for officers," and (here the schooling question crops up again), "those on the list for promotion who have not improved on their earlier defects in education have to go by the board" or, in other words, they lose the chance of getting on they otherwise would have had.

So you see I finish up where I started—to impress all you boys not to be in too great a hurry to quit school the first opportunity you get. If you have to start work early, then go to a night-school, and keep on going. You will find there is always something more to learn, whatever you may be studying or working at.

SALESMANSHIP

A. L. STRUTHERS
Representative of the Business Science Club of Winnipeg

I am glad to look into your faces this afternoon, boys. You are to be congratulated on working in harmony with a school system which is sufficiently progressive to prepare you here and now for the work which many of you will do for the rest of your lives. A number of you will become salesmen and you are wise to lay hold of anything that will enable you to become scientific salesmen.

We are living in a scientific age, one in which all lines of useful effort are rapidly becoming reduced to a scientific basis. Salesmanship is a science because the facts of successful salesmanship have been gathered together, classified, and arranged for easy study by young men who wish to make it their life's profession. We are living in an age of the survival of the fittest. It means more to be fit today than it did ten years ago. It will mean more to be fit ten years from now than it does today.

We shall consider some principles that will point the way to sound preparation for the work of salesmanship so that you will be "fit" for the struggle for success in business.

I shall speak this afternoon of a few ways in which a school boy can prepare himself for high-grade salesmanship while he is still at school. I say "while he is still at school," because I meet hundreds of salesmen every week who bemoan the fact that their parents allowed them to leave school too soon. These men sell quite a lot of goods, but they feel every hour of each day that they could sell so much more goods if they were better educated.

Salesmen drawing large salaries tell me that they lose big sales through not being able to write a convincing letter or on account of making some slip in their speech. Many of these salesmen tell me that they have to do business with highly educated people and they feel handicapped because their own education has been neglected. They cannot talk to a well-educated man in his own language. Then, again, some of their customers have highly trained minds and strong reasoning powers. These men seem so far above the unequipped salesman that the latter's confidence in himself is not sufficient to enable him to close deals with men of superior mentality.

To be ready for some of these conditions, I have a few suggestions to make to you, boys, this afternoon. One is, endeavor to enjoy every hour you put on such subjects as arithmetic, algebra, and Euclid, because they train your reasoning powers. They also train your power to concentrate. Every good salesman must be able to concentrate or hold his mind down to one thing for a long time. I would say, also, endeavor to enjoy the study of literature and poetry because it trains your imagination, your memory, and your power to express yourself in convincing word-pictures.

I mentioned memory just now. Many sales are lost through lack of a good memory. You have an opportunity here and now to train your memory while at school. Better practice now than have to do it when you should be busy studying your goods and studying your customers.

One other thing I must mention, and that is, to study the laws of health, so that you will not poison your bodies with the food you eat and by the way you eat it. A great many sales are lost by good men just because they are sick through being careless in their eating. Take breathing exercises first thing every morning. Bathe your chest in cold water every single morning. Keep the muscles in splendid trim by easy exercise during several parts of the day. All this will help you make good salesmen.

Now here is one thing I want to say about what you can get here in school, so that you will not be sorry for having neglected it later on. Many salesmen close deals by being able to write good letters or good advertisements. Other salesmen lose fine sales by being ignorant of how best to state their points on paper. To avoid this condition of affairs later on, boys, make the most of the composition period, polish up your language in order to make it more forceful. To this end, study the rules of rhetoric so that you can make your language more convincing and clear. Do it now, boys, while you have the chance, and in later years you will have more time to study your goods and to study your customers. If you do what I have just advised, you will be well equipped to tackle the selling game.

Now I am going to speak of a part of salesmanship that you should pay a great deal of attention to. It is this: Sizing up customers, and then rubbing customers the right way, as it were—being tactful. To do this you should cultivate a pleasing personality. Be in earnest in everything you do. Cultivate gracefulness of walk, and when standing. Read books about great men who have these qualities. Fill your mind with such stories. Broad study will make you open-minded, which is a necessary quality of a good salesman. A narrow-minded salesman is so because he is ignorant, and you want to do everything you can now to equip yourself with knowledge, so that people will never accuse you of being narrow-minded. Such qualities as refinement, regularity, and thoroughness will enable you to get on well with different types of customers. These qualities you have the chance of developing now while mastering your studies in school. Do everything to persuade your parents to keep you in school for a number of years, in order that you may be highly equipped for rendering high-class service to your firm and its customers.

Closing a sale means the ability to get another mind to look at the thing in your way. He must be persuaded. You can do this by a careful selection of words and sentences when at the critical point of the sale. So study this matter of language-mastery. It will help in every single move of a business deal.

Now, boys, this means a lot of effort, I know. Many men sell goods without the equipment I have spoken about, but they could sell a great deal more if they had more of such equipment. I know of one furniture salesman in the city who often sets his customers laughing at him by saying "Them's fine chairs." "That's some sofa." Many women do not like his way of talking. They have no respect for him. They lose confidence in his judgment. They do not take his advice about things, because they feel that if he is not careful in his words he will not be careful in his dealings with them. Remember, boys, women are the most numerous buyers in the world.

Some salesmen get $50.00 a month. Some earn $150.00 a month. Why? The first one sells goods, but needs a lot of correcting—supervision or oversight. The second one sells much goods and needs less correcting and overseeing. No one else is paid part of his salary to do his thinking for him. The thought may be represented with some degree of accuracy by these lines:

Much supervision needed	Little efficiency
Less supervision needed	More efficiency
Little supervision needed	Greater efficiency
No supervision needed	Highest possible efficiency

These two things—needed supervision and efficiency—vary. That is, each grows less or greater as the other grows greater or less. If, then, you wish to measure the grade of your work as to quantity and quality, study carefully to find out how much supervision is really needed. And mark well: the test—the real test—is not how much it *gets*, but how much it *needs*.

UNIVERSAL APPLICATION OF THE LAW

The law applies to everyone from the ruler of the nation down to the humblest employee. Even the ancient king in an absolute monarchy was sometimes greatly in need of supervision, although by virture of his position there was no one to administer it directly. When that need became too great, he was sometimes removed or even beheaded through the exercise of indirect supervisory power by his subjects.

Your opportunity for fitting yourselves for high-grade salesmanship is right here at school. Avoid envying those who are at work in business places. They have not the chance you now have. You will be able to apply all you learn here out in the whirlpool of business competition. The best equipped man wins out.

I repeat that your opportunity for obtaining the equipment is here and now.

THE BUILDING TRADES

W. H. CARTER
President of the Carter-Hall-Allinger Co.

I represent the building business, one of the largest industries in our country, in which I am sure there are more opportunities for you, boys, than any other business. A boy that makes good in the building business finds so many different avenues open to him. A successful building superintendent can go out as superintendent or foreman on railroad construction, concrete work of all kinds, such as dams, bridge piers, etc., road building, street paving, water works, and sewer construction. Numerous jobs with big pay await the man who knows the business.

To learn the building business there are several ways, but I would advise you to finish your high-school education, then, at about 16 or 17, apprentice yourself to some contracting firm as a carpenter or bricklayer, if you feel you cannot afford a college education such as structural or civil engineering. Of course you can afford this if you try, as many of our best engineers have worked their way through college and come out quicker and with higher honors than the boy whose dad furnished the money.

While there are all the different trades connected with the building business, I suggest the bricklaying or carpenter trades, as you come in contact with all branches of the work from the foundation up, and have an opportunity of becoming familiar with all classes of construction work under more different foremen or more difficult buildings, and have a chance to talk to different mechanics, from all of which you gain your entire knowledge of the building trade.

I can say to you that all I know of the building business I have learned from close observance of the different methods employed by other contractors and from conversation with different mechanics.

However, although this is your principal source of knowledge, there are many ways for you to get help as you go along. When you start your apprenticeship, get hold of different books to read on different kinds of construction. We have a library in our office from which we loan our boys books on the trade they are learning. Take a course of architectural drawing at the Y.M.C.A. or night school, or by correspondence. This will help you to understand plans and specifications prepared by architects, and when you understand and know them and can lay out work, the one hard thing to learn is to work your men to the best advantage.

This knowledge can only be obtained by applying good horse sense and watching the other fellow when you are working under him, and ever waiting for a chance to show what you can do; and when you get that chance don't let anything prevent you from making good. If you have to disappoint social friends, miss a ball game or taking your girl to a show, go in and make good—run the work as if it were your own. When that job is done another will be waiting for you, and your career as a building superintendent is well under way. It all means hard study and hard work and large responsibilities. When you are placed in charge of work, your men's lives are protected by your judgment as to the placing and erecting of scaffolding and equipment. Your firm's reputation is up to you and their money, perhaps. One bit of poor work or of misplaced judgment in some respect might lose them much money.

Now, in serving your apprenticeship and learning a trade, you do not have to do as perhaps your father did in the Old Country—pay for a chance to learn a trade. To learn to be a bricklayer or mason, you apprentice yourself to some firm of contractors for four years. The first year you are paid $6.00 per week; the second, $12.00; the third, $18.00, and the fourth, $24.00. After the four years and your apprenticeship are completed, you make 75 cents per hour for eight hours as a journeyman, or you should be able to run a job at a salary of $40.00 to $50.00 per week. A carpenter is much the same, only the wages are not as much.

Carpenters make $5.00 a day, but they get in more days' work in a year than a bricklayer, which makes their year's pay about the same.

Now, boys, the reason I have told you all this is to show you that while you are learning a trade which will bring you a good salary always, a trade for which you will always be in demand somewhere, you are at the same time making the first year as much per week as the boy who runs messages, runs an elevator, or drives a delivery wagon—a work in which there is no possible future, except from $6.00 to $12.00 or $15.00 a week as long as you live. See the difference? One leads to a job of $50.00 a week, one to a job of $15.00; one to a position in which you do things, erect buildings to which you can point in your old days with pride, the other to just a job of long hours and small pay.

The building business or any construction work is very fascinating; you see each day something done, something new accomplished; you meet all kinds of people, travel in different lands, work out of doors, which makes you strong and healthy, and each job completed, if done well, will stand for years as a monument to your handiwork.

As I said before, the highest positions in any firm of builders are open to each of you, boys, if you are square and honest and willing to work hard and apply your whole energy to the job you are on and to your employer's interest.

You do not require a college education to become a building superintendent, although no boy should miss the opportunity of getting a college education if it is within his reach.

The pay of a building superintendent depends entirely on his ability to do work quicker and cheaper with the same number of men than the other fellow. We have superintendents in our employ making from $30.00 to $60.00 per week. The $60.00-a-week man is a fellow who has applied himself closely to his business, knows all the quick ways of doing things, is capable of handling men to good advantage, looks after his work day and night if required, and goes out with one aim in view—to erect the building he is sent out on quicker and cheaper than any other man can. That is what you want to be, and you have perhaps a better opportunity to succeed than some of the men with us.

We have about thirty superintendents and foremen and several under-foremen in our employ, and about 1,500 workmen during the busy season. Most all of our superintendents or foremen have been promoted from the ranks. If we want a brick foreman, I go to the superintendent on some job and ask if he has a bricklayer on the job who would make a good foreman. If he has a man who seems interested in his work and wants to get ahead, we give him a trial. If he makes good, he possibly goes on up to general superintendent. The same with a carpenter foreman or any other trade. We have a good superintendent who started as water-boy, went up as labor foreman, who is now making $40.00 to $50.00 per week. Some started as timekeepers. That is a good way, as you can get a good knowledge of the business or bookkeeping side as well as the practical side.

That is the way I started in the building business. About sixteen years ago I was keeping time and checking material under construction at $5.00 per week. I soon became assistant to the general superintendent and in a short while was placed in charge of some small work. I worked hard, made good, and they gave me a larger job, and so on, always on the job and working for the interest of the firm I was with, until I went into the company I am a part of today.

Now, boys, I could tell you a lot about the building game that would interest you if I were more used to talking to you or acting in this position, as it is an interesting business. I could tell you of men I know in some of the larger cities who are recognized as the best men in the business, men who carry out large undertakings, build twenty- and forty-story buildings, and things like that—men who are making a success of the business financially, and not one of these men had any special training or any special opportunities that are not open to you in Winnipeg today.

Boys, every opportunity to become great in any business or profession is offered you in Winnipeg today; it is up to you to make good, and I hope that some of you boys here this afternoon will be strong factors in the building business in the years to come, and any time I can be of any service to you in the way of advice or information I trust you will come to see me. Come to my office or my home any time.

PATTERN-MAKING

E. STEWART
Mechanical Superintendent Manitoba Bridge and Iron Works, Ltd., Winnipeg

We are now living in the age of extreme specialization of trades and industries, consequently the older and more typical handicrafts are rapidly being broken up.

Fifty or sixty years ago, the old race of millwrights were "all-round" men in the engineering firms. They could fit up a mill throughout, design its arrangements, make the patterns, weld a shaft, forge levers, fit up the bearings, turn and bore the wheels, line the shafting, and, in fact do all the work that is now divided among half a dozen separate and distinct trades. Necessarily they were not so skilful in any one branch as the individual tradesman of today, but they were better craftsmen, because more complete than the mechanics who now do one thing and one thing only. This race of craftsmen, except in some isolated localities, has nearly died out.

Now the pattern-maker constructs the wooden models; the fitter chips, files, and fastens the different parts together; the planer, slotter, and shaper save the fitter's muscles; and the iron-turner prepares the shafts and bores the wheels. The fitter and erector occupy distinct positions, while each individual workman usually excels only in some special branch of work.

But this division of labor has its advantages. Machinery has been cheapened; there is more beauty and finish about it; and it is capable of being turned out much more rapidly than was possible under the old style.

Let us now consider for a few moments the subject of this paper, "The Art and Trade of Pattern-Making." I need not waste valuable time describing to you the various tools required by a pattern-maker, nor yet the various uses they are put to, as I am well aware you receive valuable instruction along that line at the manual classes in connection with the schools. There is only one tool which I cannot overlook, as it is most necessary in pattern-making, viz., the contraction rule. Now the contraction rule, as the name implies, is a rule which is made longer than the standard rule by the amount which metals contract in cooling from the molten state to the ordinary temperature of the atmosphere. Though a standard rule is required for the measurement of castings, it would be obviously inconvenient to use it in pattern-making, because the workman would be perpetually making approximate allowance for contraction in fractional parts of a foot. So the contraction rule economizes his time and insures something more accurate than approximations.

A two-foot contraction rule for cast iron is $\frac{1}{4}$ inch longer than the standard rule, $\frac{1}{8}$ inch in two feet for steel, $\frac{1}{8}$ inch in ten inches for brass, and so on. Of course this contraction varies in accordance with style and weight of article being made, and the proper allowance can only be learned by careful study and years of practice.

Next we come to the timber used for patterns. Yellow pine is the most extensively used timber for large patterns. It is light, soft, easy to work, comparatively free from liability to warp and twist, and it is cheap. Of course it must be perfectly dry, as wet lumber is useless for patterns, because the pattern would warp and shrink out of shape when drying. For small patterns mahogany is the best timber. It is hard, strong, and not liable to warp. Its price, however, precludes its use except for small patterns or standard patterns which have to be molded repeatedly. Other woods are sometimes used, but these are the best and are the ones most commonly used.

To fully explain the various methods of constructing patterns would incur much labor and occupy many volumes, so I will content myself at present by explaining to you what a pattern really is. A pattern is a duplicate of the article required, but made larger than the casting by the amount of contraction which that metal will have when cooling. It must also have allowance made for machining where required, and be so constructed that it can be withdrawn from the sand. It must also be so constructed as to make the pattern as strong as possible and least likely to warp. I have here a pattern of a sheave wheel. You will notice that it is split through the center of the groove; this is necessary in order to withdraw the pattern from the sand. The pattern is first placed on a straight board, bottom side upward, and a suitable box placed around it. This box is then filled up with sand and rammed up. The whole is then rolled over and the sand dug out to the bottom edge of the groove, and a tapering ring put in position. This ring is then rammed with sand and a parting made to the upper edge of the groove. Next, the top half of the box is placed in position and rammed with sand, provision having been made for the running metal. The top box is then lifted off, one-half of the pattern withdrawn, next the ring is withdrawn and then the other half of the pattern. The ring is then replaced and the top half of the box put on, clamps are then put in position to hold the top and bottom boxes together and the mold is ready for receiving the metal. The drawing on the board will fully explain what I mean. This is an example of a sheave with a solid web, but sheaves of a larger size are very often made with arms, the construction of which the models before you will explain. Time will not permit of my explaining the construction of any other style of pattern at present, but I have with me several examples which I shall be only too pleased to explain to any of the boys interested at the end of the lecture.

We will now dwell for a little time on the "Qualifications of a Pattern-Maker."

Now I am not going to frighten any of you boys who have the ambition of becoming a first-class craftsman, whether it be pattern-making, molding, engineering, or a trade of any description, or a profession of any kind, by laying down to you a long list of studies. Book knowledge is indeed not really necessary, for many a first-class workman has been comparatively illiterate; but then such a man is generally incapable of ever becoming anything more than a mere man at the bench. Now I am sure very few of the boys before me wish to drudge along day by day, year by year, content with a mere journeyman's wages. Now is the time to start and expand the mental horizon. Spend your spare moments in enjoying the pleasures of literature and in gaining an insight into the marvels of the Wonderland of Science, instead of idling away the most valuable time of your life on the streets or in the pool rooms. Everyone cannot reach the top of the ladder; everyone will be appreciated who has learned the fundamental reasons of things and so can proceed intelligently at his task. Even when working at the bench no man knows when he may be thrown upon his own resources. There is many a shop where there is no foreman kept to instruct you, so the man who can cope with emergencies as they arise and can do h's job quickly and substantially without assistance generally finds employment as long as he cares to keep it.

There is no use to think of becoming a good pattern-maker without becoming also, to some extent, a good engineer. If you are ill-informed in the principles of design you will hesitate how to proceed with a new piece of work, or whether to proceed with it at all without consulting the foreman or superintendent. It is therefore necessary to have a knowledge of the elements of geometry or mensuration; with that knowledge you can mark out and cut away your stuff at once without working slowly and doubtfully in the dark.

A knowledge of drawing is one of the chief requirements of the pattern-maker. By drawing I mean the principle of projection as applied to geometric figures in plane, elevations, sections at various angles, and so forth. The mere copying of mechanical drawings is of little or no value, but the student that has thoroughly mastered the principles of projection will never experience any serious difficulty either in making or in understanding an intricate drawing. You should also be proficient in arithmetic; by that I mean the elementary rules, together with proportion, decimals, and the evolution of the square and cube roots.

Lastly, there is that experience which in the course of time bears the semblance of intuition—that experience which comes of close and long-continued observation and which is invaluable to its possessor. So, boys, I would advise you to be always on the lookout for something new. Study well everything you see; you will learn much more in this way than by many book studies.

Pattern-making is a trade which I would recommend to any boy who is energetic. You will always find it most interesting, for it is one of the very few trades where such a variety of work can be got. To any who wish to become pattern-makers or tradesmen of any kind, I can only say, be industrious, study hard while at school, stay at school as long as possible. Nothing will be gained by leaving school too early, as what you are learning now will be forgotten before you start work if you run around the streets for a few years.

[*To be continued*]

FACTS ABOUT THE WORKING CHILDREN OF CINCINNATI, AND THEIR BEARING UPON EDUCATIONAL PROBLEMS—*Concluded*

HELEN T. WOOLLEY
Cincinnati, Ohio

WAGES

(Table VII; Chart VII)

The educational return to the children is, then, a small factor. How about the financial return? Table VII gives the wage statistics for a series of 2,067 children. At the time these statistics were tabulated, half of these children had held but one position, 32.3 per cent had held two, 11 per cent had held three, 2.6 per cent had held four, and 4 per cent had held five or more positions. No account is taken in this table of the length of time the positions had been held.

Almost 40 per cent of the children had taken the first position without even asking what they were to be paid. The wages stated in the table are those promised the children when their contracts were signed. In most cases the office has no assurance about wages except the word of the child, but a long experience has taught us that their statements are surprisingly accurate.

There is a decided sex discrimination from the start. More than eight-tenths of the girls receive less than four dollars a week, while only one-half of the boys are paid less than four dollars. Three dollars is a medium weekly wage for the girls, although more than half of them receive less than that in their first positions. The medium weekly wage for boys is three dollars and seventy-five cents. These sums do not represent average weekly earnings for the year, but merely wages paid at the start in each position. For a limited series of children—474 at the present time—we have a complete industrial history for one year, stating all the rates of pay received, and the time employed. From these facts, an average weekly wage for the year has been figured out for each of

TABLE VII

WAGES OF CHILDREN UNDER SIXTEEN IN CINCINNATI

	Position I				Position II				Position III				Position IV				Position V			
	Boys		Girls		Boys		Girls		Boys		Girls		Boys		Girls		Boys		Girls	
	No.	Percent-age	No.	Percent-age	No.	Percent-age	No.	Percent-age	No.	Percent-age	No.	Percent-age	No.	Percent-age	No.	Percent-age	No.	Percent-age	No.	Percent-age
Less than $3.00	85	12	317	55	27	7	150	40	1	0.5	46	36	1	1.5	16	35	1	2	11	31.0
$3.00–$3.99	347	51	198	34	206	49	174	46	72	47.5	63	49	31	46.5	20	45	13	30	17	49.0
$4.00–$4.99	193	28	49	8	133	32	42	11	60	40.0	17	13	27	40.0	9	18	18	42	4	11.5
$5.00 and over	62	9	15	3	50	12	13	3	19	12.0	3	2	8	12.0	1	2	11	26	3	8.5
Total	687	100	579	100	416	100	379	100	152	100	129	100	67	100	46	100	43	100	35	100.
Had not asked	340	.....	461	.....	106	.....	130	.....	35	.....	50	.....	7	.....	19	.....	3	.....	4	.....
Total	1,027	.....	1,040	.....	522	.....	509	.....	187	.....	179	.....	74	.....	65	.....	46	.....	39	.....

these children. It is an interesting fact that the medium wage on this basis is also three dollars for girls, and three dollars and seventy-five cents for boys. Apparently the increases in pay balance the time unemployed, and leave the average yearly earning about equal to the initial wage.

Another interesting fact revealed by the table of wage statistics is that the rate of pay increases with mere change of position (Chart VII). The proportion of children in the lower rates of pay decreases with successive changes, and the proportion of those in the higher rates increases. The children have, then, some justification for changing positions. They better themselves financially by doing so. It may still be true that the occupations which hold out the best permanent future are most poorly paid in the early years. The children may be short-sighted in their policy, but one judges their apparent instability less harshly when he knows the immediate profit which it brings them.

ECONOMIC NECESSITY AS A FACTOR IN CHILD LABOR

We have seen that the educational value of the work open to children under sixteen is very small. A child does not profit much intellectually, or in manual skill in general, by running errands, basting sleeve seams, or lacing shoes for two years. Small as the wages are, the first supposition is that these children must be going to work because of economic necessity. Before adopting any definite educational policy in the matter, it is essential to know how large a proportion of the families really need the earnings of the children under sixteen. In our own office, we have made the best estimate we could of the economic necessity in a series of over six hundred families. A visit had been made to the home in only half of the cases. Our estimates were based on all the facts we preserved about the family—such as the number of wage earners, their occupations, their earnings, if known, the number of children under fourteen, the rent paid, the number of rooms occupied by the family, the amount of spending money given the child, and the child's own statement of a preference for work or school. The estimates were made separately by more than one person, and the judgments compared. Very doubtful cases were omitted. The point we tried to decide in each case was whether the family, without the child's earnings, would need outside assistance. The final estimate was that 73 per cent of the families did not need the child's earnings, while 27 per cent did. This estimate, of necessity, is very nearly the same as that made in the government investigation (29.3 per cent),[1] but is a little more than that of Massachusetts towns (24 per cent),[2] or of New York (20 per cent).[3] The only estimate very much higher than this is the one made by Mr. Talbert[4] in the Stockyards district of Chicago (53 per cent), where the conditions are exceedingly bad. Economic necessity is not, then, a compelling force of child labor in the majority of cases.

The real force which is sending the majority of these children out into the industrial field is their own desire to go to work, and behind this desire to go to work is frequently the dissatisfaction with school. The children who tell us that they would have preferred to stay in school are a minority. Most of them are quite frank in saying that they are tired of school and anxious to leave it. The dissatisfaction with school is doubtless in part the restlessness and desire for change, adventure, and independence characteristic of the age of puberty, but perhaps an even more potent factor is the large amount of retardation among working children. Two-thirds of the children leaving our public schools are the failures—and, like the rest of humanity, they are tired of the things in which they fail.

APPLICATION TO EDUCATIONAL PROBLEMS

Here are the facts—a large army of children leaving our public schools before they have completed even a grammar-school educa-

[1] *Woman and Child Wage Earners in the United States*, Vol. VII, "Conditions under Which Children Leave School to Go to Work," Washington, 1910; Senate Document No. 645, p. 57.

[2] *Report of the Commission on Industrial and Technical Education* (Massachusetts), Columbia University, Teachers College; *Educational Reprints*, No. I, New York, 1906, p. 92.

[3] Barrows, Alice P., "Report of the Vocational Guidance Survey," *Bulletin No. 9, Public Education Association*, New York, 1912.

[4] Talbert, Ernest L., *Opportunities in School and Industry for Children of the Stockyards District* (University of Chicago Press, 1912, p. 39).

tion—leaving, not because they must, but because they wish to—entering occupations which do not aid in their development—receiving wages so small that they would not furnish the barest necessities of life. Shall we allow it to go on?

Suppose we agree, for a moment, that the state of affairs ought

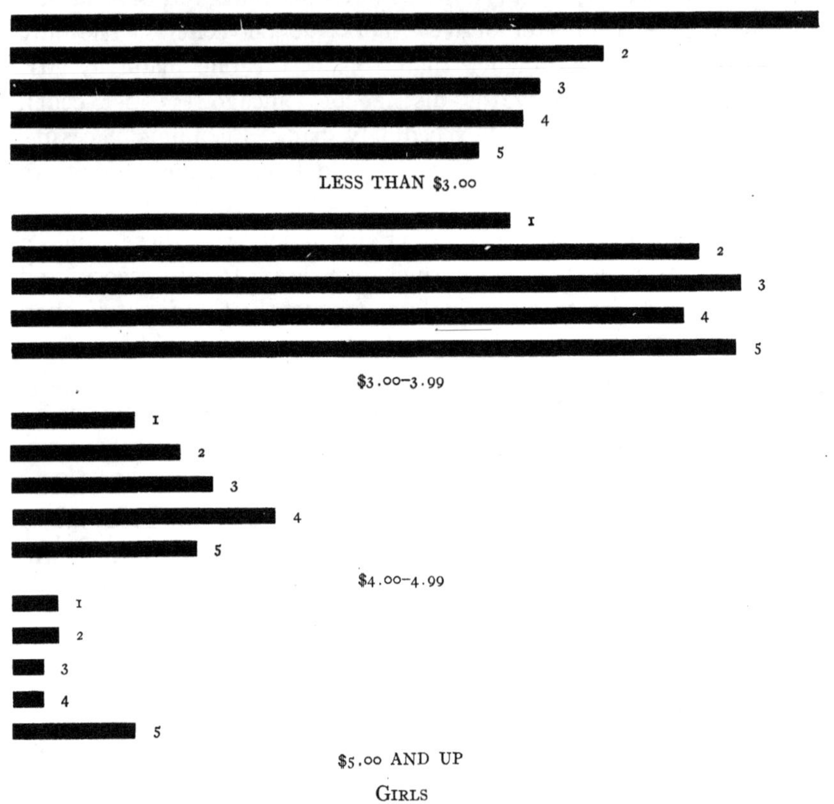

GIRLS

CHART VII—WAGES

not to continue, and consider what ought to be done about it. It is hopeless at present to expect industry to modify the conditions of employment sufficiently to insure educational work to children. The problem must be attacked by the schools, if at all. Until recently, the public schools have felt that their responsibility ended when the children who were not capable of succeeding were simply dropped from the rolls, but they are beginning to feel that turning out every year an army of children who have merely failed, and have not been helped to find out in what direction, if at all, they might succeed, cannot be regarded as satisfactory educational work. The most obvious suggestion for a remedy is to raise the age require-

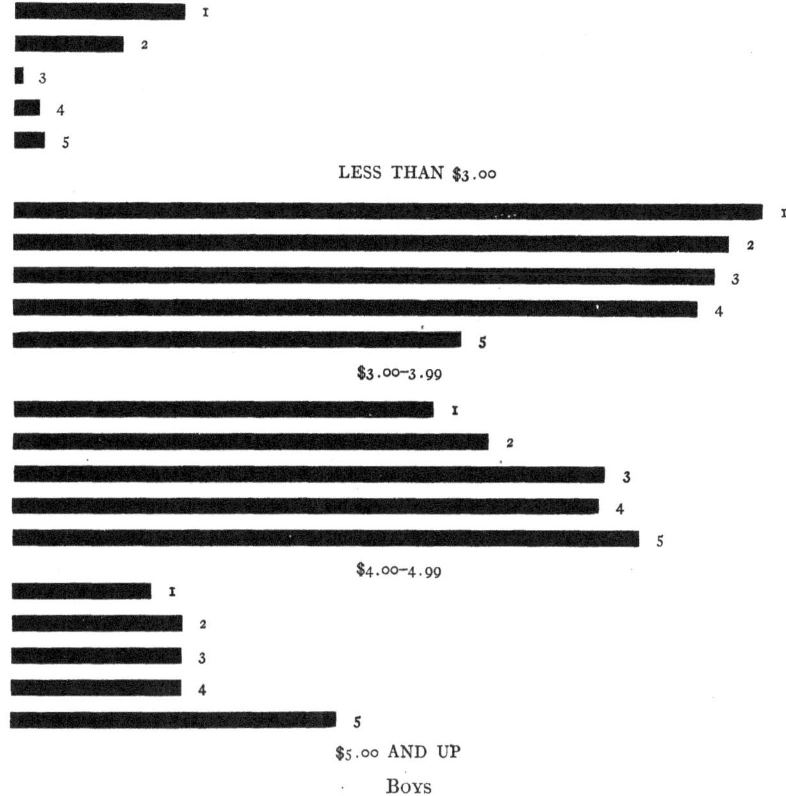

CHART VII—WAGES—*Continued*

ment to sixteen years, when the openings for children in industry are more advantageous. But to force children, who have already failed, to endure two more years of a kind of training for which they have shown themselves unfitted, seems barbaric.

The problem cannot be really met by the schools until they provide a different type of training—a type of training which would make possible an appeal to the children's desire to work with their hands, and to their longing for economic independence. Those who feel most intensely the necessity for such a modification of the school curriculum are tempted to urge an immediate increase of the age requirement to sixteen years, because it would bring the schools at once face to face with the imperative necessity for providing a more nearly adequate kind of education for those who are failing in the present academic régime.

But the recognition of the need of the children for more vocational education is only the first step in the complex problem before us. For what occupations in particular shall the schools undertake to prepare children? It is safe to say that not one of the trades or occupations on our list, as it is at present conducted, offers enough in educational and financial return to the children to warrant the public school in training them for it. It ought to be laid down as a basic principle in devising any system of industrial education, that the state will never take over the preparation of workers for a specific trade until that trade can show that it offers its employees a chance for *physical* and *mental* development, and a fair financial return for their labor.

It seems the part of wisdom, then, for the public schools to go very slowly in the matter of establishing courses of training designed to prepare young children—even as young as sixteen—for specific industries. As industry itself becomes more socialized, and the welfare of the individual worker becomes a matter of much greater concern to it than at present, it may be safe for the schools to take over the preparation of workers for a larger number of industries. Indeed the schools may have a very powerful influence in hastening the development of this more social spirit in industry, provided they make the training of workers for any craft depend directly upon the conditions of employment, and the educational and financial returns of the craft itself.

But even though specific trade training for the younger group of working children seems inadvisable at present, it does not follow that there is nothing the schools can do at once to assist them. We have seen that most of the children who are leaving the schools are those who do not succeed with work in which the stress falls—

as it does in our present system of instruction—on the purely intellectual method of presentation. If they are to succeed at all, it must be in some calling where work with the hands is of paramount importance. If the schools could lay more stress from the start on training manual dexterity of various kinds, and through many media, children of the class who leave the schools early—and perhaps the others also—would be the gainers in many ways. Not only would the mere possession of greater manual dexterity be an asset in industrial work and indeed in most pursuits in life, but the process of trying various kinds of occupations would be the most effectual way of helping a child decide for what type of work he is best fitted. Then, too, many children who are now failing in the schools, fail not so much because they lack mental ability, as because the kind of instruction offered does not succeed in stimulating their intellectual processes. Experiment has shown that many of these same children can be held in school, and that they can do the theoretical part of the school work, when their interest is maintained by making some sort of constructive work with the hands, a central feature in instruction.

In addition to general training in manual dexterity and the use of tools, the children who are to enter industry early would be much better equipped if they received elementary instruction in industrial history, social and industrial legislation, and simple business methods. There seems no good reason why a child should leave the public schools without knowing what the provisions of the child labor law are, or with so little idea of business method that he takes his first position—as 40 per cent of our children do—without even asking what he is to be paid.

One is often asked what is the use of providing better training of any sort for children who enter industry early, so long as the jobs remain the same. Perhaps there would be little use in it, if the jobs were sure to remain the same, but it seems a reasonable hope that more skilful and more intelligent workers may improve, faster than any other agency, conditions of industry.

BOOK REVIEWS

New Ideals in Rural Schools. By George Herbert Betts. Boston: Houghton Mifflin Co., "Riverside Educational Monograph Series," 1913. Pp. x+128. $0.60 net.

In this volume, Professor Betts discusses three of the major problems of rural education: the social organization and relationships of the rural school, the curriculum, and the quality of the teaching. Under the first of these topics, after showing the nature, opportunities, and characteristics of the rural population, he discusses the need of a community social center and the possibility of using the rural school for this purpose. The advantages of consolidation on both the social and instructional sides are presented, and the financial problems discussed.

He shows the meager, antiquated character of the rural-school curriculum and the crying need of modernization and adaptation to rural conditions. He presents recommendations as to the content of each of the elementary and secondary subjects, so as to fit them for their purposes in rural education.

In the last chapter, he portrays the inefficient character of the teaching in the rural schools, the inadequacy of the training, the salaries, and the supervision. He presents recommendations as to modes of remedying the deficiencies.

J. F. Bobbitt

University of Chicago

The Education of Tomorrow: The Adaptation of School Curricula to Economic Democracy. By Arland D. Weeks, with an introduction by M. V. O'Shea. New York: Sturgis & Walton, 1913. Pp. xii+232. $1.25 net.

It can safely be asserted that in the present transitional stage of education, there is no single body of rational opinion, lay or professional, that is generally convincing and accepted as to what should be the content of the curriculum of public education. Partial interpretations and conflicting opinions make up the literature of the topic. Popular and professional dissatisfaction with the work of the schools is the note now universally heard. These voices of discontent usually spend themselves in pointing out defects; constructive suggestions of fundamental import are rare.

The present volume, while still but a partial and hastily organized interpretation of the needs, is wholly constructive. Taking the social, particularly the economic, point of view, the author discusses the kinds of knowledge that men need for efficient living under the three headings, Productional Knowledge, Distributional Knowledge, and Consumptional Knowledge. The first refers chiefly to vocational education on the productive side; in his suggested curriculum he includes practical mathematics, elements of manufacturing, mechanical drawing, manual training, agriculture, productional phases of the various sciences, conservation of wealth, and the practice of trades.

By distributional knowledge, he refers apparently for the most part to commerce and government, as shown by the series of suggested topics: current political events, economic history, distribution of wealth, war, peace, slavery, feudalism, elective franchise, taxation, political parties, socialism, money, graft, corporations, charity, and as many others of the same nature. Consumptional knowledge is to show men how most profitably to spend their wealth and their time, and to give the necessary tastes and habits for doing so. Consumptional knowledge, following his list, includes literature, history, music, other fine arts, ethics, foreign languages, non-productional aspects of sciences, sports and games, travel, and a dozen others. The book urges a closer relation between education and the life-interests and life-work of a community.

J. F. BOBBITT

UNIVERSITY OF CHICAGO

What Children Study and Why. By CHARLES B. GILBERT. Boston: Silver, Burdett & Co., 1913. Pp. vi+332.

This is a discussion of the curriculum of the elementary school. It deals chiefly with the program of work, not with the methods and processes. After a short introductory chapter discussing the problems involved in drawing up an effective printed course of study as a teacher's manual, the book is given up almost entirely to discussions of the various values of each of the subjects taught in the elementary school. It is clear from the general tone and spirit of the text that the book represents the crystallized results of long practical contact with the subjects as they are taught in our schoolrooms, rather than the theoretical contacts of the pedagogical student in his study, armed with his psychological and pedagogical "authorities." It is the kind of discussion of the curriculum that one would expect from the practical superintendent of long and successful experience.

J. F. BOBBITT

UNIVERSITY OF CHICAGO

Human Behavior: A First Book in Psychology for Teachers. By STEPHEN SHELDON COLVIN and WILLIAM CHANDLER BAGLEY. New York: Macmillan, 1913. Pp. xvi+336. $1.00 net.

This is, in the main, a brief untechnical book of general psychology, with the special cast indicated by the subtitle. The authors accept the functional point of view, and formulate all psychological principles in terms of human behavior. Greatest attention is given to those general topics that lie nearest to the teacher's practical labors; illustrations are drawn from classroom procedure; and application is made to teaching problems. The book is clearly intended for immature students: materials are organized upon the "spiral" plan; it is written in easy English, employing a simplified terminology; to each chapter is appended a glossary of all psychological terms used, and also a rather full list of "Questions and Exercises." The authors have emphasized more than is usual in textbooks for teachers the matters of instinct, habit, feeling and emotion, memory, and economical methods of learning.

J. F. BOBBITT

UNIVERSITY OF CHICAGO

Industrial Education. By JAMES E. RUSSELL and FREDERICK G. BONSER. New York: Teachers College, Columbia University, 1912. Pp. 50. Paper. $0.30.

This bulletin is a reprint of an article published by Dean Russell in the *Educational Review*, December, 1909; and of another by Professor Bonser which appeared as *Technical Education Bulletin, No. 10.* Both articles consider mainly the selection and organization of industrial materials in the vocationally undifferentiated elementary schools. Both suggest the consolidation of manual training, drawing and design, household science, and household arts into a single subject to be called industrial arts. In connection with such studies made as real and practical as possible, they would develop the related mathematics, science, history, and geography. They point out clearly the necessity of the school's concerning itself quite as much with the general *character* of the workingman as with technical information and skill. The articles are well worth the republication.

J. F. BOBBITT

UNIVERSITY OF CHICAGO

CURRENT EDUCATIONAL LITERATURE IN THE PERIODICALS[1]

IRENE WARREN
Librarian, School of Education, University of Chicago

Abbott, Helen L. The responsibility of the schoolroom. Educa. 34:27–30. (S. '13.)
Asterisk, John. The reorganization of the University of London. Educa. R. 46:109–34. (S. '13.)
Bell, Catherine F. Another experience with the Binet test. Train. School M. (N.J.) 10:77–78. (S. '13.)
Bennett, Charles A. Impression gained from a day's visit to the Mississippi Industrial Institute and College. Voca. Educa. 3:11–23. (S. '13.)
Bok, Edward. Is the college making good? Outl. 104:851–57. (16 Ag. '13.)
Brown, Marion Frances. The creed of an American schoolboy. Educa. 34:45. (S. '13.)
Cholmeley, R. F. Secondary education: the next step towards a national system. Educa. T. 66:375–78. (S. '13.)
Church, H. O. The use of scientific material in the high-school course in English. School R. 21:461–66. (S. '13.)
Claus, Henry T. The problem of college chapel. Educa. R. 46:177–87. (S. '13.)
Colby, Elbridge. Value of the college fraternity. Educa. R. 46:157–67. (S. '13.)
Cooley, Edwin G. Professor Dewey's criticism of the Chicago Commercial Club and its Vocational Education Bill. Voca. Educa. 3:24–29. (S. '13.)
Crawshaw, F. D. College entrance and advanced credits for manual arts. School R. 21:467–74. (S. '13.)
Dorey, J. Milnor. Public speaking and dramatics in high schools. Educa. 34:31–38. (S. '13.)
Education that educates. Outl. 104:845–46. (16 Ag. '13.)
Eikenberry, W. L. First-year science in Illinois high schools. School R. 21:542–48. (O. '13.)
Gathany, J. Madison. Teaching practical politics in our schools. Educa. 34:20–26. (S. '13.)
Goldfarb, A. J. The teaching of college biology. Science 38:430–36. (26 S. '13.)
Grupe, Mary A. A review of the pedagogical studies in the teaching of spelling. Educa. 34:1–19. (S. '13.)
Hargitt, Charles W. A problem in educational eugenics. Pop. Sci. Mo. 83:355–67. (O. '13.)

[1] *Abbreviations.*—Educa., Education; Educa. R., Educational Review; Educa. T., Educational Times; J. of Educa. Psychol., Journal of Educational Psychology; Lit. D., Literary Digest; Outl., Outlook; Pop. Sci. Mo., Popular Science Monthly; School R., School Review; Train. School M. (N.J.), Training School Magazine (New Jersey); Voca. Educa., Vocational Education.

Hollingworth, H. L. Correlation of abilities as affected by practice. J. of Educa. Psychol. 4:405–14. (S. '13.)
Host, Arthur G. First-year work in modern languages. School R. 21:549–59. (O. '13.)
Irwin, Elizabeth A. A study of the feeble-minded in a west side school in New York City. Train. School M. (N.J.) 10:65–76. (S. '13.)
Is the college making good? Outl. 104:991–95. (30 Ag. '13.)
Jessup, Walter A. The shifting school population. School R. 21:513–22. (O. '13.)
Judson, Harry Pratt. Economy in education. School R. 21:441–45. (S. '13.)
Kenwood, Sydney H. The real problem in education. Educa. T. 66:379–80. (S. '13.)
Library theory and practice. Dial 55:131–33. (1 S. '13.)
Lyttleton, Edward. Instruction in matters of sex. Educa. R. 46:135–42. (S. '13.)
McVey, Frank L. The matter of college entrance requirements. Pop. Sci. Mo. 83:286–93. (S. '13.)
Manny, Frank A. Bibliography of sex hygiene. Educa. R. 46:168–76. (S. '13.)
Misused mathematics. Lit. D. 47:467. (20 S. '13.)
Moore, E. C. Indispensable requirements in city school administration. Educa. R. 46:143–56. (S. '13.)
(The) next college president; by a near professor. Pop. Sci. Mo. 83:265–85. (S. '13.)
Potter, George M. Relative efficiency of public and private secondary institutions. School R. 21:523–37. (O. '13.)
Reavis, W. C. An experiment in the teaching of high-school composition. School R. 21:538–41. (O. '13.)
Redfield, William C. A plea for practical education: excerpts from recent addresses. Voca. Educa. 3:1–10. (S. '13.)
Rust, Annie Coolidge. Economy in the kindergarten. Educa. 34:46–49. (S. '13.)
Sachs, Felix. Preliminary study of the relative efficiency of inductive and deductive teaching of logical reasoning. J. of Educa. Psychol. 4:381–92. (S. '13.)
Shideler, Samuel Ervin. Qualifications, salary, and tenure of the teachers in the commissioned high schools of Indiana. School R. 21:446–60. (S. '13.)
Short, R. L. The institutional high school and what it does for the community. School R. 21:475–77. (S. '13.)
Starch, Daniel. Correlations among abilities in school studies. J. of Educa. Psychol. 4:415–18. (S. '13.)
Stearns, Wallace N. What does it cost to build a college? Educa. 34:39–42. (S. '13.)
Stratton, George Frederic. The man behind the child. Outl. 105:137–40. (20 S. '13.)
Strong, Edward K., Jr. Psychological methods as applied to advertising. J. of Educa. Psychol. 4:393–404. (S. '13.)
Vocational Bible-schools. Lit. D. 47:475. (20 S. '13.)
Wallace, J. A. A plan for outside reading. School R. 21:478–85. (S. '13.)

VOLUME XIV NUMBER 4

THE ELEMENTARY SCHOOL TEACHER

DECEMBER 1913

EDUCATIONAL NEWS AND EDITORIAL COMMENT

School Tests Are Popular

The development of standard methods of testing the results of teaching in the various subjects of the curriculum has taken place within three or four years. Within that short time standard tests have come to occupy a very prominent place among methods of supervision, and the construction of test methods has become a frequent subject of investigation. The most widely used test is probably Mr. Courtis' arithmetic test, which he reports to have been given to two hundred thousand children. Wide currency has also been given to the Thorndike and Ayers handwriting scales and to the Hillegas-Thorndike scale for merit in English.

The New Courtis Tests

Mr. Courtis has now published two new tests. The first of these is a new arithmetic test based upon the experience gained with the earlier form of the test. It was found that the ability which was measured by the speed tests in the simple addition, subtraction, multiplication, and division problems did not closely correspond to the ability to use these processes in complex problems. The new test accordingly includes only complex problems in the four processes. The reasoning problems were omitted because it was found that success with them was too much a matter of ability to read.

Mr. Courtis also presents a group of entirely new tests which he classes under the general term "English." The same material is used ingeniously to serve as the basis for a variety of tests. The first part of a simple story is read for a dictation exercise. The children then compose an ending to the story. A second and a third section are then read by the pupils to test rate and accuracy of reading and a fourth section is read aloud by the teacher to test memory by free reproduction. The material thus obtained is to be used to measure the quality and rate of handwriting; ability in composition, including avoidance of mistakes in spelling and punctuation; and the ability to gain and reproduce words and ideas from reading or from listening to oral presentation. In addition there is a speed test in copying letters.

It is highly desirable that these new tests be given a trial. Mr. Courtis displays great ingenuity in devising his tests so that they can be conveniently applied by a large number of people under widely different conditions, and by this means a large amount of representative material is gathered. School administrators can therefore gain experience which will be of great value to them in their supervisory duties and at the same time be of service in standardizing the tests if they will take the small amount of trouble necessary to apply the tests in their schools.

Some Questions for Investigation

The critical student may put some questions concerning these new tests which experience should answer. It is a question, for example, whether the same material can be used advantageously for all the grades above the second, whether conditions under which the handwriting is produced give a true measure of speed (the quality is measured by the Thorndike or the Ayers scales), whether the verbal memory measured in the first reading test is significant, etc. Doubtless some parts will prove to be of more value than others and possibly the test will have to be made somewhat less complex. We shall await with interest the results of the use of the tests.

F. N. F.

Economy of Time in Education

The problem of saving two years in American schools is discussed in the report on economy of time in education by the committee of the National Education Association which has been at work upon the problem for five years. The report is published by the United States Bureau of Education for free distribution.

For the most part the discussions contained in the report are merely expressions of theoretical opinions to the effect that some means should be provided for solving the problem, accompanied by very *general* recommendations concerning how it *might* be done. A reader who is well acquainted with the plan of Comenius described in his *Great Didactic* as early as 1649, with the discussions by President Eliot of Harvard concerning the enriching of the grammar-school period which were published during the eighties and nineties, and with the suggestions by President Butler of Columbia published in 1903, will find little that is new in this publication.

For years we have been told that we take two years longer to achieve the educational results that are achieved in Europe by the age of eighteen. What we need most is not to be continually reminded of this unpleasant fact, but to be shown specifically how the time may be saved. What we need is detailed accounts of how the problem is being solved in various places in the country; for example, how Superintendent Morrison of New Hampshire and other New England educational leaders, beginning with a *nine*-year elementary course instead of one of eight years, have instituted almost marvelous economies in a few years, so that they are well on the way to a ten-year course for the combined elementary- and high-school periods. Similarly we might be informed in detail how some of the Texas schools get along with a seven-year elementary course and a four-year high-school course. Educational progress is best stimulated by actual object-lessons showing how the suggested innovations are actually administered.

The discussion in the report of economy in elementary education, by Superintendent Van Sickle, may be contrasted with the general theoretical character of the report. Thus he tells us in the following paragraph that the needed reforms for brighter children have been already accomplished in certain places.

> One of the conspicuous causes of waste in elementary education is the attempt to give the same preparation to all, regardless of wide differences in aptitude and the character of the life to be led. Classifying the grades above the sixth as secondary will facilitate a differentiation in the upper grades which will permit some pupils to make more direct preparation for business or the industries than is now possible while others continue to follow the more strictly academic program as far as may be necessary in preparation for managerial positions or professional life. Without accurate and detailed accounts of the results of actual trial under such an organization, positive

assertions as to economy of time could not be made, yet the probability that time would thus be saved would seem strong. But enough communities have made progress in this important field to place the matter beyond the stage of mere probability. Worcester, Indianapolis, Baltimore, Lincoln, Harrisburg, and Rochester, by maintaining special classes for exceptionally capable children, have shown that it is possible for able pupils to save one year between the sixth grade and the twelfth, with other advantages to themselves besides the saving of time.

Similarly Superintendent Van Sickle makes reference to the report of the Cleveland six-year course of study and quotes a part of its schedule of standards of achievement.

Moreover, he emphasizes the crux of the administrative situation in securing economy in his discussion of the importance of the principal, in the following words:

> It is upon the principal that large responsibility for improvement must be placed; so in a certain sense we are justified in modifying the well-known expression, "the teacher is the school," and in saying instead, "the principal is the school." The right kind of a principal will help weed out poor teachers, will make teachers of uncertain value into good teachers, and good teachers into better teachers. One prominent cause of waste in elementary education is the existence of inertia among school principals. Soon after the position is secured there comes a tendency to settle down into an easy routine. This tendency the superintendent, county or city, must counteract, if the waste under the heading "poor teaching" is to be materially lessened. What a laboratory a school principal has, and what an opportunity for the study of educational problems! No university possesses equal facilities in this field. The principal needs to feel more keenly his responsibility as a supervisor, but responsibility is not real unless coupled with a large degree of freedom. How to secure the amount of individual initiative that is desirable in principals and teachers without impairing the unity of the school system is an important problem in school administration. Teachers associated with routine principals are apt to become routine teachers, while, on the other hand, an alert and professional-minded principal always inspires his teachers with zeal. In considering waste in education, therefore, no problem looms up larger than the preliminary and after-training of suitable principals. Given a salary that will enable the superintendent to select persons of tested strength and character for these positions, no effort is expended to better advantage in checking waste than that which the superintendent devotes to conferences with his principals. The principal can either make or mar the most carefully planned scheme, and in his hands rests the success or failure of any plans that may be formulated for economizing time in elementary education.

Increased Professional Requirements Encourage Extension Courses for Teachers

Professional standards for teachers were advanced very materially in Illinois by a greatly improved certification law passed at the last legislature. One immediate effect of the law is seen in the organization of extension courses for teachers in some of the cities, in order to enable teachers who have not had professional training to take courses that will enable them to meet the requirements of the new law. Springfield and Joliet are among the most active cities in organizing such extension courses. In Springfield the instructors are secured from the state university and in Joliet from one of the state normal schools. The new law will probably also have the effect of sending many more Illinois teachers or prospective teachers to summer schools.

Similar experimentation in organizing extension courses for teachers is under way in Ann Arbor, Mich. In this case the instructors are also secured from the state university. While only 120 were enrolled there by October 18 and the superintendent was disappointed in the numbers, the experiment ought to succeed if any professional premium is placed upon the taking of the courses. The success of such work in cities where there are local universities to furnish the instructors would indicate that it ought to succeed eventually in centers where the instructors need to be imported from neighboring institutions.

Objective Supervisory Tests Needed

One of the most pressing needs in the administration of public-school systems is an objective scheme for grading the efficiency of teachers. If a teacher's record of efficiency can be secured without depending upon the extremely valuable personal opinion of supervisors, and the teacher can be shown in black and white how her efficiency compares with others in the system, the supervisor or principal need not be afraid of being perfectly open and frank in discussing with the teachers his reports to the superintendent on their efficiency. In New Orleans Superintendent Gwinn is working in the direction of such publicity, as shown in the following report from the *New Orleans Picayune:*

"If a teacher is rated as of low efficiency by the principal, she has a right to know why," was the statement made by Superintendent Gwinn at yesterday's meeting of third-, fourth-, and fifth-grade teachers. "Can a teacher request to see the report turned in by a principal as to her rating in efficiency?" he was asked. "She certainly can," admitted Mr. Gwinn. "In fact, the objects of the report would be lost if a teacher could not know in what she was deficient. The rule specifically states, however, that the representations to the board, on the teacher's efficiency, and consequent rating in salary, must be made by the superintendent."

S. C. P.

Professional Work in the Louisville Schools

The latest development in the elementary schools of Louisville, where so much progress has been made during the past two years, is the establishment of a prevocational class in the Seventeenth and Madison Street school.

The three lines of industrial work introduced thus far are printing, bookbinding, and woodworking.

The time is divided equally between the industrial work and the book subjects, or so-called "academic work." This latter has been carefully correlated with the shop problems, the teacher in charge of it, Miss Ethel M. Lovell, having spent several weeks in studying the scope of prevocational work and in visiting the printing plants and binderies of Louisville. She states that the opinion of the practical men was that the vitalized academic work is of greatest importance. She says also that from the teacher's point of view it is most interesting and encouraging to "watch the children as they grasp the 'reason' for things," that is, for their formal school studies. "Our library," she says, "is growing and our little librarian solemnly checks off books after school for the waiting children."

Mr. Louis A. Bacon, head of the industrial department of the school and director of manual training for the city, says that one of the great advantages of the school is that the work itself holds the children because they like it. One reason for this is that the work is made intensely practical and that the time element is emphasized.

Although in the early weeks of its existence, the school has attracted much public interest and appreciative comment.

One circumstance which ought to contribute to the success of the printing class is that the Typographical Union of Louisville has recently adopted a rule making graduation from the elementary school a condition of apprenticeship in the printing trade. This is another indication of the possibility of improving our schools by means of co-operation with trade and business organizations.

Vocational Bureau to Be Formed for Philadelphia Schools

Two years ago the Public Educational Association of Philadelphia outlined plans for developing a department of vocational guidance in the public schools. This was done after their investigation and report on the economic conditions relating to children entering the business and industrial world between fourteen and sixteen years of age which was so ably presented in Mr. James S. Hiatt's article, "The Child, the School, and the Job."

The plan has had more recently the approval of Dr. Martin G. Brumbaugh, superintendent of schools, and finally of a special subcommittee on the Committee on Elementary Schools of the Board of Public Education. Dr. Brumbaugh says:

> Society suffers, particularly in the economic world, by reason of the fact that in America the transition from school life to a wage-earning relation to society is sudden, sharp, and abrupt. Whatever the school has done for the child it suddenly ceases to do, and the next day he must begin the struggle for bread.
>
> We have endeavored for some time to find means of establishing a vocational bureau as part of our public-school obligation to society. The purpose of this bureau would be to know (1) the capabilities and aptitudes of the pupils at the time they leave school; (2) the form of training they have had in school; and (3) the types of industrial occupations promising the largest return for good to the individual. This later phase of equipment would carry with it a knowledge of the several employers of labor, to the end that only those who endeavor to deal fairly and helpfully by their employees should be allowed to receive the assistance of the bureau.

The Committee on Elementary Schools has unanimously agreed to the creation of a Department of Vocational Education and Guidance and submitted to the Board of Public Education the following resolution, which has been adopted:

> *Resolved*, That a new department in the office of the superintendent be and is hereby created, to be known and designated as the Department of "Vocational Education and Guidance" and that a director for this department together with two clerical assistants be elected in conformity with the rules of the Board of Public Education, said director to be paid a salary not to exceed

four thousand dollars ($4,000) per year; and to have general supervision over all vocational activities for boys in the elementary schools; to secure definite articulation of said work and correlate it with the manual-training work in the high schools for boys; to organize and direct a bureau of vocational guidance for all pupils leaving the public schools and to have the same general relation to the superintendent as now pertains to other directors of special branches.

A New Idea in Vocational Work

A clipping from the editorial page of the *Union*, published in Ft. Atkinson, Wis., says that "vocational work took an advance step in a new direction in Wisconsin last summer." The movement came through the initiative of the boys of the manual-training department of the Waukesha high school. The students organized a co-operative manufacturing establishment, and with the advisory help of the superintendent of city schools rented the manual-training rooms for the summer months.

The work consisted of the manufacture and sale of mission furniture, the building of coal sheds, chicken coops, farmers' gates, and such articles. The boys paid for all their material, paid rent for the school plant, and still made a profit for themselves.

If the work was done faithfully, as it must have been, judging from the results, the boys should have some high-school credit for this work. If they do not get credit there are still three distinct advantages to be gained from such work. First, it gave the boys experience in work approaching real labor conditions which they are to meet in life. Second, it will develop, in some of them at least, the power of initiative, a very essential thing in those who are to make much progress in industrial life. And lastly, it may help to show teachers and school boards that manual training may be made intensely practical and at the same time be less a burden on the financial resources of the school.

F. M. L.

The Newburgh Survey

Our cities are coming to realize that there are other functions which they may well perform outside of the individualistic production and distribution of commodities. They are coming to understand the possibility of an efficient and sufficient production and an equitable distribution of human welfare to all elements of the city population.

The first labor that suggests itself after this realization develops is taking stock of all the human welfare assets and liabilities possessed by the city. Then there must be a consideration of the effectiveness with which the assets are employed, and an equally careful study of the success in warding off the harmful effects of the social liabilities. This stock-taking is coming to be called the city survey. One of the latest published instances is that of Newburgh, N.Y., a city of some 30,000 inhabitants.

This survey was a community undertaking, initiated entirely by the citizens. On the survey committee were representatives appointed by the Chamber of Commerce, Merchants' Association, Central Labor Union, Ministerial Association, and the Associated Charities. The survey covered schools, public health, housing, delinquency, public library, recreation, charities, industrial conditions, and municipal administration. The survey was made by specialists from the Russell Sage Foundation, and the report is published as one of their bulletins.

In examining into the situation as regards the schools they pursue the excellent plan of comparing the various aspects of the Newburgh schools with those of the other cities of similar size in the state, or with the absolute standards set up by the office of the State Commission of Education. Things studied in this fashion are: school expenditures per pupil; adequacy of buildings and equipment in the matters of lighting, cubic feet of air space per pupil, sanitaries, school desks, washing facilities, wardrobes and lockers, fire-escapes, heating; the division of administrative functions between school board and superintendent; the teaching force as regards salaries, system of appointment, ratings, stimulation to effort, and supervision. The city is compared with the rest of the group as to the presence or absence of the following provisions, to the discredit of Newburgh in all cases but one: half-yearly promotions, supervisor of physical training, medical training, school doctor or nurse, supervisor of penmanship, domestic science, school yards used for playgrounds, class for backward children, class for truants and incorrigibles, kindergartens, evening schools, open-air classes, industrial education, and the social use of the school buildings.

The survey of the schools is very slight as compared with what the city superintendent ought himself to make and publish in his annual report to the community. Where conditions are unsatisfactory, however, due to the school board rather than to the superintendent, under present conditions, there is sometimes for obvious reasons a decided advantage in having the work done by some disinterested outside agency.

A more complete survey of a school system has recently been made in Portland, Ore. This city has grown large; but the form and methods of the school organization remain the same as when Portland was but a rural village. As a result, the city has to use the same textbooks as the rural schools, although many are entirely unsuitable; taxes are still voted in town meeting, though the method is an impossible one for a large city; the Board of School Directors is still unduly powerful in the control of matters that rightly belong to the professional experts. Owing to this lack of professional initiative, the curriculum has failed to grow and keep pace with the demands of modern progress. Full recommendations are made for remedying these maladjustments. J. F. B.

Rural Life and the Rural School

The decrease and change in the nature of rural population is constantly introducing further complications in the rural school problem. In a "Social and Economic Survey of a Rural Township in Southern Minnesota," Thompson and Warber show that the township population is composed as follows: American, 11 per cent; German, 30.8 per cent; Norwegian, 24.2 per cent; mixed, 21.3 per cent; English, 5.8 per cent; Irish 3.7 per cent; and Swedish 2.9 per cent. Although the foreign population in rural districts in general is increasing in many regions, the total rural population is decreasing. Iowa had fewer people in 1910 than in 1900, and the same statement would hold true for some other states, if the cities were left out of consideration.

During the time while this relative, and sometimes actual, decrease of population has taken place, it is commonly known that there has been a great increase in rural wealth. In the survey in Minnesota it is shown that the township investigated had in

1860 a lands and buildings valuation of $985,955 and in 1910 a valuation of $19,504,914. Farm machinery in 1860 was valued at $59,971 and in 1910 at $727,941. Farm animals in 1860 were valued at $179,817 and in 1910 at $2,345,138. Other farm materials and products show similar increase in value.

It is a notable fact that rural school expenditures and rural school efficiency have not kept pace with the value of rural properties. The change in rural population and lack of advanced ideals of rural education are important factors in this situation. Consolidation of rural schools has been urged and has taken several forms. In some cases where there has been a decrease in the number of pupils in adjoining districts the pupils are brought together in one school, all being taught by one teacher with little or no increase in school efficiency. This is a means of keeping the school alive, but not necessarily a means of increasing its efficiency. In other cases several districts are consolidated and grade schools, sometimes high schools, established. Too often these are attempts to establish city schools in the country, but in some cases these schools are developing types of work that are fitted to rural life. It seems fairly clear that the rural education problem must be solved by the development of schools which shall consider the needs of rural life rather than city life. Many things are common to both kinds of schools, but rural life must be intellectualized through rural schools, as city life is through city schools. All over the United States this change in emphasis is now being recognized. Experimentation in the development of this new type of rural education is second to none in importance, for successful rural life is fundamental to the occupation upon which city people live.

Another phase of rural life is admirably set forth in Gill and Pinchot's book *The Country Church*, in which they present the results of a prolonged and careful study of the rural churches in Windsor County, Vt., and Tompkins County, N.Y. In many ways until recently the rural church has been the social center of rural life. In the two counties studied there has been a decline of rural population of 19 per cent in Windsor County between 1830 and 1910 and of 34 per cent in Tompkins County between 1840 and 1910. In Windsor County the church attendance of

Protestant persons has declined from 26 per cent in 1888 to 19 per cent in 1908; and in Tompkins County there has been over 5 per cent decrease in church attendance of Protestant rural population between 1890 and 1910. In Tompkins County there has been a decrease of Protestant rural population from 16,805 in 1890 to 13,743 in 1910. The salary, education, and efficiency of the rural preacher have declined and the rural church has well-nigh lost its place as a social center. The change in the nature of rural population helps to make the school the logical rural social center. Difference in religious views, or absence of positive religious views, makes it unlikely that churches can gather together all the persons of one community. Common educational interests if aroused should enable the country school to serve as a social center. Many attempts are under way to make the school an instrument for securing a social unification of the community. O. W. C.

The Gary Schools

At the request of the Board of Education of the Gary public schools the announcement is made that visitors who wish to see the school system are asked to time their visits so as to come within the weeks of March 16 to 20, June 8 to 12, and July 27 to 31. The fact that the Board has found it necessary to restrict the time of visiting to these weeks when especial attention will be given to visitors is a result of the very great interest which the innovations made in the schools at Gary have awakened.

Scientific Experimentation by Teachers

A notice in the *Zeitschrift für pädagogische Psychologie und experimentelle Pädagogik* reports that the Swiss Association of Teachers has decided to undertake systematic experimentation in the field of experimental pedagogy. A number of European teachers' associations have undertaken work of this character in the past. The Teachers' Association of Leipzig, for example, has for a number of years maintained a laboratory for research and a series of lecture courses under the expert direction of Dr. Brahn, of the University of Leipzig. Teachers in Berlin, Breslau, Dresden, and Stuttgart have also carried on work of this nature. So far as the writer is aware, no such systematic, organized effort to maintain scientific research in the field of education has been undertaken by bodies of teachers in the United States. Large associations have from time to time discussed or maintained researches of a less comprehensive nature. Such efforts as this may serve as a stimulus to educators in the United States.

Regularity of Attendance and Promotion

A study made under the auspices of the Committee on School Inquiry of New York brings out clearly one of the factors in the rate of promotion of children. This study is reported in a bulletin of the Public Education Association of New York. It shows that 17.10 per cent of the children between the ages of seven and fourteen were absent from school from eleven to twenty days in a term of a half-year, that 6.63 per cent were absent from twenty-one to thirty days, that 3.12 per cent were absent from thirty-one to forty days, and that 4.10 per cent were absent forty-one days and above. The significance of these results may be seen from the following quotation:

> Nearly one-half of the pupils who failed of promotion were absent over two-fifths of the school term, and 70 per cent were absent from school at least thirty days during the half-year. These data, furthermore, took account only of the pupils who failed of promotion on June 30; the 70,000 children who left school during the year being disregarded.

The report then discusses at length the need for more efficient organization for the purpose of reducing this large amount of non-attendance. This study confirms the results of less extensive investigation upon the importance of regularity in attendance for the advancement of the child through the school.

F. N. F.

LITERATURE IN THE ELEMENTARY CURRICULUM

J. F. BOBBITT, A. C. BOYCE, AND M. L. PERKINS
University of Chicago

In what school grade should any given piece of literature be read? Obviously, it ought to be used in that grade where, as shown by practical experience, it works best. Our questions can therefore be asked in terms of practical experience: Into what school grade has any given piece of literature tended to gravitate in the country-wide "trial-and-error" experimentation that is going on? By examining the courses of study used in the various cities and states, it is possible to locate the grade in which the given piece is most frequently used at the present time. This is the best evidence that we can now have as to where it belongs.

It must be remembered, however, that the experimentation is not ended. Certain pieces have got their present position through tradition and custom, and have not fully gravitated to the place where they belong. Others have found their place in the curriculum as the result of special systems of educational thought; these in many cases will be shifted as the systems of thought are modified or discarded. Notwithstanding these and other similar disturbing factors, it can still be safely said that the consensus of experience in the country, as shown by a full tabulation of courses of study, is the surest authority as to the rightful position in the elementary school of any particular literary selection.

The present study was undertaken for the purpose of ascertaining what readings were used in the elementary schools of the United States and in what grades. Our supply of printed courses was incomplete. Of those at hand, very many suggested only the general lines of work, and apparently left to principals and teachers a large amount of freedom in the selection. It was possible, however, to select fifty printed courses which presented reasonably full statements as to what was to be read and the grade in which it was to be used. Of these, thirty-six were of cities, among which were to be found New York City, Boston, Washington, D.C., Cincinnati, Minneapolis, Detroit, Tacoma, and San Francisco. Fourteen were state courses representing states in all portions of the country, from Massachusetts and New York on the Atlantic seaboard to Washington on the Pacific side. It is believed that the consensus of these fifty courses will approximate the results which would be obtained were it possible to know what is being done in every city and state.

The inaccuracy with which printed courses of study represent the work actually done is sufficiently well known. Still, it is believed that the readings most often recommended in the printed courses are the ones most often to be found in actual practice; and those least often referred to in the courses are the ones that will least often be used in practice. Our aim, therefore, under the circumstances, is to show accurately the relative frequencies of recommendations as an approximate index of the relative frequencies of use. Our aim is relative emphasis, not absolute number. It is believed that the tabulations fairly present relative emphases.

The following lists include only the longer readings—books, long stories, and the longer poems. Short stories and poems have been tabulated separately and conclusions concerning these will be published in a later issue.

In the first of the following lists, the readings are alphabetical, by authors. In the original tabulation of the fifty courses, 138 authors, represented by 296 titles, were found. Obviously a book that occurred but once or twice in the fifty courses, however, represented special circumstances; and in tabulating consensus of practice, it could well be omitted from the list. The 113 titles that occurred only one, two, or three times have been eliminated. The list as given below includes the 183 titles that are recommended four or more times in the fifty courses.

The number of times a title was recommended in the fifty courses is stated in the first tabular column. The second column represents the grade for which the piece was most often recommended. In case a title was recommended equally often for two grades, the figure chosen was the one that lay nearest the majority-practice, as shown by the entire array of recommendations. The third column shows the range of grades for which the title is recommended in the fifty courses of study.

GENERAL LIST

Author	Title	Times Recommended	Grade	Range of Recommendations
Anonymous	*Arabian Nights*	22	6	1–8
Aanrud	*Lizbeth Longfrock*	5	4	3–7
Abbott	*Boy on the Farm*	5	4	3–5
Aesop	*Fables*	18	4	1–8
Alcott	*Eight Cousins*	6	5	4–8
	Jack and Jill	4	6	5–6
	Little Men	17	6	3–8
	Little Women	18	5	3–8
	Old-Fashioned Girl	7	7	5–8
	Under the Lilacs	9	6	3–6
Aldrich	*Story of a Bad Boy*	12	6	4–8
Amicis	*Cuore*	4	5	5–8
Andersen	*Fairy Tales*	28	4	1–6
	Ugly Duckling	4	1	1–5
Andrews, G.	*Each and All*	11	4	2–5
	Seven Little Sisters	23	3	1–4
	Ten Boys	15	5	3–6
Andrews, M. R. S.	*Perfect Tribute*	4	......	7–8
Arnold	*Sohrab and Rustum*	4	8	7–8
Baldwin	*Discovery of the Old Northwest*	6	7	5–8
	Fairy Stories and Fables	13	3	1–4
	Fifty Famous Stories Retold	30	4	3–7
	Hero Stories Told in School	5	5	5
	Old Greek Stories	24	4	1–7
	Story of Roland	9	7	5–7
	Story of Siegfried	13	7	4–7
	Thirty More Famous Stories	9	4	3–6
Beckwith	*In Mythland*	8	3	1–4
Bennett	*Master Skylark*	4	7	7–8
Brooks	*Stories of the Red Children*	6	2	1–4
Brown, A. F.	*In the Days of Giants*	12	5	1–6
Brown, G.	*Rab and His Friends*	15	4	2–8
Browning	*Pied Piper of Hamelin*	11	3	2–7
Bunyan	*Pilgrim's Progress*	9	7	4–8
Burnett	*Little Lord Fauntleroy*	14	5	3–7
Burroughs	*Birds and Bees*	18	7	6–8
	Sharp Eyes	11	7	6–8
	Squirrels and Other Fur Bearers	10	6	5–8
Carpenter	*Africa*	7	6	4–7
	Asia	9	5	4–7
	Australia	7	6	4–7
	Europe	9	6	4–7
	How We Are Clothed	5	6	4–8
	How We Are Fed	6	8	4–8
	North America	9	5	4–6
	South America	7	6	4–7
Carroll	*Alice in Wonderland*	27	4	3–7
	Through the Looking Glass	9	5	4–7
Carter	*Story of Brave Dogs*	5	4	3–5
Church	*Story of the "Iliad"*	8	5	4–8
	Story of the "Odyssey"	9	5	3–8

GENERAL LIST—*Continued*

Author	Title	Times Recommended	Grade	Range of Recommendations
Clarke	*Story of Ulysses*	9	5	3–6
	Story of Troy	4	5	4–6
Clemens	*The Prince and the Pauper*	10	7	5–8
	Tom Sawyer	6	7	6–8
Collodi	*Pinocchio*	9	4	1–7
Cooke	*Nature Myths and Stories*	5	2	1–3
Coolidge	*How the Leaves Come Down*	4	2	2–3
Cooper	*Deerslayer*	7	7	5–7
	Last of the Mohicans	17	7	6–8
	The Spy	13	7	6–8
Craik (Mulock)	*Adventures of a Brownie*	21	4	2–6
	Little Lame Prince	17	3	2–6
Craik	*Bow-wow and Mew-mew*	6	2	1–2
Dana	*Two Years Before the Mast*	11	7	6–8
Defoe	*Robinson Crusoe*	29	4	1–7
Dickens	*Christmas Carol*	25	7	3–8
	Cricket on the Hearth	14	8	6–8
	David Copperfield	11	7	5–8
Dodge	*Donald and Dorothy*	5	5	3–7
	Hans Brinker	19	6	4–8
Dopp	*Early Cave Men*	8	3	1–6
	Tree Dwellers	7	3	1–6
Du Chaillu	*The Land of the Long Night*	4	7	6–7
Dutton	*In Field and Pasture*	5	3	1–3
Eddy	*Friends and Helpers*	7	4	3–5
Eggleston	*First Book in American History*	8	5	4–6
	Hoosier School Boy	11	6	3–8
	Hoosier School Master	5	7	5–8
	Stories of American Life and Adventure	7	4	3–6
	Stories of Great Americans for Little Americans	13	3	3–4
Eliot	*Silas Marner*	8	8	8
Ewing	*Jackanapes*	11	5	3–6
Franklin	*Autobiography*	12	7	5–8
Frost	*Court of King Arthur*	5	6	5–7
Goldsmith	*Deserted Village*	7	8	7–8
Grimm	*Fairy Tales* (for young children)	16	1	1–4
	Household Stories	6	3	3–4
Grover	*Overall Boys*	7	1	1–2
	Sunbonnet Babies	8	1	1–2
Guerber	*Story of the English*	7	6	6–8
	Story of the Greeks	6	6	5–8
	Story of the Romans	8	6	5–9
Hale, L. P	*Peterkin Papers*	5	5	2–5
Hale, E. E.	*The Man Without a Country*	31	8	6–8
Hall	*Four Old Greeks*	4	5	3–5
Harris	*Uncle Remus*	12	5	1–7
Hawthorne	*Grandfather's Chair*	11	7	6–8
	Snow Image	5	7	3–7
	Tanglewood Tales	22	5	1–7
	The Great Stone Face	12	7	4–8

GENERAL LIST—*Continued*

Author	Title	Times Recommended	Grade	Range of Recommendations
Hawthorne (*cont.*)	*Twice-Told Tales*	6	6	6–8
	Wonder Book	27	5	3–7
Holbrook	*Nature Myths*	11	2	1–5
Hopkins	*Sandman*	4	3	1–3
Hughes	*Tom Brown at Rugby*	6	7	6–8
	Tom Brown's School Days	13	8	4–8
Irving	*Alhambra*	5	8	7–8
	Rip Van Winkle	16	6	2–8
	Sketch Book	19	7	6–8
	The Legend of Sleepy Hollow	11	7	5–8
Johonnot	*Ten Great Events in History*	5	8	6–8
Kingsley	*Greek Heroes*	11	5	5–7
	Water Babies	17	4	3–6
	Westward Ho!	4	7	6–8
Kipling	*Captains Courageous*	11	7	6–8
	Jungle Books 1 and 2	20	5	2–7
	Just-so Stories	17	5	1–8
Lamb	*Adventures of Ulysses*	7	6	6–8
	Tales from Shakespeare	28	7	5–8
Lang	*Blue Fairy Book*	4	1	1–4
Lear	*Nonsense Songs and Stories*	4	3	1–6
Long	*Secrets of the Woods*	6	5	5–7
	Wilderness Ways	12	5	3–7
Longfellow	*Evangeline*	23	7	5–8
	Hiawatha	27	2	1–6
	Miles Standish	23	7	5–8
	Tales of a Wayside Inn	8	7	6–9
Lowell	*Vision of Sir Launfal*	13	8	7–8
Mabie	*Norse Stories Retold from the Eddas*	16	5	2–8
Macaulay	*Horatius at the Bridge*	11	7	4–8
McDonald	*At the Back of the North Wind*	5	5	3–7
McMurry	*Classic Stories*	6	2	1–3
Monroe	*Flamingo Feather*	5	5	5–8
Nicolay	*Boy's Life of Abraham Lincoln*	4	8	4–8
Otis (pseud.)	*Toby Tyler*	7	4	3–6
Page	*Two Little Confederates*	9	5	3–8
Parkman	*Oregon Trail*	5	8	5–8
Pratt	*Legends of Norseland*	4	5	5–7
	Legends of the Red Children	10	3	1–4
Pyle	*Men of Iron*	4	7	6–7
	Merry Adventures of Robin Hood	17	5	4–8
	Story of King Arthur and His Knights	11	5	4–8
Radford	*King Arthur and His Knights*	14	6	4–8
Ramée	*Moufflon*	6	4	1–5
Rice	*Mrs. Wiggs of the Cabbage Patch*	4	8	6–8
Ruskin	*King of the Golden River*	30	5	3–7
Schwatka	*Children of the Cold*	6	5	3–6
Scott	*Ivanhoe*	14	8	6–9
	Kenilworth	7	8	6–8
	Lady of the Lake	20	8	6–9
	Lay of the Last Minstrel	4	.....	7–8

GENERAL LIST—*Concluded*

Author	Title	Times Recommended	Grade	Range of Recommendations
Scudder	*Book of Legends*	5	4	3–5
	Fables, Folk Stories and Legends	15	3	1–4
Seton	*Lives of the Hunted*	9	5	4–6
	Lobo, Rag and Vixen	9	5	4–6
	Wild Animals I Have Known	18	5	1–7
Sewell	*Black Beauty*	31	5	3–8
Shakespeare	*Julius Caesar*	18	8	6–9
	Merchant of Venice	14	8	8–9
Shaw, C.	*Story of the Ancient Greeks*	4	6	6–8
Shaw, E. R.	*Big and Little People of Other Lands*	11	3	2–4
Smith	*Eskimo Stories*	8	2	1–3
Snedden	*Docas, the Indian Boy*	9	4	3–6
Spyri	*Heidi*	15	6	3–6
	Moni, the Goat Boy	8	5	4–6
Stevenson	*Child's Garden of Verses*	14	3	1–7
	Kidnapped	6	8	7–8
	Treasure Island	17	8	3–8
Stockton	*Fanciful Tales*	19	5	1–6
Stoddard	*Little Smoke*	5	5	3–6
Stowe	*Uncle Tom's Cabin*	10	8	6–8
Swift	*Gulliver's Travels*	14	6	4–8
Tennyson	*Idylls of the King*	4	8	8
Thaxter	*Madame Arachne*	4	3	2–4
Turpin	*Classic Fables*	4	3	1–3
Van Bergen	*Story of China*	5	7	6–8
Van Dyke	*First Christmas Tree*	4	6	6–8
Waterloo	*Story of Ab*	6	1	1–8
Whittier	*Snow-Bound*	24	7	6–8
Wiggin	*Birds' Christmas Carol*	23	4	1–8
	Rebecca of Sunnybrook Farm	7	8	5–8
	Story of Patsy	7	8	2–8
Wiltse	*Folklore Stories and Proverbs*	5	2	1–3
Wyss	*Swiss Family Robinson*	23	5	3–7

No school can use all this list of 183 titles. Selection must be made. One must not blindly follow consensus of practice. But in this field, at least, it is the safest single guide. The second list shows the selections most frequently used in each grade, in the order of their frequency.

SELECTED LIST OF TITLES IN ELEMENTARY SCHOOL LITERATURE

INCLUDING THOSE APPEARING NINE TIMES OR MORE IN THE COURSES STUDIED

	Title	No. Times Recommended	Most Frequent Grade	Range of Grades
GRADE I—				
Grimm	*Fairy Tales* (for young children)	16	1	1–4
GRADE II—				
Longfellow	*Hiawatha*	27	2	1–6
Holbrook	*Nature Myths*	11	2	1–5
GRADE III—				
Andrews	*Seven Little Sisters*	23	3	1–4
Craik	*Little Lame Prince*	17	3	2–6
Scudder	*Fables, Folk Stories and Legends*	15	3	1–4
Stevenson	*Child's Garden of Verses*	14	3	1–7
Baldwin	*Fairy Stories and Fables*	13	3	1–4
Eggleston	*Stories of Great Americans for Little Americans*	13	3	3–4
Browning	*Pied Piper of Hamelin*	11	3	2–7
Shaw	*Big and Little People of Other Lands*	11	3	2–4
Pratt	*Legends of the Red Children*	10	3	1–4
GRADE IV—				
Baldwin	*Fifty Famous Stories Retold*	30	4	3–7
Defoe	*Robinson Crusoe*	29	4	1–7
Andersen	*Fairy Tales*	28	4	1–6
Carroll	*Alice in Wonderland*	27	4	3–7
Baldwin	*Old Greek Stories*	24	4	1–7
Wiggin	*Birds' Christmas Carol*	23	4	1–8
Craik	*Adventures of a Brownie*	21	4	2–6
Aesop	*Fables*	18	4	1–8
Kingsley	*Water Babies*	17	4	3–6
Brown	*Rab and His Friends*	15	4	2–8
Andrews	*Each and All*	11	4	2–5
Baldwin	*Thirty More Famous Stories*	9	4	3–6
Collodi	*Pinocchio*	9	4	1–7
Snedden	*Docas, the Indian Boy*	9	4	3–6
GRADE V—				
Sewell	*Black Beauty*	31	5	3–8
Ruskin	*King of the Golden River*	30	5	3–7
Hawthorne	*Wonder Book*	27	5	3–7
Wyss	*Swiss Family Robinson*	23	5	3–7
Hawthorne	*Tanglewood Tales*	22	5	1–7
Kipling	*Jungle Books*	20	5	2–7
Stockton	*Fanciful Tales*	19	5	1–6
Alcott	*Little Women*	18	5	3–8
Seton	*Wild Animals I Have Known*	18	5	1–7
Kipling	*Just-so Stories*	17	5	1–8
Pyle	*Merry Adventures of Robin Hood*	17	5	4–8
Mabie	*Norse Stories Retold from Eddas*	16	5	2–8
Andrews	*Ten Boys*	15	5	3–6
Burnett	*Little Lord Fauntleroy*	14	5	3–7
Brown	*In the Days of Giants*	12	5	1–6
Harris	*Uncle Remus*	12	5	1–7
Long	*Wilderness Ways*	12	5	3–7
Ewing	*Jackanapes*	11	5	3–6

SELECTED LIST OF TITLES IN ELEMENTARY SCHOOL LITERATURE—*Continued*

	Title	No. Times Recommended	Most Frequent Grade	Range of Grades
Kingsley	*Greek Heroes*	11	5	5–7
Pyle	*Story of King Arthur and His Knights*	11	5	4–8
Carpenter	*North America*	9	5	4–6
	Asia	9	5	4–7
Carroll	*Through the Looking Glass*	9	5	4–7
Clarke	*Story of Ulysses*	9	5	3–6
Church	*Story of the "Odyssey"*	9	5	3–8
Page	*Two Little Confederates*	9	5	3–8
Seton	*Lobo, Rag and Vixen*	9	5	4–6
	Lives of the Hunted	9	5	4–6
GRADE VI—				
Anonymous	*Arabian Nights*	22	6	1–8
Dodge	*Hans Brinker*	19	6	4–8
Alcott	*Little Men*	17	6	3–8
Irving	*Rip Van Winkle*	16	6	2–8
Spyri	*Heidi*	15	6	3–6
Radford	*King Arthur and His Knights*	14	6	4–8
Swift	*Gulliver's Travels*	14	6	4–8
Aldrich	*Story of a Bad Boy*	12	6	4–8
Eggleston	*Hoosier School Boy*	11	6	3–8
Burroughs	*Squirrels and Other Fur Bearers*	10	6	5–8
Alcott	*Under the Lilacs*	9	6	3–6
Carpenter	*Europe*	9	6	4–7
GRADE VII—				
Lamb	*Tales from Shakespeare*	28	7	5–8
Dickens	*Christmas Carol*	25	7	3–8
Whittier	*Snow-Bound*	24	7	6–8
Longfellow	*Miles Standish*	23	7	5–8
	Evangeline	23	7	5–8
Irving	*Sketch Book*	19	7	6–8
Burroughs	*Birds and Bees*	18	7	6–8
Cooper	*Last of the Mohicans*	17	7	6–8
Baldwin	*Story of Siegfried*	13	7	4–7
Cooper	*The Spy*	13	7	6–8
Franklin	*Autobiography*	12	7	5–8
Hawthorne	*The Great Stone Face*	12	7	4–8
Burroughs	*Sharp Eyes*	11	7	6–8
Dickens	*David Copperfield*	11	7	5–8
Hawthorne	*Grandfather's Chair*	11	7	6–8
Irving	*The Legend of Sleepy Hollow*	11	7	5–8
Kipling	*Captains Courageous*	11	7	6–8
Macaulay	*Horatius at the Bridge*	11	7	4–8
Dana	*Two Years Before the Mast*	11	7	6–8
Clemens	*Prince and the Pauper*	10	7	5–8
Baldwin	*Story of Roland*	9	7	5–7
Bunyan	*Pilgrim's Progress*	9	7	4–8
GRADE VIII—				
Hale	*The Man Without a Country*	31	8	6–8
Scott	*Lady of the Lake*	20	8	6–9
Shakespeare	*Julius Caesar*	18	8	6–9
Stevenson	*Treasure Island*	17	8	3–8

SELECTED LIST OF TITLES IN ELEMENTARY SCHOOL LITERATURE—*Concluded*

	Title	No. Times Recommended	Most Frequent Grade	Range of Grades
Dickens	*Cricket on the Hearth*	14	8	6–8
Scott	*Ivanhoe*	14	8	6–9
Shakespeare	*Merchant of Venice*	14	8	8–9
Hughes	*Tom Brown's School Days*	13	8	4–8
Lowell	*Vision of Sir Launfal*	13	8	7–8
Stowe	*Uncle Tom's Cabin*	10	8	6–8

SOME PRACTICAL STUDIES OF HANDWRITING[1]

FRANK N. FREEMAN
University of Chicago

THE RELATION BETWEEN SPEED AND QUALITY

In an article in the *Journal of Educational Psychology* for 1912 the writer, in describing a number of problems in psychology and pedagogy of handwriting, emphasized the question of the relationship between the speed and the quality of writing. From investigations which have been made in connection with the School of Education and from some of the published articles from other sources, material can be gathered which bears upon this and other questions. The purpose of this article is to present such data as exist as a basis for certain tentative conclusions and as an incentive to further research on the same problems.

In order that the relationship of speed and quality might be set forth from as large variety of sources as possible, the results of a number of investigations have been brought together in Table I. Part of the figures of this table are borrowed from other sources, but they are put into new relationships. The table shows the average quality (which may be interpreted as legibility or as general merit), and the average speed for as many of the grades as have been reported upon or measured in the various investigations. The notes at the bottom of the table give the sources from which the figures were drawn.

In order that the averages representing the quality of writing might be made comparable, it was necessary to transmute the figures which were obtained by using the Thorndike and the Ayers scales into a common measure. This was done by using the Ayers scale as the basis and transmuting the results obtained with the Thorndike scale by multiplying the figures by five. This procedure is not entirely accurate. It presupposes that Grades 20 and 90 of the Ayers scale correspond with Grades 4 and 18

[1] The author acknowledges with thanks the assistance of Messrs. J. R. Young and R. M. Tryon in making many of the tabulations.

respectively of the Thorndike scale and that the intermediate grades correspond in like manner. It is probable that the Thorndike scale has a greater range than the Ayers scale and that therefore the lower figures obtained in this way will be too high and

TABLE I

The Quality and Speed of Writing in Several School Systems

Grade	Quality						Speed					
	A	B	C	D	E	F	A	B	C	D	E	F
1B	46.0	....	....	....	....	....	22	....	....	....	....	....
1	....	....	....	....	30.0	....	....	....	....	....	19.3	....
1A	47.5	....	....	....	....	22	9	....	....	....	....	....
2B	50.5	....	....	....	....	34	17	....	....	....	....	....
2	....	....	....	....	37.0	....	....	....	....	....	33.1	....
2A	52.0	....	....	....	....	37	14	....	....	....	....	....
3B	49.5	....	....	....	....	41	20	....	....	....	....	....
3	....	38.5	....	....	39.0	....	....	52.0	....	....	34.0	....
3A	51.5	....	....	....	....	44	36	....	....	....	....	....
4B	51.0	....	....	36.8	....	46	48	....	....	56.0	....	....
4	....	42.5	38.0	....	43.0	....	....	82.1	62.4	....	40.2	....
4A	50.0	....	....	43.4	....	48	60	....	....	75.0	....	....
5B	51.0	....	....	42.0	....	44	51	....	....	64.0	....	....
5	....	43.0	36.0	....	46.0	....	....	83.2	46.4	....	50.6	....
5A	51.5	....	....	48.1	....	46	52	....	....	65.0	....	....
6B	57.0	....	....	51.6	....	47	71	....	....	73.0	....	....
6	....	49.0	46.6	....	49.0	....	....	114.9	77.3	....	61.6	....
6A	58.5	....	....	53.7	....	50	60	....	....	71.0	....	....
7B	57.0	....	....	....	....	54	58	....	....	....	....	....
7	....	....	34.7	57.0	51.0	....	....	....	103.1	69.0	79.4	....
7A	58.5	....	....	....	....	56	55	....	....	....	....	....
8B	56.0	....	....	....	....	59	86	....	....	....	....	....
8	....	63.0	49.4	52.3	52.0	....	....	71.4	80.2	71.5	84.8	....
8A	55.0	....	....	....	....	58	74	....	....	....	....	....

School A: Connersville, Ind., schools. Figures taken from Superintendent Wilson's report in *Elementary School Teacher*, Vol. XI (1911), 540–43 (Thorndike scale).

School B: Large city school (Thorndike scale).

School C: System of a town in Illinois (Ayers scale).

School D: University Elementary School (Ayers scale).

School E: Madison, Wis., schools. From report by D. Starch in *Journal of Educational Psychology*, IV (1913), 445–64 (Thorndike scale).

School F: Iowa City schools. From report of Irving King in *Journal of Educational Psychology*, III (1912), 514–20.

the upper figures too low, but since the majority of the figures are in the intermediate parts of the scale, this error is not of great consequence.

Another difficulty arises from the fact that the figures as to quality are obtained by different judges. No attempt has been made to determine exactly how much error is due to this fact.

Some allowance then must be made in the case of quality for chance error in comparing different school systems with one another. In the cases in which different grades of the same school or the same grades at different times are compared the determinations were made by the same judges.

In order to display the results in Table I graphically they are represented upon Chart I. The graphs upon the various charts are made comparable by introducing a line which may be taken to represent a tentative standard in quality and in speed. In order to interpret the charts from the point of view of quality the figures upon the left margin should be used. The figures in the right margin represent speed. Thus a single line may be used to represent both characteristics. For example, for Grade 1A the standard for quality found by reading from the left margin is 35 (upon the Ayers scale). The standard for speed represented by the same point and found by reading the right margin is 30 letters per minute. Similarly the standard for Grade 8A is 70 for quality and 100 for speed. The graphs upon the various charts then are compared with the same standard.

We may first compare the different relations between speed and quality which are found to obtain in the various schools and school systems. In some cases the speed is relatively above the quality, as, for example, in Schools B, C, and part of the grades in School D. In School A, on the other hand, the speed is relatively below quality, while in School E they run closely together. It is evident that some schools place much greater emphasis upon one of these characteristics in relation to the other than do others. Furthermore, in some schools the speed is not only above the quality with relation to the standard, but it is absolutely equal to or above the standard, whereas in others it is considerably below. The same remark holds true for quality except that it is above the standard only in the case of the first four grades of School A.

It further appears that there is variation in the time of the pupil's school life in which quality or speed is particularly emphasized. An example of the emphasis of quality at the expense of speed in the lower grades is seen in School A. A high standard of quality is maintained throughout the first five grades, whereas

CHART I

Quality
Speed
School A
Quality
Speed
Grade 1B 1A 2B 2A 3B 3A 4B 4A 5B 5A 6B 6A 7B 7A 8B 8A
School B
Speed
Quality
Grade 3 4 5 6 8
School C
Speed
Quality
Grade 4 5 6 7 8

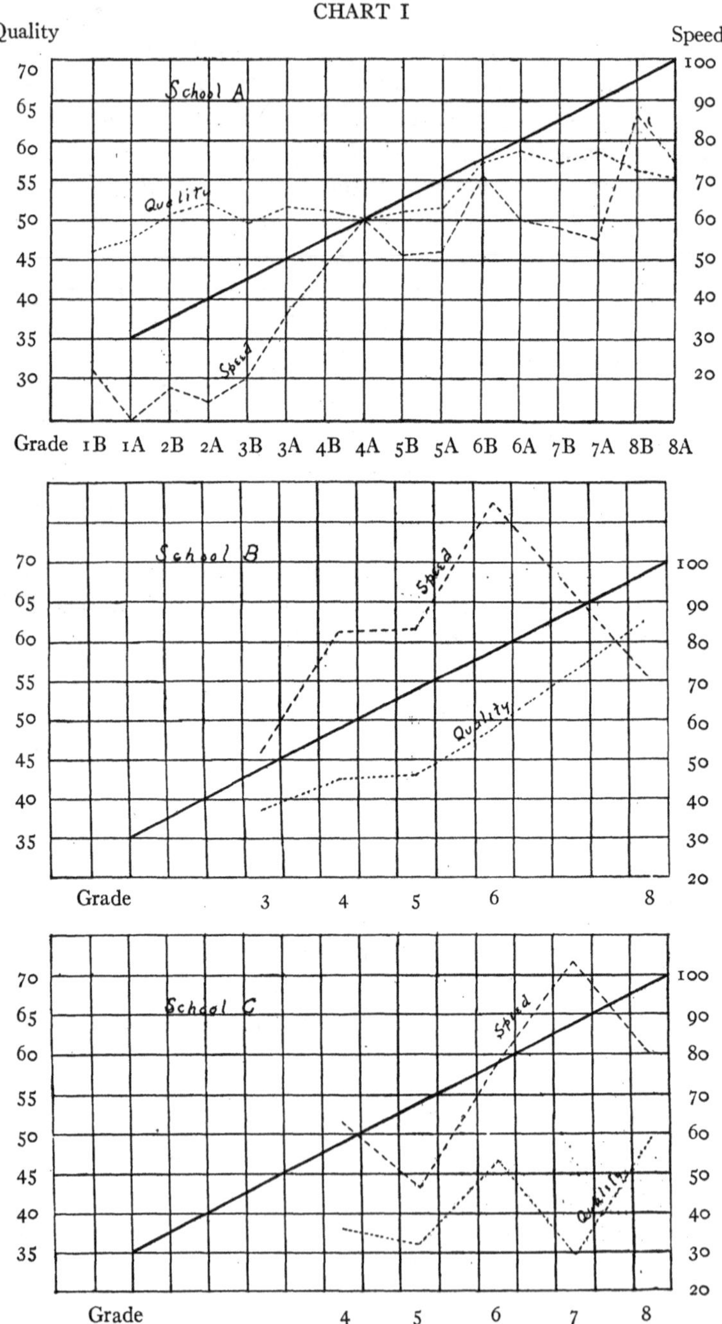

CHART I—*Continued*

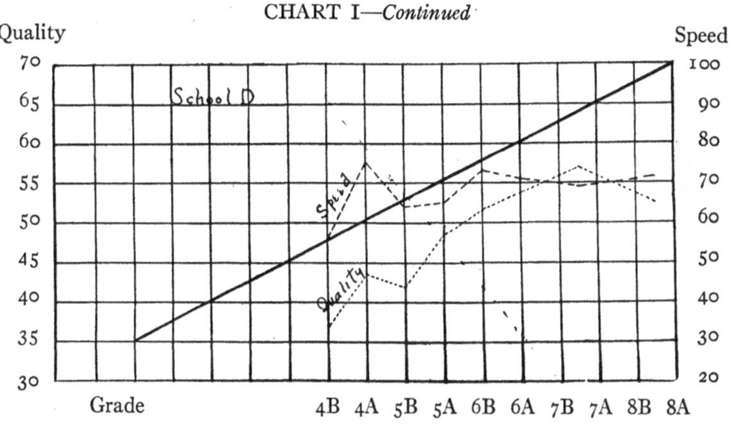

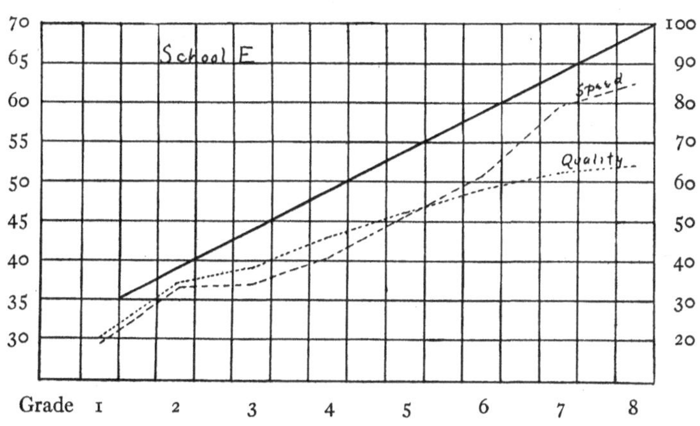

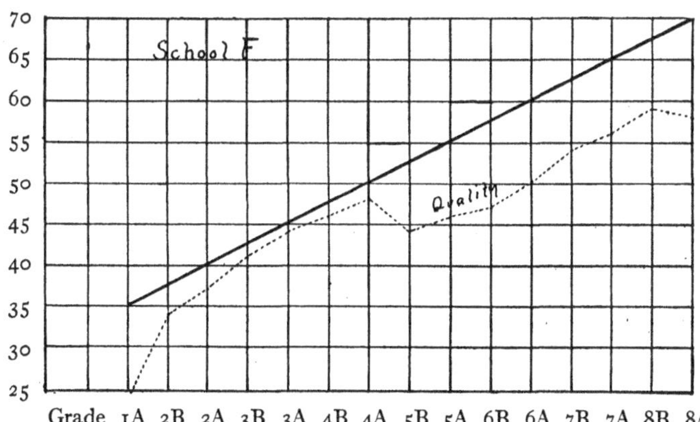

the speed in the lower grades is very low and only increases gradually. In School D, on the other hand, quality is inferior to speed in the lowest grades of which we have record and approaches it only in the upper grades. In School E, on the other hand, both speed and quality progress alike from the lowest to the highest grades.

A variation in the standard of attainment in these two characteristics, speed and quality, appears also in the different grades of the same school. A very striking example of this is seen in School C. In grade seven speed is emphasized so greatly that it exceeds the standard by 16 letters a minute, whereas the quality is inferior to the standard by nearly 30 points of the scale. In school B again in the sixth grade there is an extreme emphasis upon speed which raises it to 15 letters a minute beyond the standard for the eighth grade, whereas there is no corresponding variation in quality. Some differences in emphasis, which are not so extreme, may be found in Schools A, D, and E. Table IV and Chart II indicate further that the emphasis in the same grade varies from one part of the year to another.

The relationship between quality and speed may be studied in another way by requiring the pupils to write under three sorts of instructions: first, with instruction to write both rapidly and well; second, to write as well as possible; and third, to write as rapidly as possible. The writing obtained by the first instruction we may call the normal writing. The results from such an experiment are shown in Table II. The first columns under "Speed" and "Quality" represent the normal writing, the second column the writing which was to be done as well as possible, and the fourth column the rapid writing. The columns which are headed "Percentage of Difference" represent the effect of trying to write as well as possible and trying to write as rapidly as possible. It is clear from an inspection of the figures for each grade and of the averages at the bottom of the table that trying to write well improved the quality of the writing at the expense of speed, although the speed is decreased by only 3.7 per cent, while the quality is improved by 6.2 per cent. Trying to write as rapidly as possible, on the other hand, increased the speed by 27.2 per cent at the expense of a loss in quality to the extent of 9.1 per cent. There is then a certain degree of inverse relationship between these two characteristics if we base our conclusions upon the averages. The same relations hold in varying degrees for

CHART II

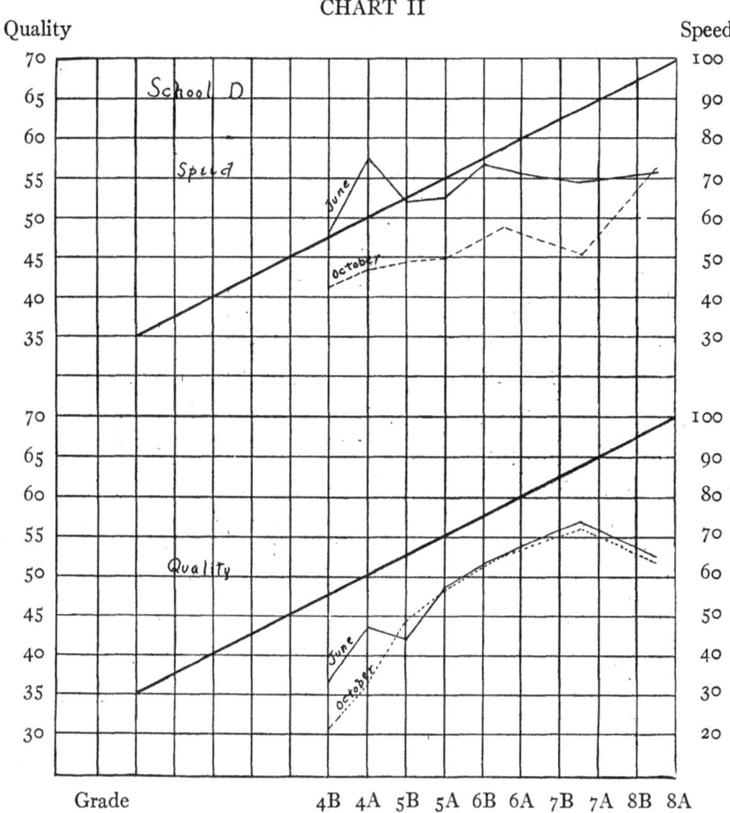

each grade, but in some cases the increase in quality is accompanied by only a very slight decrease in speed or the increase in speed is accompanied by only a small decrease in quality. Some of the grades are able to improve their writing in one respect or the other with less sacrifice than are other grades. It follows then that an improvement in both respects is to be looked for where the teaching is efficient.

There is still another means of testing the relationship of these two characteristics. We may compare the standing of different individuals in these two regards and determine whether or not there is correlation between them; that is, we may determine

TABLE II

COMPARISON OF THE QUALITY AND SPEED OF WRITING UNDER INSTRUCTIONS WHICH GIVE DIFFERENT EMPHASIS TO QUALITY AND SPEED

Grade	Quality					Speed				
	Normal	Well	Percentage of Difference	Rapid	Percentage of Difference from Normal	Normal	Well	Percentage of Difference	Rapid	Percentage of Difference from Normal
4B.......	37.6	39.7	+5.6	36.0	− 4.3	57.3	57.1	− .3	71.5	+24.8
4A.......	38.9	40.0	+2.8	36.6	− 5.9	55.3	55.1	− .4	64.3	+16.3
5B.......	36.8	40.0	+8.7	35.0	− 4.9	59.2	58.7	−2.5	68.0	+15.5
5A.......	50.8	53.6	+5.5	46.8	− 7.9	53.5	50.4	−5.8	78.8	+47.1
6.........	52.0	56.4	+8.5	41.7	−19.8	73.0	66.0	−9.6	89.6	+22.1
7.........	59.7	63.2	+5.9	56.5	− 5.4	65.0	63.8	−1.8	86.7	+33.4
8.........	52.3	55.6	+6.3	44.3	−15.3	71.5	67.5	−5.6	94.0	+31.5
Average			+6.2		− 9.1			−3.7		+27.2

whether a pupil who writes more rapidly than the average also writes better. The correlation between speed and quality was calculated for the children of School C and the results are given in Table III. It was, of course, necessary to calculate the correlation separately for each grade. As will be seen from the table,

TABLE III

CORRELATION BETWEEN SPEED AND QUALITY OF WRITING OF CHILDREN OF SCHOOL C

	Grade IV	V	VI	VII	VIII
Coefficient of correlation...	+.08(±.02)	−.10(±.04)	−.14(±.04)	−.34	−.15(±.05)

there is in all cases except that of Grade 4 a negative correlation between speed and quality. The coefficient for Grade 4 is so low as to be negligible. It appears then that there is some opposition between speed and quality so that some pupils emphasize the one and others the other characteristic. The practical conclusion would seem to be that different pupils require different sorts of teaching so as to lead to improvement in the feature of their writing in which they are weak.

STANDARDS OF ATTAINMENT IN HANDWRITING

The results which are presented in the charts before us make possible some consideration of the standards in speed and quality which should be attained in the various grades. A general form of standard may be arrived at by comparing the different grades within the same school. Barring special conditions, we should expect that the successive grades should show an improvement over those which preceded them. At least there is nothing in the results before us which indicate that there should be a drop in any particular grade. The possible exception is found in the fact that the fifth grade in all cases except that of School E does not show an improvement over the fourth grade. With this possible exception then we may take for granted the principle of progression. It is apparent that there are many exceptions to this principle. The most frequent exception appears in the low standard of the eighth grade. In many cases it is inferior to the seventh grade and in some cases to the sixth. In general, the upper grades do not progress as rapidly as the lower grades. For example, in School A there is very little progress after the fifth grade. In School C the progress is slight and very irregular. In School D there is practically no progress after the fifth grade.

Whether this fact is due to a decline in the teaching in the upper grades or to some more fundamental fact does not appear from the results, but the fact that there are exceptions to this rule, as, for instance, in the case of School E, particularly in speed, and in the case of Schools B and F in quality, would seem to indicate that the fault is due to teaching rather than to an inability of the pupils to progress farther. That this is the true interpretation is also indicated by the rapid progress which pupils in business courses make and by the degree of attainment far above that presented in these charts which they reach.

The lack of continued progress may be taken to indicate that there is not a due sense of the importance of training in handwriting. The other subjects of the curriculum tend to crowd out this one and under-emphasis upon it is further brought about by the low repute in which so-called drill subjects are held. It may be also that the pupils become less inclined to drill in handwriting as they reach the upper grades. Some new motive to good writing beyond the pleasure in drill and in improvement itself needs to be found. If attention were paid to the quality of the pupil's writing in the other subjects of the curriculum and if he were given a grade based upon his writing in these subjects, this motive would be furnished and the continuance of mechanical drill beyond a sufficient amount to retain what had been learned in the lower grades would be avoided.

A more particular question regarding standards relates to the degree of attainment which should be expected of the average of a class. Any standard which may be set up is bound to be in some degree arbitrary and variations according to particular conditions must be allowed, but the possession of a standard is of great importance as furnishing stimulus and as giving a basis for self-judgment on the part of the teacher and of judgment by supervising officers. In general, we may lay down the principle that the attainment of the best grades should furnish the standard instead of the average attainment. If the average attainment were used, the grades or schools which now exceed that standard would be content with poorer results than they attain unaided by any criterion. As a general principle, it is better for a standard to be too high rather than too low. If, for example, Grade 4A in School A can attain the tentative standard which we have laid down, why should the same grade of School E be content to remain below it, unless indeed undue time and energy are expended in handwriting in the first school? That this is the case there is no evidence.

The final determination of standards cannot be made without further investigation. It may be that the tentative standard here suggested will be modified both in the relative emphasis which it gives to speed and to quality and in the demands which are made in both of these characteristics. This determination can be made after we are satisfied that the best has been attained by a certain school or school system. It cannot be too often said that it is this best which should serve as a standard, however, and not a mere average attainment.

THE IMPROVEMENT IN ONE SCHOOL THROUGHOUT THE YEAR

In School D tests were taken four times during the school year in order to find out what improvement was made and whether or not improvement was greater in certain grades in which special instruction was given. The results of this study are given in Table IV. The results for the October and the June tests are shown graphically in Chart II.

TABLE IV

THE QUALITY AND SPEED OF WRITING OF THE GRADES IN SCHOOL D FROM TESTS TAKEN AT DIFFERENT TIMES THROUGHOUT THE YEAR

	QUALITY					SPEED				
	October	December	March	June	Gain or Loss	October	December	March	June	Gain or Loss
3A	36.5	36.2	......	......	......	36.5	41.6	......	......	......
4B*	......	*30.6*	*35.4*	*36.8*	+6.2	......	*42.0*	*45.5*	*56.0*	+14.0
4A	**36.3**	**37.6**	**41.1**	**43.4**	+7.1	**46.5**	**57.3**	**67.5**	**75.0**	+28.5
5B	*44.1*	*38.9*	*40.0*	*42.0*	−2.1	*49.0*	*55.3*	*69.0*	*64.0*	+15.0
5A^2	46.6	36.8	39.9	49.0	+3.6	52.8	59.2	73.4	68.0	+16.0
5A^1	50.0	50.8	49.4	47.2	−2.8	47.0	53.5	61.1	62.0	+15.0
6C	......	......	51.6	53.7	......	......	......	75.2	76.0	......
6B	......	......	51.9	49.4	......	......	......	71.2	70.0	......
6A	......	......	49.5	53.7	......	......	......	71.0	71.0	......
All	52.8	52.0	51.0	52.3	−0.5	57.5	73.0	72.4	72.3	+14.8
7	56.0	59.7	53.4	57.0	+1.0	50.5	65.0	71.0	69.0	+18.5
8	51.9	52.3	......	......	+0.4	72.5	71.5	......	......	−1.0

* In October and December the classes which now go by the names 4B to 5A were half a grade lower in each case. These pupils are represented in the table by their present rather than their former grade name.

It is apparent from the chart that the greatest improvement was made in speed, but that practically no improvement was made in quality except in Grades 4B and 4A. The reason for this lack of improvement in quality is not clear, unless it is due to the fact that the whole emphasis of the teaching was put upon speed. There was, however, no special instruction in writing given in Grades 6 to 8 and if this explanation is the correct one the emphasis must have been given incidentally in these grades. It is also possible that the sixth and seventh grades improved so greatly in speed because the children at the beginning of the year were writing much more slowly than they were capable of. At any rate, the conclusion seems justified that it is easier to bring about improvement in speed than in quality without special training given in special handwriting lessons.

The grade in which the longest continued special training was given was 4A and it is noteworthy that this grade made the greatest improvement of all. In speed particularly it finally rose superior to every other grade in the school. At the same time the quality was raised from an inferior rank to one which was comparable to that of the other grades. Grades 4B, 5B, and 5A were also given special training, though only for half of the year. Two of these grades, on the whole, also made satisfactory progress, but Grade 5B showed the slump which was found above to be a general phenomenon. It is apparent that too great emphasis was placed upon speed in the teaching. Such a result can now be corrected on the basis of such an array of figures as these. If greater emphasis had been placed upon quality or if in the succeeding year these same grades are taught in such a way as to emphasize quality, their writing can undoubtedly be raised sufficiently to approach, if not equal, the tentative standard. There is no doubt, at least, that it can be brought to a higher degree of efficiency by the time these children reach the eighth grade than is possessed by the writing of the present eighth grade. If excellence in writing is worth while at all, then it certainly pays to set aside periods for it and to give particular attention to the methods of teaching it.

CONCLUSIONS

The main conclusions from the paper may briefly be summed up.

The belief that it is necessary to give separate attention to the two characteristics of speed and quality and to study their relationships is amply justified by the results presented in this paper.

The wide variation both in the relationship of speed and quality and in the general efficiency of writing indicates a need for the determination of standards.

A tentative standard in speed and quality is offered for further verification or modification.

There is especial need of attention to writing in the upper

grades in order that it may continue to improve beyond the intermediate period.

The value of special instruction in writing and of keeping records of the progress of the pupils in a particular school or school system is apparent from the study of School D.

The question whether speed and quality should progress together or whether one characteristic should be emphasized above the other in certain grades is a matter for further investigation.

Finally, upon all of these points the data at our command should be extended by studies from other school systems.

THE INTERESTS OF CHILDREN OF THE PRIMARY AND INTERMEDIATE GRADES IN THE USE OF COLOR

W. C. REAVIS
St. Louis, Missouri

The following study is an attempt to find out the primary interests of children of the lower grades in the use of color. It deals with three questions: (1) In what colors are children of the primary and intermediate grades most interested? (2) In their undirected representations, do they give major consideration to accuracy of representation, or to playing with favorite colors? (3) In following their own initiative, do they make use of color primarily as a means of representation, or for the pleasurable sensations derived?

In order to ascertain with some degree of certainty the colors that give children the most delightful sensations, the following test was arranged. Colored squares of paper were prepared, representing each of the spectrum colors, and sets were given to each child of the first three grades to mount in the order of his preference. The pupils of the fourth and fifth grades were given the spectrum colors, and after they had used them, each one was asked to designate his favorite color and his second choice. Tables of frequency were compiled from these data, and the results are shown in surfaces of frequency in Chart I. An examination of the data for the first three grades showed that it was not worth while to compute tables beyond the second choice. Color as the expression of a third, fourth, fifth, or sixth choice was merely a perfunctory matter.

In the surfaces of frequency of Chart I, the first- and second-choice colors of 74 children of the first grade, 50 of the second grade, 60 of the third grade, 42 of the fourth grade, and 39 of the fifth grade are given. The ordinate shows the percentage of children, and the abscissa the spectrum colors in the following order: red, blue, yellow, violet, orange, green. Figs. 1 to 5 inclusive show the favorite colors of the first five grades respectively; and Figs. 6 to 10 inclusive show the second-choice colors of the same pupils. The curves indicate that red and blue are the colors in which the large majority of children are most interested. However, the color interests of the children of the intermediate grades appear to have widened.

CHART I

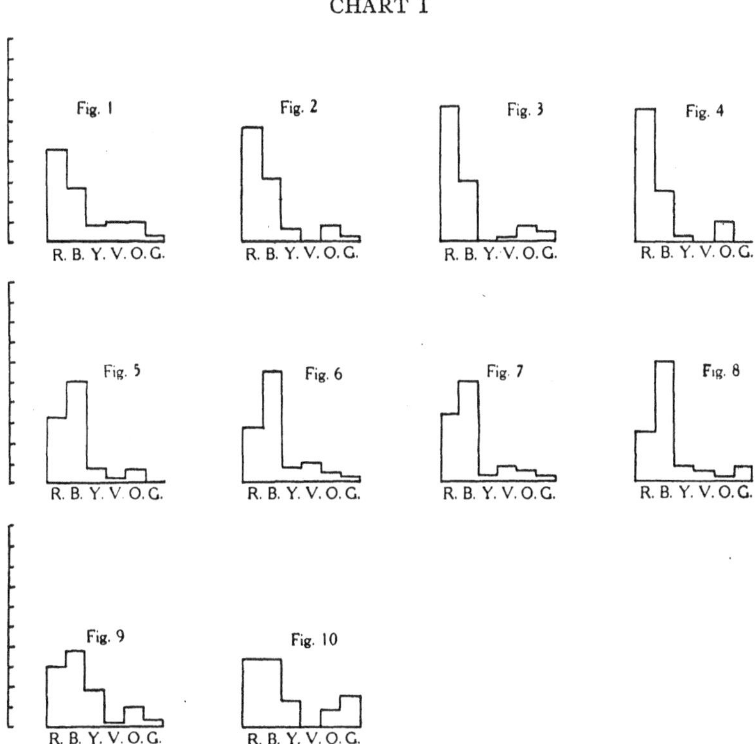

There was no doubt regarding the expression of individual choices of colors by the pupils of the fourth and fifth grades in the foregoing test. However, as the pupils of the first, second, and third grades did have an opportunity to see how other pupils of their grade arranged the colors, it was thought that they might have been influenced to some extent by imitation. Hence, as a check on the validity of the results obtained from these grades, thirty children of the same grades in another school were given the same test, individually. The surfaces of frequency obtained by compiling the choices of this group were then compared with the surfaces of frequency obtained by combining Figs. 1, 2, and 3 of Chart I, and likewise Figs. 7, 8, and 9, when it was found that the curves were almost identical. These curves are shown in the following Chart II in which Fig. 1 gives the distribution of the favorite colors of the group of thirty children, and Fig. 2 shows that of the composite group; while Figs. 3 and 4 show the distribution of second-choice colors of the same groups respectively.

CHART II

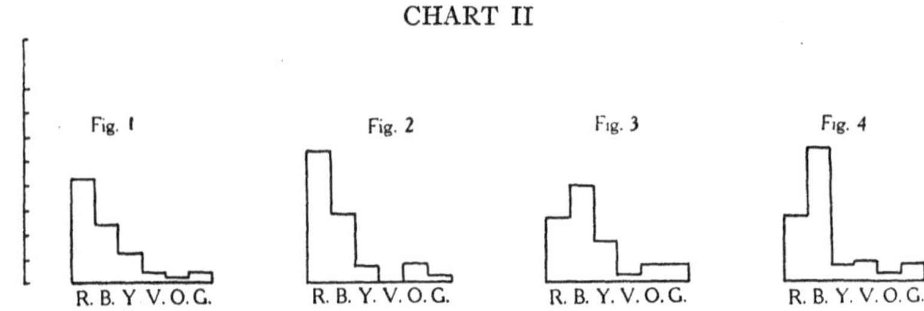

Hectographed outlines of birds were next given to the children with the instructions that they were to fill in the outlines just as they pleased. The birds chosen for the test were those common to the vicinity. In fact, they were seen daily in the trees on the school ground, and were the subject of nature-study lessons several weeks before the tests were given. All of the pupils recognized the birds, as was ascertained by holding the outlines before the class, before giving them to the children with the instructions mentioned above.

Figs. 1 to 5 of Chart III show the way in which the outlines of the bluejay were colored by the pupils of the first five grades, respectively. The abscissa indicates the percentage of children, and the ordinate the following colors (reading from left to right): red, blue, yellow, brown, any combination of two different colors designated in the chart by M, and conglomerate mass of colors.

Chart IV shows the coloring of the outlines of the woodpecker, and is similar in every respect to Chart III, as is Chart V that follows, which shows the coloring of the outlines of the English sparrow.

A careful examination of the data shown in Figs. 1, 2, and 3 of Charts III, IV, and V reveals several interesting facts regarding

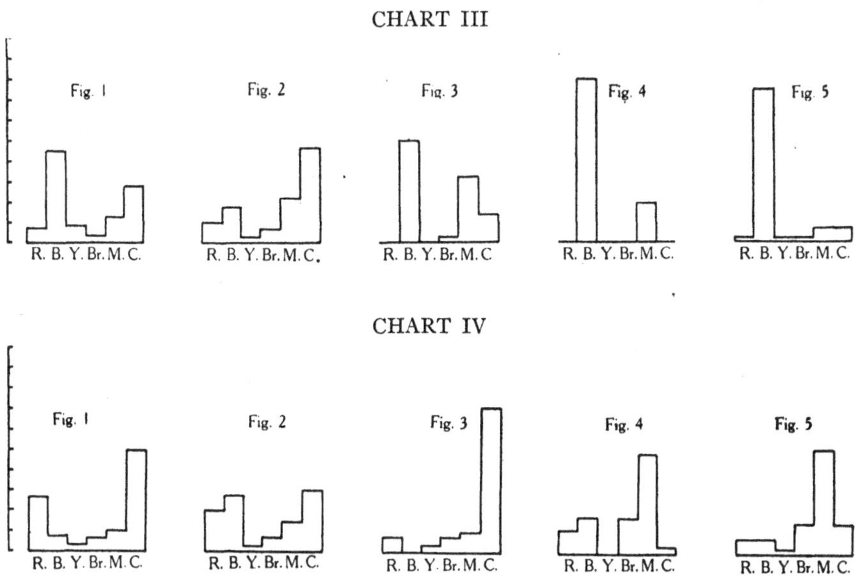

NOTE.—In every drawing of the pupils of the fourth and fifth grades the head of the woodpecker is colored red. For percentage of pupils of the other grades who colored the head the same way, see Chart VI. Hence, the colors shown in Chart IV refer to body, wings, and tail. For example, the pupil may have colored the head correctly and the body, wings, and tail a single color, a combination of two colors, or a conglomeration of colors.

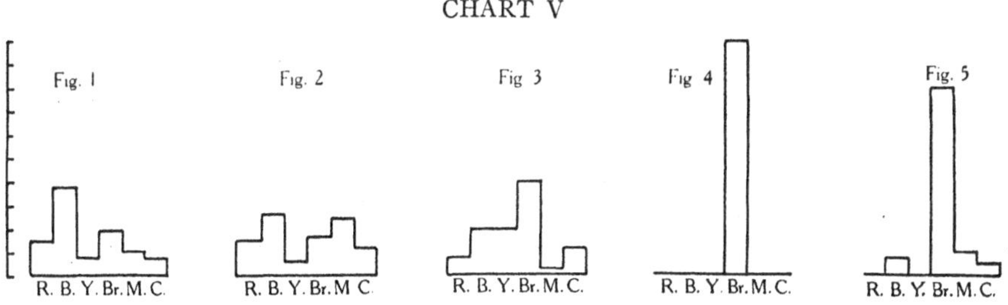

the use of color by the pupils of the primary grades: (1) A considerable number filled in the outlines without manifesting any concern whatever in exact representation, as was evidenced by the indiscriminate use of all the colors of the spectrum in painting a single bird. (2) Some of the children seemed to take a cue from the most striking detail, and filled in the outline with that color only. For example, they colored the jay with a single shade of blue and the woodpecker red. (3) Another group made serious attempts at truthful representation, indicated by their attention to the proportions of the different details. However, their interest in strong color seemed to have caused them to err grievously in the choice of colors necessary to make even the semblance of a truthful representation.

The work of the fourth and fifth grades differed markedly from that of the lower grades, although a few of the pupils appeared to be just as erratic and indifferent to correct results as the younger children. (1) A majority of the pupils made use of tones of color in representing a bird, a fact that was not observed in a single drawing of the primary children. (2) The pupils of the intermediate grades, excepting the erratic ones referred to above, consumed much more time in filling in the outlines, thus showing the presence of external standards in contrast with the spontaneity and absence of standards in the minds of most of the children of the first three grades. (3) The intermediate-grade pupils greatly increased their percentages in the selection of correct colors, and in attention given to details, as is shown by the surfaces of frequency in Charts III, IV, and V, and in Chart VI that follows.

CHART VI

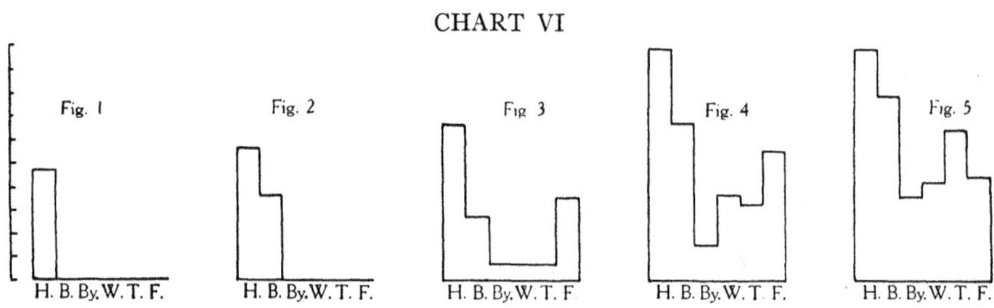

Chart VI was compiled from the drawings of the woodpecker shown in Chart IV. The ordinate gives the percentage, and the abscissa the following details (reading from left to right): head, bill, body, wings, tail, feet. The woodpecker was chosen for the reason that its details are most marked, and it had been closely observed by the classes in their nature-study lessons several weeks before the tests were given.

The surfaces of frequency for the pupils of the first three grades point out that only the most significant details were represented with any degree of accuracy. Even these were ignored in many instances by children who apparently became intoxicated with the bright colors they were permitted to use in free and undirected play. With the fourth and fifth grades the drawings were altogether different. They represented significant details with great accuracy, and truthfully portrayed the minor details in almost 50 per cent of the cases.

Another noticeable fact in the drawings was the relative development of the power to grasp and give attention to details as the pupil advanced through the primary into the intermediate grades. This appeared to be the rise of a new interest in more exact representation due to the consciousness of an objective standard of form and color appropriateness resulting from age readjustments, and instruction. This observation was further corroborated by the data shown in Chart IV, in which the grosser errors tended to disappear as the pupils advanced; shown by the facts that 55 per cent of the pupils of the first and second grades, and 21 per cent of the third grade colored all parts of the bird the same, while only 12 per cent of the fourth grade and 9 per cent of the fifth grade committed the same error.

A different situation was presented in the next test. The pupils were asked to paint a sled. The teachers refrained from giving any directions or suggestions, and the children had to rely upon their own initiative for the selection of color, and the form they were asked to represent. The results are shown in Chart VII, in which the ordinate shows the percentage, and the abscissa the following colors: red, blue, yellow, any of the secondary colors, brown or black, conglomeration of colors.

Excepting two facts, the results of the above test do not differ essentially from those of previous tests: (1) The decrease of red as a leading color in the first two grades and the large use of neutral were certainly the result of a complication of the problem of form with the free use of color. Favorite colors seemed to be forgotten by many of the pupils in their efforts to meet the requirements of form, and as a result they reacted in the way they had been taught to react in drawing objects, i.e., by employing light and dark. Some left the drawing simply in outline done with the black or brown pencil, thus showing that the problem of form had deprived them of the pleasure accruing from a free use of color; while others proceeded to fill in the outlines with the color or colors that pleased

CHART VII

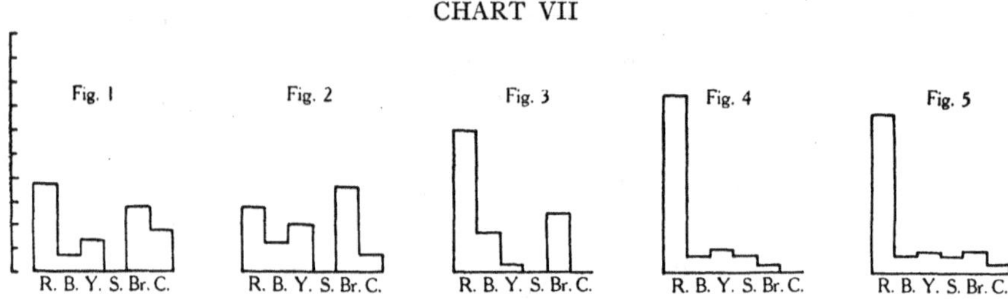

them. (2) The decrease of the use of blue by all the pupils, especially those of the third, fourth, and fifth grades, was evidently due to psychological reasons. Blue is a color of rest, while red is a color of action. Therefore, the association of a color of rest with the drawing of a sled, which suggests one of the favorite and most active sports, could hardly be expected.

Without taking into consideration the pedagogy of color in relation to the art work of our public schools, we believe that this study at least warrants the following answers to the questions at issue: (1) Children of both primary and intermediate grades are interested in strong colors, chiefly red and blue. (2) The majority of children of the primary grades are interested more in the sensations derived from a free use of color, than in exact representation. They paint with great freedom, and apparently take little interest in the perfection of details. On the other hand, most of the children of the intermediate grades draw with less freedom but pay greater attention to accuracy of details, and manifest greater interest in the character of their results. They seem to realize the importance of objective standards, and put forth serious efforts to master the external facts that lead to a realization of their standards. (3) The interest of most of the children of the primary grades centers around sensation, while the intermediate-grade children appear to employ color primarily for purposes of representation.

BOOK REVIEWS

Plant and Animal Children, and How They Grow. By ELLEN TORELLE. Boston: D. C. Heath & Co., 1913. Pp. 230, 325 figures. $0.50.

The preface states that this book is written especially for the pupils of the elementary school. "It aims to make clear the ideas of evolution, heredity, variation, effect of environment, and the evolution of sex, without once mentioning these names." Most biologists would gasp at the idea of presenting these subjects in so brief a compass, and give a second gasp at the mention of making them clear to children. However, "the author has demonstrated in practical work in the schools . . . . that children are also able to comprehend the subject-matter when this is expressed in language suitable to their comprehension." The book is a simple and lucid account of an evolutionary series of plants and animals. The forms studied, however, are not sufficiently numerous to make the steps of evolution appear plausible. To jump, for instance, from "Hydra and its children" to the worm family, dealing primarily with the earth-worm, would be an impossible step for an adult, much less a child, trying to comprehend the evolution process. The reviewer fails to see wherein the laws of heredity are presented, and certainly the evolution of sex would not be understood by an adult who reads the book without previous biological knowledge.

The book is a good presentation of some facts and principles of growth. Reproductive processes are stressed out of due proportion, it seems, though it must be borne in mind that it is the intention of the book to serve as an introduction to sex hygiene. It would be an exceptional public school that would have facilities to study reproductive processes, for instance, in the molds, the algae, the early stages of the moss, and in such animals as amoeba, worms, etc. Such a book put into the public schools inevitably means that it will be simply a reader, that the information will be inaccurate, because there are no clear concepts of the things discussed, and such method of procedure in a science subject is necessarily vicious. It is wise to approach sex hygiene by way of biology, and the simple reproductive processes of animals and plants can readily lead up to a knowledge of the matter in man, but such a detailed biological approach as presented here is not essential, and the book in the hands of an ordinary teacher must lead to a mere memorizing of unintelligible materials instead of natural inductions from the child's observations.

E. R. DOWNING

UNIVERSITY OF CHICAGO

Farm Arithmetic. By C. W. BURKETT and KARL D. SWARTZEL. New York: Orange Judd Co., 1913. Pp. 280.

Farm Arithmetic is a most interesting attempt to relate the fundamentals of arithmetic to practical farm problems. The first-named author of the book is editor of an agricultural magazine; the second, a professor of mathematics in a state university. The book is not intended as an introduction to the principles of arithmetic, but as a text for the upper grades in the elementary schools, or as a supplement to any other text which may be used in these grades. It attempts to present the quantitative side of farm life, and to teach many facts of modern agriculture. The nature and arrangement of the topics and problems indicate that the book is designed primarily to teach agriculture by means of arithmetic, rather than to teach arithmetic. The pupils must know arithmetic fairly well in order to solve the problems presented.

The chapter headings are similar to those of an elementary text on agriculture; as, Plant Feeding, Animal Feeding, Human Feeding, Dairy Products, Soil, Field Crops, Farm Animals, Farm Mechanics, Forestry, etc. The Animal Feeding chapter may be taken as an illustration of the nature of the problems. A preliminary discussion of the source of food states what the foods are and gives the percentages of different substances which green pasture grass contains. Similar tables of contents of other foods are given. Upon these percentages the pupil is asked to calculate the amounts of different substances in given quantities of animal food, as one ton of green grass, or of clover hay, corn, or corn stover. The amounts of different kinds of food substances—protein, carbohydrate, and fat, etc.—needed in a properly balanced ration of different farm animals are then given. These are made the basis for calculations upon the amounts of feed necessary to maintain or to fatten different kinds of farm animals.

The book is full of most interesting and important information for agricultural communities. The problems should help greatly in fixing this information. As a source of profitable and concrete supplementary problems the book should find a wide use.

O. W. C.

UNIVERSITY OF CHICAGO

Moral Training in the School and Home. A Manual for Teachers and Parents. By E. HERSHEY SNEATH and GEORGE HODGES. New York: Macmillan, 1913. Pp. 219. $0.80.

The Golden Deed Book. A School Reader. By E. HERSHEY SNEATH, GEORGE HODGES, and EDWARD LAWRENCE STEVENS. New York: Macmillan, 1913. Pp. 351.

The first of these two books discusses the moral training of children during the age period of the grades. The chief method advocated is the use of the story, and lists of stories for illustrating the virtues and duties of life are given. These lists will be valued by some who may be a little dismayed at the somewhat formidable number of virtues set down. The authors' remarks on the bodily, intellectual, social, political, aesthetic life are sensible and likely to be helpful.

The second of the two books contains a selection of stories for the eighth grade. Many of them are familiar classics, but some are new and tell of deeds which thrill even the grown-up reader. I think boys and girls will like them.

The Moral Education of School Children. By CHARLES KEEN TAYLOR. Philadelphia: C. K. & H. B. Taylor, 1913. Pp. 77. $0.75.

Part I contains some useful comments on the necessity of proper physical conditions in the school as a preliminary for any moral training. Part II gives lists of topics for discussion with children in elementary grades, with brief suggestions for their treatment. Part III is a plea for the use of school premises in the evening for the entertainment and teaching of working girls and boys. The author's statement that his endeavor is "to furnish a complete outline which will make it unnecessary for the individual teacher to do much original work" seems over-optimistic.

The Way to the Heart of the Pupil. By HERMANN WEIMER. Translation by J. REMSEN BISHOP and ADOLPH NIEDERPRIEM. New York: Macmillan, 1913. Pp. 178.

The translators state in their preface that "there is afoot a subtly devised reactionary movement in educational experiment that concerns itself with the mechanical measurement of the results of the teacher's work." "This little book is a protest against mechanical methods in the general relationship of teacher and pupil." No leader can fail to be impressed by the sympathetic tone of the author. Parents would like to have their children in a school pervaded by such a personality. Some of the points treated are of value to all beginning teachers; some are less necessary in this country, e.g., the elaborate arguments against indiscriminate thrashing. Probably few, even of a "reactionary movement," would wish to revive intimidation on a general scale as an educational principle. In general the atmosphere of the book is, to some degree, that of a country which suffers from the formalism and conservatism often attendant upon the very excellence of administration and technic.

J. H. TUFTS

UNIVERSITY OF CHICAGO

Backward and Feeble-Minded Children. By E. B. HUEY. "Educational Psychology Monographs." Baltimore: Warwick & York, 1912. Pp. xii+213. $1.40.

This little volume has for its purpose the delineation of the mental status of 35 cases of children who occupy a borderline position between normality and feeble-mindedness. The cases are chosen from the "brightest" children who could be found among the 1,300 inmates of the Lincoln State School and Colony. The author believes that this class of mentally deficient children is particularly worthy of study because of their great number, because of their peril to society due to the fact that they constitute a large proportion if not all of the instinctive criminals, and because they propagate their kind at a rapid rate if not prevented by some form of social institution.

The study is of value to students of mental deficiency and to all who have to deal with high-grade defectives in the schools, because of its full and clear presentation of a variety of typical cases. In this respect it supplements the statistical studies which give information regarding the ability of children of various grades of intelligence to pass certain tests by furnishing concrete pictures of individuals. These pictures give the reader a notion of the various types or forms by which the defect may be represented, for the author distinguishes ten types of cases. The most interesting distinction he makes is between children who are dull and those who are unstable. Among the latter group are some who are characterized by moral instability.

Besides the description of cases the author gives an introduction in which he discusses the classification of defectives and the terms used to describe them, and a chapter consisting of a syllabus for clinical examination.

A Cyclopedia of Education. Edited by PAUL MONROE and OTHERS. Vol. IV. New York: Macmillan, 1913. Pp. 740. $5.00.

The general comments which have been made upon this work in the reviews of the previous volumes apply equally to this fourth volume. The work is one which is proving to be of great value to educators of every sort. The information which is contained in these volumes is in a compact, well-organized form which makes it suitable not only for reference, but also for the systematic study of a subject. Much of the material is in a form in which it has not been previously available, and hence is virtually new.

A feature of the *Cyclopedia* which is very prominent in the present volume is the series of articles upon the systems of education in the various states, contributed by Professor Cubberley. This volume contains articles on Maine, Maryland, Massachusetts, Michigan, Minnesota, Missouri, Mississippi, etc., up to and including Oklahoma. Besides these state systems the volume contains accounts of the systems of various countries and important cities.

The authoritativeness of the majority of the articles is made apparent by a glance at the names of the contributors. Some of the longer articles of this volume, besides those mentioned in the preceding paragraph, which may serve as examples of this fact are the articles on "Medical Education" by Dr. A. Flexner, on "Medical Inspection," by Dr. L. P. Ayers, on "Memory" by Professor Pillsbury, on "Mental Measurement" by Professor Tichener, and the article on "Mission Education" by Secretary J. L. Barton of the American Board of Commissioners of Foreign Missions.

While it would not be difficult to make criticisms upon matters of minor importance—as in the case of any pioneer work—educators will acknowledge great indebtedness to the editors of this valuable work.

F. N. F.

BOOKS RECEIVED

AMERICAN BOOK CO., CHICAGO

Hin und Her: Ein Buch für die Kinder. By H. H. Fick. Cloth. Pp. 90. Illustrated. Price $0.30.

Philip of Texas. By James Otis. Cloth. Pp. 153. Illustrated. Price $0.35.

The Barnard Language Reader. By Marion D. Payne. Cloth. Pp. 142. Illustrated. Price $0.30.

Business Speller and Vocabulary. By Edward H. Eldridge, Ph.D. Cloth. Pp. 219. Price. $0.25.

Advanced Algebra. By Jos. V. Collins, Ph.D. Cloth. Pp. 342. Illustrated.

Principles of Bookkeeping and Farm Accounts. By J. A. Bexell and F. G. Nichols. Cloth. Pp. 180. Price $0.65.

Webster's Secondary-School Dictionary. Full buckram. Pp. 864. Illustrated. Price $1.50.

Sixty Lessons in Agriculture. By Burt C. Buffum, M.S., and David Clement Deaver. Cloth. Pp. 272. Illustrated. Price $0.80.

The Teaching of Arithmetic. By Alva Walker Stamper, Ph.D. Cloth. Pp. 284.

Essentials of Business Arithmetic. By George H. Van Tuyl. Cloth. Pp. 272. Price $0.70.

A Short Course in Commercial Law. By Frederick G. Nichols and Ralph E. Rogers. Cloth. Pp. 304. Price $0.80.

Essentials of Physics. By George A. Hoadley, C.E., Sc.D. Cloth. Pp. 556. Illustrated. Price $1.25.

New Medieval and Modern History. By Samuel Bannister Harding, Ph.D. Cloth. Pp. 800. Illustrated. Price $1.50.

New English Literature. By Reuben Post Halleck, A.M., LL.D. Cloth. Pp. 562. Illustrated. Price $1.30.

Little Dramas for Primary Grades. By Ada Maria Skinner and Lillian Nixon Lawrence. Cloth. Pp. 176. Illustrated. Price $0.35.

WARWICK & YORK, BALTIMORE

How I Kept My Baby Well ("Educational Psychology Monographs"). By Anna G. Noyes. Cloth. Pp. 193. Illustrated. Price $1.25.

Inductive versus Deductive Methods ("Educational Psychology Monographs"). By W. H. Winch. Cloth. Pp. 146. Price $1.25.

A Syllabus for the Clinical Examination of Children. By Edmund B. Huey. Paper. Pp. 45. Price $0.35 each, $2.50 per dozen.

Record Blanks ($0.40 per dozen):

Binet-Simon Test for Intelligence Age.

Home Record and History.

School Report.

A Point Scale of Tests for Intelligence.

Directions for Giving and Scoring Point Scale Tests.

Clinical Reference Cards. $0.30 per dozen.

THE MACMILLAN CO., NEW YORK

Pinocchio under the Sea. Translated from the Italian by CAROLYN M. DELLA CHIESA. Edited by JOHN W. DAVIS. Cloth. Pp. 201. Illustrated. Price $1.25 net.

The Pupils' Arithmetic, Book Six. By JAMES C. BYRNES, B.S., PH.M., JULIA RICHMAN, and JOHN S. ROBERTS, A.M., PH.M. Cloth. Pp. 432+ix. Price $0.50.

Materials and Methods in High School Agriculture. By WILLIAM GRANVILLE HUMMEL, M.S., and BERTHA ROYCE HUMMEL, B.L.S. Cloth. Pp. 385. Illustrated. Price $1.25.

The People's Health. By WALTER MOORE COLEMAN. Cloth. Pp. 307. Illustrated. Price $0.70.

Educational Resources of Village and Rural Communities. Edited by JOSEPH K. HART, Cloth. Pp. 277. Price $1.00.

HOUGHTON MIFFLIN CO., BOSTON

The Teaching of Spelling ("Riverside Educational Monographs"). By HENRY SUZZALO. Cloth. Pp. 129. Price $0.60.

Interest and Effort in Education ("Riverside Educational Monographs"). By JOHN DEWEY. Cloth. Pp. 101. Price $0.60.

Teaching the Common Branches. By W. W. CHARTERS, PH.D. Cloth. Pp. 355. Price $1.35.

Representative Cities of the United States. By CAROLINE W. HOTCHKISS. Cloth. Pp. 212. Illustrated. Price $0.65.

WORLD BOOK CO., YONKERS-ON-HUDSON

Barbara's Philippine Journey. By FRANCES WILLISTON BURKS. Cloth. Pp. 199. Illustrated.

Stories of Woods and Fields. By ELIZABETH V. BROWN. Cloth. Pp. 192. Illustrated. Price $0.40.

Stories of Childhood and Nature. By ELIZABETH V. BROWN. Cloth. Pp. 223. Illustrated. Price $0.40.

When the World Was Young. By ELIZABETH V. BROWN. Cloth. Pp. 160. Illustrated. Price $0.40.

GINN & CO., CHICAGO

The See and Say Series, Book One. By SARAH LOUISE ARNOLD, ELIZABETH C. BONNEY, and E. F. SOUTHWORTH. Cloth. Pp. 128. Illustrated. Price $0.35.

Manual for Teachers: To Accompany the See and Say Series, Book One. By SARAH LOUISE ARNOLD, ELIZABETH C. BONNEY, and E. F. SOUTHWORTH. Cloth. Pp. 214. Price $0.50.

TEACHERS COLLEGE, COLUMBIA UNIVERSITY

Spelling Ability: Its Measurement and Distribution. By B. R. BUCKINGHAM, PH.D. Cloth. Pp. 116. Price $1.25.

Practice in the Case of School Children. By THOMAS JOSEPH KIRBY, PH.D. Cloth. Pp. 98. Price $1.00.

UNIVERSITY OF CHICAGO PRESS, CHICAGO

List of Approved Colleges and Universities in the North Central Association of Colleges and Secondary Schools for 1913 ("School Review Monographs," IV). By CHARLES H. JUDD. Paper. Pp. 32. Price $0.25 net.

HENRY HOLT & CO., NEW YORK

Rhetoric and the Study of Literature. By ALFRED M. HITCHCOCK. Cloth. Pp. 410. Price $1.00.

Tom Brown's School Days. By THOMAS HUGHES. Edited by W. HUSTON LILLARD. Cloth. Pp. 383. Price $0.45.

GOVERNMENT PRINTING OFFICE, WASHINGTON

Annual Report of the Board of Regents of the Smithsonian Institution: Showing the Operations, Expenditures, and Condition of the Institution for the Year Ending June 30, 1912. Cloth. Pp. 780. Illustrated.

CAMBRIDGE UNIVERSITY PRESS, CAMBRIDGE

Steps toward Educational Reform. By C. W. BAILEY, M.A. Cardboard. Pp. 111. Price $0.25.

RAND McNALLY & CO., CHICAGO

Globes and Maps in Elementary Schools, A Teachers' Manual. By LEON O. WISWELL. Cloth. Pp. 64. Illustrated.

MANUAL ARTS PRESS, PEORIA

Paper and Cardboard Construction. By GEORGE FRED BUXTON and FRED L. CURRAN. Cloth. Pp. 191. Illustrated. Price $1.50.

REGINA BOOK SHOP, LIMITED, REGINA

English for the Non-English. By NORMAN FERGUS BLACK, M.A., D. PAED. Cloth. Pp. 211.

ORANGE JUDD CO., NEW YORK

Farm Arithmetic. By CHARLES WILLIAM BURKETT and KARL DALE SWARTZEL. Cloth. Pp. 280. Illustrated.

DOUBLEDAY, PAGE & CO., NEW YORK

The Children's Book of Christmas Stories. Edited by ASA DON DICKINSON and ADA M. SKINNER. Cloth. Pp. 335. Price $1.25 net.

THE A-TO-ZED, BERKELEY

Elementary General Science, Book I. By PERCY E. ROWELL, M.S. Cloth. Pp. 198. Illustrated. Price $0.60.

D. C. HEATH & CO., BOSTON

A History of the United States. By HENRY ELDRIDGE BOURNE and ELBERT JAY BENTON. Cloth. Pp. 534+lxi. Illustrated. Price $1.00.

B. D. BERRY & CO., CHICAGO

English Grammar. By JOSEPH VILLIERS DENNEY and SILAS B. TOBEY. Cloth. Pp. 250.

FREE PUBLIC LIBRARY, JERSEY CITY

Monographs on Anniversaries and Festivals. By EDMUND W. MILLER. Paper.

CURRENT EDUCATIONAL LITERATURE IN THE PERIODICALS[1]

IRENE WARREN
Librarian, School of Education, the University of Chicago

Abbott, Allan. A high-school course in periodical literature. English J. 2:422–27. (S. '13.)

Addresses by citizens to school boys. El. School T. 14:117–31. (N. '13.)

Alton, Margaret. The mental value of the study of English grammar. Educa. 34:78–80. (O. '13.)

Anderson, L. F. The manual labor school movement. Educa. R. 46:369–86. (N. '13.)

Babcock, E. B. The use of phonetics in teaching elementary French. School R. 21:608–17. (N. '13.)

Bawden, William T. Agricultural education thru home projects: the Massachusetts plan. Voca. Educa. 3:86–105. (N. '13.)

Bennett, Charles A. Newcomb school of art: its relation to art industries. Voca. Educa. 3:119–25. (N. '13.)

Blaine, Anita McCormick. The ideals which led to the founding of the School of Education. El. School T. 14:73–81. (O. '13.)

Bowder, Witt. Education for the industrial advance of the wage-earner. Educa. 34:69–77. (O. '13.)

Bristol, George P. High school graduation and college entrance. Educa. R. 46:325–29. (N. '13.)

Brooks, E. C. Seven, eight, and nine years in the elementary school. El. School T. 14:82–92. (O. '13.)

Coover, J. Edgar. The Union High School questionnaires. Educa. 34:81–94. (O. '13.)

Corbin, John. The struggle for college democracy. Cent. 87:80–87. (N. '13.)

Crawshaw, F. D. The relation between and the control of manual arts and vocational education. El. School T. 14:107–116. (N. '13).

[1] *Abbreviations.*—Atlan., Atlantic Monthly; Cent., Century; Colum. Univ. Q., Columbia University Quarterly; Educa., Education; Educa. Bi-mo., Educational Bi-monthly; Educa. R., Educational Review; El. School T., Elementary School Teacher; English J., English Journal; J. of Educa. Psychol., Journal of Educational Psychology; Lit. D., Literary Digest; Pop. Sci. Mo., Popular Science Monthly; Psychol. Clinic, Psychological Clinic; R. of Rs., Review of Reviews; School R., School Review; Voca. Educa., Vocational Education.

Curtis, Henry S. The rural church as a social center. Educa. 34:111–18. (O. '13.)

Dingee, Gertrude P. The value of Latin in the high school. Educa. Bi-mo. 8:23–27. (O. '13.)

Earle, Samuel Chandler. The organization of instruction in composition. English J. 2:477–87. (O. '13.)

Egbert, James C. Extension teaching at Columbia. Colum. Univ. Q. 15: 366–71. (S. '13.)

Flexner, Abraham. The German side of medical education. Atlan. 112: 654–62. (N. '13.)

Gaston, George H. A bibliography for the study of the history and government of Chicago. Educa. Bi-mo. 8:81–87. (O. '13.)

Glenny, Mrs. Bryant B. How may a community make a study of its schools as opportunities for vocational education? Voca. Educa. 3:79–85. (N. '13.)

Greenwood, James M. How New York City administers its schools. Educa. R. 46:217–28. (O. '13.)

Groszmann, Maximilian P. E. A tentative classification of exceptional children. Child (London) 4:33–39. (O. '13.)

Grupe, Mary A. How the problems of the rural schools are being met. Pop. Sci. Mo. 83:484–90. (N. '13.)

Heniger, A. Minnie Herts. The drama's value for children. Good Housekeeping 57:636–43. (N. '13.)

Hooper, Cyrus L. The Cornman and Wallin spelling tests. Educa. Bi-mo. 8:28–41. (O. '13.)

Hosic, James Fleming. The advance movement of teachers of English. Educa. 34:99–103. (O. '13.)

———. Co-operation of all departments in the teaching of English composition. School R. 21:598–607. (N. '13.)

Howerth, Ira W. The apportionment of school funds. Educa. R. 46: 273–84. (O. '13.)

Hughes, Helen Sard. "Literature for children": a protest. English J. 494–99. (O. '13.)

Inglis, Alexander. The distribution of pupils in the public high schools. Educa. R. 46:344–50. (N. '13.)

Jennings, H. M., and Hallock, A. L. Binet-Simon tests at the George Junior Republic. J. of Educa. Psychol. 4:471–75. (O. '13.)

Jones, Adam Leroy. Some new methods of admission to college. Educa. R. 46:351–60. (N. '13.)

Klapper, Paul. A judgment of the New York City schools. Educa. R. 46: 335–43. (N. '13.)

Lewis, J. C., Hoke, K. J., Welles, J. B., and Wilson, G. M. Accuracy of pupil reporting. Psychol. Clinic 7:135–41. (O. '13.)

Long, Percy W. Grades that explain themselves. English J. 2:488–93. (O. '13.)

(The) lost years of the schoolboy. Lit. D. 47:681. (18 O. '13.)

McKitrick, May. The adaptation of the work in English to the actual needs and interests of the pupils. English J. 2:405-16. (S. '13.)

Maclear, Martha. The Froebel fetich. Educa. R. 46:330-34. (N. '13.)

McManis, John T. Chicago schools and child welfare. Educa. Bi-mo. 8:42-50. (O. '13.)

Mardorf, Mae F. Contributions to nature-study from the Chicago schools. Educa. Bi-mo. 8:78-80. (O. '13.)

Miner, James Burt. The scientific study of child development. Pop. Sci. Mo. 83:506-13. (N. '13.)

Molter, Harold. Practical suggestions for the teaching of sex hygiene. Educa. 34:95-98. (O. '13.)

(The) Montessori schools in Italy—an account based on personal visits by two Americans. Lit. D. 47:637-38. (11 O. '13.)

(The) need of more romantic mathematics. Current Opinion 55:260. (O. '13.)

Otis, Margaret. The Binet tests applied to delinquent girls. Psychol. Clinic 7:127-34. (O. '13.)

"Peopleizing" the museums. Lit. D. 47:757. (25 O. '13.)

Roberts, William M. Classes for apprentices in the Chicago Public Schools. Educa. Bi-mo. 8:16-22. (O. '13.)

Rounds, C. R., and Kingsbury, H. B. Do too many students fail? School R. 21:585-97. (N. '13.)

Schinz, Albert. Difference between the work of the high school, college and graduate school. Educa. R. 46:237-51. (O. '13.)

Schroeder, H. H. A real problem for educational psychology. J. of Educa. Psychol. 4:465-70. (O. '13.)

Sex education as its friends and its foes view it. Current Opinion 55:261-62. (O. '13.)

Starch, Daniel. The measurements of handwriting. J. of Educa. Psychol. 4:445-64. (O. '13.)

Sykes, Marion. Failures in the high school. Educa. Bi-mo. 8:8-15. (O. '13.)

Venable, Francis P. A question of morals. Educa. R. 46:361-68. (N. '13.)

Wells, Dora. An experiment in applied household science. Educa. Bi-mo. 8:1-7. (O. '13.)

Winter, John G. Greek and Latin in the schools of Belgium. School R. 21:618-26. (N. '13.)

Woolley, Helen T. Facts about the working children of Cincinnati, and their bearing upon educational problems. I. El. School T. 14:59-72. (O. '13.) II. 14:132-39. (N. '13.)

Young, Karl. High-school courses in the history of English literature. English J. 2:500-504. (O. '13.)

VOLUME XIV NUMBER 5

THE ELEMENTARY SCHOOL TEACHER

JANUARY 1914

EDUCATIONAL NEWS AND EDITORIAL COMMENT

Meeting of the Department of Superintendence

The Department of Superintendence of the National Education Association will meet in Richmond, Virginia, February 23–28, 1914. A preliminary program has been sent out, from which the following general account of the character of the meetings has been compiled.

Three committees are scheduled to report to the meeting. The subjects of the reports are "Economy of Time in Education," "Health Problems of the American Public School," and "Standards and Tests of Efficiency." Rural-school problems occupy a prominent place in the program, two sessions being given over to this subject. A report is to be presented upon it by the United States Bureau of Education, and Mr. John H. Finley, commissioner of education in New York, will present a discussion of the rural schools in that state. Vocational training also occupies a prominent position. One session upon part-time, continuation, shop, and trade schools is to be held, and the relation between vocational and cultural education is the subject of discussion of another session. There are, as usual, a number of papers on various subjects by prominent educators, and the group of round tables for superintendents of the various sorts of administrative unit.

Besides the National Society for the Study of Education and the Society of College Teachers of Education, which are announced below, the following associations will meet with the Department of Superintendence: National Committee on Agricultural Education; Educational Press Association of America; National Council of Teachers of English; conferences of state superintendents of education and of teachers of education in state universities with Commissioner Claxton; conference of teachers in city training schools; American School Peace League; International Kindergarten Union; National Congress of Mothers and Parent-Teacher Association; School Garden Association of America; National Association of Collegiate Registrars.

F. N. F.

The following is an announcement of a tentative program for the meeting of the Society of College Teachers of Education, to be held in conjunction with the meeting of the Department of Superintendence in Richmond, Virginia, in February, 1914.

I. Session Devoted to Report of Committee on Rating, Placing, and Promotion of Teachers.
   1. "The Rating, Placing, and Promotion of Teachers; Introduction," Frank E. Thompson, University of Colorado, Chairman.
   2. "The Rating of Prospective Teachers," William H. Kilpatrick, Columbia University.
   3. "The Rating of Teachers in Service," Lotus D. Coffman, University of Illinois.
   4. "The Placing of New Teachers," A. S. Whitney, University of Michigan.
   5. "The Promotion of Teachers," Ellwood P. Cubberley, Stanford University.
   6. "A Plan for Co-operation between States or Sections for the Placing and Promotion of Teachers," Edward C. Elliott, University of Wisconsin, and W. S. Sutton, University of Texas.
   7. "The Advantages of a State Teachers' Agency," George P. James, University of Minnesota.
   8. "Plans for the Betterment of Conditions," the Committee.

NOTE.—These papers will appear in the *Yearbook* and will be discussed at the first session.

II. Luncheon.

III. Session Devoted to Educational Surveys and Business Meeting.
   1. "The Significance of City School Surveys for Departments of Education in Colleges and Universities," Paul H. Hanus, Harvard University.
   2. "The Significance of State Educational Surveys for Departments of Education in Colleges and Universities," M. B. Hillegas, Columbia University.

NOTE.—These papers will appear in the *Yearbook* and will be discussed at the second session.

IV. Bibliography on School Surveys.
G. D. Strayer, Columbia University. This will be printed in the *Yearbook.*

V. Classified List of Educational Investigations now under way by Members or their Students.
Compiled by the Secretary. This will be printed in the *Yearbook.*

VI. Report of the Committee on Rating of Normal Schools in Relation to Departments of Education in Colleges and Universities.
Chairman, W. A. Jessup, Iowa State University.

This committee will report at the second session on a definite plan for concentrating the work of the Society for the 1915 meeting on the investigation of this problem.

The final program and full details of the time and place of the meetings will be sent later.

CARTER ALEXANDER, *Secretary-Treasurer*

PEABODY COLLEGE FOR TEACHERS
NASHVILLE, TENNESSEE

The annual meeting of the National Society for the Study of Education will be held in connection with the sessions of the Superintendents' Section of the National Education Association, in Richmond, Virginia, on Monday, February 23, at 8:00 P.M. The program will consist of discussions of the *Yearbook*, which will be organized as follows:

GENERAL TOPIC: "SOME PROBLEMS IN HIGH-SCHOOL INSTRUCTION."

1. "Reconstructed Mathematics as an Example of the Adaptation of Instruction to the Needs, Interests, and Capacities of High-School Students," by H. C. Morrison, superintendent of public instruction for New Hampshire.
2. "Supervised Study as a Means of Providing Supplementary Individual Instruction," by E. R. Breslich of the University High School, the University of Chicago.
3. "The Character of the Teaching Population as Influencing the Possibility of Improved Instruction," by L. D. Coffman, professor of education, the University of Illinois, and W. A. Jessup, professor of education, the University of Iowa.

The *Yearbook* will be distributed about February 1.

S. C. PARKER, *Secretary*

UNIVERSITY OF CHICAGO

In recent discussions regarding state-aided vocational education little has been said about the progress of the work in Maine. The fact should not be overlooked that here is a state which has been working at the most important phase of the problem, namely, the preparation of teachers who understand the vocational conditions obtaining in their own state and who are prepared to meet those conditions. State Superintendent Smith, in speaking on this point, says:

"Vocational" Branches in Teacher Training in Maine

> No teacher can now graduate from any state training or normal school without having studied the elements of agriculture, and without having taken courses in manual training and housekeeping. This year nearly eight hundred young persons are in the normal schools getting ready to teach school. Every one of them before he goes to a school of his own will understand the underlying principles of these subjects, and many of them will be sufficiently expert to take full direction of special courses. Every year there will be added to our teaching force those who can teach through the work of the hand as well as through the words of the book.

Vocational Training in Corporation Schools

The meeting of the National Association of Corporation Schools at Dayton, Ohio, is not without its significance in the field of public education. No amount of discussion can determine the extent to which the public industrial school can give efficient trade preparation, but these corporation schools will unquestionably help in fixing standards and in defining limits within which the public school may legitimately work. There are certain types of technical training which the corporation schools can give better than the public school, and in this training the public school should not compete. This will not relieve the public school of its duty to provide genuine vocational training, but will make its problem clearer and more specific.

F. M. L.

Credit for Outside Work

Experiments in which credit has been given by the school for work done outside the school have been reported in recent numbers of the *School Review*. In one case credit was given for music lessons and for time spent in practice. In the other case a Minnesota superintendent gave credit for a great variety of home work, from milking a cow to sleeping with the windows open. *School Progress* reports an experiment similar to the one last mentioned which was carried on for two years by Mr. A. I. O'Reilly at Spring Valley, Oregon. The general nature of the plan may be seen from the following quotation:

The plan worked out by Mr. O'Reilly was in the form of a contest, a certain number of minutes being allowed for specified duties discharged at home, and the six children earning the greatest number of minutes at the close of the school year receiving prizes. The prizes were cash furnished by the school board and consisted of $3 each for the three pupils earning the highest number of credits, and $2 each for the three children having the next highest. This money was placed in the savings bank to the credit of the pupils winning it.

Each morning the children brought signed statements from their parents itemizing work done, and each morning Mr. O'Reilly carefully registered these items. Although no pupil was obliged to enter the contest, all did so eagerly; even the little tots proudly presented their notes each morning, and happily told Mr. O'Reilly how they had fed the chickens, watered the flowers, cleaned their teeth, slept with the window board in, and so on.

Perhaps the most unique thing about the list of duties for which Mr. O'Reilly offered credit was his original method of obtaining personal neatness and sanitation. For instance, thirty minutes were allowed children for each bath; ten minutes for reaching school with clean hands, face, teeth, and nails, and with hair combed; ten minutes for washing teeth; five minutes for sleeping with window board in, and five minutes for retiring at or before nine o'clock.

The plan is reported to have been attended with success if the enthusiasm of the people of the district and of a wider circle of observers may be taken as a test. At the close of the year a picnic was held at which the prizes were distributed and addresses were delivered by the state superintendent of schools, who first suggested the experiment, and by the governor of the state. A similar project is being carried on in the Junction City High School, where the credit takes the form of exemption from the final examination, provided an average grade of 85 per cent in class work has been maintained.

Doubtful Propriety of This Practice

The popular acclaim with which such practices are rewarded makes it likely that they will become more widespread and it is therefore worth while to consider how far they may be regarded as legitimate forms of school endeavor. It is a familiar fact that the modern home, especially in the city, is not equipped to furnish the child the same opportunity for doing tasks which have educative value that the home of a generation or more ago offered. It is pretty generally admitted that the school should accept as part of its duty the responsibility of making good this lack to the child. The cases here described, however, do not come under this principle. The opportunities for work exist in the home, and the school seeks to induce the child to perform his legitimate home tasks by offering rewards, which sometimes take the form of exemption from school duties which would otherwise be required. That the school should cultivate closer relations with the home may be freely granted. Further, it may be conceded that the school should use its influence to induce the child to perform his duties, whether at home or elsewhere; but that the school should relieve the parent of the responsibility of directing the conduct of his child at home, unless indeed conditions such as are found in city slums render it difficult for the parent to supervise the conduct of his child, or the parent is incompetent, is to be questioned. Where changed conditions have not made it necessary, it may be doubted whether it is desirable for the school to encroach upon the authority and responsibility of the home.

School Credit for Sunday-School Work

A different principle underlies the plan which has been proposed in a resolution adopted by the recent convention of the Colorado State Teachers' Association as reported in the *Pueblo Chieftain*. After dwelling upon the need of religious training, on the strong organization which has this as its aim, and of the unstandardized nature of Sunday-school work, the resolution reads:

> We therefore recommend that this Association approve of the strong effort now being made by the churches and the Colorado Sunday-School Association to elevate the standards of teaching in the Sunday schools, to improve their courses of study, and to secure on the part of the pupils the same grade of lesson preparation work as is demanded in public-school work; that with this object in view, it commends to the Sunday school for classes of high-school grade the recognized standards of the North Central Association of Secondary Schools and Colleges; that when these standards have been attained it recommends that high schools give credit for Bible-study of corresponding grade in the Sunday schools, to an extent not to exceed one-fourth unit for each year's work; and that this body appoint a permanent committee to co-operate in prudent and legitimate ways for all the foregoing purposes with a similar committee from the Colorado School Association.

The proposal which is here made merits thoughtful consideration. The details of such a plan, including the amount of credit to be allowed, would need to be fully discussed. To those who believe that religious instruction is not a legitimate form of public concern, and to those at the opposite extreme who believe that it is so much a matter of public concern that it ought not to be delegated but should be given to all pupils together and in the same form, the proposal will not commend itself. In those inclined to a compromise position, on the other hand, it may awaken interest. It has the advantage that it would be likely to raise the standard of Sunday-school work and it seems probable that the better character of the work offered, together with the credit which would be obtained, would attract a number of the young people who now drop out of the Sunday school. If some school system should adopt the plan as an experiment, the result would be watched with interest.

The Training of Teachers of the Manual and Industrial Arts

A group of ten men recently met at the Bradley Polytechnic Institute, Peoria, Illinois, in an informal three-day conference on questions relative to the training of teachers of the manual and industrial arts. These men were heads of manual arts departments in as many state normal schools, colleges, or universities located in the following states: Ohio, Tennessee, Indiana, Illinois, Wisconsin, Iowa, and Missouri.

The conference discussed in considerable detail the content and organization of a four-year training course of college grade for teachers of the manual arts. While it was agreed that the four-year course is highly desirable, it was commonly accepted as inevitable that the great demand for manual-training teachers would render the two-year course both popular and necessary. Consequently the conference decided upon desirable standard requirements for such a training course. In working out these requirements, due regard was had for the fact that such a course should afford sufficient technical and professional work to render the graduate immediately efficient in certain types of schools and, at the same time, should serve as good foundation for further collegiate work leading to a degree.

A session was given to a discussion of the best means of meeting the insistent call for teachers equipped to give instruction in the new vocational schools. In most of the states represented, legislation of some kind has stimulated the introduction of vocational work and this influence is already felt in the teachers' training classes.

Perhaps the most important question discussed was how the educational institutions represented could best make known to suitable young men what excellent opportunities were offered to well-trained manual arts teachers by this new and growing demand. The testimony of all present was to the effect that this demand far exceeded the supply from all available sources. So valuable did the conference prove that it was decided to hold a meeting next year at the University of Chicago.

Provision for Childen Retarded Because of Remediable Physical Defect

There are many signs that school boards and school administrators are attacking the problem of the discovery and treatment of defective children in the schools. In Louisville, Kentucky, the public-school system is taking over a school for defective children which was started a year ago under private auspices. The *Louisville Herald* gives the following account of the situation:

The special school for retarded children which will be opened at the Second and Gray Street school next week, will be the continuation of the work begun last year at Cathedral House, under the auspices of the Cathedral House Guild.

The Board of Education is enabled, by the indorsement of the school bond issue, to take up the cases which come to it demanding special training. A trained teacher will be employed, and the work will be conducted according to the best methods.

The special school was opened last November at the Cathedral House. Only those children were taken into the school who had a physical defect which could be improved by proper medical and surgical attention. For this reason it was necessary that every child undergo a physical examination. Four general clinics were held at the Cathedral House.

The children of this school, "marred in the making," have been tremendously helped by the school. After their lunch at 9:30 in the morning and after dinner, a tooth-brush drill was given. Then they rested for half an hour in the reclining chairs on the roof garden. Before they went home there was another period of work and play. A printed form was kept for every child and duplicates were made for the public school, the city health office, and the mental examiner, Dr. Trawick. This record gives a complete history of the case, and the children are still being visited in order to keep the data up to date.

Whether the purpose which is declared in the following quotation from the *Chicago Tribune* will be authorized by the Board of Education of Chicago remains to be seen, but in any case it is one which cannot fail to be regarded as entirely worthy of approval.

Centers for the Care and Teaching of Epileptic Pupils and Crippled Children

The epileptic children of Chicago will be taken care of by the board of education as far as the school laws will permit. Mrs. Ella Flagg Young, superintendent of schools, will open centers for epileptic children at a number of schools. It is expected that all will be ready by January 1, and part of them probably will be started before the Christmas vacation.

The rooms, according to Mrs. Young's idea, will be in charge of a teacher who is to be paid a somewhat higher salary than the regular grade teacher. The rooms will be ungraded, as the subnormal rooms, and the children will receive individual instruction.

Each center will have one or two couches and screens, so that children who are overcome during school hours can be taken care of away from the rest of the children. Mrs. Young has had a number of urgent requests from parents of epileptic children asking that the school board do something, and a number of cases have come to her personal attention.

"From time to time children come to the office," she said, "who necessarily are sent out of the schools because they are afflicted with epilepsy. There ought to be some provision for them. I expect it will be difficult to get teachers for the rooms, although the salary will be greater. One of the district superintendents will be in charge of the rooms. The district superintendent and the teachers will be given instruction in the proper method of handling epileptic children."

We learn also from the *Milwaukee Sentinel* of the opening of a school in Milwaukee for crippled children:

"The school for crippled children, Scott Street and Sixth Avenue, will open in about two weeks," said Acting Superintendent of Schools, A. E. Kagel, on Sunday.

The committee of finance of the Board of Education, at its meeting last Tuesday, appropriated money for the purchase of an automobile, for the renovating of the rooms, and for the hiring of a matron and chauffeur, who will have the care of the unfortunates in, from, and to the school. The automobile will cost about $800 and the funds necessary to clean and paint the new school, which is one of only a few similar in the United States, will be about $125.

A New School for Defectives Planned for Detroit

Superintendent Chadsey, of Detroit, according to a notice in the *Detroit Free Press*, plans to ask the legislature for an appropriation for a new school exclusively for the training of defective children. This is a more elaborate provision than is commonly made by even large city systems, and from the point of view of efficiency in studying and handling cases of atypical children, at least, the centralization of the work in a well-equipped building instead of trying to deal with the defective children in single rooms scattered throughout the various schools is an experiment worth trying. It would call attention to the magnitude and seriousness of the problem and make it more likely that specially trained experts, with equipment particularly suited to their task, would be employed. The notice follows:

> Declaring that a school for backward and subnormal children is needed in Detroit, Dr. C. E. Chadsey, superintendent of public schools, Judge Hulbert, of the Probate Court, and Frank Cody, head of the special training classes and social center work, will endeavor to have a state law passed granting the city the right to establish such a municipal school.
>
> Detroit school officials say that time is ripe to build a special school, at a cost not to exceed $100,000, where such children may be educated and trained along special lines.
>
> Mr. Cody declares he has found that many children, after a year in these special classes, respond to special training and treatment, and fit themselves to enter on the work in regular school grades with normal pupils.
>
> "We need a municipal or county school in Detroit, for the children we are now handling in special classes," said Mr. Cody. "These subnormal children must be taught in classes where special courses are arranged to fit each individual case, or set of cases."

F. N. F.

State Textbooks

Should a state publish its own books? California raised the question a number of years ago and has been trying to settle it ever since. During the first nine months of 1913, this state published 1,231,681 volumes of school texts. Since the California books are published from plates used by textbook companies which print books for other states, it is possible to compare relative costs of the two plans in connection with the same books. If these books had been purchased from the book companies at the list price to dealers, they would have cost the state $485,169.84, according to W. G. Eggleston, writing in *The Public.* The cost of manufacturing at the state plant, plus royalties, was $219,681.95, a saving to the state of $265,487.89. The book company's price for the fifth reader, he tells us, is 75 cents. California's printing plant manufactures it for 15.2 cents and pays a royalty of 9 cents, making a total cost of 24.2 cents a copy. The total cost of manufacturing the introductory history is 30.5 cents, while the company's retail price is 60 cents.

It must be remembered that the company's price is for the book delivered into the hands of the pupil; therefore the costs of distribution and perhaps other costs should be added to the state cost. Nothing is said as to the relative quality of the paper used in the state books, or of the press work and binding. Before one can make secure judgment as to relative success of such state publication, one must have certain fundamental *facts.*

An act of the last legislature in Kansas provides that the state, beginning with 1914, publish and distribute all common-school textbooks. The new printing plant will be ready for work by March. The first book to be published will be the Kansas primer. This was selected from among an offering of eighty manuscripts from Kansas teachers. They are attempting to secure all manuscripts from their own teachers, a feature of the plan that in California proved a distinct failure.

A compromise suggestion comes from the province of Ontario. In this province the school authorities draw up the manuscripts of books that they wish to have for their schools, and also plans and specifications for the finished books. Independent publishing houses are then asked to bid for the publishing contract, which is awarded to the lowest responsible bidder. The school authorities claim a saving of about 50 per cent on the cost of the books. Not so often is it mentioned that the successful bidder carries on a mail-order business and is willing to bid very low in order to secure the additional favor of running some advertising matter in the school books.

J. F. B.

LITERARY SELECTIONS MOST FREQUENTLY MEMORIZED IN THE ELEMENTARY SCHOOL[1]

LEWIS ATHERTON
Educational Adviser, Swift & Company, Chicago

The course of study for the elementary schools of New York City provides that "at least four lines of poetry per week, or an equivalent amount of prose, should be memorized by every pupil" during the first four grades. For the fifth and sixth grades, the amount is placed at six lines per week; and for the seventh and eighth grades, at eight lines per week. The total thus prescribed for the entire elementary school course is the quite considerable amount of 1,720 lines. This is more than 100 poems of sixteen lines each. Very many cities require, or at least recommend, similar amounts.

Where so much is prescribed, it is important that selections be made with care. The present writer is of the opinion that, in this field at least, the things that have stood the test of successful practical experience in many cities are the ones that can be chosen with the greatest confidence. In the nation-wide experimentation that is now going on, selections that are best adapted to needs and interests of children of the different ages tend, after trial, to keep their place, and to become established; inappropriate selections naturally tend to disappear. The present study was undertaken for the purpose of finding out what memory materials have stood the test of practical experience in our various cities and states.

About 125 state and city courses of study were examined. It was found, however, that but one out of every four published courses yields material upon this point in sufficiently definite form to be available for the purposes of this study. Thirty-four courses were found in which recommendations and prescriptions were intelligible,

[1] This is the report of an investigation which was made in connection with the course on the curriculum conducted by Assistant Professor J. F. Bobbitt, in the University of Chicago.

and apparently fairly complete. These were the courses used in the following cities and states:

Cities:

New York City	Berkeley	Evansville	Paterson
Chicago	Beloit	Jersey City	Schenectady
Boston	Brookline	Johnstown	South Bend
Cincinnati	Columbia	McKeesport	Williamsport
Minneapolis	Dayton	Nashua	Worcester
Washington City	Decatur, Ill.	Oakland	
Tacoma	Detroit	Omaha	

State and county courses:

New York	Massachusetts	Idaho	Tennessee
California	Pennsylvania	Maine	Baltimore County

A very complete list of memory materials was found recommended in Hosic's *Elementary Course in English.* Since this was developed in connection with the practical work of the training classes of the Chicago Teachers College, his recommendations have been included in the tabulations.

With Granger's *Index to Poetry and Recitations* taken as authority upon the verse-portion—this makes up 99 per cent of the entire list—it was found that many errors in exact title and more mistakes in assignment of titles to authors occur in the several courses of study used. While the entire elimination of these and other errors from the list of authors and titles is extremely improbable, much has been corrected. It is very difficult to trace down each error and know exactly where it arose, and how it crept into its present place. Wherever there has arisen a question regarding any selection in this study, a safe course has been followed, and the study eliminated from the list. This procedure cut the list of titles found in the thirty-four published courses from 1,050 to 834 titles. And further, for the sake of brevity in publishing the gist of the results of the study in this journal, it has been thought well to eliminate from the list all titles appearing less than three times. There remain, after the two prunings, 140 authors and 382 titles. It is believed that the list as it now stands indicates in a general way the relative valuations placed upon these 382 titles by the practical workers in the field.

TABLE I

MATERIAL FOR MEMORIZATION

Author	Title	1	2	3
Addison, J.	Spacious Firmament on High, The	10	8	6–8
Alden, R. M.	Lost, The Summer	3	.....	1–4
Aldrich, T. B.	Before the Rain	11	6	2–6
	Marjorie's Almanac	12	3	3–4
Alexander, Mrs. C. T.	All Things Bright and Beautiful	15	1	1–2
	Burial of Moses	6	.....	6–7
Allingham, W.	Fairies, The	10	2	2–4
	Robin Redbreast	8	2	1–2
	Wishing	10	3	2–4
Allison, Joy	I Love You, Mother	3	2	1–2
Arnold, M.	Self-Dependence	4	8	7–8
Bates, Mrs. C.	Who Likes the Rain?	3	1	.....
Bennett, H.	The Flag Goes By	19	6	1–7
Bible, The	Psalm 1	4	4	3–4
	Psalm 23	10	3	2–5
	Psalm 24	5	3	1–5
Bjornson, B.	Tree, The	18	3	1–5
Blake, W.	Lamb, The	8	.....	1–5
	Nurse's Song	4	3	1–3
	Tiger, Tiger, Burning Bright	3	5	2–5
Bland, Mrs. E. N.	Baby Seed Song	4	2	2–3
Boyle, Mrs. Sarah	Voice of the Grass	4	3	3–5
Branch, Mrs. M. L.	Petrified Fern	3	6	.....
Brooks, Rev. P.	Christmas Everywhere	4	7	3–7
	O Little Town of Bethlehem	13	3	2–6
Brown, K. L.	Little Plant Seed, The	11	1	1–3
Browning, R.	Herve Riel	3	8	7–8
	Home Thoughts from Abroad	6	7	4–7
	How They Brought the Good News	7	6	6–8
	Incident of the French Camp	9	5	5–8
	Pied Piper of Hamelin	7	3	1–7
	Pippa Passes	8	4	3–7
	Pheidippides	3	.....	6–8
	Year's at the Spring	15	5	1–7
Browning, Mrs. R.	Child's Thought of God	9	4	1–4
	Romance of the Swan's Nest	3	7	.....
Bryant, W. C.	Antiquity of Freedom	5	8	7–8
	Death of the Flowers, The	7	7	5–8
	Gladness of Nature	13	5	3–8
	Hurricane	3	6	6–7
	Hymn to North Star	4	8	.....
	Love of God	3	8	.....
	March	7	.....	2–8
	Planting of the Apple Tree	18	5	2–8
	Robert o' Lincoln	22	5	1–8
	Song of Marion's Men	12	6	4–7
	Thanatopsis	12	8	7–8
	To a Water Fowl	20	7	6–8
	Yellow Violet	6	5	5–6
Bunner, H. C.	One, Two, Three	9	2	2–4
Burns, R.	Auld Lang Syne	4	8	6–8
	Bannockburn	5	7	5–8
	Field Mouse, To a	3	.....	2–8

TABLE I—*Continued*

Author	Title	1	2	3
Burns, R. (*cont.*).....	Man's a Man for a' That..............	13	6	6–8
	My Heart's in the Highlands..........	6	5	5–7
	Mountain Daisy, To a................	4	.....	5–8
Byron, Lord.........	Destruction of Sennacherib............	7	6	6–8
	Ocean............................	6	8	6–8
	Waterloo..........................	7	.....	5–8
Campbell, T.........	Hohenlinden.......................	6	.....	5–7
	Lord Ullin's Daughter................	3	6	.....
Carlyle, T...........	Today............................	21	5	2–7
Cary, Alice..........	Nobility..........................	12	6	4–7
	November.........................	15	3	1–4
	Order for a Picture, An..............	5	.....	4–8
	Three Little Bugs in a Basket.........	6	.....	1–4
Cary, Phoebe........	Don't Give Up......................	6	3	2–3
	Suppose..........................	15	2	1–4
	They Didn't Think..................	5	1	1–3
Child, Mrs. L. M.....	If Ever I See.......................	3	3	1–3
	Thanksgiving Day...................	15	2	1–3
	Who Stole the Bird's Nest?...........	9	2	1–3
Coleridge, S. T.......	Answer to a Child's Question..........	10	2	2–4
	He Prayeth Best....................	10	3	3–4
	Hunting Song......................	3	5	2–5
Collins, W...........	How Sleep the Brave................	3	.....	5–7
Cone...............	Dandelions, The....................	3	4	2–5
Coolidge, S..........	How the Leaves Come Down..........	16	2	1–4
Cooper, G...........	Wind and Leaves...................	9	1	1–2
Cornwall, B. (B. W. Procter)..........	Sea, The	8	5	4–7
Cowper, W..........	Cricket, The	3	6	4–6
	Nightingale and the Glowworm, The....	4	.....	4–6
Dickens, C..........	Ivy Green, The.....................	4	5	.....
Drake, J. R.........	American Flag......................	14	6	5–8
Edwards, M. B......	Child's Prayer, A...................	5	3	.....
Emerson, R. W......	Concord Hymn.....................	24	7	5–8
	Duty.............................	3	.....	4–8
	Each and All......................	7	8	6–8
	Forbearance.......................	3	7	4–7
	Humble-Bee, The...................	3	7	6–7
	Mountain and Squirrel...............	24	4	1–5
	Rhodora, The......................	9	7	6–8
	Snow-Storm, The...................	10	7	6–8
	We Thank Thee.....................	7	.....	1–3
Field, Eugene.......	Christmas Eve......................	4	1	1–2
	Duel, The.........................	3	3	2–3
	Japanese Lullaby...................	7	.....	2–5
	Little Boy Blue.....................	9	2	1–4
	Nightwind, The.....................	20	4	2–5
	Norse Lullaby......................	14	3	2–5
	Rock-a-by Lady.....................	10	2	1–2
	Why Do Bells of Christmas Ring?.....	8	1	1–2
	Wynken, Blynken, and Nod...........	29	2	1–4
Fields, J. T.........	Captain's Daughter..................	6	3	3–5
Finch, F. M.........	Blue and the Gray, The..............	9	6	5–8
Follen, Mrs. E. L.....	New Moon, The....................	8	1	1–2

TABLE I—*Continued*

Author	Title	1	2	3
Follen, Mrs. E. L. (*cont.*)	Stop, Stop, Pretty Water	4	.....	1–2
French, F.	Waiting to Grow	3	1	1–3
Garabrandt, N. M.	Dandelion	3	2	2–3
German, The	Lullaby	22	1	1–2
Goethe	Rest	5	8	4–8
Gould, Mrs. H. F.	Frost	12	4	2–7
Gould, S. B.	Now the Day is Over	3	.....	2–3
Grey, T.	Elegy in Country Churchyard (sel.)	8	8	7–8
Hale, Mrs. S. J.	Mary's Lamb	9	1	1–2
Halleck, F. G.	Marco Bozarris	4	.....	6–8
Hemans, Mrs. F. D.	Casabianca	8	4	4–5
	Landing of the Pilgrim Fathers	29	5	3–7
	Voice of Spring	3	7	.....
Henry, P.	Liberty or Death	3	7	.....
Herrick, R.	Succession of the Four Sweet Months	3	2	2–4
Higginson, Ella	Four-Leaf Clover	4	.....	4–5
Hogg, J.	Boy's Song, A	16	3	1–4
	Skylark, The	6	4	2–7
Holland, J. G.	Gradatim	14	7	5–8
	Lullaby	4	2	2–4
Holmes, O. W.	Chambered Nautilus	26	7	6–8
	Deacon's Masterpiece	5	7	5–7
	Grandmother's Story of Bunker Hill	3	7	.....
	Last Leaf	27	8	6–8
	Old Ironsides	25	6	4–8
	Union and Liberty	8	7	6–7
Hood, T.	I Remember, I Remember	4	3	3–4
Hopkins, J.	Hail Columbia	4	6	6–7
Houghton, Lord	Good Night and Good Morning	10	.....	1–3
	Lady Moon	17	2	1–2
Howe, J. W.	Battle Hymn of the Republic	12	8	4–8
Howitt, M.	Northern Seas	3	4	3–4
	Spider and the Fly	5	3	2–3
	Use of Flowers	3	.....	4–7
	Voice of Spring	5	3	.....
Howitt, W.	Wind in the Frolic	3	2	2–4
Hugo, V. M.	Good Night	5	1	1–3
Hunt, J. H.	Abou Ben Ahdem	30	6	4–7
	Grasshopper and Cricket	3	5	5–6
Ingelow, Jean	Seven Times One	30	2	1–5
Jackson, Mrs. H. H.	"Down to Sleep"	10	5	3–6
	October's Bright Blue Weather	25	4	2–6
	September	25	4	1–5
Janvier, Margaret T.	The Sandman	9	3	1–3
Jewett, S. O.	Discontent	6	2	1–3
Jones, Sir W.	What Constitutes a State?	6	.....	7–8
Jonson, B.	Noble Nature	3	5	5–7
Keats, J.	Autumn	4	.....	6–7
	Grasshopper and Cricket	6	6	4–6
Keble, J.	All Things Bright and Beautiful	3	2	1–2
Key, F. S.	Star-Spangled Banner	15	7	4–7
Kingsley, C.	Farewell, A	8	5	2–5
	Lost Doll, The	16	2	1–3

TABLE I—*Continued*

Author	Title	1	2	3
Kingsley, C. (*cont.*)	Sands o' Dee	3	.....	4–7
Kipling, R.	Ballad of East and West	3	8	7–8
	L'Envoi	3	8	6–8
	Recessional	17	8	7–8
	Seal Lullaby	7	2	2–7
Krout, M. H.	Little Brown Hands	10	3	1–4
Lang, A.	Scythe Song	5	6	6–7
Lanier, S.	Song of the Chattahoochee	8	.....	4–8
Larcom, L.	Brown Thrush	19	2	1–5
	Calling the Violet	5	3	2–3
	Golden-Rod	3	6	5–6
	If I Were a Sunbeam	4	2	.....
	Rivulet	5	2	2–4
	Sir Robin	2	2	2–3
Lear, E.	Owl and the Pussy Cat	13	2	1–3
Lincoln, A.	Address at Gettysburg	20	8	6–8
Longfellow, H. W.	Arrow and Song	23	5	3–8
	Bell of Atri	5	6	2–8
	Builders	20	6	5–7
	Building of the Ship	8	8	6–8
	Children	4	3	3–5
	Children's Hour	24	4	1–7
	Christmas Bells	4	.....	3–6
	Day Is Done	17	5	4–8
	Daybreak	11	7	2–8
	Excelsior	11	5	4–6
	Fiftieth Birthday of Agassiz	5	5	1–7
	Hiawatha	14	4	1–7
	Hiawatha's Childhood	13	1	1–3
	Hiawatha's Friends	3	.....	2–4
	Hiawatha's Sailing	10	3	3–5
	King Robert of Sicily	5	6	6–8
	Ladder of St. Augustine	3	8	7–8
	Lighthouse	3	6	.....
	Legend Beautiful	4	6	6–8
	Miles Standish	6	7	7–8
	My Lost Youth	4	7	3–7
	Old Clock on the Stairs	12	5	3–7
	Paul Revere's Ride	17	5	4–8
	Psalm of Life, A	18	5	5–8
	Rain in Summer	9	4	3–5
	Sandalphon	5	8	6–8
	Santa Filomena	5	.....	5–7
	Ship of State	16	8	5–8
	Skeleton in Armor	3	.....	6–8
	Snow-Flakes	6	.....	3–6
	Village Blacksmith	29	4	2–6
	Windmill	3	3	3–4
	Wreck of Hesperus	9	4	3–6
Lover, S.	Angel's Whisper	3	3	1–3
Lowell, J. R.	Aladdin	6	8	7–8
	Commemoration Ode	6	8	7–8
	Courtin', The	3	8	.....
	Day in June	7	8	6–8

TABLE I—*Continued*

Author	Title	1	2	3
Lowell, J. R. (*cont.*)	Finding of the Lyre, The	9	7	4–8
	First Snow-Fall	23	6	2–7
	Fountain	13	4	3–6
	Heritage	14	7	5–8
	Shepherd of King Admetus	3	6	5–6
	Singing Leaves	3	7	7–8
	Stanzas on Freedom	4	8	5–8
	Vision of Sir Launfal	9	.....	5–8
	Vision of Sir Launfal, Prelude	3	6	6–8
	Yussouf	4	5	5–6
Mabie, H. W.	"Value of Literature"	3	8	...
Macauley, T. B.	Horatius	8	7	6–7
MacDonald, G.	Baby	15	1	1–2
	Little White Lily	4	.....	1–2
	Wind and the Moon	9	4	1–5
Mackay, C.	Miller of Dee	6	.....	3–4
	Tubal Cain	5	6	3–6
Markham	Lincoln, the Man of the People	4	8	6–8
Miller, E. H.	Little May	3	.....	2–5
	Blue Bird	15	4	2–4
Miller, J.	Columbus	19	7	4–8
Milton, J.	Evening in Paradise	3	8	.....
	May Morning	4	6	6–8
	On His Blindness	6	8	.....
Montgomery	Arnold von Winklereid	4	8	6–8
Moore, C. C.	Visit from St. Nicholas	11	3	1–4
Moore, T.	Minstrel-Boy	4	3	3–6
Morris, G.	Woodman Spare That Tree	12	5	4–7
Mother Goose	Selections	52	1	1–2
Moultrie, J.	Violets, The	5	2	2–3
Newman, J. H.	Lead, Kindly Light	4	8	7–8
Payne, J. H.	Home, Sweet Home	12	5	3–6
Perry, Nora	Coming of Spring	6	6	2–6
Pierpont, J.	Warren's Address at Bunker Hill	16	8	5–8
Poe, E. A.	Bells, The	3	7	7–8
Poulsson, A. E.	Sunbeams, The	7	1	1–2
Procter, A. A.	One by One	5	6	5–6
Procter, B. W.	Sea	8	5	4–7
Rands	Great, Wide, Beautiful World, The	8	.....	2–3
Reade, T. B.	Sheridan's Ride	7	6	6–8
	Windy Night, The	3	5	5–6
Riley, J. W.	First Blue-Bird	4	5	5–7
	Knee-Deep in June	3	5	4–5
	Life Lesson, A	4	.....	3–8
	Old Aunt Mary's	3	.....	3–7
	Song, A	4	6	4–6
Rossetti, C. G.	Consider	3	6	3–6
	Green Cornfield, A	4	5	3–5
	"O Lady Moon"	5	1	1–2
	Uphill	3	8	6–8
	White Ship	3	8	.....
Scott, Sir W.	Breathes There the Man?	12	8	5–8
	Christmas	3	6	.....

TABLE I—*Continued*

Author	Title	1	2	3
Scott, Sir W. (*cont.*)	Coronach	3	8	7–8
	Douglas and Marmion	3	8	6–8
	Hie Away	4	3	2–4
	Lochinvar	9	7	5–7
	Love of Country	10	6	4–8
	Lullaby of an Infant Chief	3	2	2–4
	My Native Land	5	6	5–8
	Soldier Rest	3	.....	6–8
Shakespeare, W.	Blow, Blow, Thou Winter Wind	5	5	.....
	Farewell, a Long Farewell	4	7	.....
	Good Name in Man and Woman	6	7	7–8
	Hark, Hark, the Lark	8	7	3–8
	Neither Borrower nor Lender Be	8	8	6–8
	Noblest Roman of Them All	8	8	.....
	Orpheus with His Lute	4	6	5–6
	Over Hill, Over Dale	5	2	2–4
	The Quality of Mercy	13	8	6–8
	Under the Greenwood Tree	13	5	3–5
	Who Is Sylvia?	3	8	5–8
Shelly, P. B.	Cloud, The	12	8	7–8
	Skylark, To a	9	.....	3–8
Sherman, F. D.	Clouds	6	.....	3–5
	Daisies	16	2	1–3
	Dewdrop, A	6	1	1–2
	Four Winds	17	2	2–3
	March	3	3	3–4
	May	3	6	3–6
	Real Santa Claus	4	2	.....
	Shadow Children	4	2	2–3
	Vacation Song	3	3	.....
	Wizard Frost	3	2	.....
Sill, E. R.	Opportunity	11	8	5–8
Smith, S. F.	America	13	2	1–5
Southey, R.	Battle of Blenheim	3	.....	4–7
	Inchcape Rock, The	5	5	4–5
Stedman, E. C.	What the Winds Bring	11	.....	1–4
Stevenson, R. L.	Autumn Fires	10	1	1–3
	Bed in Summer	16	1	1–2
	Cow, The	9	1	1–2
	Foreign Children	5	1	1–2
	Foreign Lands	4	3	.....
	Good Play, A	3	1	.....
	Happy Thought	7	1	1–2
	Lamplighter, The	3	1	.....
	Land of Counterpane, The	7	.....	1–3
	Land of Story Books, The	10	2	2–4
	Moon, The	3	.....	1–4
	My Bed is a Boat	7	1	1–3
	My Shadow	28	2	1–3
	Rain	13	1	1–2
	Sun's Travels, The	5	1	1–3
	Swing, The	28	1	1–2
	Time to Rise	4	1	.....
	Where Go the Boats?	12	3	1–3

TABLE I—*Continued*

Author	Title	1	2	3
Stevenson, R. L. (*cont.*)	Whole Duty of Children	9	1	1–2
	Wind, The	25	1	1–4
	Windy Nights	7	2	2–3
	Winter-Time	4	2	1–4
Swett, S. H.	Blue Jay	3	5	....
Tate, N.	While Shepherds Watched	11	4	2–4
Taylor, B.	Song of the Camp, The	7	8	5–8
Taylor, Jane F.	Thank You, Pretty Cow	6	1	1–2
	Twinkle, Twinkle, Little Star	15	1	1–2
	Violet, The	5	3	2–4
Tennyson, Lord	Break, Break, Break	7	5	5–7
	Brook, The	26	4	3–8
	Bugle Song, The	26	7	2–8
	Charge of the Light Brigade, The	17	6	4–7
	Crossing the Bar	6	7	6–8
	Death of the Old Year, The	4	7	4–8
	Eagle, The	7	....	2–8
	Flower in the Crannied Wall	6	8	6–8
	Owl, The	10	3	2–4
	Revenge, The	3	....	6–8
	Shell, The	6	8	6–8
	Sir Galahad	9	7	6–8
	Sweet and Low	23	4	1–4
	Trostle, The	4	4	3–6
	What Does Little Birdie Say?	23	1	1–2
	Winter	4	4	2–4
Thaxter, C.	Little Gustave	6	2	2–3
	March	3	3	....
	Piccola	3	5	3–5
	Sandpiper, The	25	4	3–7
	Wild Geese	3	2	....
Thomas, E. M.	Talking in Their Sleep	4	5	3–5
van Dyke, H.	Angler's Reveille	4	8	....
Wadsworth, O. A.	Over in the Meadow	9	1	....
Warner, A. B.	Daffy Down Dilly	4	....	2–5
Watts, I.	Cradle Hymn, A	3	3	1–3
Webster, D.	Reply to Hayne	5	8	7–8
Westwood, T.	Little Bell	3	2	2–4
Whitman, W.	O Captain, My Captain	19	8	5–8
Whittier, J. G.	Abraham Davenport	3	8	7–8
	Barefoot Boy	23	5	2–8
	Barbara Frietchie	11	....	3–8
	Corn Song, The	15	5	3–8
	In School-Days	13	5	2–7
	Palm-Tree, The	5	3	3–6
	Pipes of Lucknow, The	4	6	....
	Skipper Ireson's Ride	3	7	5–7
	Snow-Bound (sel.)	10	8	5–8
	Telling the Bees	3	7	3–7
	Thanksgiving Ode	3	7	6–7
	Three Bells	6	4	3–5
Wolfe, C.	Burial of Sir John Moore, The	10	6	5–8
Wordsworth, W.	Happy Warrior, Character of the	3	8	....
	Lines Written in Early Spring	4	2	2–4

TABLE I—*Concluded*

Author	Title	1	2	3
Wordsworth, W. (*cont.*)	Lucy Grey	10	4	3–6
	Pet Lamb, The	6	.....	1–4
	Solitary Reaper, The	4	7	3–7
	To a Butterfly	5	3	2–3
	To a Child	3	3	.....
	To Daffodils	22	6	3–8
	To the Rainbow	3	6	5–6
	To a Skylark	3	7	4–7
	We Are Seven	8	4	2–5

In Table I, which precedes, in the first column following the title is the number of times it is recommended by the systems studied. In the second is the school grade for which it is recommended the largest number of times. In the last the lowest and highest grades for which it is recommended are shown.

This list of 382 selections is a very generous one from which to choose. Obviously only a comparatively small fraction of the whole can be prescribed for any school system. A safe plan is to choose those selections that occur the greatest number of times. The following select list of about 100 titles includes all that occur ten or more times. They are grouped according to the grades in which they occur most frequently.

TABLE II

AUTHORS AND TITLES MOST POPULAR IN THE SEVERAL GRADES AND THE RANGE OF THEIR RECOMMENDATION

Author	Title	No. Times Recommended All Grades	Range of Grades for Which Recommended
	FIRST GRADE		
Alexander	All Things Bright and Beautiful	15	1–2
Brown	Little Plant Seed	11	1–2
The German	Lullaby	22	1–2
Longfellow	Hiawatha's Childhood	13	1–3
MacDonald	Baby	15	1–2
Mother Goose	Selections	52	1–2
Stevenson	Autumn Fires	10	1–3
	Rain	13	1–2
	Swing	28	1–2
	Wind	25	1–4
Taylor	Twinkle, Twinkle, Little Star	15	1–2
Tennyson	What Does Little Birdie Say?	23	1–2
	SECOND GRADE		
Allingham	The Fairies	10	2–4
Cary, P.	Suppose	15	1–4
Child	Thanksgiving Day	15	1–3
Coleridge	Answer to a Child's Question	10	2–4
Field	Rock-a-by Lady	10	1–2
	Wynken, Blynken, and Nod	29	1–4
Houghton	Lady Moon	17	1–2
Ingelow	Seven Times One	30	1–5
Kingsley	Lost Doll	16	1–3
Larcom	Brown Thrush	19	1–5
Lear	Owl and Pussy Cat	13	1–3
Sherman	Daisies	16	1–3
	Four Winds	17	2–3
Smith	America	13	1–5
Stedman	What the Winds Bring	11	1–4
Stevenson	Land of Story Books	10	2–4
	My Shadow	28	1–3
	THIRD GRADE		
Aldrich	Marjorie's Almanac	12	3–4
Allingham	Wishing	10	2–4
Bible	Twenty-third Psalm	10	2–5
Bjornson	Tree	18	1–5
Brooks	Little Town of Bethlehem	13	2–6
Cary, A.	November	15	1–4
Coleridge	He Prayeth Best	10	3–4
Field	Norse Lullaby	14	2–5
Hogg	Boy's Song	16	1–4
Krout	Little Brown Hands	10	1–4
Longfellow	Hiawatha's Sailing	10	3–5
Moore	Visit from St. Nicholas	11	1–4
Stevenson	Where Go the Boats?	12	1–3
Tennyson	Owl	10	2–4

TABLE II—*Continued*

Author	Title	No. Times Recommended All Grades	Range of Grades for Which Recommended
	FOURTH GRADE		
Emerson	Mountain and Squirrel	24	1–5
Field	Night Wind	20	2–5
Gould	Frost	12	2–7
Jackson	October's Bright Blue Weather	25	2–6
	September	25	1–5
Longfellow	Children's Hour	24	1–7
	Hiawatha (selections)	14	1–7
	Village Blacksmith	29	2–6
Lowell	Fountain	13	3–6
Miller	Blue Bird	15	2–4
Tate	While Shepherds Watched	11	2–4
Tennyson	Sweet and Low	23	1–4
	Brook	26	3–8
Thaxter	Sandpiper	25	3–7
Wordsworth	Lucy Gray	10	3–6
	FIFTH GRADE		
Browning	Year's at the Spring	15	1–7
Bryant	Gladness of Nature	17	3–8
	Planting of the Apple Tree	18	2–8
	Robert o' Lincoln	22	1–8
Carlyle	The Day	21	2–7
Hemans	Landing of the Pilgrims	29	3–7
Jackson	"Down to Sleep"	10	3–6
Longfellow	Arrow and Song	23	3–8
	Day is Done	17	4–8
	Excelsior	11	4–6
	Old Clock on the Stairs	12	3–7
	Paul Revere's Ride	17	4–8
	Psalm of Life	18	5–8
Morris	Woodman Spare That Tree	12	4–7
Payne	Home, Sweet Home	12	3–6
Shakespeare	Under the Greenwood Tree	13	3–5
Whittier	Barefoot Boy	23	2–8
	Corn Song	15	3–8
	In School Days	13	2–7
	SIXTH GRADE		
Aldrich	Before the Rain	11	2–6
Bennett	The Flag Goes By	19	1–7
Bryant	Song of Marion's Men	12	4–7
Burns	Man's a Man for a' That	13	5–8
Cary, A.	Nobility	12	4–7
Drake	Our Flag	14	5–8
Holmes	Old Ironsides	25	4–8
Hunt	Abou Ben Ahdem	30	4–7
Longfellow	Builders	20	5–7
Lowell	First Snowfall	23	2–7
Scott	Love of Country	10	4–8

TABLE II—*Concluded*

Author	Title	No. Times Recommended All Grades	Range of Grades for Which Recommended
Tennyson	Charge of the Light Brigade	17	4–7
Whittier	Barbara Frietchie	11	3–8
Wolfe	Burial of Sir John Moore	10	5–8
Wordsworth	To Daffodils	22	3–8
	SEVENTH GRADE		
Bryant	To a Waterfowl	20	6–8
Emerson	Concord Hymn	24	5–8
	Snow-Storm	10	6–8
Holland	Gradatim	14	5–8
Holmes	Chambered Nautilus	26	6–8
Key	Star-Spangled Banner	15	4–7
Longfellow	Daybreak	11	2–8
Lowell	Heritage	14	5–8
Miller	Columbus	19	4–8
Riley	Old Glory	10	5–8
Tennyson	Bugle Song	26	2–8
	EIGHTH GRADE		
Addison	The Spacious Firmament	10	6–8
Bryant	Thanatopsis	12	7–8
Holmes	Last Leaf	27	6–8
Howe	Battle Hymn of the Republic	12	4–8
Kipling	Recessional	17	7–8
Lincoln	Address at Gettysburg	20	6–8
Longfellow	Ship of State	16	5–8
Pierpont	Warren's Address	16	5–8
Scott	Breathes There the Man?	12	5–8
Shakespeare	The Quality of Mercy	13	6–8
Shelly	Cloud	12	7–8
Sill	Opportunity	11	5–8
Whitman	O Captain, My Captain	19	5–8
Whittier	Snow-Bound (selections)	10	5–8

ADDRESSES BY CITIZENS TO SCHOOL BOYS.—*Concluded*

PHYSICAL CULTURE

R. M. SIMPSON, M.D.
Of Drs. Simpson and Halppenny, Sterling Bank Building, Winnipeg

The object of physical culture, as applied to you young people, is to develop your bodies in such a way as to bring them into that condition which we know as most favorable for perfect health. Just as the general education you get in school is not designed to fit you for any particular walk of life, so the object of these exercises is not to train you to do any special feats of strength or agility, but to produce healthy, symmetrical bodies; and this symmetry, if you think a moment, really means the same thing as beauty.

Before going into any special profession or occupation, the wisest thing for you to do is, of course, to get a good, sound, general education as a foundation, and if any of you wish to go into any particular line of athletics with a view to excelling in it, you should not do so until all your muscles have been evenly developed and growth has practically been completed.

For anyone to lay down a set of rules for physical exercises and intelligently apply them it is plain that he should have some knowledge of the structure of the human body and of its functions; that is, he should know some anatomy and some physiology. The same is also true of you, if you are rightly to understand and appreciate the value of these exercises.

Each of your bodies has, as you know, a strong framework made of bones, and these bones are joined together by tough membranes and bands called ligaments, these often being arranged so that between two adjoining bones there is a hinge-like movement possible. Outside these bones and attached to them are the muscles which make up the greater part of the bulk of our bodies. These muscles are generally spindle shape in form and are able to shorten in one direction, and it is by this property we are able to move; and even when we are not moving they, by having a certain tone, support the different parts of the body. Outside these muscles is the tough skin that serves a very important purpose in protecting our other tissues.

There is, besides, the little muscular pump, called the heart, that pumps the blood to every part of our anatomy, and this blood carries with it certain substances to feed and nourish our bodies, which substances it picks up from the digestive tract and the lungs.

Then there is the most wonderful part of all, the nervous system, which rules the whole body and which may be compared to an electric battery, which is the brain, and from this battery run little tubes or fibers, to all parts of our bodies. When we wish to move an arm, from our brain goes an impulse down one or more of these little nerves and certain muscles shorten and the limb moves.

This is, of course, a very crude description, but perhaps it will help you to understand better what I am going to tell you. To begin with, Nature has made a law that all the muscles or organs of our bodies must be exercised or used if they are to remain normal and healthy; so that if you bandage up an arm in such a way as to prevent movement, even for a few weeks, you will find when you remove these bandages that it is much smaller and weaker than its fellow, because the muscles have wasted away from non-use. And the same thing occurs over a large part of the body if the patient is simply put to bed and kept from exercise. Even higher organs than muscles come under the same rule. I am sure most of you have heard of the little fish in the great cave of Kentucky. These fish have become totally blind because they have lived for generations in perfect darkness, and as they could not use their eyes they gradually became quite sightless.

Now that very young children and animals may get this needful exercise, there is implanted in them a desire for play, and that they may not do this to excess, Nature has provided that when they have had enough they get tired and want to rest or sleep. From this a very useful lesson can be learned, for, especially when we are growing, we should not indulge in any muscular effort to excess, but should heed the warning that comes to us from feeling tired. If by will power we force our muscles to do too much work, they may not become sufficiently refreshed during the next period of rest to be in the best possible condition when required for use again.

The wise Mother Nature has also arranged that if a muscle

or group of muscles is used more than others, that is, within reasonable bounds, it gradually increases in size and strength. This is a very fortunate thing, for you know how necessary strong arms are to a blacksmith and strong legs to a soldier. These changes come very gradually, and this is a very important thing to remember, for Nature needs time to increase the size and number of the muscle cells. If a boy wishes to do any feat, such as running a certain distance or throwing a weight, the proper way is to fit himself by gradually increasing exercise for it. This seems to have been known to people long ago, for you have read of the famous athlete who commenced to lift the calf every day until finally he was able to lift it even when it had become a full grown ox.

Here I would like to again impress on you these simple facts:

1. That a muscle must be regularly exercised to keep up its strength and condition of health.

2. That if a muscle or group of muscles is exercised so that gradually more and more work is imposed on it, and ample intervals allowed for rest, it will increase in power, often to a wonderful extent.

3. That if, on the other hand, it has too great a task imposed on it, and is not given sufficient rest, it may become chronically tired and even weaker.

Sometimes a boy or girl, by getting into careless habits, may not give certain of his or her muscles a chance to develop; for instance, if he sits continually in an improper position, he may not exercise certain of the muscles of his chest properly and these may become weaker than those that are used, and this may go so far as to interfere with the proper expansion of the chest, a very important thing; or some of these muscles that support the spinal column may be affected in the same way and you may even get a deformity which may be very hard to cure. The same thing applies to all the muscles of the body, and it is the part of the instructor to pick out these defects and decide the proper exercises for their correction.

Another result obtained from proper physical exercises is the education of the nervous system. You all know how difficult it is to do even simple things, such as drawing a straight line or sharpening a lead pencil, when you try it for the first time. This is because the little paths or tubes through the nervous system are not used to carry the impulse to the particular muscles, but after you practice these actions for a time they soon become easy, and then so that you hardly know that you are doing them; that is, automatic, all because the nerve paths have been educated, or perhaps, as some think, new ones formed. So you see these exercises may be of use in training you to precise and graceful movement.

One thing I would like to leave clearly impressed on you, even though by doing so I may be wandering away from the exact subject of this talk, and that is the very serious injury you may do yourselves from excess in your sports and games.

This damage falls particularly on the circulatory system, which consists as you know of the heart and blood vessels, and whose function is to carry the nutrient blood to all parts of our bodies. The heart is nothing more than a little pump whose walls are a peculiar kind of muscle, but which obeys the same laws as those we mentioned in connection with the skeletal muscles. That is, if it is given extra work to do over a considerable period, the muscular wall thickens and it becomes much more powerful and pumps the blood along with greater ease. This is why athletes who are in training feel so well and are able to run great distances or play long, hard games without being exhausted. A Marathon runner who would be in perfect condition would have the muscles of his legs well developed and firm, and, more important, his heart developed so that it would keep pumping the blood more rapidly through the lungs and tissues of the body. If this were not so, he would soon fall exhausted.

This desired condition he brings himself into by daily practice, gradually increasing the distance until he is equal to the task of running the whole odd twenty-five miles. Now if he were to force himself to run this great distance without any preparation, what would likely happen would be that the muscular wall of his heart, not being gradually prepared for the prolonged strain, would weaken and stretch and the cavity of the heart be dilated, with the result that the runner might even die or at least damage himself very seriously. And this is exactly what often happens to boys who play hard games of hockey or lacrosse without proper preparation.

And it is not only the heart that may suffer from excessive or irregular strain, but these elastic tubes, the arteries, and especially the large one next the heart may be damaged. So that it is not uncommon for porters and others who have to lift great weights at irregular intervals to have the walls of this artery give way, forming a little sac or pouch which grows and which often, by rupturing, causes sudden death; or the wall may not be so seriously damaged and the effects may be noticed only later on in life.

While training and getting into condition within reasonable bounds is not a bad thing, it is to be remembered that if a boy has been playing lacrosse or football all season he should not stop exercise suddenly, but as he should prepare himself gradually, so he should also gradually diminish his exercise. The reason of this is that his heart wall has become thicker and stronger during his training by the muscle cells becoming larger and perhaps more numerous. When he gives up his sport he has no use for the extra muscle, and Nature, as we said above, always adapts a muscle, even the heart, to the amount of work required of it, so that these heart muscles return to their normal size. And if this is allowed to occur too quickly the heart may become temporarily weaker than normal while these changes are going on, and harm may be done. In fact, every doctor sees such a case now and then.

In a little talk like this it is of course impossible to tell you many things I would like to, but if I have succeeded in exciting your interest in your own bodies I will be very much pleased; and I am sure you will be able to get any special information from your teachers. You will also, I hope, take more interest in the instruction given you in physiology, for what can be more important for a man or woman than to know all about his or her body and how to care for it?

THE TRAINING OF AN ELECTRICAL EXPERT

PROFESSOR E. P. FETHERSTONHAUGH
University of Manitoba

I am here today to tell you something about electricity and the electrical industry and also to talk to you about the education that a man must have if he is to become an expert in this line of work. At the age you have now reached you should be beginning to plan your training for some branch of work, and I must impress on you the necessity of taking advantage of every opportunity in the way of education that is available, no matter what kind of work you are going in for. In these days of strenuous competition it is only the man with the highest qualifications who can reach the highest positions. In electrical work there are many such positions to be had, and, if we look forward to the future of this Province with its magnificent water powers and the many systems of electrical railways, city lighting, power plants, and industries to be operated by electricity, we cannot fail to realize that a high degree of training will be required by the men who are to occupy the best positions in these industries.

In order that you may have some definite idea of what electricity can be made to do, I have brought with me some simple pieces of apparatus which can be made by any boy at home, and which illustrate the fundamental principles of electrical science. I will first show you how an electric battery can be made. If you take a glass jar about the size of this one I have, and place in it six ounces of sal-ammoniac, and then fill it about two-thirds full of water, and place in it a piece of carbon and a piece of zinc, you have a simple electric battery, and if you take two wires and connect one to the zinc and the other to the carbon and touch them together, a current of electricity will flow through them. This current may be made stronger by connecting two cells together, that is, connecting the carbon of one to the zinc of the other, and then connecting the outside carbon and zinc to whatever you are going to use the electricity on.

Now let us see what we can do with this current that we have available. You will notice that this needle, which is a piece of hard steel which has been magnetized, always points in one direction, that is, toward the north pole. This is because the earth is a magnet and the north pole of the earth attracts one end of this needle, and the south pole attracts the other. The end of the magnet which points toward the north pole is called the north pole of the magnet and the other end is called the south pole. This needle is a permanent magnet, but we can also make magnets which are not permanent, these being made from soft iron instead of steel. If I take this coil, which consists of 200 turns of insulated copper wire, and place it around this U-shaped piece of soft iron, and then send a current of electricity from the battery through the coil, the U-shaped iron will become a magnet and you will see that it can lift a piece of iron of considerable size. If I disconnect it from the battery it loses its magnetism immediately and the piece of iron will fall. This is called an electro-magnet. One of its ends will be a north pole and the other a south pole; but if I connect the coil to the battery in the reverse direction so that the current flows in the opposite direction around the magnet, the end which was previously a north pole now becomes a south pole. A north pole of one magnet will attract a south pole of another magnet and will repel a north pole of another magnet and it is on this principle that all electric motors are operated. An electric motor in its simplest form consists of two magnets, one of which is always magnetized in the same direction and is called a field magnet, and another which is arranged to revolve between the ends of the field magnet and has an arrangement called a commutator which, as it revolves, changes the direction of the current passing through its winding in such a way that just as its north pole has reached a south pole of the field magnet, the polarity is reversed and therefore the south pole of the field magnet repels the south pole of the revolving magnet, or armature as it is called, and thus it is made to revolve continuously. A motor built on this principle can be made very powerful and will drive machinery by connecting its shaft directly to the machine to be driven or by means of a pulley and belt.

A peculiar fact about this machine is that if it is driven by some outside force, for instance if you revolve it by hand, it would generate or produce a current of electricity. So you see a dynamo or generator is just the same machine as a motor, the only difference being that the motor is supplied with electricity and produces mechanical power and the generator is supplied with mechanical power and produces electricity. It would be too expensive to generate electricity for large lighting systems by means of batteries such as I have described above and consequently we get all our electricity from these machines called generators, which are driven either by steam engines, by hydraulic turbines, or by gas engines. In the electric plants at Lac du Bonnet and at

Point du Bois, from which we get our city supply of electricity, very large generators of thousands of horse-power capacity are used and as the voltage which these generators supply is very high, and the mechanism by which the current is conducted from the generators to the transformers and from the transformers to the transmission line is very intricate and complicated, and since the one essential in a plant such as this serving a large community is to avoid a shut-down or interruption to the service, you will realize the necessity for having such plants designed by very competent experts and operated by highly skilled engineers. The same applies to motors in machine shops and to all sorts of electrical machinery on which our various industries depend, and if you are thinking of going in for electrical work the question is "How is the necessary knowledge to be obtained?" In answer to this my first advice would be to stay at school until you have finished your school course and taken every advantage that the schools in our city are now so well able to afford. The next step would be to take a course in electrical engineering at a university if this is possible, as such a training affords the best opportunities for getting a knowledge of all the underlying principles forming the foundation of this profession. If you cannot take a university course you can enter the services of some electrical company and learn by experience a great many of the practical applications of electrical principles, and if you study at home and take advantage of night classes and read the technical papers you can acquire a very fair knowledge of the subject, but let me impress upon you the fact that whether you gain your knowledge through a university course or through the school of experience, it is only by hard work and continuous study that you can become an expert in electrical work.

THE POSSIBILITIES FOR SUCCESS IN RAILWAY WORK

GEORGE BURY
Vice-President and General Manager of Canadian Pacific Railway

Ordinarily, every boy is fitted to attain success in some walk of life. Before deciding on his life work, a boy should endeavor to learn for himself what thing he is best adapted for and then follow that line. Should he feel that his future lies in railway work there are many avenues he might enter and follow to success.

Before entering the service of the railway, a boy should have a good common school education, and if he determines to be successful, he should, at the outset, endeavor to make himself master of the details of the position he enters upon.

A straightforward, manly disposition counts for almost more than anything in attaining success in life. Every man having a reputation for integrity, thoroughness, perseverance, and loyalty is eagerly sought after by all employers.

Having determined to enter railway service, there are many avenues which might be followed. If a boy determines that his natural inclination is for mechanics, he might enter as an apprentice and, depending on the trade selected, would in the course of four or five years become a full-fledged mechanic.

Having learned the mechanical trade, if ambitious, he would in a short time be promoted to an assistant foreman, from that to foreman, district master mechanic, master mechanic, superintendent of motive power, and finally general manager, as is witnessed by the career of Mr. Hall, the present General Manager of Western Lines.

Now, it would naturally occur to you that while there are thousands of mechanics, there is only one general manager, but it must be remembered that there are a great many foremen, assistant foremen, master mechanics, etc., and that a number of men having reached the position of tradesman are satisfied to remain there, because, following the lines of least resistance, it is easier to be free of responsibility at the end of the day's work rather than to attend night school and study with a view to fitting oneself for the higher positions.

If engineering appeals to a boy, and his parents are not in a position to afford a regular college course, he might enter the service as a rodman, at a salary of forty dollars per month and his board, and work up to the position of civil engineer, studying mathematics and engineering generally in his spare time, so that his actual and technical experience would in time fit him for the position he was aiming at. Once having become a civil engineer, every position on a railway is open to him.

If the train service appeals to him, he might enter the yard office in a clerical capacity until he was twenty-one years of age, when he could adopt yard or train work, beginning as a brakesman. The wonderful growth of Canada is such that the number of men in train service will be continually added to, and as the Canadian Pacific Railway follows the practice of promoting its own men, it would be only three years, or four at the outside, before he would be promoted to the position of freight train conductor, or, if he entered the yard service, the position of yardmaster. Having arrived at the position of yardmaster or trainmaster, every position in the railway service is within his reach.

If a boy prefers an outdoor life entirely and thought of entering the maintenance of way department when becoming full grown, he could enter the service as a section man and quickly be promoted to section foreman, and if he studied, was observant, and fitted himself, would quickly be promoted to the position of roadmaster, or, if he entered as a carpenter, might find himself promoted to the position of bridge and building master.

If instead of an outdoor life he preferred indoor work, there are two channels by which he might enter. He could either fit himself as a stenographer or enter as an agent's assistant and learn telegraphy. If he determines that he has a natural aptitude for clerical work, having perfected himself in stenography, he would have no trouble in securing a position in the railway service. Once having secured a position as a stenographer, if he studied and determined to succeed, his promotion in the West, where the growth is so great at the present time, would be very fast. Having entered the service as a stenographer, if he had a good address, became proficient in taking notes and transcribing them accurately, he would very quickly be picked up as secretary to some officer, and in that position he would learn the details of the work of administrative duties, and quickly fit himself for an official position, his ability, honesty, perseverance, and personality being the only limit to his advancement.

Should he determine to climb the ladder through the station service, he would begin work as a station assistant. During his spare hours he would learn telegraphy, and inside of a year from entering the service, he would be fitted to take a small office as operator. From that he would in turn be promoted to a station agency at a small station, then advance to the larger stations, and, if he displayed the necessary qualifications, would be picked up and placed in the traffic department, beginning as a traveler and winding up as a chief officer.

Or if the transportation side appealed to him more than the commercial, he would in time be transferred from station agent to the position of train dispatcher, and from that to chief train dispatcher, trainmaster, superintendent, and so on.

It will naturally be said that there are few official positions and that the opportunities are few and far between for advancement. I would point out, however, that the President of our Company, Sir Thomas G. Shaughnessy, began work as a clerk in the Stores Department, that the General Manager of Western Lines, Mr. Hall, began his career as a machinist's apprentice. We have four General Superintendents: Mr. Coleman, who has just recently been appointed in charge of the Manitoba Division, began as a stenographer, and his salary twelve years ago was $40 per month. The General Superintendent of the Saskatchewan Division began as a clerk in the Mechanical Department. The General Superintendent of the Alberta Division began as a telegraph operator. The General Superintendent of the British Columbia Division began as a clerk. Every officer on the Canadian Pacific Railway began in the service in a junior position and worked his way to his present position.

It will probably surprise you to know that I am continually looking around for officers and that most of the other Western Railways are doing the same thing. If there is a vacancy for a superintendent, for instance, a list of all the trainmasters, district master mechanics, roadmasters, chief train dispatchers and chief clerks is made out, with their age, the date they entered the service, etc. This list is then gone over with a view to determining which would be the most suitable man for the position.

First, the characters of the different men are discussed and those who are known to be lacking in courtesy are struck off the list. Of the remainder, it is determined that some have not endeavored to fit themselves for promotion to the vacant position, not having improved on earlier defects in education, and their names have to go by the board. Of the names left, it is found that some are lacking in the moral courage necessary to handle large bodies of men, or are without initiative, resourcefulness, or are lacking in ambition, and their names are struck off, so that it finally comes down that there are but a few considered eligible. When it is narrowed down to this, the man who is senior in the service is given the position.

It may be truthfully said that a man's future rests almost entirely with himself. There is no use in denying that luck sometimes enters into a man's success, but I am not much of a believer in luck, because opportunity, in the West at any rate, will come to all boys, and those who have fitted themselves to take advantage of the opportunity that presents itself will be thought to be lucky.

I think that all boys should stay at school until they are well grounded. It is, of course, to be expected that through unfortunate circumstances some boys will have to leave school earlier than is good for them—too early to receive a good grounding, but then these boys who are so unfortunately placed should take advantage of their spare hours to make up for the loss in their education from having been compelled to leave school too early.

The world is certainly becoming better all the time, and the relations generally between men and their employers are better than ever before.

THE LITHOGRAPHING TRADE

W. J. BULMAN

Of Bulman Bros., Ltd., Winnipeg, President of the Winnipeg Industrial Bureau

Now, boys, I want to tell you about a business that depends upon something which was known from the beginning of the world but was never applied to printing until the year 1789. You all know grease and water will not mix, don't you? Well now, just because they don't mix, lithographers can make the colored pictures you see and a great many other forms of printing which you would never guess depend entirely upon that one fact. Don't you think it strange that thousands of years should elapse, and millions of men live and pass away with this fact known to them, and yet the great industry of lithography had to wait for a German named Aloys Sennefelder to discover how to use it, and while improvements in machinery and methods have taken place, still the great idea of how to use the fact was his? And, boys, upon just such little facts most of the great industries find their base, and maybe some one of you when you grow up will adopt some little truth you learn and discover an invention upon which some great industry employing thousands of men will grow up, and the world be richer for your having lived. I have brought with me a little piece of what we call lithographic stone. It is a limestone and is found in Bavaria. This stone is of a fine grain, and if you put grease upon it, it is able to absorb enough of it to make a greasy spot, and then if water is put upon it, it also absorbs a little of that where it is not greasy. Now, you can imagine what takes place. Here is a greasy line, the rest of the stone is damped with water and we take a roller covered with printing ink and roll it over the stone; what happens is this: the ink being of a greasy nature adheres to the greasy line but will not stick to the damp parts of the stone because the water is there. The part of the roller which touches the line gives up some of its ink, but on the part which touches the damp places, the water comes between and the ink does not dirty the stone, it just stays on the roller. Now, the line having ink on it, it only remains to put paper on that and something to squeeze it down hard, and when we lift it off there is a print of the line on the paper. That is the process. But, boys, it takes great skill to take greasy ink and draw beautiful things on the stone, so it is hard to get lithographic artists. That is a trade by itself, and if you ever learn to be a lithographic artist you can be certain that if you are very skilful every employer in the land will try to obtain your services, and you can command a very good salary. But if you are an ordinary workman you will get about $20.00 per week and if you are a poor one you will not get any more than you could earn with a pick and shovel. The same is true of the engravers, the men who with a tool, very like a lead pencil, but having steel instead of the lead, cut lines, etc., into the stone's surface, and fill them in with ink. This is the way all the finest stationery is printed. In this art there is a very great demand for good men and they are as well paid as the artists; but again if you are only an incapable workman the result is "pick-and-shovel" wages. The same is true in every department of lithography, and, boys, when you grow up you will learn it to be true of every trade or calling. Whether you can make life pleasant and comfortable not only for yourself, but for all that may depend upon you, depends right now upon your earnest effort to study, and a little later, on choosing a calling and then applying what you have learned, giving your whole self to your work. If you do this, your reward is sure.

I am very anxious that you will grow up earnest workers to make this, your home city, famous as the place where the best workmen are found. It can be done only by forming the habit of being perfect in your work. Remember that you will commit the greatest crime possible if you leave school too soon, for you then kill your own possible future. Think of what must be learned in this trade. Every engraver ought to know enough geometry to make the perspective correct when he has to engrave a building or other picture. Every artist must also have some knowledge of geometry, and if he is to be a superior workman he should read a great deal to gather ideas and fit himself to apply suitable designs to all sorts of business. The man who prints what the artist draws should have a knowledge of chemistry, an understanding of mechanics to take care of his machine, and a knowledge of color mixing. Then there is a trade we call that of the transferrer. He is a man that can take prints from the artists' and engravers' work and transfer them to another stone. I will show you a sheet of labels. You see the artist drew only one label, but the transferrer has made a great many prints of that and stuck his prints upon a sheet of paper in the form required to fill this large sheet. He then turned them face down onto a clean stone and applied pressure, so transferring the wet ink to the new stone. After preparing it is then printed by the printers as you see it.

I will explain how the printing of colored pictures is done. The artist first paints a picture complete, which is submitted to the man who wants to buy such a picture. After the buyer approves of it, the artist lays upon the painting a sheet of transparent gelatine and traces with a sharp point an outline, the point making a scratch in the gelatine. This scratch is then filled in with ink by the transferrer and the gelatine is damped, then squeezed upon a stone so as to transfer the outline. This outline is then printed on a few sheets of paper and while the ink is wet a red chalk is dusted over it; this sticks only to the wet ink and is shaken off every other part of the paper. Next these sheets are placed each upon a clean stone and squeezed so as to make a chalk mark of the outline, and these stones are given to the artist, who proceeds to draw carefully to these outlines all the yellow there is in the picture, like the sheet I am showing you, then he draws all the red on another stone, all the blue on another until he has all the colors needed to perfect this picture and make it just like the original painting. The printer prints from these stones one at a time, namely, all the yellow first, the red next, and so on. You remember what I said before about grease and water; well, the presses have flannel rollers which are kept damp and they run over the stone, then after these, rollers covered with leather and the leather covered with printing ink also run over the stone. The water not going where the greasy design is, and the ink not going where the water is, leaves it so that when the work is all inked, a cylinder pressing a sheet of paper on the stone makes the ink mark the paper as you see. It is very simple, but, boys, most things men work at are simple, that is, each operation is a simple one. Men grow up from boys and, strange to say, they don't change much. It only seems that the able, useful, and successful men are boys that are willing to plug hard and work hard practicing, who are not soft-headed enough to let fun and pleasure take all the time, but study hard and work earnestly at whatever they undertake. The Bible says "Whatever your hands find to do, do it with your might." That is the key to success today, and remember, boys, you have not only to use your might of muscle, but the more important might of brain; for it is of little use to have the muscular power of an elephant, but of tremendous use to have the power of mind of a Newton. This immensely valuable faculty of mind you are cultivating in school and as your time is short, your teachers are trying to give you the keys to many departments of knowledge, so that you can use them in after life and get at what you want to make success. I have one thought I want you to remember: Without knowledge you cannot be a good workman, and if you are not a good workman, you and all depending upon you are condemned to that horrible life of the inefficient, filled with unspeakable irritations and despair.

A TEACHER-TRAINING EXPERIMENT EVOLVED BY THE SCHOOL AUTHORITIES OF LIMA, OHIO

JOHN DAVISON
Superintendent of Schools

A plan has been evolved at Lima, Ohio, for the special training of elementary teachers for the city schools, which has been in practical operation under my personal supervision for more than eight years. By this plan the preparing of young and inexperienced teachers for their work in the primary grades is carried on successfully without any additional cost to the city. Two separate rooms in the Garfield Building, containing the second and third grades respectively, are under the direct personal supervision of a special instructor who receives the combined salaries of the two grades and acts as training teacher.

Since the beginning of the present school administration at Lima, nearly nine years ago, from eight to twelve apprentice teachers have been selected from the training class each year, the requirements for admission being as follows: (1) The applicant must be a graduate of the Lima High School, or of some other school of equal rank with that of Lima, or have had an education equal to the four-year course given in Lima High School. (2) The applicant must have passed satisfactorily the Lima city teachers' examination for an elementary certificate. (3) The applicant must be appointed to membership in the training school by the Superintendent of Schools and the appointment must be regularly confirmed by the board of education.

The training course is one year in length. During this time each student spends at least two months in each of the two grades, one month as assistant, and one month in actual practice teaching. The assistant must observe the teaching of the training teacher, assist in directing seat work, and become familiar with all reports required by the superintendent and with the ordinary routine of the classroom. After the student-teacher has mastered these requirements so that she feels free in the presence of the class, she begins to teach under the close supervision of the training teacher. Outlines of every lesson given must be prepared at first with the direct help of the training teacher, but later without assistance. These lesson plans are always carefully criticized before they are used in the class. After the lesson is given, the training teacher indicates the causes of success or failure, placing special emphasis on all the good points, thus giving all the encouragement that may be necessary in order to secure the best results.

When the student-teacher is not engaged in teaching or assisting, she is required to spend her time in observing the work of some of the best teachers in the city. She spends two or three days with the same teacher, writing out in full a lesson plan of each branch taught in that grade. The training teacher reads all these plans, discusses them in class, and answers such questions as the training class may ask regarding the work observed.

One hour each day is given to class recitation in the training school throughout the entire year. During the year, thirty-five hours are given to psychology, forty hours to school management, twenty hours to the history of education, thirty-five hours to public-school music, and the remaining time, about fifty-five hours, to lectures and discussions by the training teacher on methods of teaching the various subjects in the first four grades.

The two classrooms under the supervision of the training teacher are adjacent, so that the work of the apprentice-teachers can be easily observed and, if not well done, corrected before any harm is done to the children in the school.

After completing the year's work in the training school, the apprentice-teachers are appointed by the superintendent to regular and substitute positions in the instruction corps, according to the degree of proficiency shown in the training class and attested by the results of the city teachers' examination.

In my judgment this experiment may be regarded as having been very successful in this city. The children are taught fully as well in the training school as in other rooms of the same grades throughout the city. In fact, better results are often secured there than elsewhere, so far as the children are concerned. In the course of my term as superintendent, I have had the opportunity to try out a number of groups as regular teachers, made up of those who had served the apprenticeship in the training school. I have discerned in my regular visits of inspection to the schools under their charge ample evidence in their teaching that they have profited largely by that apprenticeship. We are greatly pleased with the results of the experiment and intend to continue the plan.

A HOME GEOGRAPHY LESSON FOR A CITY SCHOOL

HOW THE PEOPLE OF A LARGE CITY ARE SUPPLIED WITH WATER

R. C. PECK
McKinley Manual Training School, Washington, D.C.

[The following article comprises the notes on a lesson which has been used in elementary science in the first semester's work in the high school. It is typical of the attempt which is being widely made in the elementary science work of both the high school and the elementary school to correlate and unify the various branches of science by basing the lessons upon concrete situations. The lesson here described shows in detail how one particular situation may be used as an occasion for the discovery and application of laws of physics, biology, economics, geology, etc. It may serve as an example, not to be followed in detail, but to furnish a stimulus to each science teacher to work out his own problem so as to meet the needs of his community.—EDITOR.]

When hunters are choosing a site for camp, they try to find one near a spring or stream of clear water and this is one of the things the early settlers always had to think about when they built their cabins and made their clearings. When the water of the spring was not easy to dip up, it was found a great help to dig a hole and set a barrel in it with the bottom knocked out. This kept the dirt from filling the hole and made a deep hollow which soon filled up with clear water. If no spring was convenient, they sometimes reached underground water by digging the holes deeper and lining them with stones. Thus every farm house had its own spring or well.

Would you like to live in a city that had to depend on such wells? What inconvenience would this cause us, especially when the well was deep? Are shallow wells safe, especially when a stable is near?

In villages people often have high tanks which they fill by means of pumps which are driven by windmills or engines of some sort. From these tanks the water runs to the faucets in pipes, the pressure of the water outside pushing that within the house up as high as the water in the tank. (Illustrate with a funnel with tube and nozzle attached.) Would this do for a large city? Would the water rate your father pays dig such a well and buy an engine and pump? Could several neighbors save expense by building one large tank together? Could a tank be built large enough for a whole town? What is a standpipe?

Tanks large enough to supply a town with water are sometimes built, but if there are hills, there is a better way. What could a farmer do if he had a hill full of springs near his house? Is there a large reservoir in your city? Is it in the upper or lower part of the town? How is it kept full of water?

What never-failing source of water supply has Washington near at hand? Is the Potomac River water at the wharves fit to drink? Would it not be a great saving of expense if we could get the water into the reservoir without pumping it? Would we have to go far upstream to find the water as high as most of the city? Why are there so many locks in the canal which skirts the river? Why are there so many rapids? Where is the descent so rapid that locks had to be built even in Washington's time to let the flat boats get up the river?

In Roman times great cities were often supplied by aqueducts or overhead canals bringing the water from some distant mountain lake or river. Some such idea seems to be suggested in a little book written by the private secretary of George Washington, in which it is proposed to bring the water from above Great Falls by a canal kept high up back among the hills and then extended out over the city. May not Washington have had this in mind in choosing the site of the city? Nothing was done about it until shortly before the Civil War when a conduit or covered canal was built, sometimes by tunneling through the hills and in one place by crossing a stream at Cabin John Bridge. The canal ended in the Macmillan Park reservoir, from which the water is drawn to be filtered and distributed to the city.

A comparison with the water-supply of other cities naturally follows, especially with those similarly located on the "fall line." Interest is aroused in the cause of the remarkable change in the character of the river and surrounding country at Washington, and in the historical geology of the region. Opportunity for the discussion of a number of economic and social problems is given. A further study of the filtration problem introduces the question of disease prevention, and the pumping plant and distribution system prepares the way for some elementary physics.

BOOK REVIEWS

Story Telling in School and Home. By EMELYN NEWCOMB PARTRIDGE and GEORGE EVERETT PARTRIDGE. New York: Sturgis & Walton Co. Pp. 319. $1.25.

One author has selected a large number of well-chosen children's stories; the other has evolved the elements of a science of story-telling. The book is exceedingly helpful and suggestive for grade teachers and for mothers.

The Swallow Book. By DR. GUISEPPE PITRE, University of Palermo. Translated by ADA WALKER CUMEHL. New York: American Book Co. Pp. 158. $0.35.

This supplementary reader for the upper grammar grades consists of an introductory chapter describing the swallow, followed by a collection of interesting myths, legends, fables, folk-songs, proverbs, and superstitions of many lands about swallows. The aim is to teach the story of this particular bird and to cultivate the imagination and the power of observation of the reader.

A Dickens Dramatic Reader. By FANNY COMSTOCK. Boston: Ginn & Co. Pp. 338. $0.60.

In this book the author has dramatized many scenes from the *Pickwick Papers*, *Nicholas Nickleby*, *The Cricket on the Hearth*, and *A Christmas Carol.* Stage directions are full and explicit; but the characters speak the language Dickens gave them. With the possible exception of Pickwick, the works chosen are the most appropriate of Dickens for junior readers. The dramatic form, eliminating as it does much description, serves as an attractive introduction to young readers.

Primary School Reader III. By WILLIAM H. ELSON. Chicago: Scott Foresman & Co. Pp. 287. $0.45.

A primary reader with many fresh stories. The grouping is especially suggestive. The tales are grouped as follows: Fairies, Fables, Folk Tales, Children, Legends, Festivals, Patriotism, Heroes, Nature, Fairy Tales.

Little Dramas for Primary Grades. By ADA MARIA SKINNER and LILLIAN NIXON LAURENCE. New York: American Book Co. Pp. 176. $0.35.

Plays for the third school year derived largely from well-known prose and poetical selections. The plays may be acted by the children or may be used simply as reading-lessons. The book is well illustrated for children.

Stories from the Far East. Translated by ROLAND G. KENT and I. FREEMAN HALL. New York: Charles E. Merrill Co. Illustrated. Pp. 153. $0.30.

A unique story book. The stories are two thousand years old, translated from the Sanskrit, each dealing with some sort of animal life. The book is suitable for the lower grades and for the nursery.

Southern Literary Readings. Edited by LEONIDAS WARREN PAYNE. Chicago: Rand McNally & Co. Pp. vii+487. $0.75.

A reader for grades 7 to 11, selecting the best in southern literature that is suited to the interests of young readers. This is a book that should find wide use in the public schools of the South. The full notes make this book suitable even for classes in college English.

The Dramatic Method of Teaching. By HARRIET FINLAY JOHNSON. Edited by ELLEN M. CYR. Boston: Ginn & Co. Pp. v+199. $1.00.

This book ought to be in the hands of every elementary-school teacher. It is a vigorous exposition of vitalizing methods which are rapidly making their way into our schools. The characters of history, of literature, are made to live again in the eyes of the children.

The Second Book of Stories for the Story Teller. By FANNY E. COE. Boston: Houghton Mifflin Co. Pp. iii+209. $0.80.

A book full of delightful stories well selected for variety and interest: folk tales, modern fairy tales, myths, and stories from real life make up the contents. The *moral virtues* are emphasized by the subject-matter.

The Jatakas, Tales of India. Retold by ELLEN C. BABBITT. New York: Century Co. Pp. vii+92. $0.40 net.

Miss Babbitt has selected some of the tales of the sacred books of the Buddhists, and retold them in style suitable for children. A distinctive feature of the book is the method of illustration. It includes forty-two illustrations in silhouette by Ellsworth Young.

R. L. LYMAN

UNIVERSITY OF CHICAGO

The Posture of School Children. By JESSIE H. BANCROFT. New York: Macmillan. Pp. xii+327. $1.50.

At first thought it seems impossible to fill a book with a discussion of this subject and not deal with technical details. Yet when you turn over the twelve pages of bibliography at the close of the volume, citations of titles that deal with varying phases of it, the manifold bearings of posture on health and efficiency are apparent at a glance. "Erect carriage of the body is necessary (1) for full vigor and health, (2) to prevent waste of energy in maintaining the upright position in any of the activities of life, (3) with children, to admit of proper growth and development." In chap. ii, on "How to Judge of Correct and Incorrect Posture," the vertical line test is advocated: "The long axis or diameter of the trunk of the body is a perfectly vertical line; the long axis of the neck and head taken together is also a vertical line. In poor postures the axes of these main segments of the body, instead of forming one continuous, vertical line, are broken into two or three zigzag lines." To assist the eye in detecting these poor postures "a line may be dropped from the front of the ear to the forward part of the foot." The long axes of head, neck, and trunk should parallel this vertical line. The directions for assuming the correct standing position are simple: "Stretch the arms directly sidewise at shoulder level, with the palms turned downward, and holding the arms there, sway forward from the ankle so that the weight is nearly or quite over the balls of the feet, not, however, rising on the toes, but keeping the heels on the ground." Draw the chin inward. Keep head, chest, and shoulders as this places them and drop the arms to the side. This will leave the body in correct standing position. Attention is called in chap. iii to the fact that man in the course of his evolution has only recently (speaking in geological terms) learned to assume the erect position. There are still many of his anatomical features that make it a difficult task. Hence the necessity for teaching children how to do it. Chapters iv–x inclusive discuss the correct attitudes of spine, head, chest, shoulders, abdomen. Chaps. xiii and xiv are on methods of correcting poor posture; xv on the hygiene of posture. Then several chapters are devoted to achieving correct postures of children in school, and the hygiene of school postures. Many illustrations are repeated in the book, and considerable subject-matter. The impression is left that the book might have been condensed without losing any of its value. Otherwise it is a valuable presentation of an important matter. Not the least valuable part of it is the appendix in which are quoted summaries of several recent investigations of attitudes, dress, and pathological results of wrong postures.

An Introduction to the Study of Social Evolution, the Prehistoric Period. By F. Stuart Chapin. New York: Century Co. Pp. xxii+306. $2.00.

"The object of this book is to present in elementary form a summary of the most generally accepted evidence and theory of social evolution." The book opens with a presentation of some of the biological evidences of man's evolution and of a modified Darwinism as the probable method. The book shares the fault of all social and educational works that attempt to present a biological foundation. Biology advances with such rapidity that before chapters can be printed they are erroneous. Thus on p. 8 in discussing variation the author says: "A consistent increase in asymmetry or skewness of the curve . . . . must mean that the species is moving in a definite direction." This in connection with a discussion of the heights of American school boys. Now we know that Johannsen's work on pure line cultures quite discredits such an interpretation. The author adopts Darwinism. "This in brief is Darwin's famous doctrine of the origin of species by descent under the influence of natural selection. It is the core of the theory of evolution." He is aware of de Vries's work and Mendel's results and discusses them, but does not appear to realize their bearing upon modern biological thought. To avoid the difficulty of the non-inheritance of acquired characters, he adopts the antiquated theory of organic selection. Orthogenesis is apparently an unconsidered possibility. With so weak an introductory discussion of the biological factors involved, a biologist hesitates to commend in point of accuracy the rest of the book. It is interesting, however, and stimulating. The chapter (iii) on the origin and antiquity of man includes Dawson and Woodward's discovery at Pittdown, England, in 1912, of the skull fragments of a man, and this whole chapter is very clearly and ably written. Through the Paleolithic and Neolithic ages man is traced by the remains of his utensils and implements, his dwellings and monuments. The remainder of the book deals rather with mental and social evolution than with the material basis. Chap. iv is on associations, showing how gregariousness produced necessary changes in social structures. Chap. v deals with the influences of environment on society and the direction of historic events. Chap. vi deals with social heredity. Chap vii, one of the most interesting chapters, traces the origin of races. The author adopts Giddings' notion that the white race "is the variable plastic race coming down from the earliest paleolithic times." From maps showing present distribution of the races there appears to be a zone extending from Java on the southeast to the valley of Thames on the northwest which marks their separation and which also includes the regions where have been found the remains of the primitive races. This seems the probable original habitat of primitive man. Finally, chaps. viii and ix deal with tribal society and the transition from this to the modern social organization. On the whole, the book is an attractive presentation of man's social progress from the beast that has just arrived at human level to man who begins to make history. Its accuracy is all that could be expected in a book dealing with such unsettled matters.

E. R. D.

UNIVERSITY OF CHICAGO

The Marking System in Theory and Practice. By J. E. FINKELSTEIN. ("Educational Psychological Monographs.") Baltimore: Warwick & York, 1913. Pp. 2+88. $1.00.

A brief theoretical discussion of the marking system and a display of the distribution of a large number of marks given in Cornell University. Among the distinctive conclusions of the author are the belief that the marks should be based upon accomplishment (performance in examinations plus other evidence of the student's real knowledge or skill) rather than ability; that effort or zeal is to be regarded as a separate factor from ability and as one which when present produces a proportionately greater effect in the upper than in the lower ranges; and that as a consequence of these facts and of the fact that greater incentive to effort is present in the case of the mediocre than of the superior student, the curve of distribution should be skewed to the right. To the reviewer it would appear that the assumed disproportionate effect of effort and the different power of incentives with poorer and better students should neutralize rather than reinforce each other. Many interesting and typical illustrations of deviations in practice in the marking of different instructors or departments are given.

F. N. F.

BOOKS RECEIVED

AMERICAN BOOK CO., CHICAGO

Die sieben Reisen Sinbads des Seemannes. By ALBERT LUDWIG GRIMM. Edited with notes, exercises, and vocabulary by K. C. H. DRECHSEL, A.M. Cloth. Illustrated. Pp. 188. Price $0.40.

John Bunyan's Dream Story. By JAMES BALDWIN. Cloth. Illustrated. Pp. 198. Price $0.35.

Kwahu: The Hopi Indian Boy. By GEORGE NEWELL MORAN. Cloth. Illustrated. Pp. 237. Price $0.50.

The Art of Writing English. By ROLLO WALTER BROWN and NATHANIEL WARING BARNES. Cloth. Pp. 382. Price $1.20.

LITTLE, BROWN & CO., BOSTON

Colette in France. By ETTA BLAISDELL MCDONALD. Cloth. Illustrated. Pp. 120. Price $0.45.

Indian Child Life. By CHARLES A. EASTMAN (OHIYESA). Cloth. Illustrated. Pp. 160. Price $0.50.

Twilight Town. By MARY FRANCES BLAISDELL. Cloth. Illustrated. Pp. 173. Price $0.40.

The Wide Awake Fourth Reader. By CLARA MURRAY. Cloth. Illustrated. Pp. 329. Price $0.50.

THE MACMILLAN CO., NEW YORK

The Facts about Shakespeare. By WILLIAM ALLAN NEILSON, PH.D., and ASHLEY HORACE THORNDIKE, PH.D., L.H.D. Cloth. Pp. 273. Price $0.60.

Principles of Secondary Education. Vol. I. *Basic Ideals: The Studies.* By CHARLES DE GARMO. Cloth. Pp. 338. Price $1.00 net.

ORANGE JUDD CO., NEW YORK

Soils and Crops. By THOMAS FORSYTH HUNT and CHARLES WILLIAM BURKETT. Cloth. Illustrated. Pp. 541.

UNIVERSITY OF PITTSBURGH, PITTSBURGH

Psychological Aspects of the Problem of Atmospheric Smoke Pollution. By J. E. WALLACE WALLIN, PH.D. Paper.

TEACHERS COLLEGE, NEW YORK

School Health Administration. By LOUIS W. RAPEER, M.A., PH.D. Cloth. Pp. 360. Price $2.15.

THE W. E. RICHARDSON CO., CHICAGO

The Montesorri Manual. By DOROTHY CANFIELD FISHER. Cloth. Pp. 126. Price $1.25 net.

CURRENT EDUCATIONAL LITERATURE IN THE PERIODICALS[1]

IRENE WARREN
Librarian, School of Education, University of Chicago

Army and navy condemnation of football. Lit. D. 47:941. (15 N. '13.)

Backward children and forward teachers. A symposium. Train. School M. (N.J.) 10:97–104. (N. '13.)

Bidwell, Alice T. A course in letter-writing. English J. 2:562–66. (N. '13.)

Bobbitt, J. F., Boyce, A. C., and Perkins, M. L. Literature in the elementary curriculum. El. School T. 14:158–66. (D. '13.)

(A) book-mark to save eyesight. Lit. D. 47:1003. (22 N. '13.)

Bostwick, Arthur E. The making of an American library. III. Bookman 38:399–404. (D. '13.)

Brown, Horace G. Efficiency in teaching by pictures. Educa. 34:171–78. (N. '13.)

Canby, Henry Seidel. The luxury of being educated. Harper 128:68–74. (D. '13.)

Carpenter, D. F. Mental age tests. J. of Educa. Psychol. 4:538–44. (N. '13.)

Child-life in Palestine. Liv. Age 269:437–41. (15 N. '13.)

(A) Chinese Helen Keller. Lit. D. 47:876–77. (8 N. '13.)

Churchman, P. H. The place of study on the curriculum. Pop. Sci. Mo. 83:567–80. (D. '13.)

Coover, J. Edgar. The Union High School questionnaires. Educa. 34:153–61. (N. '13.)

(The) Daniel Boone idea in education. A school system based on voluntary work. Sci. Am. 109:361, 370–71. (8 N. '13.)

Eliot, Charles W. Governmental mothering. Harp. W. 58:14. (15 N. '14.)

Fee, Mary Helen. Teaching English to Filipinos. English J. 2:539–45. (N. '13.)

Freeman, Frank N. Some practical studies of handwriting. El. School T. 14:167–79. (D. '13.)

Gosling, Thomas Warrington. Tobacco and scholarship. School R. 21: 690–93. (D. '13.)

[1] *Abbreviations.*—Atlan., Atlantic Monthly; Educa., Education; El. School T., Elementary School Teacher; English J., English Journal; Harp. W., Harper's Weekly; J. of Educa. Psychol., Journal of Educational Psychology; Lit. D., Literary Digest; Liv. Age, Living Age; Pop. Sci. Mo., Popular Science Monthly; Psychol. Clinc., Psychological Clinic; School R., School Review; Sci. Am., Scientific American; Train. School M. (N.J.), Training School Magazine (New Jersey); U.S. Bur. of Educa. Bull., United States Bureau of Education Bulletin.

Grady, William E. Measuring efficiency of instruction. Psychol. Clinic 7:145–52. (N. '13.)

Hoffman, Frederick L. Some vital statistics of children of school age. School R. 21:657–69. (D. '13.)

Huey, E. B. The education of defectives and the training of teachers for special classes. J. of Educa. Psychol. 4:545–50. (N. '13.)

Inaccessible museums. Lit. D. 47:1005–6. (22 N. '13.)

Locard, Frederic. The study of French in the public high schools of the United States. School R. 21:682–89. (D. '13.)

Mauller, C. T. A solution for public speaking in the high school. Educa. 34:162–68. (N. '13.)

Melbourne, Margaret. Children and the theatre. Home Progress 3:68–71. (O. '13.)

Miller, Kelly. Moral pedagogy. Educa. 34:133–44. (N. '13.)

Minnick, J. H. An experiment in the supervised study of mathematics. School R. 21:670–75. (D. '13.)

Moore, Charles Leonard. On education. Dial 55:395–97. (16 N. '13.)

Parker, S. Chester. Bibliographies, briefs, and oral exposition in normal schools. English J. 2:546–50. (N. '13.)

Paton, Stewart. The essentials of an education. Science 38:758–62. (28 N. '13.)

Reavis, W. C. The interests of children of the primary and intermediate grades in the use of color. El. School T. 14:180–86. (D. '13.)

Rihbany, Abraham Mitrie. At the feet of my teachers. Atlan. 112:791–801. (D. '13.)

Scott, Colin A. General intelligence or "school brightness." J. of Educa. Psychol. 4:509–24. (N. '13.)

Shall we harden our children? Lit. D. 47:942. (15 N. '13).

Starch, Daniel, and Elliott, Edward C. Reliability of grading work in history. School R. 21:676–81. (D. '13.)

Strong, Frank. Some educational problems in Kansas. Science 38:730–34. (21 N. '13.)

Taft, L. E. The recitation as a factor in producing social efficiency. Educa. 34:145–52. (N. '13.)

Thorndike, Edward L. Notes on the significance and use of the Hillegas scale for measuring the quality of English composition. English J. 2:551–61. (N. '13.)

Winch, W. H. Experimental researches on learning to spell. J. of Educa. Psychol. 4:525–37. (N. '13.)

Wolcott, J. D., ed. Monthly record of current educational publications. U.S. Bur. of Educa. Bull., 1913, No. 45. (N. '13.)

VOLUME XIV NUMBER 6

THE ELEMENTARY SCHOOL TEACHER

FEBRUARY 1914

EDUCATIONAL NEWS AND EDITORIAL COMMENT

The Chicago Banquet

On Wednesday evening, February 25, alumni and students of the University of Chicago in attendance at the meeting of the Department of Superintendence in Richmond, Virginia, will meet for the annual Chicago banquet. The place and exact time of the meeting will be announced by placards posted at headquarters.

The Chicago School Controversy

The school system of Chicago is suffering from an acute attack of politics. For some time the Board of Education and the Superintendent have been at odds. During the summer the disagreements of the two parties came to the surface through the resignation of the Superintendent and an acrimonious discussion about the adoption of certain textbooks. The Superintendent took the position in which the educational profession would unqualifiedly support her, that the choice of textbooks is a professional matter and that she could not advantageously continue in office if deprived of the power of selecting textbooks. So strong was the expression of public sentiment at that time that the Board of Education went through the form of assuring the Superintendent of its warmest support; and the resignation having been gracefully refused, the Superintendent resumed her office.

The pretense of harmony was not long maintained. In December the Superintendent once more expressed her willingness to withdraw if she could not command the support of the board and the board elected a successor.

At this point the Mayor of the city took a vigorous part in the proceedings. It seems that he had demanded and received at the hands of a number of his appointees, before they entered upon their exalted duties as members of the board, their resignations. These resignations, or pledges of good behavior, had been carefully preserved in the Mayor's office against the date when the members of the board should prove unfit in the eyes of the Mayor for the further discharge of the duties which belong to the lay directors of the school system. To the Mayor the acceptance of the withdrawal of the Superintendent seemed bad business. So he brought out the resignations of board members from their storage and accepted them, thus affecting a sudden reorganization of the board. Unfortunately the Mayor had only a few documents of this type and he could not mold the board into a perfect instrument of his will. He secured a board which was able, however, to re-elect the Superintendent; the sometime successor resigned and once more became first assistant superintendent. The ousted members of the board entered upon a clamorous discussion of the intricate problem of the validity of their resignations, even entering legal suits to prove their contentions. In the meantime the board resumed its work divided, as it would appear, into two factions, one of thirteen and the other of seven.

Other developments came on apace with the new year. It seems that a high price has been paid for certain school sites and this matter is to be investigated. The problem of teaching sex hygiene has been much discussed and has been variously voted upon. Just at present it is not to be taught, according to the latest action of the board, and the Superintendent expresses the complaisant view that perhaps people are not ready for such courses. The air is thick with rumors of good and evil, and the common man wonders what will happen next.

The situation has at times been discussed in the public press as though it involved primarily personal elements. The memory of man reaches back, however, to earlier controversies in this school system not dissimilar to this, and one is disposed to believe that the personal factors in the present situation do not explain the fundamental difficulty.

Some have tried to use the occurrences of the last few months in the interests of the woman's movement. This effort has complicated the situation somewhat; it has hardly contributed to its explanation or solution. There are those who say that the anxiety of the political leaders to keep up the pretense of peace is connected with their fear lest the candidacy for higher municipal office of some of the women involved may issue from this unfortunate controversy between the board and a woman superintendent.

Stripped of its incidental complications the spectacle is that of a school system distracted by uneducational politics, used by interested parties for ends other than those which are legitimate. A board of education at the beck of the mayor is no board. Any superintendent who has to go into politics or enter upon a political career from choice is just in that degree distracted from the functions of his office. Chicago is a little worse than most other places merely because it is larger and more complicated.

It is idle, however, merely to indulge in condemnation. What is the cure? The cure is to be found in the development of a professional control of schools. This means that school people must know what is efficient in education and they must be able to make clear to the communities which they serve that they know what is efficient. There is a body of fact about the Chicago schools which would make it perfectly clear that in these and these respects the administration is efficient and in these and these respects in need of improvement. The collection of such objective information about schools is a professional, scientific problem. When school people make it their business to get such material together the politicians will be less eager and less able to interfere with them. It is the opinion of the present writer that the school administration of Chicago can be taken out of politics through the development of scientific professional methods and only in that way. The politicians will sooner or later overcome every agency which does not meet them with a definite professional body of fact and with a clear objective body of evidence. The life of any administration depends on its ability to replace personal and political control by objective, scientifically justified methods and principles.

C. H. J.

The Ohio State School Survey

On December 5 and 6 there was held at Columbus, Ohio, a congress of education, consisting of some two thousand five hundred delegates representing the local communities of the entire state. The meeting was called by the governor of the state for the purpose of considering, in town-meeting fashion, the report of the Ohio State Survey Commission as to the condition of the schools of Ohio, and the remedial legislation that was being proposed by this commission.

The report shows the need of: (1) a more extended training of teachers; (2) more adequate supervision of the school plant and the classroom teaching; (3) more systematic expenditure of money for school purposes; (4) simpler and more effective methods of certificating teachers; (5) more adequate buildings, equipment, and financial support; (6) consolidation of rural schools, especially where they are small. In connection with each of these shortcomings, the commission points out the necessary remedial legisative program, as they conceive it.

The report was adopted with practically no opposition; and the speaker of the House, referring to the legislation recommended, said: "In the special session, if you give us nothing better, we shall pass this." The extensiveness and thoroughness of the survey, together with its popular nature, gives the leaders of educational reform in Ohio a tremendous leverage upon the legislature.

Many other states have had small expert educational commissions make intensive study of conditions for purposes of legislation. Their work is often done without much contact with the workers in the field, and may or may not receive popular support. Ohio has shown a method of arousing the entire profession of the state by means of such a survey, and making its recommendations far more certain of passage.

Other states are proposing similar surveys. At the recent meeting of the State Teachers' Association of Illinois, for example, a resolution was passed proposing for Illinois a state-wide survey to be carried forward by the superintendents and teachers of the state in co-operation with the state department of education, the state university, the state normal schools, and such other colleges and universities of the state as would be willing to assist in such an undertaking. This plan of organization and leadership has a number of points in its favor not possessed by the method pursued in Ohio. Tremendous good could be accomplished for the schools of the state if it could be carried through in a thorough manner. Where the fifteen thousand teachers of the state are all voters, as in Illinois, if once aroused and organized for action, they might easily carry through any rational legislative program.

A State Survey Proposed in Illinois

J. F. B.

One who desires to know the most progressive principles of school management as applied to all phases of a modern complex city school system could not do better than to read the recently published report of the school survey of Portland, Oregon. The survey was intrusted to as expert investigators as are to be found and they were given free hand. Professor Ellwood P. Cubberley, of Stanford, was in general charge and was assisted by Professors Fletcher B. Dresslar, of Peabody College for Teachers, Edward C. Elliott, of the University of Wisconsin, and Lewis M. Terman, of Stanford, and Superintendents J. H. Francis, of Los Angeles, and Frank E. Spaulding, of Newton, Massachusetts. Each of these men is recognized as an expert in some phase of school management. The feature of their report which makes it of interest, not merely to the citizens and school men and women of Portland, but also to educators and citizens of other communities, is the fact that the authors do not "offer merely a critical report, or summarize the merits and defects and cast up a balance, and stop with such." On the contrary, they go much farther in the direction of positive recommendation than they would be justified in going if their purpose were primarily

The Portland School Survey

criticism, and outline a constructive program for the organization of the whole system in accordance with the best ideal which has been formulated on the basis of present-day experiment and thought. This ideal is one which is not realized in all its elements in any single school system and therefore no school system can be criticized for not measuring up to it in all respects. Each part of it has been made actual in some system, however, and in some of the more progressive systems much of it has been reduced to practice. The aspect of the Portland situation which makes it serious is that in nearly every regard it is inferior to the best practice in other places.

It is not in place here to detail the criticisms which are made in the report. The responsibility for the condition which was found is believed to rest not so much upon the average personnel of the system as upon the general administrative situation which was developed when the city was small and which has not changed to keep pace with the city's extraordinary growth. The responsibility for the administration of the schools, even in the details of its educational side, was found to be largely in the hands of the board, and the superintendent and his subordinates did not, therefore, have either the opportunity or the stimulus to initiate progressive measures. The modern plan of administration by which the conduct of an institution is concentrated in the hands of an expert or experts who are given large freedom and are held accountable for results is the obvious remedy. The result of the plan in which the non-expert board of education interferes in the conduct of the educational aspect of the schools is at the best—as the present survey proves—that the conduct of the schools degenerates into a lifeless routine. The school board of Portland was conceded to be public spirited and conscientious. When it is composed in whole or in part of appointees who owe their position to their political influence we have the intolerable situation which is referred to in another column in the comments on the Chicago situation.

The scope of the Portland report may be seen from the subdivisions of which it is composed. The first part consists in an illuminating description and discussion by Professor Cubberley of the organization and administration of the schools, and includes chapters on the selection and tenure of teachers, and the salary of teachers. The same author also contributes an outline of the needs of the educational system of the city based upon an analysis of its social and economic position. Superintendent Spaulding follows this outline by a detailed survey of the curriculum and methods which are at present employed and of the improvements which should be made. Professors Cubberley and Dresslar contribute chapters on school buildings in answer to the questions: "(1) How can they [the Board of School Directors] secure the construction of the best, safest, and most economical school buildings; and (2) How can they make those already constructed meet most helpfully the educational and hygienic demands of school life?" Professor Terman gives a constructive program for health supervision, Professor Elliott a survey of attendance statistics and of records, and Professor Cubberley a discussion of the costs of the system.

Such a survey as this, made by disinterested experts outside the school system, ought to be initiated by the school board or superintendent of every large school system. The advance of every school system is retarded in some measure by practices which are inherited from a past in which the conditions were different from those which prevail at the present time. Those who have grown up within the system cannot realize the discrepancy between the present demands and the opportunities offered by the school. Furthermore, the personal relations which exist between the various members of a school organization make a thorough survey by members of the system itself difficult. The demand for a survey by outsiders is therefore no disparagement of the ability of the members of the school organization.

When a situation arises such as that which confronts the citizens of Chicago, where strong evidence of a corrupt relationship between the board of education and the prevailing political faction is presented, it becomes all the more evident that strong light should be thrown upon all the recesses of the organization. In such a case plans should be laid not merely to detect and punish the present offenders but also, if possible, so to reorganize the whole system that corruption will be very difficult. Either for making the financial administration of the schools free from taint and public spirited, then, or for keeping the educational administration up to the level of the best practice and theory of the time, an impartial, expert survey is an essential instrument.

F. N. F.

Bureau of Research of Upper Peninsula Educational Association

There appeared recently a report of the Bureau of Research of the Upper Peninsula Educational Association (Michigan). This bureau, of which James H. Kaye, Marquette, Michigan, is chairman, is maintained by the associated teachers of this part of the state to conduct research regarding the educational conditions that maintain in the schools. The report is divided into three parts, one on the rural schools, another on the city grade schools, and the third on the high schools.

The number of teachers sending in reports is almost the same for the rural schools as for the city schools, so that comparisons are easily made. In all, 1,412 grade teachers, 24 superintendents, and 7 commissioners reported, representing twelve of the fifteen counties; 702 rural teachers reported, 710 city teachers. Of the rural teachers, 137 are without any training for their work and 172 are normal or college graduates. The cities and towns all demand normal or college graduation as prerequisite for grade teachers' certification.

The average number of pupils per teacher in the city and village schools is 37; the average in the rural schools is considerably less, although there are 37 rural schools with more than 50 pupils. The pupils are a surprising mixture of nationalities: the single town of Ironwood reporting 22 nationalities.

The region is devoted to mining, lumbering, and agriculture; the schools consequently make prominent manual-training and agricultural instruction—16 out of the 24 towns reporting give manual training, seven give agriculture. Six of the towns have trade schools, taught by instructors who have practiced the trades. Trades taught include carpentering, plumbing, blacksmithing, bricklaying, machine-shop, metal work, and pattern-making; two schools have trade courses for girls in dressmaking. The city schools are giving more manual training, trade work, and agriculture than are the country schools.

The city teachers report that 77 out of the total of 710 are performing experiments in physiology along with their instruction. Ninety-nine of these same teachers report taking geography classes on field trips. In the country 152 teachers are performing experiments in physiology; 151 are taking their classes on field trips in geography. These are interesting evidences of progress, especially when the writer recalls that in these same regions field trips in geography and experiments in physiology were an unknown factor during his boyhood experiences in these schools. The report on the whole is an interesting one, and in view of the fact that the region is something of a natural geographical unit, it is worth while.

Bulletins on Health of School Children

Three exceedingly valuable bulletins on the health of school children were issued during 1913 by the United States Bureau of education. One (No. 16) is a *Bibliography of Medical Inspection and Health Supervision, 1909–12 inclusive*, of 136 pages. It is an annotated and classified list of available books, pamphlets, and magazine articles covering practically everything of prime importance recently published on the subject.

Another (No. 44) is entitled *Organized Health Work in Schools*. It is by Ernest B. Hoag, M.D., director of school hygiene for the Minnesota State Board of Health. It outlines the three types of organization for the administration of health supervision, (1) with school medical officer, nurse or nurses; (2) with school nurse only; (3) with simple and non-technical health survey on the part of the teachers only. Under each heading there is described clearly just how the work is conducted in one or more cities in which the particular plan has been successfully tried, except that under (3) detailed suggestions and directions are given for a survey with the printed forms and questionaires that are to be used.

Briefly, the subject of health supervision in rural schools is discussed, as is also the study of exceptional children.

Part II of the pamphlet describes the state organization of

school hygiene in Minnesota, which until last year was the only state to undertake such work.

The third bulletin is No. 48 and is a report of the Fourth International Congress of School Hygiene, held at Buffalo, New York, August 25–30, 1913. Part I is a brief introduction; Part II gives abstracts of many important papers; Part III describes the scientific exhibit.

These bulletins mark the wide-spread and increasing interest in medical supervision of school work in the interest of greater efficiency. In 1900 only 8 cities in America had any organized health work in schools. The school nurse was an unknown, the world over. It was only in 1909 that the first open-air school for tubercular children was opened in Providence. Now some eight hundred cities have departments for health supervision and school nurses are employed by the hundreds while open-air schools are provided by the score in many cities for many pupils besides the tubercular.

> Last year [1911–12] Boston's eighty-seven school physicians under the direction of Dr. W. J. Gallivan, examined 118,781 school children. Of these 40,850, one-third, were without defects and 77,931 had defects that needed medical attention. In 1912–13, 121, 832 were examined, 69,332 were defective.
>
> The special feature of the work of the year was an attempt to find out how many defects were corrected through the initiative of parents, after they had been notified by the school physicians.
>
> Result: At the end of the year another examination was made and it was found that 70 per cent of the defective palates had been attended to, 74 per cent of the skin diseases, 25 per cent of the defective teeth, 43 per cent of the bad tonsils, 66 per cent of the malnutrition, 65 per cent of the nervous diseases.

In New York, 1909 to June, 1912, 727,750 children in the public schools received a complete physical examination. In round numbers, 60 per cent were found defective.

> In the schools alone the efforts of the division of child hygiene have resulted in an immense gain in school time for those children who were affected with contagious skin and eye diseases, the necessary exclusions for these reasons being reduced from over 57,000 in 1903 to slightly over 3,000 in 1911. . . . . Without an effective follow-up service conducted by the visiting nurses, medical inspection is ineffective. Until 1908 New York City relied upon postal cards sent to parents of defective children, and was able to secure

action in only 6 per cent of the cases where treatment was recommended. Immediately on placing the follow-up service in the hands of school nurses the percentage increased to 84.

Similarly in Philadelphia 21.1 per cent of the cases reported were found to have had action when not followed up by a nurse, 80 per cent when so followed up.

Fall River, Massachusetts, in its school report for 1911 states that the percentage found defective in 1907 was 4.1; in 1908, 3.3; in 1909, 2.9; in 1910, 2.9; in 1911, 2.2. Everywhere there is the fight through the schools against such diseases as tuberculosis, the hook-worm disease, and the communicable diseases of childhood. Systematic recreation is receiving attention, play under guidance as a means of achieving health. Dental clinics are adjuncts of the school. Trained oculists are employed by the school boards, and experts on nose, ear, and throat diseases.

In Saginaw, [Michigan] the work begins [1913] with seventeen east-side dentists volunteering to co-operate and give of their services freely. Besides this, the dentists are providing the equipment to give the free clinics a suitable start, and this means a great deal. Free dental treatment will be given the school children attending the clinics, and they will be taught the proper methods of caring for their teeth, as well as general hygiene pertaining to the dental science. It is proposed to throw the clinics open to all school children, including those of the parochial schools.

Defective and retarded children are segregated, studied, and treated. More than that causes are traced and if possible eradicated.

At the Congress on School Hygiene, held recently in Buffalo, Dr. Walter M. Roach, district supervisor of school medical inspectors in Philadelphia, reported the results obtained among school children of ages from six to fourteen years after the establishment of a food clinic in certain schools in his district. Many of the children were found to be coming to school with insufficient or no breakfasts.

The children were fed for a period of four weeks in the spring of 1913, at the morning recess period, with some form of cereal and milk, the form of cereal being changed daily. In all, 113 children were fed in this manner.

In a group of fifty, who were carefully weighed, measured, and physically examined before the beginning of the feeding and afterward, it was found that there was an aggregate gain of over 252 pounds.

The average grades for the whole school, 350 pupils, including the 113 who were given the feedings, increased in spelling from 76.4 to 82.3, and in arithmetic from 69 to 72. For the same period the averages of the pupils of the second grade attending the clinics increased from 71 to 87 in spelling, and from 59.6 to 71.3 in arithmetic.

E. R. D.

Faults of the District Unit

The faults of the district school unit are presented on the basis of very illuminating statistical evidence in an article in the *Missouri School Journal* by Dean Charters of the University of Missouri. The situation is put vividly in the following concrete illustration:

> The first weakness of the system is the inequality of opportunity for boys and girls.
>
> Let me illustrate this inequality in country districts lying side by side. Presumably if John lives on one side of the road in this imperial state of Missouri and his cousin James lives on the other side of the road, they should have the same chance to get an education. But if you will consult Table I, you will see that sometimes, if they happen to be in different school districts, they have far from equal opportunities. If John lives in the $110,000 district and James in the $36,000 one, John gets a chance to go to school eight or nine months in the year, while James must be satisfied with six months. John, while at school eight months, will be likely to have a first- or second-grade teacher at a salary of over $400; while James will probably be given a second- or third-grade teacher at a salary of less than $400.

That this is not an isolated case is shown by the comparison of two groups of districts in each of eighty-four counties. In each case the two districts which are compared in each county are adjoining. The average assessed valuation of the wealthy districts is $110,594 and of the poor adjoining district is $36,674. The median tax levy of the wealthy districts is 40 and of the poor districts over 60. Seventeen per cent of the teachers in the wealthy districts have the third or lowest degree of certificate, while 52 per cent of the teachers of the poor district have these lowest-grade certificates. Seventy-eight per cent of the teachers in the wealthy districts receive over $400 in salary and 76 per cent of the teachers in the poor districts receive less than $400. It is evident, then, that the various points which Dean Charters makes are well taken. Not only is there an inequality in opportunity in the adjoining districts, but the rate of taxation and the returns are "unequal and inequitable." Furthermore, there is a very unequal return for the amount which is spent in the better and the poorer districts. This may be expressed in the per capita cost. In Columbia County, for example, where the length of term is nine months and where twelve grades are maintained, the per capita cost is $37, whereas in District 42, where the length of term is only seven months and only eight grades are maintained, the per capita cost is $66. This indicates that in some districts the administration is very much more economical than in others. In general, then, it may be said that the poor districts suffer through a larger tax levy and through a smaller return for the money which is spent.

A further difficulty with this system is the great multiplication of school directors which it entails. There are in the various districts of Missouri 30,000 school directors. It is obviously impossible for a state superintendent to exercise any adequate supervision over such a large number of individuals and it is further obvious that some form of concentration is necessary to make possible an efficient administration. Professor Charters shows that the county school unit exists in twelve states and points out that it is therefore a practical plan. The theoretical basis for the union of the smaller districts into larger administrative units is, as Dean Charters points out, the fact that the school exists for the purpose of furnishing adequately equipped citizens for the state and that the responsibility for the support of the school inheres in the state and not in the local units. The equalization of opportunity and the distribution of the burden according to ability to meet it are therefore fundamental principles of education and ones which are obviously grossly violated in the conditions which are shown to exist under the district system.

Education of the Immigrant

A recent bulletin of the United States Bureau of Education entitled *The Education of the Immigrant* presents in a convincing fashion the educational responsibility and the opportunity which result from the large tide of immigration which has come to this country in recent years. The unusual character of this responsibility is indicated in the following paragraph from the bulletin:

The instruction of the immigrant child is a problem with which few nations have had to deal in any but a meager way. Colonies are usually settled by homogeneous bodies of people agreeing in language, customs, political ideas, and religious beliefs. Settled countries generally receive accretions of small bodies which are readily absorbed. For a time, however, these bodies naturally seek association with those who have come before them and who have, to a great extent, adopted the language and customs, as well as the political ideas, of the country in which they have sought a home. As long as the immigration is comparatively small in quantity, the problem is not serious. But when what may be called "the saturation point" has been reached, the most serious consideration must be given to the problem. Such a point has been reached in some parts of the United States, especially in New York City.

There are certain characteristics of the immigrant child which make his education a peculiar problem. The fundamental problem in connection with the foreign-born children, of course, is that of language. In New York City this problem has been met by the formation of special classes in which instruction in the English language is a very prominent part of the work. A further condition which limits the usefulness of the school to the immigrant children is the fact that the tendency to leave school at the age of fourteen, which is a general characteristic of the school population, is still more marked in their case. These children, then, besides being more difficult to teach because of their language disability are in the school for a shorter period of time. Another of the problems which confronts the teacher of the immigrant and his children is the readjustment to the social ideals of the new country which the immigrant is required to make. The conflict between the new and the old points of view is brought out very clearly in the second generation. It is pointed out that the second generation underestimates the value of the culture which existed in the old countries and therefore grows out of sympathy with its parents and beyond their control. This presents a situation in the home which has grave social consequences, as is shown by statistics of crime.

The number of male prisoners per 1,000,000 of the population of voting age in 1890 was as follows: Native white of native parents, 3,395; native white of foreign parents, 5,886; foreign whites, 3,270. In this analysis, age for age, the foreign-born show a lower rate than the native-born. Besides, the table shows criminality among the native-born of foreign parents twice as high as either of the other groups.

The school is attempting to meet this situation both by leading the child to appreciate the value of the older culture and also by bringing to the parents some of the opportunities which are open to the child and which will prevent too great a gulf between the points of view and the attainments of the child and the parent. This education of the parents is carried on in evening schools and in a most interesting type of work which has been recently inaugurated in New York state. A recent law has been enacted which authorizes the creation of temporary schools in labor camps where the construction of public work is going on. A great many of the immigrants go directly to these labor camps, and it is therefore necessary to take the school to them if they are to be reached by its influence. The form of training consists pretty largely, of course, of language work and includes also something of arithmetic and geography. Besides the formal studies the life of the laborers is relieved from monotony by forms of recreation such as the radiopticon and the phonograph. It is reported that this work is of great value in preventing the formation of the drinking-habit, and its importance to the immigrant and to the nation can scarcely be overestimated.

F. N. F.

A STUDY OF RETARDATION AND CLASS STANDING ON THE BASIS OF HOME LANGUAGE USED BY PUPILS

EVERETT EVELETH CAMPBELL
American Mission, Sialkot, India

Does the use of some foreign vernacular as the home language of pupils have any causal connection with their acceleration or retardation in our public schools, or with their relative standing in the classroom?

The extent of the problem which is presented in this question is measured, on the one hand, by the exceedingly large foreign-speaking population which we have come to have in America, especially in our cities, and, on the other hand, by the heavy percentage of retardation that prevails in our schools. To cause this retardation many factors are operating. Whether or not the use of a foreign language in the home is one of these is the subject considered in this investigation.

The percentage of the foreign element is indicated by the tables given in the United States Census Reports of 1910, showing that of the 91,972,256 inhabitants in the continental United States, 14.7 per cent are foreign born, while 20.6 per cent more have foreign-born parents. In distribution throughout the states the percentages vary from 2.4 per cent of foreign born in the South Atlantic Division, and 2.6 per cent in the South Central Division, to 15.6 per cent in the North Central Division, 19 per cent in the Western Division, and 25.6 per cent in the North Atlantic Division. Those with foreign-born parents vary from 3.6 per cent in the South Atlantic Division, and 4.8 per cent in the South Central Division, to 24.5 per cent in the Western Division, 27.8 per cent in the North Central Division, and 29.5 per cent in the North Atlantic Division.

Within these various divisions a few of the typical states vary as follows:

TABLE I

	Percentage Foreign Born	Percentage Foreign Parents
Massachusetts	31.2	34.8
New York	33.0	29.9
Illinois	21.3	30.6
Wisconsin	22.0	44.0
California	21.8	26.7
North Carolina	0.3	0.7
Indiana	5.9	13.0

These figures indicate a wide variation, yet in a majority of the states the percentages are high. In many of them from one-half to two-thirds of the people are either foreign born themselves or have foreign-born parents. In our large cities, where the population is densest, this condition is most pronounced.

When we turn our attention to retardation in the schools we find figures that are equally striking. In *Bulletin No. 5*, 1911, of the United States Bureau of Education, prepared by Dr. Strayer, of Teachers College, New York, tables are presented showing the results of an investigation in 318 cities. Counting children six or seven years old in Grade I as of normal age, seven or eight in Grade II, eight or nine in Grade III, and so on, the tables give the following percentages:

TABLE II

	Normal Age	Over Age					Under Age
		1 Yr.	2 Yrs.	3 Yrs.	4 Yrs. and Over	Total	
Chicago boys	61.7	19.9	9.7	3.8	2.2	35.6	2.7
" girls	66.8	18.1	7.6	2.7	1.4	29.8	3.4
Indianapolis boys	63.5	20.0	9.5	2.3	2.1	33.9	2.6
" girls	65.9	18.2	8.7	2.9	1.0	30.8	3.3
Philadelphia boys	53.6	21.9	12.5	6.2	3.6	44.2	2.2
" girls	57.2	21.1	11.7	5.0	2.5	40.3	2.5

The variation in the percentage of those entered as of normal age extends from Savannah, Ga., (colored) boys 25.6 per cent, girls 25.8 per cent; Houston, Tex., boys 25.8 per cent, girls 30.5 per cent; and Erie, Pa., boys 38.9 per cent, girls 46.3 per cent, up to Aurora, Ill., boys 73.7 per cent, girls 76.1 per cent. The variation in the enrolment of under-age pupils extends from boys 0.3 per cent, girls 0.2 per cent, in Birmingham, Ala. (Columbia, S.C., is reported blank), to boys 35.7 per cent, girls 39.4 per cent, in Haverhill, Mass.

For cities with a population of less than 25,000 the figures are similar.

Here again, just as in the tables presented above giving the foreign element percentages, there is a wide range of variation, yet a condition that is widespread, pronounced, and serious.

Other investigations, more limited in extent, and varying somewhat in method, but made with equal care, have netted approximately the same results.

This present study to discover whether the first of these conditions, viz., the presence of a large foreign-born and foreign-speaking element in our population, has an active influence in producing the second condition, is not the first that has been made. Many educators have suggested that such a relationship exists, and have been desirous of ascertaining the actual facts. Dr. Leonard P. Ayres conducted in New York City an investigation of 20,000 children in fifteen schools. The results were negative. These he sums up in his *Laggards in Our Schools*, and also refers to the experience of the department of education in Porto Rico in changing its schools from the Spanish to the English basis with little or no loss of time on the part of pupils, and again to the investigation conducted by Superintendent James E. Bryan, of Camden, N.J. This last also gave negative results.

So far as known to the writer, however, no extended investigation has been made in Chicago or anywhere in the North Central Division, though the percentages given above indicate that the two factors are as acute here as elsewhere. Nor can it be questioned that the problem is of sufficient importance to warrant the gathering and considering of more extensive data than we have yet had before conclusions can be reached that may be called final.

Further, it appears that the preceding investigations, notably that of Dr. Ayres, have been based on differences in *nationality*. This is not identical with difference in language. Many Germans use English exclusively in their homes while still entered in school registers as German in their nationality. The same is true of immigrants from all other countries. The present study undertakes to differentiate on the basis of the language used by pupils as their home language.

METHOD OF INVESTIGATION

The method followed has been:

1. On printed cards, as shown here, the individual records of over 3,000 pupils have been entered. These have been secured by copying them carefully from the school registers and enrolment cards in seven different schools widely scattered in the city of Chicago.

School.......................................Room.............
Pupil's name...
Language...
Date of birth..
Home conditions..
Age entering this school.....................................
Grade..
Date of entering grade...........................Age.............
Half-years below grade...........................Age.............
Half-years above grade...........................Age.............
Mentality.........Interest.........Industry.........Scholarship.......
Remarks..
....

2. By arrangement with the principals the pupils were given blank slips on which they were asked to write their names and the home language used. With the envelope in which the blank slips were handed to the teachers, or more frequently sent to them by the principal from his office, the following directions were given:

Please have each pupil enter on one of the inclosed slips:

(1) Name.

(2) Language ordinarily used at home *with parents.*

Please emphasize that it is the language used with parents, or those with whom the pupils live, that is to be given, since many use English with brothers and sisters and playmates, who use some foreign language with their parents.

Kindly check over the slips to see that the answers given agree with your own knowledge of the facts.

3. The language entry was then transferred from the pupils' slips to the corresponding printed cards on which the register records had been entered.

This use of two separate sets of cards with the transfer of entries involved much extra work, but it was felt that it was necessary in order to avoid the distribution of the full printed cards in the schools, with the consequent danger of pupils objecting to such a laboratory study. Principals and teachers might well object to this. No such objection holds against the method used.

4. For the children of the lower grades, who could not be expected to fill out their own slips, the method followed was to enter the nationality of each pupil on the cards, together with the other entries from the school enrolment cards, and then have the principal send these to the teachers with the accompanying request:

> Will you kindly check "Language," as entered on inclosed slips, and make corrections as necessary? The entry made is the nationality of father and mother as shown by the record cards, and may or may not indicate the language spoken. Some pupils speak English with brothers and sisters but a foreign language with parents or guardians. It is this latter that is wanted if it can be given.

5. Extensions were made on the cards which were then arranged by grades, and these subdivided into language groups, and the number in each entered in the tables of frequencies which present the data used in this study, and on the basis of which its conclusions are reached. It was found that the enrolment card entries for "above grade" and "below grade" could not be used on account of inaccuracies and variations in method of computation, so only age was entered as an extension on the cards. Acceleration and retardation were computed in the frequency tables. The blanks on the cards for "mentality," "industry," and "interest" were inserted to correspond with the enrolment card entries in Schools A and B. No use of them has been made in these tables. In the registers of the other five schools there were no corresponding entries.

6. In computing ages the nearest half-year has been taken.

7. In computing acceleration and retardation the usual method is to count all six- and seven-year-old children as normally graded when in Grade I, seven- and eight-year-old children as normally graded when in Grade II, and so on. But for the purposes of comparison between various groups within each grade, this two-year range of variation is too wide. Accordingly an arbitrary standard has been established, and children of all groups have been measured by this. Those of age six have been considered normal only in

Grade I, of age seven, only in Grade II, of age eight, only in Grade III, and so on up to Grade VIII, in which only those of age thirteen have been counted as normal.

As in computing ages the nearest half-year has been taken, it follows that acceleration and retardation have been figured on the same basis.

Certain difficulties encountered in securing accurate data need to be noted:

1. Register and enrolment card records are often incomplete. The date of original entry into the school can usually be found on the enrolment cards where this system is used, but not in the register, where the register system is used, except by a hopelessly interminable tracing-back to the year when the pupil first entered, and then back a year or two farther to find a time when he was not present.

For some schools, moreover, up until within the last four or five years, the grades of pupils were not entered in the register, but only the number of their room. The grade now in this room may or may not indicate the grade that was in the room five years ago. These conditions prevent an investigator from tracing individual pupils and basing his conclusions on their progress through the grades.

2. The forms in which records are kept are dissimilar. In five of the seven schools studied there are registers. In two there are enrolment cards, filed in card catalogue system. The register entries give the number of the pupil's room, his father or guardian's name, his birthplace, age, age entering grade, grade, weeks in grade, and promotion, with one or two other columns giving information not germane to this study. The column headed "Promotion" is ordinarily not filled in.

The enrolment card entries include all that is given above, together with nationality of father and mother, home conditions, school from which received, or certification when dismissed, original date of entering the school, half-years below grade, half-years above grade, and columns for entering letters to indicate mentality, interest, industry, scholarship, etc. Much of the material, then, that might be secured from the enrolment cards cannot be secured from the registers.

The dissimilar nature of the records is found again in the variation in methods of making entries that obtain in different schools, or among different persons in the same school.

3. The nomadic character of the population is an added difficulty that renders a study of the progress of individual pupils very unsatisfactory. Often children are moved from one district to another several times during their years in school.

4. Variation between given names entered in the register and those written by the pupils prevented the completion of some cards. Absences, too, left many cards without language entries, while promotions during the year without corresponding changes in the room numbers on the register made the finding of corresponding slips in large numbers of cases exceedingly tedious.

These difficulties have been overcome by the adjustment of method to suit the available data. The ages and languages of pupils now enrolled in each grade have been considered rather than the progress of individual pupils through the grades, and cards on which the data are incomplete have been rejected.

5. A still more important consideration remains, however, in the problem of singling out this factor of language and dissociating other factors from it. Racial differences, individual differences, and social and economic conditions are so intimately connected with language that a complete separation is scarcely possible. Approximately to eliminate them the study has been carried on in districts where, with possibly one exception, similar social and economic conditions prevail. Wealthy residential sections of the city have not been included. Nor have schools in which English-speaking children largely predominate been compared with schools in which foreign-speaking children predominate. Moreover, the foreign-speaking pupils have been segregated in their own national groups and these, as well as the totals, have been compared with English-speaking pupils in the same school. Finally, the totals of each group in all the schools have been combined for the purpose of deducing more general conclusions.

The enrolment and the number of grades studied in the various schools are shown in the following table, together with the number of foreign-speaking and English-speaking pupils:

TABLE III

School	Total Attendance	Grades for Which Data Were Secured	Foreign Pupils	English-Speaking Pupils
A...........	897	I–VIII	545	197
B...........	829	III, V, VIII	155	140
C...........	500	III–VIII	....	....
D...........	1,903	III–VIII	586	75
E...........	1,614	III–VIII	556	163
F...........	520	II–VIII	112	89
G...........	1,151	III, V, VIII	125	193
			2,113	900
Total pupils..............			3,013	

In School A and School B it was possible to determine the nationality of the pupils from the enrolment cards. A comparison between nationality and home language for 881 pupils of other nationality than those for whom English is the mother-tongue shows 677, or 77 per cent, using their foreign vernaculars; 167, or 19 per cent, using English, and 37, or 4 per cent, using both. The complete table is as follows:

TABLE IV

Nationality	Using English	Using Mother-Tongue	Using Both	Total
Austrian..................	....	1	....	1
Bohemian..................	1	3	....	4
Belgian..................	1	....	....	1
Danish..................	8	1	2	11
Dutch..................	6	11	1	18
French..................	3	2	....	5
German..................	50	58	7	115
Hungarian..................	....	41	1	42
Italian..................	5	82	....	87
Jewish..................	13	32	1	46
Lithuanian..................	....	5	....	5
Norwegian..................	6	4	1	11
Polish..................	11	318	5	334
Russian..................	....	5	1	6
Servian..................	....	1	....	1
Slavish..................	1	46	1	48
Swedish..................	62	66	12	140
Yiddish..................	....	1	3	4
Welsh..................	....	....	2	2
	167	677	37	881

Of the Germans, Swedes, Danes, and Norwegians, a large percentage use English; of the Poles, Hungarians, Italians, and Slavs, a low percentage.

EXPLANATION OF TABLES AND CHARTS

In the first column are given the half-years of age for pupils in each grade; in the second column, the half-years under age (marked −), and over age (marked +), measured from the arbitrary standard of six for Grade I, seven for Grade II, and so on. In the third column (marked A) is given the number of pupils of the language indicated at the head of the column for each half-year of acceleration or retardation. In the fourth column (marked B) are given the products of columns two and three, with plus and minus signs preserved. Under languages represented by but few pupils the B column is omitted. The algebraic sum of column B divided by the sum of column A gives the average acceleration or retardation per pupil measured in half-years. Below the average the mode in half-years of retardation has also been entered. This indicates the age at which the largest number of pupils are found.

In all cases throughout the tables the average and mode are found in retardation, not in acceleration, since the accelerated pupils, measured from the arbitrary standard, are few.

Subjoined to many of the retardation tables are tables indicating the class standing of pupils in the various language groups. The letters E, G, F, and P stand for excellent, good, fair, and poor. At the bottom of the table the mode for each group is shown.

In preparing the charts percentages have been used for the frequencies instead of absolute figures. The ordinate in all the charts represents frequencies. The abscissa in the retardation charts represents acceleration and retardation in half-years (+ and − respectively); in the class-standing charts, it represents relative ranks as indicated by the letters. The figures in parentheses, placed before the names of the various groups, give the number of pupils represented in the curve.

For the purposes of this article only a few of the individual class tables and charts need be given. The combined class tables, which will be presented in full in the next number, furnish a basis for drawing more general conclusions than could safely be drawn from these of the separate classes.

SCHOOL A

In Grade I of this school (Table V) the Polish pupils are in the majority. Their average retardation falls a little below that of the total foreign group, but is a half-year in excess of the retardation of the English-speaking group. This is indicated by the difference in the mode as well as in the average. In the mode with the English pupils are the Germans, Swedes, and Hungarians. The Slavs fall into the mode of the Poles.

No doubt the prevailing similarity in the tables is due to the fact that age six is the time when most children are started to school, and differentiation in ages and class ranks has not yet been established. In both the graphs prepared for this class (Chart I) the uniformity of the various curves is apparent.

In Grade II the English-speaking group was found to pass above all the others in retardation except the Hungarians. The Jews, with but half a dozen pupils, showed the least. In class standing there was essential similarity, the foreign pupils receiving a larger percentage of G's, and the English pupils more E's.

In the succeeding tables and charts of this school the advantage was decidedly with the English pupils, except in Grade VIII. In that grade the average retardation for them was 2.37 half-years; for the others, it was only 2.0 half-years. The English pupils, however, had two half-years advantage in the mode. Only at one other point were they surpassed in average, viz., by the Swedes in Grade IV, where all the groups, except the Swedish, were abnormally high in their retardation. The Polish children in the class had an average retardation of 6.66 half-years.

Several of the charts, notably those for Grades VI and VIII, showed decided difference in mode in favor of the English children.

CHART I

Retardation
Grade I.
(49) Eng.
(181) Total For.
(16) German
Class Standing
P
F
G
E

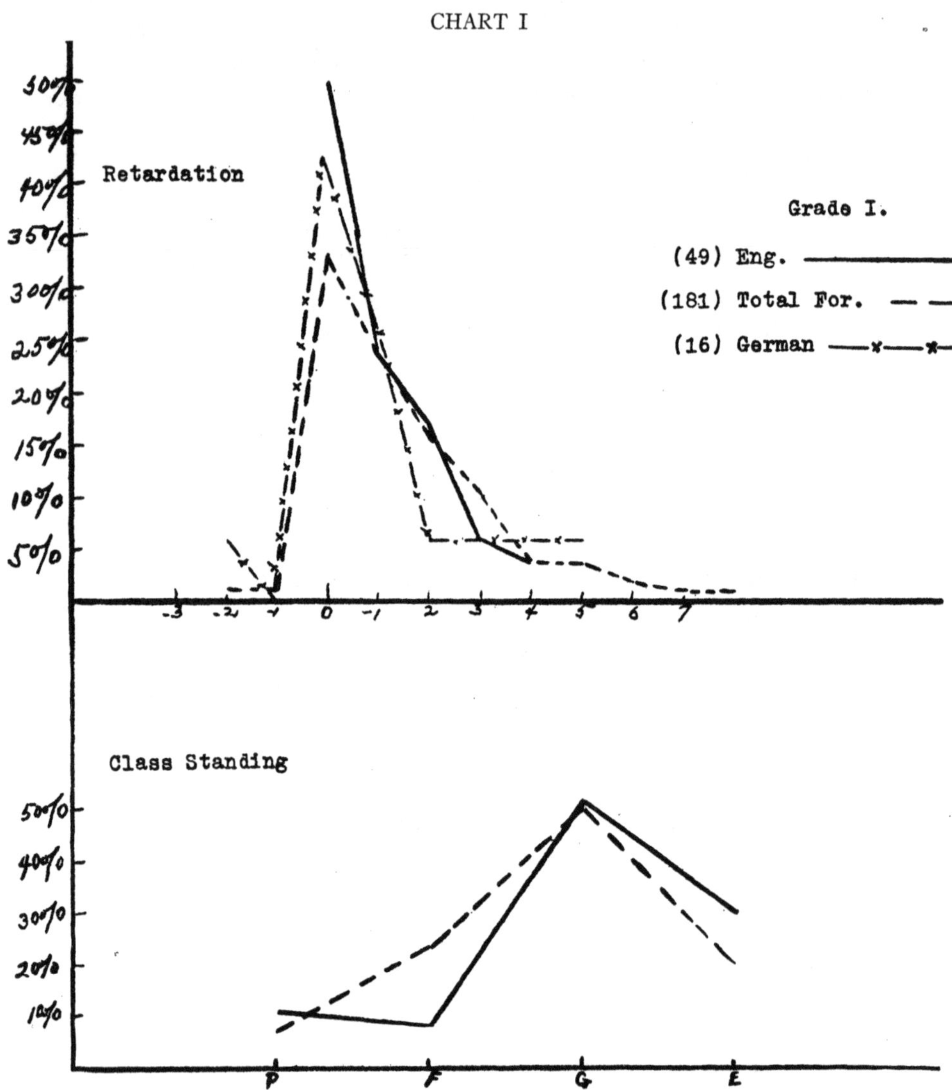

TABLE V

School A—Grade I

Ages	Half-Years Under and Over Age	Polish		German		Slavish		Swedish		Hungarian		Misc.	Total Foreign		English Speaking	
		A No. of Pupils	B Total Half-Years Accelerated and Retarded	A	B	A	B	A	B	A	B	A	A	B	A	B
5....	−2	1	−2	1	−2	....	....	....	....	....	....	....	2	−4	....	....
5½...	−1	2	−2	....	....	....	....	....	....	....	....	....	2	−2	....	....
6....	0	38	....	7	....	2	....	6	....	4	....	3	60	....	24	....
6½...	+1	34	34	4	4	4	4	....	....	2	2	....	44	44	12	12
7....	+2	22	44	1	2	3	6	2	4	3	6	....	31	62	8	16
7½...	+3	14	42	1	3	2	6	1	3	1	3	1	20	60	3	9
8....	+4	4	16	1	4	2	8	1	4	....	....	....	8	32	2	8
8½...	+5	5	25	1	5	1	5	....	....	....	....	1	8	40	....	....
9....	+6	2	12	....	....	....	....	1	6	....	....	....	3	18	....	....
9½...	+7	1	7	....	....	....	....	....	....	....	....	....	1	7	....	....
10½...	+9	....	....	....	....	1	9	....	....	....	....	....	2	18	....	....
Totals		123	176	16	16	15	38	11	17	10	11	5	181	275	49	45
Average ret. in half-years....			1.43		1.0		2.53		1.54		1.1			1.52		0.92
Mode of ret. in half-years....			1		0		1		0		0			1		0

Class Standing

	German	Slavish	Polish	Swedish	Total Foreign	English Speaking
E..............	5	4	17	5	34	15
G..............	5	7	65	2	89	25
F..............	3	1	32	3	40	4
P..............	2	3	6	1	13	5
Mode..........	G	G	G	E	G	G

SCHOOL B

This is a community in which there is a large percentage of Italians. The English group was surpassed by all the others in Grades III and VIII as regards average. In all three of the grades

CHART II

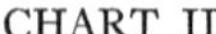

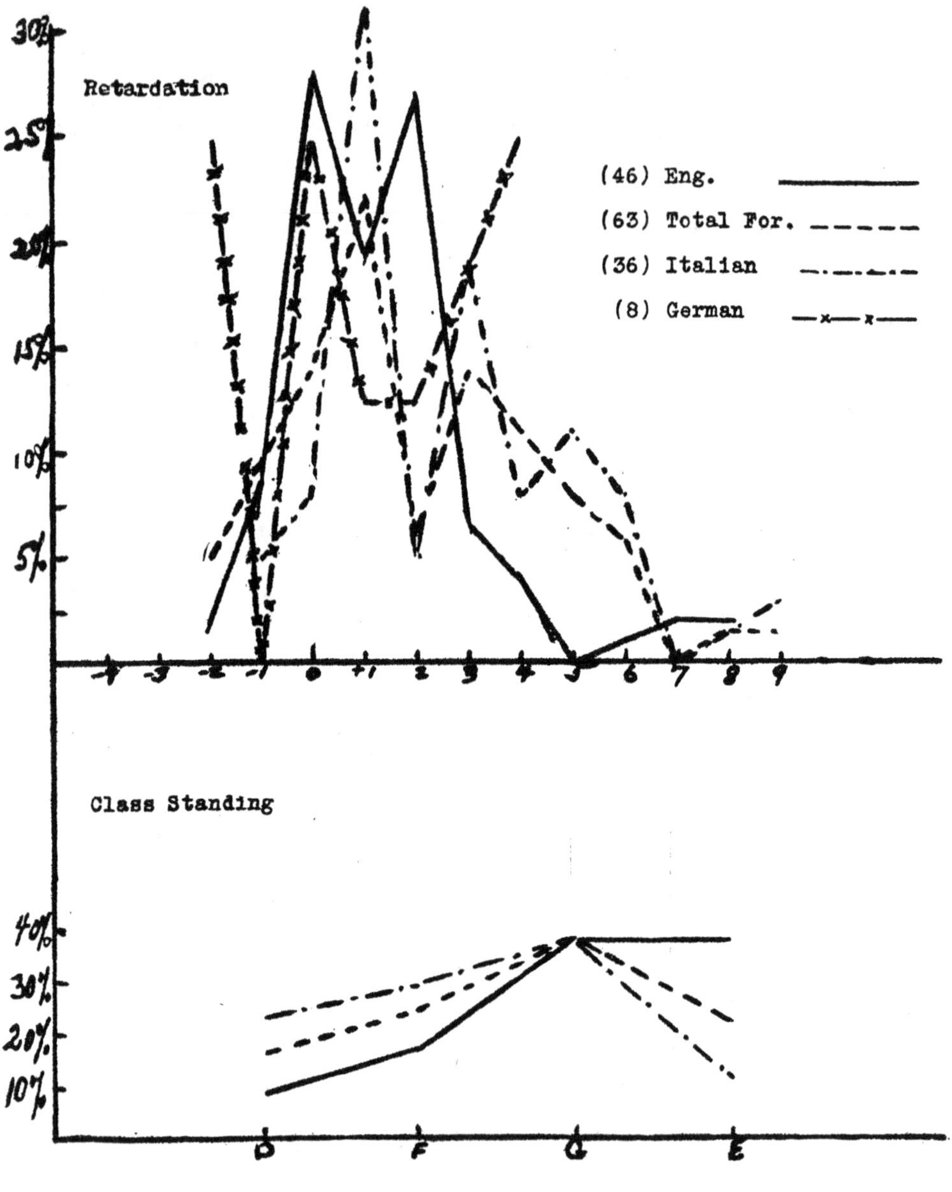
30%
25%
20%
15%
10%
5%
Retardation
(46) Eng.
(63) Total For.
(36) Italian
(8) German
-4
-3
-2
-1
0
+1
2
3
4
5
6
7
8
9
Class Standing
40%
30%
20%
10%
D
F
G
E

measured it was equal or ahead in mode. As shown by the charts, it was really bi-modal in each case. Chart II shows Grade V.

The heavy elimination of the foreign element in the successively higher grades was shown by the relation between its numbers and those of the English-speaking: in Grade III, 63 of the former to 26 of the latter, in Grade V, 63 to 46, in Grade VIII, 29 to 68. The Swedes and Germans held their own, but the Italians dropped from 36 in V to 9 in VIII.

SCHOOLS G, E, AND D

In each of the three grades investigated in School G the English-speaking pupils were found to have the least average retardation, and in each grade except VIII the lowest mode. In this grade there was a clearly marked difference of one-half year. More Germans were found in this district than in any other; of Italians, Poles, and Hungarians, there were very few; of Swedes, an average number.

School D is in an overwhelmingly Italian section of the city. School E is in an equally overwhelming Jewish section. The averages and modes of the total foreign column, accordingly, are determined entirely by the averages and modes of these two respective groups.

In Grades III and VII of School D only one more pupil was found in the total foreign group than in the Italian. In VIII there were only Italians. In each grade except Grade VI the English-speaking children showed less average retardation than the others. Their mode in this grade showed less, and in each of the others showed the same or less.

In School E some have given Yiddish as their language, but aside from this there are only seven that appear outside of the Jewish or English columns. Those who have entered Yiddish have been included with the Jewish in the final classification. In Grades V and VI the English group proved to be more retarded than the Jewish and Yiddish groups. In Grade IV it was more retarded than the total foreign group. This last differed from the Jewish by but one pupil. As regards mode the English pupils ranked even, or ahead, in each grade. The results for Grade VIII are shown in Table VI and Chart III.

CHART III

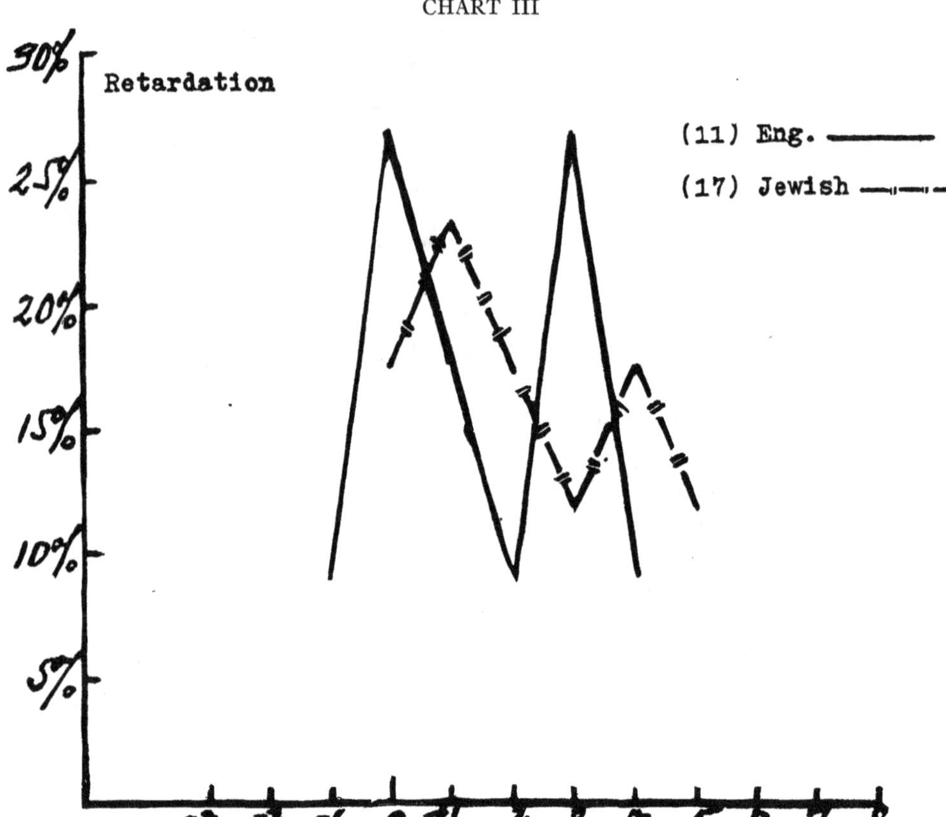

TABLE VI

School E—Grade VIII

Ages	Half-Years Under and Over Age	Jewish		English Speaking	
		A No. of Pupils	B Total Half-Years Acc. and Ret.	A	B
12½	−1	....	....	1	−1
13	0	3	....	3	....
13½	+1	4	+4	2	+2
14	+2	3	6	1	2
14½	+3	2	6	3	9
15	+4	3	12	1	4
15½	+5	2	10	....	....
Totals		17	38	11	16
Average retardation			2.24		1.45
Mode			1		0

SCHOOLS C AND F

These two schools have a majority of their pupils Italians, though many other nationalities are represented. Of School F it may be said in general that irregularity of relative standing was found to be the most characteristic feature. In School C the English-speaking children showed less retardation than the others in each grade except VII. Only twelve cards all told were secured in this class. This is too few for anything approaching accurate comparison.

The following tables and charts will illustrate the conditions that obtain. Vable VII and Chart IV represent Grade III in School C and Table VIII and Chart V represent Grade IV in School F.

Throughout the tables and charts of the separate classes in each of the seven schools there has been much variation. In the larger percentage of cases the English-speaking pupils have shown least retardation. There have, however, been a number of marked exceptions. Five times they have been excelled in average by the Italians, once by the Germans, twice by the Swedes, three times by the Jews, once each by the Poles and Slavs, and six times by the total foreign group. In mode many groups have been equal to the English. Twice the Italian and total foreign groups have

TABLE VII

SCHOOL C—GRADE III

Ages	Half-Years Under and Over Age	Italian		Chi-nese	Jewish	Yiddish	Total Foreign		English Speaking	
		A No. of Pupils	B Total Half-Years Acc. and Ret.	A	A	A	A	B	A	B
8	......	......	......	1	......	......	1	......	......	......
8½	+ 1	2	2	......	......	......	2	2	......	......
9	+ 2	6	12	......	......	......	6	12	3	6
9½	+ 3	9	27	......	1	......	10	30	2	6
10	+ 4	7	28	......	......	......	7	28	3	12
10½	+ 5	4	20	......	......	1	5	25	2	10
11	+ 6	1	6	......	1	......	2	12	2	12
11½	+ 7	4	28	......	......	......	4	28	1	7
12	+ 8	1	8	......	......	......	1	8	......	......
12½	+ 9	2	18	......	......	......	2	18	1	9
13	+10	1	10	1	......	......	2	20	......	......
14	+12	3	36	......	......	......	3	36	......	......
Totals		40	195	2	2	1	45	219	14	62
Average ret.			4.87					4.87		4.43
Mode			3					3		4

CHART IV

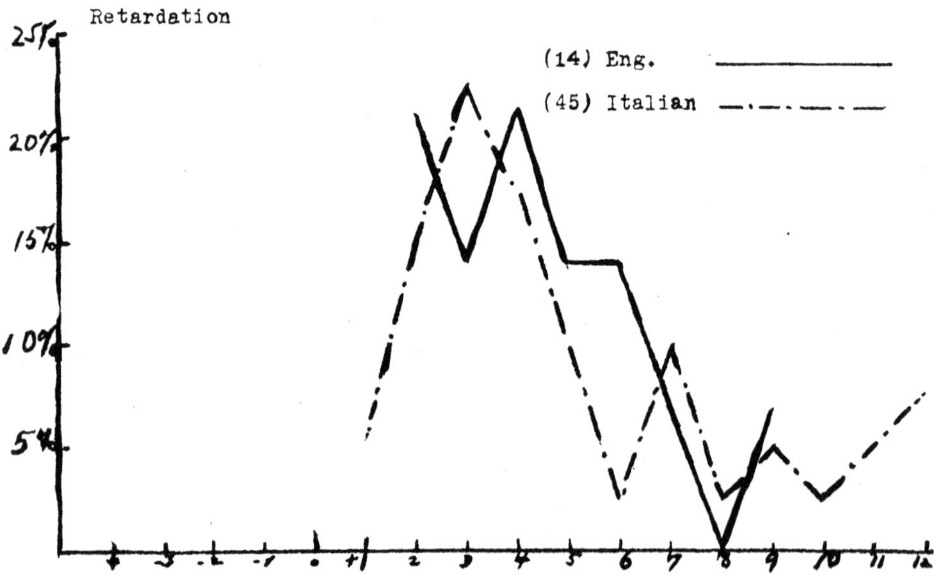

CHART V

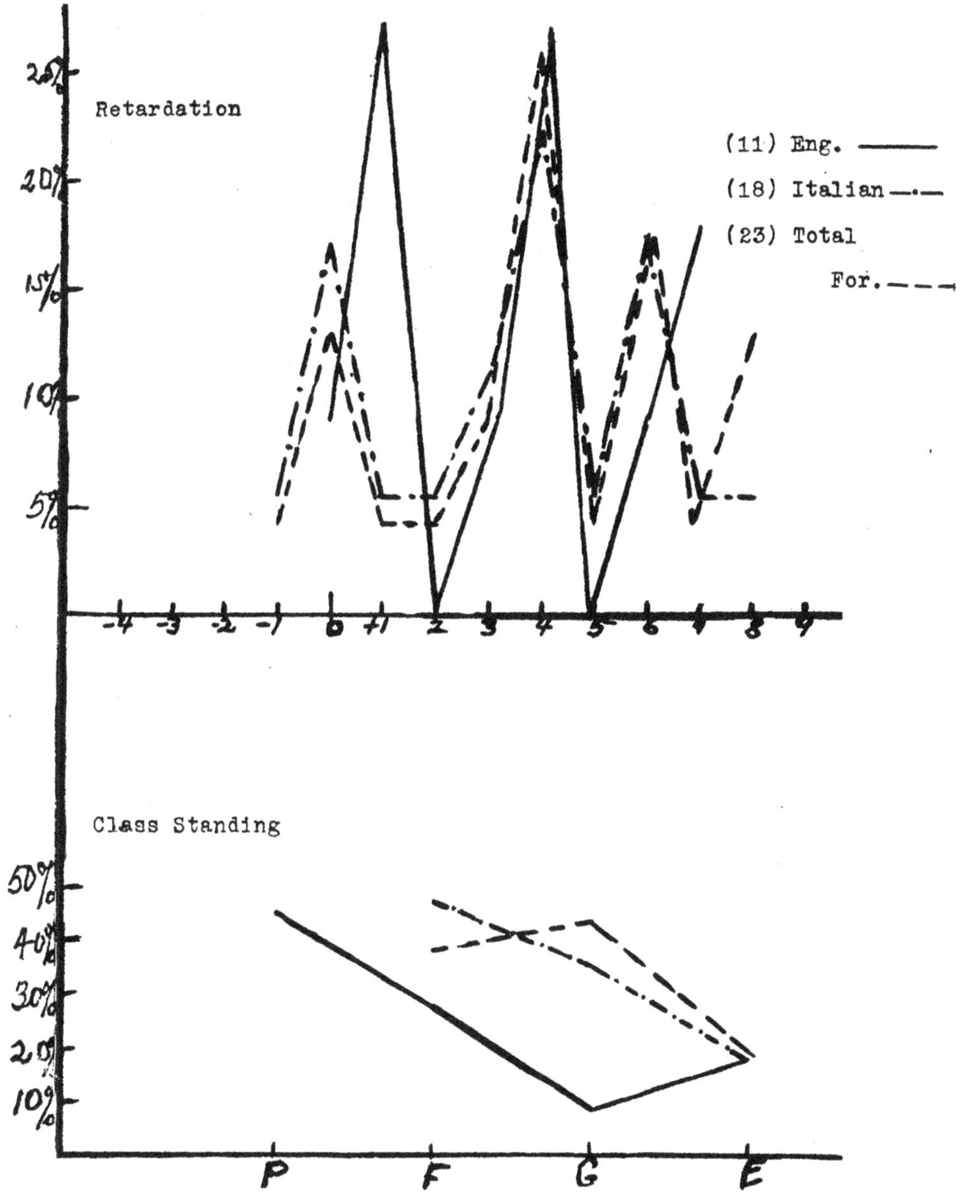

Retardation

25%
20%
15%
10%
5%

(11) Eng. ———
(18) Italian —·—
(23) Total
For. — — —

-4 -3 -2 -1 0 +1 2 3 4 5 6 7 8 9

Class Standing

50%
40%
30%
20%
10%

P F G E

TABLE VIII

SCHOOL F—GRADE IV

Ages	Half-Years Under and Over Age	Italian		Greek	Jewish	Persian	Total Foreign		English Speaking	
		A No. of Pupils	B Total Half-Years Acc. and Ret.	A	A	A	A	B	A	B
8½	−1	1	−1	......	......	......	1	−1	......	......
9	......	3	......	......	......	......	3	......	1	......
9½	+1	1	1	......	......	......	1	+1	3	+3
10	+2	1	2	......	......	......	1	2	......	......
10½	+3	2	6	......	......	......	2	6	1	3
11	+4	4	16	1	......	1	6	24	3	12
11½	+5	1	5	......	......	......	1	5	......	......
12	+6	3	18	......	1	......	4	24	1	6
12½	+7	1	7	......	......	......	1	7	2	14
13	+8	1	8	......	1	1	3	24	......	......
Totals		18	62	1	2	2	23	92	11	38
Average ret. in half-years			3.44					4		3.45
Mode of ret. in half-years			4					4		4

CLASS STANDING

	Italian	Total Foreign	English Speaking
E	3	4	2
G	6	9	1
F	8	8	3
P	......	......	5
Mode	F	G	P

shown a better mode; once the Germans have been ahead. In class standing there has been equal irregularity.

It will be of advantage, therefore, in deducing general conclusions to have the data for the separate classes presented in the form of combined tables and charts. These will be given in the next section of the study.

[*To be continued*]

RETARDATION, ACCELERATION, AND CLASS STANDING

V. A. C. HENMON
University of Wisconsin

During the past decade, retardation, acceleration, and elimination have been in the forefront of discussion as important social and educational problems. Compulsory school laws have brought into the school system hosts of children of widely varying ability and maturity. This legislation and the growing consciousness of social responsibility for education, of which it is an evidence, have resulted in extensive provisions for defective and backward children, on the one hand, and in an influx of pupils who might otherwise not be in the system, on the other. These conditions have enormously complicated the problem of internal organization and adaptation of schools and curricula to the so-called normal child. Genetic psychology and child-study, the study of individual differences, and the practical experience of teachers have all shown that the concept of the normal child is a rather useless fiction. Pupils of the same age are strung out all along a vertical scale of maturity, on the one hand, and are distributed perhaps quite as widely on a horizontal scale of ability, on the other. Recent publications in popular journals of cases of unusual precocity have called attention afresh to this variability in rate of mental development. These cases have been wrongly interpreted as evidence of the inefficiency of the school system rather than as cases of unusually rapid maturity which the laws of variability would lead us to expect on rare occasions. If there is this variability, then chronological age is not an adequate index of mental or pedagogical age, and age-retardation statistics will give no satisfactory evidence of mental or pedagogical retardation. To furnish some data on this point and to indicate a method of inquiry which seems fruitful is the purpose of this paper.

Retardation is an ambiguous term that has come to be applied to three very different things: (1) Retardation is used, e.g., by Witmer, to mean slow or arrested mental development. The retarded child is one the functions of whose brain are not developed up to the normal limit for his age. (2) Retardation refers merely to age-in-grade. The retarded child is one who is over-age, or behind the grade for his age, regardless of whether it is due to late entrance, absences from school, slow mental development, or lack of ability. (3) Retardation relates solely to the progress of the child in school. The retarded pupil is one who makes slow progress, the repeater, who takes more than the normal time to complete a prescribed course. The relation between these different conceptions of what retardation means has not been satisfactorily worked out and the reader of the already voluminous literature finds it hopelessly confusing.

Most of the numerous statistical investigations by Thorndike, Ayres, Strayer, Falkner, Lurton, etc., have been concerned with age-retardation, the determination of the percentage of pupils over-age, under-age, and of normal age in the various grades. In some of the studies there is an apparent assumption that age-retardation is indicative of mental retardation, that the retarded or over-age pupil is also a backward or a maladjusted pupil. Ayres, e.g., says: "The child of nine acts and thinks differently from the child of seven. Put the two in the same class and the work of the teacher is increased. The amount of attention which can be given to each is diminished, and the effect of the teaching is therefore lessened. No one can doubt that it would be a very great advantage if children could be so classified that the classes would be more homogeneous with respect to age." This assumption that growth in maturity is closely correlated with age is unwarranted. The child of nine may be mentally a child of seven or one of eleven. It may well be that the age-retarded pupil who is only a year or two over-age is classified with the group where he can work to the best advantage. If so, then retardation is not the serious evil it has been claimed to be. The good of the school and the good of society may best be served by having the child of nine years classed with children of seven or of eleven. Homogeneity in classes is of course greatly to be desired but it is not necessarily accomplished by placing children of like chronological age together, but by placing together children of like mental age. Classification by size would probably be as useful for purposes of securing homogeneity as classification by chronological age.

The real problem of retardation is thus psychological rather than administrative and economic. What is needed for purposes of gradation of pupils is some measure of mental maturity, such as, for example, the much-discussed Binet scale of intelligence, which will enable us to determine mental age more accurately. Such tests are being applied in various sections of the country and the results will be awaited with interest.

In the meantime, it seemed worth while to study the school records of retarded, normal, and accelerated pupils to determine what qualitative differences are shown by each of the groups in school work measured by the schools' own standards of capacity and attainment. It is only by such a study that the real significance of retardation can be discovered. From the pedagogical and psychological points of view the important problem is whether there is actually such maladaptation as the age statistics suggest and whether age-retardation is correlated in any way with mental retardation. The specific questions raised were: What are the class standings of the retarded, accelerated, and normal pupils? Are the standings of the retarded pupils lower than those of the normal pupils? How are the standings distributed among the different kinds of retarded, normal, and accelerated pupils? Is there any alteration in the distributions up the age-scale?

Data on the amount of retardation and acceleration were obtained for 2,023 pupils in elementary schools of Madison through the kindness and co-operation of Superintendent Dudgeon. For assistance in the collection and tabulation of the data I am indebted to Mr. J. A. Stevenson, of Chicago, Illinois, and Mr. B. F. Adams, of Cambria, Wisconsin.

Table I gives the distribution of the children through the grades, the number accelerated, the number retarded, and the number of normal age.

TABLE I

	1	2	3	4	5	6	7	8	Total
Total number	286	315	326	275	225	226	206	164	2,023
Normal	178	157	160	112	79	93	75	66	920
Retarded	48	99	111	138	112	90	86	77	761
Accelerated	60	59	55	25	34	43	45	21	342

Table II gives the distribution in percentages.

TABLE II

	1	2	3	4	5	6	7	8	Total
Normal	62.2	49.8	49.1	40.7	35.1	41.1	36.4	40.2	45.5
Retarded	16.8	31.4	34.0	50.2	49.8	39.9	41.7	47.0	37.6
Accelerated	21.0	18.8	16.9	9.1	15.1	19.0	21.9	12.8	16.9

The age-standard for each grade has occasioned much controversy. Ayres[1] considers a pupil of normal age if, in the first grade, he is under eight years, in the second grade, under nine, etc. The Ayres standard thus allows an extra year for each grade. Its effect may be to conceal one year of retardation or repetition. On this standard, as applied to schools of the Middle West, it would be possible for every pupil in the system to enter at six years, the most frequent entering-age, to repeat a year, and still not be retarded according to the age statistics.

Lurton[2] in a study of retardation statistics from smaller Minnesota towns notes this point. He says that in every system covered by his investigation the children are admitted at six years of age or younger. He therefore reckoned the entering-age at six. Further, in every one of the schools studied, promotions are made once a year, in June. Each grade, by definition, means a year's work. Therefore, the child who enters the first grade at six should enter the second grade at seven, the third grade at eight, and so on. From the administrative point of view, the child who enters at seven is behind the prescribed schedule.

[1] L. P. Ayres, *Laggards in Our Schools.*

[2] F. P. Lurton, "A Study of Retardation in the Schools of Minnesota," *Science,* N.S., XXXIV, No. 884, December 8, 1911.

This age-standard is practically the one employed in this study. The date of birth and the average of the marks assigned for the school year 1910–11 were obtained for all pupils from the school records. The pupils were then classified into three groups according to the following age-standard:

	Retarded	Normal	Accelerated
First grade....	If born before September 1, 1903	If born between September 1, 1903, and September 1, 1904	If born after September 1, 1904
Eighth grade..	If born before September 1, 1896	If born between September 1, 1896, and September 1, 1897	If born after September 1, 1897

On this basis the amount of retardation in the Madison school system is much less than that reported by Lurton.[1] For fifty-five city systems in Minnesota with the same age-standard, so far as I can judge from his statement, he finds 58.9 per cent retarded, 34.2 per cent normal, and 7.1 per cent accelerated pupils. The corresponding figures here are 37.6 per cent, 45.5 per cent, and 16.9 per cent, showing less retardation and more acceleration. The legal entering-age in Minnesota is five years, with the further provision that school boards may exclude children under six years, while that of Wisconsin is four years, though the most frequent entering-age in both states is six years. This may in part account for the difference in the results.

Charts 1 and 2 give the median class standings and the distribution of these standings for the three groups of pupils by grades.

An inspection of the medians and of the distribution-curves shows very clearly that, while the median standings are highest for the accelerated pupils and lowest for the retarded, the differences are not great and the overlapping in the curves is so marked that the differences lose significance. The noteworthy thing is that the range of variability is in general quite as great for one group as for the other or for all the pupils of a grade. Age-retardation is no index of inferior mental ability nor is acceleration an index of superior ability. Greater homogeneity in these classes would not,

[1] *Ibid.*

Chart I.—The comparison of the distribution of the marks received by pupils who have progressed at the normal rate (N), are retarded (R), or advanced (A) with the median standings.

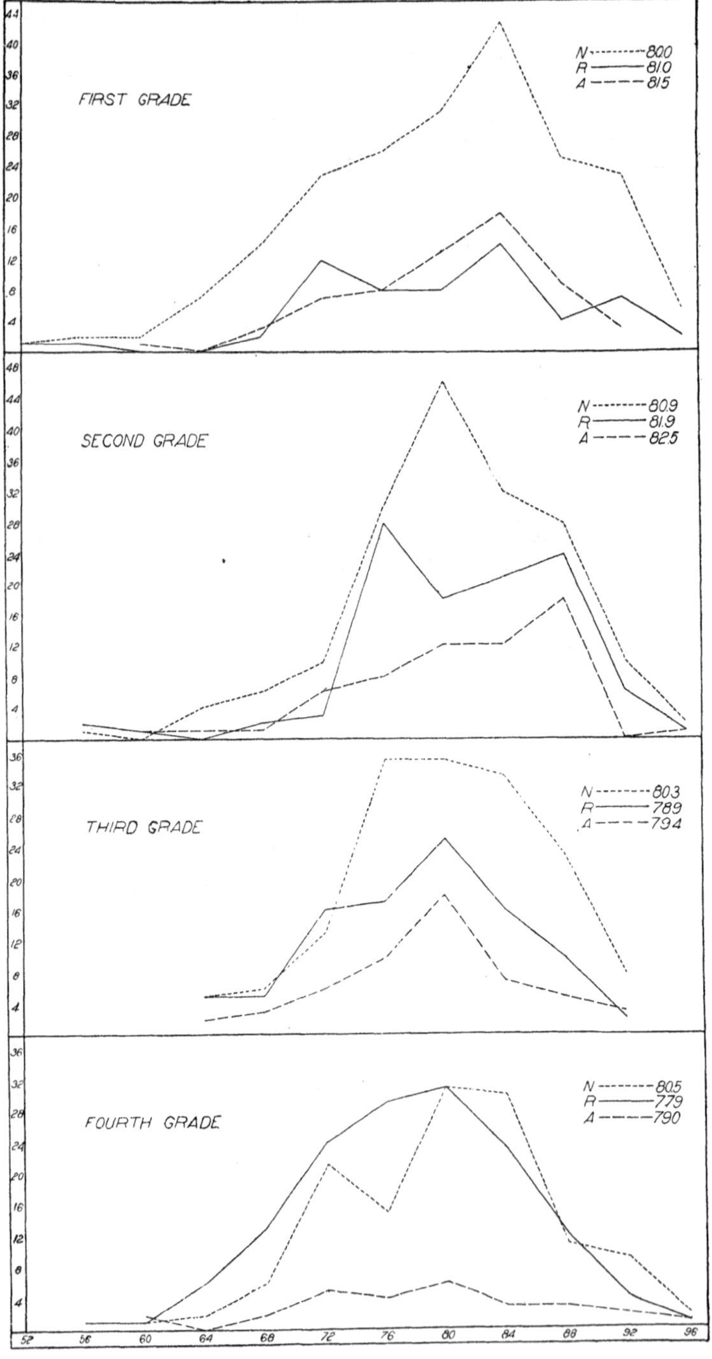

CHART I.—*Continued*

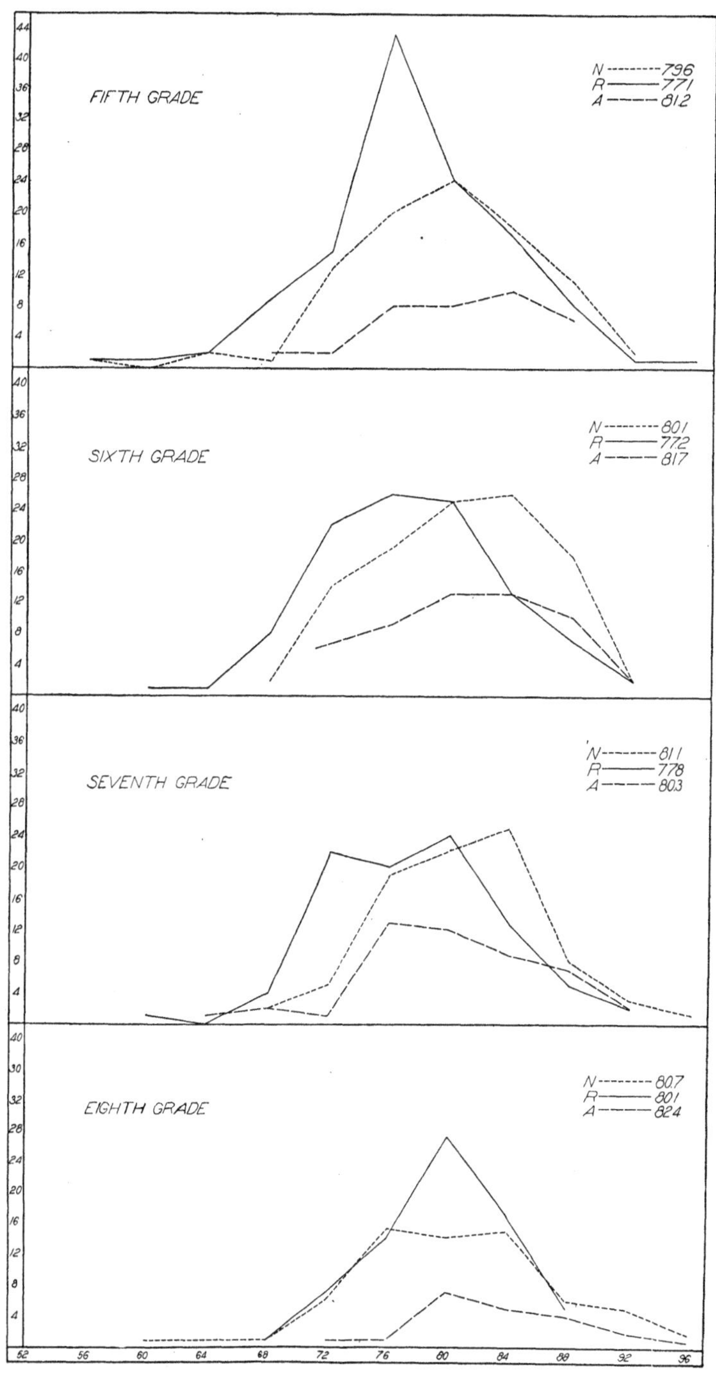

therefore, be secured on a basis of greater likeness in age-in-grade. Classification by similarity in ability or attainment, moreover, would include relatively about as many from one group as from either of the others, except in the sixth and seventh grades. There is a tendency to a sharper differentiation between the retarded and normal pupils beginning in the fifth grade and culminating in the seventh where the differences in the medians are considerable. Greater difficulty in work, greater rigor in the assignment of marks, and the accumulation of repeaters and over-age pupils who are but waiting to escape the operation of the compulsory school law account in large part for this fact.

The classification of pupils as retarded, normal, and accelerated, and a study of their average performances do not carry us very far. The retarded group may include (1) those who entered late but who may have made normal progress or even faster than normal progress; (2) those who entered at the normal age but who have been put back in change of schools, or who may have been kept out a year because of illness; (3) those who have repeated because of slow development or because of lack of ability, etc. Similarly, the normal group may include (1) those who entered at the normal age and progressed at the normal rate; (2) those who entered late one or more years and have gained one or more years; (3) those who entered early and repeated, etc. With a view to such detailed analysis of the performances of the different types of retarded, normal, and accelerated pupils, it was necessary to know the number of years the pupils had been in school. The school records unfortunately did not give this information and it could not be obtained until September, 1911. In the meantime, transfers, withdrawals, etc., reduced the number for whom complete data could be secured to 1,301 pupils from the first to the seventh grades, inclusive.

Table III gives the number of pupils and the average standings for all of the different types of retardation, normality, and acceleration.

The table is self-explanatory; a word only with reference to the effect of age of entrance on standings will make its meaning clear. There were in all 347 pupils of normal age and normal progress, i.e., a year for each grade, with an average standing of 79.7 per cent. It is particularly interesting to compare with this group those pupils who have made normal progress in school but who are over-age or retarded one or more years. There were 180 such pupils who entered a year late, or who dropped out for a year and then re-entered, with an average standing of 78.7 per cent; 47 pupils retarded two years, with an average standing of 78.6 per cent;

TABLE III

	Accelerated		Normal Age	Retarded					
	2 Yrs.	1 Yr.		1 Yr.	2 Yrs.	3 Yrs.	4 Yrs.	5 Yrs.	6 Yrs.
Advanced 3 years........				2 79.5					
Advanced 2 years........		2 85.0	1 86.0	1 75.0					
Advanced 1 year.........	1 87.0	14 81.9	23 79.2	14 82.0	3 78.3	3 77.7	2 83.0		1 69.0
Normal progress..	13 81.4	142 78.9	347 79.7	180 78.7	47 78.6	13 78.7	5 75.8	2 79.0	1 60.0
Repeated 1 year.........	5 78.4	18 80.0	83 78.5	130 78.6	67 77.5	41 76.8	16 77.8		
Repeated 2 years........		1 82.0	12 79.6	20 77.7	26 77.1	34 78.8	8 74.6	3 77.0	1 73.0
Repeated 3 years........				2 74.5	6 76.3	5 72.0	4 79.2		
Repeated 4 years........						1 81.0			
Repeated 5 years........									1 70.0

13 retarded three years, with an average standing of 78.7 per cent. In other words, the pupils who were one, two, or three years older, and hence, supposedly more mature, and who had been in school the normal number of years for their grade, do no better, but rather a little worse, than those of normal age. Similarly, the 142 pupils who entered a year early and progressed at the normal rate had an average standing of 78.9 per cent, a little less than the standing

of those of normal age and progress and identical with that of pupils retarded one, two, or three years. So far as one is able to judge from teachers' estimates of performance as indicated in assigned marks, and I know of no other method by which a better judgment can now be secured, the pupils are classified with considerable accuracy. One finds here in fact 750 pupils who have made normal progress distributed over a range of seven age groups (two pupils retarded five years and one retarded six years being disregarded), with substantially the same class standings for each age group.

TABLE IV

	No. of Pupils	Standings	P. E.
1. Accelerated and advanced	17	82.6	±1.3
2. Accelerated but normal progress	155	79.2	±0.4
3. Accelerated but repeated	24	79.8	±1.0
4. All accelerated	196	79.5	±0.35
5. Normal age but advanced	24	79.5	±1.0
6. Normal and normal progress	347	79.7	±0.25
7. Normal but repeated	95	78.2	±0.5
8. All normal age	466	79.4	±0.25
9. Retarded but advanced	26	79.9	±1.0
10. Retarded but normal progress	248	78.6	±0.35
11. Retarded and repeated	365	77.7	±0.25
12. All retarded	639	78.1	±0.2
13. Repeated 3 or more years	19	75.5	±1.2
14. Repeated 2 years	105	77.9	±0.5
15. Repeated 1 year	360	78.2	±0.25
16. All repeaters	484	78.0	±0.25
17. Normal progress	750	79.8	±0.20
18. Advanced 1 year	61	80.3	±0.65

The average standings of the various classes of pupils, which the classification by age and progress make it possible to analyze, together with an indication of the range within which the standings are statistically reliable, are shown in Table IV.

The noteworthy feature of the table is the slight difference in the average standings of the different classes of pupils. Aside from the first group, which includes the bright and precocious children (and their standings are not high enough to indicate serious maladjustment), there are nine groups with substantially the same average standings. Exception should be made of group 7, the repeaters of normal age, but the difference, while significant, is not great. Such close agreement in standings was unexpected by the writer. It will be interesting to discover whether it prevails in other school systems as well. Objection can, of course, be made that statistical averages obscure the evils of bad classification, but such detailed analysis as is presented here should have shown any significant differences if they existed. At any rate, this inference from statistical averages is sounder than from individual cases of maladjustment.

The average performances of the retarded pupils are lower than those of the normal and accelerated pupils but the differences are again so slight as to be of little significance. Even the repeaters, on the average, attain marks but little below the normal except in the case of those who have repeated three or more years. School marks are notoriously unreliable but they are the best estimates we have of a pupil's ability to do the work of the school.

The general impression which the writer and his collaborators have obtained from the study of the average performances of the different types of pupils as well as from the individual marks is one of surprise, in view of current opinion, at the smallness and the character of the differences in scholarship. We should have expected the distribution-curve for the accelerated pupils to be skewed positively, and that of the retarded pupils to be skewed negatively. While such is the case, the differences in the character of the curves is not great. Even the repeaters who are supposed to be a drag upon a class keep approximately much closer to the average than is usually supposed.

A study of this character in a school system with three thousand or four thousand pupils in which careful records were kept of age, progress, and performance would permit a detailed analysis for the various classes of pupils in each grade. The number of cases in this investigation unfortunately does not make possible with sufficient reliability such a separate treatment by grades. If, in addition, separate marks were secured for ability, attainment, and effort or diligence, valuable information would be available. One pupil of A ability may do B work because of C diligence or effort. Another may be of C ability, but do B work because of A diligence or conscientiousness. Teachers commonly estimate pupils in this way but make no separate records of such estimates. Marks assigned are often, if not usually, compounded from such judgments. So a pupil of C ability and C attainment may, and often is, given a mark of B because of his superior conscientiousness in work. The significance of school marks is therefore obscure. With complete records from a large school system we should obtain much better information than we now possess concerning the various classes of accelerated, normal, and retarded pupils, the significance of the entering-age, the relation of work in the kindergarten to progress in the elementary school, and the adjustment or maladjustment of the curriculum to the pupils.

BOOK REVIEWS

The German System of Industrial Schooling. By RALPH C. BUSSER, American Consul, Erfurt, Germany. Philadelphia, Pa.: Published by Public Education Association. Pp. 63.

The report is timely, coming, as it does, when educators and the general public alike are anxious to know what can be learned from the German industrial schools which will be pertinent to the American problem of education. The author states that his purpose is not to describe the organization and methods of these schools in detail, but rather to set forth the general principles on which the system is founded. He states, at the outset, the most significant of these principles when he says: "This system represents the result of many years' study and experience of the German people in endeavoring to solve the problems involved in the education of the *industrially employed youth* of the manufacturing communities."

He shows that Germany has, in truth, a "system" and that it is nicely adjusted to the purpose above mentioned. This system includes the common schools themselves, general trade schools, special trade schools, and engineering and scientific schools, thus offering progressive education for every grade of industrial worker.

Industrial continuation schools are generally a "part of the public-school system" and are supported by the local community, usually with state aid. "The total expenditures in Prussia for the industrial continuation schools amounted in 1911 to $2,304,792, of which 52 per cent was borne by the municipalities, 35 per cent by the state, 2 per cent by associations and gilds, and 11 per cent by employers' contributions consisting of tuition fees which they are bound to pay for the employes, together with the sum which some of them contribute voluntarily."

The common schools lead naturally to the continuation schools in which not only trade subjects are given, but also physical, business, and civic training.

One chapter discusses "Trade Schools as a Substitute for Apprenticeship," another "Auxiliary Educational Facilities," while the final chapter deals with the relation of the schools to national industry. This shows that the splendid industrial success of Germany has not been a mere accident, but it also makes it clear that neither is it due to the industrial schools alone, or perhaps even mainly, but rather to the appropriateness of these schools to the whole social, economic, and political structure of the Empire.

Paper and Cardboard Construction. By GEORGE FRED BUXTON and FRED L. CURRAN. Peoria, Ill.: Manual Arts Press. Pp. 191. $1.50.

This is a handbook for teachers desiring to give instruction in paper and cardboard work suitable for children in the primary grades, though the work is capable of application as high as the fifth grade. It contains just the kind of information which the grade teacher needs to enable her to carry on the work with pleasure and profit, both to the pupils and to herself. The information is both technical and general, serving to secure accurate and purposeful methods of work and also to show the relations which may be established between this work and everyday life.

A considerable variety of material is introduced and the problems are presented in the form of finished projects which are grouped under four heads: books, boxes, cards, and envelopes. These four types of problems involve a variety of processes including cutting, measuring, folding, pasting, gluing, sewing, punching, tying, and also the planning and application of suitable decorations.

The book also contains valuable chapters on the organization of courses, and on the purchase, distribution, and handling of supplies and equipment. The chapters are both technical and informational and give hints for correlating the work with other school subjects.

The volume itself is an excellent example of "paper and cardboard construction," being well printed and profusely illustrated. It will be a boon to grade teachers who are required to give instruction in manual training in the grades covered.

FRANK M. LEAVITT

UNIVERSITY OF CHICAGO

Social Forces. A Topical Outline, with Bibliography. By MRS. A. L. QUACKENBUSH. Portage, Wis.: Published by the Education Committee of the Wisconsin Woman's Suffrage Association. Pp. 83. $0.15.

This text, prepared not for propaganda but for education in the problems of present citizenship, will be useful to teachers who want to know where to look for information, and how to direct others in the community who may come for suggestions. Its value for the layman as a select bibliography is great, and even the well-informed teacher will find himself much aided by the material here brought together. Some of the topics are "Government," "Labor," "Woman," "Educational Problems," "Lessons Other Countries Teach Us."

J. H. TUFTS

UNIVERSITY OF CHICAGO

A Text Book on the Teaching of Arithmetic. By ALVA WALKER STAMPER, Head of the Department of Mathematics, State Normal School, Chico, Cal. New York: American Book Co., 1913. Cloth. Pp. 284. $1.00.

This volume is designed for those who are giving instruction or supervising the work in arithmetic in the elementary schools. It is especially designed for teachers new in the service.

The author devotes a small portion of his book to the history of arithmetic and to the reasoning involved in arithmetic. The chapter on "Preliminary Steps in Arithmetic" is especially helpful for the beginning teacher. Much emphasis is placed upon the principal operations in arithmetic. The application side of arithmetic as well as the place for algebra and geometry in the elementary school, as presented by the author, deserve special attention.

The author's views on lesson plans, course of study, character of problems, etc., will be of help to the reader. All in all, this book seems to be a very helpful guide to the teacher of arithmetic.

D. W. WERREMEYER

FORT WAYNE, IND.

A Cyclopedia of Education. Edited by PAUL MONROE, PH.D., and OTHERS. Vol. V. New York: Macmillan, 1913. Pp. 892. $5.00.

This volume completes the series of volumes of the *Cyclopedia of Education* and enables one to make a general survey of the whole work. This survey is materially aided by the analytical index which is a feature of the present volume. In this index all of the articles of the *Cyclopedia* are classified according to the general topic under which they come. Thus there is a section for history of education, for philosophy of education, psychology, etc. This index makes evident the fact, which has impressed the reader already, that the work is a comprehensive one. The index forms a very valuable part of the work, since it enables the student to follow systematically some subject by reading the articles as they appear in the classification.

There is nothing especially new to be said, aside from this, in regard to the present volume. It strikes one as having a particularly large number of articles upon psychological topics, as the fourth volume had many on state school systems. This of course, is the accidental result of the alphabetical arrangement. A few of these articles on the psychological aspects of education may be mentioned. On account of the growing application of laboratory methods to the study of educational problems, the article upon laboratory equipment in psychology will prove to be of value. The general article upon psychology gives an orientation in the subject, and the special discussion of educational psychology is timely in view of the great divergence of opinion and practice as to what should be included in this subject of the curriculum. There are three fairly long articles upon the psychology and pedagogy of the subjects of the elementary curriculum, namely, upon reading, spelling, and writing. Reading and writing have been the subjects most extensively investigated by psychological methods, and these articles present summaries of the results in these fields.

In addition to the above-mentioned there are a number of articles treating of the application of psychology to education. An article upon sense-training indicates the value of this form of discipline on the one hand and at the same time rightly warns against the uncritical attempt to train the senses without regard to the value of the result. The value of space perception and its training is the subject of another article. Social psychology in its various forms is shown to be of direct application to education. There is a very interesting article upon the education of children among primitive peoples. Contrary to common belief, this education is rather elaborate, although it is directed merely to the activities which are characteristic of the tribe in question. That is, the education is shown to be of a rather specific nature and to be conservative in its tendencies.

These may serve merely as illustrations of one type of article. There are, of course, a great many upon other topics, but it would be impossible to attempt anything like a review of the wealth of articles in this volume. In closing the notice of this final volume it may be said that the statement made in reviewing the first volume, that the work is one of the highest importance to all who are at all concerned with education, is entirely justified by the work as it now stands complete.

FRANK N. FREEMAN

UNIVERSITY OF CHICAGO

Essentials of Business Arithmetic. By GEORGE H. VAN TUYL. New York: American Book Co., 1913. Pp. 272. $0.70.

This book is suitable for use in classes in arithmetic in business schools and high schools, and especially for advanced classes in the elementary school. Short methods of solution are a valuable feature. The treatment of aliquot parts is adequate. The problems are practical and sensible, and most of them admit of variation to meet the conditions of the industrial and civic community. Business practices in calculation are explained clearly. The many definitions are adequate, but simple and brief. While the work is too advanced for most elementary-school classes, teachers of the upper grades will find the book of value as a reference book of modern business practices in computing.

Arithmetic by Practice. By D. W. WERREMEYER. New York: The Century Co., 1913. Pp. iii+80.

The teacher of mathematics in the upper grades will find in this book a great variety of practical problems that are full of content. They are in general not grouped according to mathematical principles involved, but the problems of each set call for the expression of number relations between facts which are related in business and home life. This is not a textbook, but is excellent for supplementary work.

HARRY O. GILLET

UNIVERSITY ELEMENTARY SCHOOL

BOOKS RECEIVED

AMERICAN BOOK CO., CHICAGO

Reading, Writing, and Speaking Spanish for Beginners. By MARGARET CAROLINE DOWLING. Cloth. Pp. 256. Illustrated. Price $0.75.

BOARD OF EDUCATION, CLEVELAND

Seventy-sixth Report of the Superintendent of Schools. Paper. Pp. 107.

BOARD OF EDUCATION, NEW ORLEANS

Annual Report of the Superintendent of Schools. Paper. Pp. 207.

GINN & CO., BOSTON

The Beacon First Reader. By JAMES H. FASSETT. Cloth. Pp. 160. Illustrated. Price $0.35.

HOUGHTON MIFFLIN CO., BOSTON

Songs and Stories for the Little Ones. By E. GORDON BROWNE. Melodies Chosen and Arranged by EVA BROWNE. Cloth. Pp. 143. Price $0.80.

The Teacher and Old Age ("Riverside Educational Monographs.") By CHARLES A. PROSSER. With the collaboration of W. I. HAMILTON. Cloth. Pp. 140. Price $0.60.

RAND McNALLY & CO., CHICAGO

Five Messages to Teachers of Primary Reading. By NETTIE ALICE SAWYER. Cloth. Pp. 219. Price $1.00.

The Four Wonders: Cotton, Wool, Linen, Silk. By ELNORA E. SHILLIG. Cloth. Pp. 137. Illustrated.

UNIVERSITY PRESS, CAMBRIDGE

Outlines of Victorian Literature. By HUGH WALKER, LL.D., and MRS. HUGH WALKER. Cloth. Pp. 224. Price 3*s*.

J. BIELEFELDS VERLAG, FREIBURG, BADEN

The Little Yankee. By ALFRED D. SCHOCH, PH.D., and R. KRON, PH.D. Cloth. Pp. 192. Price M. 3.

CURRENT EDUCATIONAL LITERATURE IN THE PERIODICALS[1]

IRENE WARREN
Librarian, School of Education, University of Chicago

Allen, I. M. Some experiments in high-school instruction. School R. 22:26–44. (Ja. '14.)

Bell, Clair Hayden. Experiences of an American exchange teacher in Germany. Educa. R. 47:28–56. (Ja. '14.)

Benson, C. E. Some thinking processes of grade children. Psychol. Clinic 7:189–97. (D. '13.)

Beyer, Thomas Percival. Creative evolution and the woman question. Educa. R. 47:22–27. (Ja. '14.)

Boas, Ralph Philip. The introduction to English literature. English J. 2:630–36. (D. '13.)

Bole, John A. The organization of a large high school. School R. 22:1–11. (Ja. '14.)

Bostwick, Arthur E. The making of an American's library. Bookman 38:531–36. (Ja. '14.)

Briggs, Thomas H. Formal English grammar as a discipline. Teach. Coll. Rec. 14:1–93. (S. '13).

Brown, Elmer Ellsworth. The need of better preparation of teachers for secondary schools. Educa. 34:201–6. (D. '13.)

Cohen, Helen Louise. The foreigner in our schools: some aspects of the problem in New York. English J. 2:618–29. (D. 13.)

Cubberley, Ellwood P. Politics and the country-school problem. Educa. R. 47:10–21. (Ja. '14.)

Curtis, John W. Manual and vocational education. Man. Train. M. 15:89–104. (D. '13.)

Davidson, Percy E. Professional training of school officers. Educa. R. 46:463–91. (D. '13.)

Doll, E. A. Mental and physical development of normal children. Train. School M. (N.J.) 10:113–20. (D. '13.)

[1] *Abbreviations.*—Atlan., Atlantic Monthly; Cent., Century; Educa., Education; Educa. Bi-mo., Educational Bi-monthly; Educa. R., Educational Review; English J., English Journal; Lit. D., Literary Digest; Liv. Age, Living Age; Man. Train. M., Manual Training Magazine; Outl., Outlook; Pedagog. Sem., Pedagogical Seminary; Pop. Sci. Mo., Popular Science Monthly; Psychol. Clinic, Psychological Clinic; School R., School Review; Teach. Coll. Rec., Teachers College Record; Tech. World M., Technical World Magazine; Train. School M. (N.J.), Training School Magazine (New Jersey); U.S. Bur. of Educa. Bull., United States Bureau of Education Bulletin.

Draper, Ernest G. The college man in business. Outl. 106:27–30. (3 Ja. '14.)

Dresbach, M. Ocular defects and their relation to the health and work of the student. Educa. R. 46:492–509. (D. '13.)

Dutton, Samuel T. The investigation of school systems. Educa. R. 47:57–64. (Ja. '14.)

Edgerly, Joseph G. A co-operative industrial course. Educa. R. 46:438–49. (D. '13.)

Edson, Andrew W. The New York school inquiry. Educa. R. 46:450–56. (D. '13.)

Experiments in dramatization. Educa. Bi-mo. 8:106–22. (D. '13.)

Keith, Kate. Dramatization in third grade.

Stellar, Florence. Making of a play in third grade.

Fuller, Robert J. Co-operation between the National Education Association and the National Society for the Promotion of Industrial Education. School R. 22:12–19. (Ja. '14.)

Gilbertson, A. N. Contributions of the Danish anthropological survey to child study. Pedagog. Sem. 20:542–48. (D. '13.)

Good and bad in the New York schools. Educa. R. 47:65–79. (Ja. '14.)

Guild, Thacher H. Suggestions for the high-school play. English J. 2:637–46. (D. '13.)

Hart, Joseph K. The democratic organization of a state university. Pop. Sci. Mo. 84:91–100. (Ja. '14.)

Hastings, Wells. Our children. Cent. 87:345–47. (Ja. '14.)

Hibben, John Grier. The type of graduate scholar. Educa. R. 47:1–9. (Ja. '14.)

Hill, Herbert Wynford. The problem of harmonizing aesthetic interests with the commercial and industrial trend of our time. English J. 2:609–12. (D. '13.)

Hill, L. B., Rejall, A. E., and Thorndike, E. L. Practice in the case of typewriting. Pedagog. Sem. 20:516–29. (D. '13.)

Hinkle, E. C. Tests for efficiency in arithmetic. Educa. Bi-mo. 8:123–35. (D. '13.)

Keene, Charles H. The effect of conditions of schoolroom heating and ventilating on schoolroom attendance. School R. 22:20–25. (Ja. '14.)

Lowell, Abbott Lawrence. Measurements of efficiency in college. Educa. 34:217–24. (D. '13.)

McFarland, Raymond. Present facilities for the training of secondary school teachers in New England. Educa. 34:207–12. (D. '13.)

MacLear, Martha. The teacher's need of a community life. Pedagog. Sem. 20:539–41. (D. '13.)

McManis, John T. The locus of studies. Educa. Bi-mo. 8:95–105. (D. '13.)

Mason, Gregory. Educating a democracy. Outl. 105:742–44. (6 D. '13.)

Massal, Joseph A. Sending the convict to school. Tech. World M. 20:698–99. (Ja. '14.)

Mead, Cyrus D. The age of walking and talking in relation to general intelligence. Pedagog. Sem. 20:460–84. (D. '13.)

Mirrors in school. Lit. D. 47:1273. (27 D. '13.)

Morse, Josiah. A comparison of white and colored children measured by the Binet scale of intelligence. Pop. Sci. Mo. 84:75–79. (Ja. '14.)

Mrs. Young and her enemies. Lit. D. 47:1263–64. (27 D. '13.)

Orr, William. Aims and standards for preparation of secondary school teachers in New England. Educa. 34:213–16. (D. '13.)

Passano, L. Magruder. The college as a commercial factory. Educa. R. 46:457–62. (D. '13.)

Program of New England Association of Colleges and Preparatory Schools. Educa. 34:197–200. (D. '13.)

Repplier, Agnes. Popular education. Atlan. 113:1–8. (Ja. '14.)

(A) "school of country life." Lit. D. 47:1160. (13 D. '13.)

Scott, Jonathan F. Education and social conditions. Pedagog. Sem. 20:530–38. (D. '13.)

Sechrist, Frank K. Psychology of unconventional language. Pedagog. Sem. 20:413–59. (D. '13.)

Spaulding, Frank E. Measurements of efficiency in college. Educa. 34:225–48. (D. '13.)

Strayer, George Drayton. Is scientific accuracy possible in the measurement of the efficiency of instruction? Educa. 34:249–58. (D. '13.)

Strong, Alice C. Three hundred and fifty white and colored children measured by the Binet-Simon measuring scale of intelligence. A comparative study. Pedagog. Sem. 20:485–515. (D. '13.)

Sylvester, R. H. Clinical psychology adversely criticized. Psychol. Clinic 7:182–88. (D. '13.)

Terman, Lewis M. A report of the Buffalo conference on the Binet-Simon tests of intelligence. Pedagog. Sem. 20:549–54. (D. '13.)

Thompson, Oliver S. The minimum essentials of the school curriculum. Educa. Bi-mo. 8:136–43. (D. '13.)

Titchener, E. B. Psychology: science or technology? Pop. Sci. Mo. 84:39–51. (Ja. '14.)

Webster, Edward Harlan. Preparation in English for business. English J. 2:613–17. (D. '13.)

Welby, Désirée. The child and the nation. Liv. Age 274:707–12. (20 D. '13.)

West, Andrew F. The household of knowledge. Educa. R. 46:433–37. (D. '13.)

Witmer, Lightner. Children with mental defects distinguished from mentally defective children. Psychol. Clinic 7:173–81. (D. '13.)

Wolcott, J. D., ed. Monthly record of current educational publications. U.S. Bur. of Educa. Bull., 1913, No. 53. (D. '13.)

VOLUME XIV NUMBER 7

THE ELEMENTARY SCHOOL TEACHER

MARCH 1914

EDUCATIONAL NEWS AND EDITORIAL COMMENT

The Bureau of Education has issued a monograph entitled *Teaching Material in Government Publications*. In the introduction to this monograph Commissioner Claxton says:

Valuable School Material in Government Publications

One of the greatest needs of our elementary and secondary schools, both public and private, is the need for suitable material to supplement the meager outlines and brief statements of the textbooks in geography, history, hygiene, nature-study, agriculture, and other subjects. This need is greatest in country and village schools, which are without access to public libraries. Among the publications of the federal and state governments, reports, bulletins, circulars, and special documents are thousands of pages of matter of highest value for this purpose. Frequently these are published under titles that in no way indicate their fitness for this use.

The monograph makes an effort to place before the teachers of the country this large body of material. One finds the general divisions of the monograph under such heads as agriculture, geography, nature-study, hygiene, history, economics, including domestic economy. If one turns to the details he finds references which show where one can secure series of maps and geological studies of different parts of the United States. Under history one finds the accounts of some of the Indian tribes, accounts of the big trees of California, together with the historical events which parallel the climatic conditions indicated by the development of these trees at different ages. There are studies of the boundaries of the United States. Under hygiene there is a long list of subjects dealing with the uses of milk, dust preventives, etc.

These chance examples selected from the list of titles presented in the monograph will make it clear to every teacher that there is information of great value in public documents. In some cases the monographs can be secured without charge. In other cases the documents can be secured at a relatively very slight cost. Any teacher who makes application for this monograph will receive it as long as the supply lasts.

The Vermont State Survey

Vermont is the first state to have a comprehensive state-wide investigation of its school organization. The committee which was appointed about a year ago undertook to make an examination not only of the higher institutions, but also of the elementary schools of the state, together with the relation between these different members of the school system. The following extract from the *Journal* of Montpelier, Vermont, sets forth the results which have just been published:

The State Commission to Investigate the Educational System and Conditions of Vermont is distributing through the press Part II of the report made to it by the experts of the Carnegie Foundation based upon their recent educational survey. Part I, which was given to the public the latter part of December, attracted wide attention, as it deserved to do, and was read with keen and sympathetic interest by all desirous of seeing the schools of the Green Mountain State attain their greatest possible degree of efficiency and success. The comprehensive and accurate view of educational conditions as they actually exist, which this report furnishes, is of the highest value and its recommendations and suggestions may well be given the best thought of every friend of the public schools.

In the part of the report made public at this time there is contained a summary in tabular form of the conclusions reached which relate to general policies, legislative measures, and the State Board of Education's administrative policy. In Section 3 of Part II elementary schools are dealt with. The experts explain that the conclusions reached are based almost entirely on impressions gained through visits to 200 schools, observation of the work of 220 teachers, from a study of the registers in all schools in 202 towns, from printed reports of the state and towns, and from interviews.

It is clear, however, that the investigation of the experts was even more searching than shown by this summary, for they say in the report "a form calling for certain information regarding their training, salary, and experience was sent to each elementary-school teacher in the state, and 200 replies were received and studied. Finally, there were the suggestions of nearly 1,000 representative citizens sent in response to inquiries from the commission."

Discussing the state course of study the Carnegie experts say that, though the course given in the *Teachers' Annual* is not essentially different from most other state courses, the fact that it is not followed in any of the schools visited to any considerable extent indicates it is not suited to their needs. It is pointed out that this course of study recognizes to a small extent only the varying abilities of children and that here as well as elsewhere pupils who complete the school course are unable to do satisfactory work in positions in which the use of arithmetic and English is required.

The course in English, it is explained, is based on a supposition "that the child will enter the high school and that the work given is that which is best calculated to prepare for that end. The fact that only a few of these boys and girls will ever enter high school is constantly ignored." As to the course in arithmetic the experts declare "the situation is but little better."

It will be seen in this part of the report of the experts, as it was made plain in the part that preceded it, that the aim has been to suggest changes that will provide the most practical education for the children of Vermont, the kind of education that will give them the greatest degree of efficiency in the place in life they are destined to occupy.

The *Morning Journal* has heretofore expressed the belief that the recommendation of the Carnegie foundation experts that state subsidies be withdrawn from institutions of higher learning and devoted to the strengthening of the elementary and secondary schools, in which 95 per cent of the children of Vermont obtain their entire education, will meet the hearty approval of an overwhelming majority of the citizens of the state. It is as strongly convinced that the recommendations concerning elementary schools will be given similar widespread indorsement.

More School Surveys

School surveys are the order of the day. Laymen and teachers recognize the value of such studies of the school situation. The following report, which is reproduced from the *Times* of Leavenworth, Kansas, shows how general is the interest in this type of inquiry:

Leavenworth will set a good example to the less progressive cities of the state and give this city a position to render educational aid to the state as the result of the school survey which will be held the second and third weeks in March. That was the opinion given yesterday by Dr. W. R. Monroe, of the School of Education of the Emporia Normal, who is to have charge of the survey.

W. W. Charters, of the School of Education of the University of Missouri, Mr. Monroe, W. R. Smith, of the sociology department of the Normal, and Miss Minnie E. Porter, of the English department, came to Leavenworth yesterday morning for the purpose of gathering data for foundation of the survey work. The observations will be continued today. Yesterday the educators did not visit any of the institutions, simply driving about the city, paying particular attention to the educational needs of Leavenworth.

OUTLINES PURPOSE

At the high school yesterday afternoon short talks were delivered by Dr. Monroe, Dr. Smith, and Miss Porter to the teachers of the city. Dr. Monroe outlined the purpose of the survey and said that it would show the educational needs of the community, and make a graphic presentation of the present efficiency of the system. He said that it was impossible to have ideal education without all agencies working together.

Miss Porter outlined to the teachers the relation of the child in the classroom to the organized life of the school and the world of men and affairs. Dr. Smith said that the school survey is yet in its infancy and that this city should be complimented for having the first in the state.

A fairly large crowd was in attendance at the high school last night to listen to a talk delivered by W. W. Charters. The Missouri University man proved an interesting talker. He explained the purpose of the survey and forecasted that much good would result if the teachers and patrons of the school lent the proper co-operation in the movement.

Another school survey which has been completed is reported by the Bureau of Education in its *City School Circular No. 26* in the following terms:

The board of education at Grafton, West Virginia, a city of 8,000 population, not being satisfied that they were expending the school funds to the best advantage, invited three practical school men of their own state to make a survey of the schools of that city, and to make a definite report regarding the needs of the schools and the best method of economizing on the funds available so as to provide for these needs.

The committee, composed of Dr. J. N. Deahl, head of the department of education in the State University; Mr. Joseph Rosier, superintendent of schools, Fairmont; and Mr. Otis Wilson, superintendent of schools, Elkins, were asked to make the survey, and accepted on condition that their report should in no way affect the standing of the superintendent. The board assured these men that the superintendent was leaving, and that it was desired to have an investigation before the election of a new superintendent.

The investigation covered the following points: educational needs of the community from an industrial standpoint, the professional training and equipment of the teachers employed, the course of study in use in the schools, the methods of teaching and the plan of school organization, methods of administration as related to the assignment of teachers, possible consolidation of departments and grades, current expenditures, the purchase of supplies, and high-school equipment.

The committee made no attempt to discuss theories, but recommended among other things that a co-operative industrial course similar to that at

Fitchburg, Massachusetts, be instituted; that night classes be formed for the boys and girls employed in the glass factories; that the present organization of the high-school work into four curricula should be made less restrictive; that the grades below the high school be reorganized so that the average enrolment for each teacher would be between 30 and 40 pupils and that the money saved be applied to the employment of instruction of manual training and domestic science; that the grade work could be improved by giving less time to the formal study of United States history, geography, physiology, and arithmetic, the time assigned for arithmetic being excessive.

The Powers of the Board of Education

Several controversies have recently brought to the front the question of the relative positions in matters of school administration of the school superintendent and the board of education. In many of these discussions it has been assumed by the board of education that it has supreme control of the school system. It is therefore interesting to see the problem of the school board's functions brought out from an entirely different point of view. The following news item, taken from the *Gazette* of Schenectady, New York, calls attention to the fundamental fact that the functions of the school board have not been clearly defined:

The situation in this city, with reference to the administration of the school system, presents some very awkward and very undesirable features and a condition of affairs exists in regard to it that should be changed.

The public assumes, generally speaking, that all matters in relation to the schools are within the jurisdiction of the board of education. Actually, however, such is not the case and the limitations imposed upon the board by amendments to the supplemental city charter—the charter itself dealing very little with educational matters—tend to handicap those nominally responsible for the direction of this exceedingly important branch of municipal affairs.

The board of education, it is true, prescribes courses and employs teachers and in general has authority over the teaching and the teachers. But, strangely enough, it has no authority over the school janitors, who are under the control of the commissioner of public works. Hence in the simple matter of even maintaining a suitable temperature in a schoolroom not only does the principal of a school theoretically have no power to issue orders to the janitor of the building, but not even the superintendent of schools or the board of education itself has such authority. The impracticability and the foolishness of such an arrangement is plainly apparent.

When it comes to new school buildings, the board may determine where they shall be located, but the authority to choose the plans for them is given to the city engineer. The board has not even the authority to compel the making of repairs. In reality it can only suggest and advise that they be made. It does not even have charge of the cleaning of the school buildings.

There is no system of bookkeeping for the board outside the comptroller's office. When it wants to know the condition of its finances, just how much it has expended and how much it has remaining to expend, it must go to the latter to learn the condition of affairs.

There is still another factor in the situation. The superintendent of schools does not change with a change of administration. Neither does the personnel of the board of education, entirely; that is to say, there are enough hold-over members to make it a continuous organization, and its policies and plans are continuous ones. On the other hand, the superintendent of public works and the city engineer, both of whom have charge of different matters relating to the school system under the present arrangement, nearly always change with every change in the administration. The incumbent of either of these offices may modify or overturn the plans of his predecessor. Furthermore, it has a tendency to bring politics into the school system.

The board is quite justified in feeling that this system is unwise and that it is unfairly handicapped. Certainly such a method of conducting the affairs of the school system does not tend to promote efficiency. On the contrary, it imposes difficulties and obstacles in the way of a satisfactory administration.

The necessary legislation to change it and to give the board control of the schools in fact as well as in theory should be sought. It will, if secured, place the entire matter on a more practical and common-sense basis.

This clipping illustrates perhaps more clearly than the disputes between superintendents and boards of education the fact that our organization of school systems in this country is by no means completely worked out. Perhaps this item is a better text for school men to preach from than their own personal disputes with boards of education. This text certainly furnishes good ground for the contention that we ought to have a final and expert re-examination of the whole problem of the functions of the board of education.

The following report, clipped from the *Free Press* of Milwaukee, Wisconsin, indicates a type of extension of the public-school system which may help to solve one of the gravest city problems:

School for the Unemployed

Kenosha has opened a school for the unemployed. There are no limitations of age, color, or nationality. The Deming School, one of the smaller buildings of the city, has been partially given over and in a week twenty students have been enrolled. Nearly all are men and women who have been employed as machine operators in the factories.

It is planned to offer something which will be of distinct benefit to every student. Some of the men, who have been driven from the bench in machine-shops, are studying the common branches of "readin, 'ritin', and 'rithmetic," while at an adjoining bench another man is learning the rudiments of book-keeping and commercial arithmetic.

Typewriters have been installed and some of the students are studying stenography. It is probable that some of these men and girls will never return to the bench, but will be graduated into office positions.

The students are given thirty hours of schooling each week and some have shown so high an appreciation of the new school that they are also attending the evening schools of the city.

The following editorial, clipped from the *Herald* of El Paso, Texas, states briefly the case for compulsory education as it is viewed in one of the progressive cities of Texas:

Compulsory Education in Texas

Compulsory education in Texas is being talked of again. Texas is one of the very few states not having such a law, the others all being in the south. It is time that Texas, with her enormous resources for public education, should provide school facilities for all her children, and compel them to come in.

El Paso educators have long wanted such a law. If the state legislature again refuses to enact a general law to this effect, it is probable that an effort will be made to procure the passage of a special act applying to this city alone, as an independent school district.

Compulsory education in El Paso, enforced, would mean between 2,000 and 3,000 more children in school than are now attending. Provision would have to be made for them, in rooms and teachers. But our failure to provide schooling for these thousands of children is a kind of failure that curses this community in many different ways. It is costly every way, far more costly than the schools would be; it is a menace to the health and welfare of the community; it greatly curtails our producing power as a city; and it sets us back in the race of the cities for industrial and commercial development.

The following quotations are from an article published in the *New York Tribune:*

Visiting Teachers in New York

The visiting teacher was added to the machinery of the New York public schools in 1906 by private charity, under the auspices of the Public Education Association. The success of the eight teachers they have maintained since then has been so great that it is now proposed to add two more to the force. For this purpose an association known as the Visiting Teachers' Auxiliary to the Public Education Association has been formed within the last few days.

One of the members of this association in an interview discussed the functions of these visiting teachers:

What do they do? Well, they discover that very often the "stupid" child is not stupid at all, but merely misplaced. I remember one Tommy, who had been given up by several teachers as hopeless. He simply could not learn his lessons, and they were about to advise that he be sent to an institution for the feeble-minded when the visiting teacher heard of him. She went to his home, and found the family admiring a little baby's chair the boy had made from pieces of old boxes. It was an excellent piece of work, and the visiting teacher realized at once that the boy was a mechanical genius. She recommended that he be transferred to a school where he could study carpentry. This was done, and now this Tommy is a shining member of society.

Sometimes the visiting teacher finds that the fault lies not with the school or the child, but with the home. It may be that he has no proper place to study. Then the neighborhood is searched until a quiet room is found, either in a settlement or in a public library. Sometimes the child seems dull and listless in school not because he is feeble minded, but because his sleep is impaired. Perhaps his mother has sewing to do late into the night, and must work in the one little room where Tommy is trying to sleep; or perhaps his diet is composed largely of tea and coffee, and he does not sleep soundly. In this case his mother is taken aside and instructed in the health and feeding of children.

Women in the Cincinnati and Philadelphia Schools

The *Cincinnati Enquirer* reports that the small board of education of the city of Cincinnati adopted unanimously the recommendations of Superintendent Condon in which sweeping changes were recommended in the rules of the Cincinnati school system with regard to the employment of women. Superintendent Condon made the following recommendations with regard to the salaries of women:

While lack of funds will prevent any favorable consideration of the subject at this time, yet that I may make my position perfectly clear I wish to say that when expenses will warrant such a move I propose to recommend to the Union Board that they amend the regulations which discriminate in the matter of salary between men and women holding positions of similar responsibility and performing work of the same grade with the same degree of success. I cannot reconcile such a discrimination with my idea of justice.

Furthermore, Superintendent Condon recommends that the board revise its rule which provides that "any female teacher shall forfeit her position by marrying during the term of her appointment." Superintendent Condon further recommends that teachers be chosen for the high school even if they are not university graduates, provided they have shown themselves to be successful in their school work. The list which has formerly been drawn upon for high-school appointments is made up exclusively of university graduates. Superintendent Condon devotes several paragraphs to his statement that he is entirely in favor of a university education for teachers, but he believes that success in teaching should not be rated below academic training.

These sweeping changes in the attitude of the board of education if they are really made operative will furnish another evidence of the movement in American schools in the direction of a more complete recognition of women. A report comes also from Philadelphia to the effect that the women teachers of that city have secured a favorable vote in that the women are now to be placed upon the same list as the men so far as their eligibility for appointment to principalships is concerned. Formerly two distinct lists were kept, one of the men and one of the women. From this time on the appointments are to be made without discrimination.

Outside Credits Supervised by Schools

The topic of school credit for work done at home has several times been the subject of comment in the *Elementary School Teacher*. In the January number attention was drawn to the difficulty of organizing such work in a way to justify school credit and also in a way to justify the expenditure of the energy of the school in this direction. That note has brought from several quarters reports of the success of plans of the type under discussion. In some cases the courses that have been favorably reported are courses in music. These are especially successful when conducted in connection with high-school organization. The following comments from Superintendent Shideler, of Junction City, indicate the success of that type of work in one city:

> I wish to state that the plan of the outside study of music is very successful on the part of the high school, as it meets a long-sought need in this community. It is successful on the part of the private teacher, as it shifts the responsibility somewhat and encourages her pupils to do regular work. The parents are satisfied in that it compels the pupils to practice and also to keep up with their lessons in order to conform to the requirement of reporting to the superintendent's office, and thus receive high-school credit. The pupil is pleased, since she receives high-school credit for work which she would like to complete regardless of such credit. In truth, the plan is meeting with more

success than we had anticipated. Six private teachers are instructing pupils outside of school in piano, voice, violin, and cornet, for which high-school credit will be granted.

The plan is successful in that it measures in quality and quantity with any other high-school subject, it affords training in instrumental music where high schools cannot offer it, and the supervision is entirely within the control of the school authorities.

The following from Spokane, Wash., also gives the opinion of the community with regard to the experiment being tried in that state:

So popular has become the system of giving school credits for chores and household work performed by the pupils of Spokane County at their homes that County Superintendent E. G. McFarland is making a second distribution of the credit blanks, and has ordered 100,000 of them printed to supplement a 5,000 order which was exhausted in one month from the time the plan was started. Mr. McFarland states that 80 out of the 176 schools of the county are now giving this credit and that new ones are adopting the plan each week.

"The teachers say the system has greatly aided their work," said the superintendent, "and the parents are delighted with it. Instances have come to our attention where children who could hardly be compelled to do any work before now eagerly perform the tasks around their homes and take the credits to school to get the monthly half-holiday for perfect records. Several schools have reported that not a pupil was tardy or absent during the month."

The system allows one or two credits for certain listed home tasks performed on school days. The perfect month's record consists of five such tasks performed every day, making 25 for each school week and 100 for each month. In conjunction with the work, which must be done cheerfully, not under compulsion, the pupil must be at school every day and never be tardy. Parents fill out the blanks according to the excellence of the child's performance.

At the end of the term 10 credits are given on examination, so that a pupil who has done the outside work and has never been tardy or absent will have a few credits to make up any deficiency in examinations.

Another feature that Mr. McFarland is now extending is the giving of diplomas to each perfect pupil making a perfect year's record. He says that one thousand such diplomas will have to be issued if the interest continues.

The success of these two experiments in outside credit does not in any wise modify the opinion of the writers of the January editorial. The general question which was raised and is here reiterated is the question of the organization of this work in such a way as to make it a genuine part of the school activity. It should be recognized that the school activity is not synonymous with home work and that there is grave danger of distracting students from the legitimate problems of school work unless both kinds of work are carefully planned and made genuinely educative.

SOME FACTORS AFFECTING INDUSTRIAL EDUCATION

LEONARD P. AYRES, PH.D.
Director, Division of Education, Russell Sage Foundation

During the past six months the Division of Education of the Sage Foundation has been conducting a series of studies with the object of securing a fact basis for some parts of our thinking and acting with regard to vocational education and vocational guidance. One of our investigations consisted of a study of certain facts concerning all of the thirteen-year-old boys in the public schools of 78 American cities and the fathers of the boys. The total number of cases amounted to 22,027. We chose the thirteen-year-old boys because those are the ones that are in the last year of compulsory school attendance. Soon large numbers of them will leave school to enter money-earning occupations.

Thirteen-year-old boys in each grade from kindergarten through high school.—The first fact that we learned about these boys was that they are scattered through all the grades of the school course from the kindergarten to the last year of the high school.

More significant still, we found that one-half of them were in the sixth grade or below. Since, in general, the children who drop out of school earliest are those who are seriously retarded and are found in the lower grades at relatively advanced ages, this fact is most important. It indicates that large numbers of these boys may be expected to leave school soon and go to work with an educational preparation so inadequate that they cannot enter the ranks of industry with profit either to themselves or to the community.

Another fact brought to light by this part of the investigation was that there is a wide range of conditions in the different cities. In those making the poorest showing, scarcely one in ten of these thirteen-year-old boys was in the seventh grade or above, while in the cities at the other end of the list eight boys out of every ten were within sight of completing the common-school course.

The lesson of these figures is that in many cities the problem of securing a reasonably complete elementary schooling for all the children is far more pressing than that of instituting specialized industrial training. The data show too that, since this has been accomplished by some of the cities, it may be hopefully undertaken by all.

Only one father in six now lives where he was born.—The next set of data secured give the birthplaces of these boys and their fathers. This inquiry showed that only about one father in six is now living in the city of his birth and that among the boys only a few more than one-half are now living where they were born. These facts are significant because it is often urged that the schools should develop courses of industrial education that will directly prepare the children to enter the local industries. But if present conditions maintain in the future, the great majority of adults are not going to work in the same communities in which they received their schooling.

Industries in which the fathers work.—Another portion of the investigation showed for each of the fathers the nature of the trade or business in which he was engaged and also what kind of work he was doing at that trade or business. The occupations of these fathers were studied in the hope that they might furnish an index to the sorts of life work that the young people now in city schools may be expected to go into. A double classification of the data was made first by industries and second by occupations within the industries. The industrial classification was the one adopted by the United States Census Bureau and included the following five main divisions:

I. Industries of Extraction—Agriculture, Forestry, Mining, etc.
II. Industries of Transformation—Building Trades, Manufacturing, etc.
III. Industries of Transportation and Communication—Railroads, Telegraph, etc.
IV. Industries of Trade—Wholesale and Retail Trade, Real Estate, etc.
V. Service—Government, Professional, Domestic, Personal, etc.

The tabulation of the returns showed that the fathers were distributed in these five main industrial divisions as follows:

TABLE I

INDUSTRIAL DISTRIBUTION OF FATHERS

Industrial Group	Percentage
Extraction	4
Transformation	52
Transportation	13
Trade	19
Service	12
Total	100

One surprising fact shown by these returns is that only about one-half of these men are found in the industries of transformation which include the building trades and all classes of manufacturing. This is important, because plans for inaugurating systems of vocational education are commonly based on the proposition that a large majority of the young people in our city schools will find their life work in these industries.

Occupations of the fathers.—The occupational classification of these workers was made under six heads, of which the first three relate to occupations primarily manual in nature, while the remaining three groups are primarily mental. The distribution of the fathers in these groups is shown in Table II.

TABLE II

OCCUPATIONAL DISTRIBUTION OF FATHERS

Occupational Group	Percentage
Unskilled laborers	4
Semi-skilled laborers and machine operatives	22
Artisans and industrial foreman	40
Clerks and salesmen	9
Managers, superintendents, and proprietors	21
Professional and financial	4

One-third in headwork, two-thirds in handwork.—Three significant facts are brought to light by the figures in Table II. The first is that more of these men are in professional work than there are engaged in unskilled labor. The second is that the group of managers, superintendents, and proprietors is practically as large as that made up of semi-skilled laborers. The third is that the mental workers constitute more than one-third of all the workers.

Constant and variable occupations.—The analysis of the data concerning the industries and occupations by which these men earn their livings brought to light the significant fact that there are some occupations which are common to each community and which we may term "constant occupations." Other occupations are found in some localities and not in others, and these we may term "variable occupations." The constant occupations are those which are necessary to maintain the many branches of that enlarged municipal housekeeping which must go on wherever large numbers of people live together in one place. For example, house painting must be carried on in the city where the house is, while paint may be manufactured anywhere. The baking of bread must be carried on by each community, but crackers can be baked somewhere else and brought into the city.

In making our analysis of constant and variable occupations, we enlarged the scope of our inquiry so as to include all of the cities of the United States of more than 50,000 population. We discovered the facts concerning the number of people engaged in each of 140 separate occupations in each one of those cities. As a result, we found that there are 20 constant occupations in which the number of men workers is always at least equal to one for each thousand people in the population. We discovered, for example, that in any city in the United States of 50,000 population, you will always find more than 50 barbers, and that in the average city of that size you will find 150 barbers. It so happens that this is the most constant of all occupations, so that, if anyone knowing these facts had been able to foresee that Gary, Indiana, for example, would be a city of 40,000 population, he would have been able to prophesy ahead of time that the city would employ approximately 120 barbers. These constant occupations with the number of people engaged in them in the average city are shown in Table III.

It is almost certain that if these data were entirely up to date, two, and only two, additional occupations would be included in the list—those of stenographer-typewriter and chauffeur. These occupations include in the aggregate more than half of all the people engaged in gainful occupations in all of our cities. These facts appear significant. They seem to indicate that if all other conditions are equal, vocational education should give preference to occupations that are everywhere constant over those that are not.

TABLE III

CONSTANT OCCUPATIONS IN CITIES OF 50,000 POPULATION AND OVER

Occupation	Average Number Workers per Thousand Population
Men—	
Bakers	2
Shoemakers	2
Street railway men	3
Plumbers	3
Barbers	3
Masons	4
Blacksmiths	4
Printers	4
Engineers	5
Waiters	6
Bookkeepers	6
Painters	7
Machinists	8
Steam railroad men	11
Carpenters	11
Salesmen	12
Teamsters	12
Clerks	15
Storekeepers	15
Laborers	37
Women—	
Housekeepers	2
Nurses	3
Laundresses	4
Saleswomen	4
Teachers	5
Dressmakers	9
Servants	25

Summary.—The findings that have been so briefly reviewed are preliminary and tentative. It is hoped that the studies now under way will produce results more final and definite in character. Meanwhile we believe that these studies already furnish material which should lead us to proceed with caution in our thinking and acting with respect to vocational education and vocational guidance. We may summarize our findings as follows:

1. A study including 22,027 thirteen-year-old boys in 78 city school systems shows that these boys are scattered through all of the grades of the school course from the kindergarten to the last year of the high school.

2. One-half of the boys are in the sixth grade or below. They need a common-school education more than they need specialized industrial training.

3. In some cities nearly eight of each ten boys were in the seventh grade or above, while in other cities only one boy in ten was in the seventh grade or above. What some cities have accomplished others may hopefully strive for.

4. Only one father in six was born in the city where he now lives, and only a few more than one-half of the boys were born where they now live. This has an important bearing on the proposition that the schools should shape their courses with the predominant aim of preparing the children to enter the local industries.

5. Only about one-half of the fathers are engaged in industries of the building trades and manufacturing.

6. More of the fathers are engaged in the professions than are in unskilled labor.

7. Mental workers constitute more than one-third of all the workers. This fact, and the two preceding ones, indicate the inaccuracy of the common generalization to the effect that only one child in ten in our public schools will find his life work in an intellectual occupation, while the other nine are destined to do handwork.

8. In American cities of 50,000 population and above there are twenty "constant occupations" in which the number of men workers is everywhere at least equal to one for each thousand in the population, and seven "constant occupations" in which the number of women workers is at least equal to one for each thousand people in the population. Other conditions being equal, vocational education and vocational guidance may well consider favoring "constant occupations" over localized ones.

REPORT OF EXPERIMENT ON THE VALUE OF PLAYS AND GAMES IN ARITHMETICAL DRILL[1]

PAULINE E. MATTHEWS
Los Angeles, California

The experiment which is reported in this paper was conducted by a student teacher and extended over a period of nine weeks. The grade was the Fourth "A." At the beginning of the work there were twenty children in the class. Soon after, six more entered, giving a total of twenty-six in the end. However, none of the data in this report, with the exception of the statement of the training-teacher, was taken before the entrance of the last six pupils.

The aim of this experiment was (1) to prove that more ground may be covered than is required by our course of study, (2) to determine the effects of plays and games in arithmetical drill.

The following is the statement of the teacher in whose room the experiment was conducted, as to the condition of the class at the time the work began and her general criticism of the work as conducted.

> At the beginning of the last nine weeks the children knew their multiplication tables and the first case in long division. At the end of the eighth week they had completed long division and had started fractions as far as addition.
>
> During this period all the children took an active part in the arithmetic games, which were carefully and skilfully carried out by the teacher in charge. The interest was keen and the children worked hard and cheerfully when a game was in view.
>
> The period following was a period of relaxation. This was necessary in order to have the children ready for further work. I believe the arithmetic games are an excellent motive to interest children in arithmetic and to make the work seem alive to them. An increased efficiency in word problems was noticeable.
>
> LILLIAN LOCKETT

[1] This experiment was outlined and supervised by Myrtie Collier, teacher of mathematics in the Los Angeles State Normal School.

The ground covered was the last half of Case 1 in long division, through long division to the addition of fractions. This was done in the time allowed by the course of study to drill in long division. During this period considerable work in word problems was taken up which was almost entirely a review and application of simple operations in the fundamental processes. When this work began, the class was doing long division problems in which the division was of two numbers, the first being greater than the second. At the close of the term they were able to handle any divisor consisting of two or three integers and seemed much more capable of handling word problems than formerly. In advance of this, which was the regular work for the Fourth Grade, they had acquired a good concept of fractions, were able to add fractions having the same denominator, and to multiply a whole number by a fraction.

The part of interest lies in the "how," rather than the "what," however, for the latter will vary according to the grade and locality in which one teaches. The work was accomplished by the use of plays and games with formal drill. In the nine weeks games were used seven times, which does not include two smaller play devices used in the more formal periods of drill.

The games were (1) the baseball game, (2) the "Santa Monica" Road Race, and (3) the "Grand Avenue Department Store." The play devices were a clock face with movable hands, for each child, and a card game. A description of the games follows.

BASEBALL

Preparation for the game.—

1. Selection and making two copies of problems, one for the pitcher, other for the umpire (teacher).

2. Choosing of team and team names by the children.

Scheme of game.—

Captains compete on problems to decide which team has first "bats." The first correctly finished wins "bats" for his team. Captains choose at signal, "Play ball." The successful captain then works on paper, competing with the batter at board, who is also competing with the catcher. If the batter is the first one finished and correct, he passes on to "first," where he competes with the first baseman and the right fielder at the same time that another of his team is working at bats. If the batter is the first one finished and correct, he passes on to "first," where he competes with the first baseman and the right fielder at the same time that

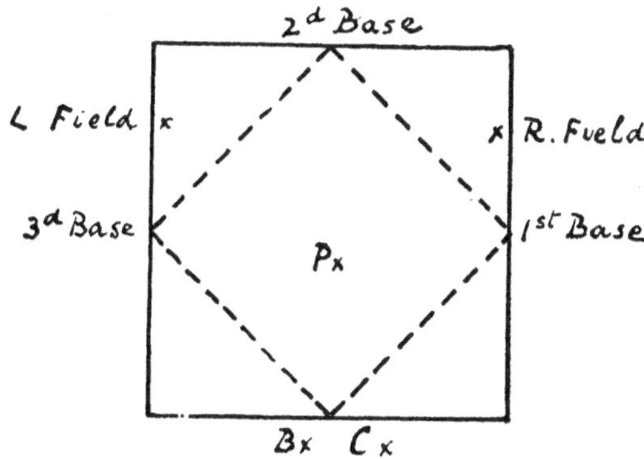

another of his team is working at bats. If the batter is not the first one finished and correct, he has been put out. Three outs means change of team at bats and two changes make an inning. A "run" consists of a player having successfully passed the third base and counts 1 for his team.

COMPARATIVE TABLE

Table of Baseball	*Formal Drill*
(NUMBER OF PROBLEMS)	
Problem worked in game:	
First game = 7	Average = $8\frac{2}{3}$ problems per game
Second game = 9	
Third game = 10	
Problems in formal drill	Average = $4\frac{2}{3}$ per day

This means, of course, that $8\frac{2}{3}$ problems were correctly worked by *different* pupils, during the game, those who were running for their team, as opposed to an average of $4\frac{2}{3}$ for each child during the formal drill. However, by the time of the third game all the children were working all the problems, which gave each child ten problems during that hour.

ROAD RACE

Preparation: 1. Teacher.—

1. Selection of problems.

2. Selection of familiar names for stations.

3. Writing of problems on board (one or two) under name of each station.

4. Working of problems before class so that *all* the answers may be had at once.

5 (desirable but not necessary). Making of pennants, one for each child, a different color for each machine, each pennant bearing initial of his machine and his individual number. These are quickly and easily made from any art paper at hand.

Preparation: 2. Pupils.—

1. Choice of names for machines (one for each row).

2. Numbering down rows for individual machine's number.

Scheme of game.—

One of *each* kind of *machine* starts at *each* station. Work on paper. Take problems from board. As soon as anyone is finished he goes to the teacher who tells him if he is correct; if he is, he goes on to the next station to the right; if not, he goes back and works that problem over again. When he does get right he goes immediately to work on his new problem at the next station, and another machine of his same make takes his place at the old station. In this way the whole class is soon on the floor and at work. The score is made by the number of players on each side who complete the circuit, the machine having had the greatest number being accounted the winner.

When the game starts one will have as many as eighteen on the floor starting to work and inside of five minutes will be able to put on ten more, for the work in this game is very rapid. This is in the teacher's opinion the best way of keeping *every* child working *every* minute.

COMPARATIVE TABLE

Road Race v. *Formal Drill*

	Road Race	Formal Drill
Average No. problems correct	$4\frac{10}{13}$	$3\frac{25}{26}$
" " " incorrect	$1\frac{4}{13}$	$\frac{19}{26}$
" " " worked	$6\frac{1}{13}$	$4\frac{9}{13}$

It is shown here that the number of problems worked in the road race was greater, and that the number worked correctly was greater than on the day of the formal drill and that despite the fact that the degree of inaccuracy is greater on the day of the game. This inaccuracy is due, I believe, wholly to the fact that the children had not yet accustomed themselves to the excitement. The only criticism that might be offered here is that things move so rapidly that the teacher has no chance to give any individual help. Still, that also has its advantage, for it gives the child the chance to find his own mistakes and profit by them.

STORE

Preparation.—

1. To decide kind of store—grocery or department.
2. To have children bring things.
3. To have children make invoice, prepare store, and help them determine prices.
4. To prepare lists for the class's first trip to store.
5. To select clerks, bookkeepers, head bookkeeper, have children make signs, play money, and price lists for their customers. The latter are put on the board.

Scheme of game.—

Clerk makes sale, writes slip and duplicate. Slip goes to buyer and duplicate to bookkeeper who makes change and O.K.'s the slip. Buyers go in relays. When through making purchases or when told to take seat, buyers go "home," make out a statement of money on hand when game started, purchases made, total amount spent, money on hand at present. This shows whether they have accepted wrong change and if the clerks are making wrong change. They then figure out where the mistake was made and go back to that department and state their case. At the end of about twenty minutes' buying the store closes, the clerks begin putting away the goods, while the bookkeeper checks up his slips. He makes out a statement which he hands in to the head bookkeeper with his cash drawer, showing money in drawer at beginning of hour, sales made and amount, money in drawer at close of period. His account must balance. This is determined by the head bookkeeper, who makes out the report of the store by departments and hands it into the manager (teacher). All reports go to the teacher.

This game is particularly valuable in teaching how to make a sales slip, beginning of bookkeeping, denominate numbers, i.e., money, linear measure, weights and values, practical fractions, etc.

To be able to tell the effect of this game one should use it for about a week at first, then omit it for six or seven lessons and repeat it. It was impossible to do this at this time, for the end of the year was at hand, so it was used on only two successive days. On both days the work went very well, but especially so on the second day. The storekeepers had learned to make the change for $12\frac{1}{2}$ cents or any sum with half-cents, on the first day, and the board price lists showed many articles on special sale at $7\frac{1}{2}$ cents, $12\frac{1}{2}$ cents, $87\frac{1}{2}$ cents, etc. As a whole the work was accurate and it was decidedly a success.

Probably the most noticeable effect of these games was the joy the children gained from the games which they carried over into the formal drills. They seemed to feel that since the games were "fun," all number work was, and they worked with a will. There was never a day after a game that I found the discipline at all difficult and never a game where the children seemed inclined to take advantage of their freedom. And they were *free*, they laughed and ran to their bases or stations, and jumped and clapped when their team or machine scored. There was nothing stiff or formal about the work.

The fact that the class went farther than the work assigned by the course of study, in even such a short time as was allowed for this work, proves the first point stated in the aim. In the second place, it is shown that *more work* and that *more accurate work* is accomplished through the use of plays and games as drill devices than by the ordinary methods of formal drill.

THE TEACHING OF HYGIENE BELOW THE HIGH SCHOOL

J. MACE ANDRESS
Instructor in Hygiene, State Normal School, Worcester, Mass.

I. THE FAILURE OF HEALTH INSTRUCTION IN THE GRADES

That the health instruction in the public schools has improved within the last few years is not to be doubted; but its effectiveness is still to be questioned. Dr. McMurray, a member of the Hanus commission which investigated the schools of New York City, found that the health instruction was wooden and far from practical.[1] Rapeer, who made a careful investigation of the educational hygiene in twenty-five leading cities, says of the teaching of hygiene:[2] "And yet the subject is a tail-end subject, little emphasized, and furnished with poor textbooks for the most part, and very frequently with poor teachers in the grades and high school. Colleges do not usually give credit for, nor demand a knowledge of, this vitally essential subject of health and how to get and maintain it, much to their disparagement, and consequently we find many schools almost entirely neglecting it."

The writer wishes to propose the following reasons for the failure of the teaching of hygiene in the grades below the high school:

1. The teachers as a class are not well prepared to teach hygiene. The training received in the normal schools has too often emphasized anatomy and physiology rather than hygiene. As a result the teachers are deficient in the right kind of knowledge. They have not yet learned to appreciate the importance of health instruction.

2. The psychology and pedagogy of hygiene have as yet not been worked out, because hygiene is really one of the newest subjects in the curriculum. The disadvantage of teaching hygiene rather than arithmetic is obvious when one considers the splendid devices

[1] Frank M. McMurray, *Elementary School Standards*, 1913 (World Book Co.), pp. 51–54, 148–54.

[2] *School Health Administration* (Teachers College, Columbia University), p. 25.

involving play and construction now in use in the teaching of arithmetic, and the dearth of these devices in the teaching of hygiene.

3. Many of the textbooks still in use devote altogether too much space to anatomy and physiology. Much of the material in these books is too difficult for children, and in some cases the way in which it is presented leads to prejudice against any further study of the subject. The writer has known of cases where the children referred to lessons in hygiene as "nasty." Such an attitude can scarcely be expected to inspire a love for health or result in hygienic practices. Fortunately there are a number of good books on hygiene that have recently appeared that could be put into the hands of children with profit.

4. The hygiene that has been taught has been too general and abstract and has aimed at knowledge rather than practice. For example, teachers often spend much time on the anatomy and physiology of the digestive system to the neglect of such topics as food values, the hygiene of eating, how to preserve food, how to keep it from becoming contaminated, etc.

5. The instruction in hygiene is not well organized through the grades, hence repetition and tedium both for teachers and for pupils are common.

6. The aims in teaching hygiene have not been clearly formulated. Few principals of the elementary schools have clearly in mind what results they ought to get by the time the children get through the eighth or ninth grade; consequently there has been little systematic planning for results.

7. The teachers do not like to teach hygiene. It is only natural to expect that such vagueness as to aims, values, and methods tends naturally to dull the teacher's zeal, spontaneity, and efficiency. She realizes her failures in teaching hygiene, has a hearty dislike for it, and slights the subject whenever possible.

The psychology and pedagogy of hygiene are still crude and unsystematic. This paper is written with the idea of helping hygiene to find itself by suggesting some principles for guidance. The brevity and scope of this paper make some of these assertions sound dogmatic. At best they can be regarded only as tentative.

The old-fashioned instruction has been a failure. We must have a program for further experimentation.

II. FUNDAMENTAL FACTS AND PRINCIPLES INVOLVED IN THE TEACHING OF HYGIENE

It is the belief of the writer that methods of teaching hygiene should take into consideration the following facts and principles:

1. *The fundamental aim in teaching hygiene should be the inculcating of habits necessary for health rather than knowledge.* It is better to have the habit of cleaning one's teeth than to have all the information on the teeth which is available. To make the instruction in hygiene really effective the teacher should have a good knowledge of the psychology of habit formation, and how to apply it. Whenever possible the instruction should be correlated with action. If, for example, the teacher wishes the children to clean their shoes when entering the schoolroom, she should see that a place is provided for that purpose, and she must then insist that the shoes be cleaned, until the habit has been gained.

2. The child has no appreciation for health which serves as a motive for future action.[1] In the stirring dramatic world in which he lives there is almost no inclination to consider the consequences of his behavior on health. To say to the small boy, "Now, Johnny, if you do not get plenty of fresh air, you will not be strong," has little or no effect on Johnny. He is concerned with his immediate world, and not with the problems that he is likely to have six months or ten years hence. Minor illnesses, which might be expected to serve as motives for action, are soon forgotten, and it is doubtful whether the more serious ones offer anything more than specific motives. The boy who is dangerously ill because of the eating of green apples may be forever cured of such action, but such an experience would not deter him probably from overeating.

3. Health being inadequate as a motive, one of the teacher's great problems is to discover motives that will be effective. What is going to happen in some far-distant time does not interest the child in the least. The younger the child, the truer this is. All the instruction must center around the child's interests. The child is

[1] See "Health Instruction in the Elementary School," *Teachers College Record*, May, 1912, pp. 10–14.

interested in the approval of the teacher, in activity, in competition, and in imitation. To such instinctive sources the teacher must turn for the forces which will assimilate her instruction, and make for action. To illustrate, a child may have no desire to keep his desk neat and clean but if there is competition among the pupils of a school he is likely to develop a new interest in the appearance of his desk.

4. Activity is one of the essentials for health. The first law of the child's nature is action. Every stimulus around him moves him to act. There is little use in telling children about the great need of exercise. The problem is to give the children plenty of opportunity to exercise so that this tendency may not atrophy. It needs also to be directed along the right channels. If the teacher gives the child opportunity to express his playful activities in the schoolroom and on the playground, she will have accomplished more than would have been possible through any amount of formal instruction. A permanent interest in physical activity, rather than knowledge, should be one of the goals of instruction.

5. The structure of the body—something which the child cannot see, and a knowledge of which is not necessary for the solution of his immediate problems—is not interesting. Before the child leaves the grades, he ought to have some kind of common-sense knowledge of how his body is made and how it works. Such knowledge should generally be free of technical terms, and should in every case be presented to satisfy his curiosity or to support his knowledge and practice of hygiene. The Gulick "Hygiene Series" (Ginn & Co.) presents in an interesting manner all the hygiene that the child needs to know.

6. There is grave danger in isolating the instruction in hygiene so that the child is led to think of hygiene as coming at a certain time of the day but having no further relation to his life-activities. The teacher should seize opportunities in other lessons to give information in hygiene and whenever there is occasion in the play or work of the pupils. Especially desirable is individual instruction when it is needed. The teacher who advises a pupil who is anemic to walk to school rather than to ride in a closed car, and who afterward follows this up to see that it is done, has no doubt

accomplished more for the good of the child than would have been possible through any given class instruction for a year.

7. In matters pertaining to hygiene children should be taught and be led to act for the good of the group. To obey the laws of health is desirable, not merely for one's own sake, but for the good of others. Mere word knowledge about such things is largely worthless unless children live it in the school. For example, children may and should be taught that there is danger in catching or communicating a disease through the common drinking-cup; but in addition to this the teacher must see that individual drinking-cups are provided and used. Every teacher should be able to teach children how to make a drinking-cup out of a piece of paper.

8. Instruction relative to the effects of tobacco and alcohol on the bodily health has probably accomplished but little. These topics when considered in the upper grades should emphasize particularly the economic and social loss to the person who has these habits. To tell boys that good football players do not smoke and that nobody who drinks can be an engineer or a conductor is probably more effective in influencing action than to show the boys pictures of ulcers in the stomach due to the excessive use of alcohol.

9. While a knowledge of sex hygiene is desirable for children, the ordinary teacher who has had no special scientific training, and has little or no sympathy with the matter, is not at all fitted to teach the subject with success, and the probability is that she may do more harm than good. The proper place for this instruction is in the home. Teachers should lend their influence toward the distribution of good literature on such instruction to parents, and toward the encouraging of meetings for parents where such matters can be talked over.

10. Instruction in hygiene to become effective must plan to make the pupil personally responsible. This responsibility cannot be expected unless the pupils are trained in habits that make for health. The school life of the child offers many opportunities for cultivating the right kind of action. Let us take a single example. Children who eat their midday lunches in the schoolroom are likely to leave much of the remains on the floor and desks. The teacher should insist on food remnants being properly taken care of until

finally, through pupil organization if necessary, pupil responsibility is assumed.[1] A schoolhouse and grounds that have been planned from the point of view of hygiene make it easier, of course, for the teacher to inculcate the right kind of habits. A poorly lighted, badly ventilated schoolroom, furnished with non-adjustable seats, and a muddy schoolyard do not make for good habits. An investigation of the rural schools of Worcester County, Massachusetts, conducted by the State Normal School at Worcester, shows that the hygiene and sanitation of these schools are deplorable. But even under the most unfavorable conditions, the ingenious and intelligent teacher can devise many ways for training the children in good habits.

11. In the selection of subject-matter, stress should be laid particularly on the most important health problems of the community. The teacher in the rural schools should lay particular emphasis on topics in rural hygiene, such as the "Danger of Infection from Surface Water, Springs," etc. A teacher in city schools would find topics like "Why It Is Better to Walk Short Distances Rather than to Take a Car" and "The Danger from a Leaky Gas Tube," etc., more valuable.

[1] For an illustration of this sort of training, see Hunter, "An Experiment in Student Control of School Sanitation and Hygiene," *U.S. Bureau of Education Bulletin*, 1913, No. 48.

[*To be continued*]

A STUDY OF RETARDATION AND CLASS STANDING ON THE BASIS OF HOME LANGUAGE USED BY PUPILS.—*Concluded*

EVERETT EVELETH CAMPBELL
American Mission, Sialkot, India

To eliminate as far as possible the effect of exceptional individual cases, and also the influence of special conditions that may have affected certain classes, the data presented for the separate grades of the various schools, in the preceding tables and charts, are combined in Tables IX to XV, and in Charts VI to XII.

All the pupils of each language group for each grade have been brought together. Grade I is represented by only one school. This has been presented in Table V and Chart I. Within these summarizing tables the extensions have been made exactly as in the preceding part of the study. The mode in age has been added.

There is again much variation. The English-speaking pupils rank well, but entirely fail to stand uniformly above the other groups. In Grade II they are surpassed in average by all the others, and in mode are equaled or passed by all. In Grade III they are surpassed in average by the Swedes only, and are equal with, or ahead of, all in mode. In Grade IV the Swedish group again excels, this time in both average and mode. In Grade V the Germans join the Swedes in averaging better than the English-speaking pupils. The Swedes alone pass the English in mode.

In Grade VI the Yiddish are ahead. The Italians, Jewish, Polish, and total foreign are behind the English, while the Swedes, Germans, and others are too few in number to be brought into the comparison. In mode the Jewish and Yiddish surpass the English, while the Polish fall behind. In Grade VII, on the contrary, the Polish forge ahead of all except the English in average, while the Swedish drop behind. The English excel in both mode and average.

In Grade VIII the Germans and Swedes stand better in average than the English, while the total foreign is the same until the third decimal place is reached. The Jews are not far behind in average, and stand with the English, Germans, and Swedes in mode.

As in the preceding charts, the numbers in parentheses before the names indicate the number of pupils in the respective groups.

CHART VI

35%
30%
25%
20%
15%
10%
5%
Retardation
II Grades
(44) Eng.
(112) Total For.
(13) Italian
(52) Polish
(13) Hungarian
-2
-1
0
1
2
3
4
5
6
7
8
9
10
11
12
13
14

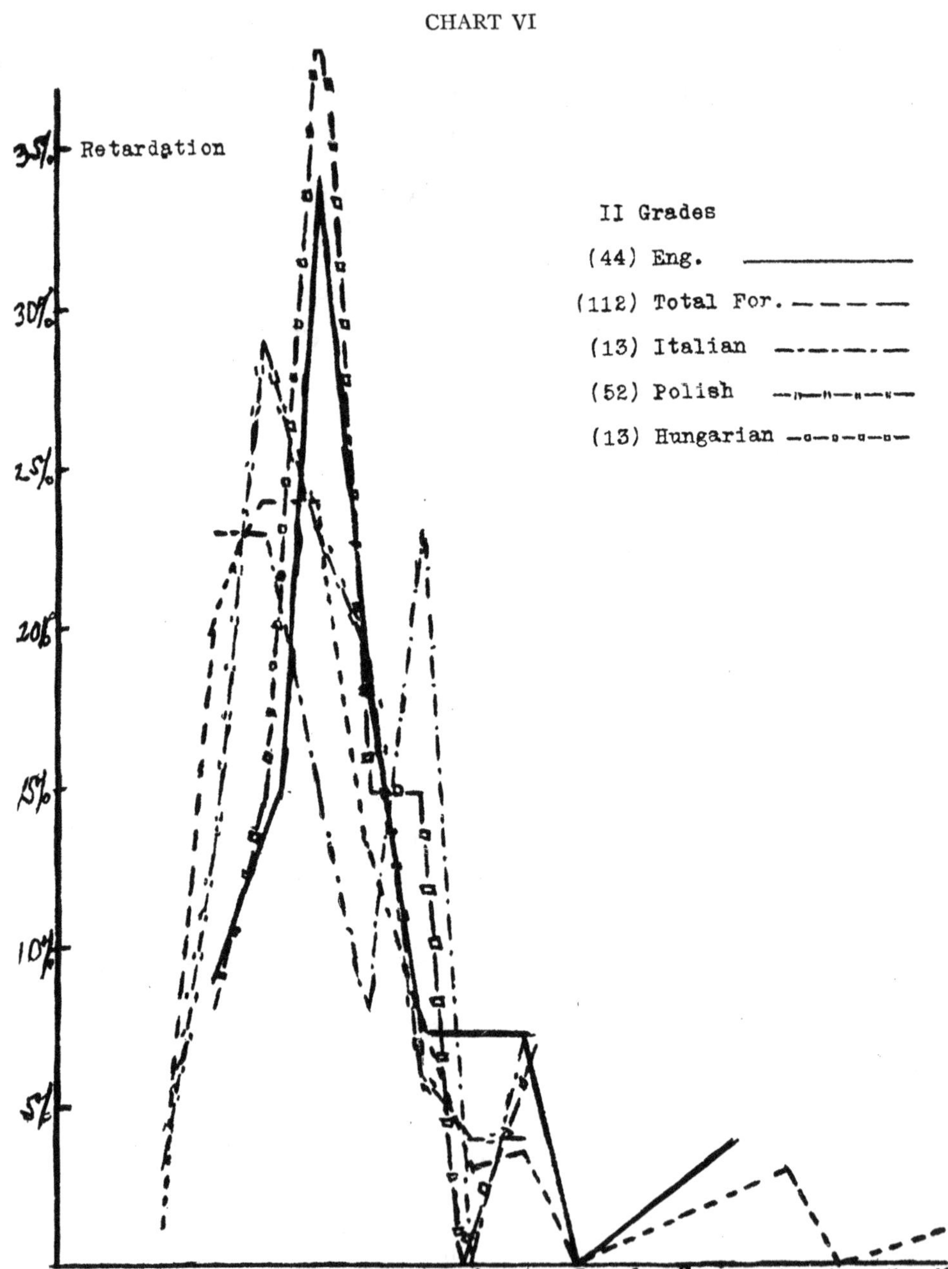

CHART VII

Retardation
35%
30%
25%
20%
15%
10%
5%
III Grades
(206) English
(609) Total For.
(267) Italian
(183) Jewish
(54) German
(42) Polish
(26) Swedish
-4
-3
-2
-1
0
1
2
3
4
5
6
7
8
9
10
11
12
13
14

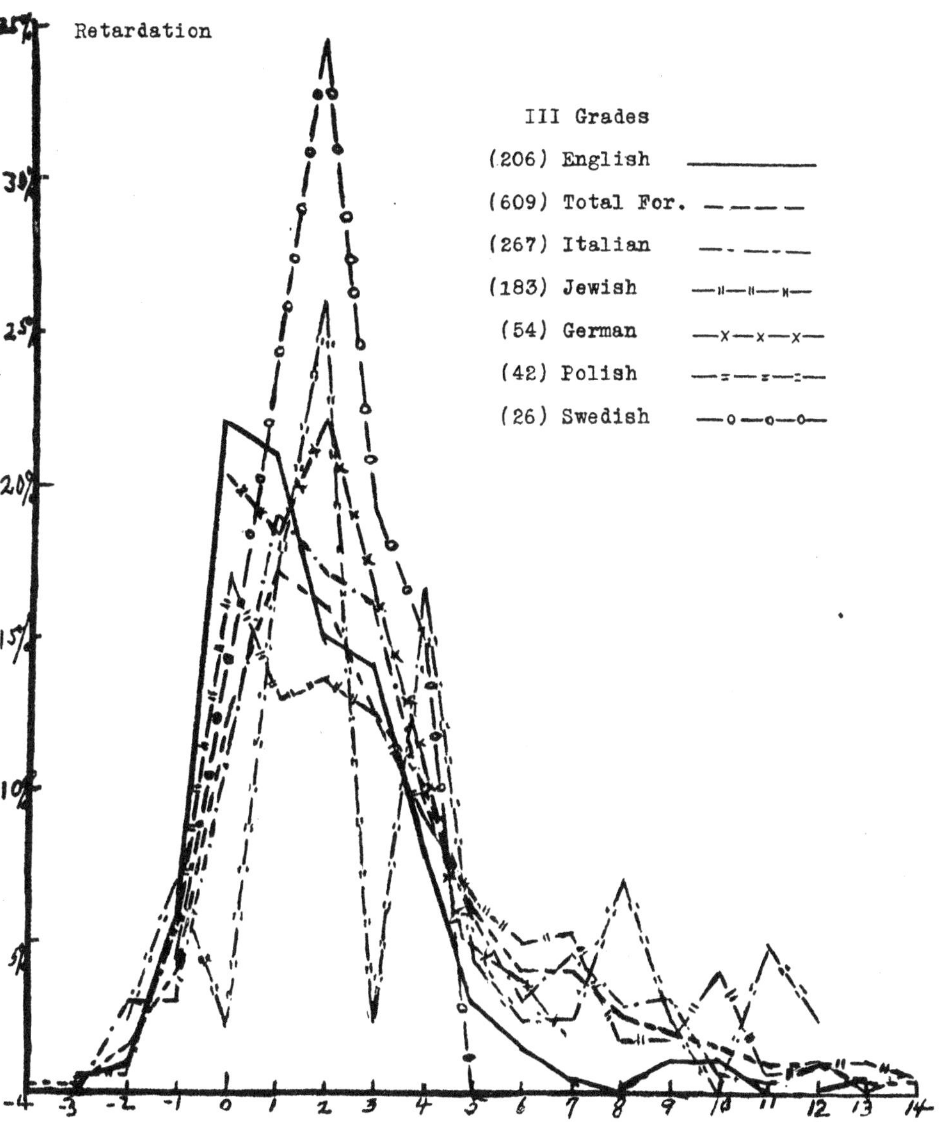

CHART VIII

Retardation
IV Grades
(103) English
(469) Total For.
(202) Italian
(179) Jewish
(47) Polish
35%
30%
25%
20%
15%
10%
5%
-3
-2
-1
0
+1
2
3
4
5
6
7
8
9
10
11
12
13

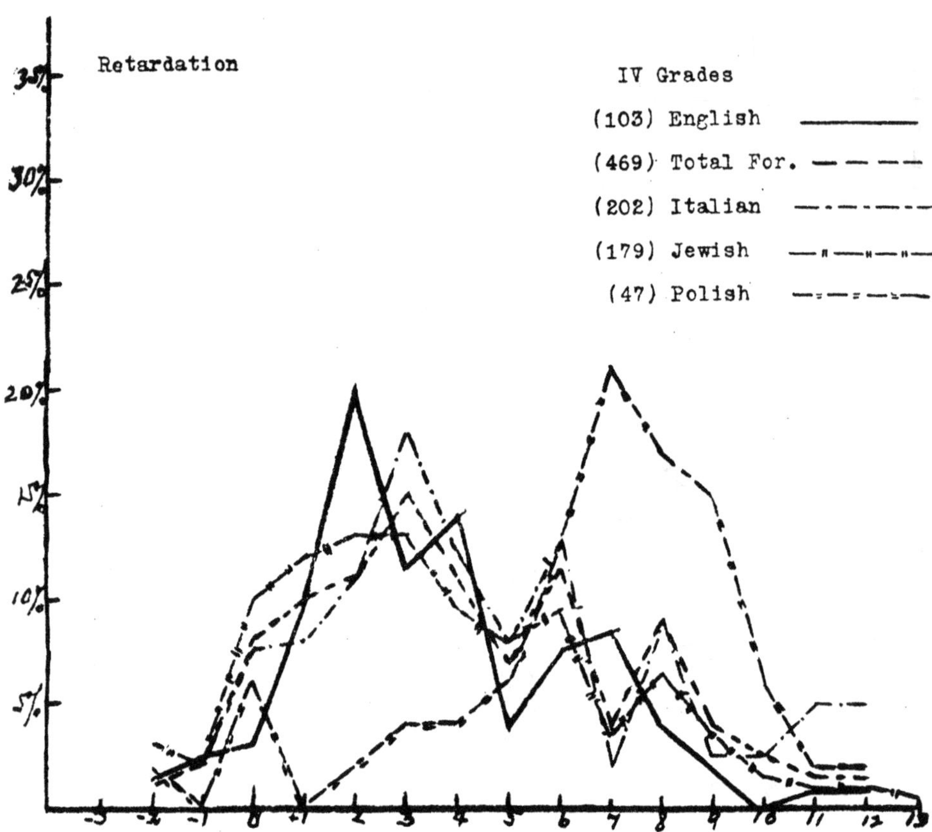

CHART IX

Retardation
V Grades
(23) Polish
(117) Jewish
(208) Italian
(19) Swedish
(39) German
(436) Total For.
(196) Eng.
30%
25%
20%
15%
10%
5%
-4
-3
-2
-1
0
+1
2
3
4
5
6
7
8
9
10
11

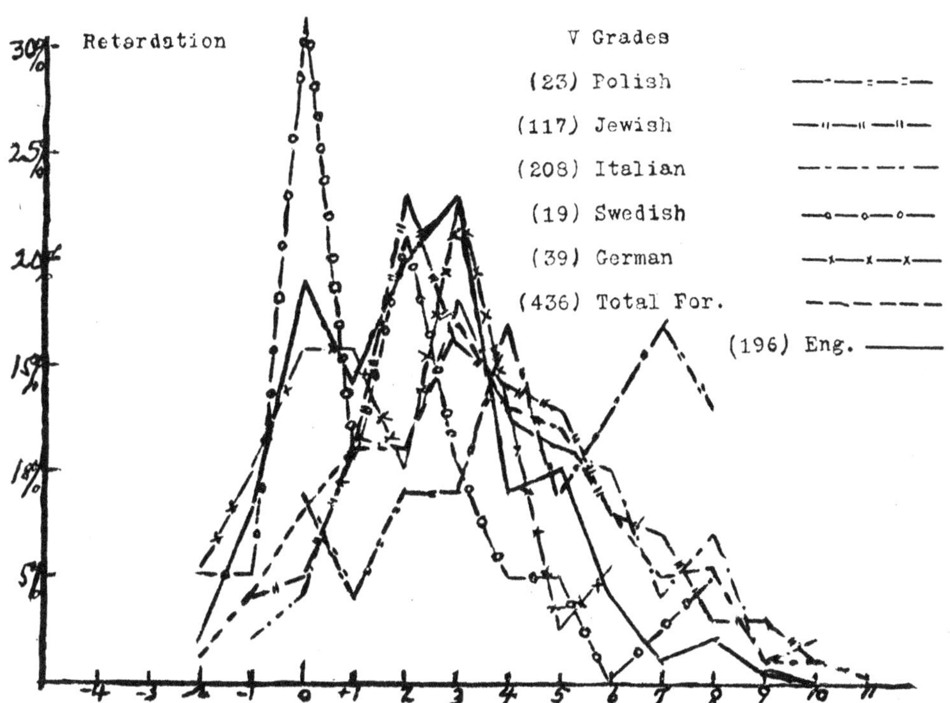

CHART X

Retardation
VI Grades
(82) Eng.
(152) Total For.
(77) Italian
(31) Jewish
35%
21%
15%
10%
5%
-4
-3
-2
-1
0
+1
2
3
4
5
6
7
8
9
10
11

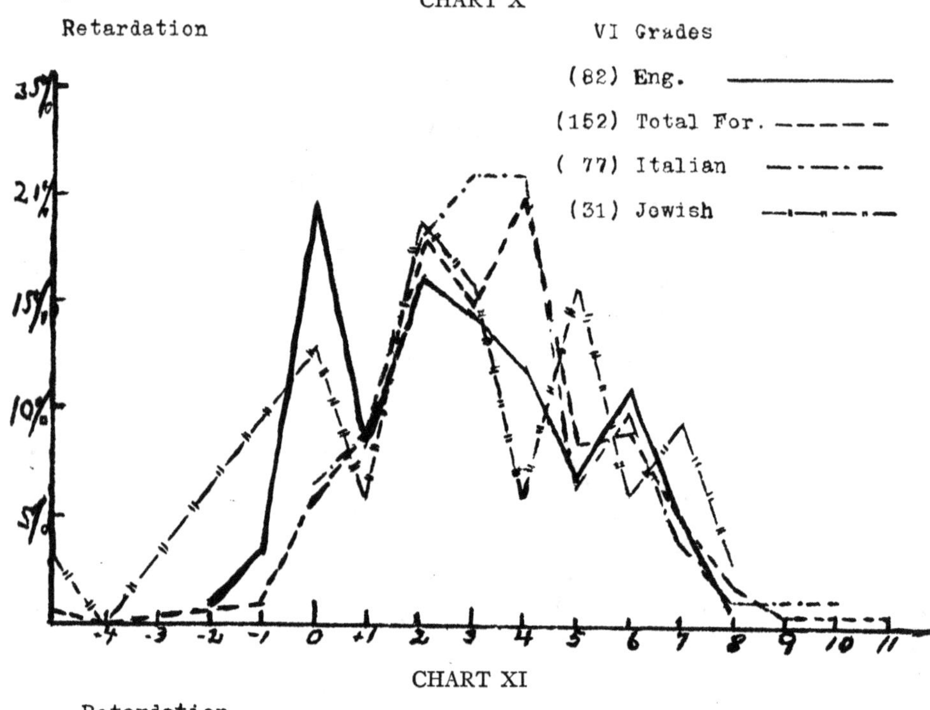

CHART XI

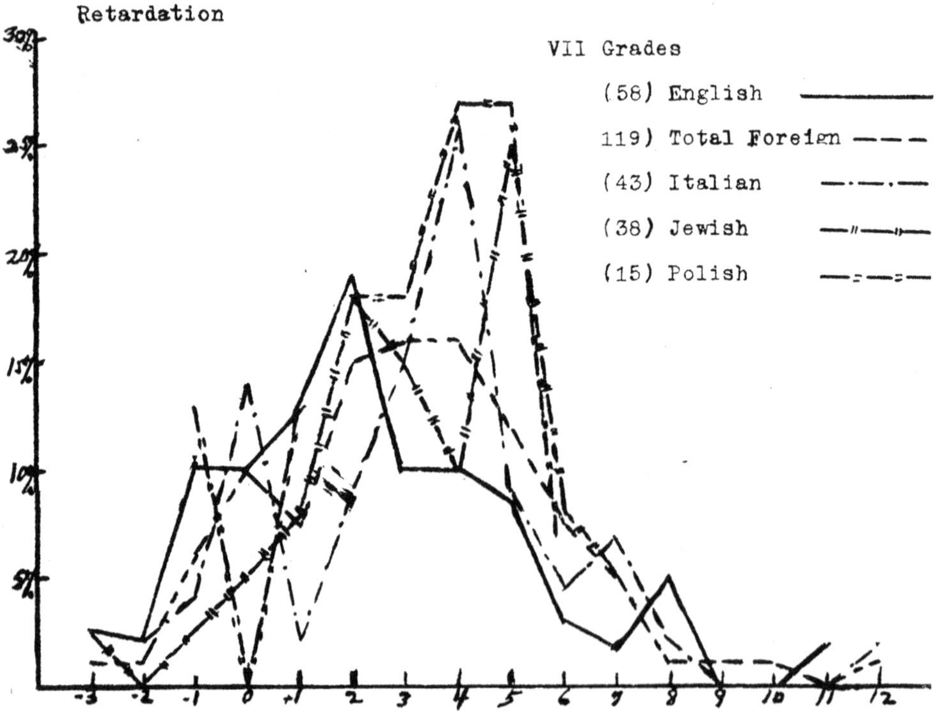

Retardation
VII Grades
(58) English
119) Total Foreign
(43) Italian
(38) Jewish
(15) Polish
30%
25%
20%
15%
10%
5%
-3
-2
-1
0
+1
2
3
4
5
6
7
8
9
10
11
12

CHART XII

Retardation
VIII Grades
(162) English
(114) Total Foreign
(35) Italian
(22) German
(19) Jewish
(15) Swedish
5%
10%
15%
20%
25%
30%
35%
40%
-4
-3
-2
-1
0
+1
2
3
4
5
6
7
8
9
10
11

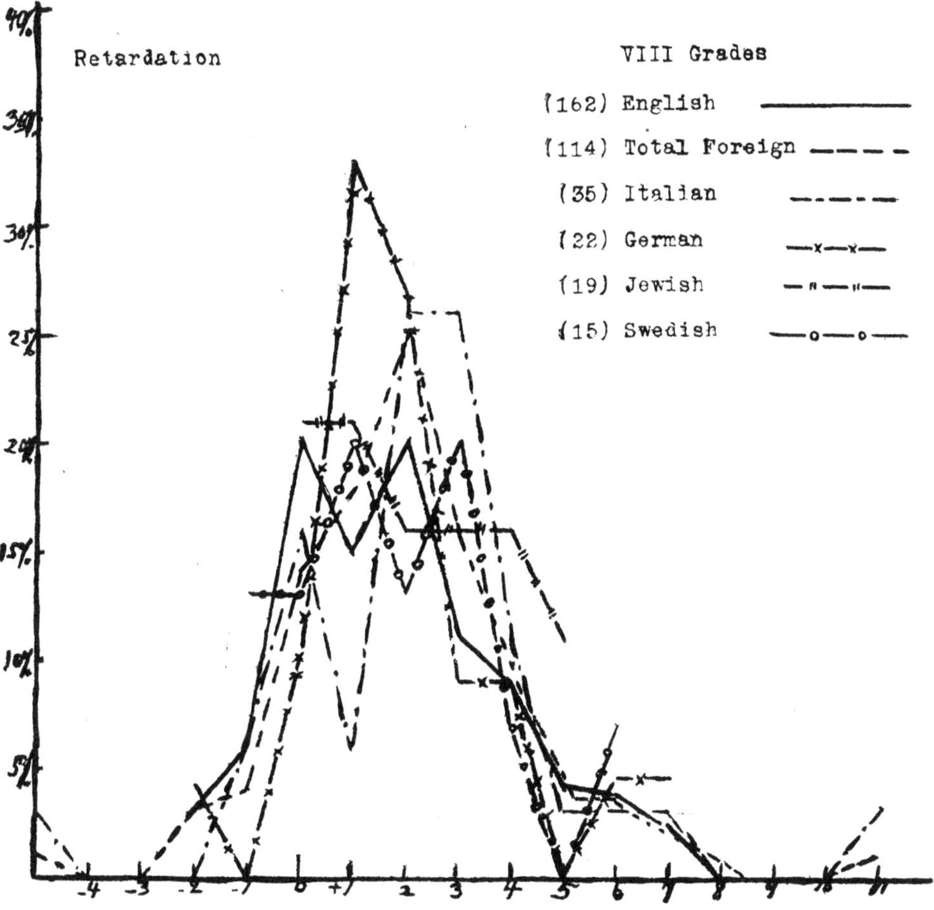

TABLE IX

COMBINED SECOND GRADES

Ages	Half-Years Under and Over Age	Polish		Italian		Hungarian		German		Slavish		Swedish		Jewish		Greek		Norwegian		Total Foreign		English Speaking	
		A No. of Pupils	B Total Half-Years Acc. and Ret.	A	B	A	B	A	B	A	B	A	B	A	B	A	B	A	B	A	B	A	B
6½	−1	1	−1																	1	−1		
7	0	7		3		1		3		2		2		4						22		4	
7½	−1	15	+15	3	+3	2	+2	1	+1	3	+3	3	+3							27	+27	6	+6
8	+2	12	24	2	4	5	10	3	6	1	2			2	4	1	2	1	+2	27	54	15	30
8½	+3	10	30	1	3	2	6			1	3	1	3							15	45	8	24
9	+4	3	12	3	12	2	8					1	4							9	36	3	12
9½	+5	2	10									1	5							3	15	3	15
10	+6	2	12	1	6	1	6													4	24	3	18
10½	+7																						
11	+8																						
11½	+9																						
12	+10																					2	20
12½	+11							1	11							2	22			3	33		
13	+12																						
13½	+13															1	14			1	14		
Totals		52	102	13	28	13	32	8	18	7	8	8	15	6	4	4	38	1	2	112	247	44	125
Average ret. inhalf-years			1.96		2.15		2.46		2.25		1.14		1.87		0.67		9.5		2.0		2.2		2.84
Mode of ret. in half-years			2		1		2				1		1		0						1		2
Mode in age			8		7½		8				7½		7½		7						7½		8

TABLE X

COMBINED THIRD GRADES

Ages	Half-Years Under and Over Age	Italian A (No. of Pupils)	Italian B (Total Half-Years Acc. and Ret.)	Jewish A	Jewish B	German A	German B	Polish A	Polish B	Swedish A	Swedish B	Slavish A	Hungarian A	Dutch A	Bohemian A	Misc. A	Total Foreign A	Total Foreign B	English Speaking A	English Speaking B
6	−4	1	−4	....	....	....	....	....	....	....	....	....	....	....	....	....	1	−4	....	....
6½	−3	....	....	1	−3	....	....	....	....	....	....	....	....	....	....	....	1	−3	1	−3
7	−2	7	−14	1	−2	....	....	1	−2	....	....	....	....	....	....	....	9	−18	2	−4
7½	−1	8	−8	11	−11	....	....	3	−3	1	−1	....	1	....	....	1	25	−25	12	−12
8	0	30	....	32	....	11	....	1	....	6	....	....	....	1	....	5	86	....	43	....
8½	+1	50	50	26	24	10	10	7	7	9	9	2	....	3	....	1	106	106	53	53
9	+2	45	90	25	50	12	24	11	22	5	10	....	2	....	....	....	100	200	32	64
9½	+3	43	129	23	69	9	27	1	3	4	12	1	1	1	....	3	86	258	30	90
10	+4	26	104	16	64	6	24	7	28	....	....	1	1	....	1	2	60	240	16	64
10½	+5	15	75	12	60	3	15	2	60	....	....	....	....	....	1	2	35	175	6	30
11	+6	8	48	9	54	2	12	1	6	....	....	2	....	....	....	2	24	144	3	18
11½	+7	12	84	10	70	1	7	1	7	....	....	....	....	....	....	1	25	175	1	7
12	+8	7	56	3	24	....	....	3	24	1	8	....	....	....	....	....	14	112	....	....
12½	+9	8	72	3	27	....	....	1	9	....	....	....	....	....	....	....	12	100	2	18
13	+10	2	20	7	70	....	....	....	....	....	....	....	....	....	....	1	10	100	2	20
13½	+11	1	11	1	11	....	....	2	22	....	....	....	....	....	1	....	5	55	....	....
14	+12	3	36	2	24	....	....	1	12	....	....	....	....	....	....	....	6	72	....	....
14½	+13	....	....	2	26	....	....	....	....	....	....	....	....	....	....	....	2	26	1	13
15	+14	1	14	1	14	....	....	....	....	....	....	....	....	....	....	....	2	28	....	....
Totals		267	763	183	571	54	119	42	145	26	38	6	5	5	3	18	609	1749	206	358
Average half-years of ret			2.86		3.15		2.2		3.45		1.46							2.87		1.74
Mode of ret. in half-years			2		1		2		2		1							1		1
Mode in age			9		8½		9		9		8½							8½		8½

TABLE XI

COMBINED FOURTH GRADES

Ages	Half-Years Over and Under Age	Italian A No. of Pupils	Italian B Total Half-Years Acc. and Ret.	Jewish A	Jewish B	Polish A	Polish B	Swedish A	Swedish B	Slavish A	Hungarian A	German A	Bohemian A	Chinese A	Persian A	Danish A	French A	Greek A	Total Foreign A	Total Foreign B	English Speaking A	English Speaking B
8	−2	....	....	5	−10	1	−2	....	....	....	....	....	....	....	....	....	....	....	6	−12	1	−2
8½	−1	4	−4	4	−4	....	....	....	....	....	....	....	....	....	....	....	....	....	8	−8	2	−2
9	0	15	....	18	....	3	....	....	....	....	....	....	1	....	....	....	....	....	37	....	13	....
9½	+1	16	+16	22	+22	....	....	5	+5	....	2	1	1	....	....	....	....	....	47	+47	10	+10
10	+2	23	46	23	46	....	....	4	8	1	....	....	....	1	....	1	....	....	53	106	21	42
10½	+3	40	120	24	72	2	6	1	3	1	1	2	....	....	....	....	1	....	72	216	12	36
11	+4	26	104	17	68	2	8	....	....	4	....	....	....	1	1	....	....	1	52	208	15	60
11½	+5	16	80	15	75	3	11	....	....	....	....	....	....	....	....	....	....	....	34	170	4	20
12	+6	27	162	17	102	6	36	1	6	1	2	....	1	....	....	....	....	....	55	330	8	48
12½	+7	4	28	7	49	10	70	....	....	....	....	....	....	....	....	....	....	....	21	147	9	63
13	+8	19	152	12	96	8	64	1	8	....	1	....	....	....	1	....	....	....	42	336	4	32
13½	+9	5	45	7	63	7	63	....	....	2	....	....	....	....	....	....	....	....	21	189	2	18
14	+10	5	50	3	30	3	30	....	....	....	....	1	....	....	....	....	....	....	12	120	....	....
14½	+11	1	11	2	22	1	11	....	....	....	....	....	....	....	....	....	....	....	4	44	1	11
15	+12	1	12	2	24	1	12	....	....	....	....	....	....	....	....	....	....	....	4	48	1	12
15½	+13	....	....	1	13	....	....	....	....	....	....	....	....	....	....	....	....	....	1	13	....	....
Totals		202	822	179	668	47	313	12	30	9	6	4	3	2	2	1	1	1	469	1954	103	348
Average ret. in half-years		4.07		3.73		6.66		2.5												4.1		3.38
Mode of ret. in half-years		3		2		7		1												3		2
Mode in age		10½		10		12½		9½												10½		10

TABLE XII

Combined Fifth Grades

Ages	Half-Years Under and Over Age	Polish		Jewish		Italian		Swedish		German		Yiddish	Hungarian	Bohemian	Slavish	Chinese	Russian	Lithuanian	Dutch	Misc.	Total Foreign		Total English Speaking	
		A No. of Pupils	B Total Half-Years Acc. and Ret.	A	B	A	B	A	B	A	B	A	A	A	A	A	A	A	A	A	A	B	A	B
9	−2	...	...	...	...	...	...	1	−2	2	−4	...	...	...	...	...	...	...	...	1	4	−8	4	−8
9½	−1	...	...	5	−5	5	−3	1	−1	4	−4	...	...	1	...	...	1	...	1	...	16	−16	15	−15
10	0	2	...	6	...	9	...	6	...	6	...	1	...	1	1	...	1	...	...	2	35	...	38	...
10½	+1	1	1	13	13	26	26	2	2	6	6	...	...	...	...	...	...	...	...	1	49	49	28	28
11	+2	2	4	15	30	22	44	4	8	4	8	1	...	...	...	...	...	...	1	...	49	98	40	80
11½	+3	2	6	19	57	38	114	2	6	9	27	...	1	...	1	1	...	1	1	...	75	225	26	78
12	+4	4	16	17	68	27	118	1	4	5	20	...	2	...	1	...	...	...	1	1	59	136	19	76
12½	+5	2	10	16	80	33	165	1	5	...	...	1	...	...	...	...	...	...	...	...	53	165	10	50
13	+6	3	18	9	54	20	120	...	...	1	6	...	...	...	...	...	1	1	...	2	37	222	8	48
13½	+7	4	28	8	56	9	63	...	...	2	14	...	...	...	...	...	...	...	...	...	23	161	2	14
14	+8	3	24	4	32	15	120	1	8	...	...	...	...	...	...	...	...	1	...	...	24	192	4	32
14½	+9	...	...	4	36	2	18	...	...	...	...	...	...	...	...	...	...	...	...	...	6	54	1	9
15	+10	...	...	1	10	4	40	...	...	...	...	...	...	...	...	...	...	...	...	...	5	50	...	...
16½	+13	...	...	...	...	...	...	...	...	...	...	...	...	...	...	1	...	...	...	...	1	13	...	...
18½	+17	...	...	...	...	...	...	...	...	...	...	...	...	...	...	...	...	...	...	...	...	...	1	17
Totals		23	107	117	431	208	815	19	30	39	73	3	3	2	3	2	3	3	4	7	436	1565	196	392
Average ret. in half-years			4.65		3.68		3.87		1.58		1.87											3.30		2.0
Mode of ret. in half-years			7		3		3		0		3											3		2
Mode in age			13½		11½		11½		10		11½											11½		11

TABLE XIII

Combined Sixth Grades

Ages	Half-Years Under and Over Age	Italian A No. of Pupils	Italian B Total Half-Years Acc. and Ret.	Jewish A	Jewish B	Yiddish A	Yiddish B	Polish A	Polish B	Norwegian A	German A	Slavish A	Swedish A	Chinese A	Albanese A	Total Foreign A	Total Foreign B	English Speaking A	English Speaking B
9½	−5	…	…	1	−3	…	…	…	…	…	…	…	…	…	…	1	−3	…	…
10	−2	…	…	…	…	…	…	…	…	…	…	…	…	…	…	1	−2	…	…
10½	−1	…	…	…	…	1	−1	…	…	…	1	…	…	…	…	2	−2	3	−3
11	0	5	…	4	…	…	…	…	…	…	…	…	…	…	…	9	…	16	…
11½	+1	7	+7	2	+2	5	+5	…	…	…	1	…	…	…	…	15	+15	7	+7
12	+2	14	28	6	12	4	8	…	…	…	2	…	1	…	…	27	54	13	26
12½	+3	16	48	5	15	3	9	…	…	…	…	…	2	…	…	26	78	12	36
13	+4	16	64	2	8	2	8	5	20	1	1	1	1	1	1	31	124	10	40
13½	+5	5	25	5	25	1	5	…	…	…	1	1	…	…	…	13	65	6	30
14	+6	8	48	2	12	2	12	2	12	…	…	…	…	…	…	14	84	9	54
14½	+7	3	21	3	21	1	7	1	7	…	…	…	…	…	…	8	56	4	28
15	+8	1	8	1	8	…	…	1	8	…	…	…	…	…	…	3	24	1	8
15½	+9	1	9	…	…	…	…	…	…	…	…	…	…	…	…	1	9	…	…
16½	+11	1	11	…	…	…	…	…	…	…	…	…	…	…	…	1	11	…	…
17	+12	…	…	…	…	…	…	…	…	…	…	…	…	1	…	1	12	…	…
Totals		77	269	31	98	19	53	9	47	1	6	2	4	2	1	152	525	82	226
Average half-years of ret.			3.49		3.23		2.39		5.22								3.44		2.73
Mode of ret. in half-years			3		2		2		4								3		3
Mode in age			12½		12		12		13								12½		12½

TABLE XIV

COMBINED SEVENTH GRADES

Ages	Half-Years Over and Under Age	Italian A No. of Pupils	Italian B Total Half-Years Acc. and Ret.	Jewish A	Jewish B	Polish A	Polish B	Swedish A	Swedish B	Hungarian A	Hungarian B	German A	Slavish A	Misc. A	Total Foreign A	Total Foreign B	English Speaking A	English Speaking B
10½	− 3	....	....	1	− 3	....	....	....	....	....	....	....	....	....	1	− 3	2	− 6
11	− 2	1	− 2	....	....	....	....	....	....	....	....	....	....	....	1	− 2	1	− 2
11½	− 1	2	− 2	6	− 1	2	− 2	1	− 1	....	....	1	....	....	7	− 7	6	− 6
12	0	6	....	2	....	....	....	1	....	....	....	2	....	1	12	....	6	....
12½	+ 1	1	+ 1	3	+ 3	2	+ 2	1	+ 1	1	+ 1	....	....	1	9	9	8	+ 8
13	+ 2	4	8	7	14	2	4	1	2	1	2	1	1	....	17	34	11	22
13½	+ 3	7	21	6	18	4	12	....	....	1	3	....	....	1	19	57	6	18
14	+ 4	11	44	4	16	4	16	....	....	1	4	....	....	....	20	80	6	24
14½	+ 5	4	20	9	45	1	5	....	....	....	....	....	....	....	14	70	5	25
15	+ 6	2	12	3	18	....	....	1	6	1	6	....	1	1	9	54	2	12
15½	+ 7	3	21	2	14	....	....	1	7	....	....	....	....	....	6	42	1	7
16	+ 8	1	8	....	....	....	....	....	....	....	....	....	....	....	1	8	3	24
16½	+ 9	....	....	....	....	....	....	....	....	....	....	....	1	....	1	9	....	....
17½	+10	....	....	....	....	....	....	....	....	....	....	....	....	1	1	10	....	....
18	+11	....	....	....	....	....	....	....	....	....	....	....	....	....	....	....	1	11
18½	+12	1	12	....	....	....	....	....	....	....	....	....	....	....	1	12	....	....
Totals		43	143	38	124	15	37	6	15	5	16	4	3	5	119	363	58	137
Average ret. in half-years			3.32		3.26		2.46		2.50							3.13		2.36
Mode of ret. in half-years			4		5		3									3		2
Mode in age			14		14½		13½									13½		14

TABLE XV

COMBINED EIGHTH GRADES

Ages	Half-Years Under and Over Age	Italian		German		Jewish		Swedish		Polish		Dutch	Greek	Hungarian	Slavish	Misc.	Total Foreign		English Speaking	
		A No. of Pupils	B Total Half-Years Acc. and Ret.	A	B	A	B	A	B	A	B	A	A	A	A	A	A	B	A	B
10½	−5	1	−5	....	....	....	....	....	....	....	....	....	....	....	....	....	1	−5	....	....
12	−2	....	....	1	−2	....	....	1	−2	....	....	....	....	....	....	1	3	−6	5	−10
12½	−1	2	−2	....	−2	....	....	2	−2	....	....	....	....	....	1	....	5	−5	10	−10
13	0	....	....	2	....	4	....	2	....	1	....	1	1	....	....	1	16	....	33	....
13½	+1	2	+2	7	7	4	4	3	+3	1	1	....	1	1	....	2	21	+21	25	+25
14	+2	9	18	6	12	3	6	2	4	3	6	2	....	1	1	1	28	56	33	66
14½	+3	9	27	2	6	3	9	3	9	1	3	....	....	....	....	....	18	54	18	54
15	+4	4	16	2	8	3	12	1	4	....	....	....	....	....	....	....	10	40	14	56
15½	+5	1	5	....	....	2	10	....	....	....	....	1	....	....	....	....	4	20	15	75
16	+6	1	6	1	6	....	....	1	6	1	6	....	....	....	....	....	4	24	5	30
16½	+7	1	7	1	7	....	....	....	....	1	7	....	....	....	....	....	3	21	4	28
18½	+11	1	11	....	....	....	....	....	....	....	....	....	....	....	....	....	1	11	....	....
Totals		35	85	22	42	19	41	15	22	8	23	4	2	2	2	5	114	231	162	334
Average ret. in half-years			2.43		1.91		2.16		1.47		2.87							2.063		2.061
Mode in half-years			3		1		1		1		2							2		1
Mode in age			14½		13½		13½		13½		14							14		13½

FINAL SUMMARY

Table XVI and Chart XIII give a summary of the final totals, bringing all the grades together for each group. The average retardation per pupil for each language group in the seven schools is thus found. In this final classification the Swedes stand at the top with an average retardation of only 1.77 half-years. The

CHART XIII

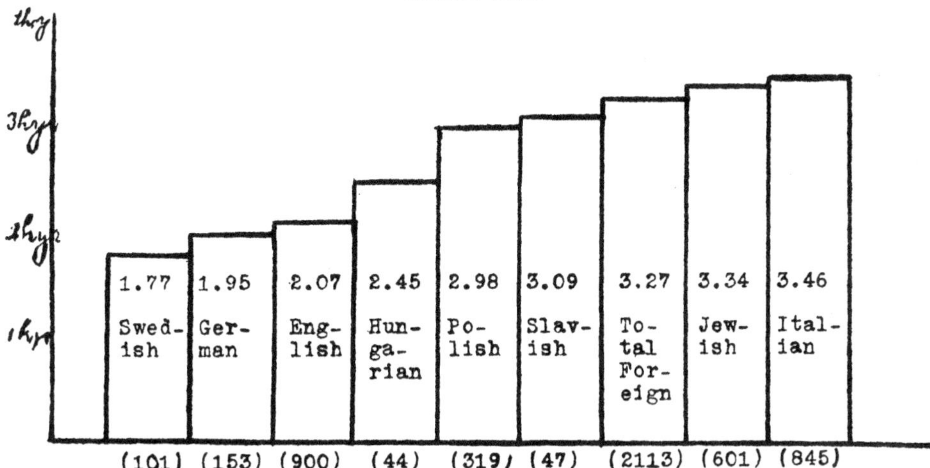

Germans come second with an average of 1.95. The English-speaking pupils rank third. These are followed in order by the Hungarians, Yiddish, Polish, Slavish, total foreign, Jewish, and Italian groups. The last has an average retardation of 3.46 half-years. In Chart XIII the Jewish and Yiddish groups have been combined.

ELIMINATION OF MIXED CARDS

Since pupils who gave "English and Swedish," "English and German," "English and Italian," and so on, for their home language were counted with the Swedish, German, and Italian groups, respectively, it was decided to test the German and Swedish groups to see what the effect of this had been. By eliminating these mixed cards the Swedish average was lowered 0.07, while the German average was raised 0.03. This factor thus proved entirely negligible.

TABLE XVI

General Summary

Grade	Italian		German		Swedish		Polish		Jewish		Yiddish		Slavish		Hungarian		Total Foreign		Total English Speaking	
	A	B	A	B	A	B	A	B	A	B	A	B	A	B	A	B	A	B	A	B
I.	.....	.....	16	16	11	17	123	176	2	.....	.....	.....	15	38	19	11	177	253	49	45
II.	13	28	8	18	8	15	52	102	6	4	.....	.....	7	8	13	32	107	207	44	125
III.	267	763	54	119	26	38	42	145	182	571	2	8	6	20	5	10	585	1674	206	358
IV.	202	822	4	17	12	30	47	313	179	668	.....	.....	9	45	6	25	459	1920	103	348
V.	208	815	39	73	19	30	23	107	117	431	3	7	3	7	3	11	418	1781	196	392
VI.	77	269	6	13	4	12	9	49	31	98	19	53	2	9	.....	.....	148	501	82	224
VII.	43	143	4	1	6	15	15	37	38	124	2	4	3	17	5	16	116	347	58	137
VIII.	35	85	22	42	15	22	8	23	19	41	.....	.....	2	1	2	3	103	217	162	334
Totals...	845	925	153	299	101	179	319	952	575	1937	26	72	47	145	44	108	2113	6905	900	1963
Average ret. in half-years		3.46		1.95		1.77		2.98		3.37		2.77		3.09		2.45		3.27		2.07

CLASS STANDING

The total results for class standing are equally negative. Of the English-speaking pupils 67 per cent are in ranks E and G; of the German pupils, 62 per cent; of the Swedish pupils, 57 per cent; of the Hungarian pupils, 47 per cent; of the Italians, 56 per cent; of the Slavs, 52 per cent; of the Jews, 80 per cent; of the Poles, 55 per cent. These percentages are based on the class ranks in Schools A, B, and F.

HOME CONDITIONS

To separate further the language factor from other factors, the home conditions entered on the enrolment cards in School A have been arranged on a percentage basis for the various nationalities, with the following results:

TABLE XVII

	Percentage German	Percentage Swedish	Percentage Polish	Percentage Hungarian	Percentage English
E.	. . . .	2.2	0.9	. . . .	4.13
G.	50	66.7	24.7	17.8	52.07
F.	40	28.9	59.7	50.0	39.67
P.	10	2.2	15.0	32.1	4.13

Thus 50 per cent of the Germans are in home conditions that are good or excellent, 56 per cent of the English-speaking, 69 per cent of the Swedes, 26 per cent of the Poles, and only 18 per cent of the Hungarians.

If superior home conditions were assigned as the cause of the Swedes overcoming any language difficulty and surpassing the English-speaking pupils, the same reason could not be given for the Germans. Nor would it account for the average retardation of the Hungarians being but a trifle higher than that of the English-speaking pupils.

CONCLUSION

Summing up the whole investigation, we find that the language factor is not of sufficient importance to be considered as one of the causes of retardation, or as determining relative class standing of pupils.

A MEASURE OF PROGRESS IN THE MECHANICAL OPERATIONS OF ARITHMETIC

J. W. GRAHAM
Clarkston, Washington

It seems difficult to secure a measure which will allow a careful record to be kept of the progress of different pupils in the mechanical operations of arithmetic. A simple means is here suggested. The device is valuable for other purposes also, since it stimulates pupils to learn number combinations and helps to bring them up to a definite standard of efficiency.

All that is needed in the way of materials is a cord about four feet in length, a weight sufficiently heavy to serve as pendulum bob, and a support that will allow the pendulum to swing clear of the wall. Interest in the use of the device is easily aroused. The teacher suspends the pendulum, having its initial length such that it will vibrate slowly. By way of concrete example, let us consider its use in a fourth grade where the multiplication tables are still troublesome, and the simple number combinations are still unmastered. The pendulum is set in motion, at first at its maximum length, therefore at its maximum time periods. If the drill desired is in addition, let the teacher announce a *constant*, as six. After the class has the constant well in mind, some starting-point is announced, as nine. In concert the class gives the results of successive additions of six, starting with the base nine: "Nine, fifteen, twenty-one, twenty-seven," etc. It will be surprising how many drop out as the numbers grow larger. Here is a sifting process. If this were the only value, it might be worth while; but the greatest value of the device lies in the accurate measure of attainment at any period of arithmetical work. The pupils who drop out early in the concert recitation are urged to suspend such pendulums at their homes and drill themselves, shortening the pendulum as fast as possible. The *length* of the pendulum is recorded and furnishes a measure both accurate and universal in application.

It may appear to some that this is a mere drill device. It does furnish suggestions for different drills to the teacher of original mind, but the greatest value in its use is the accurate measure afforded of both class and individual advancement. If the drill be in subtraction, some such base as thirty-five is announced, with four as the constant to be subtracted. The recitation proceeds: "Thirty-five, thirty-one, twenty-seven, twenty-three," etc.

In multiplication this drill or test can be used in various ways. Only one will be given here. Let a constant, as eight, be announced. The pendulum is set vibrating slowly. As the bob reaches its left-hand limit the variables are announced by the teacher, the class giving the products as the pendulum approaches its right-hand limit.

The teacher will see many ways to vary the use of this simple device, both as a means for drill and as an accurate measure of results. The device has proved also to be a welcome aid in this part of arithmetic work which is so often a drag to the teacher and the grade.

BOOK REVIEWS

The School System of Norway. By DAVID ALLEN ANDERSON. Boston: Richard G. Badger, The Gorham Press, 1913. Pp. 232. $1.25.

The appearance of Dr. Anderson's book is very timely. Our pedagogical literature is well provided with comparative studies of education in foreign countries. Unfortunately, however, the Scandinavian countries have remained, if not entirely unrepresented, at least represented only by fragmentary and misleading accounts. This is greatly to be regretted, since we could not but have received stimulating impulses from these countries where general education is of such a high standard and which socially, morally, and politically are among the most progressive countries in the world.

By his very able and accurate presentation of the school system of Norway, Dr. Anderson has very satisfactorily supplied a part of this deficiency, and it is to be hoped that he may find occasion in subsequent volumes to deal with the school systems of the sister-countries, Denmark and Sweden.

Dr. Anderson's book contains a wealth of information, technical and general, presented in a direct and logical manner with the greatest possible clearness and a commendable brevity, characteristics which render his book especially convenient both for reference and for class use. Here and there in the interpretive conclusions one might have desired a little less brevity, since the pedagogical clear-sightedness and independence of views of which the author has manifested his capability render these conclusions very valuable.

The book is an interesting, stimulating, and reliable presentation of the educational tendencies in Norway.

E. J. VICKNER

UNIVERSITY OF WASHINGTON

Animal Communities in Temperate America. By VICTOR L. SHELFORD. Chicago: The University of Chicago Press, 1913. Pp. xiii+362. $3.00.

Animal Communities in Temperate America is a serial account of the animal groups found in various spots about Chicago; it is just as true an account of those occurring in any similar district in the Northern United States or Southern Canada, and hence it answers many questions which have asked themselves of a great many people. Among the chapters are descriptions of certain economic phases and of the animal communities of large and of small lakes, of ponds, of streams, of forests, of thickets, and of prairies, and of their conditions and controlling factors. Although Dr. Shelford has taken the college viewpoint and has made his work most appealing to higher students, yet throughout there is a readableness, a simplicity of style, and a suppression of technicality which puts the book well within the comprehension of the general reader or even of high-school pupils.

In the description of conditions in a shallow lake one reads: "One of the most distinctive and characteristic forms of such lakes is a transparent true shrimp (*Palaemonetes paludosus*), about 2 inches long, which is a close relative of some of the edible marine shrimps. In spring they are found carrying numbers of green eggs attached to the appendages of their abdomens. Another common animal in these situations is the large polyzoan (*Pectinatella magnifica*). This is a colonial form which reproduces by budding in several directions. It also secretes a clear and transparent jelly. As the number of animals increases, the amount of jelly increases on all sides and the animals are arranged on the outside of the more or less spherical mass of jelly; the necessary increase in surface for the growth of the colony is supplied through additional secretion by each new animal added. Some of these masses of jelly reach a size of 6 inches in diameter."

Again, quoting from the account of conditions in a hickory woods: "The walking-stick (*Diapheromera femorata*) is common on the tree trunks in the fall. The red oak supports the tree cricket (*Oceanthus angustipennis*), the stinkbug (*Euschistus tristigimus*), and the oak-leaf beetle (*Xanthonia 10-notata*). Felt records several insects injurious to the red oak alone. From the white oak we have taken the katydid (*Cyrtophillus perspicillatus*), the larvae of sawflies and moths (*Anisota senatoria*), and various galls. Several weevils occur on acorns, and the twig-borer (*Elaphidion villosum*) in the twigs. The hickory supports many larvae, including a *Phylloxera* which forms galls on the leaves.

"The red-tailed and red-shouldered hawks, the red-headed woodpecker, the wood-pewee, the crow, bluejay, robin, and bluebird nest in the trees. The panther and wildcat (*Lynx rufus*) were former residents."

Many nature students have long awaited such a work as this, for there is an ever-growing movement which reverts to Agassiz's outdoor laboratory for its material, its method, its inspiration. Dr. Shelford has furnished a text-manual for this work which can be appreciated only through first-hand perusal and by the nature-lovers who really want to know. "It marks an epoch in the study of life."

The illustrations are mostly half-tones; they are original, profuse, and well explained.

H. B. S.

Schurz High School
Chicago

BOOKS RECEIVED

AMERICAN BOOK CO., CHICAGO

Deutsche Lieder. By PETER SCHERER and LOUIS H. DIRKS. Cloth. Pp. 110. Price $0.25.

Peter and Polly in Winter. By ROSE LUCIA. Cloth. Pp. 160. Illustrated. Price $0.35.

EDWARD E. BABB & CO., BOSTON

The Ideal Sound Exemplifier. By a SISTER OF SAINT JOSEPH. Paper. Pp. 64. Price $0.15.

BOBBS-MERRILL CO., INDIANAPOLIS

Better Rural Schools. By GEORGE HERBERT BETTS and OTIS EARLE HALL. Cloth. Pp. 512. Illustrated.

T. Y. CROWELL & CO., NEW YORK

The Religious Value of the Old Testament. By AMBROSE WHITE VERNON. Cloth. Pp. 81. Price $0.90.

HOUGHTON MIFFLIN CO., BOSTON

Art Education. ("Riverside Educational Monographs.") By HENRY TURNER BAILEY. Cloth. Pp. 102. Price $0.60.

The Concrete and Practical in Modern Education. ("Riverside Educational Monographs.") By CHARLES W. ELIOT. Cloth. Pp. 57. Price $0.35.

MACMILLAN, NEW YORK

Intensive Studies in American Literature. By ALMA BLOUNT, PH.D. Cloth. Pp. 331. Illustrated. Price $1.10.

RAND McNALLY & CO., CHICAGO

The Teachers' Story Teller's Book. By ALICE O'GRADY and FRANCES THROOP. Cloth. Pp. 352. Price $1.00.

STURGIS & WALTON CO., NEW YORK

The Old Testament Phrase Book. By LOUISE EMERY TUCKER, M.A. Cloth. Pp. 148. Price $1.00 net.

Readings from the Old Testament. By LOUISE EMERY TUCKER, M.A. Cloth. Pp. 260. Price $1.25 net.

THE UNIVERSITY OF CHICAGO PRESS, CHICAGO

The French Verb: Its Forms and Tense Uses. By WILLIAM A. NITZE and ERNEST H. WILKINS. Paper. Pp. 40. Price $0.35.

UNIVERSITY OF MISSOURI, COLUMBIA

The University of Missouri Bulletin. Education Series. Vol. II, No. 1. Paper. Pp. 139.

WARWICK & YORK, INC., BALTIMORE

The Socialized Conscience. By JOSEPH HERSCHEL COFFIN. Cloth. Pp. 247. Price $1.25.

CURRENT EDUCATIONAL LITERATURE IN THE PERIODICALS[1]

IRENE WARREN
Librarian, School of Education, University of Chicago

(The) alliance between Harvard University and the Massachusetts Institute of Technology. Sci. Am. 110:81. (24 Ja. '14.)
(The) apprentice problem. Print. Art 22:361–2. (Ja. '14.)
Athletics and morals. An introduction. Atlan. 113:145–60. (Fe. '14.)
Stearns, Alfred E. Athletics and the school.
Stewart, C. A. Athletics and the college.
Balliet, Thomas M. Points of attack in sex hygiene. J. of Educa. (Bost.) 79:87–90. (22 Ja. '14.)
Boynton, F. D. "College domination" of the high school. Educa. R. 47:154–64. (Fe. '14.)
Bruce, H. Addington. New theories in education. Outl. 106:144–48. (17 Ja. '14.)
———. The boy who goes wrong. Cent. 87:542–46. (Fe. '14.)
Cattell, J. McKeen. Science, education and democracy. Science 39:154–64. (30 Ja. '14.)
Chadwick, F. E. The woman peril in American education. Educa. R. 47:109–19. (Fe. '14.)
Childs, W. L. How can physical training be made of greatest value to the high-school boy? School R. 22:103–5. (Fe. '14.)
Comstock, Sarah. Byways of library work. Outl. 106:201–5. (24 Ja. '14.)
———. The story corner. St. Nich. 41:308–13. (Fe. '14.)
Curtis, Henry S. Educational extension through the rural social centre. Educa. 34:283–94. (Ja. '14.)
Farrington, Frederic Ernest. A unique industrial school. Educa. R. 47:134–38. (Fe. '14.)
Fuess, Claude M. Phillips Academy, Andover, Massachusetts. School R. 22:73–81. (Fe. '14.)
Goldwasser, I. E. Shall elective courses be established in the seventh and eighth grades of the elementary school? Psychol. Clinic 7:205–21. (Ja. '14.)
Greenwood, J. M. Elementary schools and standards. Educa. R. 47:139–53. (Ja. '14.)

[1] *Abbreviations.*—Atlan., Atlantic Monthly; Cent., Century; Cur. Opinion, Current Opinion; Educa., Education; Educa. R., Educational Review; J. of Educa. (Bost.), Journal of Education (Boston); J. of Educa. Psychol., Journal of Educational Psychology; J. of Home Econ., Journal of Home Economics; Lit. D., Literary Digest; Liv. Age, Living Age; Outl., Outlook; Pop. Sci. Mo., Popular Science Monthly; Print. Art, Printing Art; Psychol. Clinic, Psychological Clinic; School R., School Review; Sci. Am., Scientific American; St. Nich., St. Nicholas; Teach. Coll. Rec., Teachers College Record; Train. School M. (N.J.), Training School Magazine (New Jersey).

Heck, W. H. Parents' part in school hygiene. Educa. R. 47:127–33. (Fe. '14.)

Herzberg, Max J. The educational value of a dramatic museum. Educa. R. 47:120–26. (Fe. '14.)

Inadequacy of scientific teaching in our schools. Lit. D. 48:199. (31 Ja. '14.)

King, Irving. Physiological age and school standing. Psychol. Clinic 7:222–29. (Ja. '14.)

Kohnky, Emma. Preliminary study of the effect of dental treatment upon the physical and mental efficiency of school children. J. of Educa. Psychol. 4:571–78. (D. '13.)

Kohs, Samuel C. The Binet test and the training of teachers. Train. School M. (N.J.) 10:113–17. (Ja. '14.)

McLaren, A. D. The German child in the German school. (With special reference to child-suicide in Germany.) Liv. Age 280:295–302. (31 Ja. '14.)

Maxwell, William H. On a certain arrogance in educational theorists. Educa. R. 47:165–82. (Fe. '14.)

Mitchell, H. Edwin. The distribution of high-school graduates in Iowa. School R. 22:82–90. (Fe. '14.)

Myers, G. W. A plan for testing methods of teaching secondary mathematics. School R. 22:91–97. (Fe. '14.)

Portland survey. J. of Educa. (Bost.) 79:63–64. (15 Ja. '14.)

Price, William R. One cause of poor results in modern-language teaching. School R. 22:98–102. (Fe. '14.)

(The) professorship of philosophy and psychology of Lafayette College. Science 39:164–68. (30 Ja. '14.)

Ruckmich, Christian A. Is myopia inherited or acquired? J. of Educa. Psychol. 4:593–606. (D. '13.)

Sanders, Frederic W. The organization of education. Educa. 34:273–82. (Ja. '14.)

(The) Society of College Teachers of Education. School R. 22:108–17. (Fe. '14.)

Strout, Joseph Woodbury. The rural opportunity and the country school. Pop. Sci. Mo. 84:176–83. (Fe. '14.)

(A) syllabus for a three-year high-school course in German. School R. 22:118–20. (Fe. '14.)

Thatcher, Oliver J. Educational reforms that set a whole state in turmoil. Survey 31:494–95. (24 Ja. '14.)

Thorndike, Edward L. The measurement of achievement in drawing. Teach. Coll. Rec. 14:1–39. (N. '13.)

Vaughan, Victor C. The doctor's dream. Science 39:149–54. (30 Ja. '14.)

Webster, Arthur Gordon. The physical laboratory and its contributions to civilization. Pop. Sci. Mo. 84:105–17. (Fe. '14.)

Wellman, S. T. The industrial need of technically trained men. IX. Sci. Am. 110:78. (17 Ja. '14.)

What a college year costs. Lit. D. 48:207. (31 Ja. '14.)

What America thinks of Montessori's educational crusade. Cur. Opinion 56:127–29. (Fe. '14.)

What kills the school children? Survey 31:514. (31 Ja. '14.)

Winch, W. H. Experimental researches on learning to spell. II. J. of Educa. Psychol. 4:579–92. (D. '13.)

Woods, Robert. College extension in domestic science. J. of Home Econ. 6:41–43. (Fe. '14.)

VOLUME XIV NUMBER 8

THE ELEMENTARY SCHOOL TEACHER

APRIL 1914

EDUCATIONAL NEWS AND EDITORIAL COMMENT

The Department of Superintendence and Affiliated Meetings

The Department of Superintendence of the National Education Association together with its affiliated societies met in the city of Richmond, Virginia, during the week of February 23. The actual sessions of the Department of Superintendence began on Tuesday evening and continued until Friday noon. Some of the affiliated societies, such as the National Society for the Study of Education, began a day earlier. The Society of College Teachers of Education had a full day's session before the opening of the general meeting. The National Council also met the day before the Department.

Cultural and Industrial Education

The meetings were significant because of the large and representative group of school men and women in attendance, and also because of the character of material presented. Two or three of the discussions may be referred to in detail. The program on industrial education which was given on Thursday morning developed a sharp contrast between the views of Commissioner Snedden, of the state of Massachusetts, and Professor Bagley, of the University of Illinios. Commissioner Snedden represents, as does the state of Massachusetts, the general policy of separation between the industrial education to be given to workers and the general education to be given to those who are going forward to higher schools. Mr. Bagley's contention, on the other hand, was that there should be no separation; that those who are going into the trades deserve a very large amount of cultural training, and those who take cultural training should in turn be given some insight into the practical activities of life.

The discussion of these contrasts is, of course, one of the vital problems of current education and the differences between the two points of view led to much discussion in lobbies as well as at the various meetings. There can be little doubt that it is the hope and expectation of the progressive school men and women of this country that some solution of the industrial problem will be found which shall operate to the advantage of the common schools and of the high schools, and not merely to the advantage of a separate industrial school; so that there shall ultimately be one democratic system of education in this country rather than a subdivision of a sort which shall separate any child from the possibilities of culture or from the possibilities of securing an insight in a practical way into the industries of the country.

The Committee on Standards

Another important meeting was that of the National Council, at which the Committee on Standards and Tests of Efficiency made its report. Last year this committee was continued only after a heated discussion in which the possibility of measuring efficiency was stoutly called in question by many of the conservative members of the Council. This year the committee presented a general statement regarding the nature of school surveys and the organization of these surveys. The statement of the chairman of the committee is to be issued by the Bureau of Education, so that it will be accessible to all who are interested in the general problem. The members of the committee then followed with brief statements of constructive programs of work through which it will be possible for the teachers to participate in general educational studies. Elsewhere in this issue of the *Elementary School Teacher* attention is given to one of the detailed programs of investigation.

It is to be hoped that this committee may now have an opportunity to work out through the co-operation of many school people its important problem of organizing a general survey of the educational community through its own activities. It is to be noted that the report made by Superintendent Blewett, of St. Louis, of his own experiences on the Committee on Standards and Tests contributed very largely to the continuation of the committee and to the enthusiasm which was expressed for the work of the committee. Superintendent Blewett gave an account of his original skeptical attitude toward surveys and of the development in his own mind as he sat with the committee of an attitude more favorable to such educational research. At the end of the report of the committee the Council continued the committee and voted to recommend an appropriation to carry on its work. The time is past, it would seem from this discussion and from the general temper of the meeting of the Department of Superintendence, when anyone needs to be afraid of a school survey. Such a survey organized by school authorities and conducted in the interests of improved education is not unfriendly to the school system and is not uncertain or dangerous.

The General Education Board

A third session which developed much interesting material was that in which Mr. Buttrick and Mr. Flexner, of the General Education Board, made detailed reports of the activities of this foundation. This report is one of the first public reports that has been made by the General Education Board of its activities. All through the South the board has been co-operating in the development of various forms of practical activity in and outside of the school. The secondary schools of the South have been aided by the establishment of professorships in secondary education through the funds furnished by this board. Extension work has been organized in the form of corn clubs and tomato-canning clubs. The board promises to be an important factor in the development of the elementary and secondary schools of the country and it is interesting that the Department of Superintendence should receive from the leaders in this movement some account of the general expectations of the board and its general program of activities. This program of activities is avowedly not definitely formulated, but it is obvious that the General Education Board is interested in working out productive experiments of a type which shall enlarge the usefulness of the individual to the community. The program of socialized education was the program set forth by both of the speakers.

Other programs deserve discussion, but the limits of space and the freedom with which the Association distributes its publications make it inadvisable to attempt any general review of all the programs.

Significance of the Winter Meeting

Anyone who visits these meetings from year to year certainly is impressed with the representative character of the attendance. Superintendents come from all parts of the country. Many of them have their expenses paid by their boards, and the question is sometimes raised whether this is a paying investment. Even the casual observer can hardly fail to realize that the solidarity of American education is very largely promoted through the social intercourse that this meeting permits. In addition to the social advantages there are very obvious educational advantages. The growth of a scientific attitude toward educational inquiries and the wholesome attitude of interest in economy and efficiency are certainly fostered by these gatherings as they could not be if there were no annual gatherings of representatives of the teaching profession.

There was some discussion, from the floor, on one occasion, of the desirability of giving to the teachers who come to the summer meeting some of the results of the committee reports and discussions presented at the meetings of the Department of Superintendence. It is probably a mistake to assume that the summer meeting can distribute adequately the important results of these winter conferences. Much better would it be for these winter conferences to organize through their committees programs of work which can be carried out during the whole year and can be brought to a focus at the winter meetings. After subjecting themselves to criticism at the winter meetings these programs and the results derived from the actual experiments in the field can then be very much more adequately distributed, not through a single meeting, but through the publications of the Association which reach the hands of most of the teachers in all parts of the country. The winter meeting is a representative meeting. It is not an effort to bring together all the teachers, but rather it brings together all the interests under one roof and makes it possible for these representative school people to carry back to their several systems some of the best and most critical results of education work.

It is hardly necessary to add the remark that southern hospitality was evident at the Richmond meeting on every hand. The Association was well entertained and the opportunities for interesting historical excursions which were offered to those in attendance were so numerous that they sometimes threatened to distract the members from the regular programs.

The next meeting, under the presidency of Superintendent Snyder, will be held in the city of Cincinnati, Ohio.

The Chicago School Situation

The school situation in the city of Chicago continues to attract public attention. The members of the Board of Education whose resignations were accepted by the mayor of the city some time ago succeeded in establishing their right through court proceedings to a reconsideration of their resignations. The court that gave first judgment on their plea ruled that their resignations were not valid. Legal complications may prevent these ousted trustees from regaining their seats, for if the matter cannot come up very soon, their terms of office will expire automatically in June. The autumn session of the court where the cases would then be heard will come too late to give the ousted members any actual advantage from the ruling of the lower court.

It is interesting to note, however, that the lower court took definitely the position that a resignation placed in the hands of the mayor is not good law and not good policy. The school board would become, if such resignations were valid, a mere political tool and could not exercise properly the functions vested in it.

In the meantime the course of events within the Board of Education itself is turbid. The budget of the superintendent is held up for the time being and was subjected to an examination by the Bureau of Efficiency. The course of study is also held up for a time on the ground that it is not adequate and that it contains "fads." This led to an acrimonious discussion of what constitutes a "fad" in a course of study. The superintendent indicated that the course of study had been organized through the joint efforts of principals and teachers and not through any special activities of her own office.

Again one can only repeat the comments that school people are making everywhere in the country. If a superintendent cannot formulate the course of study with the co-operation of the educational staff and be sure that it will not be subjected to rejection or tinkering by the board of education, there is radical need of revision of relations within the school system.

One wonders how it would be possible for a superintendent to avoid this kind of clash. A vague and somewhat general answer is that it is the business of the superintendent to educate a community as well as to educate the children in the schools. The problem of educating a great community like the city of Chicago is no small undertaking. There undoubtedly ought to be in every superintendent's office additional machinery above and beyond what now exists—machinery that will collect information about the course of study and have it in such form that the public can be made aware instantly of the actual changes which are proposed in any new scheme of recitations submitted to the board. At the present moment the ordinary layman in the city of Chicago is wholly unable to decide from his own personal knowledge whether the Board of Education or the superintendent is in the right. Would it not be well to expend a part of the school money in presenting to the citizens of a great municipality the actual content of the present course of study and the significance of every change made? Certainly with the large innovations which are constantly being made in any living course of study such an exhibition of the actual content of the course would be a matter of large public interest.

Again, the holding-up of the salary budget indicates a very vital interest of the modern school community. The contention was set forth that this budget was not scientifically made. Probably the charge was only partially true. In all probabilities the superintendent would have been refused the necessary clerical force if she had asked for an opportunity to present a truly scientific budget of salaries. Now is the time, however, to make clear the fact that such clerical and expert assistance is indispensable. It ought to be possible from this time on to forestall actual controversy by an intelligent development in the Chicago school system of agencies which shall continually submit expenditures to careful scientific scrutiny. There ought to be no board of education without its financial experts, and those financial experts ought to be in a position to answer instantly any question with regard to finances. This means, of course an enlargement of the administrative offices of the schools, but the kind of enlargement of administrative offices here demanded is the kind which every great corporation has come to recognize as necessary and legitimate.

The present situation in Chicago certainly cannot long continue. Whatever the outcome in detail, it is to be hoped that this deplorable controversy will lead to the creation of agencies competent to answer definitely and scientifically all the questions raised. If, then, these questions are mere evasions of the real situation and if they are efforts to antagonize and blockade the machinery of public education in this city, they would soon be set aside through the force of information actually in the hands of the school administration. If they are sincere questions expressing public opinion, they ought to be fully answered.

The National Association of Audubon Societies makes the following announcement, to which we are very glad to give currency:

Bird Pictures for Distribution

Any teacher or other person who will interest not less than ten children in contributing a fee of ten cents each to become junior members and will send this to the office of the National Association, will receive for each child ten of the best colored pictures of wild birds which have ever been published in this country. With each one of these ten pictures goes an outline drawing intended to be used by the child for filling in the proper colors with crayons. Each picture is also accompanied by a four-page leaflet discussing the habits and general activities of the bird treated. Every child also receives an Audubon button. The cost of publishing and mailing this material is a little more than twice as much as the child's fee.

The teacher who forms such a class receives without cost to herself one full year's subscription to the beautiful illustrated magazine *Bird-Lore*. This is the leading publication in the world on bird study. To the teacher also there is sent other free literature containing many hints on methods of putting up bird boxes, feeding birds in winter, and descriptions of methods for attracting birds about the home or schoolhouse.

The Leipzig Book and Educational Exhibit

The city of Leipzig, in Germany, has long been famous as one of the great seats of the book trade of the world. This is the center of the organization known as the Book Exchange which makes it possible for the dealers in the remotest towns of Germany to be in direct contact with all the publishers who are turning out scientific and literary material. The city is preparing to hold, during the coming summer, a great exposition of books and school materials. The circular which has been sent out indicates that a variety of different interests will be represented in this exposition.

The first division will deal with drawing. Books, pamphlets, and actual school materials are being collected to show the development of the child's interest and ability to represent objects in space. This school exhibit will also be accompanied by historical books and collections that will show the development of art.

A second group of exhibitions will deal with the problem of writing. The stages of writing will be exhibited in a concrete way by examples of different kinds of penmanship. Furthermore, the problem will be taken up with reference to the psychology of the practice and the results that have been attained in the school.

A third group of exhibits will deal with singing and music. The high development of music in Germany has long been known to American students. The discussions of this kind of training in the school and the materials employed in carrying on the work will be presented.

The next division will make a study of language in a scientific way and will show the relation of the development of language to the various subjects of instruction.

The fifth group of exhibits will be made up of photographs. There will be photographs which show school work in its different aspects, others showing the buildings and material equipment of the schools. In addition the exhibits will aim to show how photography can be used, for example, in mathematical instruction and natural scientific instruction. How the subject of photography itself can be made a suitable subject for school training will also be shown.

The sixth group of exhibits will show what has been done in

child-study. The seventh group will give the books on school history and statistics, showing how the methods of scientific inquiry have been applied to school problems.

In short, there promises to be a very large exhibition of all the manifold applications of the printing and engraving art to the different aspects of school life. The material of instruction, the results of instruction, and the efforts that are being made to improve both the teachers and the children will find here an expression that ought to be of interest to visitors from across the water as well as to visitors who come from various parts of the German Empire.

A Shorter Elementary Course

In an interview which is published in the *Hartford Times* of February 28, Secretary Charles D. Hine, of the Connecticut State Board of Education, discusses the shorter elementary course which has been put into operation in the town of Wethersfield in the state of Connecticut. The schools of this town are organized under the direct supervision of the state board. The state appoints the superintendent, who has charge of the schools. In this town children who have been in the elementary school up to their twelfth year are now allowed to enter the high school. This innovation is commented upon at length by State Secretary Hine. He points out that there is a disposition on the part of some high-school authorities to oppose the admission of children before they are fourteen years of age. These high-school authorities contend that the age of twelve is one of too great immaturity; that the children cannot take up the work of the high school with proper experience behind them. On the other hand, Mr. Hine points out that the long elementary course, filled with a great variety of subjects that are badly organized, very frequently leads to a kind of mental dissipation which is not good for the child and is not a suitable preparation for the higher work of the secondary school.

Certainly there are many children who ought to be able to carry on the work of an ordinary high school when they are twelve years of age. The fact that this is being done in Wethersfield, that the children are securing, in spite of this more economical turn of education, the essentials of elementary-school training makes the secretary of the Connecticut board optimistic in the belief that the practice will become very much more general and that shortly many other children will benefit by this abbreviation of the elementary course.

Languages in the Elementary Schools

The tendency appears in many quarters to undertake in the elementary school types of work included heretofore only in high-school programs. Certainly there is much to be said on the psychological side in favor of the introduction of languages into the schools at an earlier period than at the present time. The city of Portland, Oregon, has recently undertaken a number of radical changes in its school organization. The commission which investigated these schools recommended certain changes and these changes are going forward rapidly. One of the changes which is to be made in an experimental way is described in the following article:

> Within the next few days an absolute innovation in the curricula of the public schools of the city will have its inauguration—that of teaching languages in the grade schools. Experimental classes will be started in the Irvington, Ainsworth, and Ladd schools in Latin and German. Teachers of English who are qualified to teach these two languages will assume these duties in addition to their regular work.
>
> The plan has been broached to the pupils themselves and they have unanimously expressed a wish to join the classes, and under the direction of Professor A. P. McKinley language teaching in the grades will soon form a part of the regular grammar-school work.
>
> In these introductory classes, however, it is hoped to work out and to solve many of the problems that will face the teaching of languages to younger students and also to try out textbooks. The plan is expected to prove a success because grade-school children are of the age that learns readily and assimilates easily. With the ground work of language received in the grades the pupils will pass on to high school able to take up moderately advanced work and later go to college with language requirements largely satisfied, thereby allowing more time for other studies.
>
> "We hope at some future date to add French and Spanish to the list of languages," said the teacher in charge. "Spanish will be most important because the Panama Canal will increase our trade relations with Central and South America and Spanish will prove exceedingly useful to the business man of the Pacific Coast.
>
> "We Americans are behind Europeans in learning foreign languages and starting the study in the grades will stimulate interest in them. It will also make language work easier in the high schools and colleges.
>
> "We hope to start a normal class for training teachers in the teaching of languages. For the present we shall teach the language in 25-minute halves of the regular 50-minute period, each half of the class studying and reciting in turn."

READING TESTS

CHARLES H. JUDD
University of Chicago

The Committee on Standards and Tests of the National Council of Education has authorized its individual members to seek the co-operation of school officers in different parts of the country in collecting materials. This paper was prepared with a view to securing such co-operation in testing reading. The author of the paper invites correspondence from anyone who will undertake this type of work. Fortunately Mr. Courtis' paper which follows this came to hand in time to appear in the same issue. Mr. Courtis has followed a somewhat different method from that here suggested. The author of this paper wishes to lend all support possible to Mr. Courtis. If school officers can carry out the work more easily by that method, the results will be quite as useful to the Committee on Standards. The chief purpose of both papers is to get work along this line started at many centers.

Many teachers are prejudiced against the measurement of school work because they assume that such measurement means the imposition of arbitrary outside standards on their pupils. They assume that someone believes that he has a definite yardstick by which he can determine the efficiency of all the children in the United States in their reading or arithmetic. Such prejudices would disappear entirely if the distinction between social standards and physical standards of measurement were clearly apprehended.

The fact is that every teacher is employing standards in judging the efficiency of various children in his or her class. If a given boy in the fourth grade reads poorly as compared with the other members of the class, if he shows no ability to understand the passage which the other members of the class easily understand, the teacher grades this boy as inefficient in the work of the class. In this case the boy has been measured by comparison with other members of his own class. The standard to which he has been subjected is a social standard. It is not held by his teacher that he ought to have the mental ability of an older boy, and the teacher would not be satisfied with this fourth-grade boy on the ground that he shows great efficiency in reading the primer used by the first grade. In other words, the boy must prove himself to be like the other members of the group with which he is associated. If he can do this he is judged to be efficient; if he cannot he is judged to be in some sense deficient.

The kind of comparison which the teacher is able to make within the limits of her own class ought to be extended in such a way that the class as a whole may be compared to larger units of school organization. That is, the efficiency of a fourth-grade class can be determined by comparing it with classes above and below, exactly as the efficiency of a single boy can be determined by comparing him with the other members of his class; or a fourth grade in one school building can be compared with similar grades in other school buildings, or other school systems. This comparing of one class with another is also a common fact in school experience. A certain boy comes to a given school, transferred from a neighboring school. We have no hesitation whatever in condemning the school from which he comes if this product of the school does not succeed in taking his place with the class which he enters. In other words, we judge schools by their products, and we formulate our judgment in detail by comparing one product with another product. In the same way the students who come to a given high school from several neighboring elementary schools are all compared with each other and judgments are formed by the high-school teacher regarding the efficiency or deficiency of the various elementary schools which contribute their students to the high school. Here again standards are social standards rather than absolute standards.

Even when the child's ability is measured by what seems to be an absolute standard, as by his actual solving of certain problems which are set for him, there are certain variable characteristics of the standard which must be taken into consideration. Thus the difficulty of solving the problems chosen is an important consideration in any case. If, for example, the ten problems set are very easy, the child who fails in one of these problems is not as efficient as the child who fails in several problems of a difficult set. In other words, the level at which the work is done becomes a matter of importance, and the level which is expected is determined by comparison, not by some absolute measure. Other considerations are, of course, of equal importance. How long were the children allowed to work on the problems? Was their preparation immediately before the test directed toward this particular examination or was it general in character? In other words, though a test seems at the outset to be an absolute test of the child's ability, it turns out on analysis to contain many elements which differ with the social setting in which the pupil works, and the absolute character of the standard is seen to be a mere fiction. The standard is in reality a social standard and its value depends upon comparison with other school situations and with other groups of individuals who are undertaking similar work.

With this definition of the meaning of standards in mind, let us consider some of the comparative problems which are of importance in the teaching of reading in the elementary school. In the first place, it is obvious that a comparison of different grades in the same school system is a matter of great importance. If the child shows adequate progress as he passes from the second to the third grade, from the third to the fourth grade, and so on, we may be satisfied that the school is doing efficient work even if the ability to read at any given point is in the absolute not great. Or, to put the matter in another way, the grade which is steadily improving shows a higher degree of efficiency than a grade which is improving less rapidly, even though the grade which is improving less rapidly shows a fair degree of ability. In preparing our test, therefore, we should aim to determine the rate of improvement during the different grades.

Second, there are two fundamentally different types of reading. There is reading which is oral and reading which is silent. If one notes the sharp contrast between little children and adults, he finds that oral reading is the common mode of reading among little children and the very exceptional form of reading in adult life. The ordinary adult finds it so much more convenient and easy to read to himself that he does not read aloud except under the most unusual circumstances. This distinction between oral and silent reading is not one which has been clearly recognized in school work. School work has for the most part dealt with oral reading. A comparison of the two types of reading will soon convince even the casual observer that oral reading is a rather slow and inconvenient form of reading as compared with silent reading. Furthermore, oral reading does not exhibit the highest training given in the schools, therefore a comparison of oral and silent reading will help in making a systematic comparison of the mental development of children at different stages of school work.

Third, reading is after all merely a secondary form of activity. What we want primarily in the reading class is ability to understand the passages which are read. In the lower grades the mastery of words is itself so difficult a problem that the child is able only very slowly to take in information from the passage which he reads. In the upper grades, on the other hand, the comprehension of the passage is so fully developed that the chief value of reading in these later grades is the information which it gives. Little or no time is required in the upper grades for the formal process of pronouncing words or mastering sentence forms. The mechanics of reading, if we may use that phrase to distinguish the process of reading from the process of understanding, are mastered and the whole attention may now be concentrated on the significance of the passage. We have here an important contrast between pupils in different stages of advancement. If the little child expends most of his mental energy in reading the sentence and the older child expends most of his mental energy in getting the significance of the passage, we may, therefore, test the various children in different grades by inquiring into their ability to get the meaning of the passages which they read. We shall have to choose passages with different kinds of ideas and with different degrees of complexity; simple ideas and ideas which are easy to formulate will be given in the lower grades; more complex and difficult ideas in the upper grades. It would indeed be possible in some cases to use exactly the same passage all through the school for the purpose of finding out how the ability to get at the meaning progresses at different stages in education, but it will usually be found to be more practical to arrange an overlapping series of tests so that comparisons between the extremes may be made indirectly through intermediate tests which are applied only to smaller units of the school population. For example, we may make a comparison of the first three grades with each other. Then compare the third, fourth, and fifth grades with each other, and finally the fifth, sixth, and seventh grades. The overlapping of the third and fifth grades, each appearing in two groups, will make it possible to get an idea of the relative ability of the first and eighth grades, or any other two grades in the series.

Another type of variation in the reading matter to be used is suggested by a consideration of the changing interests of children. There is a period in the intermediate grades when children exhibit a marked interest in the things in the physical world about them as contrasted with the people who go to make up the social world. Later in the adolescent period the social interests are renewed, and there is a marked interest in romantic or social literature. By testing the ability of children to get the meaning of different kinds of reading matter we gain some insight into the kinds of reading matter best suited to different stages of development. Children at one stage will get the meaning of one kind of reading matter most easily, while children at another stage of development will take up readily a totally different type of matter.

It would undoubtedly be advantageous in the interests of direct comparison if tests could be made all over the United States with the same material, that is, if the same passage could be presented to every third grade in the United States and the results carefully tabulated. We should then have a very illuminating study of the whole American school system. The disadvantage with such an effort at absolute uniformity is that while the passage itself might be the same, it would undoubtedly relate itself to the preparation of the different third grades in very different ways. It is conceivable that a third grade otherwise relatively inefficient would have just the preparation in words and ideas that would make it possible for that particular third grade to stand well in the test on the passage selected. Conceivably a third grade which had had an entirely different type of training might show very little ability with the particular passage chosen. We shall accordingly lose little by foregoing the use of a single passage. Each school system may select its own material, provided only the material is thoroughly analyzed and the results accompanied in every case by a statement of the material thus employed. After a number of tests of this sort within single school systems have been carried out, we shall perhaps be prepared to undertake a more systematic and unified test of many school systems.

The first step in making tests is to select some simple phase of the reading process which can be clearly described and definitely determined. One such phase which offers itself as the simplest characteristic of most mental processes is the rate of speed. The rate at which a child reads is a very useful indication of efficiency. One has only to observe little children who are just learning to read to be impressed with the slowness of their mental operation. On the other hand, the fluent reading of an upper-grade child is a sign of his mastery of the mechanical side of the process. Furthermore, this test of rate will bring out very effectively the contrast between silent reading and oral reading. In the lower grades silent reading is a very slow, if not indeed an impossible, process. In the upper grades silent reading is a very rapid form of reading, much more rapid indeed than any form of oral reading. With the adult, oral reading is from two to three times as slow as silent reading.

With these suggestions regarding rate and the general character of comparative tests in mind, let a test in silent reading be carried out as follows. The teacher selects a passage to be read. She reads it silently herself and notes the time which it requires. It will be in the interests of later comparison if a group of teachers will select the same passage and all test first their own rate of silent reading. After selecting a suitable passage each child to be tested is supplied with a copy. The passage should of course be new to the child. He is told before he looks at the passage that he is to read it, getting as much of its meaning as he can, because he will be asked to tell on paper what is in the passage. At a given signal the reading begins. After three minutes, or whatever period the teacher's own test shows to be well within the time required to read the passage, a signal is given and the children mark how far they have gone and at once set about writing down all that they remember. They should be allowed as much time as they need for this part of the exercise. Sometimes, instead of asking the children to write down what they can recall, a series of questions may be given which will bring out definitely the ability of the child to recall certain particular ideas.

Such a test as this should be made repeatedly and a continuous record should be kept for each child. A test is of little value if given as a single examination. It is of great value if it is used as a common routine of instruction.

Different kinds of reading matter should be used and different degrees of difficulty should be sought in the different passages.

The making and tabulating of the record does not involve as much labor as might be anticipated by one not acquainted with experimental methods. If each child indicates how far he has gone, the number of lines can readily be recorded. It is better in the interests of future comparisons for the teacher to reduce the record to number of words read, because lines are so different in different books. This reducing of the pupil's report in lines to number of words requires only a single counting. A check for the number of lines read is, of course, supplied by the number of ideas reproduced.

In order to measure a child's efficiency in getting meaning the passage should first be analyzed into ideas presented. The following is a passage thus analyzed by Professor Freeman for such a test. With this analysis the child's report can easily be rated. He has so and so many of the ideas presented in the original passage; or, as suggested above, suitable questions can be made up to draw out the ideas.

A BOY'S PET

In our town, | when a boy had a coon, | he had to have a box turned open side down | to keep it in, | and he had to have a little door in the box | to pull the coon out through | whenever he wanted to show it to other boys | or look at it himself, | which was forty or fifty times a day | when he first got it. |

He had to have a collar for the coon, | and a chain, | because a coon could gnaw through a string | in a minute.

The coon liked to stay inside his box, | where he had a bed of hay, | and whenever the boy pulled him out, | he did his best to bite the boy. | He knew no tricks; | his temper was bad; | he wouldn't even let a fellow see him eat, | and there was nothing about him, except the rings round his tail, that anybody would care for.

My boys' brother had a coon | that got away two or three times. | He ran up the tall locust tree | in front of the house, | and in a few minutes all the boys of the town would be there | telling his owner how to get him down.

Of course the only way was to climb for the coon, | which would be out at the point of a high and slender limb, | and would bite you awfully, | even if the limb didn't break under you; | while the boys kept yelling to you what to do, | and the dog just howled with excitement.

The last time the coon got away | he was discovered by moonlight | in the locust tree. | His owner climbed for him, | but the coon kept going higher and higher, | and at last he had to be left till morning. | In the morning he was not there, | or anywhere.

The test of oral reading is more difficult to conduct as a part of the regular work of the school. Individual oral reading tests are relatively easy and may be carried out like the silent test above described.

A teacher can, however, train herself to carry on the oral test in connection with the regular lesson. The teacher should call upon successive members of the class to read orally and should indicate the length of time that is consumed in the reading of each passage. A little training in noting the time of such reading will make it possible to check up a whole class very rapidly. The work will be much more efficiently done if one can use a stop watch, but, without this added convenience, illuminating information can be secured with regard to the rate of oral reading as contrasted with the rate of silent reading by noting the number of seconds required for each passage and the number of words in the passage.

It is not easy to determine the value of oral reading as a means of getting ideas when the work is done in class, for the simple reason that while one child is reading orally, the rest are either supplementing the test by reading silently or are neglecting the class exercise while the slow process of oral reading is going on. One way of avoiding this difficulty and of making at the same time a very interesting test of ability to understand matters heard rather than seen is to pass the single copy of the text from pupil to pupil allowing only the one who is reading to see the text and requiring all to reproduce the ideas. The pupil who reads the passage will of course be in an entirely different relation to the passage from those who hear. With reference to the different passages the various children will be successively readers and listeners.

The only satisfactory way of getting a test of the ability to understand meanings through oral reading is through individual tests. If a teacher will test two or three pupils daily, however, the burden of such a test will not be great and a tabulated result will be of great value in checking up the other types of results which have already been discussed.

Further utilization of this test would be possible by allowing the children to read the same passage several times. Some very illuminating tests have been made of the ability to recognize simple geometrical figures after successive attempts, and so undoubtedly with the reading of passages it would be possible to get in the second or third reading great improvement over the first reading. The test would thus grow naturally into an examination of the way in which children assimilate ideas. For example, in studying the lesson in geography or history silently at his seat, the boy undoubtedly reads over certain passages several times. In some cases he reads over selected passages which offer especial difficulty, in other cases he reads over the whole lesson several times in succession. We ought to be able to determine which of these two methods of study is the more economical so that we may help children in their silent reading.

Mr. Courtis has shown in his tests the importance of the child's rate of writing as an element in any test which calls upon the child to reproduce ideas that he has acquired through reading. The child who writes slowly is disadvantaged in comparison with the child who writes rapidly, so that our definition of a child's ability to reproduce ideas should undoubtedly include ultimately his ability to write. The difficulty which is here encountered can be overcome so far as individual tests are concerned by allowing children to reproduce orally the ideas acquired. The teacher has now to note those ideas which are correctly reproduced and those which are omitted. Part of the difficulty can also be eliminated by giving the writer plenty of time. Even if he has plenty of time, however, the rate of writing will enter into the situation, because the child who writes slowly and laboriously will be distracted by the mere process of writing and his recollection of ideas will be in a measure distracted by this mere process of setting down on paper what he has recalled.

STANDARD TESTS IN ENGLISH

S. A. COURTIS
Liggett School, Detroit, Michigan

Standard tests in education are rulers for the measurement of educational products; tools for research work. They should be differentiated from the ordinary examinations on the one hand and the more rigid and formal measurements of the experimental psychologists on the other. An examination, for instance, is supposed to show whether or not the individual has successfully completed a prescribed course of work. Examinations are complex, are usually made afresh each time they are given, and only in the most general sense may the conditions under which they are given said to be controlled.

The tests of the psychologists are "pure science" tests. The test itself often deals with a single elemental phase of mental action, and the conditions under which the test is given are rigidly controlled. For this reason the learning of nonsense syllables, crossing out of *A*'s, and other tests of this character, while of value from the point of view of scientific study of the mind, have little connection with actual classroom work.

Day by day, however, the school is attempting to make certain well-defined changes in the minds and habits of the children in its care. The character and the amount of these changes is not determined by chance, but in accordance with laws which, in their operation, are as constant as those which determine other phenomena of the natural world. Until these laws are known, scientific control of the efficiency of the educational process will be impossible. The greatest need of the educational world today, from the point of improvement of the efficiency of teaching, is scientific yet *practical* measures of the fundamental abilities actually being developed by school work. For it is the possession of such measures that makes possible the study of the development of these abilities from grade to grade and the evaluation of the effects of varying conditions in method.

In the writer's thinking, the functions of standard educational tests are four: (*a*) to secure information that will enable school authorities to formulate in objective terms the ends to be attained in any educational process; (*b*) to measure the efficiency of methods designed to produce the desired results; (*c*) to determine the factors and laws which condition learning and teaching; (*d*) to furnish data that will enable comparisons of school with school, and teacher with teacher for purposes of supervisory control to be made upon *scientific, impersonal, objective* bases.

If the reader will keep these purposes in mind during the discussions of the tests described below, he will not be led into making unwarranted criticisms. For the tests are neither examinations, classroom exercises, nor measures of elementary psychological activities.

As the readers of this journal know, the writer has for some years been measuring the efficiency of teaching in arithmetic. The development of the abilities involved in work with whole numbers in the four processes has at last been brought under control; but little success has been achieved in the control of the reasoning processes. Recent experimental studies have seemed to show that the chief difficulties are closely connected with the abilities involved in reading. It has become imperative, therefore, to determine standard rates of reading and of comprehension; but in giving tests for this purpose it was found that the material secured could be scored in so many other ways of value that the group of tests has been combined into a single series under the head of "English Tests." These have been issued on the same co-operative basis followed in the arithmetic work, and are now being standardized by teachers and superintendents in different parts of the country. Definite standards cannot be formulated for some time, but it was thought that a summary of the results obtained from a single school would furnish a concrete illustration of the products of such tests and lead to a more widespread interest and a greater degree of co-operation in the work of standardization.

The tests are six in number and have been named as follows: Test 1, "Handwriting"; Test 2, "Dictation"; Test 3, "Original Story"; Test 4, "Normal Reading"; Test 5, "Careful Reading";

Test 6, "Reproduction." They are not distinct tests, but a series of related exercises grouped about a central theme.

The test sheets are printed on paper of a uniform size and bound with appropriate record sheets in pamphlet form. Exactly the same tests are given to all grades from the fourth through high school and university, and that conditions may be kept uniform, instructions for giving, scoring, and tabulating the tests have been printed in convenient form together with necessary record sheets, answer cards, and graph sheets. The tests themselves contain many devices tending to make scoring easy and to reduce the time required to a minimum. They will be supplied at cost to those who will return their results for tabulation with those of other schools. Any teacher of English, even though without previous training in educational measurement, may, at nominal cost, take part in the co-operative investigation with benefit to himself.

The series of tests is based upon the picture of a child, startled by the appearance of a hungry dog while sitting in a doorway drinking from a bowl of milk. The dictation exercises (Test 2) give the first part of a story (Part A) based upon the picture, but the story is interrupted at a critical point and in the third test the child is required to finish the story for himself. When this has been done a printed continuation of the story (Part B) is given him to read at his normal rate. This is followed by a test of verbal memory of what has been read. In the fifth test, the printed continuation of the story (Part C) is also given him to read, but this time he is cautioned that he must read so carefully that he can reproduce what he has read. The reproduction of this part of the story immediately follows. The concluding portion of the story (Part D) is then *read to* him and again the child is asked to reproduce the subject-matter. Test 1, which occurs on the last page, is called a test in handwriting, but needs considerable explanation. A portion of the test is shown in Fig. 1. It will be noted that the activity in the test is that of copying letters arranged in nonsense groups of five letters each. The actual letters used are those which occur in the dictation exercises, Test 2, and the frequency of occurrence of each letter is the same as in that test. As far as handwriting is concerned, the situation closely resembles that of the formal writing-lesson in which a copy is used. For this reason, this test has the *least* value of any for purposes of measuring handwriting. It does measure, however, very effectively, the rate of motor activity of the child, and his response to a strange situation involving no thought-content. It serves the further purpose of disposing of the question of handwriting. In this test, if anywhere, the child affects the mannerisms and style of the handwriting instruction, but, *having been tested in handwriting*, he writes

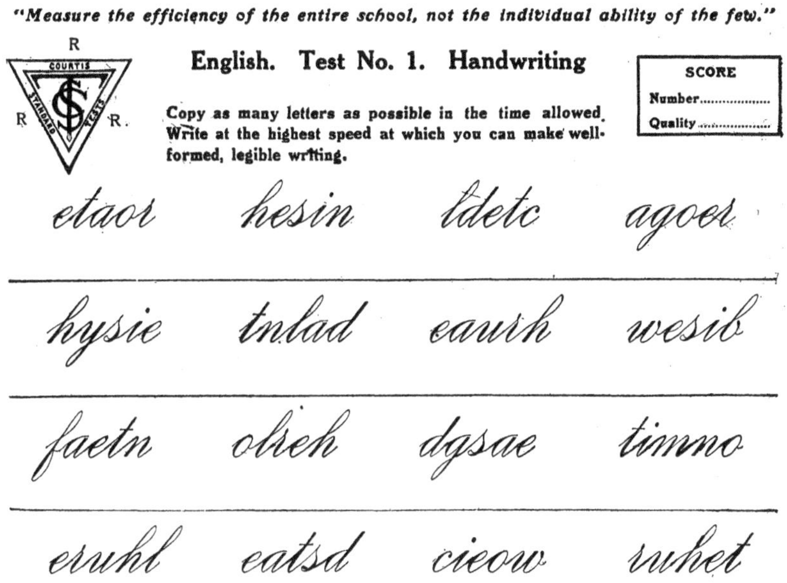

"Measure the efficiency of the entire school, not the individual ability of the few."

R COURTIS STANDARD TESTS R R.

English. Test No. 1. Handwriting

Copy as many letters as possible in the time allowed. Write at the highest speed at which you can make well-formed, legible writing.

SCORE
Number..................
Quality..................

etaoi hesin ldetc agoei

hysie tnlad eauih wesib

faetn olteh dgsae timno

eruhl eatsd cieow ruhet

Fig. 1.—Portion of Test 1. This test is called a test of handwriting, but really measures rate of motor activity.

normally and naturally in the tests which follow. In other words, comparison of the quality of handwriting in Test 1 with the average score made in Tests 3, 5, and 6 reveals any lack that there may be of transfer of the abilities generated by the handwriting lesson to the handwriting of a child when serving its normal function, that of recording thought.

The tests are scored as to quality and legibility of handwriting by the Thorndike or Ayres scales, as to number of words read or written per minute, as to the quality of the original story and of the reproductions written, following the methods adopted by Rice, Bliss, and others, as to mistakes per hundred words written in punctuation, spelling, and syntax, as to the rate and accuracy of memory of both words and sense.

The details of the scoring and of the provisions taken to insure uniformity are too many to be given here. Two of these, however, need special comment. The question is often asked, why the Hillegas scale for measurement of English composition is not used. The answers are two in number. For one thing, the writer has not found the Hillegas scale a practical tool for classroom use. In the hands of a person of sufficient training, it affords a valuable objective basis of comparison of one type of composition with another. For instance, in comparing the products of future editions of the Courtis English tests with the present edition, the values of the standards in English composition would be equated by means of the Hillegas scale, but for measurements of school efficiency in teaching English composition it seems to the writer more practical to attempt to devise a scale, all the samples of which shall have a uniform subject-matter. This the products of the present series of tests will yield, and the construction of such a scale is one of the underlying reasons why the tests are issued in the present form. The second answer must be that the purpose of the tests is not so much to measure the abilities of the children in English composition as it is to determine the variation in judgment of teachers in various parts of the country, and the factors entering into such judgment. If as a result of giving these tests a thousand sample papers are secured all of which, in the judgment of the teachers scoring them, are "Excellent," and if these are compared with other groups of one thousand papers each, scored by the teachers "Good," "Fair," "Poor," "Failure," respectively, all on material uniform in content and obtained under uniform conditions, it will be possible to determine with great exactness what weight should be given to mistakes in spelling, writing, style, etc., in determining the grade of a paper. This would reduce the formulation of standards in English composition to a scientific objective basis. For this reason the teachers are asked to score the papers as to English composition according to *their own standards.*

A second point that needs discussion is the measure of spelling, punctuation, and syntax. The tests are in no sense spelling-tests, for instance, but they do measure spelling-efficiency. For if in one school under certain conditions 10 per cent of the eighth-grade children are able to write 100 words without making a single mistake, while in another school, under precisely the same conditions and on the same subject-matter, 53 per cent of the children in the eighth grade are able to write 100 words without a single error, it is evident that the efficiency of the instruction in spelling, other things being equal, is much greater in the second school than in the first. Tabulations of the returns from many schools will, therefore, yield standards of efficiency in spelling, punctuation, and syntax.

As a concrete illustration of the types of results secured from these tests, in Fig. 2 are given the scores made by an adult. This man, a supervisor in arithmetic in a school system in Michigan, was able to make a better score in the formal handwriting than he did in the later tests. The average quality in his handwriting by the Thorndike scale was judged to be that of sample 9, and his legibility equal to that of sample 50 on the Ayres scale. In the simple copying of groups of letters the individual wrote at the rate of 30 words per minute. In reproducing material which he had just read or which had been read to him, he wrote at the rate of 25 words per minute, but in the original story his rate fell to 19 words per minute. This fall in score is significant as revealing a difficulty which this person experienced, either in creating the ideas to write, or in putting into proper form the story he wished to express. His normal rate of reading was high—378 words per minute—but when reading with care for reproduction his rate was but 128 words per minute. The quality of his original story was "Good," as judged by the standards of the teacher who scored the paper, but his reproductions were only "Fair." He made on the average of two mistakes in punctuation per hundred words written, and none in spelling and syntax. His verbal memory is poor as shown by the very low rate of three words per minute in Test 4 and by the low accuracy of his results. This fact is again brought out in Tests 5 and 6. Here his rate is higher but his

"Measure the efficiency of the entire school, not the individual ability of the few."

COURTIS STANDARD TESTS
IN
Reading, Writing and Arithmetic

ENGLISH
Series C

INDIVIDUAL SCORE SHEET.

Name Henry, BOY OR GIRL, Age last birthday 35

School ..... Grade ..... Room .....

City ..... State ..... Date .....

Tests	HANDWRITING QUALITY—THORNDIKE Trials 1st	2nd	Change	LEGIBILITY—AYERS Trials 1st	2nd	Change	RATE WORDS PER MINUTE Trials 1st	2nd	Change	COMPOSITION GRADE Trials 1st	2nd	Change
1	10			50			30					
2	10			50			22					
*3	9			50			19			B		
4							378					
*5	9			50			128 25			C		
*6	9			50			28			C		
*Av.	9			50								

Tests	MISTAKES PER HUNDRED WORDS WRITTEN PUNCTUATION Trial 1st	2nd	Change	SPELLING Trial 1st	2nd	Change	SYNTAX Trial 1st	2nd	Change	Tests	MEMORY RATE Trial 1st	2nd	Change	ACCURACY Trial 1st	2nd	Change
														WORDS		
2	2			0			0			4	3			32		
3	1			0			0			*5	8			21		
5	3			0			0			*6	12			20		
6	2			0			0			*Av.	10			20		
														POINTS		
Av.	2									5	2.2			88		
										6	3.1			73		
										Av.	2.6			80		

FIG. 2.—A sample record showing scores made by an adult.

accuracy correspondingly lower. It is to be noted that he responds more readily to auditory stimulus than he does to visual. In spite of his poor verbal memory, however, his comprehension of what was read to him is high. He was able to reproduce 75 per cent of the essential subject-matter of the two passages, after a single reading.

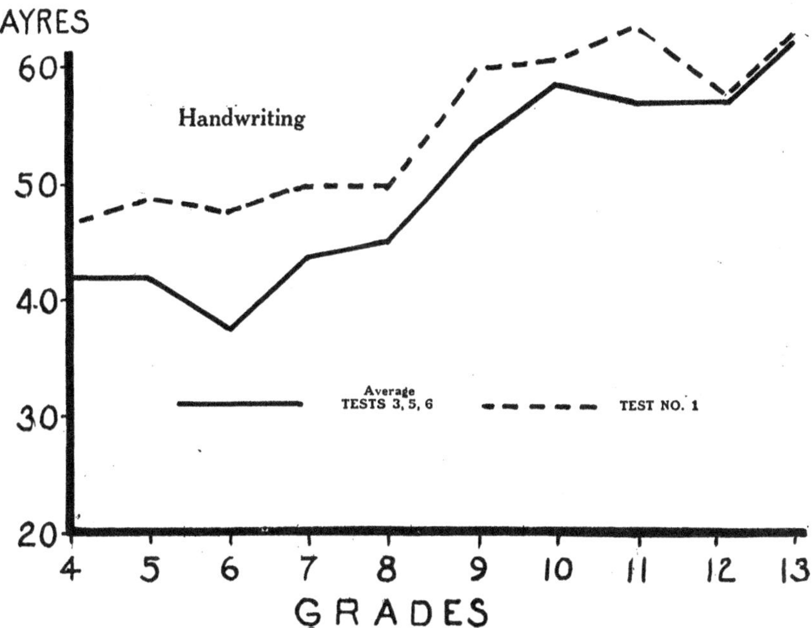

FIG. 3.—Median scores by grades in handwriting. Papers scored by the Ayres' scale. Solid line, average of median scores, Tests 3, 5, and 6. Dotted line, median score, Test 1, formal handwriting. The difference between the two curves was caused by the attempt to make good copy in the formal test.

It will be evident at once that the tests measure a number of very simple yet fundamental aspects of the ordinary products of school instruction in various phases of English work. The essential element in the interpretation of such scores, however, is standards based upon a sufficient number of cases for each grade to afford reasonable norms. These are, of course, entirely wanting at the present time, but in the graphs which follow, the results from the measurements of a single school are given. It should be particularly noted that the conditions of examination were kept uniform from the fourth grade through the high school (five-year course, hence grade 13) and that the scoring was done by one person in a uniform manner.

In Fig. 3 are given the median scores by grades in handwriting. It will be seen that the curve declines at the sixth grade, then rises to a maximum of 62 on the Ayres scale. This marks the efficiency of the handwriting instruction in this school as low, a fact which the school authorities had already recognized. The superiority

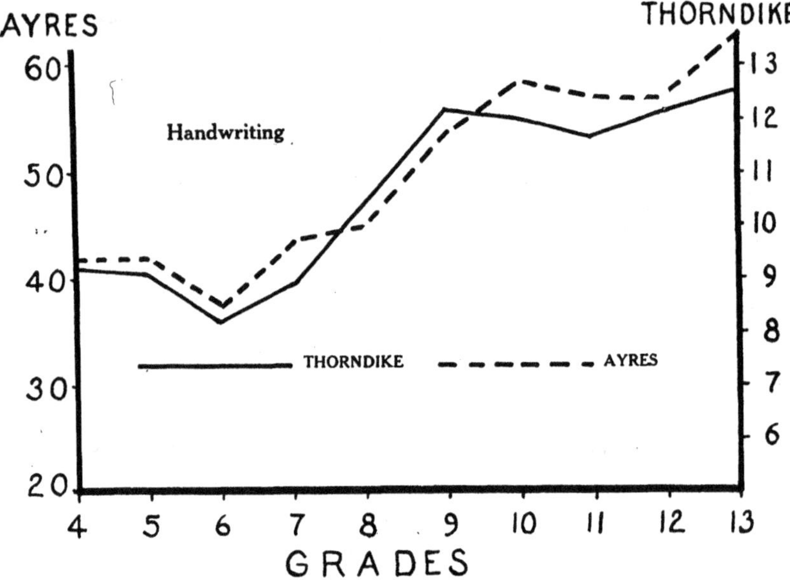

FIG. 4.—Comparison of the Development Curves for Handwriting as Determined by the Ayres and by the Thorndike scales.

of grades four and five over six indicates the effect of recent changes in the course of study with definite provision for handwriting instruction in place of the incidental training of previous years. The differences between the curves for Test 1 and the average of Tests 3, 5, and 6, differences which are fairly constant in grades 4, 5, 6, 7, and 8, indicate a lack of transfer of ability in these grades; in other words, the effort to produce good copy in a handwriting test leads to a better handwriting product than that which is obtained when the children are writing naturally. This should serve to emphasize the need of *careful control of the conditions under which specimens are secured* in any measurement of efficiency of handwriting instruction.

In Fig. 4 are given for comparison the development curves for handwriting in this school, as measured by the Ayres and by the Thorndike scales. Except for grades 8 and 9, the differences in the two curves are slight. The fact that consistent *relative* results

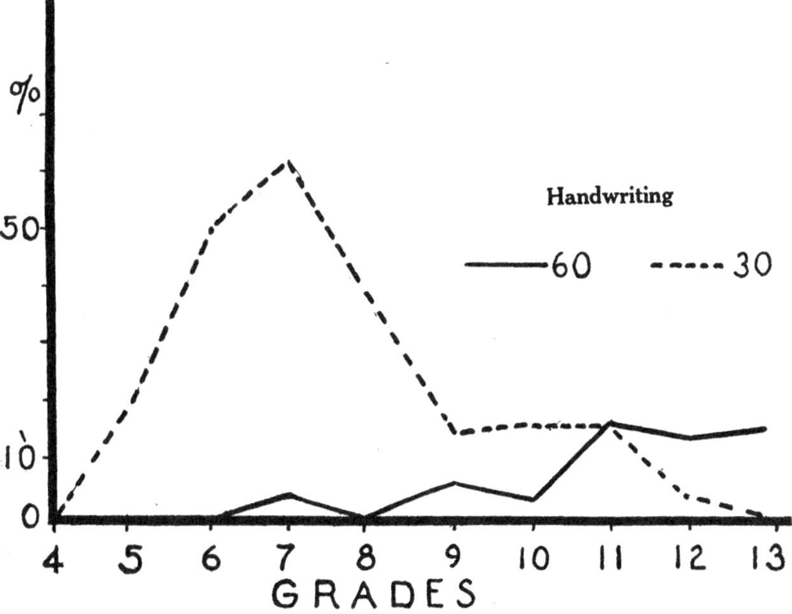

FIG. 5.—Efficiency curves for handwriting. Solid line shows the percentage of the membership of each grade that equals or exceeds sample 60 on the Ayres scale.

may be secured when samples of handwriting are measured by two different scales at different times is proof to the writer that objective measurement of handwriting rests upon no uncertain basis.

From the point of view of efficiency of instruction, however, median scores should be replaced by the percentage of the class membership that reach or exceed the desired standard. In Fig. 5 the heavy line shows the percentage of each grade's membership which equals or exceeds sample 60 on the Ayres scale. As noted before, the efficiency of the handwriting instruction in this school is very low, but at least the school now has an objective basis of comparison of present results with those which will have been reached when the present fourth-grade class shall have become Seniors. It will be remembered that a comparison of a school with itself or comparisons of methods from school to school was one of the fundamental purposes of such standard tests. In similar fashion the dotted line in Fig. 5 shows at once the percentage of each class membership whose writing equals or falls below

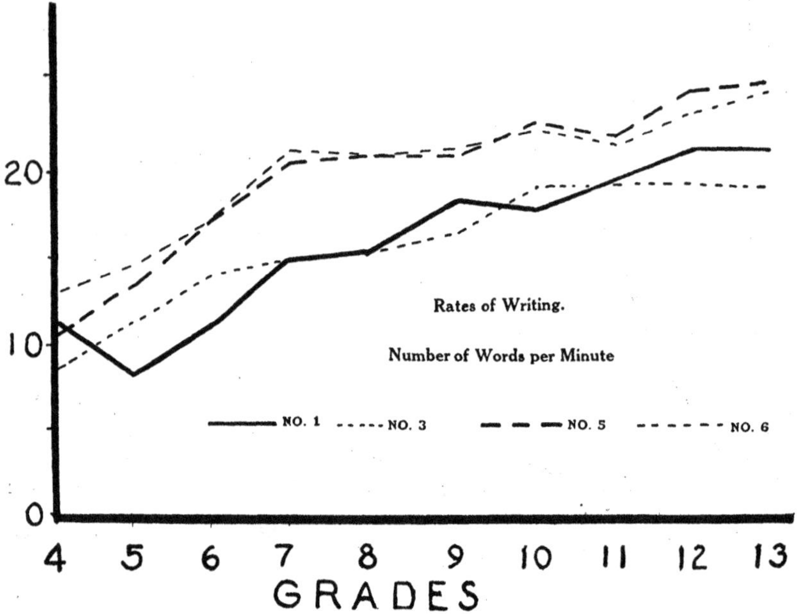

FIG. 6.—Development curves for rates of writing in Tests 1, 3, 5, 6.

sample 30 on the Ayres scale. Grades 5, 6, 7, and 8 are thus seen to have the greatest need for improvement.

In Fig. 6 are given the development curves for rate of writing, the number of words written per minute in Tests 1, 3, 5, and 6. It should be noted that curves for Tests 1 and 3 closely agree, as do those of Tests 5 and 6, but that the second set are considerably higher than the first. This means that slowing-down of speed of writing in Test 1 in the effort to produce good copy was about equal to the effect of the effort put forth in composing the original story in Test 3. In other words, the difference between the two sets of curves measures the retarding influence of mental effort. Eighth-grade children able to write at the rate of 22 words per minute when reproducing a story that they have read, or that has been read to them, were able to write but fifteen words per minute when they were forced to supply their own ideas, or when they are taking particular care to make legible writing. In this ability as in so many others, the period of rapid growth ends at the seventh grade.

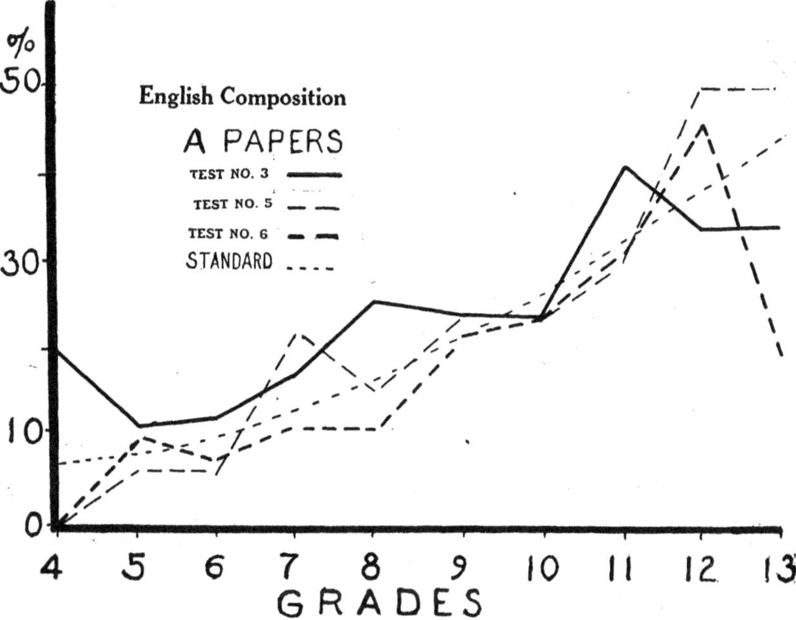

FIG. 7.—Development curves for the ability to write an "A" (Excellent) paper in the various tests.

In Fig. 7 are drawn the curves showing the percentage of A ("Excellent") papers in each grade for various tests. It is interesting to note that in nearly every grade the curve for the original story is higher than the curves for either of the two reproductions, as it should be by the doctrine of interest. The dotted line marked "standard" represents, for this school, the efficiency of present instruction. That is, the efficiency of training in English composition at the present time is such that at the eighth grade but 13 per cent of the children are able to write A, or "Excellent," papers.

Fig. 8 shows the curves based upon the mistakes in punctuation, spelling, and syntax per hundred words written. Development of these abilities, like many others, is most rapid in the early grades but continuous through to the end of the high-school years.

More interesting, however, are the efficiency curves given in Fig. 9. These are based upon the percentage of papers in each

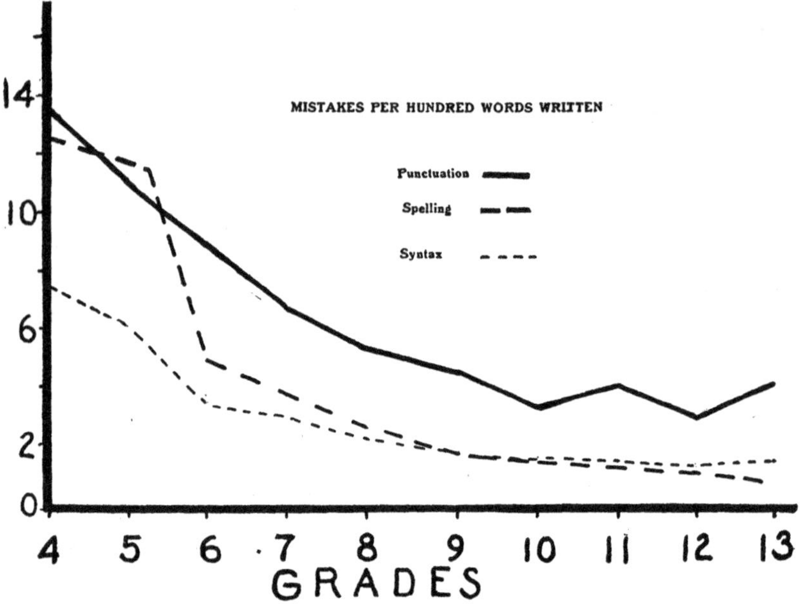

FIG. 8.—Development curves for punctuation, spelling, and syntax as determined by the number of mistakes in each per hundred words written.

grade which had between one and four mistakes in punctuation per hundred words, less than one mistake in spelling and in syntax per hundred words. Note the extremely rapid rise of the curve for punctuation and the more gradual development of the curves for spelling and syntax. It is interesting to note that while at the eighth grade but *one child in ten* is able to write 100 words without making a mistake in spelling, by the thirteenth grade the number has risen *to 55 per cent.* In this school the greater development of these abilities comes, not during the years when provision is made for active study of spelling (grammar grades), but during high-school years *when the corrective work is incidental.* If these results are confirmed by the tests of other schools, it probably means that here, as in arithmetic, training on the specific abilities of spelling, punctuation, and grammar, is nearly valueless and does not transfer, that our first concern must be to give the children experience in thinking, expressing, and recording their thoughts and later perfect the mechanical elements through repeated use.

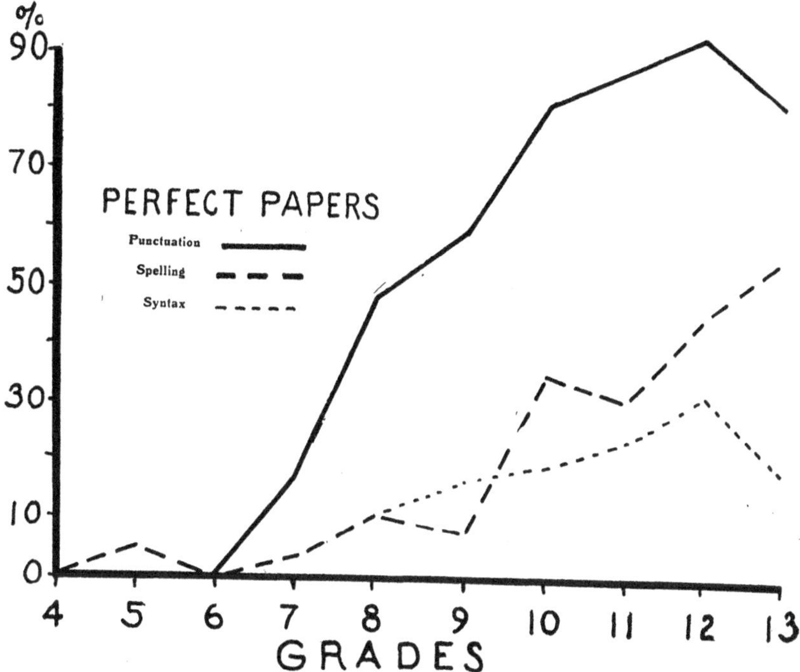

FIG. 9.—Efficiency curves for punctuation, spelling, and syntax. The curves indicate the percentage of each class membership which made but from 1 to 4 mistakes in punctuation, and less than 1 mistake in spelling and syntax, per hundred words written.

The curves in Fig. 10 give the median scores for rates of reading. It will be seen that the curve for normal reading rises to a high value and does not reach its maximum until the high-school years. The curve for careful reading, on the other hand, is practically constant from the sixth grade on. This probably means that the rate and character of one's serious reading is fixed in the early school life. The result, however, needs to be confirmed by the tests of many school systems; it may be due to purely local conditions. If this type of curve should prove general, it should be possible eventually to define the ability to read in objective terms, i. e., a child would have standard ability in reading as soon as it could read 230 words per minute of a simple narrative printed in the size of type, length of line, openness of spacing represented by Test 5. To this must be added the qualifying clause, "and be

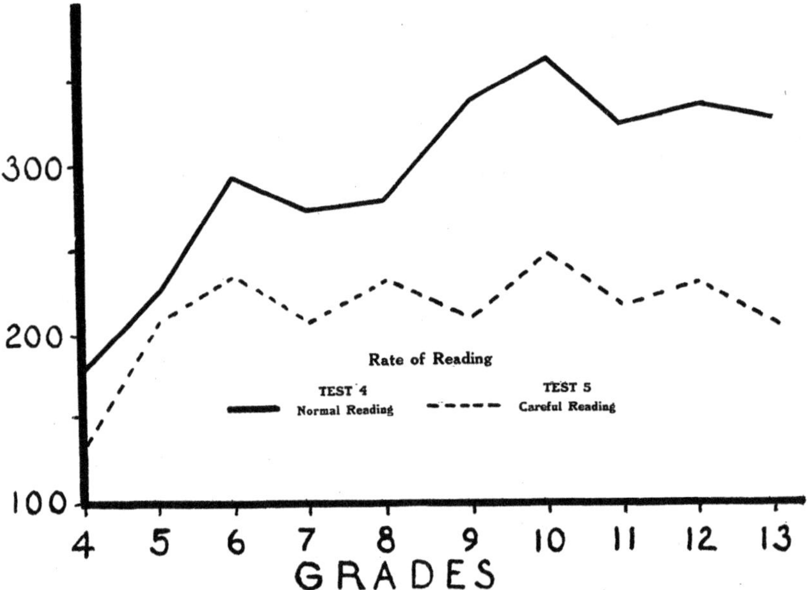

FIG. 10.—Development curves for normal and for careful reading, based upon the number of words read per minute.

able to reproduce about 50 per cent of the words and 75 per cent of the ideas after a single reading."

The results of the tests prove that the range of individual ability in reading, writing, etc., is as great as that revealed by the arithmetic tests. The performance of the more able child in any one class is usually from two to three times that of the less able child.

In the upper half of Fig. 11, for instance, the distribution of the 175 children in grades nine to thirteen are shown for Test 4 (solid line) and Test 5 (dotted line). The scale along the base of the figure represents the number of words read per minute, while the scale at the left shows the frequency of the different scores. In each test a group of 50 children exceed the limit of the test. (The experimental work upon which the lengths of the various tests were based was done mainly with adults.) Had the tests been

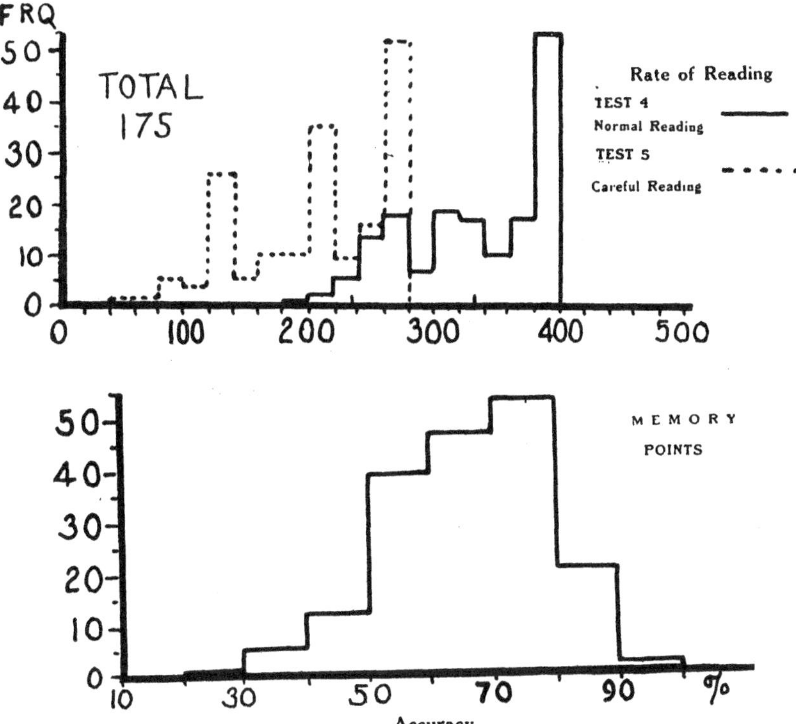

FIG. 11.—Distributions of individual scores of 175 high-school pupils as samples of the great range of individual variation in all tests. Abilities selected, the number of words read per minute in normal reading and in careful reading, and the number of ideas remembered of what was read. The more able children have scores from two to three times as large as those of the less able.

long enough, the ability of these pupils would undoubtedly have varied from 200 words per minute to 500 words per minute for normal reading, and from 60 words per minute to 400 words per minute for careful reading. When the vital nature of ability to read and understand is considered, this range of ability to read the simplest prose becomes very significant. Precisely similar results are shown for memory in the lower half of the figure where the scale along the base line shows the accuracy with which the ideas read were remembered. It is evident from this one test alone that the character of the school product in reading is precisely similar to that in arithmetic, and the writer expects to find that the same general causes operate to prevent success, that the same factors determine efficiency, and that the same changes in methods of teaching will prove effective.

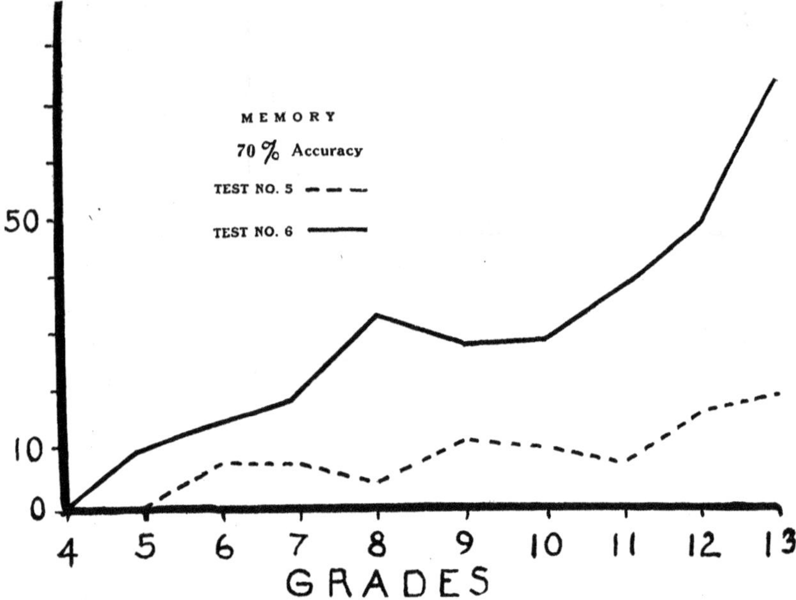

FIG. 12.—Curves showing the percentage of each class membership remembering 70 per cent or more of what was read (Test 5, visual stimulation) and of what was heard (Test 6, auditory stimulation). Note the rapid rise of the second curve, particularly in high-school years, and the very slight increase in the first curve.

The results shown by the curve in Fig. 12 were unexpected. The solid line is based upon the percentage of each class who remember 70 per cent or more of what was read to them (auditory stimulation), while the dotted line is a similar curve for the material the children read themselves (visual stimulation). It is evident from the figure that the children are steadily growing in their ability to remember the spoken word, while their ability to retain what they themselves read is much less and shows little increase during the period of school life. In this particular school, at least, the growth in the power of the visual stimulus is much less than has been supposed.

In Fig. 13 is given a graphic representation of the use of the products of such standard tests in dealing with individual children. On the basis of these tests and the requirements of the school it is possible to say that an eighth-grade child of standard ability should

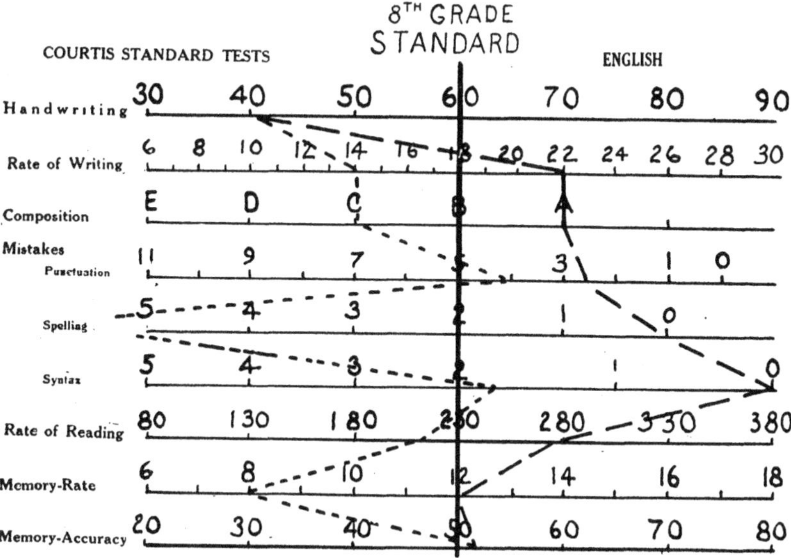

FIG. 13.—Comparative graph of standard and individual scores in the various tests. A suggestion of the possible use of scores in such tests for diagnosis of individual defects.

be able to write an original story at the rate of 18 words per minute and that legibility of the writing should be 60 on the Ayres scale, and the quality of the story "Good"; that in the story there should not be more than five mistakes in punctuation per hundred words, two in spelling, and two in syntax; that in careful reading of the given material under standard conditions, the rate should be 230 words per minute, and that in the reproduction of the material read, 12 of the original words should be used per minute and that these words should constitute 50 per cent of the words used in the reproduction. The graph shows the actual scores made by two members of the same class. One individual—represented by the heavy broken line—wrote 22 words per minute, but the quality of her handwriting was only 40. Her story, however, was excellent. She made but 2.7 mistakes per hundred words in punctuation, none in spelling and syntax. She was able to read the test material at a high rate of speed and could reproduce what she had read at the standard rate and with better than standard accuracy. The other individual made the same scores in handwriting, although her rate was but 14 words per minute in the original story and the quality of the story itself but "Fair." Her control of punctuation and syntax was above standard but she was a poor speller. Her rate of reading was nearly normal, but she was slow in reproducing what she had read, although what she actually did write was up to the standard in accuracy. It is evident from these curves that both individuals need additional training in handwriting; that the second one needs also special assistance in spelling and special practice in the control of the mechanism by which the ideas are expressed.

The work in arithmetic has proved that it is not possible radically to change the efficiency of present methods *until the actual work assigned to each pupil is based upon his measured needs.* It should be evident from the foregoing discussion that the products from these tests in English will furnish objective standards that will serve both as goals for the guidance of teachers and pupils, and as a means of detecting the peculiar weaknesses of individuals. The co-operation of all teachers and superintendents interested in the experimental evaluation of such aids to classroom work will be appreciated.

THE TEACHING OF HYGIENE BELOW THE HIGH SCHOOL

J. MACE ANDRESS
Instructor in Hygiene, State Normal School, Worcester, Mass.

III. METHODS OF TEACHING HYGIENE

a) *Incidental.*—As previously suggested, we need to judge the results of the teacher of hygiene largely by the habits which she has been able to inculcate. In one sense the schoolroom and the school grounds are to be considered as places for the practice of hygienic habits. Every opportunity that the teacher has to help the child to form the right kind of habit should be eagerly seized. It is quite absurd to think of different habits, all important to health, being taken up in certain grades in a mechanical fashion and then being allowed to drop. It is not sufficient to mention cleanliness in one grade, or to make a great crusade for cleanliness at this time, and then let it drop and begin on another habit in the next grade.

Instruction in, and practice of, habits necessary for health should take place as soon as the child enters school. In most cases this instruction should be incidental and individual. In some cases, as in the cleaning of the teeth, class instruction should be given, and toothbrush drills inaugurated. As soon as the habit is being practiced regularly, nothing further need be done except in individual instances. Sometimes the entire school may come from homes where they are taught to clean their teeth regularly. In such circumstances, the teacher would not find it necessary to give the matter any consideration. When lessons are given in the lower grades, they should be brief, simple, and in a conversational tone. The first four grades should center their forces on getting children to form essential habits, and eventually on making the pupils responsible for them. Reading and a more systematic treatment of the subject should come in the higher grades.

Among the many habits which the teacher can supervise to a certain extent in the school are: (1) cleanliness of body, and cleanliness in the schoolhouse and on the schoolgrounds, (2) cleaning the teeth, (3) ventilating the schoolroom, (4) assuming correct postures, (5) correct breathing, (6) cleaning shoes before entering the schoolroom, (7) correct use of the voice, (8) right use of the eyes, (9) care of hair and nails, (10) use of individual drinking-cups, pencils, and other materials, (11) dusting school furniture, (12) cleaning blackboards.

There are also some bad habits which should be discouraged, such as (1) putting things into the mouth, (2) expectorating on the floor, (3) biting nails, (4) thumb-sucking, (5) "swapping" gum, food, etc., (6) coughing in another's face, (7) kissing on the lips, (8) carrying soiled handkerchiefs, (9) picking the nose, and (10) licking the fingers in turning the pages of a book.

In the upper grades, say beyond the fourth, it is to be hoped that less and less effort will be necessary on the part of the teacher as the pupils assume more and more the responsibility. Incidental instruction, however, will always be necessary.

Even if pupils practice certain habits while at school it does not necessarily follow that they will practice them at home, and then there are many habits such as sleeping with the window open that cannot be practiced at school. The teacher may advise children, ask them to report, or possibly confer with the parent to get the child to act. The deep-seated prejudice and ignorance found in many homes interfere greatly with the teacher's success in this direction. Often she can do little but give advice and hope that it will function. Parent-teacher associations which bring teachers and parents together to talk over common problems should be encouraged.

The teacher in co-operation with a school physician and nurse may accomplish a good deal to make the parents feel a sense of responsibility. As the school physician is not in direct contact with the children and carries certain authority because he is a physician, both the children, and the parents in many cases, are more likely to respond. If they do not, if there is a school nurse, she may be sent directly to the home to advise the parents and to see personally that the children have proper care. To make the work of the school physician and school nurse effective, however, the teacher's intelligent co-operation is necessary. She must be quick to see that there is something wrong and refer the case to the physician. The result in most cases is likely to further the interests of school work. Often it is backwardness in school which suggests that there is something wrong with the health of a child. When that is corrected the school work invariably improves. Whenever a child is backward without any apparent cause he should always be turned over to the physician.

The Massachusetts State Board of Education has issued a pamphlet which should be very helpful to teachers. The general symptoms which would justify sending a pupil to the school physician, according to this pamphlet, are as follows: (1) emaciation, (2) pallor, (3) puffiness of the face, (4) shortness of breath, (5) swellings in the neck, (6) general lassitude, and other evidences of sickness, (7) flushing of the face, (8) eruptions of any sort, (9) a cold in the head with running eyes, (10) irritating discharge from the nose, (11) evidences of sore throat, (12) coughs, (13) vomiting, and (14) frequent requests to go out.[1]

As an illustration of the practical way the teacher in co-operation with the medical inspector may further the health of pupils, I quote from the records of the Elizabeth Street School, Worcester, Massachusetts:

WINTER OF 1912–13

H., boy of thirteen years, anaemic, nervous, undersized with greatly enlarged glands, had grippe which left him with hard cough, and in a weakened condition. His school work was so poor the teacher reported the case to the medical inspector, thinking that it might be best to take the child out of school.

A tonic was recommended, milk and fresh eggs were obtained through the Anti-tuberculosis Society, and part-time attendance was permitted for the remainder of the year. At the request of the medical inspector, and after a conference with the mother, this boy was taken to the City Hospital. An examination showed tubercular infection in one lung, and other symptoms. By appealing to a charitable organization, an arrangement was made whereby he was sent to the country for the summer.

H. returned to school in better condition than he has ever been before, is doing good work in class, receiving the last term the best report he ever had.

[1] See *Suggestions to Teachers and School Physicians regarding Medical Inspection*, issued by Massachusetts Board of Education, Boston, 1907.

As a result of conferences with the mother, the boy is now able to sleep with his windows open and be out of doors a good deal. He is examined at intervals by the school physician, who reports that he is now in an excellent physical condition.

This is a kind of work in hygiene that counts.

Medical inspection if it is to further the health of the school children must do something besides "inspect." It must follow up cases to see that they are properly treated. The ordinary notice sent to the parent, unless it is followed up as in the case mentioned above, is generally useless. Dr. Storey has demonstrated the value of a "follow-up method" in the secondary and lower collegiate department of the College of the City of New York.[1] This plan of individual instruction in hygiene, Dr. Storey says, proved effective in 90 per cent of the cases. Although there are probably many more obstacles in connection with an elementary school, yet there is no reason why a similar method should not be employed with a great improvement over the present prevalent practice.

Another way of teaching hygiene incidentally, one which is seldom made use of, is to treat all simple emergencies that arise in the schoolroom. This should be done for the sake of the health of the children and to give them some valuable ideas on hygiene. Many children have no idea of antisepsis. If a cut or burn is treated in the school, such information may be given so that it may be remembered. There is no reason why children should not be taught how to bandage a finger or hand. When skill has been gained in doing this in a class exercise they will then be able with the teacher's supervision to put on a bandage in an actual case of emergency. A simple emergency outfit can be purchased for a slight expenditure. One of these outfits should be on hand in every school building, especially in a rural school building where the home and physician are often some distance away. An inexpensive emergency outfit which can be purchased at any good drug-store is indicated below:

EMERGENCY OUTFIT[2]

Bandages: 1-inch for fingers and toes, $0.30 a dozen; 1-inch for extremities, $0.40 a dozen.

[1] See *Pedagogical Seminary*, XIX, 522–25.

[2] For suggestions on emergencies I am greatly indebted to Hannah C. Simmons, M.D., Worcester, Massachusetts.

Absorbent cotton, $0.27 a pound.

Sterile gauze pads, for use as sponges or as wet dressings, 1 dozen in a package, $0.30.

Zinc oxide adhesive plaster, to draw edges of cuts together and hold dressings on, ½ inch × 10 yards, $0.40 a roll.

Flexible collodion, 1-ounce bottle with brush to apply, $0.18.

Creolin, Pearson's, 1 pound, $0.75. (One teaspoonful in one pint of water makes antiseptic solution.)

Tincture of iodine, 2 ounces with brush to apply, $0.10.

Aromatic spirits of ammonia, 4 ounces, about $0.25. (For faintness, 15 drops in a tablespoonful of water. Repeat in 5 minutes if necessary.)

Carron oil, 6 ounces, about $0.20. (Apply to burns.)

Witch-hazel, 6 ounces, about $0.20. (For sprains.)

Rubber hot-water bottle. A common-sized glass bottle is as good and far cheaper.

Safety pins, small and large.

Scissors.

May have in addition:

Essence of peppermint. (One-half teaspoonful in one-half cup hot water, for colic, or a pinch of red pepper in hot water.)

Soda bicarbonate tablets, gr. V. (For sour stomach and vomiting.)

Spirits camphor. (To rub on swellings where skin is unbroken.)

Peroxide. (One teaspoonful in one-half glass of water as a gargle.)

Blue bichloride of mercury tablets. (One in one pint of water makes an antiseptic wash.)

This complete outfit can be purchased at any good drug-store for about $4.00. If conditions make this expense impossible, every teacher may have a simple outfit to treat cuts, burns, and bruises for a small sum. It should be put into a substantial wooden box and kept under lock and key.

Two books of invaluable assistance to every teacher in dealing with emergencies are: *Emergencies* (Gulick "Hygiene Series"), Ginn & Co. Barton, *First Aid Text-Book* (published by First Aid Association of America, Boston).

Incidental instruction which may not be directly related to immediate action should also be touched upon in other lessons. Health is so related to all the experiences of life that it may be considered in this fashion without a thought of "dragging it in." Let us note a few examples. In history, children should be taught to perceive the progress that has been made in overcoming disease, new discoveries in medicine and hygiene, and the effect of these on society; in civics, activities pertaining to public health, such as the cleaning of the streets, the disposal of garbage, and the prevention of the spread of disease, should be emphasized; in geography, the failure or success of man to conquer his environment through the neglect or practice of modern sanitation is important; in nature-study, many opportunities are offered to teach the structure and function of the human body by comparing man with the plant and animal world. Knowledge thus gained helps to make the child feel the importance of health.

b) *Systematic instruction.*—It is only fair to ask why, if habit is the real goal of instruction in hygiene, systematic instruction needs to be given. Personally I believe there is no place for it below the fourth or fifth grades, and not even in the higher ones unless it centers about the interests of the children. In the upper grades its purpose should be that of supporting the hygienic habits which the children are learning or have learned. It should also give them some sort of an appreciation of health as one of the assets of our civilization. This general purpose of appreciation must be characteristic of much that is taught in our public schools. For example, a large proportion of the children who study about the mining of coal or the manufacture of steel will never make their living in those industries, and coal would burn just as well without any knowledge of how it came into being. A knowledge of both coal and iron does help to broaden the social consciousness of the child. It enables him to see these industries in relation to the needs and achievements of the people. For a similar reason systematic instruction in hygiene should be given, only in this case hygiene is much more important as a social problem, and is something which the citizen can influence to a large extent by his voice and vote and action.

Fortunately at this time there is a number of good textbooks in hygiene available for children in the grades. Among such books the Gulick "Hygiene Series" (Ginn & Co.) seems to the writer to be most interesting to children. In this brief paper it is impossible to discuss the ways in which such books can best be used. Every teacher should have on hand some few books for ready reference. The busy teacher who wishes to get a general background of physiology and anatomy with its application to hygiene will find Coleman's *Hygienic Physiology* (Macmillan) excellent. A larger and heavier work along the same lines is Hough and Sedgwick's *The*

Human Mechanism (Ginn & Co.). Every teacher should have on her desk a good book on school hygiene. Dresslar's *School Hygiene* (Macmillan) is probably the best.

Besides such material which may be permanently available, the current newspapers and magazines contain abundant material which the teacher may inject into the lessons. Some of the magazines have excellent pictures in their regular reading-columns or in the advertising section which may be used effectively. In the upper grades the teacher may find it advantageous to have a bulletin board on which the children may put printed matter of interest.

IV. AN EFFECTIVE IDEAL OF HEALTH

The psychology of ideals is still a dark chapter in our modern psychology. Many teachers and parents are misled in the belief that mere word knowledge, even when coupled with considerable understanding, functions through ideals. A child may have a good deal of knowledge about the structure, function, and care of his teeth and still never use a toothbrush. Knowledge is useful in inculcating the right habits but it is insufficient. The idea of the care of the teeth must have back of it a desire to have clean teeth, otherwise the child's knowledge becomes mere formal intellectual propositions. Our effective ideals probably come through action, and through habits of action. It is questionable whether anybody ever gained the ideal of work after knowing the value of work. The effective ideal of work really comes through habits of industry. Likewise cleanliness is acquired through habits of being clean. The first step toward getting children to develop the ideals of health is to get them to form the right habits. Attractive knowledge of the right kind will of course tend to make the practice of the habit easier. The inspiration and example of the teacher, too, are always powerful incentives to habit formation. Out of these hygienic habits, ably supported by a knowledge of the value of hygienic living, there should grow an effective ideal of health for the pupil who is to be thrown on his own responsibility in facing the problems of life.

BOOK REVIEWS

Medical and Sanitary Inspection of Schools. By S. W. NEWMAYER, A.B., M.D. Division of Child Hygiene, Bureau of Health, Philadelphia. Philadelphia and New York: Lea & Febinger, 1913. Pp. vi+318.

Eighteen years of school medical inspection in America and almost forty years in foreign countries have made it unnecessary at the present date to raise the question as to why such public care should be exercised. The focus of attention seems to be a critical sifting and sorting of proposed methods, a determined effort to extend the scope of the work and to assist in disseminating the best available information.

Dr. Newmayer's book takes its place with several others of rather recent date in attempting "to give definite, rationalized plans to prevent epidemics of contagions in the schools, and to recognize and correct physical defects of school children." It is designed as a guide for physicians, nurses, and teachers, to meet not only the one-sided aim of better care of the physical aspects of child-life, but in addition "to develop a deeper appreciation of the relations of physical and mental development."

The table of contents indicates that besides the brief introductory chapter, the whole subject-matter of the book is presented under four main headings, viz., "Administration," "The School Buildings and Grounds," "Infections, Contagions, and Communicable Diseases," "Physical Defects." Much of the matter is fresh in point of view, clearly orthodox in information, and stated in straightforward, easily interpreted language. The chapter on infections and communicable diseases is especially well done for such a condensed presentation. Many valuable specimens of report-blanks are submitted, and the whole subject-matter is illustrated, though not too profusely, with seventy-one photo-prints and fourteen full-page plates. The construction and print of the book are excellent.

It must be remembered that the whole forecast of the book is outlined from the point of view of a director of school hygiene, and to get the real value and setting of the author's undertaking one must place it in its proper relation to the whole movement—the rise, development, and best future of medical inspection.

Medical inspection first originated under the motive of fear. Parents desired their children protected from actual or possible danger of communicable diseases. This motive soon gave place to the more enlightened and humanitarian one of parents and guardians demanding or approving the public policy of taking measures to remove physical defects that might prove serious handicaps to children's profiting to the fullest by such educational opportunities as they come in contact with. And finally, the still larger ideal emerges of uniting all examinations with prevention through its handmaiden, education, by proper methods in the community at large and through instruction in the schools. Departments of school hygiene that in some way effectively combine the work of community protection and correction of physical defects with instruction will more surely meet future programs than handbooks for the work of merely examining children.

Although, then, this limited field of endeavor, as represented by Dr. Newmayer, is in itself praiseworthy, nevertheless it is somewhat disappointing to find this promising text following in the wake of its numerous predecessors of late, in failing to indicate the larger possibilities of such an undertaking by outlining a progressive program of practical work and instruction, and thereby bringing inspection and supervision of the physical condition of children more into line with the real *raison d'être* of education in school life.

D. P. MACMILLAN

BOARD OF EDUCATION
CHICAGO

CURRENT EDUCATIONAL LITERATURE IN THE PERIODICALS[1]

IRENE WARREN
Librarian, School of Education, University of Chicago

Adler, Martha. Mental tests used as a basis for the classification of school children. J. of Educa. Psychol. 5:22–28. (Ja. '14.)

Allen, William H. Two New York health universities. R. of Rs. 49:317–20. (Mr. '14.)

Atherton, Lewis. Literary selections most frequently memorized in the elementary schools. El. School T. 14:208–20. (Ja. '14.)

Ballard, P. B. Prose preference of school children. J. of Educa. Psychol. 5:10–21. (Ja. '14.)

Barnes, Earl. Comparison of Froebelian and Montessori methods and principles. Train. School M. (N.J.) 10:145–48. (Fe. '14.)

Benson, A. C. The influence of the older universities on the curricula of secondary schools. School W. 16:45–48. (Fe. '14.)

Brown, Elmer Ellsworth. Educational interests at Washington. Science 39:239–46. (13 Fe. '14.)

Bunker, Frank F. The better articulation of the parts of the public school system. Educa. R. 47:249–68. (Mr. '14.)

Bush, Arthur Dermont. Binet-Simon tests of a thirty-nine months old child. Psychol. Clinic 7:250–57. (Fe. '14.)

Butler, Nicholas Murray. Academic freedom. Educa. R. 47:291–94. (Mr. '14.)

Campbell, Everett Eveleth. A study of retardation and class standing on the basis of home language used by pupils. El. School T. 14:264–82. (Fe. '14.)

Davison, John. A teacher-training experiment evolved by the school authorities of Lima, Ohio. El. School T. 14:237–39. (Ja. 14.)

Dewey, John. Rousseau, Pestalozzi, Froebel, and Montessori. Kind. M. 26:186. (Mr. '14.)

Dunn, Arthur Wallace. Military camps for college students. R. of Rs. 49:321–26. (Mr. '14.)

Eliot, Charles W. Present problems of education. Educa. R. 47:237–48. (Mr. '14.)

[1] *Abbreviations.*—Atlan., Atlantic Monthly; Educa. Bi-mo., Educational Bimonthly; Educa. R., Educational Review; El. School T., Elementary School Teacher; English J., English Journal; J. of Educa. Psychol., Journal of Educational Psychology; Kind. M., Kindergarten Magazine; Outl., Outlook; Pop. Sci. Mo., Popular Science Monthly; Psychol. Clinic, Psychological Clinic; Relig. Educa., Religious Education; R. of Rs., Review of Reviews; School W., School World; Sci. Am. Sup., Scientific American Supplement; Train. School M. (N.J.), Training School Magazine (New Jersey).

Harkness, Mary Leal. The education of the girl. Atlan. 113:324–30. (Mr. '14.)

Heck, William H. A third study of mental fatigue in relation to the daily school program. Psychol. Clinic 7:258–60. (Fe. '14.)

Henmon, V. A. C. Retardation, acceleration, and class standing. El. School T. 14:283–94. (Fe. '14.)

Hinkle, E. E. Experiments for efficiency in arithmetic, the Courtis tests. Educa. Bi-mo. 8:189–201. (Fe. '14.)

Keltie, J. Scott. Thirty years' progress in geographical education. School W. 16:53–55. (Fe. '14.)

Keyes, Rowena Keith. How we use our school library. English J. 3:86–93. (Fe. '14.)

Lyon, Darwin Oliver. The relation of length of material to the time taken for learning and the optimum distribution of time. J. of Educa. Psychol. 5:1–9. (Ja. '14.)

Mathews, John L. Dynamic education. Harper 128:616–25. (Mr. '14.)
Vocational and industrial training in Germany.

Otis, Alvah T. The appreciation and management of high-school debate. English J. 3:94–98. (Fe. '14.)

Peck, R. C. A home geography lesson for a city school. El. School T. 14:240–41. (Ja. '14.)

Roberts, William M. The development of part-time education for apprentices in Chicago. Educa. Bi-mo. 8:215–26. (Fe. '14.)

Sadler, M. E. Thoughts on present discontents in English education. School W. 16:42–44. (Fe. '14.)

(A) school in a prison. Outl. 106:288–89. (7 Fe. '14.)

Simpson, R. M. Addresses by citizens to school boys. El. School T. 14:221–36. (Ja. '14.)

Stevenson, O. J. The old and the new in literature teaching. English J. 3:69–77. (Fe. '14.)

Terman, Lewis M. The effects of school life upon the nutritive processes, health and the composition of the blood. Pop. Sci. Mo. 84:257–64. (Mr. '14.)

Todd, John B. Fresh air in schoolrooms. Sci. Am. Sup. 77:118–19. (21 Fe. '14.)

Tooke, Frances E. Relations among the staff in secondary schools. School W. 16:58–60. (Fe. '14.)

West, Andrew F. Greek at Princeton. Educa. R. 47:279–90. (Mr. '14.)

Williams, A. M. Philosophy and education. Educa. R. 47:269–78. (Mr. '14.)

Wilson, Woodrow. The object of the college. Relig. Educa. 9:1–3. (Fe. '14.)

Witmer, Lightner. The scope of education as a university department. Psychol. Clinic 7:237–49. (Fe. '14.)

Wolfe, A. B. Tests of college efficiency. Educa. R. 47:217–36. (Mr. '14.)

Woodward, Robert S. The Carnegie institution of Washington. Science 39:225–39. (13 Fe. '14.)

VOLUME XIV NUMBER 9

The Elementary School Teacher

May 1914

EDUCATIONAL NEWS AND EDITORIAL COMMENT

Detroit's Bureau of School Efficiency

The board of education of the city of Detroit has established a new office as part of the city equipment for the supervision of schools. This office is to be filled by Mr. Courtis, who is known for his work in arithmetic and reading tests. Mr. Courtis has been doing his work in the Home and Day School of Detroit, a private school for girls. He has, however, carried out his arithmetic tests in Detroit and has made numerous suggestions for the improvement of the courses as administered in the Detroit schools. He now becomes a part of the superintendent's office and will aid in the educational supervision of the system, making regular examinations of the efficiency of the children and teachers in the schools.

This move on the part of the Detroit board of education is similar to the move which has already been made in the city of New Orleans, where a great deal of energy is being devoted to the study of school problems by scientific methods. There is a bureau for the study of efficiency in the Boston schools also. Evidently the movement to supplement the usual administrative machinery by scientific studies is well under way. If the school surveys which have been organized in recent years have performed no other service than to lead to the establishment of these permanent bureaus of efficiency at different centers, the movement has been effective and successful.

National Education Association

The officers of the National Education Association announce in a preliminary way the outlines of the programs for the various departments of the summer meeting. This meeting will be held in St. Paul, Minnesota, July 4–11. There will be six general sessions. The first will be given over to the addresses of greeting and response, the president's address, and one other. The second session will be devoted to a discussion of the status of women. "The Educational Advancement of Women" will be discussed by four women of distinction from different parts of the United States. The third session will be given up to the discussion of the final report of the Committee on Teachers' Salaries and Cost of Living. The fourth session will have as its topic "The Principles and Aims of Education," which will be discussed by four men, one speaking from the standpoint of elementary education, one from the standpoint of the college, one from the standpoint of the university, and one from a general standpoint. The subject of the fifth session will be "Education in a Democracy." The sixth session will be given over to a series of ten-minute speeches on "The Needs of the Public School." These speeches will be chiefly from the ex-presidents of the Association.

The detailed programs of several of the sessions which will be of the largest interest to elementary teachers and supervisors are as follows:

The Kindergarten Department will have as its topics for the first session, "The Readjustment of the Kindergarten and Primary Grades to Conform to the Same General Principles"; "A Kindergarten Program Based on Problems Rather Than on Prescribed Subject-Matter." In the second session, the general topic will be "The New Developments in Kindergarten Practice." The third session will be held jointly with the Departments of Special Education and Elementary Education.

The Department of Elementary Education will have for its general topic, "The Individual Child and His Individual Needs." The first session will be devoted to a discussion of "The School Life of the Child" and the second session to "The Home Life of the Child." The third session will be a joint meeting with the Kindergarten Department and the Department of Special Education, at which will be discussed, "The Possibilities of the Kindergarten to

Reveal the Classification and the Limitations of the Child for Doing Standardized Elementary-School Work." It is the purpose of this program to make the individual child the central thought of the department. Practical school people with a real live message will present the school viewpoint, while the home side will be given by those who are not directly connected with the schools, but who have the burdens of child-welfare on their hearts, and who have had much experience in social and child-welfare problems.

The Department of Physical Education will discuss, "Motor Efficiency" and "The Relation of Normal Schools to the Teaching of Hygiene and Physical Training in the Secondary Schools." The second session will be occupied with a symposium on the subject "Shall Sex Hygiene Be Taught in the Public Schools?"

The Department of Special Education will hold two separate meetings, and one joint meeting with the Department of Elementary Education and the Department of Kindergarten Education. The general topics to be discussed are: "The Handicapped but Potentially Normal Child"; "The Dependent and Delinquent Child"; "School Clinics and Medical Inspection"; "Special and Ungraded Classes in Schools for Different Types of Children"; "Methods of Testing and Classification."

The Department of Classroom Teachers, which will hold its first meeting at St. Paul, will provide an opportunity for such teachers to have a place within the Association for the discussion of educational and professional problems pertaining to them. The term "classroom teachers" includes the teachers of the entire twelve grades. The subject of the first session will be the report of the Committee on Teachers' Salaries and Cost of Living, and the second session will be given up to the question of industrial training. These discussions will be from the classroom standpoint.

Ohio School Legislation

Important school legislation was passed by a special session of the General Assembly of the state of Ohio. This legislation followed upon the survey which was made by Dr. Brittain and those who were associated with him. The survey made in Ohio has the advantage over some of the earlier state surveys which have been made in that it covered a very large number of representative schools. When the legislature assembled it was accordingly adequately informed on the conditions existing throughout the state. Among the important items of legislation are the following:

The state funds are to be distributed on the basis of the number of teachers and the average daily attendance of pupils. There is a minimum salary for teachers. No person shall be employed to teach in any public school in Ohio for less than $40 a month. If necessary, the state treasurer must contribute to the funds of a school district in order to meet this requirement. The school district is called upon to levy the maximum tax, if necessary, but is required either independently or with the help of the state to maintain school for eight months in the year. Agriculture is to be taught in all of the common schools of all villages and rural districts. There is to be a general standardization of village and rural schools so that pupils coming from these schools shall be admitted to the high schools without examination. The schools themselves are to be examined, however, with respect to their equipment, course of study, and supervision.

Ohio has been, in many respects, a backward state in its school organization. It has been governed in school matters by the local authorities. This is changed by the new legislation. The certification of teachers is given to a state board, and supervision is provided which virtually puts the schools on a county basis.

A wholesale program of reform promises some difficulties as the new machinery is first set in operation. On the other hand, a carefully digested and coherent scheme such as arises out of a general survey is the most promising solution of a complex situation. If reform is to be made, this is undoubtedly the way to make it both intelligent and comprehensive.

Lessons in Thrift

The following article from the *St. Paul* (Minnesota) *News* tells in brief and concrete way of the degree to which a practical endeavor of the St. Paul schools has been attended with success:

St. Paul school children are learning the lesson of thrift. Figures have just been compiled showing the growth of the saving habit among the pupils chiefly of the St. Paul grade schools. The amount received up to March 1, 1914, was $13,993.66. This only covers the period from November 6, 1913, when the system was first inaugurated. There are now 49 schools participating in the savings plan, representing 56,754 deposits. Since the plan was inaugurated, the withdrawals have amounted to only $3,887.10. Certain days of the month are designated as "bank days," when pupils bring their earnings. There is intense rivalry between the various rooms to make their balances the largest.

Along with this, it is interesting to note that the newspaper printing this report advocates a "Thrift Day" for public schools.

They have "Emerson Days," "Stevenson Days," and all kinds of days which are observed by reading selections from the various authors whose work they commemorate; why not have a "Thrift Day" once in a while? The majority of students being turned out of the public schools are totally lacking in knowledge of finance, even that rudimentary part of it dealing with the importance of regular saving. It would shorten the road to success for most of them if "thrift" were taken from its obscurity and made a vital part of our educational system, as has already been done in some European countries.

E. M. H.

Reorganization of the Upper Grades

An article entitled "Latin in the Seventh and Eighth Grades in California," by H. C. Nutting, of the University of California, appears in the *Classical Weekly* of March 21. This article "attempts to form some estimate of the measure of success attending the new departure," the writer's conclusions being based upon the reports from a number of teachers directly connected with the work. The paper first reports a new grouping of classes whereby the seventh and eighth grades are cut off from the grammar school and are united with the ninth grade to form what are variously known as intermediate, introductory, or lower high schools. This movement was begun some four years ago in Palo Alto, Berkeley, and a few other cities of the state.

"While at the outset there were considerable difficulties to be faced, ... the verdict at the present time is overwhelmingly in favor of the policy of beginning the study of Latin in the seventh grade, for those who are to study the subject."

The typical results of the experiment are shown by a test given to those students who began the study of Latin in the seventh grade and those who began the study in the ninth grade. This test consisted in having high-eighth-grade pupils who had had twenty months of work in Latin and ninth-grade pupils who had had ten months' work translate Latin into English and English into Latin. "All eighth-graders passed the Latin-to-English test and all but one the English-to-Latin test. Of the ninth-graders, six failed in the first, while one-half of the class failed in the second test." In comparing the papers it was found that, from all viewpoints, the work of those who began the work in the seventh grade was far superior. After a discussion of some of the apparent reasons for this, the author says: "Viewing, in the large, the California experiment of introducing the study of Latin into the seventh grade, there is little room for doubt that the new departure is proving a conspicuous success."

E. M. H.

Lengthening the School Year

The following circular, issued by the Bureau of Education, contains so much general information and makes so vigorous a plea for the establishment of summer sessions in the public schools that it is reproduced in full:

In the cities, towns, manufacturing villages, and unincorporated suburban communities of the United States there are approximately 13,000,000 children between the ages of six and twenty. Of these, more than 9,500,000 are enrolled in the public and private schools. The average daily attendance is about 6,500,000. These children are taught by more than 300,000 teachers, at an annual cost for all purposes of about $300,000,000. The city schools are in session about 180 days in the year. The average daily session is 5 hours. Children who attend school regularly and without tardiness have 900 hours of schooling in the year. The average attendance of those enrolled is 120 days, or 600 hours. There are in the year 8,760 hours, 5,110 waking hours for children who sleep 10 hours a day. Children who attend school the full time are in the school a little less than one-third of the waking hours of 180 days and not in school at all 185 days. The average attendance is only about one-third of the waking hours of 120 days, with no attendance on 245 days. Children who attend all of the school hours of the year are in school 900 hours, and out of school 4,200 waking hours; the average is 600 hours in school and 4,510 waking hours out of the school.

Probably 5 per cent of the school children of the cities and towns and suburban communities go away during the summer to the country and summer resorts; 10 per cent or less have some useful occupation through the vacation months; and 85 per cent or more are at home without useful occupation. They spend the time in idleness on the streets and alleys without guidance, on vacant lots, or swelter in crowded houses and on superheated streets. Much that was learned in school at previous sessions is forgotten; many of the children become criminals, and still more form habits of idleness.

The schools, which are established and maintained for the purpose of educating children into manhood and womanhood, of preparing them for society and citizenship, and of giving them such knowledge and training as will enable them to make an honest living, should provide some kind of instruction for the great mass of these children through what is now, in most cities, a long, wasteful vacation. I believe no one will claim that the addition of 400 or 500 hours to the number now spent in school would be a burden to any child. The addition of 3 school months of 5 hours a day would mean only 300 hours to the school year to children attending regularly and promptly, and only 200 hours to the average child on the basis of present attendance. This would give 1,200 hours for children attending the full time and 800 hours for the average child; of course much less than this for many.

Possibly the school day in the summer session should be not more than 4 hours; that is, from 7 or 8 o'clock to 11 or 12 o'clock in the forenoon. School work can be much better done during these hours in the summer than in the present school hours of the winter months. Attendance is easier and buildings do not need to be heated. Where such a program is organized it may be found necessary to change the school work so as to give more laboratory and shopwork during the summer sessions than in the winter and less of the ordinary bookwork. Children attending the summer session under these conditions would, no doubt, be much happier and healthier than they are turned loose, with nothing to do, on the streets and alleys. It is a mistake to suppose that children do not like to work. All children do like to work at whatever is of real benefit to them until they learn to be idle.

A number of careful studies made in different parts of the country and in schools of different kinds indicate that children really do not study in school more than an average of 3 hours a day, whatever may be the length of the daily session. For children in the primary grades the time is less; for the high-school grades, somewhat more. That includes not only the time which children give to their studies out of class, but the time in which they really attend to their work in class. This indicates the desirability of reorganizing school work in such way as to give 3 hours a day for intensive school work of the ordinary type, and to provide 4 or 5 hours of productive work suited to the capacity of the child, either at home, in shops under good conditions, in outdoor gardens, or in shops provided by the school. With this kind of an organization it would be very easy for children to work at ordinary school work 3 hours a day 6 days in the week, through 11 calendar months in the year, and at the same time contribute largely to their own support by well-directed, productive educational work, either at home or in the school, thus making it possible for the great majority of children to remain in school throughout the high-school period.

The cost of adding the 3 months of school would be comparatively little. There would be no cost for fuel, the cost of attendance would be less, and the additional cost for teachers would not be in proportion to the number of days added. Whatever may be the terms of the contract, teachers are in fact employed by the year. Comparatively few of them use the vacation months in any profitable way. An addition of an average of $300 to the annual salary of the teachers would require a total of less than $10,000,000, or about 3 per cent of the total annual cost of the schools.

For most teachers the additional months would not be a hardship, especially if the school days were shortened. Certainly this is true if teachers could be relieved of a large amount of unnecessary bookkeeping, report-making, and the reading of unnecessary examination papers, with which they are now burdened. It would cost very little more to employ teachers by the year, each teacher teaching three quarters, as is now done in many universities and colleges.

Ex-Commissioner Brown on the Bureau of Education

In the issue of *Science* for February 13, former Commissioner of Education E. E. Brown, now chancellor of New York University, gives a very interesting and illuminating account of his experiences when he was head of the Bureau of Education in Washington. He opens the article by telling how he was met on every side by the greatest hospitality when he first arrived in Washington. His hopes of accomplishing large things in the Bureau grew with these manifestations of hospitality. It was not until he came in contact with the Committee on Appropriations that he learned the real difficulties. He discovered in his contact with this committee the "intrenched tradition," as he calls it, "that the federal Congress should not go deeply into expenditures for public education." The opposition which he encountered in Congress made it almost impossible for him to accomplish even the ordinary work of the Bureau. By way of interesting comparison he gives an account of the growth in appropriations for the Department of Agriculture as compared with the very meager increases of appropriations for the Bureau of Education. The latter part of this interesting paper takes up the general problem of the establishment of a national university.

The paper should be read by all school people. It is perfectly clear from what Mr. Brown has said that the Bureau of Education ought to be enlarged and its operations ought to be freed from the entanglements which at present hamper its work. The school people of the United States hardly realize that they have in the Bureau of Education a unique organization which is not paralleled anywhere in the world. Foreign nations are beginning to realize the significance of the large body of information collected by our bureau. A similar institution is just being established in Berlin and a faint imitation of the sort of thing that is done by our Bureau of Education is being undertaken by the English board. Our Bureau of Education, even with the handicaps under which it now suffers, is accomplishing much for the American educational system. But school people should not be satisfied with the relatively meager service that is rendered by the Bureau, handicapped as it is by lack of appropriations and bound up in an organization which renders it helpless. There ought to be a genuine movement in this country to enlarge the facilities which are provided by our central government for the great business of conducting schools and exhibiting their efficiency.

New York Studies of Truancy

The Teachers' Council of New York City has made a careful investigation of the causes of delinquency and truancy in the schools and has rendered a report in which its findings are classified under five different heads. Children are delinquent and truant from school first of all because of defects in home control. There is a lack of knowledge or interest on the part of parents which reflects itself in the fact that children either are allowed to remain away from school or succeed in staying away without the knowledge on the part of their parents of the school's requirements.

The second group of causes of truancy arises from the acts of teachers or principals. The teacher's contributions to truancy are perhaps worth enumerating in full: (1) undue punishment for lateness; (2) fanciful requirements of certain teachers as to pupils' clothing, as white shirts, waists, etc.; (3) ill-arranged and fatiguing daily programs; (4) too close adherence to the letter of the law in scholastic requirements; (5) excessive or impossible (for the dull pupil) requirements as to home study or bringing in written work, etc. Principals are reported to show at times lack of interest in the problem of truancy. They fail to follow up absence and they sometimes inflict unjust punishment for absence or for other causes and thus drive the timid or obstinate pupil away from school.

A third group of causes arises from the treatment given by the courts to cases brought before them. In general, it is pointed out that the courts do not treat the truancy laws seriously and are very lenient in administering them. They mishandle cases of children and do not give support to the regular officers whose business it is to promote regularity of school attendance.

A fourth group of causes is described as the street causes. In the first place, there are a great many distracting agencies on the street which furnish incidental employment to school children or offer them opportunities for gaining amusement. The junkmen and second-hand dealers induce boys to steal material or collect various sorts of waste material which has a small money value. Moving-picture shows and small candy and tobacco stores welcome truant children. Policemen are said to be indifferent to the presence on their beats during school hours of children from neighboring schools; and, finally, the agencies that should follow up children between fourteen and sixteen are said to be deficient in seeing that the labor certificates are returned to the superintendent if the child is not properly employed.

Finally, under a fifth heading are brought together numerous administrative causes for truancy. A superintendent whose office is fully occupied with the routine of educational supervision cannot furnish the energy necessary to enforce the attendance laws. If assistant superintendents and others in the different districts are called upon to do this work, the central administration finds itself embarrassed by a lack of proper education supervision and is very likely to forego the rigid enforcement of a compulsory act in favor of these more essential types of supervision.

The remedy for these difficulties seems to be more adequate machinery for the execution of the law. In this connection a circular recently sent out by the Bureau of Education of the United States is of interest because of the general summary which it presents of the requirements in different states of the Union and the specific recommendations which it makes for improving conditions.

SOME BOOKS ON CHILDREN'S READING AND STORY-TELLING

FOR TEACHERS, PARENTS, AND LIBRARIANS

IRENE WARREN
Librarian, School of Education, University of Chicago

The state superintendent of instruction and the state library commission in many states issue lists of the best books for children. The public libraries in many towns, large and small, publish such lists. These are usually distributed free of charge or for a few cents. Teachers will find it helpful to collect and keep such lists on file.

LISTS

KENNEDY, H. T., comp. Suggestive list of children's books for a small library, recommended by the League of Library Commissions. Democrat Printing Co. Madison, Wis. 25 cents.

An excellent classified list of children's books. Contains over a dozen special supplementary lists such as, Books for youngest readers, Books for mothers and teachers, Children's stories for telling and reading aloud, Sea stories, Indian stories, Camping and outdoor life, Stories for holidays.

Carnegie Library of Pittsburgh—Catalogue of books, annotated and arranged, and provided by the Carnegie Library of Pittsburgh, for the use of the first eight grades in the Pittsburgh schools. $1.00.

A well-selected annotated list of the best books for children.

POTTER, M. E., comp. Children's catalogue: a guide to the best reading for young people based on twenty-four selected library lists. H. W. Wilson Co., 1909. $6.00.

Part I contains an author, title, and subject catalogue of 3,000 books. Part II is an author and subject index to *St. Nicholas*, vols. 28–36.

CHILDREN'S LITERATURE AND STORY-TELLING

BAILEY, C. S. For the story-teller: story-telling and stories to tell. Bradley. $1.50.

The book is planned for teachers and parents. The first half is devoted to a discussion of children's literature and the second half to stories for telling.

BAILEY, C. S., AND LEWIS, C. M. For the children's hour. Bradley. $1.50.

A great variety of stories designed for the use of kindergartners, teachers, and mothers.

Boston collection of kindergarten stories. Ed. 5. Hammett. 60 cents.

Good standard work. Much used by kindergarten and primary teachers.

BRYANT, S. C. How to tell stories to children. Houghton. $1.00.

Contents: The purpose of story-telling in school. The selection of stories to tell. Adaptation of stories for telling. How to tell the story. Some specific schoolroom uses. Stories selected and adapted for telling. Sources for the story-teller. The second half of the book contains stories for the kindergarten and first five grades.

———. Stories to tell to children. Houghton. $1.00.

A collection of some fifty stories for young children.

———. Best stories to tell to children. Houghton. $1.50.

"The stories in this book, some very old and unchanged, some new and some changed from an older form, grew into their present shape by the process of being told to children many, many times. All . . . . with others, are included in one or the other of the two earlier books, How to Tell Stories to Children and Stories to Tell to Children. . . . . Some of the stories are here printed separately from these books on method, for the more ready access of children themselves and those whose interest is of a wholly untechnical sort."

COLBY, J. R. Literature and life in school. Houghton. $1.25.

Contents: A plea for literature in school. Literature and the first four years of school life. Literature and the second four years of school life. Methods of handling literature in school. Literature and life after the elementary school. Graded lists of books, poems and prose, suitable for reading in elementary school make up the rest of the book.

COLES, MRS. J. D., comp. Stories to tell. Flanagan. 35 cents.

Stories for the young children.

COX, J. H. Literature in the common schools. Little, Brown & Co. 90 cents.

A guide for teachers that presents in a clear, simple way the main problems connected with children's reading. Contains also helpful lists.

FIELD, W. T. Fingerposts to children's reading. McClurg. $1.00.

"Essays on various phases of children's reading . . . . addressed to parents and teachers, librarians, Sunday-school workers—all who are concerned with the education of the child." Appendix contains lists of books suitable for children's libraries, school libraries, and Sunday-school libraries.

HOXIE, J. L. Kindergarten story book. Bradley. 50 cents.

A collection of short, simple stories designed for the teachers, mothers, or children themselves.

KEYES, A. M. Stories and story-telling. Appleton. $1.25.

One-fourth of the book is given to a discussion of children's literature; the rest contains about seventy-five short stories that the author has repeatedly used with young children.

LINDSAY, MAUD. Mother stories. Bradley. $1.00.

Good collection of ethical stories to tell to young children.

LYMAN, EDNA. Story-telling: what to tell and how to tell it. McClurg. 75 cents.

An excellent small volume. The author was a librarian before taking up story-telling for children. She has had wide experience in telling stories to large and small groups of children in all parts of the country.

Contents: Responsibility of society for what children read. Reading aloud. Story-telling. Arranging the program of miscellaneous stories. Biographical stories. National epic tales. How to use these epic tales. List of books suggested for the story-teller.

MACCLINTOCK, P. L. Literature in the elementary school. University of Chicago Press. $1.00.

"This book had its origin in several years of experience and experiment in teaching classes in literature in the Laboratory School of the University of Chicago, when that fruitful venture in education was being conducted by Professor John Dewey; in many years of private reading with children; and in many years of lecturing to teachers of children." An excellent book for class study of children's literature.

MACY, JOHN. A child's guide to reading. Baker & Taylor. $1.25.

"This is a Child's Guide to Literature and not a Guide to Juvenile Books. The larger part of the books discussed in the various chapters and included in the supplementary lists were written for adult readers, and nearly all of them are at least as interesting to the reader of forty as to the reader of fourteen."

Contents: Of guides and rules for reading. The purpose of reading. The reading of fiction, poetry, history, biography, essays, foreign classics. The press of today. The study of literature. Science and philosophy. A list of books is appended to each chapter.

MOSES, M. J. Children's books and reading. Mitchell Kennerley. $1.50.

Contains much interesting and valuable material on the development of children's literature. One-third of the book is given over to lists of books for children.

O'GRADY, ALICE, AND THROOP, FRANCES. The teachers' story-teller's book. Rand McNally. $1.00.

"These stories, beginning with short narratives to follow the nursery rhyme and moving through more developed tales, both in structure and content, are intended to supply literature for children from four to eleven years of age; in other words, from the kindergarten to the fifth grade."

OLCOTT, F. J. Children's reading. Houghton. $1.00.

"The aim of this book is to meet in a simple and practical way the following questions often asked by parents: Of what value are books in the education of my children? What is the effect of bad reading? How may I interest my children in home-reading? What kind of books do children like? What books shall I give the growing boy and girl? Where and how may I procure books?

The author is one of the best authorities on children's literature. The material in this book is exceptionally well organized. Perhaps no other single volume contains so great a quantity of practical information on children's literature.

Olcott, F. J. Story-telling poems selected and arranged for story-telling and reading aloud and for children's own reading. Houghton. $1.25.

"There is an inexhaustible source of story-telling material to be found in narrative poetry. Fables, myths, legends, tales, romantic or historical in treatment, are told in rhythmic form, and often in a logical manner that makes it easy to retell the plot. . . . . In this volume are brought together fables, legends, tales of humor and feeling, of fairy-lore and magic, historical stories, parables, and sacred stories, all told in verse of varying merit. The rhymes and poems are selected for their story-telling qualities, for their lively interest to children, for their humorous, imaginative, and ethical values, and, as far as possible, for their literary form. The poems are grouped under subjects, and, as far as possible, are graded so that they may be used with ease in the classrooms of grades one to eight. A full subject index is added so that the story-teller may find, at a glance, lists of poems on different subjects."

Partridge, E. N., and Partridge, G. E. Story-telling in school and home: a study in educational aesthetics. Sturgis & Walton. $1.25.

"The purpose in writing this book is to be helpful to all amateur story-tellers, who, we believe, include an increasing number of parents, teachers, Sunday-school workers, instructors in playgrounds, librarians, social workers, and others who, in one way or another, teach." The first one hundred and fifty pages are devoted to the discussion of the art of story-telling and the rest of the book to "retold stories."

Poulsson, Emilie. In the child's world. Heath. $2.00.

Stories for young children.

Richards, Mrs. L. E. H. Pig brother and other fables and stories. Little, Brown & Co. 40 cents.

Thirty-five short stories adapted to telling young children.

Wiggin, Mrs. K. D. S., and Smith, N. A. Story hour; a book for the home and kindergarten. Houghton. $1.00.

Fourteen stories which need no adaptation or arrangement. Adapted to the younger children.

Wyche, R. T. Some great stories and how to tell them. Newson. $1.00.

Contents: Origin of story-telling. Interest in story-telling today. What stories shall we tell? Use of the story. Retelling of stories. The story in the Sunday school, library, playground, home and social circle, kindergarten, and in leagues and clubs. The story and the fundamental needs of the child. How to tell the story—Beowulf, Coming of Arthur, Story of Sir Gareth, Passing of King Arthur, A boy's visit to Santa Claus. The great teacher. Bibliography.

PEDAGOGY AND PSYCHOLOGY OF CHILDREN'S READING

Briggs, T. R., and Coffman, L. D. Reading in the public school. Rowe. $1.25.

"The authors have aimed to be simple and direct and soundly practical. . . . . Part One treats of the subject in a most general way. The first chapter consists largely of quotations from men who have thought deeply and have expressed themselves effectively; the second is historical of texts and methods. Part Two presents the theory and method for the first three years, carefully avoiding discussions of mooted questions. . . . . Part Three sets forth the theory and gives detailed suggestions for teaching reading in the upper five grades."

CHUBB, PERCIVAL. Teaching of English in the elementary and the secondary school. (Teachers' professional library.) Macmillan. $1.00.

"So sound in its philosophy and so practical in its helpfulness that we wish it might come into the hands of every instructor in the country who is engaged with this vastly important subject. It is based on the fundamental principle of unity and continuity in the English course from its beginning in the kindergarten up through the high school. We doubt if so good and useful a book upon the subject has before been written, and the author's treatment is charming in style and based upon the most intelligent principles of pedagogy."—*Dial.*

HALIBURTON, M. W., AND SMITH, A. G. Teaching poetry in the grades. (Riverside educational monographs.) Houghton. 60 cents.

A practical small volume which gives model lessons and a list of poems for grades one to eight.

HUEY, E. B. The psychology and pedagogy of reading: with a review of the history of reading and writing and of methods, texts, and hygiene in reading. Macmillan. $1.40.

The author has "endeavored to present the most meaningful facts, and those researches in which more or less definite results have been reached. Completeness of treatment and of reference is out of the question in a subject having such various and intricate ramifications."

MCMURRY, C. A. Special methods in reading in the grades including the oral treatment of stories and the reading of classics. Macmillan. $1.25.

The purpose of this book is "to discuss, in a practical and comprehensive way, the problem of introducing children to our best reading material and to the art of reading. The entire course of study for reading in the eight grades is included in this plan."

SHERMAN, E. B., AND REED, A. A. Essentials of teaching reading. University Publishing Co., Lincoln, Neb. $1.25.

Contents: The mechanics of reading. Interpretative reading. Methods. Selections for practice.

TAYLOR, J. S. Principles and methods of teaching reading. Macmillan. 90 cents.

Contents: The psychology of reading. The physiology of reading. Principles deduced from the psychology and physiology of reading. The ends of reading. Methods of teaching reading. A quantitative study of reading. A reading test. The hygiene of reading. Bibliography. Topics for discussion.

AN EIGHTH-GRADE NEWSPAPER

AN EXPERIMENT IN ENGLISH INVOLVING UNITY OF PURPOSE AS AGAINST INDIVIDUAL EFFORT

E. CATHERINE BURKHOLDER
State Normal School, Winona, Minnesota

Children entering the eighth grade are supposed to know the mechanics of composition work. They are also expected to be able to construct into readable shape their own thoughts and experiences, to the extent of from one hundred to two hundred words. The work of the eighth grade is to enlarge upon this. Spontaneity in thought-expression combined with proficiency in mechanical detail is the goal to be attained.

Spontaneity in expression depends upon experiences that are of vital importance to the child. Proficiency in mechanical detail depends upon practice that is frequent and varied.

Situations which lend themselves to freedom of expression must be both vital and recent. A teacher who is alert finds many such situations in the everyday life—home and school—of the children. But these are likely to be of individual interest. I find that very effective situations may be created—those which involve unity of purpose and interest in a common end. One such occasion centered around the writing of a book called "The Party." The book took the composition time for two weeks following the giving of a school party by the class. "Story-Telling" was another occasion of interest—the stories being both written and told by members of the class. The occasion that furnished the audience and the incentive was an assembly of all the elementary grades. The subject-matter—both vital and recent as a history study—was the Lewis and Clark Expedition. Another situation that was most interesting and profitable centered around the "getting-out" of a newspaper. I will describe this one in detail.

The entire composition class of thirty-nine eighth-grade pupils resolved itself into an office force and devoted its composition time for two weeks to newspaper work. The paper was to be finished by the end of two weeks and was to be read by members of the "force" before an assembly of all the grades. The time limit furnished an incentive for writing under stress and the prospective audience furnished the motive for creditable work. At the first few meetings of the force preliminary problems were considered. The most important of these were: (1) length of time for reading the paper; (2) size and form of paper; (3) audience; (4) nature of material to go into paper; (5) plan of manipulation of work. After discussion we decided to "get out" a paper that could be read to an audience in twenty-five minutes. Children from the first grade through the seventh with their teachers, supervisors, and principal made up the audience. This presented a problem as to subject-matter. We decided that articles must be written which would be of interest to little children and yet be worthy of eighth-grade effort. This led to consideration of the nature of the material: Should the paper contain town news or school news? Should it be of local or of general interest? After a frank discussion someone suggested that we consider the school as a locality or community and that the children, teachers, and all connected with the school be considered the citizens, and that the different phases of school work, as manual training, gymnasium, reading, geography, etc., constitute the enterprises of the community. This was satisfactory to all, for now we could get out a newspaper concerned entirely with school affairs. It was still left to consider under what heads our articles should appear. The children were all emphatic in holding entirely to the newspaper idea and this list of headings was decided upon:

Personal Mention	Weather Report
Editorial	Sporting News
City News	Cartoons
Story	Advertisements
Poem	Funny Column
Market Reports	

Before the force could get down to writing, there were still considerations to be disposed of. The paper was to be read the Friday preceding Thanksgiving, hence it was decided that it should be a Thanksgiving number and the President's Proclamation was added to our list. It was suggested that the story ought to be a Thanksgiving one. Cartoons appropriate and advertisements incident to Thanksgiving seemed easy.

We decided that in addition to our other topics we would write up some phase of the work connected with each room in the elementary school. We planned that these articles should make up an important part of the material of the paper, for, as one girl put it, "That will make it easy to interest the children, for even the first-grade children will like to hear what we have to say about them."

As to manipulation of the work: An editor-in-chief and two assistants were elected. The three boys at once felt the responsibility of making it a "go." Reporters were also elected—two for each room in the elementary school and two for each of the other headings in our list.

The editor-in-chief and his assistants thought it would be wise that everybody on the force should write an editorial and allow the editors to choose the best one. This plan was also suggested for the story. One meeting was taken up with a discussion on "editorials." At its close the children knew the essentials of a good one. They knew where it was to be found in the paper and they had decided that theirs should set forth the sentiments of their paper in regard to Thanksgiving. Some of the editorials were quite good, but the editors saw how it was possible to work up a fine one by putting together selected thoughts from all. This is the editorial as it went into the paper:

> This paper believes that "the best Thanksgiving is Thanksliving." We ought to make every day in the year a Thanksgiving day. Most people seem to think that a good time, a holiday, and a big dinner—with emphasis on the dinner—constitute a perfect Thanksgiving. But we would have them remember the old saying of Shakespeare, "Yet for aught I see they are sick that surfeit with too much as they that starve with nothing."

By far the most interesting feature of all the work was that in connection with the reports from the several rooms. The reporters asked the teachers for interviews and arranged for a visiting-time when they might observe the work going on. I saw in advance the different teachers and explained fully to them what we were doing. I asked them to grant the visiting-time to the reporters when there was work going on that they would like especially well to have reported. (Co-operation here meant a unifying influence so far as the school as a whole was concerned.)

At the appointed times the reporters went for their visits. They always came back scarcely able to wait until they could find time to write up what they had seen and heard. The two reporters from each room worked together and came to me with their articles or asked permission to read them to the class. All the articles that went into the paper were read to the entire class for suggestions, the class taking on the attitude of an audience to see whether or no the writing was clear and interesting. Criticism was free and often severe, but common interest in the paper made it easy to give and easy to take. The reporters were always eager to go to work at revising or rewriting. In several instances the articles were worked over the fourth and fifth time—the children never showing any signs of weariness. Here are two articles typical of room reports:

MISS STAPLES' ROOM (FIRST GRADE)

Last week on Thursday afternoon Miss Staples' room was visited by two reporters of this paper. It is a light, cheery room with large east windows. It is also made pleasant with its cream-colored walls, brown woodwork, plants, palms, and goldfish.

At half-past one the attention of the school was called by the words "Lips still." Then the children were requested to raise their hands so Miss Staples might see if they were clean. The B Reading Class got their chairs and placed them very carefully and quietly in a semicircle in the front of the room, while the C Class passed to the board to draw houses and trees that they could see out of the window. The children were very much interested in their reading and they dramatized it very well by putting a great deal of feeling into it. The general attitude of the room was very good.

The desks are placed in a sort of semicircle so that the children can watch each other while they recite. The tennis shoes are fastened on the rod under the desk. On the right side of each desk is a black pocket. The contents of this pocket are: a box of paints, a paint dish, a paint cloth, a box of crayons, a pair of scissors, a button hook, and a finger-nail cleaner. On the other side of the desk is another pocket containing a drinking-cup wrapped in a napkin to keep it clean.

As a part of the children's work, they make up dreams. They fold their arms and dream. Those who have dreams pass to the front of the room to tell them. This is good practice for them to learn to speak before an audience. One little boy dreamed this: "I dreamed it was the Fourth of July and I was a fire-cracker. Pretty soon I turned into a torpedo. I had a face and arms and legs. I was walking along the street and I tripped and fell on my side and exploded."

DOG STORIES BY MISS MARVIN'S PUPILS (FOURTH GRADE)

The pupils of Miss Marvin's room were writing stories of dogs on Thursday morning of last week. All the stories are to be typewritten by the pupils themselves, bound in a book, and then sent to the children at the hospital.

These stories were illustrated in three different ways: with kodak pictures, freehand drawings, and with tracings. Copies are to be kept also and sent to the Tri-County Fair next fall.

These are some of the best subjects: "My Old Cat on Sunday Morning," "A Story of Prince," "My Cat Tempest," "A True Story of Rover," "The Result of His Visit," "A True Story of Rags." They were all very good.

As time drew near for the paper to be finished, during office hours (composition and penmanship time) nearly all phases of the work in all stages of development could be seen going on. Interviews, writing, revising, cartoon-making, conference with the editors, etc., were in progress. The children were at work singly and in groups in the main office (our schoolroom), at the tables in the textbook library, and at the long table in the principal's office.

We called the paper the *Elementary School Weekly*. It was hand-printed on a double sheet of four pages. Each page was 15×13 inches in size and was divided into four columns—the customary margins being allowed. The cartoons were reproduced on large sheets of tag board and placed where they could be seen easily by the audience. Members of the force read to the audience the different articles in the paper, including the "Funny Column" and advertisements. Proof of its success was the fact that it held the entire attention of all the audience during the reading.

As to results: Aside from the benefits in English resulting from opportunity offered for spontaneity and freedom of expression, the children had had experience in doing team-work—they had worked together for a common end and knew they had done something worth while. This gave them confidence and assurance, which showed in greater strength of attack upon other school affairs involving sustained effort, co-operation, and power of initiative.

A PEACE PAGEANT WRITTEN AND ACTED BY THE UPPER GRADES

MILDRED WELD

Dramatization in secondary schools is rapidly securing a recognized place for itself among modern educators. But though it has received less recognition in the upper grades of the elementary school, dramatic work is well suited also to the needs and capacities of the child at this period of school life. It gives the child a hitherto unrecognized outlet of expression, which is as natural to the child's mind as speech itself; it stimulates his imagination and makes him take a lively interest in historic and literary personalities; it develops assurance in a naturally timid disposition, and it acts as a restraint upon the overbold; it affords a new field of work in composition; and it correlates with the work in art, music, and physical training, because costumes and stage-setting have to be considered, and music and dancing are often introduced.

The drama which follows was worked out in the eighth grade in a series of class exercises and presented before the other classes in the assembly hall of the school building. It was not executed with any attempt at finished acting, as only one week was given to learning the parts, arranging the costumes, and rehearsing the scenes. Had more time been given, the apparent result in presentation would have been improved; but the actual benefit to the class would have been little, if any, greater. Moreover, enthusiasm pales before prolonged work on any given exercise, and good results are diminished. The special aim in this case, aside from the general benefits mentioned above, was to interest the children vitally in the peace movement. This was certainly accomplished, and in addition other lines of interest were aroused. No child in that class will again pass lightly over references to feudal days, or costumes of that period; or the old forms of English expression, which we adopted for the sake of dignity; or articles in current literature on world-peace. That is the far-reaching result which was accomplished and which made our work a success.

The problem before us at the outset was twofold: we must write a drama to be acted by fifteen girls and only five boys, a seemingly difficult thing to do; and we must select a different theme and work upon it in a different way from any that had been worked out in our building or in neighboring buildings. Our inspiration came from an address by Justice Brewer on "The Mission of the United States in the Cause of Peace." The idea of writing our drama in the form of a pageant with abstract characters sprang into being with the reading of this pamphlet, and one difficulty was solved. The other difficulty rapidly receded, for, although the peace pageant had been used among us, we had not heard of its being worked out in this way.

The first step was to make a working plan of the entire drama, which in this case was done by the teacher and presented to the class. The notion of abstract characters was hard for some of the pupils to grasp, and the historic allusions also puzzled some. A class discussion of the plan and explanation of difficulties involved followed, and many suggestions were made with regard to the subject-matter for each scene. Books were suggested for helps in getting the historic setting; then the class divided itself into four groups to work on the four scenes of the first part. If any had a decided preference for a scene, he was put into the group which was in charge of that scene. In some cases pupils contributed to other scenes after the grouping was made, but considerable license was given in that regard. The first group used the Bible as a basis for its work; the second group used history stories; and the third and fourth groups used Scott's *Ivanhoe*, Howard Pyle's *Men of Iron*, and history reference books. It seemed more dignified to use the old-time "thee and thou" forms, so we searched the pages of *Ivanhoe* to find other expressions which might be appropriately used in the same text. Several passages from the text of *Ivanhoe* were incorporated in the first part of the pageant. We hereby make acknowledgment of that fact. The children went to work with a great deal of enthusiasm, for we even decided who should take some of the parts before we commenced to write and the parts were really, in many cases, written to fit the characters. Needless to say, the original plan was modified in many respects after we commenced writing. These changes were due to suggestions by the children, to new ideas on the part of the teacher, and also to the requirements of the text as it was produced.

After the manuscripts came from the hands of the children, they were censored by a special committee and the best of each was taken to make up the first part of our drama. The teacher was always a member of the committee and did much to make the writing seem unified in the final result. The second part was then put into the hands of groups, with peace literature as a reading background, and the work was continued as in the first part. Although the construction progressed under the eyes of the children, many suggestions as well as many modifications of the writing *were due directly to the work of the teacher.* This must be borne constantly in mind. Many variations of the plot were suggested, but the one chosen seemed on the whole the most appropriate.

It may seem incongruous to have Truth a masculine character; but, as I said before, we wrote the drama for the children who took the parts and it fitted our character and our plot better to have it so. Several children who represented minor characters had to take two parts. The ancient nations in the first part became the modern nations in the second part, the lady of feudal days became the modern woman of the second part, but these changes did not seem inappropriate. The young children who represented the blessings in their first appearance were not in our presentation, but they could easily be taken from a lower class and trained for the dancing. They add lightness and grace to the whole effect and make the pageant seem more evenly balanced.

Each person provided himself with the names of the characters he represented printed in uniform black letters upon white muslin. This was at first our only plan for costuming, but gradually suggestions came in until simple but suggestive costumes were evolved at almost no expense. For example, War wore a helmet which he borrowed, and a doublet made of old black cambric decorated with silver paper; he carried a borrowed sword and a pasteboard shield of black and silver paper; Peace was gowned in white with a gold paper crown; the New World was draped in a small silk United States flag that happened to be in our possession; the modern nations carried their own flags; and the nuns were draped in sheets. One can easily imagine from this the simple touches that completed the costuming of our caste.

The names of the parts and scenes were printed on large cards and displayed during the performance. The quotation from Lowell on the first page of our program was delivered for a prologue. Between the scenes we had music appropriate to the setting, martial music in the first part and a peace song at the end of the presentation, by the actors and the school. The stage management and the prompting were put into the hands of the children, so that they conducted their own performance. This gave them the additional lesson of meeting responsibility promptly and well.

The development of character in certainly three members of the class during the work on this drama was marked, and the other members of the class were not without its effect. The pleasure derived from witnessing such growth is in itself a recompense for the extra work that an undertaking of this sort entails.

Miss Helen Loeper, instructor in music at Calvin Fletcher School, arranged and assisted us with the music for the pageant, and Miss Ruth Stebbins, art assistant at Manual Training High School, contributed advice and assistance in the simple costuming employed.

PEACE PAGEANT

PRESENTED BY

THE 8 A CLASS OF CALVIN FLETCHER SCHOOL

Indianapolis, May 18, 1913

PLAN OF PEACE PAGEANT

PART I. DOMINATION of WAR.

Scene i: A Council of Ancient People Plan to Build the Tower of Babel.

Scene ii: Tower of Babel Destroyed. Nations Aroused by the Spirit of War to Fight for Selfish Interests.

Scene iii: The Days of Chivalry, a Social and Political Institution of War.

Scene iv: The Return of a Crusade, a Religious Institution of War.

PROPHECY.

PART II. DOMINATION OF PEACE.
Scene i: Promise of World-Peace.
Scene ii: Progress in Securing World-Peace.
Scene iii: Promise of Peace Fulfilled.

DRAMATIS PERSONAE

PART I	PART II
Old World	New World
Three Nuns	Her Handmaids:
Palmer	Democracy
Ancient Nations:	Education
Assyria	Modern Nations:
Egypt	United States
India	France
China	Germany
Babylonia	Russia
Phoenicia	Holland
Persia	Italy

England
Lady of Feudal Days becomes Modern Woman, Business, Labor } Agents of Fulfilment
Truth (hero)
Peace (heroine)
War (villain)
Justice
Religion
Blessings of Peace:
Art
Progress
Industry

PROLOGUE

New Occasions teach new duties, time makes ancient good uncouth;
They must up again and onward who would keep abreast of *truth!*

PART THE FIRST

Scene i

Land of Shinar

[*A group of primitive people, sitting on the ground and on rocks, assembled in council.*]

First Person: Go to, let us make brick.

Second Person: Yea, we can use brick for stone and burn them thoroughly.

Third Person: And slime can serve for mortar.

Fourth Person: And of this brick will we build a city which shall be indestructible, and if rains come and floods destroy all the inhabitants of the earth, we shall be safe in our city, for it shall be placed upon a hill so high that the waters of the sea can never swallow it up and the floods of the earth can never reach it.

Fifth Person: For greater safety let us build in our city a tower whose top may reach unto heaven, and then we shall surely be safe from destruction.

Sixth Person: And we will call the tower Babel, and the city Babylonia, and it shall stand for a sign of our strength in ages yet unborn.

First Person: And the blessings of our work shall extend to all generations, and long may our name be praised!

Second Person: We will go forth to all the land around and select a site for our city, and we will begin this very day to make the bricks ready for the firing.

All: Away! Away!

Third Person: To find slime!

Fourth Person: To make brick!

Fifth Person: To select a site for our city!

[*Exeunt*]

Scene ii

[Tower of Babel nearly completed. The same people as in scene i, laboring to carry heavy loads of brick and heave them up to their places on the tower. As several last bricks are added the earth shakes and the Old World shudders. A loud crash is heard and the tower is destroyed by an unseen power. The people run in terror, but, after the first shock, return as separate nations *and cautiously inspect the ruins of their hopes.*]

Egypt: All our hopes are dashed to the ground, and our beautiful tower exists no more. It is thy fault, improvident India! Behold the poor foundation!

India: Indeed, thou speakest falsely. Our beautiful tower would not have fallen had it not been for thee, who mixed the slime!

China: Methinks it is the fault of neither, but of those who laid the bricks which were not made aright.

Truth (*enters and says*): Oh, Nations, why must ye quarrel? You are stupid and know not the nature of this disaster. Your wickedness and evil ways have caused this calamity to fall upon you. Did ye not hope to rest secure in the product of your handiwork? Behold the ruins and turn from your evil ways, or worse than this may come upon you. It is not the fault of one, but of all. Cease thy fighting and understand the truth!

Phoenicia: Thy name is Truth, but thou knowest not what thou sayest, for surely we are not wicked. Did we not want to be closer to heaven? Certainly that is no base desire. Come, let us start afresh and build another tower, for 'twas but poor slime that caused the first to fall.

Egypt: It is not so. The poor foundation has occasioned this, as I have said before!

India: Tell no more falsehoods. Thou knowest what thou speakest is not true.

China: Why argue more? The same tower cannot be rebuilt. I speak for a new tower.

Persia: Who shall build it?

India: I shall not build the foundation!

Egypt: Nor shall I mix the slime!

Persia: Nor shall I make the brick!

China: Then must you all depart and leave this land to me. I can build a tower that will stand.

Babylonia: Methinks I should remain here, because I own the land on which the tower was built.

Phoenicia: But I am the most industrious and I hope to establish a trading-station on this spot.

Assyria: I am the strongest. Therefore I shall remain here.

Phoenicia: Thou shouldst for that very reason remove thyself and let the weaker nations stay to pursue in peace the arts of peace and secure the blessings of industry.

The others (*in chorus*): It is mine! It should belong to me! I was here first!

War (*slips up to Babylonia*): Tell them thou wilt fight. Thou art the strongest and I will help thee.

[*Other nations talk together, and point to* War *and* Babylonia, *and continue their quarrel in an undertone.*]

Babylonia: Thou dost make me brave. I will fight and with thy help I can but win.

War (*shakes her hand*): Bravely said, my friend. Maintain thy ground, for thou wast surely here first, as who can gainsay it? Call the boldest forth to contend the ground with thee.

Babylonia (*turns and addresses the other nations*): Come one, come all and prove by force of arms who has the right to remain.

War: Yea, might makes right. [Nations *talk together.*] Why do you hesitate? You seem to me like cowards and lily-livered milk-sops. Have you not as good a title to this land as Babylonia?

Persia: I am no coward. I will fight.

Nations in chorus: Nor I. Nor I.

Assyria: I will summon my soldiers and avenge myself on you, O hated Babylonia!

Egypt: I will also prepare for war.

Others: And I. And I. [*Exeunt* Nations]

Old World (*enters*): What is this all about?

War: This is the beginning of the wrangling of Nations over points of honor that have to be settled by war. Thy boundaries will be rent asunder and thy lands laid waste, but how else can justice and honor be established between the nations? I will help thee build thy armaments and spill the blood of thy children, but it is all for their honor and glory, and victory shall decide the right. Come, Old World, with me and prepare the Nations for War.

[*Exeunt*]

Scene iii

England—Age of Chivalry

[*One* Nun *seated in English feudal castle. Two* Nuns *enter conversing.*]

First Nun: Didst thou not say that this day the worthy Truth is to be knighted?

Second Nun: Yea, those are my very words, and worthy of being knighted is this gallant youth.

Third Nun: Forsooth he is, and thy words are truly spoken, for he is the first in honor as in arms.

Second Nun: Fain would he journey to the Holy Land and fight for the recovery of Jerusalem.

First Nun: Methinks I hear some one approaching. It is the sound of War. He is to make Truth a knight, Sister, if thy words are truly spoken.

[War *enters with helmet, sword, and shield, followed by* Palmer *with* Truth, *who kneels in front of* War. Nuns *take candles and stand in a line in rear of group.* Lady *enters and sits opposite group.*]

First Nun: A right comely youth is he!

Third Nun: Aye, and seemly too!

Old World (*enters, dragging a heavy sword*): By my beard, we need more knights!

War: Thou hast been gallant and brave, fair youth, and dost now deserve to be dubbed Knight. Thy good lance won the prize in this day's tourney and thou art accounted the victor. Bethink thee of the solemn vows thou art about to take. They are the knots which bind thee to heaven. They are the cords which bind thee and thy honor to the altar. Art thou ready to take them?

Truth: I am.

War: Wilt thou hereafter honor thy conscience as thy king, neither speak no evil—no, nor listen to it—preserve the truth, and defend the ladies?

Truth: By my troth, I will. [*Takes up cross.*] I vow before God to defend the church, to protect the ladies, to help the weak, and to succor all who are in need.

War (*makes sign of cross on* Truth's *shoulder while giving him the following blessing*]: In the name of God, I dub thee knight. Be brave, be bold, be loyal. Sir Truth, arise. There is no right of chivalry more precious or inalienable than that each knight choose a lady for whom to win honor. Is thy choice made? If not, it is now thy duty as well as privilege to name thy lady.

Truth (*bends knee in front of* Lady): Grant me thy favor, O lady fair, and give me a pledge of thy constancy. That necklace that thou wearest I fain would carry with me to give me strength in battle.

Lady: Nay, you may be a knight in rank but you are not yet a knight in deed. You have done naught in arms, you have won no fame. When your name is on all men's lips, return to me and I will grant you favor.

Truth: So be it. I will for thy sake venture my life in many battles. For thy sake I will win glory. No fear of death shall hinder me.

[*Exeunt* Truth *followed by all except* Old World *and* War]

[*Enter* Peace *and* Justice]

Justice: Didst witness the tournament yestreen? They say that the victor of the day was a coward who failed to vanquish his foe in fair fight, but took him unawares. In sooth, might is the right of the strongest.

Old World: Truth before his lance lies vanquished.

Justice: Indeed not. "Truth crushed to earth shall rise again."

Peace: And Justice shall prevail.

War (*enters*): What unprofitable debate is here? By my halidom, disperse ye all! Your prattle is ruinous to my projects. Out upon thee, I say, and thee, thou base calumniator!

[*All scatter; curtain falls*]

Scene iv

England

The Return of a Crusade

Truth: We have been exposed to great dangers by the road. Many of our number we have left in the land of the Saracens and the Crescent still waves over Jerusalem. ·

England: This holy pilgrim here, he surely has won honor for the church by his fastings and prayer.

Palmer: I bring as a sacred relic this portion of the true cross which I secured in the Holy Land. [*Hands it to* England.]

First Nun: We have said faithfully our orisons.

Second Nun: We have repented of our sins and mortified ourselves with fastings, vigils, and long prayers.

Third Nun: We have been subject to disease which has laid a heavy hand upon our strength and comeliness.

Old World: English chivalry was second to none. Many English knights won much honor, and some ran three courses, casting to the ground three antagonists.

Palmer: As Truth says, we have suffered much and left our offering of dead upon the battle-field. We have stood the trial, but our object has failed of its purpose. The flag of the Saracen still waves over the Holy Land.

Religion (*enters*): It is as true as truth itself that you have failed in your enterprise, because truth means this to me, and that to thee.

All: And what does it mean to thee, pray tell?

Religion: Service to all mankind.

Palmer: Have I not served?

Nuns: Have we not served?

Old World: What more would you ask than that we offer our sons and daughters to thy service?

War: Have I not saved the honor of the church and protected the honor of thy knights in many a bravely fought battle-field?

Religion: Ah, good pilgrims, help the poor, succor the sick, and let your sons and daughters *live* to serve; and thou, O Truth, throw aside thy veil and see the light. Join the company of Peace and Justice and work for world-progress, forgetting not the Christmas message of "Peace on earth, good-will toward Men."

[*Curtain*]

[Religion *steps in front of curtain and recites Ruskin's poem entitled "The Dawn of Peace." This partakes of the nature of a prophecy.*]

Part the Second

Scene i

America

New World: Behold my vast possessions, that extend to unknown limits beyond the setting sun! Here will I place thee, fair daughter Democracy, in charge of my people, and thou mayst train them as thou wilt.

Democracy: Well said, indeed! I shall employ as my chief helper the wisdom of Education. She shall train thy people to know that all mankind are brothers, and that Justice cannot be established by War.

Education: I will raise great men who shall be an honor to their New World home. Through them shall the Spirit of War be overcome and a better way of settling difficulties be set forth.

War (enters): Thou canst not settle questions of honor without my help. Thou knowest that. Already have I helped thee establish thyself upon this virgin soil and now thou wouldst cast me off and forget the one who befriended thee.

Education: There are those who think thy help might have been dispensed with. Recall the words of him who was first in war and first in peace. He said, "My first wish is to see the inhabitants of the whole world at peace, striving which should contribute most to the happiness of mankind."

Democracy: Our brethren dwell in every land, for we ourselves have but recently come to cast our lot with thee, our new-found Fatherland. We are through with thy service, most bloody-handed War!

Truth: Begone, old War. Thy day is past; thy sun is set. Even I, thy former friend, have no further use for thee.

Peace: And from now on thou shalt be spurned by all civilized nations.

War: I am not old, I tell thee! If I am spurned by all civilized nations I will get all uncivilized nations and make war upon thee!

[*Exit* War]

Peace: Education, get thee all of the uncivilized nations and teach them the truth of service. That is the only way of overcoming War.

Education: Yea, that will I do.

[*Exit* Education]

[*Enter* England, France, *and* Germany *running*]

New World: What now? Why are you running? Hast someone frightened you?

Nations: War has been at our heels. We can no longer avoid him.

War (enters): Ye, who dare, come fight the mighty War!

Truth: O, War, why must thou always fight? Why canst thou not let the nations rest at peace with one another? Thou filled the Old World so full of thy dread spirit that it was made weak and inefficient and needs must do as thou commanded. Pray leave the New World to go about in peace.

War: List to the coward. If he were brave, he would not speak these foolish words. Is there no one left to fight? Come, Nations, build more warships and vie with one another!

New World: We'll have no fighting here. Begone, I tell thee, and let me see thy face no more! [*Exit* War.] For the last time have we soiled our hands in thy bloody business!

[*Curtain*]

Scene ii

New World: Thrice have we fallen into conflict—to our shame be it spoken! Our parent country has been our foe and even our brethren of the South. Our daughters have scraped lint and made bandages, have nursed the wounded and buried the dead; lands have been laid waste in this fair world of promise; and waters have run red with blood! O Justice, why hast thou deserted us? O Peace, canst thou endure our sight no more?

Justice: Thou deservest no better at our hands. All men are thy brethren. Thou shouldst but remember that! Settle thy difficulties fairly between thee and thy kindred. Then we will once more dwell in thy borders and comfort thy broken-hearted daughters with a clear vision of the future, unstained by kinsmen's blood.

Peace: Indeed I, too, will bless thee in manners manifold. My blessings shall rejoice thy youth and thou shalt become powerful through them in thine age. [*Sings:*]

Hither, come hither, blessings three,
Dance a roundelay merrily,
Progress, Art, and Industry
Meet with us together.

Blessings (*enter dancing and encircle* Peace):

Here we come, O Peace, to thee,
Dance we here right joyfully;
Here we always fain would be
  Thy dear children ever!

[*They encircle* New World, *still dancing*]

May we not *thy* blessings be,
O New World? For thee we see
A distant sure prosperity,
  Thine and ours together!

[*They encircle* Justice]

Justice, too, our patron see.
Peace, she always follows thee
Wheresoever thou mayst be;
  None thy bonds may sever.

[*Dancing forward and backward*]

Hither come, and hither gone,
Dance a step and sing a song,
Shall we wander far and long
  Or stay here forever?

New World: We have entertained you many times in our midst, fair children, and tried to protect your youth and innocence, but War has each time banished you by his inroads until we despaired of seeing you more. Welcome, thrice welcome, are you to our land! Establish yourselves where you will; live and grow up in the strength of this new soil until War blanches before the face of Industry and flees from the approach of Progress. War has been entertained in our midst for the last time! [*Exeunt* Blessings.] [*To* Peace:] We have established the only unguarded boundary line in the civilized world and it has remained unmolested for a century of peace. Surely that is something to win your favor?

[*Enter* Business *and* Labor. Labor *with sleeves rolled up begins to hammer away at a piece of work.*]

Peace: I congratulate you upon that endeavor to win my esteem and I pledge my assistance in securing for you further advantages. I have just returned from South America and rejoice to tell you that I have left my standard upon the boundary line between Chile and Argentina, for both nations, after years of conflict, have sold their warships, disbanded their armies, and entered into an enduring peace.

[*Enter* Woman, *who sits sewing*]

New World: I have agents at work to secure a public sentiment in favor of Peace. Business, what has thou done to promote our interests?

Business (*at a desk piled with accounts*): I have helped the New World make treaties and maintain peaceful relations with the other countries. Our interests are so bound up with theirs that no war could be successfully carried on. Business would never permit it.

New World: And thou, mine honest workingman, what hast thou to say for thyself?

Labor: I am restless and discontented. Why? Because I know that 70 per cent of the revenue of the country—taxes that I pay and taxes that you pay—is spent for the war debt and to buy more implements of war. Thirty cents out of every dollar remain to *promote* the *life* and *welfare* of the citizens, seventy cents to destroy life and to destroy property. How much longer shall we endure this outrage?

Woman: I, too, feel strongly in this matter. Who makes up the rank and file of the army? Let me answer for you. The husbands and sons of the laboring class. Again, who cares for the dependent family at home? Aye, who? Answer me ye who can. [*Pause.*] The child that looks into my eyes may one day lie on a bloody field of battle. Is it for this I have toiled and suffered—only to see the son of my hopes snatched from his rightful place in the world of service?

Justice: Behold, a brighter future is before us. I have established the Hague Tribunal of World Peace. In it can all controversies between nations be settled without recourse to war.

All: To the Hague! To the Hague!

[*Exeunt all*]

Scene iii

[Modern Nations *and* Old World *in background with flags. Enter coronation procession,* New World *escorting* Peace, *followed by* Truth *and* Justice, Religion, Industry, Progress, *and* Art. New World *crowns* Peace. *Procession and* Nations *sing:*]

All hail, most gracious queen, to thee!
  Thy loyal subjects we shall be
From now until eternity!
  All hail to thee! All hail to thee!

[New World *steps back of throne.* Truth *and* Justice *take places on opposite sides of throne;* Religion *sits at the feet of* Peace, *and the* Blessings, *now grown to womanhood, group themselves on the opposite side of the stage.*]

Truth: Fair sister, today we grant the homage that should have been thine these many years. I groped in darkness, not knowing where I erred, and associated myself with War because I was blinded by tradition and the false standard of religion. Today the scales have fallen from my eyes and I see clearly the new vision of the future!

Justice: I, too, crown thee queen of all the earth and pledge myself thine honored slave.

Religion: Today has the ancient prophecy come true which said, "And they shall beat their swords into plowshares and their spears into pruning hooks; nation shall not lift up sword against nation, neither shall there be war any more."

Peace: As thy chosen queen, I hope to serve thee well. I appoint for my chief counselors, Truth and Justice. [*Both bow.*] And as my first duty to you all I bid you summon War to a hearing.

[*Exit* Truth, *returning with* War]

Peace: War, thou art my prisoner. Hereafter thou art banished from all people forever and may henceforth wander a fugitive without friend and without comrade. No person may be seen associating with thee, and thy days may be spent in atonement for thy heedless fighting and slaying.

Truth: Be not so hard upon friend War. We have often fought side by side. I entreat you, reconsider your sentence.

Peace: Then disarm War and replace his weapons with those of Industry. If he will never arm himself again with destructive weapons, he may remain among us a friend and comrade. His wealth must be given to Progress and his time to Art and he may then prove himself a valuable citizen in the world community.

Industry: I bestow upon thee these gifts. [*Hands him a spade and a sickle.*]

War: I relinquish my gold and promise to devote myself to Art. [*Steps to her side.*] May I have the honor of thy favor?

Art: Thy career is before thee. Do with it as thou wilt. [*Accepts the gold.*]

Peace: Behold my Blessings. Call them hither. [War *steps to rear of stage.* Blessings *come forward.*]

Peace: Go forth to bless all the nations until

"The workers afield, in the mill, in the mart,
In commerce, in council, in science and art
Shall bring of their gifts and together create
The manifold life of the firm-builded state."

[*Peace song by actors and audience*]

SOME OBSERVATIONS IN GERMAN SCHOOLS

CHARLES H. JUDD
University of Chicago

One frequently hears criticism of the lecture method of teaching when it is employed in the elementary school. Superintendents are accustomed to tell teachers that they talk too much to their classes and allow the children too little opportunity to express what they have learned at home or read out of books. The American visitor in the elementary schools of Germany is very much impressed by the fact that in those schools an entirely different attitude is assumed toward this matter of oral instruction. In fact, one may say that the German method of instruction is predominantly the lecture method.

In most of the *Volksschulen* the children are very meagerly supplied with books. For example, the only textbook which they have for the work in geography is an atlas. In many of the schools the children are not supplied even with an atlas. There is no home study of geography. The children get their information from the statements made by the teachers. The usual method of procedure is for the teacher to refer to a wall map or to the maps which lie before the pupils in their atlases and to describe some region which is the subject of consideration. Incidentally it may be remarked that for the most part the regions selected are parts of the German Empire. Relatively little attention is given to the rest of the world, and the other parts of the world that are selected are emphasized in the degree in which they afford opportunities for colonial settlements or trade with the German Empire. After the description of the region has been given by the teacher and the names have been pointed out on the map or looked up in the atlases, the teacher asks the members of the class a series of questions based upon what he has said. These questions are not unlike the questions heard in the ordinary American classroom except that they are of necessity confined very definitely to the material which the teacher has presented. From time to time in an American classroom questions arise which demand of the pupils some research in books other than the textbooks. Not so in a German classroom of the *Volksschule*. Sometimes the questioning comes at the end of the period, the first part having been devoted to the lecture by the teacher. Sometimes the questioning breaks into the recitation period and is both preceded and followed by statements made by the teacher. The latter is usually the case in the lower grades, for in general the length of a recitation in these schools is forty-five minutes.

What has been said with regard to the geography class is typical of all of the work which is done in these schools. History is taught in exactly the same way by statements from the teacher followed by recitations in which the children are required to reproduce what the teacher has said. From time to time a review is undertaken of longer periods. The individual members of the class are called upon to give lengthy descriptions of the periods they have been studying on earlier days. The recitations in history are thus sometimes different from the ordinary recitation in geography in that the pupils give a longer and more coherent statement than is common in the geography recitation.

The work in arithmetic is carried on orally. Here the method differs somewhat from the work in geography and history above described. The teacher gives sums or other problems which the children are required to work out in their heads. It is very impressive to an American visitor to see how far this work can be carried with children in the elementary school. They become rapid and efficient in solving arithmetic problems, and not only this, but they show great retentiveness for the problems dictated by the teacher. When a child makes a mistake in giving an answer he is called upon to repeat the figures given by the teacher, and even when he is mistaken about the result he succeeds in remembering the details of the problem. As a method of teaching arithmetic there can be no doubt that this is much more efficient on the mechanical side than the methods ordinarily found in American schools.

The writer had an opportunity in one of the smaller schools near Berlin, through the courtesy of one of the inspectors, to observe results in turning children who were very efficient in mental arithmetic to the task of working out some problems on paper. These children were evidently not by any means as efficient in written work as they had been in the oral work. They divided a number of five digits by nine and employed long division as a means of obtaining the result. They were slower than a similar group of American children would be in doing this work and evidently were by no means as much at home with paper and pencil as with mental arithmetic.

The instruction in the vernacular which children receive in the German elementary school is only in very small part, as contrasted with our American practice training in oral reading. Instruction in the vernacular consists very largely in learning by heart sections of the classical literature of the German language. In connection with each of these selections the children learn the name of the author and the date of composition and very frequently the circumstances under which it was written. They recite what they have learned either individually or in concert. One gets the impression that much of this is very abstract. The material is selected without any such deference to the maturity of the children as is to be seen in most American readers. When the children read orally, as they do less frequently than in our schools, the reading-material is of the most formal type.

The contrast between the American and German methods of instruction can perhaps be explained in part if not altogether by reference to the history of German schools as contrasted with the history of American elementary education.

The German school originated as a catechism school. Its chief function was to give religious instruction and the method of this religious instruction was not very different from that which is adopted now in all of the classes. Indeed one is reminded continually in visiting German schools of this fundamental interest in religion. Four periods a week are devoted in all of the elementary schools in Germany to religious instruction. Sometimes this instruction consists of church history; sometimes of a careful analysis of some portion of scripture; sometimes of a discussion of dogmatic moral beliefs. Schools are divided into Protestant,

Roman Catholic, and Jewish, and the sharpest lines of division within the class are recognized whenever religion is the subject of instruction.

The American school, on the other hand, was at its beginning and has continued to be throughout its history a reading school. The early legislation in the New England colonies shows that the Puritans wanted the children to read for themselves. So emphatic was this desire to cultivate reading that even handwriting and arithmetic came in slowly as secondary subjects of instruction. The reading school of New England has gradually extended so as to include geography and history and other subjects in which children can prepare themselves by reading textbooks at home. American schools are supplied with textbooks which cannot be equaled in point of variety and number and quality by any in the world. The class exercises in American schools refer to reading-matter while the class exercises in the German schools are catechisms based upon information supplied by the teacher.

This contrast between the two schools becomes the more interesting when one reads the criticisms that are made in Germany of the *Volksschule*. A careful German observer like Dr. Kerschensteiner, who has had an opportunity to compare from the German point of view our methods of instruction with those familiar to him in Germany, emphasizes the fact that our American children are much more independent in their ideas than are the children trained in German schools. Dr. Kerschensteiner also called attention to the fact that our children read more and rely more upon the books which they read for their ideas. In a number of German cities one finds at the present time a disposition to prepare textbook material to put into the hands of children. There is evidently a feeling on the part of the teachers in these schools that information must be given to supplement that which the teacher can present in class lectures.

As soon as an American observer becomes convinced of this fundamental distinction between the American school and the German school, he naturally asks himself what are the advantages of the German method and what are its disadvantages. Among the advantages he will notice first of all the close attention given by the children to the statements presented by the teacher. If the teacher has an impressive personality, oral instruction undoubtedly can be made very effective. The teacher always has the advantage, furthermore, of being the sole source of information. There is no disposition on the part of a child to call in question any part of any statement which is made to him. There is, therefore, none of the critical attitude so often found in American schools. Doubtless there are other and broader social reasons for the personal respect in which German children hold their teachers, but certainly these broader social grounds for respect are powerfully reinforced by the fact that the teacher is the source of information to the class.

In the second place, an advantage which is apparent, especially in arithmetic, is that the children keep in mind a great number of details. Arithmetic is perhaps the most striking example, but the same fact appears in other subjects as well. The American child has before him a book and he knows that at any time he can get the details which he has read there. There is danger that he will rely upon his book for his details and not be as keen to keep them in mind. One very striking illustration of this came under the notice of the writer in a mathematics class in one of the higher schools. The class was given instruction in plane geometry without any figure upon the board or at their seats. The instructor appeared before the class and drew a circle in the air. He then drew the diameter and tangent and proceeded to demonstrate the method of measuring the angle between these two lines, depending entirely upon the ability of the students to visualize the figure and keep it in mind. This instructor said that it was not common in mathematics instruction to rely upon students in this fashion, but that he had found it very advantageous to induce students to get the matter in their own minds rather than to rely upon the board. This is undoubtedly an extreme illustration, but it brings out clearly the advantages of removing from the student all aids outside of himself. The student is stimulated to pay close attention to the matter of presentation and he is trained in a valuable form of memory. Perhaps the training might be compared to the familiar type of memory work in American classes known as flash-writing.

The third advantage, which might be regarded as somewhat doubtful, is the advantage that comes from requiring the teachers to keep themselves fully informed on the subjects of instruction. Certainly with the demand upon him that he give the details of the geography lesson, it is obvious that the teacher must be prepared on the geography lesson somewhat more fully than if it is his duty merely to hear the recitation upon a book. It is a well-known fact that the teachers in German schools have been raised by such requirements to a higher level of academic excellence than the teachers of any other country. Without uniform and intensive requirement of training the whole scheme would be entirely hopeless.

This statement suggests the turning-point in the discussion and leaves us to comment briefly upon some of the obvious disadvantages of the German method of instruction. No one who observes the German schools can fail to recognize the fact that the teachers do not fulfil the ideal which is referred to in the last paragraph. They do not know all of the facts which they ought to know to give efficient instruction in the subjects which actually come up in the class. Sometimes they give positive misinformation to students. Such misinformation can of course appear in an American classroom as well as in a German classroom, but the safeguards which are fenced about the American teacher are much more numerous. If a mistake about a geographical fact appears in the textbook it is sure to be corrected; and if it arises in class discussion it is likely to be corrected sooner or later by some pupil who has had opportunity to read in a supplementary reader about the subject which the teacher is discussing. The present writer observed several striking examples of the inability of the German teachers to carry the full body of the information in mind. If these observations can be made by a visitor who attends somewhat less than fifty classes of the type under discussion, the actual mistakes in instruction must be fairly numerous in the course of the year in all of the *Volksschulen* of Germany.

German teachers themselves, when this difficulty is pointed out, recognize it as one of the problems of their profession and are making an effort, as indicated above, to reduce the material which they need for the schools to more definite form.

The second very noticeable disadvantage of the German method has already been referred to. Children do not learn to use books freely and they go out into later life without the preparation for reading that our American students have. To be sure, many of our American graduates of the elementary school do not read books as freely as we might desire. There is an absence of acquaintance with technical mechanical literature that would be advantageous to the ordinary mechanic or ordinary housewife, and yet the American school child has handled enough books to be familiar with that mode of getting information and he is likely to have a number of books in his home just because he is familiar with books and their use. In later life his children will certainly be encouraged to get books when they go to the elementary school and he will have an appreciation of the value of books for the education of his family. The situation is very different in the homes of the graduates of the German *Volksschule*. Here books are relatively strange and unfamiliar. When the child of the family goes to school the need of books is not as clearly recognized as it is in the American home.

The German critic of American schools might be disposed to point to our voluminous periodical literature as one of the evil consequences of this reading-habit and doubtless we should have to admit that the overuse of the printing press is one of the dangers of modern American life. Perhaps the disadvantage is not all on the side of the German schools, but to the American observer who is interested in promoting reading as one of the chief features of the American school the German *Volksschule* seems to be very meager in its training of pupils.

The third disadvantage, which can be referred to only in a somewhat vague and abstract way, is the disadvantage which the German school exhibits in that it tends to train its pupils in a very dogmatic, authoritative fashion. To be sure, the German *Volksschule* is not intended to be the training school for the leaders in German life. The boys and girls who get into the German *Volksschule* are not expected to attend any higher school and it is not expected that they will occupy positions of influence in social life or in the government. Most of the positions which would give them influence are closed because one of the requirements for admission to such positions is completion of education in one of the higher schools. Perhaps this general social fact is more significant than the method of instruction in explaining why the German child in the *Volksschule* is very much under the authority and domination of the teacher and the system which is training him. Perhaps this also justifies in the minds of the German authorities the relatively narrow course of study which is administered. On the other hand, there can be no doubt that the method of instruction is the natural outgrowth of the social attitude which is back of the school and tends to perpetuate this social attitude among the children. The teacher stands before the class as a representative of the government as well as of the older generation. The teacher is himself dominated by the system, in that the course of study which he administers is prescribed from the central school authorities. The church determines the classification of the school in which he teaches and the type of religious instruction which shall be given. Everywhere there is evidence that the individual must be subordinated to the general system. This spirit appears in the methods of instruction as well as in the general social organization surrounding the schools, and when one comes from a relatively free and undogmatic American school into one of these German schools he is instantly impressed by the subordination of the individual child to the scheme of organization.

Again, there is doubtless something to be said on the side of the German schools. Perhaps here also the German observer would hardly admit that the criticisms referred to should be classified as disadvantages of that educational system. But the American comes back to the schools with which he is familiar satisfied that much would be lost if a fundamental change were made in the methods of instruction and the spirit of enthusiasm in the American classroom to conform to that which he observed in the German *Volksschule.*

BOOK REVIEWS

Design and Construction in Wood. By WILLIAM NOYES. Peoria: Manual Arts Press, 1913. Pp. 160. $1.50.

In this volume Mr. Noyes has shown how courses in woodworking may be enriched in content and made truly educational. He has chosen such simple constructive projects as the paper-basket, candlestick, picture-frame, taboret, and small box, and carried them through the various stages of development from the first steps in design, through the constructive processes and finishing, to the completed project. He has done this in such a way as to indicate the content one might reasonably expect of almost any course in woodworking. The book also contains a brief treatment of tools, materials, and constructive processes as related to the work outlined. The distinct contribution of the book lies in its clear presentation of the content of a course in woodworking and the suggestion of the author's method of presenting shop problems to his classes.

EMERY FILBEY

UNIVERSITY HIGH SCHOOL

Vocational Guidance. By J. ADAMS PUFFER. Chicago: Rand McNally & Co. 1913. Illustrated. Pp. 306. $1.25.

This is a book intended to stimulate teachers to give more consideration to the training of pupils for occupations. In a popular and readable style the author gives examples of the needs of vocational guidance and discusses cases showing the success of such guidance. He surveys the industries of the country and gives special descriptions of several of the leading occupations and professions. He presents series of questions which he has found useful in examining individuals whom he has studied and advised. The book is profusely illustrated with cuts which show children engaged in every possible type of activity, profitable and unprofitable.

The book will probably serve to keep alive, and may serve to widen interest in, a very timely topic. The careful reader will find, however, that it reflects the somewhat unorganized state of the art of vocational guidance. For example, the chapters on the "Equipment of a Counselor" and on the "Methods of a Counselor" issue in vague general maxims rather than definite, clear-cut principles. One could wish that the book based on practical experience were somewhat more explicit. What shall we do in attacking a particular case? Perhaps there are no very definite methods; in that case the advocate of vocational guidance will have to press his plea for a universal recognition of this new aspect of education with somewhat less assurance. At all events, it seems clear that in American life we shall not make over our schools to suit writers who are so general and indefinite as is our present writer.

The foregoing comment prepares the way for an adverse criticism of the book in one of its general and constantly reiterated positions. The author has little respect for the present-day school. For example, in a most concessive moment he writes (p. 79): "We must not forget that our traditional school course—antiquated, impractical, one-sided, abstract, as we justly accuse it of being—does test to the full certain valuable types of mind." All the school pictures which the author labels with favorable legends are of the "vocational" type. Other symptoms of disrespect for the traditional could be cited without number. The discussion of this aspect of the book need not delay us long. Vocational guidance, which is to depend on the turning of schools into trade schools, seems to be a little behindhand. Vocational guidance ought to precede the choice of a trade; if it comes first in a trade school it comes too late to be of much use. Has not our author like many another become so much of an enthusiast that he has shortsightedly omitted his foundation in building his palace? Vocational guidance needs the school quite as much as the school needs vocational guidance. Will not teachers profit more by reading books which show them how the general social arts such as writing, reading, and number work may function in vocational life than by reading books which abandon the traditional social arts in favor of unformulated principles of vocational selection?

C. H. J.

Language Teaching in the Grades. By ALICE W. COOLEY. Boston: Houghton Mifflin Co., 1913. Riverside Educational Monographs. Pp. 88. $0.35 net.

This book is a plea for the use of literature as the sole basis of all language work in the grades. A number of available poems and prose selections are mentioned and some detailed suggestions are given as to the method of their use. The book can hardly be regarded as more than a series of suggestions, since it does not give any systematic outline of work and its references are not adequate to fill out the whole course in the grades.

Another and more general respect in which the book seems to the reviewer fundamentally defective is in its failure to recognize that language work is much more than literature. To one who believes that the great amount of time allotted to English in the present-day course of study brings to the English teacher a responsibility for teaching the vernacular in its common as well as its literary uses, many of the extravagant statements about literature in this book sound like the intemperate exaggerations of a narrow partisan. Professional English teachers are usually more familiar with literary selections than with science or common life. They do well to recall that a very small percentage of their pupils will attain to any complete acquaintance with literature. A sixth-grade boy discontented with school can hardly be induced to stay by being obliged to learn poems. In the interests of the fine art of reading in later life it might be well to consider giving that boy a little plain shop English or some business English or some other kind not known as literature.

C. H. J.

Elementary General Science. Book I. By PERCY E. ROWELL. Berkeley, Cal.: The A-to-Zed Co., 1914. Pp. xv+198. $0.60.

This book is the first of a series of four, intended to be used in the teaching of science in the grades. It is designed for about the fifth grade. The bulk of the book is devoted to physical science and the attempt is made to teach by the use of common objects and common phenomena. Most of the apparatus suggested is very simple, and all of it can be made in the ordinary schoolroom out of common household utensils. The book looks as if it would enable children to follow its simple directions and learn a good deal of elementary science. What interest it would arouse and what results it would achieve can only be told by trial. The book would certainly make the trial easy for any grade teacher. We have had so little experimental work in the grades that we are not ready yet to answer offhand just how much pupils can learn from experiment or how complicated an experiment they can follow. Repeated trial with a book of this sort is probably the best means that we have of answering some of these nature-study problems. Doubtless many of the experiments suggested will be found better adapted to other grades, and many of the directions that are given will be modified by continued experience. On the whole, the book is a welcome addition to our literature of nature-study, especially since it deals with the physical side of nature-study, which heretofore has not been put into book shape.

E. R. D.

UNIVERSITY OF CHICAGO

BOOKS RECEIVED

GINN & CO., BOSTON

Catalogue of Textbooks for Common Schools. Cloth. Illustrated. Pp. 312.

The Beacon Second Reader. By James H. Fassett. Cloth. Illustrated. Pp. 192. $0.40.

The See and Say Series. Book II. By Sarah Louise Arnold, Elizabeth C. Bonney, and E. F. Southworth. Cloth. Illustrated. Pp. 149. $0.35.

HOUGHTON MIFFLIN CO., BOSTON

Adrift on an Ice-Pan. By Wilfred T. Grenfell. Cloth. Illustrated. Pp. 69. $0.25.

Stickeen: The Story of a Dog. By John Muir. Cloth. Pp. 74. $0.25.

Sinopah the Indian Boy. By James Willard Schultz (Ap-I-Kun-I). Cloth. Pp. 155. $0.45.

Play Day Stories. By Sarah Orne Jewett. Selected and Edited by Katharine H. Shute. Cloth. Pp. 102. $0.25

The Hygiene of the School Child. By Lewis M. Terman. Cloth. Illustrated. Pp. 417. $1.65.

G. P. PUTNAM'S SONS, NEW YORK

Introduction to the Study of English Literature. By W. T. Young, M.A. Cloth. Pp. 238. $0.75.

The Irish Twins. By Lucy Fitch Perkins. Cloth. Illustrated. Pp. 196. $0.50.

TEACHERS COLLEGE, NEW YORK

Some Attempts to Standardize Oven Temperatures for Cookery Processes. By May B. Van Arsdale. Paper. Pp. 15. $0.10.

WESTON ELECTRICAL INSTRUMENT CO., NEWARK

Elementary Electrical Testing. Monograph 2, Joint Committee Series. Contributed by the Technical Staff of the Weston Electrical Instrument Co.

NATIONAL EDUCATION ASSOCIATION

Journal of Proceedings and Addresses of the Fifty-first Annual Meeting, Held at Salt Lake City, Utah, July 5–11, 1913. Cloth. Pp. 827.

CURRENT EDUCATIONAL LITERATURE IN THE PERIODICALS[1]

IRENE WARREN
Librarian, School of Education, University of Chicago

Andress, J. Mace. The teaching of hygiene below the high school. II. El. School T. 14:325–30. (Mr. '14.) III. 14:393–99 (Ap. '14.)

Bagley, W. C. Fundamental distinctions between vocational and liberal education. J. of Educa. (Bost.) 79:339–43. (26 Mr. '14.)

Bawden, William T. The administration of state aid for vocational education. Voca. Educa. 3:287–94. (Mr. '14.)

Boyd, William. The development of a child's vocabulary. Pedagog. Sem. 21:95–124. (Mr. '14.)

Bush, Arthur Dermont. The vocabulary of a three-year-old girl. Pedagog. Sem. 21:125–42. (Mr. '14.)

Caldwell, Otis W. Home economics and rural extension. J. of Home Econ. 6:99–109. (Ap. '14.)

Campbell, Everett Eveleth. A study of retardation and class standing on the basis of home language used by pupils. El. School T. 14:331–47. (Mr. '14.)

Catlin, Claiborne. Incorrigibility due to mismanagement and misunderstanding. Psychol. Clinic 8:12–24. (Mr. '14.)

Clark, Lotta A. Pageantry in America. English J. 3:146–53. (Mr. '14.)

Edwards, Charles Lincoln. Nature play. Pop. Sci. Mo. 84:330–44. (Ap. '14.)

Elliott, Edward C. State school surveys. Am. School Bd. J. 48:9–10, 62. (Mr. '14.)

Fauver, Edwin. A suggestion for making required physical training of greater value to the college graduate. Am. Phys. Educa. R. 19:200–203. (Mr. '14.)

Fish, Susan Anderson. What should pupils know in English when they enter the high school? English J. 3:166–75. (Mr. '14.)

[1] *Abbreviations.*—Am. Phys. Educa. R., American Physical Educational Review; Am. School Bd. J., American School Board Journal; Cur. Opinion, Current Opinion; Educa., Education; Educa. R., Educational Review; El. School T., Elementary School Teacher; English J., English Journal; Hist. Teachers M., History Teachers Magazine; J. of Educa. (Bost.), Journal of Education (Boston); J. of Educa. Psychol., Journal of Educational Psychology; J. of Home Econ., Journal of Home Economics; Lit. D., Literary Digest; Pedagog. Sem., Pedagogical Seminary; Pop. Sci. Mo., Popular Science Monthly; Psychol. Clinic, Psychological Clinic; R. of Rs., Review of Reviews; School Arts M., School Arts Magazine; School R., School Review; Sci. Am. Sup., Scientific American Supplement; Teach. Coll. Rec., Teachers College Record; U.S. Bur. of Educa. Bull., United States Bureau of Education Bulletin; Voca. Educa., Vocational Education.

Goodwin, Frank P. Vocational guidance in Cincinnati. Voca. Educa. 3:249–59. (Mr. '14.)

Hahn, H. H., and Thorndike, E. L. Some results of practice in addition under school conditions. J. of Educa. Psychol. 5:65–85. (Fe. '14.)

Hamilton, A. E. Eugenics. Pedagog. Sem. 21:28–61. (Mr. '14.)

Hill, Patty Smith, ed. Experimental studies in kindergarten theory and practice. Teach. Coll. Rec. 15:1–70. (Ja. '14.)

Is the Montessori school based upon a misconception of the child mind? Cur. Opinion 56:284–85. (Ap. '14.)

Jones, G. E. Tuberculosis among school children. Pedagog. Sem. 21:62–94. (Mr. '14.)

Lee, Joseph. Restoring their play inheritance to our city children. Craftsman 25:545–55. (Mr. '14.)

(The) limitations of the Montessori method from a religious point of view. Cur. Opinion 56:292. (Ap. '14.)

Lyon, Darwin Oliver. The relation of material to time taken for learning and the optimum distribution of time. II. J. of Educa. Psychol. 5:85–91. (Fe. '14.)

Miller, Elizabeth Erwin. Progressive drawing for little children. School Arts M. 13:502–7. (Mr. '14.)

Page, Edward C. A working museum of history. Hist. Teachers M. 5:77–80. (Mr. '14.)

Payne, E. George. Commercial education in Germany. Voca. Educa. 3:271–76. (Mr. '14.)

Sayre, Harriet. The artistic value of the Montessori geometrical insets. Psychol. Clinic 8:6–11. (Mr. '14.)

Smith, Theodate L. The development of psychological clinics in the United States. Pedagog. Sem. 21:143–53. (Mr. '14.)

Souder, Charles David. The state industrial school. Survey 31:715–18. (7 Mr. '14.)

Strayer, George Drayton. The Vermont educational survey. Educa. R. 47:325–42. (Ap. '14.)

Thompson, George. Prevocational education in England. Voca. Educa. 3:239–48. (Mr. '14.)

Tuttle, Edith M. Vocational education for girls. Educa. 34:445–58. (Mr. '14.)

Witmer, Lightner. The Montessori method. Psychol. Clinic 8:1–5. (Mr. '14.)

Wolcott, John D. comp. Monthly record of current educational publications. U.S. Bur. of Educa. Bulletin, 1914, No. 3. (Fe. '14); No. 7. (Mr. 6, '14.)

VOLUME XIV NUMBER 10

THE ELEMENTARY SCHOOL TEACHER

JUNE 1914

EDUCATIONAL NEWS AND EDITORIAL COMMENT

A Rural-School Inquiry

Last fall a commission was appointed by resolution of the Minnesota Educational Association to investigate rural-school conditions in Minnesota. The first of a series of lists of questions to collect information from different available sources has been reported in the *Minneapolis Tribune*. This list is addressed to patrons of the rural schools in each of the eighty-six counties. As a preliminary step in an investigation such an action commends itself. It furnishes an opportunity to determine in a rough way the real feeling of the patrons in regard to the much-discussed question of the efficiency of their schools. Moreover, the questions will have the tendency to make such criticisms as may be given somewhat specific. And not least of all, attention is called through the questions to the possibility of helpful service on the part of the patrons themselves in making their schools what they should be.

The list of questions follows:

Are you satisfied with the progress your children are making in your rural school?

If not, why not?

Is your teacher properly trained?

Is your school well heated, ventilated, and equipped?

What are *you* doing to improve your school?

H. T. M.

In view of the large amount of federal legislation which is projected for the aid of vocational education, Congress created a Commission on Vocational Education. This commission is charged with the duty of finding out the needs for vocational education and whether or not national grants to stimulate the state are necessary to promote any of the desirable forms of vocational education. The members of the commission are Senator Hoke Smith, of Georgia, *chairman;* Senator Carroll S. Page, of Vermont; Representative D. M. Hughes, of Georgia; Representative S. D. Foss, of Ohio; John A. Lapp, director of the Bureau of Legislative Information, Indianapolis, Indiana; Miss Florence Marshall, principal of the Manhattan Trade School, New York City; Miss Agnes Nestor, president of the International Glove Workers' Union, Chicago; Charles A. Prosser, Secretary of the National Society for the Promotion of Industrial Education, New York; Charles A. Winslow, Bureau of Labor, Washington, D.C.

The National Commission on Vocational Education

This commission will report about June 1. In the meantime it has been holding meetings in Washington collecting information of all sorts from different departments of the government and from various national organizations that are interested in the problem. A brief was submitted by Commissioner Claxton, of the Bureau of Education, giving an account of the work of that bureau. The Bureau of Domestic and Foreign Commerce also contributed a report. The Department of Agriculture, which has long been engaged in vocational training in agriculture, presented a full report. The Department of Labor has also for many years been gathering information, and this bureau gave its findings to the commission. Of particular interest to the commission were the facts from the Navy and War Department presented by Commander C. B. Brittain, of the navy, and Captain Douglas MacArthur, of the Engineer Corps of the army, concerning the way in which the army and navy are preparing their men for vocations in the army and navy, which preparation the men carry with them into civil life when their terms of enlistment expire. Both departments have for many years developed this service in order to prepare men for their immediate needs in the vocations directly connected with the army and navy. It was stated that fully 10 per cent of the enlisted men of the army get training in vocational work.

The commission also has the assistance of many educational organizations, including the National Education Association, the Association of State Universities, the National Manufacturers' Association, etc.

The outcome of this investigation will certainly be a very much larger intelligence about our national problems of vocational education. Practically all of those who have appeared before the commission have been very urgent in their plea that the central government support and co-operate in the development of vocational education. But whatever may be the outcome in the way of legislation of this commission's work, it is certain that we shall have a most interesting report dealing with the general problem.

Children between Fourteen and Sixteen

The following statement of investigations made in Boston with regard to children between fourteen and sixteen years of age is taken from the *City School Circular* of the Bureau of Education:

Superintendent F. B. Dyer, of Boston, has just completed a study of the distribution of Boston children between fourteen and sixteen years of age.

As a result of this study it is made quite evident:

That the number of Boston children between fourteen and sixteen years of age who are attending school somewhere is at least 20 per cent greater than has been generally estimated. The general conclusion reached, from investigations in other large cities and from state-wide studies and reports hitherto made in Massachusetts and elsewhere, has been that about 50 per cent of all children of this age are in school and that about 50 per cent are out of school. It appears from this report that 70.4 per cent of all Boston children of this age are in school and only 29.6 per cent are out of school.

Summarized, the distribution of Boston children fourteen to sixteen years of age is shown to be as follows, based on a canvass made in January, 1914:

1. Attending school: (*a*) in the Boston public schools, January 1, 1914—13,509; (*b*) in the Boston parochial schools and all other Catholic educational institutions in Boston, January 1, 1914—1,705; (*c*) children resident in Boston attending other private schools (61 schools and institutions), January 1, 1914—1,278. Total—16,492 (70.4 per cent).

2. Legally employed in business houses or permitted to remain at home: (*a*) different children holding employment certificates, January 1, 1914—4,555;

(*b*) children holding permits to engage in profitable employment at home, January 1, 1914—86. Total—4,641 (19.8 per cent).

3. Unaccounted for: This number represents the difference between the probable whole number of fourteen- to sixteen-year children in the city and the number known to be in school or legally employed. It includes all of those who were remaining at home prior to September 1, 1913, and who have not returned to school as required by the present law; those who are presumed to be illegally employed; and those who may be classified as "on the streets"—2,298 (9.8 per cent). Total—23,431 (100 per cent).

The assumed number of fourteen- to sixteen-year children in the city, namely, 23,431, varies hardly at all from an estimate based on the average yearly increase (Boston and Hyde Park) for the ten years immediately preceding the period 1910–14 (United States census 1900 and 1910). Taking the latter as a basis of calculation the estimate would be 23,456.

The Los Angeles Situation

The city of Los Angeles is contributing another item to the history of controversies between boards of education and superintendents. It will be remembered by those who have followed the history of this school system that the last superintendent of schools had a good many difficulties in carrying on the work of public education in that city. The present superintendent has been re-elected for a term of years by a majority of the board, but the minority members of the board think it wise to make a public statement in which they charge various deficiencies and lay various irregularities at the door of the present superintendent.

Certainly the outcome of such a controversy as this is not advantageous to education. There ought to be some method of settling these problems of administration in our American schools. One begins to look with some admiration upon the English teachers' organization which would follow up a case of this sort through its representative and have a corporate opinion with regard to the justice or injustice of the position taken on various sides. We have had too many exhibitions in recent years of unjustifiable political meddling with the work of the schools. If teachers cannot defend themselves individually against such political interference, then there ought to be some court of decision including teachers who can bring support to any individual member of the profession who is unjustifiably hard pressed by those who wish for personal reasons to interfere with the work of the schools.

The present writer has absolutely no knowledge of the merits pro or con of the controversy in Los Angeles. The presumption, in view of the history of that school system, is that the superintendent is being interfered with. This presumption ought certainly to bring to the assistance of this superintendent the careful and well-formulated wisdom of his fellows in the profession. He ought to have some means of getting an examination from his point of view of the situation, and the results of this examination ought to be given to the public as of more value than the public announcement made by the minority members of the board.

Tests of Summer Pupils

Superintendent L. J. Montgomery, of the schools of South Bend, Indiana, contributes the following report to the study which was made of children who attended the summer session of the elementary schools in that city last year:

The Courtis arithmetic tests were given to the 6A grade in May and the same children took an examination furnished by Courtis, which in his estimation was as different as the first one, in September. In fact, a great many of the combinations were the same, but arranged in a different order.

In the first school we found that when the entire room was considered the results in September as compared with May were very nearly alike; that is, we found that in addition, subtraction, and multiplication the September report was poorer than the May, whereas the division, the rights in speed reasoning, and the rights in fundamental were better.

To get a better comparison and a safer result we next compared the grades of those in summer school made in May with the grades made in September, and the same in regard to the class of children which did not attend summer school. Thus the children under both conditions are compared with themselves.

We found in the first school those who did not attend summer school to be poorer in September than in May in addition, multiplication, division, fundamental attempts, in copying figures, in speed reasoning, and in fundamental rights, while those who attended the summer school the eight weeks we found to be stronger in addition, multiplication, division, copying figures, fundamental attempts, fundamental rights, and reasoning attempts in September than in May. While the gain is not very great, it is at least noticeable.

In the second school those not in summer school were weaker in September in addition, subtraction, multiplication, division, speed reasoning, speed rights, fundamental attempts, fundamental rights, reasoning attempts, and reasoning rights. In fact, the only place in which these pupils excelled in

September the May grade was in copying figures, while in this same school those who attended summer school were stronger in September than in May in addition, subtraction, the same in multiplication, stronger in division, stronger in copying figures, in speed-reasoning rights, in fundamental rights, and in reasoning rights, while they had depreciated in speed-reasoning attempts, and in fundamental attempts.

We know that ordinarily poorer work is accomplished for the first few weeks in the fall than is done in the spring, and this was proved by the tests given to those children who did not attend summer school. This result is due, of course, to the long summer vacation. Upon consideration of the tests made upon the children who attended the summer session of eight weeks, we find that they were better prepared in September to take up the arithmetic work than they were in May.

The conclusion drawn from this, of course, is that the summer session increased the arithmetical ability of these children, whereas the ability of children usually declines during the summer months.

The following item is clipped from the *Post* of Houston, Texas:

"Chamber of Commerce Day"

"Chamber of Commerce Day" was celebrated in the Houston public schools Monday, talks being made by citizens of Houston in every school.

Twenty-one speakers accepted commissions to address the students on civic patriotism topics, and for a half-hour in every schoolroom in the city the speakers told about civic pride, civic loyalty, and the future in store for the coming men and women of Houston.

The day was arranged by the Chamber of Commerce in conjunction with Superintendent P. W. Horn, and great interest was manifested by everyone concerned.

Gardening by School Children

From numerous clippings which refer to school-garden activities three may be selected which show how widespread the movement is. These items are timely, too, because they set forth very clearly the possibilities of carrying on some regular work during the coming summer. At Erie, Pennsylvania, as reported by the *Dispatch* of that city, sixty garden plots have been donated by owners and more than forty families have applied for membership in a garden club. Before spring is fairly begun it is believed that seventy-five families will belong to the club and more than one hundred and fifty lots will be in use. The work is being conducted under the general supervision of the Associated Charities, and a representative of this organization is carrying on the work of instructing the children. The children from the sixth, seventh, and eighth grades of schools No. 1 and No. 2 are becoming, it is reported, practical gardeners.

In the Middle West, the city of Indianapolis is setting a good example in this matter. The new Technical High School is organizing the work of the high-school students and is in a general way supervising agricultural education throughout the city, but "in the common schools the simplest elements of gardening are being taught," as reported by the *Indianapolis Star*, "and the students are made familiar with the common garden plants and how to grow them. Simple lessons in fertilization are given and the students raise tomatoes, cabbage plants, lettuce, beans, and other vegetables." Throughout the summer this work is to go on, being somewhat definitely systematized by a summer agricultural course in connection with the Technical High School. There a small rental is to be charged for the use of the garden lots, which rental will be used in improving the ground for later work.

In Portland, Oregon, as reported by the *Journal* of that city, 10,600 boys and girls have enrolled this year in the school-garden contest. This represents a substantial increase over last year. The large amount of gardening which is done in Portland has often been commented upon. The following details show how the ground is secured for this work:

> The work in some places is taking on the character of regular school work. In rooms where the entire school is interested children come for garden work and study twice a week. In other schools most of the work is done outside of school hours. In a great many places ground is limited and can be used only for school-garden demonstration purposes. Thus the children are taught how to conduct their home gardens more efficiently. Ground near other schools is of area sufficient to provide each pupil above the third grade with an individual plot varying from 35 to 108 square feet. Those below the fourth grade work together by rooms. This method has been followed in several schools. Where ground is limited in connection with several other schools a section is assigned to each room and a row or part of a row to each pupil.

Other details are given in the article to which reference has been made, but each of the statements from eastern, middle, and western sections of the country shows the spread of this movement and its importance. If children who have to stay in the cities during the summer could have the advantage of a little training and also the advantage of the inspiration which comes from this general movement, they undoubtedly would use their summer vacations to much greater advantage and would at the same time be contributing to their knowledge of science and practical activities.

Reforming American Schools on German Patterns

Mr. Miles, chairman of the Industrial Commission of the State of Wisconsin, is known as a critic of the public-school system and a vigorous advocate of industrial education as a substitute for much that is done at the present time in our public schools. The *Beacon*, of Aurora, Illinois, reports an address given by Mr. Miles on March 20 in that city. In this address Mr. Miles is reported as saying: "Of the four greatest manufacturing nations of the world we of the United States are the most stupid. . . . . We can produce more than any other nation. We are the youngest and most self-reliant, but we must first of all cultivate the human resources, which give value to all other resources." He then pointed out the fact that we export great quantities of raw material, but leave it for other nations to work over this material into finished form. "We must sell brains and not materials. We ship cotton to Europe for forty cents a pound and buy it back at forty dollars a pound. We sell steel at one cent a pound and buy it back at two dollars to ten dollars." The deficiency which is here pointed out Mr. Miles would correct by the adoption of a system of industrial education which he has observed in Germany. This thesis he defends by referring to the work of the Munich schools and by repeating the criticism which Dr. Kerschensteiner made of our American schools.

One can sympathize with Mr. Miles's criticism of the American public schools without being driven to any such conclusion as that which he defends. In fact, it is a commonplace with all serious thinkers that no system of education can be borrowed or transferred bodily from one nation to another. If one is tempted to advocate the adoption of the German system for the United States, it is certainly his duty to consider carefully the whole of the German system as well as the national spirit that makes that system possible.

Before we can borrow Germany's industrial education we must consider the relation of industrial education to the other types of education in that country. Whether one wishes to develop a German spirit and system of education in this country is a large problem. In the May issue of this journal the writer of this note recorded some of his observations in the *Volksschule* of Germany. To his own mind these observations make it very certain that we cannot and ought not to adopt in America a system of schools like those which Germany has.

Shortening the Elementary Course

The following news item contributes new evidence that the elementary-school course should be shortened, at least for many pupils:

In a "rapid-advancement class" in Boston, composed of the 36 brightest pupils of the fifth and sixth grades, and placed under the direction of one teacher from entrance to completion of course, the children finished all the work of the sixth, seventh, and eighth grades in a year and a half. Only one hour a day was allowed these pupils for outside study.

School Sites in Chicago

Some time ago widespread currency was given to the charge that the board of education of the city of Chicago had paid excessive prices for certain school sites. Later a subcommittee of the School Sites Investigating Committee found there was justification for the charge. They found that in the last two years so-called "syndicates" had been speculating in school sites. The ground it was known the board wished to buy would be bought up by the "syndicates" and then sold to the board at an excessive figure. The publicity given to the matter and the investigation of the committee seem to have stopped for the time the operations of these "syndicates," but the committee sets forth some recommendations as to future purchases of school sites. They recommend:

Publicity to proposed locations of school sites.

The abandonment of the offering of absurdly low original prices, resulting in condemnation suits.

The appointment of a standing committee to deal directly with property-owners.

The appointment of a standing committee to determine the prices to be paid property-owners.

The employment of real estate experts to report on transactions.

The appointment, by the city council Committee on Schools, Fire, Police, and Civil Service, of a standing committee to report on school sites and the reasonableness of the prices to be paid for them.

H. T. M.

The following is taken from the February number of the *New Zealand Journal of Education:*

An International Book for Children

An international book for children is about to be issued from Tokyo on quite novel lines. It will contain simple articles and stories in French, English, and Japanese, and drawings and photographs of children of many nations. The idea of the editor, Mr. M. Hikosaka, of 33 Abekawamacni, Asakusa, Tokyo, is that by this means a great deal may be done to promote mutual sympathy and understanding between East and West, the period of childhood being deeply impressionable. He is anxious to receive the addresses of kindergartens and similar schools which would accept the magazine as a free gift when issued.

H. T. M.

ECONOMY OF TIME IN ARITHMETIC

WALTER A. JESSUP
College of Education, State University of Iowa

In September of 1913 a questionnaire was sent by Dr. Coffman, of the University of Illinois, and myself to the city superintendents listed in the directory of the United States Bureau of Education, which includes practically all of the cities with a population of 4,000 and over—about 1,700 in all. The same questionnaire was sent to every sixth county superintendent in the United States.

The questions were answered by 52 per cent of the city superintendents, and by 24 per cent of the county superintendents. Returns were received from practically every sized city in the country. However, the larger cities were a little better represented in the matter of replies than were the smaller cities and rural districts. Each section of the country was well represented in returns. Thus it can be said that the data here submitted represent the attitude of one-half of the superintendents distributed quite evenly over the country as to size of city and geographical location.

Questionnaire

ECONOMY OF TIME AS RELATED TO MATERIAL USED IN ARITHMETIC

City.....................State......................

Underscore once the subjects which should receive slight attention; underscore twice the subjects which should be eliminated: apothecaries' weight, troy weight, furlong, rood in square measure, dram, quarter in avoirdupois weight, surveyors' tables, foreign money, folding paper, reduction of more than two steps, long measure of G.C.D., L.C.M., true discount, cube root, partnership, compound proportion, compound and complex fractions, cases in percentage, annual interest, longitude and time, unreal fractions, alligation, metric system, progression, aliquot parts.

Others...

Underscore the subjects which should receive more attention than is usually given: addition, subtraction, multiplication, division, fractions, percentage, interest, saving and loaning money, banking, borrowing, building and loan associations, investments, bonds and stocks, taxes, levies, public expenditures, insurance as protection and investment, profits in business, public utilities.

ECONOMY OF TIME AS RELATED TO THE METHOD USED IN TEACHING

Percentage of recitation time in arithmetic which should be given over to *strictly drill* exercises in each grade.

Grade	1	2	3	4	5	6	7	8	9
Percentage	___	___	___	___	___	___	___	___	___

Percentage of recitation time in arithmetic which should be given over to *rationalization* work in each grade.

Grade	1	2	3	4	5	6	7	8	9
Percentage	___	___	___	___	___	___	___	___	___

Approximate number of minutes *per week* given over to recitations in arithmetic in *your* schools in each grade.

Grade	1	2	3	4	5	6	7	8	9
No. Minutes	___	___	___	___	___	___	___	___	___

Remarks:..
....
....
....
....

Signed.................City....................

MANIPULATION OF DATA[1]

The returns were distributed so as to reveal differences, if any, between the responses of school men in the different sections of the country and for the cities of different sizes. Some of the superintendents answered only a part of the questions; hence the totals in the various parts of the report are not all the same. All doubtful answers were eliminated or checked by means of a supplementary inquiry asking for verification of statement.

MATERIAL USED IN ARITHMETIC

The percentage of superintendents who favored elimination was calculated so as to show the difference in attitude toward each of the twenty-five topics suggested. A large percentage favored

[1] This report would have been impossible had it not been for the painstaking statistical work done by a group of students in the graduate seminar in the College of Education, State University of Iowa. The following men assumed the chief responsibility: James Richardson, Chester Buckner, H. W. Anderson.

the elimination of certain formal subjects such as alligation, cube root, unreal fractions, progression, etc., and certain more or less obsolete tables such as paper-folding, surveyors' measure, etc. Table I shows the exact distribution for each subject.

TABLE I

PERCENTAGE OF SUPERINTENDENTS WHO FAVOR ELIMINATION OF THE TOPICS, DISTRIBUTED SO AS TO REVEAL DIFFERENCES IN ATTITUDE IN LARGE CITIES, CITIES AND COUNTIES, AND FOR ALL CITIES

Topic	Cities of 100,000 and Over	Cities and Counties	All Cities
	Per Cent	Per Cent	Per Cent
Apothecaries' weight	72	51	53
Troy weight	75	40	42
Furlong	85	70	72
Rood in square measure	13	19	20
Dram	78	58	60
Quarter in avoirdupois	81	66	68
Surveyors' tables	72	43	47
Foreign money	25	27	28
Folding paper	63	34	35
Reduction of more than two steps	25	21	22
Long measure of G.C.D.	66	33	35
Least common multiple	25	20	22
True discount	66	44	47
Cube root	56	41	46
Partnership	50	23	25
Compound proportion	72	49	52
Compound and complex fractions	28	24	26
Cases in percentage	28	18	20
Annual interest	63	40	41
Longitude and time	13	7	8
Unreal fractions	72	70	74
Alligation	88	82	85
Metric system	41	19	20
Progression	88	63	67
Aliquot parts	9	19	21

Many superintendents who did not go so far as to favor absolute elimination did favor the plan of giving less attention to these subjects. Table II shows the percentage of superintendents distributed for each subject.

Chart I is made up by combining Tables I and II and reveals the attitude of 867 superintendents toward these topics. The cross-hatched portion indicates the percentage of superintendents who favor the elimination of each of these subjects; the shaded portion indicates the percentage of superintendents who favor giving less attention to each of these subjects; and the unshaded portion indicates the percentage of superintendents who are satisfied with the present status. It is seen from Chart I that the superintendents are overwhelmingly inclined to favor the elimination or at least a lessening of emphasis on these subjects.

TABLE II

PERCENTAGE OF SUPERINTENDENTS WHO FAVOR THE PLAN OF GIVING LESS ATTENTION TO THE TOPICS, DISTRIBUTED SO AS TO REVEAL DIFFERENCES IN ATTITUDE IN LARGE CITIES, CITIES AND COUNTIES, AND FOR ALL CITIES

Topic	Cities of 100,000 and Over	Cities and Counties	All Cities
Apothecaries' weight	31	37	36
Troy weight	32	46	44
Furlong	12	20	19
Rood in square measure	37	39	42
Dram	18	24	23
Quarter in avoirdupois	14	17	17
Surveyors' tables	40	40	40
Foreign money	47	57	57
Folding paper	31	34	35
Reduction of more than two steps	45	46	48
Long measure of G.C.D	47	39	40
Least common multiple	50	44	45
True discount	27	31	31
Cube root	34	39	37
Partnership	39	43	44
Compound proportion	38	33	32
Compound and complex fractions	49	42	44
Cases in percentage	36	34	35
Annual interest	35	32	31
Longitude and time	55	55	56
Unreal fractions	9	17	15
Alligation	4	10	9
Metric system	42	42	44
Progression	12	21	20
Aliquot parts	28	31	32

Analyses of these data indicate that the superintendents of the larger cities are inclined to favor more elimination than are the superintendents of the smaller cities. The returns from the county superintendents who represent the rural schools seem to reveal no striking differences in attitude.

Analyses of the replies on the basis of the geographical sections of the country indicate that there is a slight difference between the North and the South, but this is no greater than the difference to be found between the North Central division and the North Atlantic division.

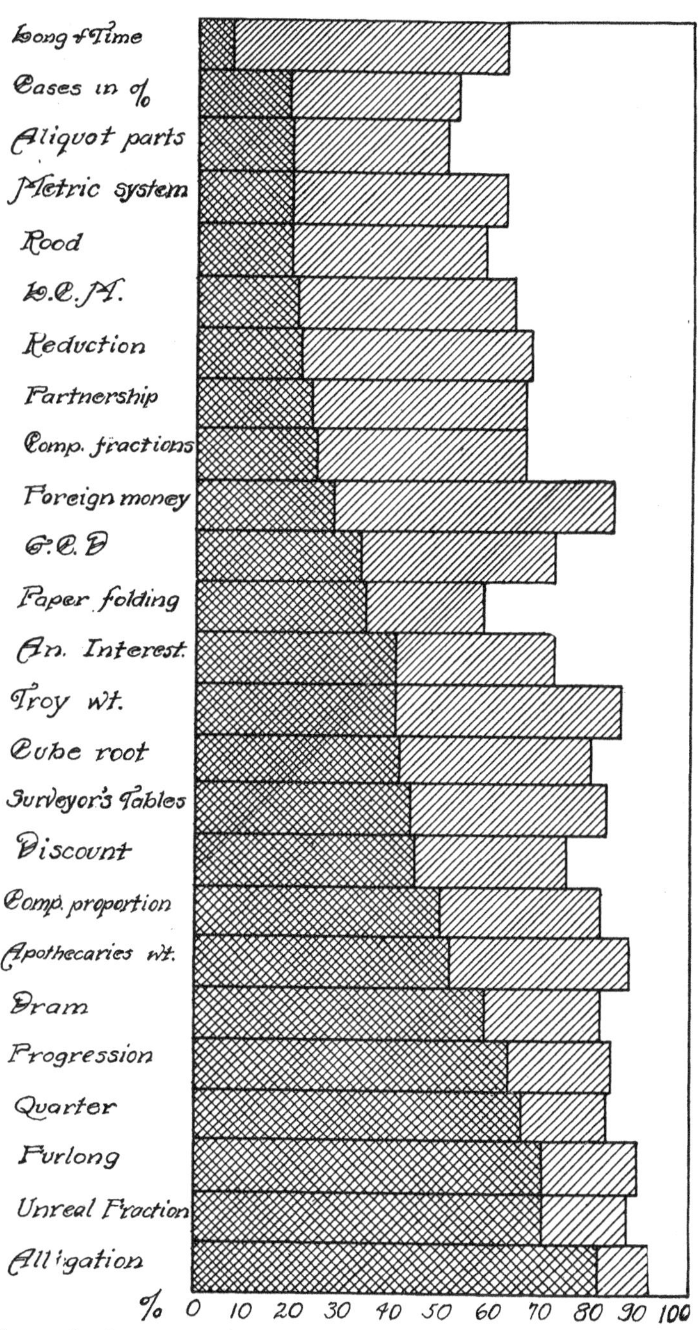

CHART I.—Percentage of superintendents who favor "elimination" or "less attention" (830 cities represented).

After distributing and tabulating the material in order to learn of differences in cities of different sizes in different sections of the country, it seems safe to say that the differences are so slight that Chart I can be taken as a representative measure of the attitude of the superintendents of the country toward the elimination or decrease of attention in regard to the different topics in the list.

ADDITIONAL EMPHASIS

The percentage of the superintendents who favored the plan of increasing the emphasis upon certain subjects was tabulated so as to show the different attitudes toward each of the subjects suggested. A large percentage were in favor of giving more emphasis to the fundamental subjects such as addition, subtraction, multiplication, and division. There was also a very strong sentiment in favor of increasing the emphasis on the applications of arithmetic to the social and economic conditions of the day; such as the saving and loaning of money, taxation, public expenditure, insurance, etc. Table III shows the exact distribution for each subject.

TABLE III

PERCENTAGE OF SUPERINTENDENTS WHO FAVOR THE PLAN OF GIVING MORE ATTENTION TO THE TOPICS LISTED, SO AS TO REVEAL DIFFERENCES IN ATTITUDE IN LARGE CITIES, CITIES AND COUNTIES, AND FOR ALL CITIES

Topic	Cities of 100,000 and Over	Cities and Counties	All Cities
Addition	59	75	75
Subtraction	50	68	69
Multiplication	59	72	72
Division	56	69	70
Fractions	56	66	65
Percentage	31	51	50
Interest	25	41	39
Saving and loaning money	50	61	61
Banking	38	40	39
Borrowing	22	37	37
Building and loan associations	13	46	48
Investments	16	44	44
Bonds and stocks	9	20	20
Taxes	25	53	53
Levies	6	36	35
Public expenditure	28	54	55
Insurance	31	54	55
Profits	28	47	46
Public utilities	34	57	57

The replies were also tabulated on the basis of size of the different cities represented. The superintendents of the larger cities seemed to be less inclined to favor an increase in attention to these subjects. This may be due to the fact that these cities are already giving more emphasis to these subjects than are the small cities.

The replies were tabulated on the basis of the geographical sections of the country. Only a slight difference was found in this particular. The South is perhaps slightly better satisfied with present conditions. This may be due to a situation similar to that in the large city. Chart II, based on the returns from all cities, seems safely to represent the present attitude toward the increased emphasis upon these topics. The shaded portion indicates the percentage of superintendents who favor giving more attention to each of these subjects.

POSSIBLE ECONOMY OF TIME

In connection with the special problem in which the committee is interested—namely, to find out if conditions are favorable for effecting an economy of time by means of the elimination of certain subjects, or by means of reducing the time being given these subjects—it seems reasonable to say that the time gained from this elimination or decreased attention to the twenty-five foregoing subjects may wisely be given to the seventeen subjects which demand more attention. While it is true that it is impossible to say how much time will be saved through this change in emphasis, it should be borne in mind that the superintendents overwhelmingly favor increased emphasis on the fundamental divisions of arithmetic—addition, multiplication, subtraction, and division. Surely, with more thorough instruction in these fundamental subjects, a distinct saving of time might be gained. It should be noted that the method of learning most of the twenty-five subjects is through memory, while the method of learning the new subjects is, with the exception of the fundamentals, largely through thinking or rationalization. It is believed that the superintendents may wisely adopt the plan of lessening the emphasis upon the twenty-five subjects and uniformly increasing the emphasis on the seventeen subjects. Surely, this is in the direction of a more *economical use* of time.

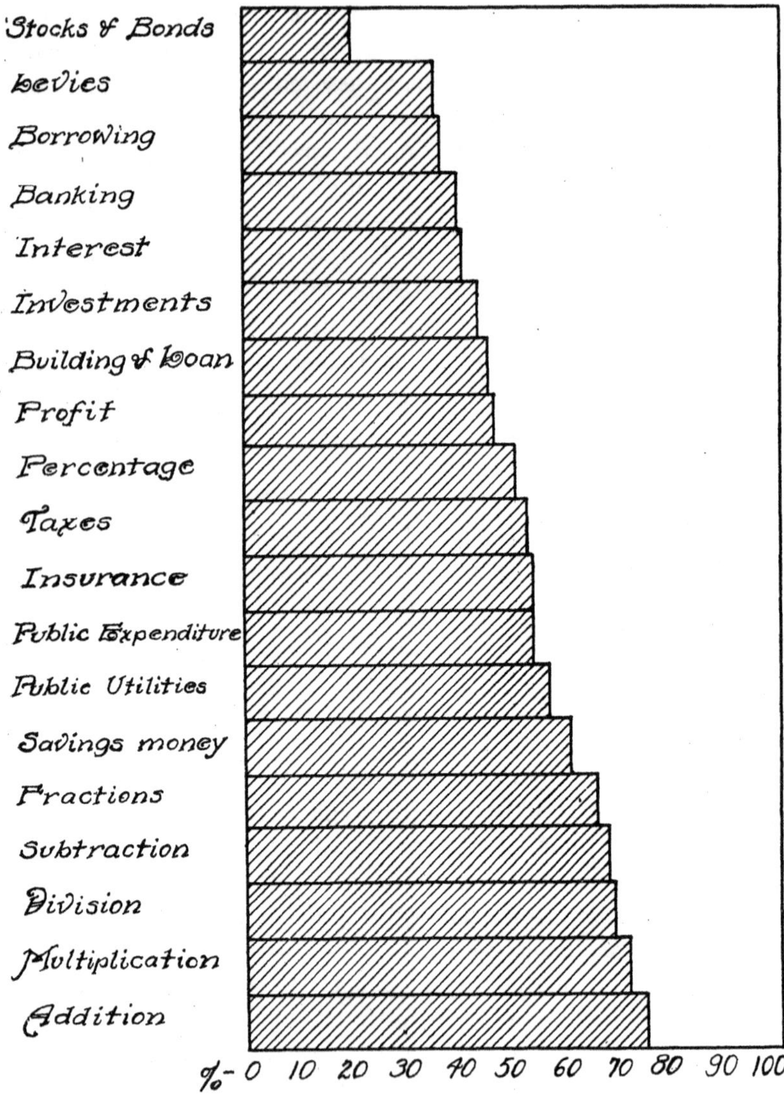

CHART II.—Percentage of superintendents who favor giving more attention to each of these topics (830 cities represented).

AMOUNT OF TIME GIVEN TO THE RECITATION OF ARITHMETIC

Reports were received from 630 superintendents showing the actual time distribution for the recitation in arithmetic in each grade in each city. The wide variation found in time expenditure is shown in Table IV. This table should be read as follows: in

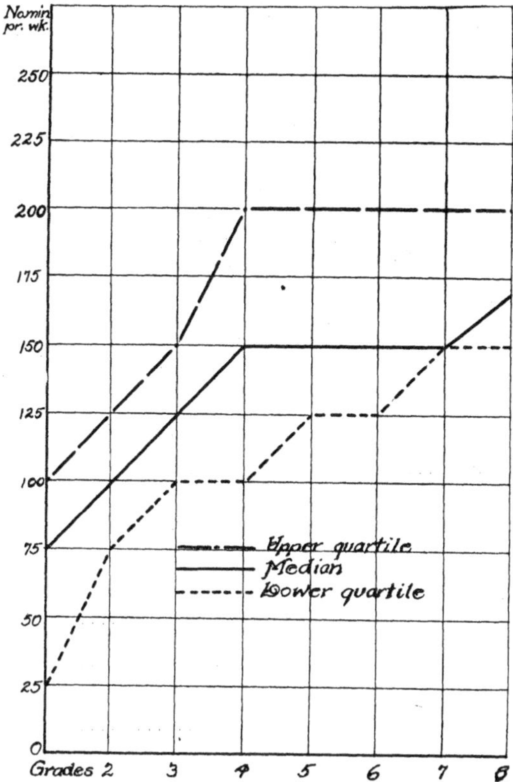

CHART III.—Showing median and quartile distribution of time per week given over to recitations.

the first grade 136 cities allow no time for arithmetic, 7 allow 15 minutes per week, 18 allow 25 minutes per week, and so on down the column. (Extreme cases were verified by supplementary correspondence, so that the variations here indicated are truly descriptive of variations in practice.)

Chart III shows graphically the variation and the central tendency in practice. It is seen that the median time spent in

TABLE IV

No. Minutes per Week	Grades								
	1st	2d	3d	4th	5th	6th	7th	8th	9th
0	136	31	4	.....	.....	.....	.....	24	439
15	7	2	.....	.....	.....	.....	.....	.....	.....
20	.....	.....	.....	.....	.....	.....	.....	.....	.....
25	18	1	1	1	1	.....	.....	.....	.....
30	10	7	5	1	.....	1	1	1	.....
35	1	.....	.....	.....	.....	.....	.....	.....	.....
40	6	4	2	5	2	1	.....	1	2
45	.....	.....	.....	.....	.....	.....	.....	.....	.....
50	99	36	3	1	4	4	2	2	.....
55	.....	.....	.....	.....	.....	.....	.....	.....	.....
60	27	22	10	5	3	4	5	5	4
65	1	.....	.....	.....	.....	.....	.....	.....	.....
70	3	3	1	1	1	1	2	1	1
75	103	127	59	12	4	.....	.....	2	.....
80	6	5	10	11	2	3	1	1	1
85	.....	.....	.....	.....	.....	.....	.....	.....	.....
90	5	6	12	3	4	2	3	3	2
95	.....	.....	.....	.....	.....	.....	.....	.....	.....
100	108	83	156	129	71	31	14	10	3
05	.....	.....	.....	.....	.....	.....	.....	.....	.....
10	1	1	6	5	3	.....	.....	2	1
15	.....	.....	.....	.....	.....	.....	.....	.....	.....
20	6	10	13	13	12	19	22	18	4
125	17	40	90	113	132	109	59	36	5
30	.....	3	4	5	6	9	3	.....	2
35	.....	.....	.....	.....	.....	.....	.....	.....	.....
40	.....	.....	2	4	6	1	9	8	2
45	.....	.....	.....	.....	.....	.....	.....	.....	.....
150	53	66	98	129	158	196	210	192	30
55	.....	.....	.....	.....	.....	.....	.....	.....	.....
60	1	2	4	4	6	2	7	8	5
65	.....	.....	.....	.....	.....	.....	.....	.....	.....
70	.....	.....	2	3	3	1	.....	2	.....
175	6	8	9	20	31	28	35	37	6
80	2	5	6	3	5	9	16	15	4
85	.....	.....	.....	.....	.....	.....	.....	.....	.....
90	.....	1	.....	.....	.....	1	.....	.....	.....
95	.....	.....	.....	.....	.....	.....	.....	.....	.....
200	11	33	54	56	52	72	96	121	60
05	.....	.....	.....	.....	.....	.....	.....	.....	.....
10	.....	3	2	.....	1	.....	2	5	7
15	.....	.....	.....	.....	.....	.....	.....	.....	.....
20	.....	1	1	2	1	1	1	2	2
225	4	10	25	19	22	28	31	38	27

TABLE IV—*Continued*

No. Minutes per Week	Grades								
	1st	2d	3d	4th	5th	6th	7th	8th	9th
30	......	......	......	1	1	2	2	2	......
35	......	......	......	......	......	......	......	......	......
40	......	4	8	8	4	4	4	7	1
45	......	......	......	......	......	......	......	......	......
250	1	9	25	39	51	51	45	34	13
55	......	......	......	......	......	......	......	......	......
60	......	1	......	1	1	2	2	2	......
65	......	......	......	......	......	......	......	......	......
70	......	......	1	1	4	3	2	1	1
275	......	2	2	8	7	9	8	5	1
To 300	......	4	14	24	30	30	38	33	5
To 350	......	......	......	3	2	3	7	8	2
To 450	1	1	1	......	......	......	2	3	......

the first grade for the United States as a whole is 75 minutes; for the second grade, 150 minutes; for the third grade, 125 minutes; for the fourth, fifth, sixth, and seventh grades, 150 minutes; for the eighth grade, 165 minutes. This means that one-half of the cities spend this amount of time or more in the various grades, and one-half this amount of time or less. The 25 percentile shows that one-fourth of the cities spend 25 minutes or less in the first grade; 75 minutes or less in the second grade; 100 minutes or less in the third and fourth grades; 125 minutes or less in the fifth and sixth grades; and 150 minutes or less in the seventh and eighth grades. Again, the upper quartile brings out the fact that another fourth of the cities spend 100 minutes or more in the first grade; 125 minutes or more in the second grade; 150 minutes or more in the third grade; 200 minutes or more in the fourth, fifth, sixth, seventh, and eighth grades. Thus, from the foregoing analysis it may be seen that some spend relatively far more time than others on arithmetic. Comparison of the 157 cities spending the greatest amount of time with the 157 cities spending the least amount of time indicates that already many of these cities are making headway in the economy of time. May we not look to these cities for suggestions? If one-fourth of the cities can get satisfactory results with an expenditure of from 5 to 20 minutes per day or less in the first to fourth grades, there is reason for inquiry as to the accomplishment of cities which spend from 20 to 40 minutes or more per day during the first to fourth grades. Again, if one-fourth of the cities are able to get satisfactory results in from 20 to 30 minutes per day or less in the fifth to eighth grades, certainly we have cause to question the reason why another fourth of the cities spend from 40 to 60 minutes or more per day in these grades. On the whole, it seems safe to say that the wide variation of recitation time in the various cities of the United States suggests the possibility of attempting to effect an economy of time by means of standardizing the number of minutes in the recitation period.

A comparison of the actual results obtained in cities giving a large amount of time to the recitations in arithmetic with the cities giving a small amount of time would be invaluable in arriving at this standard amount of recitation time for each grade. It may be said, however, that practically all of the investigations which have been made thus far on this subject indicate that there is less relation between the time expenditure and the achievement than many have supposed. In other words, from these investigations, we have no reason to expect that city A which gives twice as much time as city B to arithmetic will get results in the same proportion.

It would seem that the conservative superintendent who is spending a relatively large amount of time on arithmetic might safely reduce the time at least to the median for the country for each grade. The less conservative superintendent might reduce the time to the 25 percentile without endangering his school, while the radical superintendent might join the 157 who spend still less time on the arithmetic recitation. Thus, the 50 per cent of the cities spending the most time might simply join the 50 per cent spending the least time. Surely, this plan need not frighten even the most cautious, because half of the cities have already tried out the reduction plan.

It is noteworthy that the North Atlantic and South Atlantic states spend from 25 to 50 per cent more time in arithmetic than do the cities in the other parts of the country. It would be interesting to compare the arithmetical efficiency of the schools in the different sections.

Large cities seem to give more time to arithmetic recitations than do smaller cities, although the difference is not great. The county superintendents reporting on rural schools report a very much smaller proportion of time given to the arithmetic recitation. This is, no doubt, due to the difference in the organization of the daily program in the rural schools.

However, these differences in practice are not so great as to make it impossible for the adoption of the sliding standard suggested above. No section or city differs so much from the central tendency as to make it difficult to work toward some part of the lower half of the curve of time distribution for recitations in each grade.

DISTRIBUTION OF TIME AMONG THE DIFFERENT GRADES

It is interesting to note that the median time distribution for the grades shows a regular increase in the time given to the recitation in the classes up to the fourth grade. Chart III shows this clearly. For example, the median for the first grade is 75 minutes per week; for the second grade, 100 minutes per week; for the third grade, 125 minutes per week, and for the fourth grade, 150 minutes per week; beyond which grade there is no increase.

Certain sectional differences are found. For example, the median time in the North and South Atlantic states increases up to the seventh grade which is the maximum; while the median time in the North Central, South Central, and Western states reaches a maximum in the sixth grade. Analysis of the data indicates that the large city gives more time to arithmetic in the sixth and seventh grades than in the eighth, which is contrary to the practice in smaller cities. Such variation in practice simply emphasizes the possibility of effecting economy of time through the widespread adoption of a standard for the recitation time as suggested above.

PERCENTAGE OF RECITATION TIME GIVEN OVER TO DRILL

The superintendents were asked to make a tabular statement showing the percentage of recitation time in each grade given over to drill. Analysis of these returns revealed a wide variation in practice. Chart IV shows graphically the situation in terms of medians and quartiles for 564 cities.

It should be noted that the median percentage of time given to drill in the city schools begins in the first grade at 43 per cent, increasing to 53 per cent in the third grade, and decreasing steadily from then until the close of the eighth grade, which means that one-half of the cities spend this percentage or more of the recitation time in drill and one-half spend this percentage or less in each grade. The wide variation in practice is revealed by comparing the line which indicates the lower quartile with the line which indicates the upper quartile. That is to say, one-fourth of the cities spend 25 per cent of recitation time or less in drill in the first grade, 35 per cent or less in the third grade, decreasing to 5 per cent or less in the eighth grade; while one-fourth of the cities spend 80 per cent or more of the time in drill in the first grade, and 25 per cent or more in the eighth grade. The same variation exists in the country schools. These answers are significant in that they express the idea which the school superintendents and teachers have in regard to the emphasis which should be placed on drill in each grade. They clearly show that the distribution of time in the recitation between drill work and the so-called rationalizational work is not standardized.

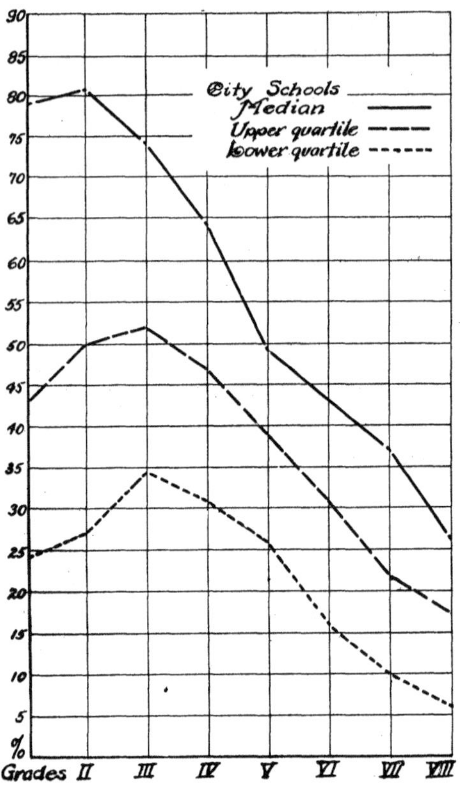

CHART IV.—Showing the median percentage of time given over to *strictly* drill work in the recitations in each grade (564 cities).

We have no adequate means of evaluating the comparative arithmetical efficiency obtained in the schools differing in the amount of time given over to drill. However, it would seem safe to say that if one-fourth of the cities are devoting 80 per cent or more of the recitation time in the third grade to drill, 50 per cent or more in the fifth grade, and 25 per cent or more in the eighth grade, we should inquire into the effectiveness of the arithmetic teaching in the 140 cities devoting 35 per cent or less of the recitation time in the third grade to drill, 26 per cent or less in the fifth grade, and 5 per cent or less in the eighth grade. In other words, such wide variation suggests the *possibility of waste in the method* at this point.

A thoroughgoing comparison of results attained in cities with widely different standards for the time given to drill would be of great value in connection with constructive recommendations. The scientific investigations on the value of drill in arithmetic have thus far been confined to a narrow range of time, grades, and other conditions. However, the results of these investigations have led to the conclusion on the part of the investigators that drill within the limits of their investigation is of decided value.

In the absence of scientific data for the evaluation of the different degrees of emphasis on drill, it is of importance to know the central tendency of existing practice based on the experience in hundreds of cities. A conservative view will no doubt tend toward the *adoption of a standard such as the median for the whole country* unless local conditions offer some specific reason to do otherwise.

Analyses of the replies on the basis of the size of cities represented revealed only slight difference in the time distribution for drill in the cities of different sizes.

Further analysis of the returns reveals the difference in different sections of the country. The North Atlantic section stands out in striking contrast to the South Atlantic section in that in the North a very much higher percentage of time is devoted to drill in the first three grades than in the South. It would be of interest to compare the arithmetical achievement in the schools of the North Atlantic division with the schools of the other sections where very much less emphasis is placed on drill in these grades.

It is significant that there is great agreement in regard to the emphasis placed on drill in the three lower grades. This is true not only for the country as a whole, but it is also true for cities of different sizes and for the different sections of the country. *Experience seems to have become standardized in regard to stage of emphasis if not as to degree of emphasis.*

SUMMARY

This study reveals the fact that there is an overwhelming tendency on the part of half of the superintendents in this country in favor of either eliminating or lessening the attention to be given to certain subjects in arithmetic such as alligation, cube root, unreal fractions, progression, and certain obsolete tables such as folding paper, surveyors' tables, etc. Again, it reveals an overwhelming attitude in favor of increased emphasis on such fundamental subjects as addition, multiplication, subtraction, and division. There is also a decidedly strong disposition to favor increased emphasis on the application of arithmetic to the social and economic conditions of the day, such as the saving and loaning of money, taxation, public expenditures, life insurance, etc.

The wide variation in the recitation time given to arithmetic as a whole, and in the different grades indicates that many cities are already effecting a large economy of time in this particular. *It is recommended that the 50 per cent of the cities spending the most time reduce this to the amount being expended by the 50 per cent of the cities spending the least time.* This plan would cut the range of practice in two, and still give opportunity for the expression of the conservative and radical points of view. This standard is shown in Chart III.

The wide variation in the percentage of time given to drill indicates the importance of scientific investigations of the relative achievements secured from the different time allotments. The median time allotment in practice now in the different grades throughout the United States most nearly represents the judgment of the school men based on their own experience. It is *suggested that this median percentage of recitation time given over to drill in each grade be adopted as a standard until scientific investigations have proven this to be in error.* This standard is shown in Chart IV.

In conclusion it should be said that this investigation clearly points to the desirability of a study of relative achievements attained in the work in arithmetic in these same schools.

THE MEASUREMENT OF THE EFFICIENCY OF INSTRUCTION IN READING

H. A. BROWN
Deputy State Superintendent, Concord, New Hampshire

One of the leading educational problems of the present day is that of measuring the efficiency of schools. In the past it has been necessary to rely upon opinion in many matters relating to the progress of children in school. There have been no adequate units until recently with which to express educational products. For this reason, the results of educational processes often have been expressed in terms of mere conjecture, which has had small scientific value. An attempt has been made during the last few years, however, to establish standards and units by which scholastic efficiency and progress in educational attainment may be measured in a definite manner and to this end experimental and statistical methods have been applied to the measurement of educational results. Since a large part of the educational practice in the past has had no scientific foundation, the results of much of the teaching have been meager, and since there have been no adequate means of measuring the efficiency of instruction, it has been impossible to determine in any precise manner what real results were being secured. To a certain extent this condition still prevails, and on that account it may be said that one of the great needs in education at the present time is the establishment of units of measurement, standards of attainment, and reliable tests in each subject by which the value of different types of instruction may be scientifically and competently measured.

There is no subject in the school curriculum in which there is a greater need that tests be devised with which to measure the accomplishment of children than reading. It is the purpose in this article to describe a test planned for this purpose which has been used by the writer to measure reading ability in seven New Hampshire school systems. A description of the test, the method of handling it, and the purpose for which it was designed are given in this article. The results of the test will be given in a future article. It was devised as an experiment to see what could be done in the way of measuring reading ability, and for the purpose of finding out how best it might be conducted. The division of educational investigation of the state educational department with the school system of the state as a laboratory is in charge of the writer and this investigation in connection with reading was undertaken as a part of the regular research work of the department.

The possibility of effectively measuring accomplishment on the part of children in school opens to the school administrator one of the most fruitful fields and one of the most promising lines of progress in the direction of the establishment of more scientific methods of teaching. With an effective means of measuring reading power it will be possible definitely to evaluate methods of teaching reading in terms of the ability of the children to read. Until this can be done the most satisfactory advance in the reconstruction of the method of instruction to secure a more efficient method will not be likely to be made. In order to attack this problem of the pedagogy of reading in a manner most favorable to progress, the method of approach must involve three distinct lines of investigation.

Reading is the greatest tool for thought-getting which an individual may have at his disposal. A comprehensive survey of the needs of the individual as a member of the social group must be made and those specific reading abilities which will function in the most serviceable way as a tool in the life of the individual must be determined. When the social needs of the individual in terms of reading power are set forth clearly in the form of certain specific reading abilities, we shall have a statement of the end to be attained by the educative process as far as this subject is concerned. This is the first great essential to progress in the right direction.

The psychology of reading has been a subject of study by a considerable group of investigators and there is at hand a respectable body of facts relating to the psychology and physiology of reading. Scientific investigation, the aim of which has been to describe the act of reading, has yielded data which are of great value to the student of experimental pedagogy. From a study of all the known facts at hand in this field the school man is able to establish certain hypotheses in regard to the method of procedure in instruction. These hypotheses will be in the form of tentative principles of teaching. We may now proceed to teach reading in accordance with the body of principles thus established. But even when a survey has been made of every known fact there is no positive assurance that the methods derived and the resulting educational practice are valid. We must have, however, working hypotheses based upon the known laws of learning and on the nature of the mental processes in children, and the most fruitful source of such hypotheses, and about the only one of great scientific value is a study of child nature in all its aspects, for it is universally recognized that knowledge regarding the laws regnant in the physical organism and predominant in the mental life of the child can furnish the only valid foundation for methods of teaching. Studies in educational psychology and experimental pedagogy have been made in large numbers and the results of these studies throw great light on many problems of teaching, especially in indicating the lines along which the most efficient and economical learning is likely to take place. The scientific school man on the basis of the data at his command is able to develop an experimental technique of instruction in the several school subjects.

A third step is necessary in establishing a valid scientific pedagogy of reading. Before we can be assured that our method is in accordance with correct principles it must be evaluated in terms of the ability of the children to read. The results of the method must be measured and it must prove its validity. As the process of evaluation proceeds, elements of efficiency will be found and elements of weakness will be discovered. A process of selection by which the former are selected and retained and the latter eliminated will now ensue, until in due time a new pedagogy of reading will be evolved which will be in harmony with the laws of the most economical learning.

This, in brief, is the method which must be pursued in all school subjects to secure satisfactory advancement in the direction of the evolution of better methods of instruction, which are so imperatively needed at the present time. The order of procedure must be: a consideration of the social needs of the individual, the formulation of an experimental technique of instruction, and the evaluation, by properly conceived tests, of the various elements which form a part of the instruction, with a constant reconstruction of method until the highest economy and efficiency are attained. The technique of teaching in every school subject must be subjected in this manner to scientific evaluation. This attitude toward problems of educational practice gives a large place to experimental pedagogy and the measurement of educational results. It is highly desirable that variations in the method of the instruction in primary reading be adopted and that systematic measurement of the results be made for the purpose of determining new elements of efficiency. This gradual rebuilding of educational practice is one of the important problems of the day as the great mass of significant facts regarding the mental processes of children and the nature of the learning process accumulates. The existence of this problem makes it imperative that a means of measuring educational products and of evaluating types of instruction be devised.

In determining reading efficiency three factors must be taken into consideration. In the first place, of two readers whose grasp of content is equally great, that reader who can read the larger amount in a given time has greater reading ability. The rate of reading, then, appears to be a very important factor. Again, of two people who can read the same amount in a given unit of time, that one whose grasp of content is greater is the better reader. In this case the reader who can reproduce the larger amount of what he has read and who can reproduce it more correctly is the more efficient. The whole question of reading efficiency reduces to this: the reader who can read the largest amount in a given unit of time, who can reproduce the largest proportion of what he has read, and who can reproduce it most correctly, is the best reader. The three things which must be accurately weighed in order to have a complete measure of reading power are: (1) rate of reading; (2) quantity of reproduction; and (3) quality of reproduction.

The reading tests prepared by the writer to determine the factors in efficient instruction in reading consisted of a printed selection for each of the grades which were tested of about a page and a half, so arranged as to have the form of the two pages of an open book when it lies before the child on the top of his desk. The two selections consisted of simple prose, easily within the comprehension of any child. The length of lines, the size of type, and the form of the page conformed to a correctly printed reading-book. At the time for the test the printed selections were given out by the teacher and placed face down on the top of each child's desk. The directions were then given and talked over until it was certain that every child understood them. Then at a signal from the teacher each child turned his paper over and began to read. At the end of a minute a second signal was given at which each child marked the word which he read last and turned his paper over. The children were now given paper and asked to write all they could remember of what they had read and for this all the time needed was given. When the directions were given the children were told that they would be asked to tell what they read but that it was desired that they read as much as they could and get the thought.

It was now possible to count the number of words which each child read and determine the rate of reading, which was expressed in words per second. Each child's written reproduction was carefully examined and the number of ideas reproduced of the total number read was determined and was expressed in the form of a percentage. For example, in the portion of the selection read by a given child there may have been forty-eight ideas and he may have reproduced twelve of those ideas. The amount reproduced of what he read was, therefore, 25 per cent. This was called quantity of reproduction. The printed selections were in a form especially adapted to the test. The sixth-grade test, for example, was chosen from a book of Indian stories and practically rewritten and put in a form which was convenient for carrying out the test. It was so arranged that the number of ideas in any portion of it could easily be determined. In ascertaining the number of ideas reproduced by each child, to get the measure of quantity, every idea was counted which was in most respects complete and in general correctly stated, even though some of the less important details were lacking. The reproductions were examined a second time and only those ideas were counted which were entirely correct in every respect and of which every detail was reproduced, though not necessarily in the words of the original. This was called quality of reproduction. We have here the three factors in reading efficiency.

But a measure of these three aspects of reading ability taken separately will not prove satisfactory. One child may have a high reading rate, a high quantity of reproduction, and a low quality. A second child may have a low reading rate and quantity and quality may both be high. It may be difficult to determine which ranks the higher. For example, suppose the averages of one grade are:

Rate of reading, 2.16 words per second.
Quantity of reproduction, 47.62 per cent.
Quality of reproduction, 39.17 per cent.

Let the averages for another grade be:

Rate of reading, 3.19 words per second.
Quantity of reproduction, 31.11 per cent.
Quality of reproduction, 29.97 per cent.

It is difficult to say at a glance just how much more reading ability one has than the other. It is necessary that some unit of measurement be established by which all reading efficiency may be measured. Accordingly a convenient unit was established. The following statement is a definition of it. One unit of reading efficiency is a reading ability in which such a rate of reading in words per second is combined with such a power of reproduction that the product of the number representing the rate and the average of the numbers representing the percentages of quantity and quality is unity. A person who can read at the rate of 0.5 words per second and whose quantity of reproduction is 3 per cent and whose quality of reproduction is 1 per cent has 1 unit of reading efficiency. A reading rate of 0.25 words per second combined with a quantity of 5 per cent and a quality of 3 per cent would also represent the same unit, as would many other variations of the three factors. Here is an entirely definite unit by which reading efficiency may be expressed adequately in a comprehensible form. There is, of course, no mathematical relation between these figures. This unit is adopted arbitrarily as a convenient means of expressing reading power in definite comparable units. Any child's reading efficiency may be found by taking the product of the number representing reading rate and the average of the numbers representing the quantity and quality of reproduction. In this computation the average of the percentages of quantity and quality, as, for example, 41.15 per cent, is regarded as the number 41.15 and is multiplied by the rate. If the rate in this case was 2.15 words per second, the number of reading units would be the product of these two, or 88.47.

Reading material of different degrees of difficulty will be found, however, and an individual who has the ability to read at a certain rate and reproduce a certain percentage of what he has read in one selection may not have the same reading rate and power of reproduction in connection with matter twice as hard. The unit of reading efficiency must be spoken of in connection with material of a certain degree of difficulty. For this reason a scale needs to be established for reading material which shall represent a considerable number of different grades from very easy to very difficult. When this has been done it will be possible to speak of a unit of reading power as the ability to read at a certain rate and recall a certain percentage of the ideas read, in connection with reading matter of a given degree of difficulty. When we have a scale of this kind it will be possible to establish standards of reading ability for each grade. Without the scale a school man may use in testing a school system prose of any grade of difficulty and it will be possible to measure growth in reading power in any given period, compare different schools in the same system and different types of teaching, and carry on various similar lines of investigation.

The reading tests were given in only the third and sixth grades and a comparatively small number of children was involved, for the reason previously stated, that the tests were given for the first time as an experiment and it was more convenient to make the first applications of the method with small numbers of children. A little over four hundred children were tested and some fairly definite pedagogical conclusions seem to be warranted from the data, which will be presented in another article. In many of the best schools divisions in reading consist of twenty-five pupils or fewer and it will always be desirable to test small groups of this size and to compare these groups in one school with similar groups in other schools.

The Tables I and II give the results of the tests.

TABLE I

GRADE III

School	Rank	Rate of Reading in Words per Second	Quantity of Reproduction	Quality of Reproduction	Reading Efficiency in Reading Units
A..........	1	2.16	41.66	35.41	83.24
B..........	2	2.71	26.94	22.49	56.98
C..........	3	2.04	27.28	23.59	51.89
D..........	4	1.94	26.35	21.70	46.61
E..........	5	2.64	19.23	15.65	46.04
F..........	6	1.47	29.73	24.11	39.57
G..........	7	1.08	42.82	27.73	38.10
Average...	......	2.01	30.57	24.38	53.20

TABLE II

GRADE VI

School	Rank	Rate of Reading in Words per Second	Quantity of Reproduction	Quality of Reproduction	Reading Efficiency in Reading Units
A..........	1	3.42	37.77	30.12	116.26
E..........	2	3.40	28.44	22.63	86.82
B..........	3	2.74	32.17	25.05	78.39
F..........	4	3.14	23.87	18.30	66.21
C..........	5	3.19	26.31	13.60	63.66
G..........	6	3.35	20.90	15.12	60.33
D..........	7	2.95	22.15	17.66	58.72
Average...	......	3.17	27.37	20.36	75.77

The object of the tests was to solve a problem in the pedagogy of reading, i.e., to determine the factors of efficiency in instruction, and it is here that tests of this kind have great value. In each of the seven school systems in which the tests were given reading is taught in a different way in certain respects, and the teaching was analyzed into its factors and an attempt made to locate those which produced rapid learning or lack of it. The object, in other words, was to test the validity of the various hypotheses on which the teaching was based. It is entirely possible, and, in fact, not difficult, to analyze the teaching of reading in any given school into its constituent elements. For example, the following is the analysis of the teaching in one school in which the tests were given:

1. The teaching of words as wholes, from the beginning, by associating the visual form vividly with the appropriate object, idea, or experience.

2. Extensive quick-perception reading of sentences from the blackboard throughout the first year.

3. Especial emphasis on concentration upon the thought rather than upon words in all the lower grades.

4. Entire absence of phonetic drill in the two lowest grades.

5. Extensive quick-perception drill with perception cards on words, phrases, and sentences as wholes in the lower grades.

6. Class reading entirely at sight.

7. Number of books read per year entirely at sight in class in first six grades as follows: first grade, 7; second, 21; third, 17; fourth, 18; fifth, 15; sixth, 16.

8. Average number of books read per year for silent reading outside of class in the five years above the first grade as follows: second grade, 19; third, 39; fourth, 75; fifth, 61; sixth, 62.

9. A large amount of oral reproduction in the pupil's own words of the thought of what is read. After several pages have been read rapidly at sight in class, various pupils are called upon to reproduce the thought without further reading or study. Practice in rapid silent reading, followed immediately by oral reproduction.

10. In the third grade, beginning about the fourth month, enough phonic analysis of words as they are met in their functional relations in sentences to give the pupils a mastery of the phonic difficulties of the language.

Here are ten entirely definite and tangible factors which are the characteristic features of the instruction in primary reading in this school. The teaching in all of the schools tested has been analyzed in this manner and the predominant features set forth. By thus analyzing the teaching into its main constituent factors in a considerable number of school systems in which the elements show important variations and by adequately measuring the products of the teaching, the pedagogy of reading can be reduced to its lowest terms and the factors of efficiency accurately determined. For example, to test the value of phonetic drill in teaching, a school system was selected to compare with that mentioned above in which the method of instruction was practically identical, with the exception that a considerable use was made of phonetic drill in the lower grades. In another school system the class reading was all prepared work, i.e., the lessons were read over several times before being read in class. After the factors entering into the instruction in reading in any school have been set forth, the resultant facts on the side of rate of reading, quantity and quality of reproduction, and number of units of reading efficiency may be represented in the form of mathematical expressions and also pictured to the eye by means of graphic curves, surfaces of frequency, and in other similar ways.

Widely different results in the three factors in reading efficiency were found as the products of the different types of teaching, and this is not surprising in view of the varying combinations of conditions which are possible. The rate of reading may be high or low and the quantity of reproduction may be large or small, with a similar variation in quality. As typical examples of what may be found we have the following: Rate may be high and combined with a large quantity and a low quality of reproduction. In another case, the same reading rate may go with a small quantity of reproduction and a quality nearly equal to the quantity. Again, rate may be low and quantity may be large and quality equal to quantity.

Another consideration which has a significant bearing on the evaluation of the method of instruction is that of the correlation of reading rate and power of reproduction. Correlation may be of three kinds: indifferent or positive or negative. Positive correlation exists when power of reproduction increases with reading rate and is complete correlation when it increases in direct proportion to reading rate. Negative correlation exists when power of reproduction decreases as reading rate increases. When reproduction remains the same regardless of increase or decrease in the rate of reading, correlation is said to be indifferent. These factors may be combined in various ways, of which the following are typical examples: (1) low reading rate, percentage of reproduction large, negative correlation; (2) high reading rate, percentage of reproduction small, negative correlation; (3) high reading rate, percentage of reproduction large, positive correlation. Correlation may be of varying degrees, both positive and negative. It is self-evident that the type of teaching which produces the highest reading rate combined with the largest quantity and the highest quality of reproduction and positive correlation is the most efficient. This means that the group of pupils who are the most rapid readers at the upper end of the curve reproduce a larger percentage of the ideas read. Indifferent correlation indicates that the more rapid readers get equally as great a percentage of the thought as the slower readers, and since they read a larger amount their reading ability is proportionately greater. In negative correlation the more rapid readers reproduce a smaller percentage of the ideas read.

Figs. 1 and 2 are given to show the method of indicating correlation or lack of it. In this particular grade the condition is apparent at a glance. In the first place, reading rate is high and shows that word pronunciation has been mastered. But, on the other hand, the actual quantity of reproduction is small and there is no marked positive correlation of reading rate and quantity of reproduction. Quality of reproduction in this grade also falls a considerable distance below quantity in most cases. In other words, it can be seen at a glance that this is the product of a poor type of teaching, everything else being equal. It is entirely evident that these children are the kind so often seen who can read readily as far as mere word pronunciation goes but who do not apperceive, assimilate, and retain the content of what is read in anything like an efficient manner. When it is remembered that reading efficiency is made up of three factors it will be seen that the deficiency of this type of reading on the side of reproduction more than offsets the high rate of reading. Had the reproduction curve been a good deal higher or had there been a gradual rise of the curve showing that assimilation was functioning efficiently, this would have been the product of good teaching, for the high reading rate enabled the pupils to read a large amount in a given unit of time.

Reading is about the most deceptive subject in the entire school curriculum and one in which mere opinion regarding efficiency has the least value. The writer recently visited a school in which the reading appeared to be highly efficient. The children could

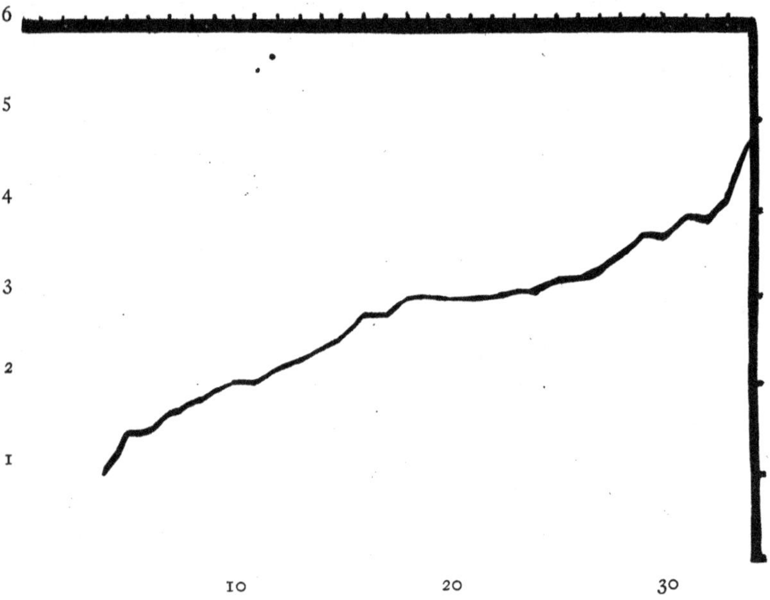

FIG. 1.—Curve representing the rate of reading in a sixth grade of 31 pupils. The scale along the base of the figure represents the number of children in the grade. The scale at the left shows the rate of reading in words per second. The papers were arranged in order of rate of reading.

stand and read a page with the utmost *apparent* ease and fluency and the casual observer would have said that it was reading of the highest competency. Word-pronunciation had been splendidly mastered. It is entirely possible and often happens that reading of this kind is in reality of low grade. Reading is essentially an apperceptive and assimilative process and when these processes do not function actively reading is not good, although mere word-pronunciation may be perfect. In such reading as this the rate will be high, but it often happens that combined with a high rate of reading are a small quantity of reproduction, a low quality, and negative correlation. Since reading efficiency is a product of

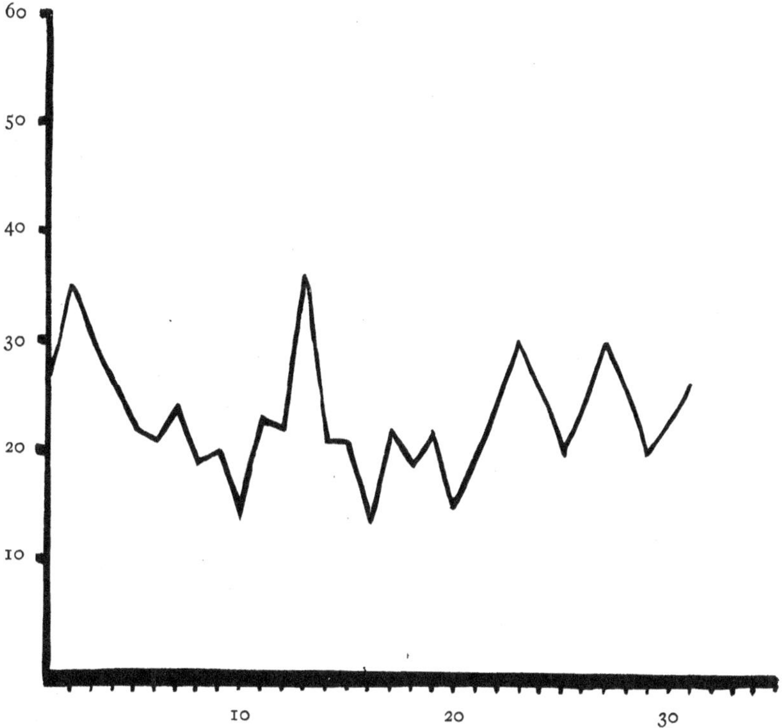

FIG. 2—Curve representing quantity of reproduction of the same children as in Fig. 1, and in the same order. Fig. 1 and Fig. 2 show the correlation of quantity of reproduction and reading rate in this grade. The scale at the left shows the percentage of quantity of reproduction.

several factors, reading of this kind is mediocre in quality. It cannot be pointed out too often that reading is more than mere word-pronunciation. It is feared that some of our prevailing methods of instruction in primary reading are faulty for the reason that undue emphasis is placed on too rapid and too complete mastery of the difficulties of word-pronunciation in the earliest stages of reading at the expense of apperceptive and assimilative activities and that this type of teaching produces a pronounced word-consciousness and a confirmed habit of reading words instead of thoughts from the printed page which the pupil never completely outgrows and which proves a real hindrance to real thought-getting in later stages of his reading.

It seems clear that by the kind of a test under discussion the factors in reading efficiency may be determined accurately and the various reading methods efficiently evaluated. The data which have grown out of these tests suggest emphatically that the prevailing pedagogy of primary reading is in need of thoroughgoing reconstruction in important particulars. Much of our educational practice in this field is based upon sheer tradition, has insufficient scientific foundation, and fails to give good account of itself under the stress of the test of scientific measurement and evaluation. A new and more correct pedagogy of primary reading must be constructed, based upon the known laws of the learning process. Never can the most satisfactory technique of instruction in this particular be developed until the laws of efficient and economical learning are known and methods of instruction based on these laws. The large question here is: How do we most efficiently and economically perceive, apperceive, and assimilate the printed sentence? The problem involved in learning to read opens the whole field of the psychology and physiology of the reading act and involves the whole question of the psychology of visual perception as related to the printed sentence. A close scientific analysis of all the known facts entering into the complete description of the reading act and the construction of a pedagogy of primary reading based on the facts, followed by a rigid evaluation of the method so established in terms of the ability of the children to read and the gradual determining, selection, retention, and elaboration of elements of efficiency in the instruction and the elimination of elements of weakness until the most effective method possible has been formulated is the only mode of attacking a pedagogical problem which insures the most rapid progress.

BOOK REVIEWS

Educational Psychology. By EDWARD L. THORNDIKE. In three volumes. Vol. I, "The Original Nature of Man." Pp. 326. Vol. II, "The Psychology of Learning." Pp. 452. Vol. III, "Work and Fatigue, Individual Differences." Pp. 408. New York: Teachers College, Columbia University, 1913.

In these three volumes Professor Thorndike has brought together a very large body of material which will be found useful by all students of education. Vol. I gives a careful and detailed account of all of the inherited modes of behavior of man. There is much incidental discussion also of the meaning and value of instincts in education. Vol. II reviews a large number of the studies which have been made of learning processes and gives a full account of the learning curve, together with a theoretical discussion of the characteristics of this curve. Vol. III repeats in the division which deals with individual differences the work that Professor Thorndike brought out a number of years ago under the title *Educational Psychology*. The first part of the volume, which deals with work and fatigue, summarizes the experiments made by Professor Thorndike and others in this field. Each volume is supplied with a copious bibliography and will be useful to anyone who is looking up the literature of education.

It is difficult to select from three large volumes of this type any particular item for special comment. Perhaps the most interesting development which appears in these volumes is Professor Thorndike's new position on the matter of formal discipline. On pp. 416–17 of the second volume he makes the following extraordinary statements: "These experimental facts as a whole, like those concerning memorizing, leave a rather confused impression on one's mind, and resist organization into any simple statement of how far the improvement wrought by special practice spreads beyond the function primarily exercised. They do, however, at least put out of court the old doctrine of a very wide spread of a very large percentage of the special improvement. Possibly nobody ever really believed that the improvement made in reasoning about Latin syntax would spread equally, or almost equally, to all or nearly all varieties of reasoning; but men wrote as if they believed substantially this. Certainly nobody can now believe it in the face of these experiments."

With regard to the future development of this matter, and especially with regard to his own frequently reiterated doctrine of identical elements, Mr. Thorndike says on p. 417: "Many more measurements of the influence of improvement in certain abilities upon the status of others must be made before psychology will be able to predict in general the disciplinary effect of any special forms of practice such as the 'studies' of schools or the industries and games of modern life. At present only rather vague protections against unwise expectations can be given. The general theory of identical elements—that one ability is improved by the exercise of another only when the neurones whose action the former represents are actually altered in the course of the exercise of the latter—is sound, and is useful in guiding thought. However, so little is known about which neurones are concerned in any ability that this general theory does not carry us far."

The changes in opinion which are represented by these statements on the part of Mr. Thorndike will be of great interest to those who all along have felt that his attack upon formal discipline was a little overdone and that the positive educational teachings which issued from his attack were very meager as contrasted with those which he attempted to overthrow.

C. H. J.

Opportunities for Vocational Training in Boston. Compiled by the Committee on Opportunities for Vocational Training; Edited by THOMAS C. McCRACKEN. Boston: The Women's Municipal League, 1913. Pp. viii+301. $1.25.

While this volume is published as a handbook of information about the opportunities for obtaining vocational training in and about Boston, it will serve a wider usefulness than its name would imply. The book is suitable for those who are seeking to promote vocational education generally, because it is illustrative of the kind of information which might profitably be collected in any considerable urban community. In this way it serves to stimulate local organizations to study their own communities and to inaugurate practical vocational courses, not only in the public schools, but in social settlements, and in the Young Men's and Young Women's Christian Associations. It also will promote home study of vocations. The volume contains a classification of vocational subjects now being taught in educational institutions, which renders it especially valuable as a reference book for students of vocational education and vocational guidance. The book is therefore commended to the attention of teachers, parents, employers, ministers, social workers, and especially to organizations planned to exercise vocational guidance in any of its phases.

FRANK M. LEAVITT

UNIVERSITY OF CHICAGO

The Fundamental Basis of Nutrition. By GRAHAM LUSK. New Haven, Conn.: Yale University Press, 1914. Pp. 62.

This book is a brief popular account of some of the scientific facts with regard to nutrition and diet. It is the work of one of the best experimental physiologists in this country and will serve admirably as a text for a part of the class exercises in home economics in high school or in the upper grades of the elementary school. It is written in a popular style and yet, at the same time, explains clearly some of the scientific terms which are used by the physiologists and dietitians.

After a brief historical introduction, there is a chapter on the constant need of fuel. In this chapter comparative tables are reported showing the amount of fuel which is used by different classes of people and the reason for these variations. Then follows a chapter on the constant need of protein. In this chapter the special importance of the protein elements is pointed out. Then follows a brief chapter on habits of diet, showing again how different peoples under different circumstances cultivate different diets. The evil effects of a one-sided diet are discussed in the following chapter, and, finally, a series of comparative tables sets forth the monetary value of foods. This discussion is followed by a bibliography which gives references to the best literature on the subject.

C. H. J.

Commercial Education in Germany. By FREDERIC ERNEST FARRINGTON. New York: Macmillan, 1914. Pp. ix+258. $1.10.

There have been frequent accounts in English of industrial education in Germany, but these accounts have usually dealt with the trades and with the type of training which prepares for participation in the different trades. Practically nothing has been written with regard to commercial education in Germany. Professor Farrington's book, therefore, makes a distinct contribution to our knowledge of an important aspect of German education.

In America, commercial education precedes in its development industrial training. The explanation of this fact is to be found in the rich natural resources of our own country. We have exported raw materials, but have, until recently, taken only a relatively small share in the manufacturing of these raw materials into finished products. As a nation which deals with the shipment of raw materials we have needed clerks and others who were interested chiefly in transportation and all that attaches to commerce in a narrow sense of that term. Germany, on the other hand, has only recently come to realize the necessity of training for commerce, but she has adopted in her commercial schools the methods which were familiar in her thorough treatment of academic subjects and in the schools which train for industry.

There are lower commercial schools intended for pupils who have enjoyed only an elementary education in the *Volksschule* and there are higher secondary commercial schools for the training of those who have gone through higher institutions. In discussing both grades of schools, Professor Farrington gives in great detail both the course of study and the methods of treating the various subjects. Commercial teachers will find this report, accordingly, very useful in working out the details of their own programs.

The book is a good example of thorough treatment of a single aspect of education. Its value in this respect is very large. If we could have a similar treatment in detail of the way in which the work is carried on in the industrial schools and even in the academic institutions of Germany, we should have a more accurate view than we now get from the somewhat vague general descriptions which are offered in the books that attempt to deal in a single volume with all phases of foreign educational systems.

C. H. J.

BOOKS RECEIVED

AMERICAN BOOK CO., CHICAGO

Essentials of Arithmetic. First Book. By L. D. HARVEY, PH.D. Cloth. Pp. 224.

Essentials of Arithmetic. Second Book. By L. D. HARVEY, PH.D. Cloth. Pp. 507.

G. P. PUTNAM'S SONS, NEW YORK

Byron's "Childe Harold's Pilgrimage." Edited by A. HAMILTON THOMPSON, M.A., F.S.A. Cloth. Pp. 286.

A Book of English Prose. Part I. By PERCY LUBBOCK, M.A. Cloth. Pp. 140.

A Book of English Prose. Part II. By PERCY LUBBOCK, M.A., Cloth. Pp. 181.

The Merchant of Venice (The Granta Shakespeare). Edited by J. H. LOBBAN, M.A. Cloth. Pp. 149. $0.30.

A Midsummer Night's Dream (The Granta Shakespeare). Edited by J. H. LOBBAN, M.A. Cloth. Pp. 118. $0.30.

Exercises and Problems in English History, 1485-1820. Compiled by W. J. R. GIBBS, B.A. Cloth. Pp. 174.

The Purpose of Education. By ST. GEORGE LANE FOX PITT. Cloth. Pp. 83. 2*s*. 6*d*. net.

Salamis. In easy Attic Greek. With Introduction, Notes, and Vocabulary. By G. M. EDWARDS, M.A. Cloth. Pp. 78. Illustrated. $0.45.

Der Zuave. Adapted from *Ein Schloss in den Ardennen.* Edited by G. T. UNGOED, M.A. Cloth. Pp. 62.

PETER REILLY, PHILADELPHIA

Hossfeld's French Grammar. By A. P. HUGUENET. Cloth. Pp. 478. $1.00.

Hossfeld's German Grammar. By C. BRENKMANN. Cloth. Pp. 453. $1.00.

Hossfeld's Gramatica Inglesa. By TOMÁS ENRIQUE GURRIN. Cloth. Pp. 335. $1.00.

Hossfeld's Italian Grammar. By A. ROTA. Cloth. Pp. 340. $1.00.

Hossfeld's Portuguese Grammar. By F. THOMAS. Cloth. Pp. 336. $1.00.

Hossfeld's Spanish Grammar. By T. E. GURRIN. Cloth. Pp. 336. $1.00.

THE MANUAL ARTS PRESS, PEORIA, ILL.

Furniture Design for Schools and Shops. By FRED D. CRAWSHAW, B.S., M.E. Cloth. Pp. 127. Illustrated. $1.00.

Handcraft in Wood and Metal. By JOHN HOOPER and ALFRED J. SHIRLEY. Cloth. Pp. 240. Illustrated. $3.00.

Kitecraft and Kite Tournaments. By CHARLES M. MILLER. Cloth. Pp. 144. Illustrated. $1.00.

HOUGHTON MIFFLIN CO., BOSTON

Summer. By DALLAS LORE SHARP. Illustrated by ROBERT BRUCE HORSFALL. Cloth. Pp. 132. $0.60.

Volunteer Help to the Schools. ("Riverside Educational Monographs.") By ELLA LYMAN CABOT. Cloth. Pp. 141. $0.60.

THE CENTURY COMPANY, NEW YORK

Beyond the Pasture Bars. By DALLAS LORE SHARP. With Illustrations by BRUCE HORSFALL. Cloth. Pp. 160. $0.50.

Practical Homemaking. By MABEL HYDE KITTREDGE. Cloth. Pp. 153.

J. B. LIPPINCOTT CO., PHILADELPHIA

Macdonald's "The Princess and Curdie." Simplified by ELIZABETH LEWIS. Cloth. Pp. 126. Illustrated.

RAND, McNALLY & CO., CHICAGO

A Little Book of Well-known Toys. By JENNESS M. BRADEN. Cloth. Pp. 105. $0.45.

THOMAS Y. CROWELL CO., NEW YORK

The Education of Karl Witte. Edited by H. ADDINGTON BRUCE. Translated from the German by LEO WIENER. Cloth. Pp. 312. $1.50 net.

THE HEER PRESS, COLUMBUS

The Evolution of the Teacher. By FRANCIS B. PEARSON, A.M. Cloth. Pp. 254.

GINN & CO., CHICAGO

Play and Recreation. By HENRY S. CURTIS. Cloth. Pp. 265. Illustrated.

SUPERINTENDENT GOVERNMENT PRINTING, CALCUTTA

Progress of Education in India, 1907-1912. By H. SHARP, C.I.E. Cardboard. Pp. 292. Rs. 2, or 3*s*.

RUSSELL SAGE FOUNDATION, NEW YORK

Some Conditions Affecting Problems of Industrial Education in 78 American School Systems. By LEONARD P. AYRES, PH.D. Paper. Pp. 22. $0.10.

TEACHERS COLLEGE, NEW YORK

Food for School Boys and Girls. By MARY SWARTZ ROSE, PH.D. Paper. Pp. 15. $0.10.

BOBBS-MERRILL CO., INDIANAPOLIS

For Girls and the Mothers of Girls. By MARY G. HOOD, M.D Cloth. Pp. 157. Illustrated. $1.00 net.

CURRENT EDUCATIONAL LITERATURE IN THE PERIODICALS[1]

IRENE WARREN
Librarian, School of Education, University of Chicago

Bawden, William T. The Richmond convention of the Department of Superintendence. Voca. Educa. 3:361–68. (My. '14.)

Beyer, Thomas Percival. Tragedy and treason in education. Dial 56:338–39. (16 Ap. '14.)

Bloomfield, Meyer. School and employment. Voca. Educa. 3:319–26. (My. '14.)

Brown, H. A. The New Hampshire type of reconstructed rural high school. Voca. Educa. 3:327–37. (My. '14.)

Brown, Henry E. A plan for the reorganization of the American public high school. School R. 22:289–301. (My. '14.)

Burkholder, E. Catherine. An eighth-grade newspaper. El. School T. 14:418–22. (My. '14.)

Butler, Nicholas Murray. True vocational preparation. Educa. R. 47: 499–501. (My. '14.)

Cates, E. E. The teaching of history in the secondary schools. Educa. 34: 491–500. (Ap. '14.)

Clark, Bertha May. Humanism and efficiency. Educa. R. 47:486–98. (My. '14.)

Davies, G. R. Elements in arithmetical ability. J. of Educa. Psychol. 5:131–40. (Mr. '14.)

(A) defeat for religious education. Lit. D. 48:829. (11 Ap. '14.)

Farrell, Elizabeth E. A study of the school inquiry report on ungraded classes. Psychol. Clinic 8:29–47. (Ap. '14.)

Ford, Guy Stanton. The library and the graduate school. Educa. R. 47: 444–56. (My. '14.)

Frailey, L. E., and Crain, C. M. Correlation of excellence in different school subjects based on a study of school grades. J. of Educa. Psychol. 5:141–54. (Mr. '14.)

[1] *Abbreviations.*—Cent., Century; Educa., Education; Educa. R., Educational Review; El. School T., Elementary School Teacher; Harp. W., Harper's Weekly; J. of Educa. (Bost.), Journal of Education, Boston; J. of Educa. Psychol., Journal of Educational Psychology; Lit. D., Literary Digest; Liv. Age, Living Age; Outl., Outlook; Pop. Sci. Mo., Popular Science Monthly; Psychol. Clinic, Psychological Clinic; R. of Rs., Review of Reviews; School R., School Review; Sci. Am., Scientific American; Tech. World M., Technical World Magazine; Voca. Educa., Vocational Education.

Gathany, J. Madison. The giving of history examinations. Educa. 34:514–21. (Ap. '14.)

Goddard, Harold C. What is wrong with the college? Century 88:49–55. (My. '14.)

Greenwood, James M. Vocational guidance in high school. Educa. R. 47: 457–68. (My. '14.)

Gruenberg, Benjamin C. Vocational guidance and efficiency. How boys are started aright in life. Sci. Am. 110:312, 318. (11 Ap. '14.)

Gustafson, Lewis. An endowed trade school in a large city. Voca. Educa. 3:351–60. (My. '14.)

Hall, Walter P. Why I have a bad education. Outl. 106:848–52. (18 Ap. '14.)

Harvey, Fred. The case of Jack the dullard. Good Housekeeping 58:224–30. (Fe. '14.)

Heniger, A. Minnie Herts. Making Bible stories plain. Good Housekeeping 58:331–38. (Mr. '14.)

Hewins, Nellie Priscilla. The doctrine of formal discipline in the light of experimental investigation. J. of Educa. Psychol. 5:168–74. (Mr. '14.)

Judd, Charles H. Some observations in German schools. El. School T. 14:437–44. (My. '14.)

Kingsley, Clarence D. New aims of the modern high school. J. of Educa. (Bost.) 79:458–59, 64. (23 Ap. '14.)

Sixth of a series of papers on the reorganization of secondary education.

Leavitt, Frank M. Co-operation of the schools in reducing child labor. Voca. Educa. 3:344–50. (My. '14.)

Lee, James Melvin. Schools of journalism. R. of Rs. 49:591–93. (My. '14.)

Lennes, N. J. Mathematics for culture. Educa. R. 47:469–77. (My. '14.)

Lennon, Margaret M. The value of play in education. J. of Educa. (Bost.) 79:431–33. (16 Ap. '14.)

Lewinski-Corwin, E. H. The practical necessity of school clinics. Pop. Sci. Mo. 84:500–6. (My. '14.)

Lyon, Darwin Oliver. The relation of length of material to time taken for learning and the optimum distribution of time. III. J. of Educa. Psychol. 5:155–63. (Mr. '14.)

McAndrew, William. The plague of personality. School R. 22:315–25. (My. '14.)

MacDougal, D. T. The measurement of environic factors and their biologic effects. Pop. Sci. Mo. 84:417–33. (My. '14.)

Magnus, Philip. Vocationalism. Liv. Age 281:151–60. (18 Ap. '14.)

Martin, Edward S. The girl that is to be. Harper 128:915–18. (My. '14.)

(A) matter of educational ethics. Outl. 106:885–87. (25 Ap. '14.)

Moore, Anne. Youth and fun. Outl. 106:936–40. (25 Ap. '14.)

Myers, Garry C. Recall in relation to retention. J. of Educa. Psychol. 5:119–30. (Mr. '14.)

Myers, Garry C. Some false assumptions in education. Educa. R. 47:478–85. (My '14.)

Nash, T. P., Jr. Standardizing the child. Tech. World. M. 21:348–52, 464. (My. '14.)

New England Association of Teachers of English, Committee. Report: the training of English teachers. Educa. 34:473–90. (Ap. '14.)

Payne, E. George. A recent educational development in Germany—the commercial college. Voca. Educa. 3:369–75. (My. '14.)

Perry, Ralph Barton. The teaching of ideals. School R. 22:334–38. (My. '14.)

Rational geography. Lit. D. 48:897. (18 Ap. '14.)

Russell, James E. Outlines of a practical education. Good Housekeeping 58:339–44. (Mr. '14.)

Sanders, Frederic W. The organization of education. Educa. 34:522–29. (Ap. '14.)

School board as banker for children. Survey 32:67. (18 Ap. '14.)

Scofield, F. A. The function of the intermediate school or the junior high school. J. of Educa. (Bost.) 79:429–30. (16 Ap. '14.)

Selvidge, Robert W. State control of entrance to the industries. Voca. Educa. 3:338–43. (My. '14.)

Senger, Harry L. A comparison of the first-year courses in Latin and German. School R. 22:302–14. (My. '14.)

(The) small college and its president by one of its professors. Pop. Sci. Mo. 84:449–58. (My. '14.)

Steffens, Lincoln. How college students can educate themselves. Harp. W. 58:18–20. (18 Ap. '14.)

Trettien, A. W. The exceptional child in school. Psychol. Clinic 8:48–51. (Ap. '14.)

Tufts, James H. The teaching of ideals. School R. 22:326–33. (My. '14.)

Warren, Irene. Some books on children's reading and story-telling. El. School T. 14:413–17. (My. '14.)

Weld, Mildred. A peace pageant written and acted by the upper grades. El. School T. 14:423–36. (My. '14.)

Wesley, Charles H. The teacher's point of view in the study and teaching of history. Educa. 34:509–13. (Ap. '14.)

White, E. M. Bergson and education. Educa. R. 47:433–43. (My. '14.)

Williams, Edward H. Temperance instruction in public schools and its results. Survey 32:74–76. (18 Ap. '14.)

Volume XIV JUNE 1914 Number 10

The Elementary School Teacher

THE UNIVERSITY OF CHICAGO PRESS
CHICAGO, ILLINOIS, U.S.A.

AGENTS
THE CAMBRIDGE UNIVERSITY PRESS, LONDON AND EDINBURGH
KARL W. HIERSEMANN, LEIPZIG
THE MARUZEN-KABUSHIKI-KAISHA, TOKYO, OSAKA, KYOTO

The Elementary School Teacher

EDITED BY
THE FACULTY OF THE SCHOOL OF EDUCATION
WITH THE CO-OPERATION OF
THE FACULTY OF THE FRANCIS W. PARKER SCHOOL

Vol. XIV **CONTENTS FOR JUNE 1914** **No. 10**

The Elementary School Teacher is published monthly from September to June. ¶ The subscription price is $1.50 per year; the price of single copies is 20 cents. Orders for service of less than a half-year will be charged at the single-copy rate. ¶ Postage is prepaid by the publishers on all orders from the United States, Mexico, Cuba, Porto Rico, Panama Canal Zone, Republic of Panama, Hawaiian Islands, Philippine Islands, Guam, Samoan Islands, Shanghai. ¶ Postage is charged extra as follows: For Canada, 30 cents on annual subscriptions (total $1.80); on single copies, 3 cents (total 23 cents). For all other countries in the Postal Union, 46 cents on annual subscriptions (total $1.96); on single copies, 6 cents (total 26 cents). ¶ Remittances should be made payable to The University of Chicago Press, and should be in Chicago or New York exchange, postal or express money order. If local check is used, 10 cents must be added for collection.

The following agents have been appointed and are authorized to quote the prices indicated:

For the British Empire: The Cambridge University Press, Fetter Lane, London, E.C., England. Yearly subscriptions, including postage, 8*s.* each; single copies, including postage, 1*s.* each.

For the Continent of Europe: Karl W. Hiersemann, Königstrasse 29, Leipzig, Germany. Yearly subscriptions, including postage, M. 8.25 each; single copies, including postage, M. 1.10 each.

For Japan and Korea: The Maruzen-Kabushiki-Kaisha, 11 to 16 Nihonbashi Tori Sanchome, Tokyo, Japan. Yearly subscriptions, including postage, Yen 4.00 each; single copies, including postage, Yen 0.50 each.

Claims for missing numbers should be made within the month following the regular month of publication. The publishers expect to supply missing numbers free only when they have been lost in transit.

Business correspondence should be addressed to The University of Chicago Press, Chicago, Ill.

Communications for the editors and manuscripts should be addressed to the Editors of THE ELEMENTARY SCHOOL TEACHER, The University of Chicago, Chicago, Ill.

Entered October 12, 1903, at the Post-office at Chicago, Ill., as second-class matter, under Act of Congress, March 3, 1879

CONSTRUCTIVE BIBLE STUDIES

The Constructive Bible Studies, illustrated above, represent a series of volumes for graded work in religious education that are accurate in scholarship, pedagogically sane, beautifully illustrated, handsome in typography, prepared by experienced and capable teachers. They are in use in two thousand churches representing all denominations, as well as in several hundred of the best day schools in the country.

An inclosure of 10 cents for postage will bring a free handbook of 160 pages, giving specimen chapters from the volumes and suggestions for the organization of graded Sunday schools.

Day-school teachers are much needed in the work of the church to supervise grading, arrange courses, choose text-books, train teachers, and to act as educational advisers. Help your local church now to prepare for better work in the autumn.

THE UNIVERSITY OF CHICAGO PRESS
CHICAGO, ILLINOIS

Recent Publications

OF

The University of Chicago Press

Unpopular Government in the United States. *By Albert M. Kales, Professor of Law in Northwestern University.*

272 pages, 12mo, cloth; $1.50, postage extra (weight 24 oz.)

This volume by a prominent member of the Chicago bar is an especially timely book, presenting with great clearness and cogency some of the political needs of the country, particularly the necessity of the short ballot. The author defines unpopular government as one of centralized power which is able to maintain itself in the face of popular disapproval. He then points out that the establishment in the United States of state and municipal governments, according to the plan of splitting up the power of government among many separate offices and requiring the widest and most frequent use of the elective principle, has cast so great a burden upon the electorate that an intelligent citizen is reduced to a state of political ignorance inconsistent with self-government. This situation has made it possible, he thinks, for a well-organized hierarchy to acquire the real power of government and to retain it, in the face of popular disapproval, for selfish ends. Such leaders the author characterizes as "politocrats."

The first part of the volume deals with the rise of the politocrats; the second discusses various expedients for restoring the American ideal of democracy; while the third considers constructive proposals like the commission form of government for smaller cities, and the application of the principles underlying this form to larger cities and the state, and to the selection of judges.

Chicago Tribune. Albert M. Kales, Professor of Law in Northwestern University, has written a book which ought to be read wherever citizens are perplexed by the intricacies and distressed by the failures of government.

NEW POSTAGE RATES

A change in the post-office regulations, effective March 16, 1914, provides for the mailing of books under the parcel-post classification. It is no longer possible to announce definite postage charges because of the variation of the rate with the distance.

We shall, however, still publish on the "net" basis, which involves a separate charge for transportation. In the following announcements the weight of each book is given, which will enable the purchaser to estimate the postage cost to his place of residence.

The French Verb: Its Forms and Tense Uses. By William A. Nitze and Ernest H. Wilkins, of the Department of Romance Languages and Literatures, the University of Chicago.

46 pages, 8vo, paper; 25 cents, postpaid 28 cents
French Verb Blanks, per pad 25 cents; postage extra (weight 14 oz.)

This little book prepared by Professor Nitze and Professor Wilkins, of the Department of Romance Languages and Literatures in the University of Chicago, will be of especial interest and value to all students and teachers of French because of the great help it gives in the mastery of the French verb. It is intended to facilitate familiarity with the verb forms and fix them in the student's memory by associating those tenses which are actually related in form. A method of classroom drill is suggested; the table and discussion of tense uses are self-explanatory; and the illustrative material, when quoted, is drawn from standard nineteenth-century writers.

Verb blanks, for the suggested arrangement of verb forms, will be supplied in pads at the prices indicated above.

The pamphlet is intended for use in both elementary and advanced courses, and is believed to be in method a great improvement over anything previously published.

Chicago and the Old Northwest, 1673–1835. By Milo Milton Quaife, Superintendent of the Wisconsin State Historical Society.

488 pages, 8vo, cloth; $4.00, postage extra (weight 46 oz.)

This book recounts, in a manner at once scholarly and dramatic, the early history of Chicago. Important as this subject is, it is not treated solely for its own sake. The author's larger purpose has been to trace the evolution of the frontier from savagery to civilization. From the point of view of Chicago and the Northwest alone the work is local in character, although the locality concerned embraces five great states of the Union; in the larger sense its interest is as broad as America, for every foot of America has been at some time on the frontier of civilization. It is believed that this book will take rank as the standard history of Chicago in the early days.

The Nation. In this monograph [on the history of Fort Dearborn] we have one of the most careful studies in Western history that has ever been made.

PUBLICATIONS OF THE CHICAGO HISTORICAL SOCIETY

The University of Chicago Press has become the publishing and distributing agent for the following books of the Chicago Historical Society:

Masters of the Wilderness. *By Charles B. Reed.* (*"Fort Dearborn Series."*)

156 pages, 16mo, cloth; $1.00, postage extra (weight 12 oz.)

In reproducing these romantic episodes of our exploration era the author has neither exaggerated the color nor distorted the facts of that intensely human period. The opening essay, which gives its title to the volume, is a highly interesting and carefully wrought account of the origin and upgrowth of the Hudson's Bay Company, with a portrayal of its powerful influence on the development of Canada. "The Beaver Club," the second essay in the volume, is closely allied to the first, and concerns a social club of Montreal the members of which were drawn from the partners and factors of the Northwestern Fur Company, for many years a rival of the Hudson's Bay Company. For forty years this club dominated the commercial, political, and social life of Canada. The concluding essay, "A Dream of Empire," recounts with many fresh details the adventures of Tonty in Old Louisiana.

The book as a whole is a successful attempt to awaken interest in some of the remarkable episodes of our early history. It is not analytical but narrative, not a sequence of annals but a series of picturesque activities.

COLLECTIONS

Vol. I. *History of the English Settlement in Edwards County, Illinois.* By GEORGE FLOWER. 402 pages, royal 8vo, cloth; out of print.

Vol. II. *Biographical Sketch of Enoch Long, an Illinois Pioneer.* By HARVEY REID. 134 pages, royal 8vo, cloth; $1.00, postage extra (weight 22 oz.).

Vol. III. *The Edwards Papers.* Edited by E. B. WASHBURNE. 662 pages, royal 8vo, cloth; $3.50, postage extra (weight 4 lbs.).

Vol. IV. *Early Chicago and Illinois.* Edited by EDWARD GAY MASON. 538 pages, royal 8vo, cloth; $3.00, postage extra (weight 57 oz.).

Vol. V. *The Settlement of Illinois.* By ARTHUR CLINTON BOGGESS. 268 pages, royal 8vo, cloth; $2.00, postage extra (weight 36 oz.).